Emma Darwin

UNIVERSITY PRESS OF FLORIDA
Florida A&M University, Tallahassee
Florida Atlantic University, Boca Raton
Florida Gulf Coast University, Ft. Myers
Florida International University, Miami
Florida State University, Tallahassee
New College of Florida, Sarasota
University of Central Florida, Orlando
University of Florida, Gainesville
University of North Florida, Jacksonville
University of South Florida, Tampa
University of West Florida, Pensacola

EMMA

DARWIN

A VICTORIAN LIFE

James D. Loy and Kent M. Loy

UNIVERSITY PRESS OF FLORIDA

Gainesville · Tallahassee · Tampa · Boca Raton · Pensacola · Orlando · Miami · Jacksonville · Ft. Myers · Sarasota

Copyright 2010 by James D. Loy and Kent M. Loy

Printed in the United States of America.

This book is printed on Glatfelter Natures Book, a paper certified under the standards of the Forestry Stewardship Council (FSC). It is a recycled stock that contains 30 percent post-consumer waste and is acid-free.

15   14   13   12   11   10   6   5   4   3   2   1

Library of Congress Cataloging-in-Publication Data
Loy, James.
Emma Darwin: a Victorian life/James D. Loy and Kent M. Loy.
p. cm.   Includes bibliographical references and index.
ISBN 978–0–8130–3478–2 (alk. paper)
1. Darwin, Emma Wedgwood, 1808–1896. 2. Women—Great Britain—
Biography. 3. Wives—Great Britain—Biography. 4. Darwin, Emma
Wedgwood, 1808–1896–Family. 5. Darwin, Emma Wedgwood, 1808–
1896—Marriage. 6. Darwin, Charles, 1809–1882. 7. Great Britain—
History—Victoria, 1837–1901—Biography. 8. Great Britain—Biography.
I. Loy, Kent M. II. Title.
CT788.D25L69 2010   941.0810929–dc22
[B]   2010007785

The University Press of Florida is the scholarly publishing agency for the State University System of Florida, comprising Florida A&M University, Florida Atlantic University, Florida Gulf Coast University, Florida International University, Florida State University, New College of Florida, University of Central Florida, University of Florida, University of North Florida, University of South Florida, and University of West Florida.

University Press of Florida
15 Northwest 15th Street
Gainesville, FL 32611–2079
http://www.upf.com

*This book is dedicated to our
matriarchs, Aileen Woolsey Loy
and Margaret Kent Matthews,
whose wisdom and love continue
to inspire us.*

Contents

Preface ix

Genealogies xii

1. The Family Circle 1

2. The Two Dovelies 8

3. A Woman of the World 24

4. A Traveling Cousin, a Doveley's Death, and the Abolition of Slavery 40

5. The Return of the *Beagle* and "The day of days!" 57

6. Bride, Mother, Nurse 77

7. Narrow Lanes and High Hedges 97

8. The Old Order Changeth 109

9. A Dear and Good Child 121

10. The Great Exhibition, War in the Balkans, and the Last of the Barnacles 133

11. For Better or Worse, in Sickness and in Health 148

12. Midwiving the *Origin* 164

13. A Banker in the Family 178

14. Lives Lived, Lives Lost, and Closure at Malvern 193

15. A Book about Man, and Henrietta Takes a Husband 209

16. Two Weddings, Four Funerals, and the Fiendish Mr. Ffinden 227

17. An Irreparable Loss 242

18. "Our Secure Happiness . . . Shattered" 267

19. Life at a Lower Pitch 284

20. *The Life and Letters* 302

21. Banting, Books, and the Queen's Jubilee 320

22. The Leos Abroad, and the Last Maerite Left Standing 339

23. The Last Wind of the Watch 354

Acknowledgments 371

Notes 375

Bibliography 413

Index 423

Preface

> You all know well your Mother [who] has been my greatest blessing. . . . I marvel at my good fortune that she, so infinitely my superior in every single moral quality, consented to be my wife. She has been my wise adviser and cheerful comforter throughout life.
>
> —*The Autobiography of Charles Darwin*

In 1876, as part of a little autobiography he was writing for his children and grandchildren, Charles Darwin praised his wife, Emma, with these loving words. By that date, Darwin had earned international recognition for his scientific theories and books, the latter including *On the Origin of Species* and *The Descent of Man*, and he was well on his way to becoming the scientific icon known to every schoolchild today. His fame would ultimately be celebrated in dozens of biographies and tributes, and in these works Darwin's "greatest blessing, wise adviser, and cheerful comforter" would usually be mentioned, albeit only as a supporting character as the author moved on to the main event: the life of the great man. Yet all lives have stories to tell, connections to trace, and lessons to teach. Thus it is not unusual, when supporting characters are viewed individually, for them to prove entertaining and worthwhile in their own right, rather than simply sources of information about some more famous person.

This is precisely the case with Emma Wedgwood Darwin. Born last into the large family of second-generation English potter Josiah Wedgwood II, Emma grew from a messy little girl to be the matriarch of her own large family and the independent-minded helpmate of Charles Darwin, the famous evolutionist. Educated, intelligent, informed and active politically, well connected socially, and tireless as a caring mother and wife, Emma's life history not only reveals a lively and outspoken woman but also provides a gentry-level window on the Victorian Era in Britain. From the days of "grand tours" on the Continent, through the abolition of British slavery, Victoria's coronation and golden jubilee, the Crimean and other wars—with her husband's famous *Origin* and *Descent* published along the way—Emma witnessed and commented on most of the events of a remarkable century. Bored by science and devoutly Christian, she somewhat surprisingly entered into marriage with a man who was a rising star in geology and biology and whose faith was fast disappearing. Their differences were mitigated, however, by mutual devotion and extensive genealogical ties, and for more than forty years Emma not only stood by her man but also served as his rock and refuge as well as the moral cynosure of their large family. To be sure, through a process of "growing together" common in long-married couples, Emma changed over her years with Charles, a lessening of her own religious orthodoxy being one example of this. But mainly she was true to herself and her original values, and the story of this plainspoken and pragmatic woman is by turns interesting and amusing and, not infrequently, inspirational.

Navigating through Emma's story does require a bit of work by the reader, however, and it would be remiss not to mention this at the very start. Hers was a potentially bewildering network of family relations: at birth Emma had seven siblings, seventeen aunts and uncles (including those by marriage), and dozens of cousins, all making up a complex web of Wedgwoods, Allens, Mackintoshes, and Darwins. And while it makes sense to begin this book at Emma's beginning, doing so inevitably cuts abruptly into the ongoing lives of many other people whose own histories provide essential background material. Thus, the reader's patience is requested during the gradual introduction of this large cast of kinfolks. To aid in mastering the family connections, genealogical charts are provided.

One final prefatory note is in order. To let the characters speak for themselves as much as possible, the book contains extensive quotes from family letters. This practice carries some risk of confusion, given the vagaries of spelling and punctuation over the centuries and the fact that many of the letters appear to have been dashed off in haste and in semi-shorthand style using such abbreviations as "wd" for "would," "shd" for "should," and "v" for "very." Nonetheless, in general, there has been little attempt to adjust the spelling or punctuation of quotations to match modern usage, nor has the notation "[*sic*]" been used regularly to draw attention to what would today be considered a writing error. In almost all cases, the meaning of the quoted material is adequately clear and, if anything, the nineteenth-century style adds an element of charm. Where words abbreviated in the original have been spelled out, these modifications are shown in brackets. Endnotes are indicated throughout the book to direct interested readers to the original sources.

And now it is time to let Emma Wedgwood Darwin tell her story.

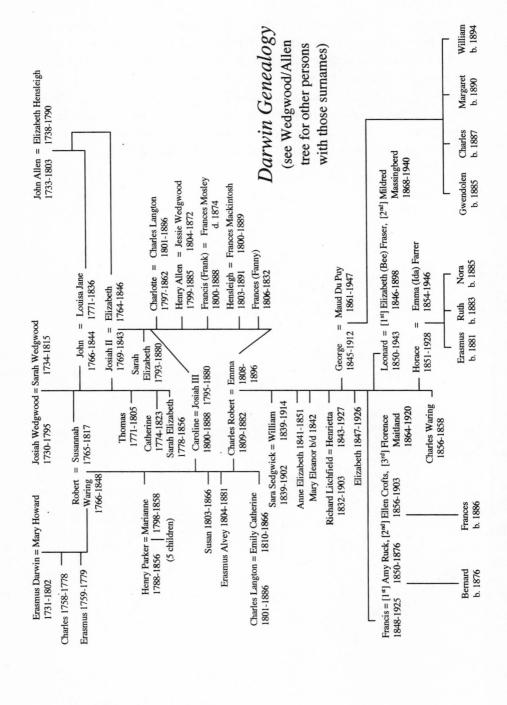

Darwin Genealogy
(see Wedgwood/Allen
tree for other persons
with those surnames)

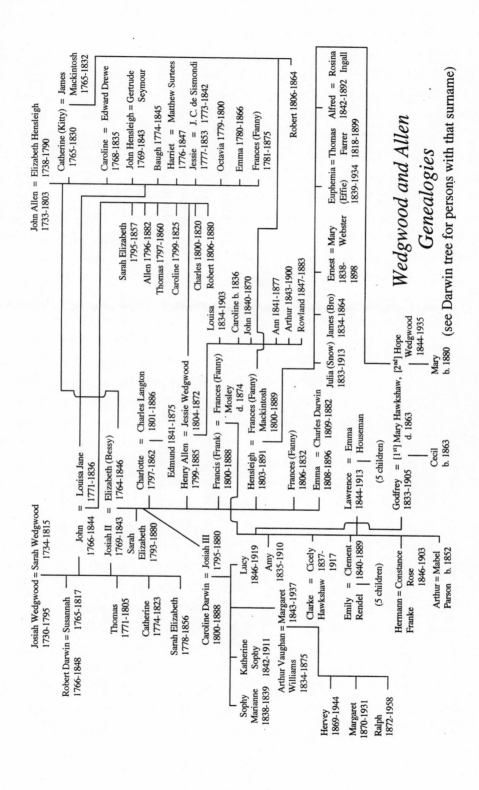

Wedgwood and Allen
Genealogies

(see Darwin tree for persons with that surname)

1 The Family Circle

THE LITTLE VILLAGE OF MAER is nestled among the rolling hills of Staffordshire in England's northern Midlands. Maer Hall, an Elizabethan manor house locally believed to have been built atop a Saxon settlement, dominates the village architecture and sits just east of the small lake, or mere, that gives the village its name. The Hall is an impressive stone structure whose gray solidity is softened by decorative plantings, latticed windows, ornate third-floor dormers, and an arched entryway. Outside the house one finds outbuildings including stables and a dovecote, as well as inviting terraces that overlook the lawn and lake. Stone stairways lead idle strollers from the terraces to scenic gardens designed, in part, by Lancelot "Capability" Brown. Sheep graze contentedly on the gentle slope opposite the Hall, while on the steeper hillside immediately behind the house stands St. Peter's Church, with its occasionally ivy-covered tower. Rebuilt in 1610 and again in 1877, St. Peter's shows Norman features that suggest a much earlier origin. All in all, Maer is a lovely and bucolic spot, equaling in beauty, if not in grandeur, any country house in England. And it was here that the last child of Josiah Wedgwood II (hereafter Jos), a little girl named Emma, was born on May 2, 1808.[1]

One can easily imagine the scene at Maer on that birthing day. Jos's beloved wife, Elizabeth, called Bessy, was in the midst of her ninth confinement. At forty-four years of age, she already had three daughters (a fourth had died in infancy) and four sons, and her oldest child was fourteen. Like many women living before the advent of widespread and effective contraception, Bessy had been pregnant most of the time since her marriage, and she must have faced this latest confinement with a sense of resignation and familiarity. Perhaps she was attended by a physician—certainly the family was affluent enough to afford one—or perhaps simply by her maids and a midwife. Possibly some of her Wedgwood in-laws came to lend support: Jos's mother, Sally (née Sarah Wedgwood), and his two unmarried sisters, Kitty (Catherine) and Sarah Elizabeth, lived together not far away at Parkfields. Jos himself most likely stayed out of the way, which was just as well since, despite his being a kind and indulgent man, his silent and reserved nature rather intimidated his wife, who believed that in general men were "dangerous creatures who must be humored." Under the circumstances, Jos's main contribution was probably to wait anxiously in the well-stocked library. Still, he was undoubtedly relieved and pleased when told of the safe arrival of his new daughter. Eight children; yes, that was a family that befitted the master of Maer.[2]

The world of 1808 into which the new baby was born included a relatively new United Kingdom; Great Britain and Ireland had been legislatively joined only eight years earlier. King George III was still in his right mind and on the throne, ruler of a population of some seventeen million souls in the United Kingdom alone. His playboy son the Prince of Wales, the future George IV, was estranged from his second wife, Caroline of Brunswick. (The prince's first marriage, to the Catholic widow Maria Fitzherbert, had been declared invalid some years earlier under the Royal Marriage Act of 1772.)[3] On the Continent and at sea, Britain was at war with Napoleon Bonaparte's France. In that struggle the British had won a key naval victory at Trafalgar in 1805, and in August 1808, three months after little Emma Wedgwood was born, Arthur Wellesley, later the Duke of Wellington, would land with his army in Portugal to begin the Peninsular War. Napoleon's final defeat at Waterloo was still seven years away, as was the settlement of the Congress of Vienna, which would restructure Europe and add Ceylon, Trinidad, Malta, and the Cape of Good Hope to Britain's already extensive overseas empire.[4]

Like the world around it, the Wedgwood family was experiencing ups and downs in 1808. The first Josiah Wedgwood, founder of the business that carries his name to this day, had died in 1795 leaving the bustling pottery works at Etruria in Burslem and an estate worth £500,000—close to $42 million in modern currency.[5] Working first with Thomas Bentley as his partner and later with Thomas Byerley, Josiah I had perfected his creamware, developed a healthy domestic and overseas trade, and even been allowed by Queen Charlotte to style himself Potter to Her Majesty. Understandably, therefore, he was bitterly disappointed in 1793 when his oldest son John announced that, while happy to inherit a share of the Etruria profits, he had no interest in actually managing the family business, preferring instead to become a partner in the banking house of Alexander Davidson & Company. Accordingly, Josiah I passed the directorship of the factory and ownership of the accompanying mansion, Etruria Hall, upon Jos, his second son.[6]

In truth, Jos had little more interest in running the pottery than did John, and he tried his best to slide out of it. Only a few months after his father's death, Josiah II moved with Bessy and their two young children to an estate in Dorset in the south of England where Jos set himself up as a country squire, leaving Byerley to manage both the Etruria pottery and the company's London showrooms. Not for Jos was the image of a tradesman; he much preferred the role of landed gentleman. Not to be outdone, brother John, whose partnership carried no active duties in the running of Davidson's Bank, left London around 1796 and settled as squire at Cote House near Bristol. Unfortunately for the Wedgwood fortunes, the brothers had other traits in common besides a distaste for manufacturing: both overdrew on their anticipated profits from the potteries while contributing little or nothing (Jos and John, respectively) to the day-to-day operation of the business. John in particular was a spendthrift who lacked a head for either business or personal finances. Although charming, he had few skills other than a talent for horticulture. He put that skill to good use at Cote House, however, developing extensive gardens and even exchanging botanical advice with George III's gardener, William Forsyth. Along with Forsyth and others, John Wedgwood founded what would ultimately become the Royal Horticultural Society.[7]

In addition to Jos, John, Kitty, and Sarah Elizabeth, the first Josiah left two other adult children: a married daughter, Susannah Darwin, and the unmarried youngest son, Thomas. Tom Wedgwood showed occasional signs of genius and might have made a creative manager for the Etruria works except for chronic ill health and, latterly, an addiction to opium. The best-known example of Tom's genius was his invention in 1802 of the first photographic technique, "[A] Method of Copying Paintings upon Glass and of Making Profiles by the Agency of Light upon Nitrate of Silver."[8] Additionally, he spent time trying to devise a scientifically based system of education. Unfortunately, Tom's brilliance came to very little in the end. In 1792 he suffered a nervous collapse that was soon followed by an incapacitating physical breakdown. Over the next few years he consulted several doctors, including his brother-in-law Robert Darwin, who prescribed foreign travel, and Thomas

Beddoes, who was experimenting with the medicinal properties of "airs" and told Tom to inhale the breath of cows to relieve his symptoms. Sometime later Beddoes also recommended opium, thus starting a practice that would become an addiction for Tom. In addition to Beddoes, Tom developed a set of lively and talented friends including the poet Samuel Taylor Coleridge (a fellow opium user and Tom's partner in numerous drug sessions) and the Wordsworth siblings, Dorothy and William.[9]

In 1801 Tom experienced a brief remission of his illness, but the symptoms returned with a vengeance after a few months, and by December 1802 he was considering suicide. Despite everyone's concern and best efforts, his condition continued to deteriorate and he died in the summer of 1805 at the age of thirty-four. The death was an enormous blow to Jos, but at least it reduced the drain on the family income, since Tom was yet another brother who had lived beyond his means. Indeed, living beyond their means was endemic among the children of Josiah I, and one had to look to their brother-in-law Robert Darwin for a contemporary example of fiscal responsibility.[10]

The son of Erasmus Darwin—poet, freethinker, and highly regarded eighteenth-century physician—Robert Waring Darwin was himself a successful doctor who had married Susannah Wedgwood in 1796 and then built her a splendid home, The Mount, overlooking the Severn River in Shrewsbury, a twenty-mile carriage ride from Maer. By 1808 Robert and Susannah had produced four children, and in May of that year Susannah conceived a fifth, a son who would be named Charles Robert after his father and a paternal uncle. Unaware that she was carrying a child destined for greatness, Susannah was simply depressed to find herself pregnant once again. Pregnancies were hard for her: she had been confined to bed for several months before the birth of her second child. Childbearing, as well as life with a brusque and easily irritated husband, was beginning to take its toll on Susannah, and not many years earlier she had remarked despondently to her brother John, "Everyone seems young but me."[11]

To be fair, Robert Darwin, while somewhat domineering and certainly imposing with a portly build and six-foot height, could also be charming and affectionate. He was a talented and caring doctor, and because he had built up one of the largest medical practices outside London, he was extremely busy. Besides being an excellent physician, Robert was a keen money manager who increased his personal fortune through shrewd investments and loans, and who was often called on by the extended family for financial assistance. For example, it was a loan from Robert Darwin to Jos that had made possible the original purchase of Maer Hall and its thousand-acre estate in 1803.[12]

Her father's people, complemented by in-laws like Robert Darwin, accounted for a good portion of little Emma Wedgwood's extended family, but to complete our initial cast of characters, we must also inventory the baby's maternal kin. Rounding off her own brood at eight in 1808, Bessy Wedgwood had come from an even larger household. Born in 1764, she was the eldest of the eleven children of John Bartlett Allen, squire of the Cresselly estate in Pembrokeshire, Wales, and his wife Elizabeth, née Hensleigh. Widowed in 1790, John Allen married a second time and fathered three additional children, all of whom died young. He then aged into a cantankerous old man whose temperamental and melancholy disposition cast a pall over Cresselly. Life with a father who would pound the table and demand entertaining after-dinner talk made the Allen daughters desperate to escape to their own married lives.[13]

Eight of the eleven Allen children ultimately married, some more illustriously than others, and five of those marriages had taken place by 1808. Bessy, the oldest daughter, married Jos Wedgwood in 1792. The next to wed was Caroline, the third child, who married the Reverend Edward Drewe in 1793. This marriage was destined to end in 1810 with Edward's death from consumption, but not before it had produced four children. The fourth Allen daughter, Louisa Jane—generally considered the beauty of the family— married Jos Wedgwood's brother John in 1794. Extravagant and gregarious, "Jane" would later develop Cote House into something of a social center for the family and their intellectual friends, and in the process compound her husband's free-spending ways. Catherine "Kitty" Allen, the second oldest child, married the widower James Mackintosh in 1798. Politician, scholar, and wit, Mackintosh seemed destined for a brilliant career, despite having a very nasal speaking voice and a weak handshake that his friend the Reverend Sydney Smith described as "mortmain"—literally, dead hand. Mackintosh's social ascendancy was confirmed in 1804 when he was knighted and then sent with his family to fill the position of Recorder of Bombay. And finally, the fifth Allen daughter, Harriet, possibly because she was desperate to escape the gloom of Cresselly, entered into a loveless marriage with the Reverend Matthew Surtees in 1799. Moody and tyrannical, Surtees was roundly disliked by his in-laws.[14]

Without a doubt, however, it was not the oldest but the three youngest Allen sisters who were destined to have the strongest and most affectionate relationships with their newborn Wedgwood niece. Jessie Allen was thirty-one and unmarried in 1808 (she eventually married in 1819). Along with her lifelong spinster sisters Emma and Fanny (Frances) and their brother John Hensleigh Allen—to whom Cresselly had passed upon their father's death in 1803—Jessie lived on at the Pembrokeshire home place. Jessie and Fanny were both more vivacious and high-spirited than their sister Emma, and considerably prettier to boot (Emma Allen once described her own face as "half-formed"). Among Fanny Allen's notable traits were her great interest in politics and her devoted admiration for Napoleon.[15]

For a member of the Wedgwood-Darwin-Allen clan to be an admirer of Napoleon in the first decade of the 1800s took considerable courage, given the indirect harm being inflicted on the family income by the French ruler. During Britain's prolonged war with France, exports of Wedgwood ware to the Continent had declined significantly and foreign debts had become difficult to collect. To make matters worse, the American market for Wedgwood products had also grown soft. Inventories at the potteries were backed up and profits had plummeted. And if all of this bad news wasn't enough, in 1800 John Wedgwood's bank had revealed to the partners that it was in serious financial trouble. This development not only threatened to bankrupt John and Jane but, because certain loans made by the bank were guaranteed by the partners' personal property, the pottery itself was at risk of being seized to pay debts owed to the Crown. Even Mackintosh far away in India was strapped for cash. Shortly after his arrival there, Sir James had to humble himself and ask Robert Darwin for a loan, but the only thing he got for his trouble was a curt refusal combined with a lecture about cutting back on his extravagant lifestyle: "A coach and four seems to be as expensive, except for the taxes, in Bombay as in England," chided Dr. Robert, adding, "Saving is an art you have to learn."[16] With Robert Darwin as the only exception, economic reforms throughout the family were clearly in order.

John and Jane's situation was the most critical. In 1805 their spendthrift life at Cote House came to an end when they were forced to sell the estate, move briefly to Maer (where they oversaw the alterations Jos was having made), and then relocate yet again to Etruria Hall. The plan was for John to become more involved in the operation of the potteries, but it was also becoming obvious to Jos that his own management responsibilities could no longer be avoided. The potential for a cash infusion into the family coffers after Tom Wedgwood's death went unrealized because closing Tom's affairs depended on reaching a final settlement of Josiah I's estate, and that had yet to be achieved. It looked as if Robert Darwin might have to stand behind his promise to Jos never to allow John's annual income to fall below the gentlemanly level of £1,000. With all this financial and business uncertainty, Jos reluctantly gave up playing the squire in Dorset and returned with his family to Staffordshire—a long move geographically and, for Jos, a long step down toward the manufacturer's life he disdained. But at least, after four years in the doing, the renovations at Maer were close to being finished. This cushioned the move considerably for Bessy, if not so much for her husband. Bessy wrote to Jessie Allen in September 1807:

> We went to look at Maer the other day; it is wonderfully improved, and will be one of the pleasantest places in the country. It does not seem to be nearly ready, but the painting is finished and the papering nearly; the walk round the pool, if they make it, will be delightful; the new road is a prodigious improvement.[17]

Maer Hall would be the Jos Wedgwoods' home for the rest of their days. Bessy was pregnant at the time of this last relocation, and the baby she was carrying would be the only truly native "Maerite" of them all.

2. The Two Dovelies

THE NEW BABY HAD RICH BROWN HAIR, gray eyes, and a fresh complexion. Doted upon by everyone at Maer—and especially by her oldest sisters, Sarah Elizabeth (called just Elizabeth) and Charlotte, fourteen and ten years old respectively in May 1808—Emma was the last addition to a lively and loving household. Elizabeth in particular was a devoted caretaker, remarking years later, "Since . . . the time [Emma] could speak, I have never had one moment's pain from her and a share of daily pleasures such as few people have it in their power to shed around." The loving bond between these two sisters, who formed the chronological bookends of Jos and Bessy's children, would last for seventy-two years and end in a tender reversal of their original roles, with Elizabeth living near her sister in Downe and being "sheltered by [Emma's] constant love and care."[1]

Inevitably, though, Emma's closest connection was with her sister Fanny, just two years her senior. Inseparable in their daily routine of tutoring and play, the two little girls, nicknamed "the Dovelies" by the family, were alike in some ways—both were happy, sweet, and amiable—but quite different in others. Fanny was the orderly and industrious one. She organized things and made "lists of temperatures . . . words in different languages, housekeeping memoranda, etc." Fanny was her mother's "Mrs. Pedigree." Emma was more spirited and considerably less tidy. (Her daughter Henrietta later described

Emma as having a "large-minded, unfussy way of taking life.") Emma was the Wedgwoods' "Little Miss Slip-Slop." Together, Mrs. Pedigree and Miss Slip-Slop enjoyed the run of Maer Hall, the beauty of the lawns and gardens, and the indulgent love of their elders.[2]

Threatening to undermine the happy life at Maer, however, was the fact that all was not well—indeed, things were getting worse—with regard to Wedgwood family finances. By 1810, trade with both Europe and America was depressed to crisis levels. At the same time, it was calculated that the potteries were carrying a total of more than £41,000 (about $3.4 million today) in unpaid accounts—money that, if collected, would have immediately relieved the cash flow problem. John Wedgwood was now nearly insolvent, and his involvement with the struggling Davidson's Bank continued to imperil the family assets. And as if these trade and banking issues weren't enough, rounding off Jos and Bessy's list of worries was the fact that expenses at Maer were skyrocketing. The oldest children were growing up and costing more: Elizabeth, although tiny and afflicted with spinal curvature, turned seventeen in 1810 and needed ball gowns; sons Joe (Josiah III) and Harry (Henry), then fifteen and eleven, needed to be educated at Eton.[3] All of this fit Jos's sense of the right lifestyle for a country gentleman, but it cost money.

Even the procrastinating Wedgwoods could no longer avoid extreme economic reforms. Jos asked John and Jane to vacate Etruria Hall so he could lease it. This was doubly devastating, since it was accompanied by the strong suggestion that they raise some quick cash by auctioning off a portion of their household goods. Trying to set an example for his spendthrift brother, Jos economized at Maer by firing three servants (leaving only fifteen). For a time, he even considered selling the Hall and moving back to Etruria himself. And finally, in 1811, to a great extent as a protective measure to preclude the Crown's seizing the potteries to pay the debts of Davidson's Bank, Jos suggested to his brother that they should dissolve their partnership in the family business. He wrote to John:

> I have thought a good deal both of your affairs and of my own. The result is that I think it desirable for both of us to dissolve the partnership. . . . The business is now not worth carrying on, and if I could withdraw my capital from it, I would tomorrow, but that is impossible; & I must continue it, if it be only to pay the interest of the money borrowed and to get a rent for my building. . . . On my side it is desirable to dissolve the partnership, to simplify the concern, to eliminate the difficulties of the settlement of my affairs in the case of my death, that would arise from a partnership, and to relieve me

from the risk, whatever it may be, arising from my partner having a share in a bank, subject to an Extent in certain cases.[4]

Ultimately John and Jane did leave Etruria, taking a leased house in the resort town of Southend-on-Sea, near the mouth of the Thames.[5]

Still there seemed to be no end to this game of "musical houses." Removing John as a partner was a prudent move, but it failed to address the chronic vacuum in management at the potteries. To correct this, in the fall of 1812 Jos reluctantly decided to leave Maer for a time, move back to Etruria, and apply what management skills he had to the floundering business. The relocation was postponed for a few months, however, when the three youngest Allen sisters, Jessie, Emma, and Fanny, came from Cresselly for a long visit. All three women were still single, and now they faced the prospect of their Cresselly home being broken up when their brother John married Gertrude Seymour, a morose woman who they suspected would resent living in the same house with spinster in-laws. After an eight-month stay at Maer, during which they grew very close to their Wedgwood nieces, the Allen sisters moved on to London to be near another brother, Baugh, the master of Dulwich College, and also Kitty and James Mackintosh, newly returned from India. Jos and Bessy, now free of guests and able to move house from Maer to Etruria, did so in 1813. It was a hard move. There is little doubt that the entire family left Maer with heavy hearts, but Elizabeth tried her best to brace her father's spirits. She wrote to him: "Mamma does not at all, I think, let the thoughts of leaving Maer harass her; she is in excellent spirits; and as for us [children], you and mamma make us so happy that where we live will signify very little to us." Emma and Fanny Wedgwood were five and seven, respectively, when they left Maer; they would not return for six years, and those years would widen their worldview considerably.[6]

Perhaps it would be useful at this point to step back from the chronology of house moves and business crises in order to give a more detailed description of Jos and Bessy's personalities and styles. These were the primary behavioral models, after all, available to the Dovelies during their formative years.

Fanny Allen once described Jos Wedgwood as a man who was "always right, always just, and always generous."[7] Being right, just, and generous, however, did not make Jos a warm or inviting man to most people. The best-known painting of Jos shows a man with penetrating eyes and a firmly set mouth. Certainly he was wise, as Robert Darwin observed, but Jos's grave personality often kept people at a distance. Sydney Smith—clergyman, wit, author, and family friend—liked to say with a chuckle, "Wedgwood's an excellent man—it is a pity he hates his friends."[8] Daunting to some, including his young nieces (but not his nephew Charles Darwin), Jos was nonetheless an indulgent and loving husband and father. His consideration for Bessy was shown in countless small ways, such as not keeping cows at Maer because she was distressed by their moaning when their calves were taken away.[9] He also wrote tender love letters to Bessy when they were apart. This excerpt is from July 1800:

> I am and will be your affectionate husband, and we are and will be tender parents to our dear children. I have no pleasures that I can compare with those I derive from you and from them. Your idea fills me, and I clasp you as the heroes of poetry clasp the shades of the departed.[10]

Both Jos and Bessy were devoted parents who delighted in their children's differing personalities and achievements, and instilled in them an appreciation for intellectual curiosity, free speech, and respect for all people. In 1819 Emma Caldwell, later a distant relation of the Wedgwoods after marrying the physician Henry Holland, observed of Maer:

> I never saw anything pleasanter than the ways of going on of this family, and one reason is the freedom of speech upon every subject; there is no difference in politics or principles of any kind that makes it treason to speak one's mind openly, and they all do it. There is a simplicity of good sense about them, that no one ever dreams of not differing upon any subject where they feel inclined. As no things are said from party or prejudice, there is no bitterness in discussing opinions. . . . The part of the intellectual character most improved by the Wedgwood education is good sense, which is indeed their pre-eminent quality. It is one of the most important, and in the end will promote more of their own and others happiness than any other quality. The moral quality most promoted by their education is benevolence, which combined with good sense, gives all education can give. . . . [In this house, doors] and windows stand open; you are nowhere in confinement; you may do as you like; you are surrounded by books that all look most tempting to read; you will always find some pleasant topic of conversation, or may start one, as all things are talked of in the general family. All this sounds and is delightful.[11]

In this lively and open atmosphere, the Wedgwood boys and girls began their educations under the guidance of governesses and tutors who taught them foreign languages (French, Italian, and German), mathematics, singing, painting, and dancing. For Emma and Fanny, their older sisters Elizabeth and Charlotte were also important teachers. The Wedgwood sons ultimately continued their studies at public schools, Eton for Joe and Harry, Rugby for Frank and Hensleigh. And despite the fact, consistent with the customs of the time, that public school education was denied the Wedgwood daughters, the girls developed into talented, knowledgeable, and sophisticated adults. Emma in particular expressed her intellectual curiosity and taste for reading quite early. At the age of five she set out to read Milton's *Paradise Lost* but, after a good start, ended up asking her mother to finish it aloud. Many years later, Emma told her own children how nice it was of Bessy not to refuse.[12]

The Jos Wedgwoods lived at Etruria until 1819, and their six-year stay there coincided with a series of important historical and family developments. In politics, Napoleon Bonaparte finally came to the end of his military and imperial career. Defeated by an alliance of European foes in 1814, Napoleon was forced to abdicate his throne and retire to the island of Elba off the Italian coast. The Bourbons then returned to the French throne in the person of Louis XVIII. In the spring of 1815, however, sensing unrest both at home—particularly within the army—and among the alliance that had been his downfall, Napoleon attempted a comeback. He reentered France in early March, was joined by the French army, and began maneuvering in an attempt to separately challenge the two enemies remaining in the field: Prussia and Britain. This Napoleon was unable to do, and on June 18 he was soundly defeated at Waterloo by the combined Prussian and British forces.[13] Another Tom Wedgwood, this time John and Jane's seventeen-year-old son, was in the thick of things at Waterloo, and six days after the battle he wrote to his mother:

> We had the post of honor and were the first to begin the attack. . . . I trusted in God and He has been pleased to spare me, for which I hope I am as thankful as I ought. The most disagreeable part was when we were on the top of our position, lying down doing nothing, with the shells and shot coming over like hailstones, and every now and then seeing 1 or 2 men killed. We had 2 officers wounded in that way. It was a very mournful sight next morning when I was on parade to see but little more than one-half the number of men that there were the morning before, and not quite one-half the officers. The Duke of Wellington was very much pleased with us.[14]

This time Napoleon was banished to the South Atlantic island of St. Helena, where he died in 1821.

The three spinster Allen sisters wasted no time, after Napoleon's final surrender and the normalization of British-French relations, in setting out on an extended tour of the Continent. Accompanied initially by brother-in-law John Wedgwood, they traveled first to Paris, where they made the obligatory visits to the Louvre and Versailles, and then moved on to Geneva and ultimately to northern Italy. While in Switzerland, thanks to some highly placed introductions provided by Sir James Mackintosh, the Allen sisters met the famous writer and political observer Germaine de Staël. Author of numerous books, lover of many men, and a captivating talker, Madame de Staël hosted a brilliant salon at her château in Coppet that was frequented by the rich and talented. Among the salon attendees was Jean Charles Léonard Simonde de Sismondi, a celebrated Swiss historian and economist, who was still a bachelor at forty-three. Sismondi was smitten virtually at his first sight of thirty-nine-year-old Jessie Allen and began to court her ardently. Despite Sismondi's reputation and prospects, his attentions were not immediately welcomed. In truth, Jessie was more than a little put off by the thought of leaving England and her family to spend her life with this physically unappealing little man. Eventually she came to return his love, however, and Jessie and "Sis" were married in 1819. Over the years, Sismondi was fully accepted into the extended family circle, although in private conversations Jessie and her husband were sometimes referred to as Beauty and the Beast.[15]

In 1816, Wedgwoods too were trickling over to the Continent. Joe, now twenty-one and a graduate of the University of Edinburgh, began his coming-of-age grand tour by escorting his younger brother Harry to Geneva, where they rendezvoused with their Allen aunts. Harry remained in Geneva and began lessons with a private tutor, but Joe was soon off to Italy, Germany, and the Netherlands. In Amsterdam Joe made contact with his shy and withdrawn cousin Allen Wedgwood, whose parents, John and Jane, hoped a sojourn abroad would help their directionless son choose a career. Sending the boy to the Continent had been done out of sheer frustration, however, since back at home the financial situation was going from bad to worse. Davidson's Bank had entered its death throes, and some of John's partners had already withdrawn large sums of money to cushion the personal bankruptcies that were coming. The dire state of affairs was reversed only when Coutts Bank took over Davidson & Company in August 1816. John and Jane were now essentially destitute, dependent for their livelihood on the support of their families. Jos and Bessy, Robert and Susannah Darwin, and Kitty and Sarah Wedgwood pooled their resources and placed £6,000 in trust for John.[16]

In March 1818, Jos, Bessy, and their four daughters took their turn traveling on the Continent. They longed not only for the amusement of new and interesting sights but also to escape depressing family circumstances beyond their control. Besides John's financial disaster, the family circle had suffered several deaths in the previous year. On Bessy's side, Caroline Drewe had lost her two youngest children to consumption in 1817, and another daughter was terminally ill.[17] On Jos's side, 1817 had seen the horrific death of his oldest sister, Susannah. Never particularly healthy, Susannah was stricken in July with severe stomach pains. Her husband and physician, Robert Darwin, watched for two days as his fifty-two-year-old wife went steadily downhill and then, realizing that the end was near, sent for her sisters, Kitty and Sarah. Kitty wrote from the sickroom to Jos:

> The Dr has not the slightest hope. . . . The pain indeed is gone that was her first illness, but she has such severe vomitings & sickness that he says he does not think her sufferings much lessened. She was today for a few hours easier, & the Dr could not help feeling some little doubt whether it was not possible she might recover. This evening she is worse, & he is very wretched. Still though so exceedingly feeble, she has such a tenaciousness of life, that he fears she may suffer for some time. . . . Her senses are as perfect as ever. From feebleness she can hardly speak. She has not seen any of the children but Marianne and Caroline since Friday. . . . The Dr has just been to tell us he does not think she will pass this night.[18]

Poor Susannah's time had not quite come, however, and she lingered for another thirty-six hours, dying on July fifteenth from what must have been peritonitis. She was buried in the chancel of St. Chad's Church, Montford, just outside Shrewsbury. Robert Darwin would join his wife there in 1848, and their two youngest daughters, Susan and Catherine, would round out the family grave in 1866.

The mood at The Mount became more and more gloomy. Robert was shattered, and it may be fairly said that he never fully recovered from Susannah's death. His usual periodic depressions now became more frequent and longer lasting. The Darwin girls were so grief-stricken that they could barely stand to mention their lost mother.[19] Eight-year-old Charles Darwin carried little memory of either his mother or her death into his adulthood. In 1838 he wrote: "I recollect my mother's gown & scarcely anything of her appearance. Except one or two walks with her I have no distinct remembrance of any conversations, & those only of very trivial nature." And years later, in 1876, he added: "It is odd that I can remember hardly anything about [my mother] except her deathbed, her black velvet gown, and her curiously constructed work-table."[20] In the place of their lost mother, Charles's older sisters Susan and Catherine would take over much of his upbringing.

In 1818 Jos, Bessy, and their daughters made straight for Paris, a city they intended to explore for several months. They settled into fashionable lodgings, and while the adults ventured out into local society—meeting, among others, Sismondi, the socialite Madame Jeanne Françoise Récamier,[21] and at that lady's salon the Queen of Sweden—the Dovelies (Fanny and Emma) began lessons in Italian, French, music, and dancing. The family also renewed their friendship with Bessy's cousin Madame Collos. This expatriate's husband was a former French army officer, now turned fishmonger.[22] Emma and Fanny were thrown in with the Collos children, one of whom features in the earliest of Emma's extant letters, written to her middle brother back in England:

> My dear Frank,
> We have got such numbers of masters. Two belong to Charlotte and two to us. I like the Coloes very except the youngest Louis who bothers one very much. At the dancing school there is a little dance every Friday and we go and dance very often they are going this moment to put in the post-office yours Emma Wedgwood.[23]

The adults may have enjoyed the high society and soirées in Paris, but the Dovelies found their greatest delight in outings such as a late May picnic at Montmorency. Elizabeth described the picnic for her father, who had returned briefly to England on business:

> The weather was delicious, we mounted our asses and went into the woods, which are the prettiest things now you can imagine. . . . Emma and Fanny were very happy on their asses, and quacked accordingly.[24]

In June, Jos returned to Paris accompanied by Frank and Hensleigh, aged seventeen and fifteen, who were on their way to Geneva for their own period of private tutoring. Leaving the Dovelies in a boarding school, the rest of the family traveled to Switzerland. Many years later, Emma still marveled at her parents' decision to leave two such young girls alone in a foreign city. She also remembered with distaste the fishy smell of the Collos' house and having to put up with the pesky seven-year-old Louis. The entire Wedgwood family returned to England in September.[25]

Back at Maer, the Dovelies continued to be loving best friends, despite Fanny occasionally lording it over Emma. Aunt Emma Allen described the girls' mutual devotion to their older sister, Elizabeth:

I marvel at the strength of the girls' spirits as much as I do at the perfection of their tempers. I feel now very sure that not only not a cross word ever passes between them, but that an irritable feeling never arises. Fanny, to be sure, is calmness itself, but the vivacity of Emma's feelings, without perfectly knowing her, would make me expect that Fanny's reproofs, which she often gives with an elder sister air, would ruffle her a little; but I have never seen that expressive face take the shadow of an angry look, and I do think her love for Fanny is the prettiest thing I ever saw.[26]

Three years later, in January 1822, fifteen-year-old Fanny and thirteen-year-old Emma were enrolled for a year of educational polishing at Greville House, a boarding school in Paddington Green (Greater London) run by a Mrs. Mayer. Both Dovelies shed a few tears when Bessy dropped them off. Interestingly, it was Fanny rather than her younger sister who seemed to be the more distressed. Naturally enough, homesickness was a problem, but eventually the girls overcame it sufficiently to settle into their studies—which, consistent with the times and the type of school they were attending,[27] do not seem to have been too demanding. They broke up their time at Paddington Green with Sunday visits to see their brother Harry, who was in London studying science with the Scottish writer and educator Mary Somerville, and with visits from cousins.[28] Bessy, in a letter to Fanny that also mentions another of the highly placed connections of the extended Wedgwood circle—in this case the result of Sir James Mackintosh becoming friendly with Lord and Lady Holland some ten years earlier—wrote these words of support and advice:

> To answer your question first my dear little Fanny, I think you had better continue to use the salt to your gums, as the best means of preventing their becoming spongy again, and as it has already done you so much good, it would be a pity to leave it off. As soon as I have done writing I will look for my Emma's manuscript music book and if I can find it (which I dare say I shall), I will send it with this letter. . . . Fanny [Mackintosh, the Dovelies' twenty-two-year-old cousin] is still at Holland House [home of the 3rd Baron Holland, Henry Richard Fox, and his family, and a noted London political and literary salon],[29] and she is so happy there, and Miss Fox [Mary Elizabeth Fox][30] is so fond of her, that they have petitioned for another week. I don't know whether I told you before how much Fanny regretted that she should not have an opportunity of calling upon you, but Miss Fox never goes out of the Gates, and as Lady Holland is in London, Fanny has no means of moving. . . . It gave me very great pleasure to hear so good a report of you

from your Cousins who paid you a visit, who reported you both to be in high health, and spirits, and that Mr Jenkins handy work was already visible in your improved carriage. I was also particularly pleased at the honourable mention you made to them of Mrs Mayer as a proof that you felt yourselves happy under her tuition, and also that you had hearts alive to kindness, when it is shewn you. It mends our hearts to feel warmth towards those that are kind to us, and this I hope will urge you never to forget how kind your Aunts always have been to you and to not forget a message, now and then, of enquiry or affection towards them. . . . You have never told me how your new gowns that Miss Shied made you looked. As the spring is coming on, you will want your straw bonnets, which I suppose will do without new trimming. I love to busy myself a little about my dear girls dress; it seems to bring them a little nearer to me. I think you will both want spencers [short jackets] as the spring comes on but it is time enough yet, as we shall now have a good deal of cold weather I dare say. You must be guided by Mrs Mayer as to this important affair with respect to the *when*, the *what*, and the *How*. Another little thing I would say before I close my letter is, that I wish your schoolfellows not to see my letters, I remember when I was at School, we were very fond of reading each others letters, and were not very scrupulous in asking each other, but we were a young set, and had not learnt that one ought never to ask to see a letter. Never, therefore my dears, ask any one to shew you a letter, and should any young lady ask you, answer them with the utmost civility, that you would, with great pleasure, [but] that I had a particular objection to it, for the same reason don't leave my letters about in your work boxes or bags, but when you have done with them burn them. Tell me how your dancing goes. . . . Blacky & Phil and Squib [Maer Hall pets] are all well and if they could speak would send their love. . . . It is time now to bid you adieu my very dear Girls.
E. Wedgwood
Is not this a long letter? God bless you.[31]

Perhaps the most memorable event of Emma's time at Greville House was being asked to play the piano for Mrs. Maria Fitzherbert, the long-estranged and legally unrecognized first wife of the newly crowned King George IV. (Why the sixty-six-year-old Mrs. Fitzherbert was visiting Greville House is not recorded, although perhaps she was considering enrolling her fifteen-year-old niece and ward.)[32] But despite such highlights, a year away from home at boarding school was enough for both the Dovelies and their parents, and early in 1823 the girls joyfully returned to Maer, where the remainder of their education was entrusted to Elizabeth, Charlotte, and occasional visiting tutors.[33]

Emma and Fanny once again flourished in the free and easy life of Maer Hall. Emma assisted Elizabeth in teaching the local children in the Maer Sunday School that was held each week in the Hall laundry. To help her young pupils learn to read, at some point in the 1820s Emma wrote a book consisting of four short stories and titled *My First Reading Book*. These little tales, written on a child's level and chock-full of moral lessons, were also used by their author many years later to teach her own children to read.[34] The first story, "The Plumb Pie," reveals Emma's strong Christian morality.

The Plumb Pie

John was a boy of ten years old, and one day his mother said to him John I shall be out all day, so you must take care of little Polly. Give her some bread and milk at dinner time, and do not let her fall and hurt herself. Here is some bread and cheese for your dinner.

When his mother was gone he played with Polly a long time till she fell asleep on his knee. As soon as she awoke, he warmed the bread and milk and fed her, and then he eat his own dinner.

Some time after this he saw part of a nice plumb tart which they had had for dinner on Sunday.

John said to himself, "my mother did not give it me and I must not have it; but then he thought, I am very hungry and I dare say my mother will never miss it. So he got upon the table and took the tart and eat it all up.

When his mother came home she said, "I hope you have been a good boy. John said not a word for he knew it was wrong of him to eat the pie.

His mother then made ready his father's supper, and as she looked upon the shelf said, Where is the rest of the pie we had on Sunday, I think I put it by on that shelf?" "I do not know said John."

His mother looked all round the room, and said she was very sorry she could not find it for his father's supper. John was very sorry too, and felt very sad because he had told a lie to his mother.

He was very sad all the next day, and at last he said "Mother I have done something very wrong." "Have you John? said she, I am very sorry to hear it, what was it?" John. "I told a story, I said I did not know where the pie was and it was

I who eat it when you were out; but I am very sorry now, and I wish I had not taken the pie, for I knew how wrong it was at the time."

Well my dear boy said his mother, I am glad you have told me, and I hope you will try never to say what is not true again. I hope you will ask God to forgive you, for a lie is a sin in the sight of God.[35]

The second story, titled "The Little Foal," took advantage of children's natural interest in animals to draw Emma's pupils into the learning process. It also provides a first glimpse of one of her lifelong concerns—the abuse of animals by humans.

The Little Foal

James and Tom were playing together one fine day.

Tom. Our ass has got a pretty foal only a month old.

James. It is a black one?

Tom. No it is gray, and it has a great bunch of hair like wool upon its head and a soft black nose.

James. How I should like to see it!

Tom. You can come some day, and we will give it some potatoes, and then it will run after us with its ears back as if it was very angry. I often play with it, and one day it gave me a kick, but I did not care, for it was only in fun and did not hurt me, you never saw such a funny little thing. One day it came into the house, and we could hardly get it out again.

James. What shall you do with it when it is grown big?

Tom. My father says he will not sell it, they get so beaten and ill used, he says he will get a small cart and then we can bring the coals, and take the potatoes to market, and he says I may drive it. I wish I was big enough to go in a cart now.

James. But when it is grown up it will not be playful any more.

Tom. Will not it? I shall be sorry for that.[36]

Emma's Christian faith was matched by, and perhaps partially modeled on, that of Fanny. Whether Emma worked as diligently on her religion as her older sister did on hers is another question, however. Two excerpts from Fanny's 1823 diary reflect an exceptionally strong desire for spiritual growth and self-improvement.

[August 17] I have not been entirely idle during this past week. I have read the Bible every day, but I think I must be more industrious. I will try to spend this day well & not to throw it away. I must be attentive to my devotions & not suffer myself to feel out of humour or jealous about any thing. I must be good natured & obliging.

[December 25] CHRISTMAS DAY . . . I took the Sacrament. I have made but small progress in the improvement which this time last year I wished to make in my character but I hope by God's assistance that at the end of another year I may look back with more satisfaction. I must take Mamma for my model & perhaps in the course of years I may become as amiable & as good as she is.[37]

As she entered her mid-teens, Emma was growing into a pretty—although, like all her sisters, bespectacled—and accomplished young woman. Her hair was glossy brown and she liked to wear it waist-length or longer. Over time, she became the hairdresser for all her sisters, creating becoming coiffures by twisting their hair into bows on top and curls that framed their faces. True to her Slip-Slop nature, however, Emma was not particularly fussy about dress or the colors she wore. In a characteristic note to Elizabeth in 1824, she asked: "If you happen to be in a ribbon shop, will you get 3 yds. of not very handsome ribbon for a turned straw bonnet. I am quite indifferent about the colour, except not straw colour."[38]

By 1824, the year she turned sixteen, Emma had begun to keep a daily diary. It was a habit that she would maintain for the rest of her life. Although her diaries are not the sort of private journal of a biographer's dreams, filled with personal reflections, but rather brief notations made in a pocket notebook, they nonetheless provide revealing information about her activities and interests. In her *Marshall's Fashionable Repository or Ladies Elegant Pocket Diary for 1824*, Emma jotted down a variety of items: visitors to Maer, trips she made away from home, church services attended, books read, significant events ("was confirmed with Jessie"), trivial events ("Frank finished spreading cow dung"), weather reports, and notes on her allowance and expenditures. She also used the diaries to record illnesses (1824 was quite a healthy year) and to note the first day of each menstrual period (this was a practice that later allowed her to keep accurate track of her conceptions and that she would teach her daughters).[39]

The 1824 diary reveals a very busy teenager. Emma made two visits that year to her Darwin uncle and cousins in Shrewsbury, staying for perhaps three weeks in all. On six occasions she traveled to the nearby village of Betley, Staffordshire, to visit with the family of George Tollet, whose seven daughters, especially Ellen and Georgina, were her dear friends. And on five occasions she visited her aunt Sarah Wedgwood at Parkfields, near Barlaston. In May, as part of a party that included her brother Hensleigh, Emma went castle viewing for ten days. From Staffordshire they traveled south to Warwickshire, where they toured the fourteenth-century Warwick Castle on one day and on another visited a "Chapel," probably the Beauchamp Chapel of St. Mary's Church. They "saw a balloon go up," did a day's touring by carriage, probably along the Avon River, and finished their stay with a trip to the Norman-era Kenilworth Castle near Coventry. Two months later Emma was sightseeing once again, this time in the Yorkshire Dales. Her party visited the sixteenth-century Bolton Abbey, Malham Cove, Thorp Arch, and Sherwood Forest. Then, swinging west into Derbyshire and the Peak District, they stayed at Matlock and hiked to the top of High Tor, a limestone crag above the Derwent River. From Matlock they traveled home, completing an approximately 270-mile round trip.[40]

The diary also shows that she didn't have to be on the road to keep herself entertained. At Maer she had her archery—an activity at which she became quite good[41]—and her reading. A bookworm all her life, Emma recorded the titles of some twenty-two books that she read in 1824, including William Paley's *Moral Philosophy*, James Boswell's *Journal of the Tour of the Hebrides*, Madame de Staël's memoirs, and Voltaire's *The Age of Louis XV.* Financial accounts at the end of the 1824 diary suggest that Emma received £5 quarterly (amounting to some $417 today) and that in September that amount was raised to £7 10s (7 pounds 10 shillings). She spent her money on clothes and various small items, haircuts, shoe repairs, and her "sacrament." She borrowed and lent small sums to family members, and won and lost small sums at cards.[42]

Finally, the 1824 diary shows that there was a steady flow of guests to Maer Hall, including casual callers, dinner guests, and overnighters; indeed, there were guests in the house an astounding three out of every four days that Emma was in residence to record the event. Many of these guests were relatives—members of the John Wedgwood and Darwin families stand out here—but visits by dozens of nonrelatives and neighbors are also recorded. One special family gathering at Maer took place on the occasion of Emma's confirmation, along with her cousin Jessie Wedgwood, into the Church of England. Interestingly, given the evidence that Emma was quite devout in her Christianity at this time, her mother apparently put little emphasis on the ceremony. Bessy wrote to her oldest daughter Elizabeth:

As the confirmation will soon take place I think it will be right in Emma to be confirmed, and therefore I hope she will feel no objection.... [She should probably read a little on the subject,] but do not let her be alarmed at that, it will be but little and the subject is simple.... perhaps one ought not to press it, any more than as an opinion that it is better done than omitted, as it is better to conform to the ceremonies of our Church than to omit them, and one does not know that in omitting them we are not liable to sin.[43]

After the confirmation service, the usual Maer crowd of Elizabeth, Charlotte, Fanny, Emma, Joe, Harry, Frank, and Hensleigh were supplemented by their cousins Jessie and Robert Wedgwood and Susan and Catherine Darwin. Emma's diary records that this spirited group of siblings and cousins, ranging in age from thirty-one (Elizabeth) to fourteen (Catherine), enjoyed five straight days of "wicked times" and "revels."[44] (Apparently the revelers were exhausted by the sixth day, when Emma simply recorded a *"quiet evening!!!!"*) One day's fun involved acting out scenes from *The Merry Wives of Windsor*, ostensibly for Jos's and Bessy's entertainment. In a letter to Fanny Allen, Bessy reported on the successes of the various performers: Elizabeth, Harry, and Frank were rated as having acted "excellently" or "very well," Emma was "very good," and Susan Darwin was "very fair." Hensleigh and the languid Joe, however, were "very indifferent" in their parts. Adding to the young folks' excitement was the fact that twenty-five-year-old Harry and twenty-year-old Jessie were obviously in love and flirting so intensely that it was wearing Bessy out keeping an eye on them. She reported (very confidentially) to Fanny Allen:

> As for Harry, he is in the highest state of excitation just now you can conceive; (*private*) very much in love, and not very cruelly treated by his mistress.... [Jessie] is looking very pretty, very merry, sitting always by him, and very much taken up with him.... After all he may forget when she is gone, but I am sure there is danger in their being together, and I don't much like mounting guard every evening till it pleases them to go to bed, or watching them talking nonsense and playing "beggar my neighbour" or other such lover-like pastimes.... In short we are just now very flirtish, very noisy, very merry, and very foolish.[45]

Susan Darwin may also have had her cap set for cousin Harry on this occasion, but she ran a poor second to Jessie,[46] and if Emma felt at all enamored of the only male cousin *she* had at the gathering, Jessie's brother Robert, it went unrecorded. Her actual future husband, Charles Darwin, was not present, despite the fact that it was partridge season and he had a passion for hunting.[47] In all likelihood, Charles was at home beginning his sixth year as a boarder at the Reverend Samuel Case's Shrewsbury School, just across the Severn River from The Mount. Mind-numbing classes in Greek and Latin prevented him from visiting Maer, a spot that he loved as well as he did The Mount. Years later, in his *Autobiography*, Charles recorded his warm memories of childhood visits to Maer:

> Life there was perfectly free; the country was very pleasant for walking or riding, and in the evening there was much very agreeable conversation, not so personal as it generally is in large family parties, together with music. In the summer the whole family used often to sit on the steps of the old portico, with the flower-garden in front, and with the steep wooded bank, opposite the house, reflected in the lake, with here and there a fish rising or a waterbird paddling about. Nothing has left a more vivid picture on my mind than these evenings at Maer.[48]

A distinctly mediocre student, Charles would no doubt have much preferred to be part of the cousins' revels, but he remained hard at his studies at his father's insistence. Charles's older brother Erasmus was already at Christ's College, Cambridge, studying to follow in Dr. Robert's medical footsteps. A career decision had not yet been made for Charles, but his lackluster performance at boarding school had definitely become a cause for paternal concern. (Probably around this time, Dr. Robert made his famous remark to Charles: "You care for nothing but shooting, dogs, and rat-catching, and you will be a disgrace to yourself and all your family.")[49] Accordingly, in early 1825, apparently concluding that further time at the Shrewsbury School would be a waste of money, Robert decided to remove Charles at the end of the academic year. This he did and then set him to work practicing small-scale medicine on some of the local poor in preparation for formal medical training. In October 1825, Charles and Erasmus traveled to Edinburgh, the former to begin attending medical classes and the latter to do hospital practicum.[50] Coincidentally, just as the Darwin brothers were headed for Scotland, Jos and Bessy and their four daughters returned to England after an eight-month grand tour of the Continent.[51] The trip had taken Emma far beyond the familiarity of Paris, and she returned a seasoned international traveler with stories to tell.

3. A Woman of the World

TO BACKTRACK JUST A BIT, the plans for a Continental tour had begun to take shape at Maer during the fall of 1824. Joe and Frank were both finished with their university studies and at work at the potteries, and Frank at least was proving to have both interest and talent for the business. This freed Jos to take time off from the manufactory to escort his ladies—Bessy, Elizabeth, Charlotte, Fanny, and Emma—to Switzerland, where they planned to visit the Sismondis, and beyond.[1] Plans were hatched to cross the Channel early in the new year.

Unfortunately, 1825 got off to a dismal start for the Wedgwoods and Allens with two deaths. Caroline Wedgwood, John and Jane's middle girl, died of consumption in January, and at Cresselly, John Allen's wife, Gertrude, also died. The deaths had widespread and unsettling ripple effects.

One result was that John and Jane now became rather fanatically evangelical in their Anglicanism. In this they were following the example of Jane's sister Caroline Drewe, who had reacted to deaths in her immediate family by turning to Evangelicism's "state of mind [and] spirit of resolution constantly invigorated by prayer, meditation, and self-searching."[2] Jos was singularly unimpressed by this new religious fervor, and he confided to Bessy: "I am rather afraid of Evangelicism spreading amongst us, though I have some confidence in the genuine good sense of the Maerites for keeping it out, or if it must come for having the disease in a very mild form."[3]

A second result was that Emma and Fanny Allen felt compelled to move back to Cresselly to live with their widowed brother, assuming, no doubt correctly, that John could use help rearing his four small children. If morose Gertrude's death had deprived her children of their mother, it at least had the silver lining of clearing the way for their aunts to come home. In an unrelated coincidence, Jos's last spinster sister, Sarah Wedgwood, was also making preparations to move. After her sister Kitty's death in 1823, it was decided that Sarah should relocate from Parkfields to a spot nearer Maer Hall. In 1825 her new home, called Camp Hill, was under construction on Maer Heath.[4]

Jos and family left Maer for the Continent on February 7, 1825. They purchased two carriages in Paris, hired local drivers, and set off for Geneva where Jessie and Sismondi awaited them. While visiting the Sismondis, the travelers took advantage of Sis's social and literary connections and enjoyed meeting the cream of Genevois society at a swirl of balls, teas, and soirées. The travelers' ultimate destination, however, was Italy, and by early March Jos and the girls were ready to take to the road once more.[5]

The Wedgwood party was now down to five: Bessy, age sixty-one and frail—she had had a bad fall from a horse three years before and was probably also beginning to suffer from adult-onset epilepsy—did not feel strong enough to continue the trip and decided to stay on with Jessie and Sis. Though saddened to leave wife and mother behind, Jos and the girls left Geneva on the eighth of March under the care of a guide and travel agent identified only as Henri.[6] Henri proved to be a reliable and accomplished guide, but a somewhat somber man. One of the rare occasions that caused him to smile was when Jos, struggling to communicate in a foreign tongue, told him to lay out all of their things on the ceiling instead of on the floor.[7]

After crossing the Alps, the Wedgwood party traveled to Turin, where Emma and Fanny were singularly unimpressed by an original Michelangelo, but Emma admired a painting by Van Dyck. From there, they proceeded to Genoa on the Ligurian Sea and thence into Tuscany, enjoying some beautiful sea views on the way. All along the route, they were concerned about bandits, and Jos wrote reassuringly to Bessy in Geneva that he would "not run with danger out of haste . . . [and] was assured on good authority that the roads were perfectly safe from robbers."[8]

They took lodgings in Florence and began the round of churches and galleries. Using the Italian they already knew plus a phrase book provided by Bessy, they were able to communicate adequately, right down to "making out [the] washing bills." This linguistic practice was particularly profitable for Emma, who had a flair for languages and returned home quite fluent in

Italian. Florence was a bit of a flop, nonetheless, as both art and architecture failed to inspire much enthusiasm. It didn't help any that the weather was cold and rainy, which made it very difficult to appreciate a stroll in the Boboli Gardens as well as works of art displayed in dimly lit buildings. Emma did muster enough energy to admire Raphael's *St. John the Baptist* in the Uffizi, but the art and Roman and Etruscan antiquities in the nearby village of Fiesole were a disappointment.[9]

By now Jos was tiring of his Italian vacation, and he regularly sought out English newspapers to catch up on politics back home. Elizabeth wrote to her mother that "Papa . . . likes his reading room, and brings us capital accounts of Mr. Peel and Mr. Canning. They are really doing all one could wish them."[10] One wonders what papers the Whiggish Jos was reading and what these two Tory politicians, Foreign Secretary George Canning and Home Secretary Robert Peel, both serving under Lord Liverpool, were doing that drew Wedgwood approval. There are some interesting possibilities. Canning had just persuaded the British government to officially recognize the former Spanish colonies of Colombia, Mexico, and Buenos Aires. This action had multiple diplomatic and economic consequences. For one thing, it brought the newly formed South American nations under the British wing and gave them important protection from the imperialistic appetites of France and the members of the so-called Holy Alliance of Austria, Russia, and Prussia. Secondly, it thumbed Britain's nose at the United States government's growing sense of hemispheric hegemony as expressed in the Monroe Doctrine of 1823. Finally, and on the economic side, recognizing the emerging South American states provided a strong stimulus to British trade with that part of the world.[11] Doubtless, as a businessman, Jos was delighted with at least the third effect of Canning's South American policy.

For his part, Home Secretary Peel was busy reforming the British legal system, and it seems likely that Jos would have favored the repeal or expiration of several laws that restricted personal liberties.[12] Canning and Peel differed strongly, however, on one such issue: Catholic Emancipation, or whether or not to grant full political rights to Catholics, including the right to serve in Parliament. This question was undergoing intense debate in the House of Commons in the spring of 1825, and Canning was a strong supporter of such legislation, while Peel was a consistent opponent.[13] Precisely which man expressed Jos's sentiments on the issue is unclear. In any event, as he sat and read the English papers, Jos daydreamed about home. In May he wrote to Bessy from Sorrento on the Bay of Naples: "All these boasted places only confirm my preference of England and of Maer. . . . I remain at least as good a John Bull as I came out."[14]

From Florence the Wedgwoods set out for Rome, suffering a plague of bad inns on the way—typical when they were traveling cross-country. Once in the Eternal City, they took lodgings on the Piazza Barberini and began their sightseeing with St. Peter's Basilica and the Vatican's Sistine Chapel. Never hesitant to voice her opinions on art, including the works of the Old Masters, Emma weighed in on Michelangelo: "I never saw anything so hideous as that last judgment of Michael Angelo. I quite dislike him for wasting his talents on anything so ugly. [He] makes his women so hideous."[15] The travelers attended Mass in the Sistine Chapel and on another occasion watched Pope Leo XII officiate elsewhere. Overall, predictably for the Anglican/Unitarian Wedgwoods, they were unimpressed by all the Catholic "mummery." In general, however, Jos's spirits seem to have gone up during his time in Rome. When not making the rounds of churches and galleries, he liked to sit at his window and watch the strollers in the Piazza Barberini. Nonetheless, he reported to Bessy that he was surprised that the Allen sisters had enjoyed Rome, for

> the filthy habits of the people and the total neglect of the police as to cleanliness, make the town very disagreeable even for a man to walk about in, and intolerable I should have supposed for English women. As one instance, towards evening you every now and then hear vessels emptied of water, or some less innocent contents, from the windows of the houses, without notice; and as far as I could perceive without the precaution of looking whether the street was clear. . . . I am afraid you will think me a very smell-fungus, but I believe there has been more humbug about Italy than any other country in the world, and travellers have affected raptures that they have not felt.[16]

Throughout the trip, travel journals were being sent back to Maer, as well as to Bessy at the Sismondis'. Frank Wedgwood, left at home to run the potteries, responded in April with a journal of his own, full of deliberately mundane tales of rainstorms and the antics of the fox terrier Squib and other family pets, and flavored with just a hint of pique at being left out of the fun.

> Dear Fanny:
> [To] be even with you, [Joe and I] have agreed to keep journals too. I will give you an extract from mine: Monday. Went to Etruria as usual; rained a little; thought at one time of putting on my greatcoat, however it went off; cauliflowers boiled crisp. Tuesday. Squib went rather farther than usual

with me, viz. to Maer field-gate. Barbara would not drink. Wednesday. Got wet. Thursday. Ditto. Friday. Ditto twice. Saturday. Counted 21 carts going to market; the fire went out; told the boy to light it again, which he did; thought the damsons tasted salt; [Joe] said "No, it was fancy." [Joe's] journal I have not seen, but I believe it is conciser than mine. Apropos to journals it would save you much trouble if you were to write a family journal, for they must all be exactly the same; do not let me find "excessively" more than once a day in it.[17]

From Rome the tourists moved southeast, encountering more bad inns on the way. In Naples Emma enjoyed an opera featuring the magnificent bass voice of Luigi Lablanche. Unfortunately, she contracted a fever that kept her from ascending Vesuvius with the rest of the party. After some three weeks in and around Naples, the travelers returned to Rome, and shortly thereafter directed their carriages toward Milan and a reunion with Bessy, who had ventured out to meet them partway. They then returned to the Sismondis' home at Chêne, near Geneva, and enjoyed a cooling two-month stay in the environs of Lac Léman before returning to England in early September 1825. They arrived back at Maer on October first.[18]

The tourists were happy to be home, but parting from the Sismondis gave them all a pang. Alone with Sis in their now empty house, Jessie wrote to Bessy that she had "never felt a parting so much and so long before; there is no describing the desolation of the house—the very cats seemed to feel it. . . . I never wanted the girls so much. . . . [Their] angelic voices . . . still sing in my ears." Bessy responded lovingly and in kind, as did Emma, who had returned home more devoted than ever to her aunt.

> My Dearest Aunt Jessie:
>   I am very glad to have this little bit to tell you what longings I have to see you again since we parted. . . . [We] *will* come and see you again. You can't think with what pleasure I think of it, but I am afraid it will be a long time first. . . . I do hope that you will quite have got over our going away by the time you get this. I cannot bear to think of you as being melancholy. . . . You and my uncle and our charming visit at Chêne are never very long out of my mind. I think it is the happiest time I ever spent, and that is saying a great deal. I will enjoy it again some time.
>   Good-bye, my own aunt Jessie, Emma W.[19]

As it happened, it wasn't long at all before Emma returned to Chêne, but some interesting events took place at Maer before her next visit to the Continent. For one thing, Jos offered his nephew Allen Wedgwood, John and Jane's eldest son, the curacy of tiny St. Peter's Church just behind the Hall. Allen made a rather eccentric addition to the Wedgwoods of Maer. Not particularly healthy—either physically or psychologically, it would seem—Allen was obsessed with his diet, his bodily functions, and maintaining rigid control over his daily routine (tea precisely at half-past eight, please). Invited by his aunt Bessy to drop in at the Hall whenever it pleased him, Allen did so three times a day for years. (Jos could never bring himself to point out that sometimes they wished to be alone.) Despite all this, Allen was an amiable enough oddball that he got along adequately in his new parish. He was destined to officiate at the marriage of his Wedgwood-Darwin cousins Emma and Charles a decade and a half after his investiture.[20]

A second item of interest from Maer in the immediate post–grand tour period involved the family's active support for the abolition of slavery. Although the slave *trade* had been outlawed in 1807, owning slaves was still legal in some parts of the British Empire, and in the spring of 1826 the Wedgwoods were busy gathering signatures on antislavery petitions to be presented to Parliament. Bessy reported in a letter: "We are exceedingly interested in the abolition of slavery. Jos has exerted himself wonderfully for a man of his retired habits in getting up a County Petition, and has succeeded and it has been presented. We have also got up a local one from the four neighbouring parishes hereabouts; and I hope shall never let the matter rest."[21] As it turned out, their efforts would not bear legislative fruit until 1833, and then it would involve the first reformed Parliament, with Jos Wedgwood as an active abolitionist member.[22]

The spring of 1826 also saw the Sismondis come to England for a reciprocal round of family visits. When they returned to Geneva in the late fall, they took back with them the grown-up Dovelies—Emma and Fanny were then eighteen and twenty—as well as the girls' twenty-one-year-old cousin Edward Drewe. Always the solicitous mother, Bessy wrote to her daughters in January 1827:

I thank my two dear girls each for a letter. I need not say how gladly I received them, or how agreeable in every way was every thing they told me. . . . I am glad Emma is already about a music Master and I hope Fanny is getting a drawing one. . . . As for singing I have no objection to that neither provided you never fancy you can sing better than you do. . . . I am glad to hear you have got your warm cloaks as I imagine it is now pretty cold with you. . . . [Given the cost of clothes in England,] it is good encouragement for you to furnish yourself well at Geneva with what you are likely to want soon. You had better get a new Corset apiece whe[ther] you want it or not made carefully by a good work woman and take some pains to make them fit at first which will save you a great deal afterwards. Don't forget to pay regularly for your letters and keep your accounts exact this is more for one of you than the other. Your consciences will tell you which. I suppose the Redoubts [dances] are begun by this time pray my dearest Girls do not take cold there and do not go with a cold already caught. Don't wait for your dear indulgent Uncle or Aunt to say "you had better refrain," but do it of yourselves if it appears necessary and save them what I know they will feel to be an unpleasant exertion. . . . I wish you would generally or always say something to, or of, your Aunt Sarah [Wedgwood] in your letter, she always enquires very kindly of you, and I should like to have something to say from you to her. . . . For my own pleasure, I should like to hear from you every day. I shall be quite satisfied if you don't let us be more than a fortnight without hearing from you. . . . Last night's paper spoke of the Duke of York as [having died], so you may get your blacks ready, which will be very convenient at the redoubts as you have your gauzes ready. . . . God bless you my dear Girls.[23]

As Bessy's letter shows, Emma and Fanny had barely gotten settled in Geneva before King George III's second son, Frederick Augustus, Duke of York, turned up his toes on January 5, 1827. In a show of respect for such a royal death, Britons at home and abroad were expected to go into some degree of mourning, thus the maternal advice to "get your blacks ready." This change of costume did not stop the young Wedgwoods from attending a series of local balls and dancing their feet off—to the delight of Aunt Jessie and Sismondi.[24] The quality of Emma's and Fanny's dance partners depended on whether the ball in question was a pay-as-you-go affair or a private by-invitation-only soirée. At a dance with a six-franc admission fee, Emma reported: "The first man I danced with was very disagreeable and vulgar, which put me rather in despair for the rest of the ball; however the rest of my partners were very tidy, so I liked it very well." At both private and public parties, the Dovelies often rubbed shoulders with the crown prince of Denmark, later King Christian VIII, who was also enjoying Geneva's social season.[25]

Emma and Fanny thoroughly enjoyed their stay with their aunt Jessie, and the delight was mutual, as always. They also grew closer to Sismondi, although Emma disliked some of Sis's Continental mannerisms ("I am afraid he will never leave off kissing our hands") and Fanny thought he was a most "anxious-looking man." For his part, Sismondi showered the girls with compliments—and white lies, like telling the rather plain Fanny that she was very pretty—and encouraged them to develop their skills at clever conversation, a talent sure to attract suitors. Fanny and Emma had inherited too much of a "disposition to silence" from their taciturn father to suit the genial Sismondi.[26]

As Bessy had hoped, Emma did find a music master in Geneva: a German whom she described as interested only in the music of his homeland and who played it "as if he was mad."[27] The precise identity of this person is unknown. Many years later Emma's daughter Henrietta Litchfield wrote, without specifying dates and places, that her mother had had music lessons from both Ignaz Moscheles and Frédéric Chopin. An April 1832 period of instruction in London by Moscheles can be traced,[28] but evidence of tutelage by Chopin is more elusive. Some two years younger than Emma—and Polish, not German—Chopin did not venture out of his native land except for visits to Prussia and Austria until he relocated to Paris in 1831. Thus we can be sure that he did not cross paths with Emma during her Continental trips of 1818, 1825, or 1826–27. Similarly, it appears certain that they did not meet in London in the summer of 1837 during Chopin's first visit to England, since the composer was vacationing incognito. It is remotely possible that they met and that lessons were taught during Emma's three-week jaunt to Paris in May 1838, but the odds seem long, given the brevity of her stay, the fact that she was busy sightseeing, and the additional fact that Chopin too was rather busy at the time—falling in love with the novelist George Sand.[29] In sum, while Mrs. Litchfield presumably knew what she was talking about, Emma's connection with Chopin is extremely hard to verify.

In late May 1827, Jos traveled to Geneva to personally retrieve Fanny and Emma. He chose as traveling companions Caroline and Charles Darwin. Charles went only as far as Paris on this, his one and only trip to the Continent, and then he returned home. Caroline Darwin continued on with her uncle even though she had always been somewhat intimidated by his stony demeanor. They reached Geneva without incident and joined the family party for a few weeks' stay that included sightseeing side trips out of Geneva. The amusing adventures during one such trip—into the Haute-Savoie region of France, east-southeast of Geneva—were recorded in Fanny's travel journal.[30]

[June 21] When we arrived at Taninge[s] we found Sismondi who had gone the right road waiting for us, after having stopped many times on the road to see if we were coming. We waited in the carriages to give the horses a feed of corn. We had about a hundred children about us with an old mad man at their head so we were very glad to leave the place.

[June 22] Found when we got up that Edward [Drewe] had joined us at four in the morning. After breakfast we mounted our mules & set off to the valley of Sixt [-Fer-à-Cheval]. . . . Caroline & I had three tumbles between us off a toad of a starting mule, the saddles we had were so insecure that the least thing would throw one off, they were merely a sort of pad with a stick for a stirrup.

[June 23] It was settled that we should go home because M[onsieur] Sismondi had the earache, we were to return by [St.-Jeoire]. The first part of our ride was the same as before. To Taninge[s] we then followed the course of the river to the right through a very beautiful country, rich in trees with fine mountains. After riding some way Aunt Jessie gained for us that we should have one more day, so we turned off toward Bellevau[x] [while the Sismondis presumably went on to Geneva], the guide promising that we should soon come to an Inn: we went on riding for a very long time after he always saying that we should arrive in a moment till at last we passed the Inn without his knowing: so he must have told us that lye to persuade us to go on another day with him. We turned back however, very cross & hungry, when we came to the Inn we found that the master & mistress were gone out & there was no bread in the house & we might not have any bacon because it was fast day. However, their maid made us some fried potatoes & omlet & we washed the plates & glasses, & had an excellent dinner. . . . We came on to Bellevau[x] in the evening. The Valley of B. is very fine, wild & rugged & barren. When we got there we rode down to M. Farras' house where M. Sis had written to ask for beds; when we came there we found that Mr. F. was gone to the mountains & had left no orders so that we were obliged to come to the Inn where we found one tolerable bed in which Papa slept [giving] his coats to us & we slept in the barn. The side of the barn was very open so that it let in a good deal of wind but we kept ourselves warm till near morning with a quantity of clothes, the worst of it was that we were kept awake half the night by a host of fleas & we had plenty of noise all round the mules beneath us eating their hay the pigs grunting next to them; our guides snoring the other side of the partition, & a cat & her kittens running around the barn.

[June 24] The road was not pretty this day, we dined at Beage [Boège?] & had an exceedingly hot ride home with the flies tormenting the horses so that we were nearly kicked off. We were very glad to get off our mules at Chine at seven o'clock.[31]

The Wedgwood-Darwin party set off for home on June 27, taking a north-northwest route along the Rhine. Fanny's travel journal recorded sights of glaciers and beautiful mountain scenes in Switzerland, picturesque castles and fine riparian views in Germany, and, on the downside, the steamboat running aground in the tidal waters of the Lower Rhine/Lek River. From Rotterdam they traveled south into Belgium, taking time for some museuming in Antwerp, where Fanny thought the Rubenses and Van Dykes were "very good," while Emma professed to be scandalized by one painting by Rubens showing two of his wives *and* a mistress. They then proceeded to Ostend for the ferry to Margate. They were back on English soil by July 28 and at home at Maer on the thirtieth.[32] After taking stock of her daughters, Bessy wrote approvingly to Jessie:

> I think you and my kind Sismondi have done them good, but I don't perceive any marks of spoilation that I rather expected from both your kindness. I perceive that they converse with much more ease than they did, and are quite as unaffected. Emma is a little bronzed, but Fanny is one degree nearer prettiness than she was; but I hope she will never make the mistake of thinking that she is pretty.[33]

The returning travelers found a large group of family visitors at Maer. In addition to the resident Wedgwoods, there were the Mackintoshes, Harriet Surtees, and Caroline Drewe. Sir James Mackintosh was hard at work on his *History of England* and was also dealing with the disappointment of not getting a cabinet post in Canning's coalition government. As a poor second choice, Mackintosh accepted a position as a privy councillor, as much out of his need of money as anything else. In the event, the Canning ministry was short-lived: it ended with the prime minister's rather sudden death in August 1827. After taking his position on the council, Mackintosh and his family relocated to Clapham in Bedfordshire, reducing considerably the bustle at Maer.[34]

Other family changes were also in the works, particularly affecting the sons in the extended family. All of the Wedgwood boys were now out of university and moving into their careers. Harry and Hensleigh—the latter being the only real scholar of his generation—were both going into law. Joe and Frank, on the other hand, were being formally incorporated into the family business, and by the fall of 1827 they had been made one-quarter partners in the potteries, with Jos retaining the remaining half interest and John having no shares but still enjoying a lifetime allowance. The name of the business was duly changed to Josiah Wedgwood and Sons.[35]

On the Darwin side of the family, other career decisions were being made, sometimes by trial and error. By early 1828 Erasmus (Ras for short) had completed his medical training and was ready to take his Bachelor of Medicine exams at Cambridge. Charles, however, had proved to be a complete failure at medicine, detesting most of his courses at the University of Edinburgh (those he attended, that is) and reacting badly to the horrors of pre-anesthetic surgery. Years later he recorded the experience in his *Autobiography*: "I . . . saw two very bad operations, one on a child, but I rushed away before they were completed. Nor did I ever attend again, for hardly any inducement would have been strong enough to make me do so; this being long before the blessed days of chloroform." Charles's reaction probably was literally visceral, judging from family comments that he had a weak stomach even as a teenager.[36]

Since leaving Edinburgh in April 1827, Charles had passed much of his time touring in Scotland and Ireland, besides making the trip to Paris with his uncle Jos. He had met James Mackintosh at Maer, and the two men had parted with mutually positive impressions. He had also spent a considerable amount of time visiting and hunting at Woodhouse, the Shropshire country estate of William Mostyn Owen. Squire Owen was as fond of Charles as the latter was of the shooting, and besides, visits to Woodhouse were sweetened by the presence of the squire's two daughters. Sarah, five years older than Charles, and the even more charming Fanny, just two years Charles's senior, were social butterflies who called eligible young men like Charles "shootables" and enjoyed being outrageously flirtatious. At eighteen, Charles was an easy target for their attentions, and by the end of the year he was thoroughly infatuated with the dark-eyed Fanny Owen.[37]

With medicine a nonstarter, Charles's career path was once again a problem. No doubt Dr. Robert could sense his early prediction—"shooting, dogs, and rat-catching"—about to come true. A paternal decision was needed, and it was forthcoming: Charles would go to Cambridge for a classical education and preparation for a career in the Church. After a bit of thought and reading of Anglican theology, Charles decided he had neither philosophical nor moral objections to a priestly career—although no burning desire for one, either—and so he acquiesced in his father's wishes. A country parish, after all, need not be too strenuous, and it would offer opportunities for family life, a bit of shooting, and even nature studies in the spirit of the Reverend William Paley's "natural theology"—the belief that one could worship God through the study of his creation. Confident that he could pledge his faith in the Church's Thirty-Nine Articles when the time came to be ordained, Charles entered Christ's College, Cambridge, in January 1828.[38]

The years 1828 and 1829 passed in a relatively uneventful fashion for the young Wedgwoods. All of Jos and Bessy's children were now grown, and although none had yet married, this did not bother their mother much—at least not with regard to the boys. Bessy did write to Jessie Sismondi in mid-1828 that her hopes of seeing her daughters "happily settled in life diminish every year, and are now grown very flat." In their "manners to men," Charlotte was "too distant, and Fanny a little stiff." Elizabeth was "agreeable . . . but [lacking in] personal attraction." Her mother judged Emma to be the most popular of the sisters, with manners toward potential suitors that were "easy and undesigning without coquetry."[39] But if the girls themselves shared Bessy's flat view of their prospects, it was not mentioned in their letters or diaries, and during visits to London they reveled in the social life of the capital.[40]

It does seem likely, however, that by this time Bessy's view of her own present and future condition had grown somewhat flat. In her mid-sixties, she was increasingly frail. Her declining health had made it impossible for her to accompany Jos and the girls on their Italian jaunt four years earlier, and in the summer of 1829 she took a serious turn for the worse. While visiting her niece Lady Gifford (Caroline Drewe's oldest daughter) in London, Bessy suffered another epileptic seizure, severe enough that at first it was feared it might prove fatal. Eventually Bessy regained sufficient strength to return to Maer, but her health would never be the same, and she was destined to have repeated seizures as she grew older.[41]

If Bessy Wedgwood's prospects were flat, her sister Kitty Mackintosh's were far worse. For Kitty, life had become a hell of loneliness and desperation. Having grown estranged from her preoccupied husband during the writing of his *History*, Kitty became further withdrawn after their move to Clapham and Mac's return to politics. Part of Kitty's problem was Mackintosh's continued inattention, but another part was the fact that Mary Rich—the oldest child of Mac's first marriage, whose husband Claudius Rich had recently died—had come to live with them. The two women did not get along, and the constant friction exacerbated Kitty's depression. In early 1829 Bessy committed her sisterly concerns to paper: "I have now and then a nameless fear about Kitty which makes me wish she should be soothed by her family as much as possible, and when I think how short a time we may some of us have together, I am desirous above all things that our last years may pass in harmony and affection." She was right to worry. Kitty had indeed had enough; in the fall of 1829 she left Mackintosh without a word and fled to Geneva to be with the Sismondis. His marriage in a shambles and his own health none too good, Mackintosh apparently made an effort to go to Kitty in Geneva, but it was too little, too late. Kitty's life was ended by a stroke in the spring of 1830.[42] Fanny Wedgwood, in London at the time for the social season, noted in her diary on May 13, 1830: "Heard of Aunt Mackintoshes death. She had an attack of Apoplexy on [April] 30th I think & died on the 6th without ever speaking."[43] The daughter of a tyrannical father and the wife of an inattentive husband, Kitty's unhappiness was over at the age of sixty-five.

The gloom cast by Kitty's death was relieved to some extent by family romances and exciting events in the world of politics. Beginning with affairs of the heart, in October 1830 the first of Jos and Bessy's children married. After years of courting and flirting, Harry had won his cousin Jessie's heart at last. Although Jos was uneasy about the meager marriage settlement he could offer the couple, an "iffy" £400 a year, or about $33,000 today, he gave the union his blessing. After their marriage, which set a pattern for their generation—the extended Allen-Wedgwood-Darwin family circle would eventually contain four first-cousin unions—Harry and Jessie settled into life at Etruria Hall.[44]

In the political realm, there was a change of monarchs and continued agitation for parliamentary and franchise reform. King George IV died at Windsor on June 26, 1830, following a series of strokes and stomach hemorrhages. His health had been declining for some time, possibly from the effects of porphyria, the same disease that had led to his father's madness. By late 1829 George IV was wheelchair-bound, partially incontinent, and heavily dosed with laudanum (tincture of opium).[45] A rather dismal specimen at the end of a life of overeating and licentiousness—one of five "fat brothers, with [an] astonishing record of gambling, gluttony, and cast-off mistresses"[46]—George IV was not well thought of by his subjects despite his undeniable intelligence and wit, and the mourning that followed his death was perfunctory at best. Charles Greville, Clerk of the Privy Council under both George IV and later Queen Victoria, described the old king's passing and his replacement by William IV in these words:

> The [new] King and his proceedings occupy all attention, and nobody thinks any more of the late King than if he had been dead fifty years, unless it be to abuse him and to rake up all his vices and misdeeds. . . . King George had not been dead three days before everybody discovered that he was no loss, and King William a great gain. Certainly nobody ever was less regretted than the late King, and the breath was hardly out of his body before the press burst forth in full cry against him.[47]

The sixty-five-year-old King William IV got off to a good start. Despite being another of those "fat brothers," he was initially more popular, and distinctly more entertaining, than his predecessor. William shed few tears for his departed brother, and those he shed were probably feigned. At the funeral, William and other "mourners" were publicly "as merry as grigs." Equally unfeeling was William's behavior following his first speech to the Privy Council. After speaking of his brother in reverently hushed tones and "with all the semblance of feeling," William blurted out as he went to sign the declaration to the dead king, "This is a damned bad pen you have given me." The new monarch, soon referred to as the "sailor king" because of his navy background, had little use for ceremony or etiquette. He went out for walks alone, gave visiting monarchs lifts around London in his carriage, and, in the words of Washington Irving, then secretary of the United States Legation in London, had "an easy and natural way of wiping his nose with the back of his forefinger, a relic of his middy habits."[48]

Altogether, "Billy IV" was initially an easy king for the average Briton to like. Unlike many of his subjects in 1830, however, he was not particularly concerned about governmental reform. While more kindly inclined toward the Whigs than George IV had been, William began his reign by placing his trust in the existing Tory government led by the Duke of Wellington. In the general election that followed the change of monarchs, the Tories retained parliamentary control, but they were soon to be undone by their general intransigence on the issue of reform.[49]

To put the demands for reform in historical perspective, the winds of political change had picked up force in the late 1820s. One significant example was the attempt by the Whigs in 1828 to permanently repeal the seventeenth-century laws that made membership in the Church of England a prerequisite for holding public office. To a great extent this move was forced by political unrest in Ireland, with its huge Roman Catholic population. Although many Tories, including the Duke of Wellington and Sir Robert Peel, were not overly pleased at the thought of Catholic Emancipation, it was clearly preferable to revolution in Ireland and therefore was duly enacted in 1829.[50]

Another Whig agenda item that gained support at about the same time was parliamentary reform. The Parliament that took office after George IV's death was a bit more open than previous governments to the idea of reform measures, including redistricting to reduce the number of "rotten" and "pocket" boroughs, and also some extension of the franchise. Thus, when Wellington as prime minister expressed his personal opposition to reform, it produced an erosion of cohesion even within his own party. By November

1830 the Tories had lost control, and their government resigned. This opened the way for a Whig government under Earl Grey to act on its agenda for parliamentary change.[51]

Grey's government—which included Sir James Mackintosh as a member of the East India Company's Board of Control, another disappointing appointment for Mac, but one he accepted because of the £1,500 annual salary—quickly put together a Reform Bill that was introduced in early 1831. The scope of the proposed changes proved too great for a good number of MPs, however, and when the bill began to be carved up in committee, Grey's cabinet decided to take their case for reform to the voters and called for the dissolution of Parliament. It was in that 1831 election that Jos Wedgwood made his first bid for public office, running—true to his liberal tendencies—as a reform candidate.[52]

Jos had two major obstacles to overcome as he wrestled with the question of whether or not to go into politics. First, he was concerned about Bessy's health and the possible ill effects of moving her to London during parliamentary sessions. On this point, Robert Darwin was reassuring:

> I think Bessy would feel uneasy if you were not to stand & might suspect your motive—and, indeed, if after one session you find any real inconvenience, either on her account, or on any other, you may withdraw from Parliament. If you are elected there must be a serious conversation with your wife that she must lead a quiet regular life in London because when she has been there hitherto [for family visits and shopping] she has I suppose been too much excited, to use the fashionable expression.[53]

The second point of concern was Jos's taciturn nature. Could a man of such reserved personality effectively sell himself to the voters? In the end, this flaw probably weighed rather heavily against him. Running against a Tory candidate sponsored by the aristocrat George Granville Leveson-Gower—soon to be created Duke of Sutherland and the controlling force in the contested "rotten" borough of Newcastle—Jos could do little better with his campaign message than to say: "My principles are those of the Reform Bill. If they are yours, you will send me to represent you. Otherwise, not." The voters opted for the "not."[54]

Understandably, Bessy and the family were disappointed by Jos's defeat, although they consoled themselves with the fact that not much money had been spent on the election and with the thought that Jos would probably run again in the future—this time for a seat from Stoke-on-Trent once reform had been achieved. During after-campaign speeches, Jos was congratulated by his supporters for running, and Harry and Frank Wedgwood were praised for being enthusiastic canvassers. Indeed, one man told Frank that if he had been campaigning on his own behalf rather than for his father, he would have been elected.[55]

Jos's loss was more the exception than the rule for reform candidates in the 1831 election. Both urban and rural voters tended to favor reformers, and the result was a comfortable majority for the Whigs in the House of Commons. A second Reform Bill was immediately introduced, this time with the predictable final approval in the Commons. Unfortunately, the Commons-approved bill encountered fatal resistance in the much more conservative House of Lords, failing to pass its second reading by 41 votes. In response to the bill's defeat, there were reform riots in Bristol and elsewhere, adding to ongoing industrial disputes and other sorts of unrest.[56]

Grey's government launched its third Reform Bill in December 1831. In order to ensure the bill's safe passage through the Lords, Grey persuaded the king to put the royal prerogative of creating new peers—in this case, reform-minded peers—at the prime minister's disposal. This tactic eventually succeeded in convincing the Lords that passing the reform measure was preferable to having the upper house flooded with new Whig peers, and the king formally assented to the Great Reform Act on June 7, 1832. The act extended the franchise somewhat and significantly redistributed parliamentary seats in favor of growing urban areas. As his family had hoped, Jos Wedgwood was elected on his second try and became an MP from the reformed borough of Stoke-on-Trent in December 1832.[57] On the sixteenth of that month Emma wrote to her aunt Jessie: "Mamma has been saying she meant to write to you every day since the election, but I think our news will be quite flat if we leave it any longer, and now I am afraid we shall not be the first to tell you that Papa was elected by a handsome majority." Bessy was delighted with the outcome, which she thought would give the family a boost in status.[58]

But if 1832 ended on a political high note, it had in fact been a bittersweet year during which the Wedgwood circle had celebrated several marriages but also suffered through two deaths. And in the midst of the nuptials and funerals, one member of the extended family had sailed off on a voyage around the world. For these important events, we must backtrack to the latter half of 1831.

4. A Traveling Cousin, a Doveley's Death, and the Abolition of Slavery

IN HIS travel journal for December 27, 1831, Charles Darwin recorded:

A beautiful day, accompanied by the long wished for E wind.—Weighed anchor at 11 oclock & with difficulty tacked out.—The Commissioner Capt Ross sailed with us in his Yatch.—The Capt Sullivan & myself took a farewell luncheon on mutton chops & champagne, which may I hope excuse the total absence of sentiment which I experienced on leaving England.—We joined the Beagle about 2 oclock outside the Breakwater,—& immediately with every sail filled by a light breeze we scudded away at the rate of 7 or 8 knots an hour.—I was not sick that evening but went to bed early.[1]

With those words Charles marked his departure on the adventure of a lifetime: an around-the-world voyage of exploration on the Royal Navy survey ship HMS *Beagle*. His university years over—he had received his B.A. in June 1831, graduating a respectable tenth out of the 178 men who had not gone in for an Honours degree[2]—Charles was now making a rather large diversion from his professed objective of ordination and life as a country clergyman. Both Charles and his extended family viewed the trip, which was projected to last two to three years, as simply postponing, not evading, a career in the Church. The invitation to join the *Beagle*'s crew had come from out of the blue.[3]

At the end of August 1831, one of Charles's Cambridge professors and his primary scientific mentor, the Reverend John Stevens Henslow, had written to inform him that an offer was on its way for him to travel as captain's companion and naturalist on the *Beagle*. The ship's commander, Robert FitzRoy, was aristocratic, unmarried, and concerned about the psychological effects of the social isolation he would face as captain during a long voyage. FitzRoy's fears for his personal sanity were based on firsthand experience of two suicides. The *Beagle's* previous commander, Pringle Stokes, had shot himself during the ship's first South American survey—thereby affording Robert his initial command at age twenty-three. And FitzRoy's own uncle Lord Castlereagh had a mental breakdown while serving as foreign secretary under Lord Liverpool and in August 1822 had ended it all by slitting his throat. FitzRoy's plan to safeguard his mental state was to add a supernumerary to the *Beagle's* crew in the form of a naturalist and gentleman messmate. Darwin fit the bill exactly.[4]

Paternal permission for Charles to go was not automatically forthcoming. Understandably, Dr. Robert Darwin felt that if this wasn't actually deliberate procrastination at the very brink of Charles's church career, it certainly had all the earmarks. Concluding that the voyage was a "wild scheme" and a "useless undertaking" that would be "disreputable to [Charles's] character as a Clergyman," Dr. Robert said no. He did leave one way out, however. As Charles was on his way to Maer for some partridge hunting, why not ask his uncle Jos Wedgwood? If levelheaded Jos thought the voyage was a good idea, the doctor would relent.[5]

To Charles's delight, Uncle Jos's opinion on the matter was the exact opposite of Dr. Robert's. Jos thought the natural history aspect of the voyage would be entirely suitable for a future clergyman; indeed, the spiritual value of such studies was a primary postulate of William Paley's *Natural Theology*. Labeling Charles "a man of enlarged curiosity," Jos gave the trip his blessing.[6] True to his word, Dr. Darwin dropped his objections at once and opened his purse for the necessary pretrip shopping. FitzRoy's personal approval of Charles took an interview or two—as a student of physiognomy, FitzRoy thought the shape of Darwin's nose indicated a lack of energy and determination—but the Tory captain soon grew to like his Whig future messmate. An official request was sent to the Admiralty adding Charles to the crew, and he was on his way. The *Beagle's* route would take them to South America, where FitzRoy was charged with mapping both coasts and the passages of Tierra del Fuego, and then home across the Pacific with stops at the Galapagos Islands, Tahiti, New Zealand, Australia, and the Cape of Good Hope. It was a trip that would change Charles's life, and the future of science.[7]

But how, one might ask, could Charles ever have qualified for a scientific position aboard the *Beagle* when his university studies had been aimed toward a career in the Church? The answer is that in addition to his classical, mathematical, and theological studies—which mostly took the form of cramming for exams: Charles was a typical undergraduate—he was exposed to a great deal of science at Cambridge, some in the lecture hall, but much of it informally. From Henslow's lectures he learned botany, including the physiology, dissection, field collection, and classification of plants. From William Whewell and others he gained an appreciation for the philosophy of science. From Adam Sedgwick he learned geology during a crash field course in northern Wales in August 1831. And from his own experiences in entomology or "beetling" Charles learned dissection, description, and perseverance. None of his old teachers considered Charles "a *finished* Naturalist," but for the *Beagle*'s voyage, he was "amply qualified for collecting, observing, & noting any thing worthy to be noted in Natural History."[8] And so the not-quite-finished naturalist sailed out of Plymouth Sound on December 27, 1831. That same day his cousins Charlotte, Fanny, and Emma Wedgwood were in London enjoying tea at the Roehampton estate of yet another cousin, Harriet, Lady Gifford. They were in high spirits because they were in town for a wedding: Hensleigh Wedgwood had finally proposed to Fanny Mackintosh.[9]

For Fanny and Hensleigh the path to the altar had been neither fast nor easy. Although they had been in love for some time, and had regularly seen each other both openly and "by accident," serious obstacles had arisen that kept marriage just out of reach. For one thing, Sir James—aided and abetted by his widowed daughter Mary Rich—was in no mood to lose Fanny's companionship and had written a letter in 1830 warning Hensleigh off. The situation was complicated by the fact that Hensleigh seemed to have decidedly low prospects for making a living. Although he had qualified as a barrister-at-law, he showed no signs of working particularly hard at his legal career *and* he had turned down Papa Jos's offer of a partnership in the pottery. Two things were needed to move the romance toward marriage: an advocate who had Mac's ear and a steady job for Hensleigh.[10]

The advocate came in the form of Fanny Allen, aunt to both Hensleigh and Fanny Mackintosh. She interceded with Mary Rich and Mac, arguing in favor of the lovers' engagement and against overzealous chaperoning. She also urged Mac to use his political connections to help Hensleigh obtain a civil service position and thus a steady salary. This Mac did—simultaneously recommending his own son, Robert, for a government job—and although the position of police magistrate that was finally offered to Hensleigh was neither as prestigious nor as lucrative as he had hoped, at £800 per year, or some $67,000 today, it did allow him to pop the question.[11]

Fanny and Hensleigh were duly married on January 10, 1832, if not without a few hitches and close calls. First, there was a problem with the churches. Though the couple had bought a house in Langham Place and planned to move there after the wedding, residency requirements prevented a ceremony in that parish's All Souls' Church. To Fanny's dismay, they had to settle for Hensleigh's old parish and the less fashionable venue of St. Andrew's Holborn. Second, and more serious, the day before the wedding Hensleigh very nearly convinced himself that he was too unwell to proceed. After consulting his doctor, however, and being told that "he was quite well" and should simply "eat a chop and drink a glass of wine" and get on with it, Hensleigh rallied—though he did conserve energy by asking Fanny to take charge of buying her own ring. And finally, Fanny's wedding gown was delivered late and she had to be married in Fanny Wedgwood's bridesmaid dress.[12] (One wonders what the latter Fanny wore.) Everything worked out satisfactorily in the end, however, as recorded in Fanny Wedgwood's diary:

> [January 10] Hensleigh & Fanny were married at St. Andrews Holborn. After a fine breakfast of more than 30 people, they went to Hasting. We then set off with all the cousins ... & had a very merry dinner.[13]

Following their honeymoon, the newlyweds set up house in Langham Place along with Sir James and Robert Mackintosh, and Mary Rich. This cohabitation was Mac's price for his approval of the marriage and his safeguard against losing the daily companionship of his beloved Fanny. It was a tactic that worked, albeit for a short time only. Unhappily, the close-knit father and daughter were soon to be separated by death.[14]

As the spring progressed, it became obvious that Cupid was only getting started with the young Wedgwoods. Two days after Fanny and Hensleigh's wedding, Charles Langton, the vicar of Onibury, Shropshire, proposed to Charlotte Wedgwood and was accepted, despite the fact that they had known each other for only two weeks. Charlotte's little sister Fanny was overjoyed, calling January twelfth "the happiest day of my life" and noting that the entire family was "in a perfect extacy."[15] The whirlwind courtship ended with Charlotte and Charles's marriage on March 22.[16]

And last but not least, Frank Wedgwood got caught up in the swirl of courting and marrying and proposed to Frances Mosley, the daughter of the rector of Rollestone in Staffordshire. They met at a ball and for Frank it was love at the first sight of his own blonde Fanny (hereafter referred to as "Fanny Frank," in order to distinguish her from "Fanny Hensleigh," Fanny Wedgwood, and Aunt Fanny Allen). In contrast to her delight at Charlotte's engagement, however, Fanny Wedgwood made a flat and almost ominous diary entry about Frank's choice: "February 13—Frank came home engaged to Miss Mosley." Other members of the family shared these misgivings about the match. Caroline Darwin wrote to Charles on board the *Beagle* that "Franks Miss Mosly by all accounts has nothing very pleasing about her," while Susan Darwin reported that Fanny Mosley was "very fat & not at all pretty, but exceedingly good tempered & a famous *scrattle* [obsessive housekeeper] so I daresay she will make him an excellent wife."[17] In the long run, the misgivings proved correct. Time would show that Frank had acted impulsively, and the marriage, which began on April 26, 1832, was not to be a happy one, although it would last for forty-two years.[18]

On April 5, 1832, just after the *Beagle's* arrival in Rio de Janeiro, Charles Darwin received a series of letters reporting on the various engagements and weddings.[19] He was interested, of course, in the fates of his cousins, but it was a wedding outside the family that interested—and pained—him most. As we have seen, Charles had been smitten for some time with yet another Fanny, namely Fanny Owen of Woodhouse. In December 1828, while at home between terms at Cambridge, Charles had described Fanny Owen to his cousin W. D. Fox as "the prettiest, plumpest, Charming personage that Shropshire possesses, ay & Birmingham too."[20] Charles and Miss Owen had played lovers' games in conversation and correspondence, with Fanny addressing him as her Postillion and calling herself his Housemaid. They also shared the dubious distinction of having been caught lying full length in the Woodhouse strawberry fields gorging together on the ripe fruit.[21] Surely, if any face arose in the traveler's imagination when he dreamed of home and a wife, it must have been that of Fanny Owen.

Thus it came as a heart-wrenching shock when he received word from his sisters that plump, pretty Miss Owen was not going to wait for him, but instead had become engaged to Robert Myddelton Biddulph, a rising politician whose family lived in Chirk Castle ten miles from Woodhouse. From Rio, a sobbing Charles wrote this rambling note back to Caroline:

> I don't know: it positively is an inconvenient fashion this marrying: Maer won't be half the place it was, & as for Woodhouse, if Fanny was not perhaps at this time Mrs Biddulph, I would say poor dear Fanny till I fell to sleep.—I feel much inclined to philosophize but I am at a loss what to think or say;

whilst really melting with tenderness I cry my dearest Fanny why I demand, should I distinctly see the sunny flower garden at Maer; on the other hand, but I find that my thought & feelings & sentences are in such a maze, that between crying & laughing I wish you all good night.[22]

Presumably Fanny Owen meant to provide comfort to the distraught Charles when she wrote to him herself on the first of March assuring him in her rather affected style "that no change of *name* or condition can ever alter or diminish the feelings of sincere regard & affection I have for *years* had for you, and as soon as you return from your wanderings, I shall be *much offended* if one of your first rides is not to see *me* at Chirk Castle." It didn't help. Charles's heart was broken and he was far from home. To compensate, he concentrated harder than ever on the wildlife of Brazil.[23]

Interspersed with weddings that winter and spring of 1832, the remaining Maer spinsters, Elizabeth, Fanny, and Emma, enjoyed a diverse mix of social, religious, and political activities, both in London and at home in Stafford-shire. During their London visit for Hensleigh's wedding, Fanny and Emma went shopping at the Covent Garden market and elsewhere, dined with nu-merous friends and relations (in particular seeing their cousins Erasmus Dar-win and Thomas Wedgwood several times), attended a christening party for another cousin, and admired the art at the National Gallery. Emma indulged her love of politics on a few occasions by going to the Ventilator, the ladies' gallery high above the chamber of the House of Commons, and listening to the debates.[24] On January 26 she heard exhortations for a day of national prayer and fasting in connection with the spreading cholera epidemic. That deadly disease had reached England in 1831 and, as the diarist Charles Gre-ville noted, it was terrifying partly because it was so poorly understood:

> [January 25, 1832] News came yesterday that the cholera had got within three miles of Edinburgh, and to show the fallacy of any theory about it, and the inutility of the prescribed precautions, at one place (Newport, I think) one person in five of the whole population was attacked, though there was no lack of diet, warmth, and clothing for the poor. This disease escapes from all speculation, so partial and eccentric is its character.[25]

Among Emma's companions in the Commons' Ventilator was Mary Rich, who was becoming increasingly obsessed with religion and who told Emma stories about attending evangelical meetings where people, including Mrs. Rich's friend Emily Cardale, spoke in tongues. Among the leaders of these prayer meetings was Edward Irving, a phenomenally popular preacher who would soon be thrown out of the Scottish Church for heresy, only to turn around and found his own Catholic Apostolic Church. Evangelical manifestations of the Spirit were too much for commonsensical Emma to brook, however, and she feared that Miss Cardale might "become quite mad soon." Aunt Fanny Allen agreed. After actually accompanying Mary Rich to an Irving prayer service and listening to the evangelical ministers and Miss Cardale "raving," Aunt Fanny wrote the whole thing off as the "extravagance of minds not quite sane." Mrs. Rich, on the other hand, thought every word had been "commanded by the Spirit."[26]

Once back at Maer, the Wedgwood women returned to their normal routine of visits to family (Shrewsbury, Etruria, Camp Hill) and friends (the Tollets in Betley village) and attendance at antislavery meetings. On May 11 Fanny Wedgwood noted in her diary how sad they had all been when told of Whig prime minister Grey's resignation. As part of his government's campaign to get a Reform Bill through the conservative House of Lords, Earl Grey had been trying to lever King William IV into creating fifty new reform-minded peers—an act that would have dramatically changed the balance of power in the upper house. When the king refused to cooperate, Grey resigned, only to be back in office within a matter of days when the Tories were unable to assemble a government of their own. The stage was now set for significant parliamentary change. Sadly, the most prominent politician in the Wedgwood family circle, Sir James Mackintosh, would play no part in these critically important events. Mac was on his deathbed and beyond caring about current affairs.[27]

Not long after his last speech in the House of Commons on February 9, 1832, Mac had got a chicken bone lodged in his throat at a dinner party. A surgeon successfully removed the bone a few days later and the incident was thought to be over, but an infection developed that led to Mackintosh's death on May 30. As he approached the end, although he was dying at a low ebb in his political career and with his *History* unfinished, Sir James was serene and focused more on religion than politics. In his edited *Life* of his father, Robert Mackintosh reported this exchange:

> I said to him at one time, "Jesus Christ loves you"; he answered slowly, and pausing between each word, "Jesus Christ—love—the same thing." He uttered these last words with a most sweet smile. After a long silence he said, "I believe—." We said, in a voice of inquiry,—"In God?" He answered,—"In Jesus."[28]

These words were no doubt comforting to all of Mac's children as they laid him in the parish burying ground in Hampstead. The entire extended family was shaken by the death, but for some—especially Fanny Allen, who had been secretly in love with Mackintosh since her teens—the loss was especially hard. The family's main politician and one of its most renowned scholars (Sismondi was the other) was dead at sixty-seven. The man whom Sydney Smith had once described in these words—"He could not hate. [He] did not know how to set about it."—would be sorely missed. Susan Darwin sent the news of the death to Charles in South America, commenting on the sadness of the unfinished *History* and the fact that Langham Place would have to "retrench very much" after losing more than £1,000 from its annual income.[29] It was a death that was hard to bear, but a worse one was coming.

By the summer of 1832 the Wedgwoods and their circle had been through three weddings and a funeral, and the year was only half over. Back home at Maer, Elizabeth, Fanny, and Emma fell into the familiar pattern of local visits. They made brief trips to Camp Hill, Betley, and Etruria, and at various times they hosted Dr. Darwin, Uncle John Wedgwood, Harry and Jessie, and Fanny Frank's parents the Mosleys. Charles Darwin's first letters from South America were beginning to trickle in, and everyone was interested in his tales of discovery and adventure. In her diary, Fanny Wedgwood described a relaxed summer after the frantic winter and spring.[30]

Then on August seventh, Fanny made an ominous entry: "A party dined at Trentham. They brought word that there had been two cases of Cholera at Newcastle."[31] Trentham, best known today for the Capability Brown–landscaped Trentham Gardens, is a mere five miles from Maer, and Newcastle-under-Lyme, to which Fanny almost certainly was referring, is only a mile farther off. Thus the deadly bacterial disease that had arrived from India in late 1831, making its first British appearance in the northern town of Sunderland in Durham County, was now in the Wedgwoods' backyard. Capable of killing susceptible victims within hours from dehydration and shock brought on by profuse diarrhea and vomiting, cholera would eventually claim 18,000 lives in London alone in 1832 and many more across the whole of the United Kingdom. Although the epidemic at Newcastle turned out to be relatively mild, it was still a serious situation.[32]

Six days after making that diary entry, Fanny Wedgwood herself was struck down with severe bowel pain, and two days later she began vomiting. Retrospective analyses have been unable to diagnose her illness definitively, and while some scholars think she had cholera,[33] others demur, since there is no evidence that she suffered the raging diarrhea characteristic of that disease.[34] At the first signs of their sister's distress, Elizabeth and Emma, aided by the Maer servants and an apothecary and a doctor from the vicinity, began a routine of nursing and watching—not realizing the seriousness of the case until nearly the end. After Fanny's death on August 20, a clearly benumbed Emma wrote a private description of the seesaw battle that ultimately proved futile.

On Monday 13th August 1832, my dear Fanny complained of uneasiness in the bowels. Eliz gave her calomel [mercurous chloride, a purgative] and jalap [a plant-derived purgative] but she would come and sit at the dinner table to save appearances as she said. The pain continued all night. Mary [a servant] and Eliz fomented her [applied medicated liquids externally] and tried to give an injection but without effect. Mr Broomhall was sent for and ordered fomentation with poppy heads, the pain gradually went off. I put on 20 leeches. On Wednesday morning he came and thought her much better but it was of great consequence to move the bowels and ordered 2 draughts which would not stay on the stomach. She had bilious vomittings all day and the next day Thursday, Mr B came and stayed all night. Her bowels did not move till 12 at night when she was much relieved. Eliz then went to bed and I sat up with her. Her bowels were much swelled and we rubbed her. On Friday she had a tolerable day but the medicine worked her too much. Saturday Dr Northen came again. She had a peaceful day and slept a good deal. She asked to have Charlotte's letter read to her. I slept in the room with her and only had to help her up once or twice. Early on Sunday morning she was low and Eliz gave her some hot drink. She revived during the day and nothing was to be done for her but to make herself comfortable. At 8 in the evening she took an injection which gave her violent pain and after that she was restless and uneasy; told Eliz to sponge her face twice and her back and chest. At 4 o'clock sent for Mr B. He found her sinking when he came and gave her brandy and she was thoroughly warmed. At 9 came on the fatal attack and in 5 minutes we lost our gentle, sweet Fanny, the most without selfishness of anybody I ever saw and her loss has left a blank which will never be filled up.[35]

In one stroke the Dovelies had been torn asunder—at least in this world. Emma immediately fastened her hope on reunion in the world to come, writing:

Oh, Lord, help me to become more like her, and grant that I may join her with Thee never to part again. I trust that my Fanny's sweet image will never pass from my mind. Let me always keep it in my mind as a motive for holiness. What exquisite happiness it will be to be with her again, to tell her how I loved her who has been joined with me in almost every enjoyment of my life.[36]

No doubt the death also reinforced for Emma the relevance of a particular prayer that had been a favorite of hers since girlhood:

Merciful God, as my uncertain life may soon be ended & I must appear before thee to give an account of my life, prepare me I beseech thee for the hour of death & for the day of judgment. Give me grace to receive with meekness thy holy word, which is able to make me wise unto salvation. Give me true repentance for my sins; teach me to delight in that which is good; enable me to love thee with all my heart & mind, & assist me to observe what thou dost command & to hope for what thou dost promise, that among the many changes of this life my heart may be fixed on true & everlasting joys. Let thy Holy Spirit help my imperfect resolutions & weak endeavors, & guide me & all belonging to me that having lived to thee here we may hereafter rise to live with thee in everlasting happiness through Jesus Christ.[37]

In Fanny's 1832 diary, two last entries were self-directed reminders that spoke poignantly of a life ended prematurely at the age of twenty-six. Looking ahead to the first week in September, she had written: "Arrange the large plants in the beds." And for the week of October 28 there was the notation "Make some Horse radish Vinegar. See Cooks Oracle."[38]

Of course, Emma was not alone in being shattered by her sister's death. The other residents of Maer and the members of the wider family circle also mourned Fanny's passing, although they varied in their resiliency and their reliance on religious faith for support. In a letter to her brother Charles, Caroline Darwin wrote (after the technical detail that Dr. Robert attributed Fanny's death to "mortification . . . in her bowels") that "Uncle Jos was terribly over come & [as for] Aunt Bessy it was some time before Elizabeth could make her understand what had happened." Once she understood what she had lost, Bessy sank into an apathetic listlessness, passing her days sitting and looking "sad & dejected."[39] Three weeks after the death, Elizabeth and Baugh Allen took Bessy on a tour into northern Wales in hopes that a change of scenery would raise her spirits.[40]

Jos rebounded fairly quickly, and so, remarkably enough, did Emma—thus showing on the occasion of her first major bereavement a resiliency that would see her through numerous deaths in later years. On September 15 Emma wrote to her aunt Jessie Sismondi:

I do not like that you should be thinking of us as more unhappy than we are. I think we all feel cheerful and susceptible of happiness. I do not expect or wish to miss our Fanny less than we do now. The remembrance of her is so sweet and unmixed with any bitter feeling that it is a pleasure to be put in mind of her in every way. . . . I am sure Papa misses his little secretary as he used to call her. She suited him so well.[41]

Emma and Charlotte both took comfort in the thought, common to the nineteenth century, that Fanny had been "taken out of the world before any distress or unhappiness came near her" and that "her life was a very happy one & closed without [her] knowing her danger or feeling the pain of separation from her family."[42] But despite these consoling sentiments, the Maer circle had lost a vital member and Emma a soul mate. As she continued to Aunt Jessie: "Sometimes I feel a sad blank at the thoughts of having lost my sweet, gentle companion who has been so closely joined with me ever since we were born."[43]

The beginning of 1833 brought a set of pleasant distractions from the sadness of the previous year. For one thing, Jos began his time in Parliament. Everyone in the family was excited by this venture into politics, even though it meant that Jos would be away from home when the House of Commons was in session. A proud Bessy confided to Jessie Sismondi that the possibility of a boost in family status due to Jos's election was "a worldly feeling I must confess, but one I find myself not able to contend with."[44] And for a second thing, the weddings of 1832 began literally to bear fruit, reversing the shrinkage of the family circle. On January 26, Fanny Frank gave birth to Jos and Bessy's first grandchild, a boy named Godfrey, who would one day become the chairman of Wedgwood and Sons, and Fanny Hensleigh followed with a daughter, Frances Julia, on February 6. Born during a heavy snowstorm, baby Frances was dubbed "Snow," a name that stuck with her for life.[45] According to her 1833 diary, Emma Wedgwood went to Etruria to help with Fanny Frank's delivery, but she remained at Maer during Fanny Hensleigh's confinement.[46]

In addition to these developments, the winter and spring of 1833 brought several proposals of marriage to Emma—rather a startling change after a girlhood without a serious love affair. Indeed, the change was so startling that Emma and the rest of the family became "quite weary" of all the attention. The identities of her suitors are not made clear in the family records, but it seems possible to sleuth out one or two names. According to the tale

Emma told her daughter Henrietta many years later, one of the suitors was a neighboring curate who, after being rejected, walked "half crying" around and around the lake at Maer, "asking [Elizabeth] what Emma found to object to in him." It seems likely that this spurned lover was the Reverend Ralph Bagot, who in 1833 was the curate of Wolstanton, Staffordshire, just five miles or so from Maer parish. This surmise is based on Emma's diary entries that show her meeting a "Mr Bagot" while she was visiting the Tollets at Betley on January 29. Also in the party that day was a "Mr. E. Mainwaring," possibly the patron of another local parish, Mucklestone. Eight days later, on February 6, the same "Mr Bagot" visited at Maer, this time accompanied by three of the Tollet women. Bagot's name then disappears from the diary, and it does not seem too far-fetched to conclude that he went away with a lover's broken heart. If this sleuthing is accurate, Emma made the right choice, since Bagot remained "unbeneficed" throughout his career, never securing an ecclesiastical "living" with a guaranteed income. He did not marry until 1845, at the age of forty-eight.[47]

The second of Emma's probable suitors is more interesting than the Reverend Mr. Bagot. It seems quite likely that Erasmus Alvey Darwin, then aged twenty-eight, floated a proposal of marriage to his cousin during the spring of 1833. Supported by a generous allowance from his father, Ras was beginning a half century of idleness and dilettantism among London's smart society. His lodgings at 24 Regent Street, just off Piccadilly Circus, were perfectly located for a well-heeled bachelor. Relatively new (built between 1817 and 1823), Regent Street was ultrafashionable and featured exclusive lodgings and high-toned shops. Indeed, it was less "a main road [than] a parade and shopping center, [with] ladies popping into drapers' before tea, while their carriages waited outside." Ras spent much of his time attending dinner parties, plays, and operas, often as the escort of either Fanny Hensleigh or, after March 1833, Harriet Martineau, who was then gaining fame as a literary apologist for Malthusian political economy. He first met Martineau at a dinner party hosted by the Hensleigh Wedgwoods on March 30, 1833. Emma was there too, as were Robert Mackintosh and Mrs. Anne Marsh, the sister-in-law of the Wedgwoods' second cousin Dr. Henry Holland. Mrs. Marsh was the person responsible for introducing Martineau, a fellow bluestocking, to most of the Wedgwood-Darwin circle, although Emma had met her about a week earlier while making a round of social calls.[48]

Ras was not only at loose ends that spring, he was also the proud owner of a stylish carriage and as a result did frequent taxi service for his various lady friends. (A year later, Ras's group of passengers had expanded to include

Jane Carlyle, the wife of the Scottish historian and essayist Thomas Carlyle, whose book *Sartor Resartus* was on everyone's reading list.) Of all his women friends, however, Erasmus always gave pride of place to his cousin by marriage and blood, Fanny Hensleigh. In fact, he paid her so much attention that it bordered on scandal and sent nervous shivers through the family. In October 1832, Catherine Darwin wrote to Charles on the *Beagle* that Ras "and Mrs Hensleigh seem to be thicker than ever; she is quite as much married to him as to Hensleigh, and Papa continually prophecies a fine paragraph in the Paper about them."[49]

Ras also made time for his other Wedgwood cousins, including Emma. When Emma came to London in March 1833 to attend a wedding, Caroline Darwin predicted that "Erasmus will be a very attentive Cavalier to [Emma] & nobody knows what will be the end of the drives in his Cab." Catherine Darwin also suspected that Erasmus had more than just cousinly affection for Emma, writing to Charles later that spring: "I think the real danger is with Emma Wedgwood, who I suspect Mr Erasmus to be more in love with, than appears, or than perhaps he knows himself."[50]

Evidence suggesting that Ras proposed marriage to Emma comes from her 1833 diary. During the spring there was a distinct flurry of interactions between the two cousins. They were together on eight occasions in March and April. They drank tea together, attended several of the same dinner parties, went to the Zoological Gardens together, and he ferried her around London in his carriage. Then on April 30, on the same day that Ras had escorted her around the Zoo, Emma made this ominous diary entry: "An awful letter." Her interactions with Erasmus stopped abruptly—his name appears in the diary only twice during May, and one of those occasions was an accidental meeting at Fanny and Hensleigh's home. Furthermore, during the last seven months of 1833 Emma saw Ras a total of only three additional times and always in the context of family gatherings.[51] What sense can be made of such a series of events at this remove? One possibility is that Erasmus proposed on April 30, only to be sent an "awful letter" rejecting his advances. We think this is the simplest explanation, although other authors think it's more likely that the lethargic Ras could never work up enough energy to propose or, alternately, felt for some reason that "marriage was essentially an enterprise for other people."[52] Certainly there seem to have been several factors that would have led Emma, though genuinely fond of her cousin, to spurn his advances. For one thing, Ras was probably too much of an idler for her taste. Also, as later comments made to his brother show, she was dismayed at Ras's loss of Christian faith.[53]

In the end, Erasmus never married—perhaps because both Emma and Fanny Hensleigh were taken. Harriet Martineau was another candidate for the role of Erasmus's wife, but she may have been a bit too intensely occupied with her politics and writing for the indolent Ras. And she may have been too self-centered. Emma described Martineau as "happy, good-humoured and conceited" in a letter to Jessie Sismondi.[54] As for Emma's actual future husband, in April 1833 he was separated by half a world from English flirtations, exploring the country around Maldonado, Uruguay. While his brother may have been laying his heart on the line with Emma, Charles was stretching his legs after weeks under sail.[55] Happily for Charles, Emma was not interested in being Mrs. Erasmus.

Two additional events from 1833 deserve mention. For one, Bessy Wedgwood, now approaching seventy, experienced another severe decline in health that year, to the great concern of her husband and children. Once again Lady Gifford's London home at Roehampton proved to be the unlucky site of an epileptic seizure, this time accompanied by a fall that broke one or more bones. Judging from Emma's diary record, Bessy's attack and fall probably occurred in mid-July. The relevant entries are: July 11, "went to Roehampton," and July 14, "M[amma] ill." Then there is a gap of nearly two weeks, during which time we can assume she was occupied in nursing her mother, before another entry indicates that Emma was moving beyond the confines of Roehampton once more: July 27, "went to Clapham . . . called at Battersea . . . went to London to shop."[56] On August fifth Emma was able to report to Aunt Jessie that Bessy was improving, although still at Roehampton:

> It is such a pleasure to send you such a good account, for I am sure nobody will feel more (or so much) joy than you at my dear Mamma's recovery. We feel impatient to be able to see the time when we can return home, but we must not think of it yet, and it is very lucky Mamma does not feel at all impatient to move. Fanny and Hensleigh have been coming constantly, and she is the nicest nurse possible, and endeared herself very much to us by her affectionate feelings for Mamma and joy at her recovery. Papa is not able to come as often as he wishes, as he is on a Liverpool Committee and the Slavery Bill in the evenings; so he is only able to come on Saturdays and stay till Monday.[57]

The diary record indicates that the trip home to Maer did not begin until August 19 and then proceeded at the gentle pace of just over twenty miles per day. Bessy, at least, traveled in some sort of carriage—her injuries were so serious that she was never able to walk again, much less ride on horseback. On August 25, Emma noted, they "came home."[58]

Back at Maer, Bessy's seizures continued, and they were accompanied by unmistakable signs of senility. Elizabeth and Emma settled into the task of nursing their invalid mother, whose worsening condition was communicated to Charles Darwin first by Catherine and later by Caroline.

> [November 27] Poor Aunt Bessy is a melancholy sight; she is perfectly helpless, and cannot stir herself the least, owing to a pain in her leg, which makes her quite powerless.—Her fits are much more frequent than they used to be, and she is excessively altered since her dangerous illness this Summer, that one would not suppose she could last much longer.[59]

> [December 30] Aunt Bessy is sadly changed since you saw her—her intellect *much* weakened & from a pain in her leg unable to stand or move herself in the least. She sits or rather lies down in the big room upstairs which is now fitted up as a sitting room & makes a tolerably comfortable one—[60]

That room was to be Bessy's universe for thirteen years. Contrary to Catherine Darwin's prediction, her aunt would live until 1846.[61]

The final big event of 1833 was the passage of the Colonial Slavery Bill by the newly reformed Parliament. At a stroke, the institution of slavery was abolished in the United Kingdom and its colonies—especially the West Indies—a reform long desired by the Wedgwood-Darwin clan. Emma's paternal grandfather, Josiah I, had been an active member of the Society for the Suppression of the Slave Trade in the late 1780s and had gained valuable publicity for the cause by producing black-on-yellow jasper "emancipation medallions" modeled on the society's seal. The medallions, or cameos, depicted a manacled black slave, kneeling and with hands raised in supplication, asking, "Am I Not a Man and a Brother?" Hundreds of these medallions were produced by the Wedgwood pottery, and they became popular items among people with abolitionist views.[62] In February 1788, Josiah I sent Benjamin Franklin, American statesman and fellow abolitionist, several of the medallions and a letter:

> Dear Sir,
>   I embrace the opportunity of a packet . . . to inclose for the use of yourself and friends a few Cameos on a subject which I am happy to acquaint you is daily more and more taking possession of men's minds on this side of the Atlantic as well as with you.
>   It gives me great pleasure to be embarked on this occasion in the same

great and good cause with you, and I ardently hope for the final completion of our wishes. This will be an epoch before unknown to the World, and while relief is given to millions of our fellow Creatures immediately the object of it, the subject of freedom will be more canvassed and better understood in the enlightened nations.[63]

Along with Josiah I, Dr. Erasmus Darwin had enthusiastically joined the eighteenth-century antislavery campaign, even inserting abolitionist sentiments into his poetical work *The Botanic Garden*.[64] And now, in 1833, Josiah II as a member of the reformed Parliament was to have a part in passing the bill that would end the abomination of British slavery once and for all.

On May 14, 1833, Edward Geoffrey Stanley, in his capacity as the colonial secretary of Earl Grey's government, moved an abolition bill before the House of Commons. That bill had five main points:

1. That slavery should be entirely abolished throughout the British colonies.
2. That emancipation should apply not only to adults but also to slave children under six and to children born to former slaves after the bill's passage.
3. That former slaves, although technically free, should serve a designated period as apprentices for their former owners.
4. That the West Indian planters should be loaned £15 million to compensate them for losses due to the abolition of slavery (rate of interest and repayment schedule to be set by Parliament).
5. That the Crown should help pay for the "religious and moral education" of the freed slaves.[65]

Two weeks later, on May 30 and 31, Emma Wedgwood visited the Ventilator high above the House of Commons and listened to the debate on Stanley's bill. She heard supporters such as Thomas Fowell Buxton argue that slaves should not be treated as cattle to be bought and sold, but as men and women with the same natural rights as members of Parliament. She also heard opponents argue that it was improper for the English Parliament to interfere in the internal affairs of the West Indies since those colonies had no direct representation in that legislative body but instead had their own local assemblies, and that abolition would result in economic loss both in the Indies and in Britain. Emma labeled the second night of speeches "very dull," but in fact they were carrying the day for the abolitionist cause.[66]

Some modifications were made to the bill as it passed through the Commons and the Lords, the most significant being increases in the sops to the soon-to-be former slave owners. These included bumping up the planters' compensation to £20 million, giving that money as a gift rather than a loan to be repaid with interest, and setting the period of forced apprenticeship at a generous five to seven years. On August 29, 1833, the *Times* (London) reported that on the previous day the House of Lords "sat at 12 o'clock; soon afterwards, the Commons having been summoned, the Royal assent was given by commission to various bills—amongst which were, the . . . Colonial Slavery Bill . . ."[67] Slavery in the British Empire had ended. It was an act that a later historian would call a show of "national virtue unparalleled in the history of the world."[68]

The news reached Charles Darwin in South America in a letter from his sister Susan. On October 15, 1833, she wrote:

> You will rejoice as much as we do over Slavery being abolished, but it is a pity the Apprenticeship does not commence till next August as that is a great while for the poor Slaves to be at the mercy of the Planters who I should think would treat them worse than ever.—I grudge too very much the 20 million compensation money: but perhaps it would never have been settled without this sum.[69]

The day Susan posted her letter, Charles was completing one of his principal inland expeditions by sailing down the Paraná River from Santa Fe to Buenos Aires. Although he would have approved most heartily the legislative events at home, at the moment he was more concerned with the danger posed by hungry jaguars and the appalling abundance of mosquitoes.[70]

5. The Return of the *Beagle* and "The day of days!"

THE MID-1830S FOUND EMMA AND ELIZABETH at Maer working patiently at the daily routine of nursing their invalid mother. They had the assistance of numerous servants, of course, but nonetheless dealing with Bessy was a full-time occupation and could have turned the sisters' lives into unalloyed drudgery if they hadn't devised a preventive. This involved making alternating trips away from Maer and thus gaining much-needed respite from their labors.

Their excursions and correspondence in 1834 can be reconstructed from Emma's diary.[1] Between February and June, Emma made trips to Derby and Shrewsbury, and then spent two months visiting kin and friends in London. Elizabeth was back at Maer during this period, and Emma's diary shows a regular flow of letters to her sister, her mother, or simply "home." While in London, Emma stayed with the Giffords at Roehampton and the Hensleigh Wedgwoods at Clapham, where she helped nurse Fanny through the birth of her first son, James Mackintosh Wedgwood, called "Mack" or "Bro." Taking advantage of London's commercial and cultural possibilities, she went shopping ("gown 2–17–4, handkerchief 4–6, cap 5–0, gloves 3–0"), dined with relatives and friends, visited gardens and art exhibitions and the zoo, and indulged her love of music and the theater. She saw Gaetano Donizetti's first international hit, the opera *Anna Bolena*,[2] on May 16, and then popped in again a month later for a repeat of the last act. She also went to Mozart's *Don*

Giovanni, an unnamed "French play," and the Philharmonic. And finally, indulging yet another love, that for politics, Emma visited the Ventilator at the House of Commons on April 30 and listened to speeches on topics including the state of Ireland and whether or not the union between that country and Britain should be repealed.[3] Although later in life she came to care passionately about the "Irish question," the younger Emma described these particular speeches as "very dull."[4]

In July and August the sisters made alternating visits to the Isle of Man, Elizabeth first and then Emma. During a short stay in Liverpool on her way to the isle, Emma attended a talk by Harriet Martineau, probably concerning the ongoing Poor Laws debate or reforming the Irish tithe system. These were both subjects about which Martineau had strong opinions, and she had been specifically asked by Baron Henry Brougham, Earl Grey's lord chancellor, to publish her views on the Poor Laws.[5] Whether Emma was simply a member of the audience on this occasion or spent time socializing with Martineau is unclear. The two women were more than mere acquaintances, having day-tripped together with two other lady friends to the newly opened Royal Beulah Spa near Clapham the year before. Still, Martineau may have been too busy to do more than give her talk and then attend to her packing, since she was due to sail from Liverpool the next day for a two-year visit to America.[6] Between London, the Isle of Man, and a few other short jaunts, Emma totaled about four months away from Maer in 1834, clearly belying the notion that she was housebound because of her ailing mother.

The following year, 1835, Elizabeth was the one who had an extended stay in London. Accompanied by the always handy Erasmus Darwin, she came to town on February 9, not to return home until mid-April. Back at Maer, Bessy was ill twice during this time, probably with seizures, and Emma kept her sister informed by mail. Emma's main trip for the year came in the fall, when she traveled to Pembrokeshire in Wales for a long vacation among a crowd of Allen kinfolks, including uncles John Hensleigh and Baugh, and aunts Fanny, Emma, and Harriet (Surtees). There were walks, picnics, and sightseeing in Tenby and nearby Penally and a never-ending flow of family gossip. This trip accounted for most of Emma's 1835 total of just over four months away from home.[7]

The mid-1830s also witnessed a considerable expansion of the extended family circle despite a round of deaths that took an infant and two senior members. Looking at the losses first, Caroline Drewe, one of the Allen sisters, passed away in 1835, never again to grace the Roehampton home of her daughter Lady Gifford. This death was felt throughout the family, but perhaps most keenly by Jane Wedgwood, close in age and affection to Caroline. Jane's own health had been precarious for years, and in April 1836 she became suddenly and fatally ill during a visit to the Darwins in Shrewsbury. Even Dr. Robert was taken by surprise by her rapid decline, and there was barely time to call the children to Jane's bedside. Eliza Wedgwood comforted her dying mother by telling her she was "going to Caroline," while Robert supported his mother's head and prayed aloud until it was all over, leaving everyone shattered. Deep in her own bodily and mental illnesses, Bessy may never have known that she had lost two sisters in less than a year; the family letters make no mention that she was burdened with the sad news. Fanny Allen, the youngest sister, was especially devastated by Jane's death. She wrote to Emma on April 25, 1836:

> We were totally unprepared for the intelligence from Shrewsbury yesterday, it seems yet to me like a painful dream that makes me restless. One's understanding as well as one's eyes are holden sometimes with regard to the illness of those dear to one; and it has been so in this instance more than in any other case I ever remember. Almost every word and action of hers during the past winter is before me, and I can think and speak of nothing else; and my own foolish blindness is before me too. There never was such ardent and unbounded affection as in her; it seemed as if her religious feelings had given her a power of loving unknown to less pious characters. The last ten months have carried away with them a treasure of affection, of tenderness, and of religious example to us. I trust the prayers of these two dear sisters for us may be heard, and that we may join them in a very few years.[8]

And lastly, through a stroke of horrendous bad luck and timing, Hensleigh and Fanny's three children all came down with whooping cough at about the time of Jane's death. Their seven-month-old baby was lost to the disease, completing the trio of family deaths.[9]

Sad though those these losses were, the deceased were soon replaced by new arrivals, most of them Wedgwoods. Harry and Jessie's first child, a girl named Louisa, was born in January 1834, and two years later along came a little sister. Fanny and Hensleigh's "Bro," born in April 1834, was followed by another son, Ernest Hensleigh, in 1838. Fanny Frank did her part, adding two daughters to the family circle, Amy in 1835 and Cicely Mary in 1837. On the Darwin side of the ledger, Charles's oldest sister, Marianne, married to the physician Henry Parker since 1824, gave birth to her fifth baby and first daughter in January 1836. Honoring both the baby's mother and maternal aunt, the Parkers named the little girl Mary Susan.[10]

Alongside the deaths and births, there were engagements and marriages as well, some affecting distant kin and others involving close members of the family. Two engagements took place in January 1834: Dr. Henry Holland chose for his second wife Saba Smith, daughter of the celebrated Sydney Smith, and the Reverend William Darwin Fox, cousin to the Shrewsbury Darwins and Charles's close friend at Cambridge, proposed to Harriet Fletcher. The Foxes were married in the spring and, after suffering one stillborn baby, they produced their first healthy child, Eliza Ann, in January 1836. She would be the first of eleven children by two wives for Fox.[11]

A third engagement added to the depression of Jane Wedgwood's last year of life. In January 1835, Robert Wedgwood, an underpaid curate of twenty-nine, startled the family by becoming engaged to fifty-year-old Frances Crewe. Catherine Darwin reported to Charles on the *Beagle* that

> the John Wedgwoods were much vexed . . . that Robert has fallen vehemently and desperately in love with Miss Crewe, who is *50* years old, and blind of one eye. [They] have tried in vain to break off this unlucky engagement, but all in vain; Robert is infatuated, and proud of his good fortune, and they will soon be married.—She is a clever woman, and must have entrapped him by her artifices; & she has the remains of great beauty to help her; it is said also that she has a violent temper, which is another bad point in this ill-starred match.[12]

In her own letter to Charles, Susan Darwin weighed in regarding Miss Crewe and, in addition, took a gratuitous shot at Fanny Frank:

> Catherine will have told you in her last letter of Robert Wedgwood's intended marriage with Miss Crewe of Muxton—just 20 years difference in their ages!—Robert came over here a fortnight ago to see Aunt Jane who is staying with us now: and talked over the matter they have given their consent much against their inclination as of course they dislike such a absurd match very much, besides all her family being very goodfornothing people.—I advised Robert to marry & go abroad as that would be much the best way of letting the *talk* subside, & he seemed very much inclined to follow my advice. People say she has a bad temper & it is impossible that she can be otherwise than very jealous of her young husband: really the Wedgwoods ought not to be allowed to chuse for themselves after Franks & Roberts specimens of wives.[13]

And finally, there were a few changes of residence in the mid-1830s, some forced and some voluntary. In the forced category, in December 1834 Charlotte and Charles Langton took leave from his parish in Onibury, Shropshire, to live for a period in Madeira in hopes that the mild climate might improve his health. There was great concern that Langton was developing life-threatening consumption, a disease that had already cost him nine brothers and sisters. On December fifth Emma noted in her diary: "Langtons sailed."[14] In the quasi-voluntary category, Harry and Jessie Wedgwood moved in with her widowed father and spinster sister at Seabridge House near Maer. Jessie was pregnant with their second child, and Seabridge offered plenty of room for a growing family.[15] And on the voluntary side, in London Ras Darwin changed houses in the winter of 1836, settling into No. 43 Great Marlborough Street, less than a half mile from his old Regent Street lodgings, in order to have more room and "a nice garden & Balcony to smoke his Cigar." Ras was back in London after a short spell of actually working for a living—as a clerk for Robert Mackintosh, who had recently been appointed one of the commissioners charged with investigating public charities. Susan Darwin's prediction that Ras wouldn't "keep his place long, at least if it requires much work," proved to be sadly accurate, although laziness wasn't the only problem: in fact, Ras didn't have sufficient legal knowledge to do the job in the first place. Certainly the brevity of his employment didn't bother Ras, who observed that "whatever people may please to say literary leisure is better than work."[16]

Throughout all of these various family affairs—births, deaths, illnesses, and relocations—Josiah II continued with his legislative duties. And his particular Parliament, the first reformed Parliament, had its ups and downs. One of its "achievements" was the so-called New Poor Law. Technically the Poor Law Amendment Act of 1834, this bill addressed the concern—which continues today—that giving food relief and other assistance to persons capable of work not only was expensive but also encouraged a culture of dependency and idleness. Thus the bill attempted to tighten up the existing system of poor relief so that the "aged and feeble poor" were the main recipients of public assistance, while the able-bodied poor were strongly discouraged from living on the dole. To achieve greater efficiency in poor relief, all such efforts were put under the control of a new nongovernmental agency, the Poor Law Commission.[17]

To the delight of Malthusians like Harriet Martineau, the New Poor Law had the teeth that the old one lacked. Strong emphasis was placed on offering relief only within the walls of workhouses, as opposed to providing "outdoor relief." And to discourage the able-bodied poor from being housed and fed at public expense, life in the workhouses was made distinctly unpleasant. Within the workhouse walls, wives were segregated from husbands in order to prevent "loading the [public] with fresh burdens," and children were separated from their parents. Additionally, when they entered a workhouse, new inmates' goods and furniture were sold to help defray the public's costs. Harsh though these measures were, they suited the spirit of the times and—after some sharp debate about the so-called "bastardy clauses," which tended to put most or all of the expenses of illegitimate children on the mother instead of the putative father, a measure designed to promote chastity among poor women—the bill passed into law.[18] As a "strong ministerial supporter" and a man with a head for business, Jos almost certainly voted for the 1834 Amendment Act in the House of Commons; at the very least, the *Times* minority list shows that he did not vote against it.[19]

Another topic of concern for the reformed Parliament—and one that ultimately contributed to its abrupt end—was the state of affairs in Ireland. Two issues in particular were the subject of lengthy debate: the status of the Established Church in Ireland, and the advisability of renewing the 1833 Coercion Act designed to deter riots and other public disruptions. The church issue revolved around two main points. First, most Irishmen—certainly the Catholics, but also many Protestants—objected to paying the obligatory tithe to support the Established Church. And second, the Church itself seemed unreasonably inflated, both in number of parishes and bishoprics and in its annual income in comparison to the number of its communicants, which was estimated at some 600,000 persons, or less than 7 percent of the island's population. Dedicated reformers brought forth proposals to change the tithe system, eliminate several bishoprics, and use the revenue from selling Church property to fund secular causes like the establishment of new schools. Unfortunately, it turned out that the Whig administration itself was deeply divided over some of these matters, especially "lay appropriation" of Church funds, which Jos opposed.[20] Four cabinet members resigned in protest. This did not kill Earl Grey's government, but in retrospect it was clearly the beginning of the end.[21]

Discussion of the Irish Coercion Act proceeded through the spring and early summer of 1834. Although the government generally felt that the 1833 bill should be renewed, there were differences of opinion about how restrictive a new version needed to be. Should, for example, the lord-lieutenant of Ireland continue to have the power to prevent public meetings that he believed were intended to cause political trouble? Prime Minister Grey said yes, and he was able to convince a majority of his cabinet on the point. Meanwhile, however, and unbeknownst to Grey, his Irish home secretary—with the assent of Grey's Commons floor leader and chancellor of the exchequer, John Charles Spencer, Lord Althorp—had intimated to Daniel O'Connell, a leading Irish Nationalist, that the public-meeting clauses would be abandoned. In July 1834, when O'Connell learned that he had been misinformed about the government's actual position on the matter, he went public about Althorp's private assurances, to the great embarrassment of Earl Grey and his administration. Both Althorp and Grey resigned, and the home secretary, William Lamb, Lord Melbourne, became prime minister (Althorp was later talked into resuming his office).[22] The Whig government was now looking very much like a legislative sick man.

The Whigs' next crisis came in November 1834 when, upon the death of his father, Althorp became the third Earl Spencer and was thereby elevated to the House of Lords. Melbourne favored naming Lord John Russell chancellor of the exchequer, but King William IV, who had no use for Russell, decided to take this opportunity to dismiss the entire reform-minded administration. For his new prime minister the king chose Robert Peel, who duly returned home from an Italian holiday. Realizing that his Conservatives, as they were now called rather than Tories, were badly outnumbered in the House, Peel called for a general election in the spring of 1835. As it turned out, the Conservatives did not gain enough seats to form a viable government, and by the spring of 1835 Melbourne and the Whigs were back in office. But Josiah Wedgwood II had chosen not to run for reelection, and so his days as an MP came to an end.[23]

Overall, Jos's parliamentary career had been both progressive and liberal. Among his causes, he had supported the abolition of slavery in the British Empire and had almost certainly cast his vote for the New Poor Law. In addition, Jos had voted to repeal the stamp duty on newspapers—a tax so heavy that, for the *Times*, the stamp duty accounted for four pence out of the sevenpence price of a day's paper—which many people viewed as hampering the diffusion of useful knowledge and/or unjustly limiting the expression of political and religious dissent. Although stamp tax repeal was a losing cause in 1834, the taxes on newspapers would indeed be lowered in 1836.[24] And finally, in full conformity with his liberal views on education, Jos had voted to support government funding for more schools and to allow Dissenters to be admitted to Cambridge and Oxford.[25] Happy to sit quietly on the back benches (he apparently never spoke in Parliament), Jos had run for office on a reform ticket and he had delivered on his promises.[26] By 1835 he was anxious to return to Maer and his ailing wife.

Thousands of miles from the zigzag history of the reformed Parliament, Charles Darwin was still beating up and down the coasts of South America aboard the *Beagle*. He was kept well informed about events at home—although the mail took four or five months to reach him—by regular letters from his three sisters in Shrewsbury. For example: February 1834, a description of Daniel O'Connell's parliamentary antics on behalf of Irish nationalism (from Susan); October 1834, news that the Houses of Parliament had been destroyed by fire (from Catherine); November 1834, the king's dismissal of the Whig government (Susan); January 1835, the end of "Uncle Jos' Parliamentary Days" and the failure of Peel's "odious Ministry" to gain significant legislative strength in the general election (Catherine); November 1835, Ras's short stint as clerk to Robert Mackintosh (Susan); March 1836, Ras's change of London lodgings (Caroline).[27] No doubt of even greater interest to Charles, his sisters sent news of the arrival of his shipments of natural history specimens from South America and their safe delivery to Professor Henslow in Cambridge. (These shipments sometimes made the papers. Caroline sent a "blundering account" from the *Times*: "several packages of specimens of fossils birds & quadrupeds skins & geological specimens have been collected by the naturalist Mr *Dawson* & sent to Professor *Hindon*.")[28] And the specimens were being examined and admired by senior scientists! At The Mount, the Darwins heard that the geologist Adam Sedgwick thought Charles was "doing admirably in S. America." Furthermore, continued the professor, Charles had "already sent home a Collection above all praise.—It was the best thing in the world for him that he went out on the Voyage of Discovery—There was some risk of his turning out an idle man: but his character will now be fixed, & if God spare his life, he will have a great name among the Naturalists of Europe."[29] This must have been heady and reassuring stuff when it was relayed to the young collector on the *Beagle*.

The *Beagle*'s voyage had pretty much gone according to plan since her arrival in South American waters in early 1832. Under FitzRoy's command, the little ship had steadily worked her way down the continent's east coast and up the west, with forays through the rambling passages of Tierra del Fuego and even out to the Falkland Islands. Whenever possible, Charles made treks into the South American interior, and wherever he went, he made geological observations and collected all manner of biological specimens. His haul of materials was quite remarkable, and it was sent back in batches to Henslow as port calls and contacts with returning ships allowed.[30] In general, Charles's physical and mental health had been excellent thus far, despite his family's constant concern and misgivings.[31]

Captain FitzRoy had not fared quite so well. In November 1834, over-worked and, from his standpoint, inadequately supported (he had just been refused Admiralty approval for the purchase of a second survey vessel), FitzRoy grew depressed and demoralized. Concerned for his sanity, he invalided himself from the *Beagle*'s command and was replaced by First Lieutenant John Clements Wickham. This development threatened to short-circuit the voyage, since Wickham's orders in such an eventuality were to end the coastal surveying prematurely and return to England by the most direct route—which would be via the Atlantic, rather than proceeding across the Pacific and Indian Oceans. Charles, who was eagerly anticipating crossing the Pacific, was greatly dismayed by the Captain's decision, as were the rest of the *Beagle*'s inmates. Luckily, after some reflection on the matter, and at Wickham's disinterested urging, FitzRoy reconsidered and resumed his command. The circumnavigation was on again. A delighted Darwin wrote home: "Hurra Hurra. . . . For the first time since leaving England I now see a clear & not so distant prospect of returning to you all: crossing the Pacific & from Sydney home will not take much time."[32]

For the rest of 1834 and into 1835, the *Beagle*'s crew continued their survey of the western coast of South America. On February 20, 1835, while the little ship was anchored in the harbor at Valdivia, the area was hit by a devastating earthquake. Charles was greatly impressed by the wreckage in Valdivia and Concepción, as well as the significant elevation of the land that the earthquake produced.[33] Observations such as these would contribute to his eventual publications on South American geology and continental change. Also during his time in Chile, Charles made a long trek into the Andes to examine the Cordilleran geology and life forms. While spending the night in the village of Luxan on the Argentinean flank of the mountains, he was bitten repeatedly by Vinchuca bugs—from which some scholars believe he may have contracted Chagas' disease. He described the episode in his *Beagle* diary:

[March 26] At night I experienced an attack, & it deserves no less a name, of the Benchuca, the great black bug of the Pampas. It is most disgusting to feel soft wingless insects, about an inch long, crawling over one's body; before sucking they are quite thin, but afterwards round & bloated with blood, & in this state they are easily squashed.[34]

Charles noted later, apparently based on personal experimentation, that the bite of the Vinchuca bug was painless, that it took less than ten minutes for the insect to drink its fill of blood, and that a single blood meal would satisfy the creature for weeks.[35] More will be said in later chapters about the possibility that these insects—or more properly the parasites they are known to carry, *Trypanosoma cruzi*—had long-term effects on Darwin's health.

On September 7, 1835, the *Beagle* left the shores of South America and started across the Pacific on her way home. She had been away from England for the better part of four years and everyone on board was desperately homesick. Charles wrote to Susan: "I trust & believe, that this month, next year, we shall be very close to if not in England. It is too delightful, to think, that I shall see the leaves fall & hear the Robin sing next Autumn at Shrewsbury.—My feelings are those of a School-boy to a the smallest point; I doubt whether ever boy longed for his holidays, as much as I do to see you all again."[36] Throughout the next year the little ship plowed along toward the western horizon, making only relatively brief stops even in the Galapagos Islands with their strange and exotic birds and beasts, and she finally reached England on October 2, 1836.[37] Charles was about to see his loved ones after an absence of nearly five years.

He arrived home to find that his travel journal—which he had been sending back to England in installments—had been greatly appreciated and was roundly judged to be worthy of publication. So vivid in places that it made Dr. Robert shudder at the risks his son had taken, it had been read and enjoyed by the family at Shrewsbury, at Maer, and in London.[38] Only Dr. Henry Holland thought that the journal was not worth publishing, an opinion that Emma Wedgwood summarily dismissed, saying, "I don't believe he is any judge as to what is amusing or interesting."[39] Charles also found, to his surprise and delight, that he was in demand in the highest scientific circles. His entrée into mainstream British science had been paved by Henslow's distribution of extracts from Darwin's letters to the members of the Cambridge Philosophical Society. Established scientists such as Charles Lyell and the anatomist Richard Owen were anxious to meet young Darwin and to discuss his observations and specimens.[40] After a reentry period of some weeks, during which he got reacquainted with family and friends, Charles eventually took lodgings in Cambridge near the Fitzwilliam Museum and began to sort out his future.[41] At least one thing now seemed clear: he was not destined for a career in the Church. Even Dr. Robert agreed that his son's destiny lay with science, not theology, and accordingly he gave Charles an allowance plus stocks that amounted to an annual income of about £400, or some $33,000 today.[42]

Charles's immediate scientific concerns were twofold: to get expert help analyzing his specimens and to write up his *Beagle* journal for publication as part of the official narrative of the voyage. On the first point he had considerable luck, for in the end Richard Owen took on the analysis of the fossil mammals, George Waterhouse the living mammals, Leonard Jenyns the fish, and Thomas Bell the reptiles. Perhaps of greatest importance for the development of Charles's evolution theories, the rising ornithologist and artist John Gould took on the bird specimens.[43] As for writing up his travel journal, Charles set to work with a will and was finished by September 1837, well ahead of Captain FitzRoy's part of the official report.[44]

Locating and consulting the various natural history experts took time and repeated trips to London, as did Charles's increasing involvement with the Geological Society, of which he was elected a fellow in late 1836 and a council member in February 1837. It wasn't long before he realized that he would be better situated in London, however "dirty" and "odious" it might be, than in Cambridge.[45] It made no sense, after all, for an ambitious young naturalist to avoid the scientific epicenter of the nation, and so in March 1837 Darwin relocated to rented rooms at 36 Great Marlborough Street, just down the road from Ras. Changing residences may have taken Charles away from frequent contact with Henslow and other friends in Cambridge, but in exchange he got a much more eclectic mix of scientific and social companions. For example, he met and rapidly became friends with Charles Lyell, and through Lyell he met other leading scientists such as the geologist Roderick Murchison, the botanist Robert Brown, and the polymath Herbert Spencer. Lyell also urged Darwin to join the Athenaeum, an exclusive West End dining club, where by 1838 Darwin was rubbing shoulders with Charles Dickens and other notables. Through Erasmus and the Hensleigh Wedgwoods, he expanded his social circle by the addition of, among others, Harriet Martineau, Thomas and Jane Carlyle, and Anne Marsh.[46]

As Charles worked away at his *Beagle* journal, organized the analyses of his various specimens, and enjoyed the social and intellectual swirl of London, he was also beginning to collect his thoughts on the subject that would define his career as a scientist: "transmutation" or, in modern terms, evolution. For Darwin, collecting his thoughts meant writing them down for later consideration, and in the spring of 1837 he began a series of notebooks containing observations, opinions, and questions about geology, metaphysics, and evolution. His interest in transmutation had been piqued during the *Beagle*'s voyage by the South American fossils he had found and how much they resembled certain living species. Furthermore, evidence for transmutation took a dramatic jump in March 1837 when John Gould determined that the Galapagos finches constituted thirteen new and distinct species, each apparently island-specific and all very similar to some of the finches on the South American mainland.[47] Was it possible that this was due to an ancestral migration followed by isolation-induced diversification once the birds were in the islands? After his enlightenment by Gould about the Galapagos finches and certain other American birds, Charles jotted an entire series of transmutation questions in his notebooks.[48] Soon his scribblings included suggestions that even humans might be the result of an evolutionary process, rather than being divinely created as taught by the Anglican Church. Three examples of these early musings on human ancestry come from Notebooks B and M:

[B, late 1837] If all men were dead then monkeys make men.—Men makes angels

[B, early 1838] the soul by consent of all is superadded, animals not got it, not look forward. [If] we choose to let conjecture run wild then animals our fellow brethren in pain, disease & suffering & famine; our slaves in the most laborious work, our companion in our amusements. they may partake, from our origin in one common ancestor we may all be netted together

[M, late summer 1838] the mind of man is no more perfect, than instincts of animals to all & changing contingencies, or bodies of either.—Our descent, then is the origin of our evil passions!!—The Devil under form of Baboon is our grandfather![49]

These were heretical thoughts. Charles was straying further and further from the Anglican orthodoxy that had once convinced him he was fit for a career in the Church.

In the larger world beyond Charles's evolutionary theorizing, 1837 was marked by a number of significant events. For one thing, Britain underwent a change of monarchs. William IV, the sailor king, breathed his last on June 20, 1837, and because he had sired only illegitimate children, the crown passed to his eighteen-year-old niece Victoria, who as the daughter of the deceased Edward, Duke of Kent, was ahead of her uncles the Dukes of Cumberland and Cambridge in the line of succession. Not quite a month past her coming of age, Victoria began the longest reign in British history and a cultural epoch that would forever carry her name. The diarist Charles Greville noted that the young queen was neither dazzled nor confounded "with the grandeur and novelty of her situation" but behaved "with a decorum and propriety beyond her years." After a full year of preparations, Victoria's coronation was held on June 28, 1838. London was filled to bursting with 400,000 excited visitors anxious to be part of the £200,000 celebration. There were bands playing in the royal parks, fireworks, and a fair in Hyde Park with a thousand booths and hot air balloon rides. Westminster Abbey was decorated with swags of crimson and gold. Charles Lyell and his wife were present for the actual coronation ceremony in the Abbey and "had a splendid view." Thomas Carlyle had a ticket for the coronation but gave it away, declaring, "Crowds and mummery are not agreeable to me." He did view the procession from a friend's window, and gave this report to his sister: "The Procession was all gilding, velvet and grandeur; the poor little Queen seemed to have been [weeping] one could not but wish the poor little lassie well: she is small, sonsy and modest,—and has the ugliest task, I should say, of all girls in these Isles." Charles Darwin missed out on the coronation hullabaloo entirely, having gone to Scotland for a firsthand look at the peculiar geology of Glen Roy. And if Ras or any of the other Darwins or Wedgwoods participated in the coronation festivities, it went unrecorded.[50]

On a much smaller scale but of significance to the family, in the fall of 1837 Hensleigh Wedgwood decided that his religious beliefs no longer allowed him to administer oaths as a police magistrate. He therefore resigned his £800-per-year job, to the considerable consternation of his loved ones. The decision forced a change of residence from Clapham back to Maer. Although his father repeatedly offered to make him a partner in the family business, Hensleigh refused, preferring to devote his time to etymological studies while seeking another government job. Such a job eventually materialized— Registrar of Cabs at half his previous salary—and Hensleigh, Fanny, and their three children moved back to a rented house in London.[51] On a happier note, 1837 was also the year that Joe Wedgwood (Josiah III) finally married his cousin Caroline Darwin. Joe was forty-two and Caroline was thirty-seven at the time of their marriage, and it was a union long hoped for by the parents on both sides. Charles Darwin called his cousin and brother-in-law "a very quiet grave man, with much to respect & like in him," but at the same time he thought Joe needed to "put himself forward more." Charles hoped the marriage would be blessed with children despite the ages of the bride and groom because, he joked, he "never saw a human being so fond of little crying wretches" as Caroline was.[52] From her sickroom at Maer, Bessy commented that she was as "pleased as if Joe had won Victoria herself."[53] Another link had been forged in the web of relationships that bound the extended family circle together.

For Charles, living a bachelor's life in London that summer of 1837 and slaving away at his writing and other scientific work, Joe's marriage to Caroline may have been the last straw. Everyone he knew was married or soon would be. His beloved "Housemaid" Fanny Owen had been married for five years, William Darwin Fox for three, and FitzRoy had married almost immediately after the *Beagle's* return. All of his Maer cousins were married or engaged, with the exceptions of Elizabeth, then forty-four, and Emma, twenty-nine.[54] Even Ras might as well have been married to Harriet Martineau, considering the time and attention he was giving her. Back in the fall of 1836, Charles had worried to Caroline about their brother's apparent fate:

> Erasmus is just returned from driving out [chauffeuring] Miss Martineau.—Our only protection from so admirable a sister-in-law is in her working him too hard. He begins to perceive, (to use his own expression) he shall be not much better than her "nigger".—Imagine poor Erasmus a nigger to so philosophical & energetic a lady.—How pale & woe begone he will look.—She already takes him to task about his idleness—She is going some day to explain to him her notions about marriage—Perfect equality of rights is part of her doctrine. I much doubt whether it will be equality in practice. We must pray for our poor "nigger".[55]

A year and a half later, Ras and Martineau were still going hot and heavy, as Charles reported to Susan in April 1838 in a letter that also described a visit to the London Zoo:

> So much for Monkey, & now for Miss Martineau, who has been as frisky lately as the Rhinoceros.—Erasmus has been with her noon, morning, and night:—if her character was not as secure, as a mountain in the polar regions she certainly would loose it.—Lyell called there the other day & there was a beautiful rose on the table, & she coolly showed it to him & said "Erasmus Darwin gave me that."[56]

Charles too was fascinated, if not attracted, by Martineau. When he first met her in December 1836, he noted "how little ugly" she was and expressed astonishment and admiration at her impressive array of projects, thoughts, and abilities.[57] He described her as "a wonderful woman" in early 1838—in the same letter that compared her to a frisky rhinoceros. Whether either of the Darwin brothers ever had marital designs on Martineau is unclear, but by 1837 the mere thought of having her as a daughter-in-law was enough to make Dr. Robert's hair stand on end. Martineau's politics were too extreme for the doctor, and her article in the *Westminster Review* calling for a Radical uprising against the Whigs to win the vote for working men was simply too much. A story circulated throughout the family that the *Westminster* piece had pitched Dr. Robert into a fit of indignation, prompting the Maer women, as well as his own daughters, to tease him about his prejudices.[58]

Although Harriet Martineau was probably never really a potential bride for Charles, other young ladies in his London crowd certainly were, and he was spotted as a very eligible bachelor—a "shootable," as the Owen sisters would have said a decade before[59]—soon after he moved to the city. Leonard Horner, a linen draper, geologist, and Charles Lyell's father-in-law, still had five unmarried daughters at home, and he and his wife Anne were quite forward in inviting Charles over for visits. Although nothing ever came of these social calls, Darwin may have been somewhat smitten with one or another of the Horner girls, as shown by his flirtatious gesture of sending them a piece of Joe and Caroline's wedding cake with a note saying he would be by on Monday to share the cake with them.[60]

Certainly Charles was not unaware of, or immune to, female charms. He had long dreamed of a quiet parsonage and a loving wife. The man who had thought Fanny Owen the "prettiest, plumpest" girl in all of Shropshire, only to lose her to another during the *Beagle*'s voyage, had also gone into raptures over the women of South America. In 1832 he had written to Caroline that in Montevideo "our chief amusement was riding about & admiring the Spanish Ladies.—After watching one of these angels gliding down the streets; involuntarily we groaned out, 'how foolish English women are, they can neither walk nor dress.'"[61] But whether English girls were outclassed by señoritas or not, by early 1838 Charles—although still up to his ears in writing and other scientific activities—had just about decided to make *some* English girl his bride. Methodical to a fault, he wrote out the good and bad aspects of marriage in preparation for making a decision. His first such note was written in April and included the worrisome likelihood that marriage might cramp his style in the following ways: reduce his ability to travel and do international scientific work; necessitate living in either Cambridge or London and taking a paying job; slash his budget for scientific books. "My destiny will be Camb. Prof. or poor man," he concluded, adding that he was probably destined to live on the "outskirts of London, [on] some small Square &c:—& work as well as I can."[62]

Three months later, in July, he was at it again, this time laying out the pros and cons of marriage in two opposing columns:

THIS IS THE QUESTION

Marry	*Not Marry*
Children—(if it Please God)—Constant companion, (& friend in old age) who will feel interested in one,—object to be beloved & played with.——better than a dog anyhow.—Home, & someone to take care of house—Charms of music & female chit-chat.—These things good for one's health.—*but terrible loss of time.*— My God, it is intolerable to think of spending one's whole life, like a neuter bee, working, working, & nothing after all.—No, no won't do.—Imagine living all one's day solitarily in smoky dirty London house.—Only picture to yourself a nice soft wife on a sofa with good fire, & books & music perhaps— Compare this vision with the dingy reality of Grt. Marlbro' St.	Freedom to go where one liked— choice of Society & *little of it.*— Conversation of clever men at clubs—Not forced to visit relatives, & to bend in every trifle.—to have the expense & anxiety of children— perhaps quarreling—**Loss of time.**— cannot read in the Evenings—fatness & idleness—Anxiety & responsibility—less money for books &c—if many children forced to gain one's bread.—(But then it is very bad for ones health to work too much) Perhaps my wife wont like London; then the sentence is banishment & degradation into indolent, idle fool—[63]

"Marry—Mary [*sic*]—Marry Q.E.D.," he finally concluded. He simply could not face "groggy old age, friendless & cold, & childless" all by himself. Marriage was the way to go. After all—and here Charles told himself something he knew to be a lie—"There is many a happy slave."[64]

Not at all romantic, but very much to the point and very much the product of an ambitious young man who hoped to fit a wife (and children, if it please God) into an already full schedule. But now, the question having been raised and proved (Q.E.D.), who would be asked to share his life?

Throughout 1837 and into 1838, Emma Wedgwood's life followed a now familiar routine of duties interspersed with the occasional respite. Her invalid mother still required nursing care at Maer, which Emma provided with assistance from Elizabeth. In January 1837, Emma made a two-month visit to Edinburgh where, along with her cousin and hostess Lady Gifford, she enjoyed a round of concerts and parties gussied up in a new muslin gown complemented by feather flowers given to her by Charles Darwin; these, she reported to the Shrewsbury women, were "much admired."[65] In the fall she traveled to Shrewsbury for a week with the Darwins, where as usual she tried to spend most of her time with her female cousins rather than the conversation-dominating Dr. Robert ("I find a week long enough . . . as one gets rather fatigued by the Dr's talk, especially the two whole hours just before dinner"). Then she went on to Onibury for a stay with Charlotte and Charles Langton.[66]

In May 1838 Emma, along with Catherine Darwin and a smattering of Allens and other Wedgwoods, joined the Sismondis in Paris for three weeks. When she returned from what would be her very last trip abroad, Emma stopped in London for a few days with Fanny and Hensleigh. While there, she enjoyed having Thomas Carlyle as a dinner companion and she saw lots of Charles Darwin, who lived right next door to the Hensleigh Wedgwoods. Although Charles was well into his mental wrestling about marriage at this time, if he was unusually attentive toward his cousin, nobody noticed—especially not Emma, who months later told her aunt Jessie Sismondi that during "the week I spent in London on my return from Paris, I felt sure he did not care about me," although, of course, he was "fond of Maer and all of us."[67] And Charles was only marginally more obvious about his interest during a short trip to Maer in late July. Although he wrote Emma a flirting letter afterwards full of chat about the "fat goose" (cozy talk) they had shared in front of the library fire and how she would soon see him again and they would have "another goose," and despite the fact that he must have been nearly at full boil with his marriage plans, still he had been afraid to pop the question. Thus, when Charles finally did work up the nerve to propose in November, it came as almost a complete surprise to Emma.[68]

The shy suitor was back at Maer on November ninth. On the eleventh he tried his luck and, perhaps to his own amazement, was accepted. "The day of days!" Charles wrote in his journal.[69] Emma's feelings—a mixture of surprise, confusion, and delight—were poured out four days later in a letter to her aunt Jessie.

[Charles] came down again last Thursday with Aunt Fanny, and on Sunday he spoke to me, which was quite a surprise, as I thought we might go on in the sort of friendship we were in for years, and very likely nothing come of it after all. I was too much bewildered all day to feel my happiness and there was a large party in the house, so we did not tell anybody except Papa and

Elizabeth and Catherine. Dear Papa, I wish you could have seen his tears of joy, for he has always had a great regard for Charles, and Charles looks up to him with the greatest reverence and affection. I believe we both looked very dismal (as he had a bad toothache) for when aunt Fanny and Jessie went to bed they were wondering what was the matter and almost thought something quite the reverse had happened. Fanny Hensleigh was 'cuter, and knew quite well what had happened. I went into their rooms at night, and we had a large party talking it over till very late, when I was seized with hunger, and Hensleigh went down to forage in the kitchen and found a loaf and 2 lb. butter and a carving knife, which made us an elegant refection. Catherine was delighted, indeed I was so glad to find that all of them had been wishing for it and settling it. It is a match that every soul has been making for us, so we could not have helped it if we had not liked it ourselves. . . .

I must now tell you what I think of him, first premising that Eliz. thinks pretty nearly the same, as my opinion may not go for much with you. He is the most open, transparent man I ever saw, and every word expresses his real thoughts. He is particularly affectionate and very nice to his father and sisters, and perfectly sweet tempered, and possesses some minor qualities that add particularly to one's happiness, such as not being fastidious, and being humane to animals. We shall live in London, where he is fully occupied with being Secretary to the Geological Society and conducting a publication upon the animals of Australia. I am so glad he is a busy man. Dear Eliz. rejoices most sweetly with me and forgets herself entirely, as, without meaning a compliment to myself, I am afraid she must miss me very much. I am sure I could not have brought myself to rejoice in her marrying. Mamma takes it very comfortably and amuses herself a good deal with planning about houses, trousseaux and wedding-cake.[70]

After gushing to her aunt for several pages, Emma finally admitted to Jessie that Charles would probably need a bit of training up in some areas: "The real crook in my lot I have withheld from you, but I must own it to you sooner or later. It is that he has a great dislike to going to the play, so that I am afraid we shall have some domestic discussions on that head."[71] She was happy, but not blinded by her new situation.

Delighted letters poured in to Emma and Charles from family and friends. From Jessie Sismondi, Emma got these congratulations and an aunt's advice about attire to a niece known in the family to care little about dress:

Dearest Emma, I conceive no greater happiness this side of heaven than that you are at this moment enjoying. Everything I have ever heard of C. Darwin

I have particularly liked, and have long wished for what has now taken place, that he would woo and win you. I love him all the better that he unites to all his other qualifications that most rare one of knowing how well to chuse a wife, a friend, companion, mother of his children, all of which men in general never think of. . . . I knew you would be a Mrs Darwin from your hands [Jessie was a believer in palmistry]. . . . Now that your person will belong to another as well as yourself, I beg you . . . pay a little more [so as to] be always dressed in good taste; do not despise those little cares which give everyone more pleasing looks, because you know you have married a man who is above caring for such little things. No man is above caring for them, for they feel the effect imperceptibly to themselves.[72]

Marianne Parker and Susan Darwin sent loving notes to Emma, and Erasmus's letter to Charles contained only brotherly affection. If, in fact, Ras's past included a failed proposal to Emma, he bore Charles no rancor:

I give you my most hearty & sincere congratulations on your good fortune, & feel very glad in what I am sure will give you so much & such certain happiness. Not less than to you, do I give my congrats to Emma though in writing to you I ought I suppose to word it somehow differently. It is a marriage which will give almost as much pleasure to the rest of the world as it does to yourselves—the best auspices I should think for any marriage.[73]

And from Betley village, the Tollet sisters sent notes of love and luck to their "dear, dear Emma." Georgina wrote:

It is seldom one thinks *two* people so enviable as we think you and Charles; we think you as lucky as you could possible wish, but we must allow that we have still better reason to *know* that he is indeed a blessed man. . . . It is very like a marriage of Miss Austen's can I say more![74]

Chief among the letters of delight, of course, were those between the parents of the newly engaged couple. Jos wrote to Robert Darwin:

A good, chearful, and affectionate daughter is the greatest blessing a man can have, after a good wife—if I could have given such a wife to Charles without parting with a daughter there would be no drawback from my entire satisfaction in bestowing Emma upon him. . . . I could have parted with Emma to no one for whom I would so soon and so entirely feel as a father, and I am happy in believing that Charles entertains the kindest feelings for his uncle-father.[75]

Interestingly, despite the solemnity of the occasion, Dr. Robert's letter to Jos and Bessy contained one of his few known jokes:

> Emma having accepted Charles gives me as great happiness as Jos [Joe] having married Caroline, and I cannot say more. On that marriage Bessy said she should not have had more pleasure if it had been Victoria, and you may assure her I feel as grateful for Emma, as if it had been Martineau herself that Charles had obtained. Pray give my love to Elizabeth, I fear I ought to condole with her, as the loss will be very great.[76]

Confirmation that the crack about Harriet Martineau was indeed the doctor's joking reply to Bessy's teasing is shown in Emma's response two days later to her own "uncle-father": "You will be glad to hear that Mamma has quite got over her disappointment about Miss Martineau & amuses herself a good deal in planning about houses cake &c."[77]

The two fathers joined together to set up the engaged couple in fine style. Jos pledged £5,000 in investment capital on Emma's behalf and a £400 annual allowance. Since according to the laws of the time Emma could not hold investments in her own name once she was married, her capital was entrusted to Ras Darwin and Joe Wedgwood as executors. Emma's dowry was matched by an investment pledge of £10,000 on Charles's behalf from the doctor—an amount expected to bring in about £600 a year in dividends.[78] Thus, thanks to their families' generosity, Charles and Emma were set to begin their married life with the modern equivalent of $1,250,000 in investment capital and an annual income of some $83,000. Now they only had to set the date and find a place to live.

6. Bride, Mother, Nurse

CHARLES WAS IN A HURRY; Emma was less so. He had only his lonely bachelorhood and rented London lodgings to give up; she would be leaving Maer, her parents, and Elizabeth. To further complicate matters, her tiny hunchbacked sister would be left alone to care for Bessy and Jos. Thus one can understand why, three days after she accepted Charles's proposal, Emma wrote to Catherine Darwin at The Mount asking for help slowing things down.

> My dear Catty
>
> Since Charles went I have been rather afraid of his being in too great a hurry so I hope you will all hold him in a little especially the Dr. I find Elizabeth would be very sorry if it was to happen very soon & that makes me wish more that things may not go too fast.
>
> She forgets herself so much that I should like her to have her wish, besides which I should wish it myself. I don't mean to insinuate that Charles would not mind what I say but if you all thought it could happen in no time as it were it would make me appear cross & disagreeable on Saturday [when he returns to Maer][1] when I mean to be particularly happy. . . .
>
> Goodbye my dearest. I am so glad you were hear. . . . You can keep this to yourself or not as you think best.

And then Elizabeth, happy for her sister but none too anxious to be left as the sole nurse for their aged parents, added this postscript to Catherine: "How I wish he would . . . wait till Spring & fine weather! F[anny] A[llen] says it is the happiest time of Emma's life & it is a thousand pities it should be a very short one—Do dear Catty clog the wheels a little."[2]

Emma's letter apparently made the rounds at Shrewsbury, and Charles, at home basking in the glow of his newly betrothed state, responded immediately with his counterargument:

> The Post has brought in your own dear note to Katty. . . . You say *truly* Elizabeth never thinks of herself, but there is another person, who never thinks of herself, but now she has to think of two people,—& I am, thank Heaven for it, that other person.—You must be absolute arbitress, but do dear Emma, remember life is short, & two months is the sixth part of the year, & that year, the first, from which for my part, things shall hereafter date. Whatever you do will be right,—but it will be *too* good to be unselfish for me, until I am part of you, dearest Emma.[3]

The reactions by both parties are understandable. The proposal had been sprung on Emma, whereas Charles had been contemplating for months making some sort of matrimonial move. And now that he had made his move, he was ready for that "nice soft wife on a sofa with a good fire, books and music." He was going on thirty, his scientific career was off and running, and most of his friends were already married. He saw no good reason to delay.

There is also evidence that Charles's libido was partly behind his eagerness to wed. He clearly had an eye for the ladies, going back at least to his days of flirting with Fanny Owen. His *Beagle* letters and travel journal contain admiring comments about the "angels gliding down the streets" of Buenos Aires,[4] and the women of Lima whose gowns "[fit] the figure closely" and who displayed "very white silk stockings & very pretty feet" and "black & brilliant" eyes.[5] And one can read multiple meanings into Charles's desire for a "nice soft wife on a sofa." Additional evidence comes from his scientific notebooks, which became increasingly erotic during the fall of 1838. To give two examples:

> [November 1838] Sexual desire makes saliva to flow yes *certainly*—curious association. . . . ones tendency to kiss, & almost bite, that which one sexually loves is probably connected with flow of saliva, & hence with action of *mouth* & jaws.—Lascivious women, are described as biting: so do stallions always. . . . No doubt man has great tendency to exert all senses, when thus

stimulated, smell as Sir. Ch. Bell says, & hearing music to certain degree sexual.

[November–December 1838] Blushing is intimately concerned with thinking of one's appearance,—does the thought drive blood to surface exposed, face of man, face, neck—upper bosom in woman: like erection shyness is certainly very much connected with thinking of oneself.—blushing is connected with sexual, because each sex thinks more of what another thinks of him, than of any one of his own sex. . . . My father even believes that the general talking about any disease tends to give it, as in cancer, showing, effect of mind on individual parts of body . . . (if you think fear you shall not have e————n ["erection," surely], or wish extraordinarily to have one you won't.)[6]

So it seems that (like most men?) Charles approached his wedding day with a mixture of love and lust. The neuter bee was about to acquire "a soft wife" whom he would enjoy physically and with whom he would experience domestic bliss. For Emma's part, any thoughts, positive or negative, about the physical side of marriage—and she must have had them—have gone unrecorded. Rather, she seems to have been preoccupied by two other concerns: first, the impact of her marriage on the people left behind at Maer and, second, the dwindling state of her groom's Christian faith.

Not long before Charles's proposal to Emma, probably during a conversation at The Mount in the summer of 1838, Dr. Robert advised his son to conceal his growing religious doubts from any future wife.[7] In the doctor's experience, marriages where the husband's disbelief was made known might go on "pretty well until the wife or husband became out of health, and then some women suffered miserably by doubting about the salvation of their husbands, thus making them likewise to suffer."[8] Charles listened carefully to his father's advice, but then, being the "most open, transparent man" Emma had ever met, he bared his soul a week into their engagement and told her the worst. She responded a few days later:

My dear Charles

. . . When I am with you I think all melancholy thoughts keep out of my head but since you are gone some sad ones have forced themselves in, of fear that our opinions on the most important subject should differ widely. My reason tells me that honest & conscientious doubts cannot be a sin, but I feel it would be a painful void between us. I thank you from my heart for your openness with me & I should dread the feeling that you were concealing your opinions from the fear of giving me pain. It is perhaps foolish of me to say this much but my own dear Charley we now do belong to each other & I cannot help being open with you. Will you do me a favour? yes I am sure you will, it is to read our Saviours farewell discourse to his disciples which begins at the end of the 13th Chap of John. It is so full of love to them & devotion & every beautiful feeling. It is the part of the New Testament I love best. This is a whim of mine it would give me great pleasure though I can hardly tell why. I don't wish you to give me your opinion about it.[9]

In the Bible passage recommended to Charles, Jesus tells his disciples that he is going to prepare a place for them in God's "many mansions." Reaching that heavenly destination, however, requires a strict faith: "I am the way, the truth, and the life; no man cometh unto the Father, but by me" (John 14:6). It seems clear, therefore, that Emma was already worried that she and Charles might be separated after death because of his lack of faith. It was a fear that would last for much of their marriage and occasion other letters. Thus while Charles's prenuptial thoughts focused solely on earthly pleasures and concerns, Emma's spanned earth and heaven.

While Emma dealt with the wedding plans at Maer, Charles threw himself into house hunting. Given his scientific needs and obligations, it was decided that they would reside in London, at least for a few years. They got advice about neighborhoods from all sides. Erasmus urged a place in central London, and Hensleigh agreed, suggesting that the houses near Regent's Park were "nice ones." The FitzRoys, on the other hand, strongly opposed a central location, and Elizabeth and Caroline also argued for the suburbs.[10] With Ras's help, Charles crisscrossed London looking for rentals and then dutifully reported back to Emma about any hot prospects. Would it be Kensington's Bayswater Road or Russell Square in Bloomsbury or perhaps one of the back lanes south of the Park? At one point, Charles was covering so much ground that Emma joked he risked going mad from house hunting and might end up wandering aimlessly about the city. They would probably have to advertise for him, she teased: "Lost in the vicinity of Bloomsbury a tall thin gentleman &c &c quite harmless whoever will bring him back shall be handsomely rewarded."[11] And then there was the issue of expense. Most of the suitable houses carried rents that were way too high to suit Charles's frugal nature, typically upwards of £150 a year. He stopped groaning about money only when cousin Robert Mackintosh sneered at him for being so cheap.[12] In the end Emma and Charles settled for a furnished house on Upper Gower Street, not far from Russell Square and less than a mile from Regent's Park. They would be within walking distance of the London Zoo and the new botanic garden,[13] and a easy carriage ride from central London.

They named the house Macaw Cottage because its previous owners had decked it out with bright yellow curtains and blue painted walls. On the advice of his legal advisor, Charles bought the contents of the house for £550—including some red plush furniture that added its own unique touch to the already garish color scheme—and then crowed to Emma that they should "not have much to buy,—even the crockery and glasses are very perfect." In modern terms a "starter house," Macaw Cottage was a two-story terraced house capable of holding a small family and a limited number of servants. There was a dining room, space for Charles's study, and a back room that overlooked a long, narrow garden where Emma planned to plant laburnums as a privacy screen. Unfortunately, the garden also came complete with a dead dog, but that was soon removed. The neighborhood was quiet and inhabited by the right class of people, but, like all the rest of London, extremely sooty.[14]

Unable to contain himself and still behaving with a bachelor's self-centeredness, Charles moved into Macaw Cottage the day after he leased it, without consulting his bride-to-be. Aided by Syms Covington, his servant since the *Beagle* voyage, Charles hauled crate after crate of books and specimens into the room he had selected for his study. This unilateral moving-in caught Emma off guard and annoyed her slightly. She wrote to Charles saying, "I was surprised indeed to find how soon you had moved into *your* new house. . . . You must have found it very interesting putting all your things away & arranging your sanctum to the greatest advantage." Picking up on her vexation, but unwilling to concede that he had acted precipitously, he wrote back "scolding": "is it not *our* house[?]" Little did Emma know how prescient she was being in labeling Charles's study a *sanctum*, an inviolable private retreat. It would be thus on Upper Gower Street and then for forty years at Down House.[15]

Among the hundred and one details Emma was dealing with was the question of her wedding dress. Taking to heart Jessie Sismondi's advice that she should smarten up her appearance, Emma reported to her aunt that she had "bought a sort of greenish-grey rich silk for the wedding . . . and a remarkably lovely white chip bonnet trimmed with blonde and flowers." She thought the silk dress, plus "a very handsome plaid satin," a "blue Paris gown," and a "blue and white sort of thing," would do "for the present."[16]

Then there was the need for servants. Emma wrote Charles about a housemaid who she thought could be hired for "Ten guineas a year & tea & sugar," or $875 today, comfortably within the salary range suggested by *Mrs Beeton's*

Book of Household Management a few years later. They would also need a manservant to replace Covington, who planned to emigrate to Australia, and a cook. Fanny Hensleigh helped out in the latter case. She vetted the cook candidates and hired an apparently suitable woman for fourteen guineas per year plus tea and sugar.[17]

The wedding took place on Tuesday, January 29, 1839, in St. Peter's Church, Maer. Charles and the other Darwins came over from Shrewsbury, whence he had written on the twenty-sixth to say "I have got the ring." He had had a pounding headache for forty-eight hours just before coming to Shrewsbury and wasn't entirely sure that he would make it to his own wedding.[18] All was well by the twenty-ninth, however, when the two families—lacking only poor bed-ridden Bessy—gathered in the little stone church to witness "Emma Wedgwood (Spinster)" being united in marriage to "Charles Robert Darwin (Bachelor, Master of Arts)." In keeping with this union of first cousins, yet another cousin, Allen Wedgwood, performed the ceremony.[19] The only dark clouds on the horizon that day were Bessy's absence and the fact that Caroline and Joe's first baby, Sophy Marianne, was dangerously ill.

The newlyweds did not tarry after the wedding. After a change of clothes and a brief rest by the fireside at Maer, they caught the train back to London. The wedding feast was sandwiches and water en route. When they arrived at Macaw Cottage, the maid had the fires going and everything was so warm and comfortable that even the garish red furniture seemed "quite tasteful." Two days later, Emma wrote a note to her mother that reduced Bessy and Jos to tears:

> My Dear Mamma,
> It was quite a relief to me to find on coming out of Church on Tuesday that you were still asleep, which spared you and me the pain of parting, though it is only for a short time. So now we have only the pleasure of looking forward to our next meeting. . . . I came away full of love and gratitude to all the dear affectionate faces I left behind me. They are too many to particularize. Tell my dear Eliz. I long to hear from her. Nothing can be too minute from dear home. . . . I don't know how to express affection enough to my dear, kind Pappa, but he will take it upon trust.
> Good-bye, my dearest Mamma,
> Your affectionate and very happy daughter,
> E. D.[20]

Bessy's response was a mixture of happiness for Emma and sadness over the death of Caroline and Joe's baby on the thirty-first.

A thousand thanks to you dearest Emma for your delightful letter which from the cheerful happy tone of it drew tears of pleasure from my old eyes. I am truly thankful to find you so happy and still more so that you are sensible of it, and I pray heaven that this may only be the beginning of a life full of peace & tranquility. My affection for Charles is much increased by considering him as the author of all your comfort. . . . Caroline has recovered her piece of mind as much as we could have expected. . . . The baby was buried yesterday. The Coffin was carried by Caroline's two maids in white gowns, hoods and gloves, and Charlotte & Susan walked after it. Joe intended to go but he was afraid he should not be able to command his feelings and was persuaded to give it up as Caroline did.[21]

Sophy Marianne joined an aunt she had never known, Fanny Wedgwood, in the churchyard of St. Peters, Maer.

Despite their somewhat unusual path to the altar—Charles being initially more taken with the *idea* of marriage than with winning a particular woman, and Emma believing that they would stay in a state of cousinly affection indefinitely—after the wedding they fell quickly and very deeply in love. Like all newly married couples, they called each other by pet names: "dear Nigger" for Charles, reflecting his "marital slavery," and "dear old Titty" for Emma, especially after the babies started to arrive. They also worked together to finish feathering their Macaw Cottage nest, buying, among other things, an armchair and a grand piano, the latter a wedding gift from Papa Jos. The piano was set up in a room overlooking the garden, and Emma's music soon became a regular part of their married life. Emma also started right in cultivating the respect of her household staff. She reported to her mother, "I have been facing the Cook in her own region to-day, and found fault with the boiling of the potatoes, which I thought would make a good beginning and set me up a little." The newlyweds began accepting invitations to tea and dinner, and entertaining in return. They also went to the theater and concerts regularly, on one occasion seeing one of Emma's favorite actors, William Charles Macready, in his new play *Richelieu*, and on another hearing Vincenzo Bellini's opera *La Sonnambula*. For his part, Charles attended regular meetings of the Geological and Zoological Societies.[22] Plays and concerts were not exactly his cup of tea, but then science wasn't Emma's. They both tried their best to appreciate and accommodate the other's interests.

One of their first dinner parties involved a number of scientific luminaries: Charles's old professor from Cambridge, the botanist J. S. Henslow, and his wife Harriet, daughter of the naturalist Leonard Jenyns; the geologist Charles Lyell, with his wife Mary and her sister Leonora Horner, daughters of another famous geologist, Leonard Horner; Dr. W. H. Fitton, physician and geologist; and Robert Brown, botanist. For Emma it was a memorable evening, although something of a hard slog. She reported afterwards to Elizabeth:

> I must tell you how our learned party went off yesterday. Mr and Mrs Henslow came at four o'clock and she, like a discreet woman, went up to her room till dinner. The rest of the company consisted of Mr and Mrs Lyell and Leonora Horner, Dr Fitton and Mr Robert Brown. We had some time to wait before dinner for Dr Fitton, which is always awful, and, in my opinion, Mr Lyell is enough to flatten a party, as he never speaks above his breath, so that everyone keeps lowering their tone to his. Mr Brown, whom [Alexander von] Humboldt calls "the glory of great Britain," looks so shy, as if he longed to shrink into himself and disappear entirely; however, notwithstanding those two dead weights, viz., the greatest botanist and the greatest geologist in Europe, we did very well and had no pauses. Mrs Henslow has a good, loud, sharp voice which was a great comfort, and Mrs Lyell has a very constant supply of talk. Mr Henslow was very glad to meet Mr Brown, as the two great botanists had a great deal to say to each other. Charles was dreadfully exhausted when it was over, and is only as well as can be expected to-day. . . . The dinner was very good.[23]

To the hostess, then, it had been a nice party but boring in spots, especially the scientific bits. And increasingly there was one aspect of Charles's devotion to science that his wife found not just boring but actually frightening: his strong turn toward materialism. Just a few months of marriage had shown her how far his evolution theories had led him from orthodox Christianity. She was terribly afraid that, following Erasmus's example, Charles was drifting inevitably into atheism and that his loss of faith would prevent them from being together in the hereafter. Desiring to express herself fully and logically and without her emotions getting in the way, she wrote out her concerns in a letter to Charles dated February 1839.

> The state of mind that I wish to preserve with respect to you, is to feel that while you are acting conscientiously & sincerely wishing, & trying to learn the truth, you cannot be wrong; but there are some reasons that force themselves upon me & prevent my being always able to give myself this comfort. I dare say you have often thought of them before, but I will write down what

has been in my head, knowing that my own dearest will indulge me. Your mind & time are full of the most interesting subjects & thoughts of the most absorbing kind, viz following up yr own discoveries—but which make it very difficult for you to avoid casting out as interruptions other sorts of thoughts which have no relation to what you are pursuing or to be able to give your whole attention to both sides of the question.

There is another reason which would have a great effect on a woman, but I don't know whether it wd so much on a man—I mean E[rasmus] whose understanding you have such a very high opinion of & whom you have so much affection for, having gone before you—is it not likely to have made it easier to you & to have taken off some of that dread & fear which the feeling of doubting first gives & which I do not think an unreasonable or superstitious feeling. It seems to me also that the line of your pursuits may have led you to view chiefly the difficulties on one side, & that you have not had time to consider & study the chain of difficulties on the other, but I believe you do not consider your opinion as formed. May not the habit in scientific pursuits of believing nothing till it is proved, influence your mind too much in other things which cannot be proved in the same way, & which if true are likely to be above our comprehension. I should say also that there is a danger in giving up revelation which does not exist on the other side, that is the fear of ingratitude in casting off what has been done for your benefit as well as for that of all the world & which ought to make you more careful, perhaps even fearful lest you should not have taken all the pains you could to judge truly. I do not know whether this is arguing as if one side were true & the other false, which I meant to avoid, but I think not. I do not quite agree with you in what you once said—that luckily there were no doubts as to how one ought to act. I think prayer is an instance to the contrary, in one case it is a positive duty & perhaps not in the other. But I dare say you meant in actions which concern others & then I agree with you almost if not quite. I do not wish for any answer to all this—it is a satisfaction to me to write it & when I talk to you about it I cannot say exactly what I wish to say, & I know you will have patience, with your own dear wife. Don't think that it is not my affair & that it does not much signify to me. Every thing that concerns you concerns me & I should be most unhappy if I thought we did not belong to each other forever. I am rather afraid my own dear Nigger will think I have forgotten my promise not to bother him, but I am sure he loves me & I cannot tell him how happy he makes me & how dearly I love him & thank him for all his affection which makes the happiness of my life more & more every day.[24]

Charles was deeply touched by the letter, full of love and concern as it was. He tucked it away for safekeeping, but not before noting at the end, "When I am dead, know that many times, I have kissed & cryed over this. C. D."[25] Whether his tears were due to Emma's touching words of love or because he knew he was causing her real pain is unknown. Furthermore, if they ever sat by the fireside at Macaw Cottage and talked about their respective faiths (and it is hard to believe that this never occurred), the conversations went unrecorded. Emma had read the signs correctly, however, and over the years Charles's Christianity would fade into a generalized theism and then finally into agnosticism.[26]

By early April, Emma was pregnant. Other than a reduction in concerts and theatergoing, however, there are few signs in her diary that the pregnancy was difficult for her. To be sure, she had her share of days when she felt under the weather, as shown by Elizabeth's remark to Aunt Jessie that Emma was "not very well" during a visit to Maer in early May. Spring turned into summer, and on August fifteenth Emma noted that she was "half way now I think from symptoms"; probably she had experienced quickening. By late October she was "poorly every other or third day . . . [but] essentially going on well & undeniably growing."[27]

Charles's first book, his *Journal of Researches into the Geology and Natural History of the Various Countries visited by H.M.S. Beagle*, was published in May as part of the three-volume *Narrative* of the voyage. It drew instant praise from such scientific notables as Richard Owen, Dr. Fitton, and—perhaps most important to Darwin—Alexander von Humboldt. In August the *Journal* was published separately, and it is still in print today as *The Voyage of the* Beagle. On April 22 Emma had made the notation "Charles Journal" in her diary, perhaps marking the arrival of a prepublication copy. Other than that, this milestone in her husband's career, the book that first made him famous and established him as an important figure in British science, went without remark. Apparently there was no book party.[28]

On October 6 Emma gave them all a scare when she stumbled and fell. No harm was done, however, and she delivered a healthy baby boy on December 27, 1839. Elizabeth came from Maer to help with the birth, and most likely Fanny Hensleigh, who since June had lived just a few doors away on Gower Street, was there as well. Predictably, Charles's stomach gave way in the face of Emma's delivery pains and he took to his own sickbed. They named the child William Erasmus and, once Charles was over his couvade, the proud father started a journal on the behavioral development of his "little animalcule."[29]

Not surprisingly, the baby—who was nicknamed Hoddy-Doddy or just plain Doddy—was a delight to both of his parents. In no sense a reserved Victorian father, Charles alternated making notes on Doddy's behavior with dispensing hugs and kisses. Emma, meanwhile, had to gain strength before she could enjoy her new son. Exhausted by the birth, she also had problems suckling the baby. Nursing brought on headaches, and for a while Doddy's diet was supplemented with ass's milk.[30] By February, however, Emma was herself again. She wrote to Jessie Sismondi extolling her son's relatively good looks:

> Now I am quite well and strong and able to enjoy the use of my legs and my baby, and a very nice looking one it is, I assure you. He has very dark blue eyes and a pretty, small mouth, his nose I will not boast of, but it is very harmless as long as he is a baby. Elizabeth went away a week too soon while he was a poor little wretch before he began to improve. She was very fond of him then, and I expect she will admire him as much as I do in the summer at Maer. He is a sort of grandchild of hers.[31]

As she convalesced, Emma had worked her way through Thomas Carlyle's latest book, *Chartism*. Now she gave Aunt Jessie the benefit of a brief review. Named for the working-class movement that arose in the 1830s in response to a deepening economic depression, bad harvests, and the perception of governmental ineptitude, *Chartism* went beyond the agitators' immediate case and examined the entire Condition-of-England Question. Carlyle agreed that the situation of the British working classes was abominable; indeed, he thought it was dangerous in much the same way as pre-Revolution conditions had been in France. He blamed the British situation on an inept do-nothing aristocratic government operating on *laissez-faire* economic policies. "That self-cancelling Donothingism and *Laissez-faire* should have got so ingrained into our Practice, is the source of all these miseries. It is too true that Parliament, for the matter of near a century now, has been able to undertake the adjustment of almost one thing alone, of itself and its own interests; leaving other interests to rub along very much as they could and would." Interestingly, Carlyle did not think granting the Chartists' demands for expanded suffrage, electoral reforms, and various parliamentary changes would correct Britain's untenable condition. Indeed, he was downright suspicious of too much democracy: "Not [that] impossibility, 'self-government' of a multitude by a multitude." Instead he longed for a "veritable" parliamentary government that would once again forcefully and wisely lead the people and inspire their loyalty. The relations between upper classes and underclasses required a system of paternalistic care and guidance reciprocated by loyalty and obedience; in short, a near return to medieval conditions when strong feudal lords led loyal and obedient serfs.[32]

Emma's reaction to Carlyle's rambling observations provides one of the earliest glimpses into her political leanings. In a word, as she told her aunt, she was unimpressed:

> I have been reading Carlyle, like all the rest of the world. He fascinates one and puts one out of patience. He has been writing a sort of pamphlet on the state of England called "Chartism." It is full of compassion and good feeling but utterly unreasonable. Charles keeps on reading and abusing him. He is very pleasant to talk to anyhow, he is so very natural, and I don't think his writings at all so.[33]

Ever a daughter of Jos Wedgwood, Emma would remain "a staunch Whig-Liberal" throughout her life.[34] While she felt compassion for the poor and working classes and always acted to relieve their distresses in small ways, she was neither a socialist nor a political reformer. Thus both the Chartists' democratic demands and Carlyle's dream of a return to the days of feudal strong men struck Emma as nonsense. Happily for the harmony of Macaw Cottage, Charles agreed.

With the return of her strength, Emma was anxious to resume a normal schedule of correspondence, social calls, and cultural excursions. She wrote to Sismondi and Aunt Jessie, who were planning a summer visit from Switzerland, that she longed to "receive you both in my own house and show you my own dear husband and child." She and Charles also bought season passes to the Philharmonic Society concerts for 1840. Emma's diary lists the full set of eight spring concerts, although as it turned out the Darwins were able to attend only about half of them.[35]

The problem was Charles's health. Only marginally well since the wedding, he took a distinct turn for the worst during the winter of 1839–40. Seeking relief from chronic nausea and vomiting, flatulence, headaches, and extreme fatigue, he consulted his distant cousin Dr. Henry Holland but "without much good effect."[36] Finally, in early April, Charles's symptoms drove him home to Shrewsbury to consult his father. Dr. Robert prescribed *ad libitum* dosing with calomel, which, in combination with the care of his father and sisters, calmed Charles's stomach dramatically.[37] And it badly needed calming; he had lost more than ten pounds in the previous six months. In fact, he was losing weight faster than Doddy was gaining it. After a week in Shrewsbury without illness, Charles returned to Macaw Cottage feeling better, but the respite would not last long.[38]

The Sismondis arrived on June 2 for their Gower Street visit, but three days later Emma was so worried about her ailing husband that she did the unthinkable and abandoned her guests in order to whisk Charles and the baby off to Maer for rest and recuperation in the country. Aunt Jessie and Sis stayed on at Macaw Cottage for another few days under the care of the maids and the new manservant, Joseph Parslow, whose talents were especially appreciated. Jessie wrote a warm thank-you note from their next stop at Tenby describing Parslow as "the most amiable, obliging, active, serviceable servant that ever breathed." She hoped the Darwins would "never part with him," and so it would prove. Parslow was destined to serve the family, primarily as their butler, for another thirty-five years.[39]

At Maer, Charles passed June and July in a state of chronic moderate illness, but nonetheless by mid-June Emma was pregnant for the second time. During the first week of August, however, he declined fairly dramatically and remained quite ill for two months, not really improving significantly until October. Dr. Darwin came over from Shrewsbury four times during this period to check on his son; Susan and Catherine Darwin came once each. Emma kept careful diary entries on Charles's energy, pulse, nausea, and other symptoms, as well as his medications (calomel, bismuth, Prussic acid) and his diet (e.g., "very good day after chicken"). In the midst of it all, Doddy cut his first tooth and his sibling-to-be continued to grow in Emma's womb. She noted in her diary on October 10, "Think I have quickened."[40]

In October, Charles showed improvement. "Brisk mornings" stretched into "good days" and he began to take some exercise by walking around the Maer estate. On November first, one day before Doddy uttered his first word (reported to have been "poor"), Charles "walked twice to the Bathing house & once to [the] gate." On November 13 the whole family returned to London and Gower Street.[41]

In order to understand Emma and Charles's relationship, one needs to pause here and examine more closely the etiology of Charles's chronic sickness and the broad effects of his ill health. Regarding the source of his affliction, suggestions are many and definitive diagnoses are few, but among the contenders are allergic reactions stemming from a dysfunctional immune system, panic disorder or some other psychological condition(s), Crohn's disease, lupus, and Chagas' disease. Taking these possibilities in order, Scottish researcher Fabienne Smith concluded that Charles inherited a vulnerable immune system from his Darwin and Wedgwood ancestors and that stress, both during and after the *Beagle*'s voyage, brought on full immunosuppression. The latter development, in turn, could have opened the way for multiple allergies including reactions to rich foods (reputedly much favored in the Darwin household), heavy metals (such as those contained in the common Victorian medications calomel and "blue pills"), and the preservative chemicals Charles used routinely in his scientific work.[42]

A second suggestion is that Charles suffered from some sort of psychological disorder that, when exacerbated by stress, resulted in his physical symptoms. Several variations on this theme were published throughout the twentieth century, among them psychoanalyst John Bowlby's suggestion that Darwin suffered from "hyperventilation syndrome," a condition that can alter blood chemistry and trigger numerous physical side effects. The origin of his psychological weakness is sometimes traced to the early loss of his mother and/or resentment toward his domineering father.[43] In their 1991 biography of Darwin, Adrian Desmond and James Moore argued that as Charles worked away at his evolutionary studies, the mental stress of developing such a controversial theory—particularly one that undercut a creationist explanation for biological diversity and human origins—could have brought on his bodily symptoms. Articles suggesting a psychosomatic component to Darwin's illness have continued into the twenty-first century.[44]

Chilean physicians Fernando Orrego and Carlos Quintana recently offered yet another diagnosis: Crohn's disease. In their view, this inflammatory gastrointestinal disorder started from a bacterial infection Darwin suffered in 1834 while in South America. Orrego and Quintana argue that the infection led to chronic Crohn's, a malady that they believe accounts for most of Charles's list of symptoms. This is an intriguing possibility, and equally intriguing is the suggestion made by D. A. B. Young, that Darwin suffered from lupus erythematosus. Young argued that Charles's nausea and vomiting, abdominal pains, eczema, and boils were all the results of systemic lupus.[45]

But in the view of the late Ralph Colp Jr., who for more than thirty years was the chief American researcher into Darwin's health problems, the most likely etiology of his symptoms is that he had Chagas' disease, a condition brought on by parasites Darwin picked up while traveling inland in South America. Charles had described being bitten by Vinchuca bugs—carriers of the Chagas' parasite—while exploring in Argentina,[46] and, according to Colp, his symptoms from about age thirty onward conform pretty well with a diagnosis of the disease "injuring the stomach and its parasympathetic nerves," thereby causing vomiting and chronic flatulence and also "increas[ing] Darwin's sensitivity to stress." The idea that Darwin suffered from Chagas' disease was first raised by parasitologist Saul Adler in the late 1950s. Colp initially dismissed Adler's theory, but in the last decade reversed his position and became fully convinced that Charles was a Chagas' sufferer.[47]

Whatever the actual etiology of Charles's complaints—and it appears likely that a universally acceptable solution to this mystery will never be worked out—there is no question that his health problems, although mitigated by his ability to remain relatively cheerful and social while ill, profoundly affected his relationship with Emma. Even before their marriage she worried about Charles's health and repeatedly expressed her desire to nurse him through all afflictions. A month before their wedding, Emma wrote from Maer:

> You have looked so unwell for some time that I am afraid you will be laid up if you fight it any longer. Do set off to Shrewsbury & get some doctoring & then come here & be idle. . . . nothing *could* make me so happy as to feel that I could be of any use or comfort to my own dear Charles when he is not well. If you knew how I long to be with you when you are not well! . . . So don't be ill any more my dear Charley till I can be with you to nurse you & save you from bothers.[48]

The sincerity of these sentiments would be demonstrated time and again throughout their long marriage. Emma positively thrived on caring for Charles, while he in turn gratefully gave himself up to her tender care. She wrote to Aunt Jessie in February 1840: "It is a great happiness to me when Charles is most unwell that he continues just as sociable as ever, and is not like the rest of the Darwins, who will not say how they really are; but he always tells me how he feels and never wants to be alone, but continues just as warmly affectionate as ever, so that I feel I am a comfort to him."[49] The "perpetual patient" had found his "devoted nurse."[50] For more than forty years, Charles would depend on Emma for peace of mind and body; for her part, Emma would never waver or grow resentful in that responsibility. Indeed, the caregiver-patient relationship would become an important channel for these two undemonstrative people to express their mutual love and devotion.

Befitting the end of the Little Ice Age, the London winter of 1840–41 was severely cold. Not as cold as that of 1837–38, perhaps, when the lowest temperatures of the nineteenth century were recorded for London, -16°C and -20°C at Greenwich and Blackheath respectively, and the Thames at Greenwich was covered with ice in January, but brutal nonetheless.[51] As they hunkered down inside Macaw Cottage, Charles's health fluctuated from good to bad, and so did Emma's as her second pregnancy entered its final trimester. One-year-old Doddy, now "a noble fat little fellow," had the family wrapped around his little finger. Doting grandfather Dr. Robert had dubbed him Sir Tunbelly Clumsy after a comic stage character. In January, anticipating the need for additional help with child care, the Darwins hired fifteen-year-old Bessy Harding from Maer to join the household as Doddy's nursemaid.[52]

Charles was struggling both with his health and with a workload that would have staggered a much stronger man. Not only was he still overseeing the piecemeal publication of the *Zoology of the Voyage of H.M.S. Beagle* and serving as secretary of the Geological Society, but now he was devoting valuable mental energy to worrying about Louis Agassiz's new glacial theory and its impact on his own sea-beach explanation of the so-called "parallel roads" of Glen Roy, Scotland. In his spare time, what little there was of it, Charles was also reading widely for information on varieties and species—that is, evolution—but his book on that subject lay far in the future. Still, he managed to free up a part of his overloaded brain to worry about his heavily pregnant wife and to wish that her confinement, always a risky time, be over.[53]

In the event, Emma delivered her second child, a little girl named Anne Elizabeth, on March 2, 1841, without any major problem. Elizabeth came down from Maer to assist with the birth, and Dr. Henry Holland was on hand as well. It appears that once again Emma found it hard to nurse her baby and that a wet nurse was hired for a short period. Annie's weight was recorded in her mother's diary in late March, mid-April, and early May, but then no more. Perhaps the baby was gaining weight satisfactorily, or perhaps the novelty of baby-weighing had simply worn off after Doddy.[54]

In late May the family set out for a month-long visit to Maer. While there, Emma's diary indicates "children christened." As there were no other young children at Maer that summer, the plural seems to refer only to Doddy and Annie. The officiating minister was undoubtedly their cousin Allen Wedgwood, vicar of St. Peter's Church next door.[55]

The month of June was devoted to family socializing in and around Maer. The usual Hall residents—Bessy, Jos, and Elizabeth—were joined by Susan Darwin and by Emma's brothers Frank and Harry and their wives. Near the end of the month Susan went back to Shrewsbury, taking Doddy with her, and then Charles followed, with Emma delaying the move to her in-laws' for an additional week.[56]

She did eventually travel to The Mount, although probably reluctantly, since Charles had warned her by post that the judgmental Darwins were lying in wait with criticisms on a host of issues. On July 3 he wrote:

> A thunder storm is preparing to break on your head, & which has already deluged me,—about Bessy [Harding] not having a cap,—"looks dirty", "like grocer's maidservant" & my Father with much wrath added "the men will take liberties with her, if she is dressed differently from every other lady's maid"!!! Both [Susan and Catherine] echoed this—I generously took half the blame, & never betrayed that I had beseeched you several times on that score—If they open on you pray do not defend yourself, for they are very hot on the subject. My Father has taken Parslow's long greasy hair into hand, which I am well pleased at, & quizzed him before the other servant, whether he was training to turn into my Lord Judge with a long wig.[57]

Dr. Robert, part concerned grandfather and part prig, was also highly critical of Doddy's care and feeding. Apparently Bessy Harding was giving the boy half a cup of cream every morning, occasionally neglecting to place water at his bedside at night, and not paying sufficient attention to whether his feet got wet during the day. These things were dangerous to the health of a grandson that the doctor already thought looked "very delicate," and he unloaded on Charles as only Dr. Robert could.[58] All in all, Charles and Emma likely had a very long fortnight at The Mount before they could decently take their leave and return to the peace of Macaw Cottage.

Significantly, between lectures about maids' caps, butlers' hair, and babies' diets, Charles had managed to sound out his father on the possibility of buying a country house and moving out of the dingy metropolis of London. The plan was to relocate about twenty miles out, but near enough to a rail line to have easy access to the city. London had become a "great Wen" full of "dirt, noise, vice & misery," and both Charles and Emma longed for a Maer-like country existence. By August they were actively house hunting. Judging from family letters and end-note entries in Emma's diaries, they searched primarily to the west and south of London, both in Berkshire, near Windsor and Hurst ("6 acres"), and in Surrey, between Chobham and Bagshot, near Reigate ("60 acres"), and in the vicinity of Lingfield. It was not until almost exactly a year later, however, that they located the property they would inhabit for four decades: Down House in Kent, a structure just over sixty years old and most recently used as the vicarage for the village church. They would be just sixteen miles from the heart of London, although initially eight and a half of that was a carriage ride to the rail station at Sydenham.[59]

The last year at Macaw Cottage passed quickly enough, although for Charles and Emma, anxious to leave the city for a cleaner, quieter country life, time must have crawled. Certainly one measure of the passing time was the undeniable fact that the children were growing up. Just a few days after her first birthday, Annie walked unaided for the first time and was heard to say the word "goat." Two-year-old Willy was now chattering away, comforting himself when told he couldn't go on a journey by saying "go when Doddy big man," but still stumbling over difficult words such as a shortened version of his Aunt Elizabeth's name, which came out as "Dziver." By the spring and summer of 1842, Willy was also displaying an independent streak; in addition to fits of temper, he made raids on the pantry for sugar and pickles, and then lied to cover up his larceny. And, in a pattern that was becoming routine, there was another baby on the way. Emma had conceived for the third time just ten months after Annie's birth, and seven weeks into this pregnancy she was already "languid & unwell." With their family growing and Emma near the end of her strength, it was clearly time to hire more help. Accordingly, a carrot-topped Scot, Jessie Brodie, was added to the household as a live-in nursemaid. Thoroughly experienced thanks to time spent caring for the children of William Makepeace Thackeray, Brodie would become a great favorite of the young Darwins.[60]

Within the extended family, the early 1840s saw other important events. On the Wedgwood side, in 1842 Josiah II finally resigned his partnership in the pottery, putting the management of the family business entirely in Frank's hands. Joe and Caroline, the latter forty-one years old and pregnant for the second time, bought Leith Hill Place in Surrey and settled down to a quiet country existence. And Charlotte and Charles Langton moved back to Maer Hall after Langton experienced such a dramatic loss of faith that he felt compelled to resign from his "living." This apparently was not uncommon among Victorian clergymen. Although undoubtedly a trying time for the Langtons, their relocation to Maer was a godsend for Elizabeth, who now had help caring for Bessy and Papa Jos.[61]

On the Darwin side, in the fall of 1841 their cousin W. D. Fox asked Charles to stand as godfather for his newborn son, Samuel William. After some hemming and hawing, during which Charles expressed his discomfort at "believing anything for another," he agreed. Both cousins understood, however, that it was purely an honorary commitment marking their long friendship. Charles made no effort to attend the actual christening ceremony.[62]

Tragically, only months later in March 1842, Harriet Fox died during her next confinement, leaving W. D. a widower with five children to care for. Charles did his best to comfort his cousin, writing that "having children . . . must make the separation appear less entire—the unspeakable tenderness of young children must sooth the heart & recall the tenderest however mournful remembrances."[63] Given Emma's own delicate condition—she was two months along at the time—Harriet Fox's passing must have haunted Charles, reminding him in the still of the night that death in childbirth was no respecter of class or position.

Nonetheless, sadness was once again balanced by happiness during the winter and spring of 1841–42. A son was born to Charlotte and Charles Langton in November 1841; christened Edmund, he would be their only child. And in February 1842 Caroline Wedgwood gave birth to a girl called Katherine Elizabeth Sophy. No doubt unnerved by memories of their lost child, also named Sophy, Caroline and Joe traveled to Shrewsbury so Dr. Robert could supervise the new baby's birth and postnatal care. Although baby Katherine's health was worrying for a few weeks, by early March she was "quite well" and Caroline was in "very good spirits."[64]

On Gower Street, although overburdened by Geological Society duties and various writing projects, with his *Coral Reefs* book nearing completion and portions of the *Zoology* still in progress, Charles found time in early 1842 to outline his ideas on transmutation. During a May–June visit to Shrewsbury and Maer, he wrote out a short "sketch" of his evolution theory and its supporting data. In thirty-seven scrawled pages, Charles touched on most of the topics that seventeen years later would serve as chapter headings in *On the Origin of Species*: variation under domestication and in the wild, natural selection, sexual selection, complex instincts, geographical distribution, classification, embryology, and rudimentary organs. He wrote about an organic world produced by means of natural laws rather than repeated and separate acts of divine creation, yet left room for the very laws themselves to be the products of an "omniscient Creator." There was still space for God in Charles's transmutationist worldview, but not for a God that acted directly on nature. Whether he showed the sketch to Emma is unknown. He was painfully aware of her misgivings about his continuing drift away from religion. Yet to share it with her would have been in keeping with his practice of full disclosure.[65]

Finally, it is interesting to note that Charles's first attempt to put his species theory into words coincided almost exactly with the appearance of a magazine that would take great delight at poking fun at it once it was published. The comic magazine *Punch* was launched in July 1841 with an initial capital of £25, and throughout the post-*Origin* years, Darwin would be one of *Punch*'s favorite targets, both in drawings and in verse.[66] The price of being an evolutionist would eventually include being caricatured as a monkey-man, a pipe-smoking ape, and a Sistine Chapel deity busily spinning worms into men.

7. Narrow Lanes and High Hedges

T
HE HOUSE THE DARWINS HAD FOUND in the summer of 1842
fit their needs adequately, if not "to a T." Down House, located just
three miles from the north edge of the Weald in the county of Kent
and village of Downe, had many features to recommend it. Most
important for Emma and Charles's rapidly growing family, it was big. "We can
hold the Hensleighs & you & Susan & Erasmus all together," Charles boasted
to Catherine. Besides numerous bedrooms on the second and third floors, the
house had a ground-floor drawing room and a dining room, a kitchen, scul-
lery, and pantry, two small rooms for hipbath bathing, and a 324-square-foot
room that Charles claimed for his study. Although hot water for bathing had
to be heated in the kitchen and carried up by the maids, cold water for the
water closet was piped down from the roof, probably from a storage reservoir
or "water butt." The house was in good repair and came with pretty plantings
in front, a kitchen garden, fruit trees, and eighteen acres of land, fifteen of
which were in use as hay fields. At £2,200, the asking price was substantially
lower than other properties Charles and Emma had considered.[1]

Initially Emma was underwhelmed. Her first tour of the house took place
on a cold and gloomy July afternoon when, six months pregnant, she was miserable from the combined effects of a toothache, a headache, and the eight-
mile carriage ride from the train station. A return visit the next day, when she
was feeling better, "worked a great change" in her opinion of the property.[2]

Part of Emma's ambivalence could have been due to the fact that she and Charles were about to move even further from Maer and her loved ones there. Whereas train travel between Staffordshire and London had been relatively easy, getting to Maer from Kent would involve two legs on the train plus the long carriage ride at the Downe end. Emma longed to see her bedridden mother and declining father *more* frequently, not less. Their generation was fast disappearing, after all, the most recent death being Sismondi's in June. In response to Emma's letter of condolence, Aunt Jessie had written to say she was sending Sis's Miltons and Camoëns to add to the Down House library.[3]

Events in August reinforced the Darwins' decision to get out of London. There was revolutionary fever in the air, and across the country the Chartists were calling for strikes by factory workers. On August 15 Emma noted in her diary "Riots in Potteries." The reference was to a confrontation in Burslem between striking workers and armed troops that left three rioters dead. Soldiers leaving London to put down the Chartist agitations passed near Macaw Cottage as they marched to their trains. For two people in search of a quiet life, it was high time to move to the country.[4]

They bought Down House in August. Although they would have preferred to rent for a year before buying, the owner was dead set on selling, and they took the advice of a local architect, Mr. Creasy, to snap up the property before someone else did. Creasy assured them that the cost of living in Downe was very low, and he even offered to tutor Charles in the raising of chickens, pigs, and cows—livestock that could be slaughtered for home use or sold to supplement the family income.[5] The purchase of Down House was underwritten by Charles and Emma's favorite family banker, Dr. Robert.[6]

Emma, the children, and some of the servants made the move to Down House on September 14, with Charles and the rest of the staff following three days later. Willy had been sickly for several days and was feverish during the move, but he soon bucked up in his new surroundings and went into ecstasies over his "country ouse." Given the advanced state of Emma's pregnancy, one of their first local contacts was the village surgeon, Mr. Cockell. And none too soon: Emma delivered her third child, a little girl named Mary Eleanor, on September 23 with Cockell in attendance (for which he was paid five guineas). Not long after the birth, Ras Darwin roused himself enough to make the train-and-carriage trip from London to see his new niece. "Uncle Ras" made it clear that it was the baby he had come to see and not the place. He disliked everything about country living and poked fun at Charles and Emma's new rusticity in the wilds of "Down-in-the-mouth."[7]

Unfortunately, the joy of Mary Eleanor's safe arrival was diluted by worrisome events at Maer. Two days before Mary's birth, Jos suffered a bad fall that everyone feared might be fatal. The family, including Dr. Darwin, now wheelchair-bound himself, gathered at Maer expecting the worst.[8] Hensleigh wrote to Charles and Emma with this description of Jos's tremors and increasing dementia:

> Yesterday . . . the shaking . . . returned in a considerable degree . . . [and he was] very restless & wanting to get up to settle affairs & by degrees getting to wander almost continually. . . . he laughed two or three times at mistakes that he made & was now & then satisfied that the things he saw were "some of his illusions." . . . He asked me last night whether his father were living, & who was in his place, what he died of, & whether by natural decay or by medicine.
>
> Elizabeth keeps up pretty well tho' she is very anxious—I do not think she is aware of what seems to me the imminent prospect of my father's end.[9]

As it happened, Jos lived on for another ten months, although fully as incapacitated as his wife. The sadness of his final decline hit everyone hard; everyone, that is, except his wife. Mercifully, Bessy was so deep into her own dementia that she was beyond worrying about her husband's last illness.[10]

But death was not to be denied a Wedgwood-Darwin victim that fall, and even as Jos stabilized, Mary Eleanor began to weaken. After a few days of going on "fairly well" under the care of a wet nurse, the baby went into a steep decline and died on October 16. In shock with grief, Emma could manage only a one-word diary entry: "died." Now she knew all too well Caroline and Joe's suffering at the loss of their first child. Four days later, and just one day after Mary's burial in the Downe churchyard, Emma wrote to Fanny Hensleigh:

> Thank you, my dearest Fanny, for your sweet, feeling note. Our sorrow is nothing to what it would have been if she had lived longer and suffered more. Charles is well to-day and the funeral over, which he dreaded very much. . . . I think I regret her more from the likeness to Mamma, which I had often pleased myself with fancying might run through her mind as well as face. . . . With our two other dear little things you need not fear that our sorrow will last long, though it will be long indeed before we either of us forget that poor little face.[11]

The death of William Fox's wife had reminded them of a woman's danger during childbirth, and now its evil twin, the death of a baby, had struck their own little family. The fact that infant mortality was commonplace—in the

1840s roughly three out of every twenty British babies died before their first birthday—did not dull the pain one bit. To society, Mary Eleanor Darwin was now just a sad statistic; to her mother, she would always be a lost "little face."[12]

By November, Emma had resumed her monthly cycles, and before the end of the year she was pregnant for the fourth time. Perhaps at about this point she might have agreed with Susannah Darwin's comment from forty years before, "Everybody seems young but me." Certainly, somewhere along the line the carefree Emma of the 1820s, the girl who had charmed friends and acquaintances with her "abounding life and high spirits," had become reserved to the point of being grave. It was Charles who told the jokes and orchestrated the merriment at Down House; Emma sympathized with the family fun, but she rarely laughed out loud. And although devoted to her husband and children, as they all knew very well, she was not given to displays of affection. She "was never a doting mother," one of the children remembered years later. As Emma entered middle age, the years full of repeated pregnancies and constant worries about her sickly husband and failing parents were taking a toll. She was becoming less and less like her extroverted mother and more and more like her strong and silent father.[13]

They began modifying Down House immediately. The drawing room on the southwest side of the house, and the second- and third-floor rooms directly above it, were enlarged by the addition of a three-window bay. This had the effect of making Emma's bedroom "truly magnificent," and Charles joked to Susan that he "quite grudge[d] it her." Additionally, they hired a crew to lower the lane in front of the house a full two feet. This improvement, combined with the construction of a six-foot-high rock wall, significantly increased privacy within the house. All of this took money, of course, and therefore worried Charles, who feared they were spending themselves into bankruptcy. But Dr. Robert came to the rescue with "a cool 300£," or $25,000 today, to cover the costs.[14]

The new year 1843 found Charles making regular trips into London, mostly to do Geological Society work. And despite suffering from morning sickness, Emma also ventured into town in January for some shopping (she considered the shops in the smallish town of Bromley next door to be "very bad") and a bit of urban culture. One of her first stops in the city was the Regent Street shop of Howell and James, where they sold everything from bathing suits to jewelry to tableware. Another was to buy "play things" for the children, and a third was to see the opera *King Arthur* by Dryden and Purcell.[15] She was then "very bad for a week" in early March with her pregnancy, but the symptoms abated somewhat in April and she "began to sit up later & be more comfortable in the evening." On May 8, two days after returning from another London shopping trip for "comfits . . . playthings . . . raisins . . . morphine . . . pencil . . . hat & [bonnet]," Emma quickened with the baby girl she was carrying.[16]

Meanwhile at Maer, Jos was in his final decline and, heavily pregnant or not, in June Emma felt the need to go to his bedside. Charles came along a month later, and they were both there alongside Elizabeth and other family members when Josiah Wedgwood II died peacefully on July 12, 1843. Emma's reaction to her father's death went unrecorded, but one can reconstruct it readily enough: deep grief borne with little outward expression. In comparison to Elizabeth's grief, however, Emma undoubtedly counted herself lucky. As the only unmarried daughter and her parents' most devoted caregiver, Elizabeth had lost one of her two main reasons for living. With an aunt's understanding of a beloved niece's devastating loss, Fanny Allen wrote these words of condolence:

> My dearest Elizabeth,
>
> I feel it almost as necessary as breathing to me now, to express to you my deep tenderness and feelings for you at this awful time. Among all his children, who have loved him so well, it is to you, who must feel his death the most, that one naturally turns with the greatest pity. I do not think the religious consolation comes immediately, but in the meanwhile you have the sweetest earthly one, the knowledge that you have been the most helpful, cheerful and affectionate child that ever father was blessed with.[17]

Once Emma was back at Down House, her pregnancy proceeded smoothly to the birth of Henrietta Emma ("Etty") on September 25. With her arrival the Darwins once again had three children, all under the age of four, and Emma had the daughter who would one day become her first biographer. The Robert FitzRoys also had three small children by that time, and September 1843 found that family under sail to New Zealand, where FitzRoy had been appointed the colonial governor. It would be a short and unhappy stay, however, and less than two years later they would make the return trip to England. Although competent in naval matters, FitzRoy proved incapable of handling colonial politics. Unable to please the settlers, the native Maoris, or the Colonial Office back in London, FitzRoy was recalled in October 1845.[18]

As 1843 came to an end, Charles and Emma and their growing brood were living contented country lives. Susan Darwin came for a visit in November and treated them to new chintz curtains, an ottoman, and other small gifts that dressed up the house nicely. Emma and baby Etty were doing splendidly. Charles reported to W. D. Fox that Emma

> has never had so good a recovery & there never was such a good little soul—as Miss Henrietta Emma Darwin—she is beginning to smile & be very charming,—though how she has any idea, except whether the milk comes fast or slow is hard to conjecture—I have now nearly got this place in order, though there is much yet to do—& I think when you next see it, you will think it greatly improved.[19]

Part of Charles's contentment that fall was due to his renewed contact and growing friendship with the young botanist Joseph Dalton Hooker. The son of W. J. Hooker, founder and director of the Royal Botanic Gardens at Kew, Joseph Hooker had recently returned to England after his own voyage of discovery, to the Antarctic aboard HMS *Erebus*. Now the younger Hooker was settling down to work up his botanical collections, and Charles hoped that in the bargain he might take on the description of his own specimens from Tierra del Fuego and the Galapagos. Professor Henslow—who would become J. D. Hooker's father-in-law in a few years—aided the scheme by passing the *Beagle* plants over to him. These specimens were important for Charles's transmutation theories, and in his cover letter soliciting help he gave Hooker very pointed directions as to which analyses he, Darwin, would find interesting. At this point their friendship was too new for Charles to tip his hand about evolution, so he simply told Hooker that a comparison of the *Beagle*'s plants with European species would be "curious" and to "the advantage of Botanical Ignoramuses" like Darwin himself. Of course, this was more than a little disingenuous, since by 1843 Charles was far from being a botanical ignoramus, although not yet an expert. Nonetheless, Hooker took the request at face value, agreed to it, and wrote back a long and enthusiastic reply.[20]

The Darwin-Hooker relationship bloomed rapidly. Hooker was flattered by the attention of the older scientist, and Charles quickly sensed that in Hooker he had found not only a source of botanical information but also a confidant and sounding board for his species theories. And Charles badly needed a confidant. He was bursting to tell *someone* about his thoughts on evolution, and the nonjudgmental Hooker seemed ideal. In January 1844 Charles ended a letter to Hooker with this confession about his post-*Beagle* ruminations:

I have been now ever since my return engaged in a very presumptuous work & which I know no one individual who wd not say a very foolish one.—I was so struck with distribution of Galapagos organisms &c &c & with the character of the American fossil mammifers, &c &c that I determined to collect blindly every sort of fact, which cd bear any way on what are species.—I have read heaps of agricultural & horticultural books, & have never ceased collecting facts—At last gleams of light have come, & I am almost convinced (quite contrary to opinion I started with) that species are not (it is like confessing a murder) immutable. Heaven forfend me from Lamarck nonsense of a "tendency to progression" "adaptations from the slow willing of animals" &c,—but the conclusions I am led to are not widely different from his—though the means of change are wholly so—I think I have found out (here's presumption!) the simple way by which species become exquisitely adapted to various ends.—You will now groan, & think to yourself "on what a man have I been wasting my time in writing to."—I [should], five years ago, have thought so.[21]

To Charles's great relief, Hooker wasn't put off at all. He fired back a letter with more botanical details and the comment "There may in my opinion have been a series of productions [i.e., creations] on different spots, & also a gradual change of species. I shall be delighted to hear how you think this change may have taken place, as no presently conceived opinions satisfy me on this subject."[22] In a phrase, Hooker was hooked, and a thirty-nine-year friendship and collaboration had begun that would shape the scientific world.

Throughout the first half of 1844 Charles worked periodically on lengthening and improving his evolution sketch of two years before. His "species work" had to be fit into a schedule already full of other, mainly geological, research projects, as well as his duties as a member of the Geological Society's governing council. Nonetheless, by July he had produced a 230-page document and—since his handwriting usually bordered on illegibility—had it copied in a clear hand by Mr. Fletcher, the local schoolmaster.[23]

And then Darwin did a most interesting thing. Instead of proceeding directly to publish his species "essay," he tucked it away with a cover letter to Emma, a note that shows the depth of his concern over his precarious health:

[July 5, 1844] My Dear Emma.

I have just finished my sketch of my species theory. If, as I believe that my theory is true & if it be accepted even by one competent judge, it will be a considerable step in science.

I therefore write this, in case of my sudden death, as my most solemn & last request, which I am sure you will consider the same as if legally entered in my will, that you will devote 400£ to its publication & further will yourself, or through Hensleigh, take trouble in promoting it.—I wish that my sketch be given to some competent person, with this sum to induce him to take trouble in its improvement & enlargement.—I give to him all my Books on Natural History, which are either scored or have references at the end of pages, begging him carefully to look over & consider such passages, as actually bearing or by possibly bearing on this subject.—I wish you to make a list of all such books, as some temptation to an Editor. I also request that you hand over [to] him all those scraps roughly divided in eight or ten brown paper Portfolios:—The scraps with copied quotations from various works are those which may aid my Editor.—I also request that you (or some amanuensis) will aid in deciphering any of the scraps which the Editor may think possibly of use.—I leave to the Editor's judgment whether to interpolate these facts in the text, or as notes, or under appendices. As the looking over the references & scraps will be a long labour, & as the correcting & enlarging & altering my sketch will also take considerable time, I leave this sum of 400£ as some remuneration & any profits from the work.—I consider that for this the Editor is bound to get the sketch published either at a Publishers or his own risk. Many of the scraps in the Portfolios contains [*sic*] mere rude suggestions & early views now useless, & many of the facts will probably turn out as having no bearing on my theory.

With respect to Editors.—Mr. Lyell would be the best if he would undertake it: I believe he wd find the work pleasant & he wd learn some facts new to him. As the Editor must be a geologist, as well as Naturalist. The next best Editor would be Professor Forbes of London. The next best (& quite best in many respects) would be Professor *Henslow*??. Dr. Hooker would perhaps correct the Botanical Part probably he would do as Editor Dr. Hooker would be very good. The next, Mr. Stickland. Professor Owen wd be very good, but I presume he wd not undertake such a work. If none of these would undertake it, I would request you to consult with Mr. Lyell, or some other capable man, for some Editor, a geologist & naturalist.

Should one other hundred Pounds, make the difference of procuring a good Editor, I request earnestly that you will raise 500£.

My remaining collection in Natural History, may be given to anyone or any Museum, where it wd be accepted.

My dear wife / Yours affect / C. R. Darwin

If there shd be any difficulty in getting an editor who would go thoroughly into the subject & think of the bearing of the passages marked in the Books & copied out on scraps of Paper, then let my sketch be published as it is, stating that it was done several years ago & from memory, without consulting any works & with no intention of Publication in its present form—

PS / Lyell, especially with aid of Hooker (& of any good zoological aid) would be best of all.

Without an Editor will pledge himself to give up time to it, it would be of no use paying such a sum.[24]

It was an extraordinary letter in many respects. First, it showed just how concerned Charles was about his health at the ripe old age of thirty-five. Just eight years before, he had been a robust seafarer returning home from an around-the-world cruise; now he wasn't at all sure he might not die in his sleep. Second, it reflected how very important he considered his species theory to be as an advance in science. For the normally frugal Darwin to pledge £500—almost $42,000 today and the equivalent of 28 percent of the 1843–44 Darwin family budget[25]—to pay an editor to polish his manuscript and arrange for its publication was quite remarkable.

But for those of us interested as much in Darwin's family relationships as in his science, the letter bears powerful witness to his faith that Emma would grant his request despite her discomfort with the essay's contents. Five and a half years into their marriage, Emma and Charles had become one in body and very nearly one in soul. Their letters reveal symmetrical and unconditional love, and therefore, despite continuing differences on religion that included the question of divine creation, Charles never doubted that Emma would honor his wishes and, if need be, assist in the publication of his species theory.

And she *was* uncomfortable with the essay, both in whole and in part. Twice already she had written out her feelings to Charles about his continuing drift away from religion. It had the potential to cause "a painful void" between them (1838) and it fed her fear that they might "not belong to each other forever" (1839).[26] Although at some level she believed "honest & conscientious doubts cannot be a sin," still the essay, with its considerable heft and detailed evidence in favor of transmutationism,[27] must have brought back all of her old worries.

Nonetheless, at Charles's request she read the manuscript and made comments. Unclear passages and questionable conclusions were brought to the author's attention; really shaky points were boldly denounced. Beside the paragraph that suggested the human eye might be the result of gradual selection for a series of "useful deviations,"[28] Emma wrote "A great assumption/ E.D."[29] Charles had asked for feedback, and he was getting it. However skeptical and reluctant she might be, for love of her husband Emma had taken the first long step toward enabling the eventual publication of the evolutionary views she so disliked.

After all of the editing, correcting, and copying was completed, the manuscript was tucked away for future publication. In that fall of 1844, Charles was not ready to go public with his evolution theory. He had work to do on various geological projects and besides, his cautious nature told him the species theory needed considerable shoring up and polishing. Transmutation was too controversial and dangerous a topic for him to publish a half-baked argument. The ideas in his essay were sure to offend many older scientists, as well as most Anglican clergymen—including several of Charles's friends, relatives, and old professors. Even worse, those ideas might feed the fires of social revolutionaries such as the Chartists. Charles might have been interested in bringing about scientific change, but certainly not societal reform.[30] It was best to wait and let his ideas ripen and allow more evidence to accumulate.

As it happened, Charles's caution was substantiated just a few months after he had tucked the essay away to ripen. In October 1844 the London firm of John Churchill published a small book titled *Vestiges of the Natural History of Creation*. The theme of the book was nature's progressive self-development, and its anonymous author, later identified as Robert Chambers of Edinburgh, covered everything from the appearance of the stars and planets to the emergence of life and ultimately the evolution of the human mind.[31] The deistic Chambers wrote of the unfolding of a divinely ordained plan that led unerringly to humans, in whose "organization" the "face of God is reflected."[32]

The reaction from established scientists and the Church was swift and predictable. Charles's old geological mentor Adam Sedgwick blasted the *Vestiges* in the pages of the *Edinburgh Review*. The book was shallow, he claimed, showed no signs of original research or scientific expertise, was full of degrading materialism, and constituted a threat to the entire social and moral fabric.[33] In a private letter Sedgwick went to graphic extremes, describing the *Vestiges* as a "filthy abortion" that should be trod upon to "put an end to its crawlings."[34] Similarly, the physician David Brewster, writing in the *North British Review*, declared that it "poison[ed] the fountains of science and sapp[ed] the foundations of religion," and John Herschel hammered away at it from the presidential podium at the 1845 meeting of BAAS, the British Association for the Advancement of Science.[35]

There were positive reviews, of course, and the *Vestiges* proved to be enormously popular on the street, selling more than 24,000 copies by 1860.[36] Significantly, Mudie's circulating library added the book to its list of offerings, and this made it readily accessible to the general public.[37] Even some scientists liked it, including Charles's new friend Joseph Hooker, who wrote to Charles in December 1844 saying, "I have been delighted with *Vestiges*, from the multiplicity of facts he brings together, though I do [not] agree with his conclusions at all, he must be a funny fellow: somehow the book looks more like a 9 days wonder than a lasting work."[38]

But Charles, sitting on his own evolutionary time bomb, saw nothing funny in the matter at all. To him, *Vestiges* was simply crackpot science, particularly in its depiction of saltatory organic evolution.[39] "I have, also, read the Vestiges," he responded to Hooker, "but have been somewhat less amused at it, than you appear to have been: the writing & arrangement are certainly admirable, but his geology strikes me as bad, & his zoology far worse."[40] In fact, the *Vestiges*' reception—especially the heat it drew from learned reviewers—gave Charles the cold shivers and confirmed in no uncertain terms the wisdom of waiting a while before going public with his own species theory.

Did Emma read the *Vestiges*? As a book of science, it would not automatically have been on her "must read" list, but perhaps she read it aloud to Charles in the evening by the fire, a habit they developed early in their marriage.[41] What would she have made of it, one wonders. It seems likely that she would have appreciated Chamber's piety but bridled at his strict adherence to ordained natural laws as the explanation for earthly developments. For her, the earth and its creatures were still the products of God's miraculous and creative powers as revealed in the Bible.

Emma conceived for the fifth time in October 1844 and gave birth to her second son, George Howard Darwin, on July 9, 1845. These repeated pregnancies were becoming a burden, as Emma admitted to Jessie Sismondi six months after George's birth. In the context of comments about whether she would hire a governess or continue to teach the children herself, Emma wrote:

I find it a great pleasure & interest teaching them & if I had but the luck to escape having another soon I should not think of a governess, as I should be quite sorry to give up teaching them myself, but when I am in that unfortunate condition I feel it too great an anxiety to be looking after them all day, or else the small quantity of lessons they do, I think I could always manage.[42]

These are the words of a woman exhausted by five pregnancies in seven years of marriage, and they make one wonder why Emma and Charles apparently never practiced any form of family planning. Early versions of condoms were available, although they have been described as "expensive, unreliable, and unpleasant to use,"[43] and of course there were always the methods of withdrawal or abstinence when Emma was near midcycle. Yet the regularity of their babies suggests that none of these methods was used. For his part, there are hints that Charles felt contraception to be somewhat immoral, even though he worried mightily about his wife during each confinement.[44] For her part, Emma—despite being the one who bore the burden of all the pregnancies—may either have agreed with her husband's views or, despite disagreeing, have lacked the assertiveness to challenge him on the matter.[45] Alternatively, it is entirely possible that Emma wanted a very large family and only wished to space the children somewhat further apart. After all, big families were common at their socioeconomic level: both Emma and Charles had numerous siblings, the J. S. Henslows had six children, Fanny and Hensleigh Wedgwood had six, and the W. D. Foxes had eleven![46] Family planning, or the lack of it, at Down House is a question we can ponder but never answer. In any event, by the mid-1840s Emma was badly in need of a respite from childbearing.

But to return to 1844 just for a moment, in December of that year Joseph Hooker made his first visit to Down House, marking the beginning of a steady flow of scientific visitors that would characterize the next thirty-eight years. As a thank-you gift after his visit, Hooker sent Emma a book on colonial missions. The next set of scientific visitors were Charles and Mary Lyell, who stayed with the Darwins twice in May and June 1845, just prior to traveling to the United States.[47] Over the years, Emma would become quite accustomed to playing hostess to scientific guests. Young and old, British and foreign, mannerly and uncouth, they would come at Charles's bidding or on their own initiative to see the sage in his country retreat.

8. The Old Order Changeth

GEORGE HOWARD DARWIN was a hungry baby. Describing her seven-week-old son to Aunt Jessie, Emma wrote:

> My new baby is very comfortable & well now & sleeps 3 or 4 hours between his meals instead of coming so often as he did before, so that I quite dreaded the sound of him & felt quite worn out by the evening. He is very smiling & fat & big & I think will be rather above an "average wean."[1]

Young George wasn't alone in his hunger: working-class people all across Britain, Ireland, and portions of Europe were feeling the pinch. The "hungry forties" found the region suffering from crop failures due to bad weather and the infamous potato blight. In Britain 1844 was one of the driest years on record, and a frigid winter and an unusually cold summer in 1845 followed in its wake. In Ireland, cold summers in 1845 and 1846 also included heavy rain, conditions ideal for spreading the spores of the fungus *Phytophthora infestans*.[2] Once invaded by *P. infestans*, potato crops soon developed blackened leaflets and stems, followed by discoloration and rotting of the tubers.[3] The potato blight spread rapidly to southern England, including to the Darwins' home county of Kent, and to the Continent, and the resulting reduction in available food was compounded by generally bad grain harvests, especially wheat.[4]

The combined effect of crop failures, the continuing Corn Law tariffs (which benefited landowners but victimized the poor by inflating bread prices), and the hated "new" Poor Law (which made poor relief as distasteful as possible in order to reduce dependence on the dole) was widespread misery and discontent, particularly in rural areas. The unrest took the form of nightly arson attacks in and around J. S. Henslow's parish of Hitcham, Suffolk, a rectorship he had taken on in 1837 in addition to his continuing professorial duties. Henslow wrote to a Cambridge colleague in 1844: "We have almost nightly fires about the neighbourhood."[5]

At precisely the same time that the English countryside was struggling with poverty and unrest, Charles and Emma became absentee landlords, purchasing (with Dr. Darwin's help) a 325-acre farm at Beesby, Lincolnshire. It appeared to be a sound investment, and they hoped to recover an annual rent of just over £400 after making some repairs to the property.[6] They strove to be landlords with a conscience, however, and following Henslow's example at Hitcham, they arranged for laborers on the Beesby farm to be provided with small allotments for personal vegetable gardens.[7] Back at home, Emma helped fight local hunger by giving beggars at Down House tokens redeemable for bread at the village bakery.[8]

To further aid his parishioners, Henslow had published directions for preparing edible flour from decaying potatoes, and Charles decided to give it a try at Downe, declaring the scheme "a pretty experiment." He also agreed with Henslow "about gentlefolk not buying potatoes," in order to save the few that were available for the poor. But social conscience or not, an investment was an investment, and although part of him detested the "infamous cornlaws," Charles was not above wincing a bit in 1846 when those laws were repealed and his Beesby rent had to be lowered by 15 percent. It was merely frugal Darwin grousing, however. By 1845 Charles and Emma had an income of about £1,400, some $117,000 today, more than enough to live comfortably.[9]

The year 1845 also saw more improvements to Down House. A schoolroom and two small bedrooms were added upstairs, while on the ground floor Parslow's butler's pantry was expanded and a new back door was built that minimized traffic through the kitchen. Additionally, in January 1846 the Darwins rented (and later purchased) a small strip of land along the southwest edge of their property that Charles turned into a quarter-mile oblong "thinking path" that was called the Sandwalk.[10]

By 1846 Bessy Wedgwood's health was going rapidly downhill from her decade-long "dreamy, dozing state."[11] In January, Emma visited Maer and had a final bedside visit with her mother. Death came to Bessy on March 31 in just the manner she had wished: earlier that evening, Elizabeth had heard her mother say, "Lord, now lettest thou thy servant depart in peace." One of God's "purest and most benevolent" souls had slipped from the world. Although deep, Emma's grief was muted by relief that her mother's long illness was over. She remarked later that the beginning of Bessy's invalidism, the seizure and fall back in 1833, "was almost a greater grief" than the final release.[12]

Sadly, Bessy's death meant that Maer was likely to be lost as well. The Hall was too big and its upkeep too expensive for Elizabeth and the Langtons, and since none of the Wedgwood brothers wanted to move back to the old home place, the decision was made to put it on the market. Emma and Charles offered to make room for Elizabeth at Down House, but she chose to accompany the Langtons to their new home. Even ancient Aunt Sarah Wedgwood had to change residences, since her home at Camp Hill was to be sold along with the rest of the Maer estate. By the end of 1847, Maer had changed hands, Elizabeth and the Langtons were living at Hartfield Grove in Sussex, and Aunt Sarah had leased a house called Petleys in Downe village, just a quarter mile across the open fields from the Darwins.[13]

At Down House, Charles kept working away at the last of his trilogy of geological volumes. *Geological Observations on South America* was published in October 1846, clearing the way for an altogether different type of project. A year earlier, in one of his botanical exchanges with Darwin, Joseph Hooker had criticized the French writer Frédéric Gérard for publishing on the "species question" without first gaining experience as "a specific Naturalist." In Hooker's view, Gérard was "a distorter of facts . . . a compiler without judgment" and only years of careful descriptive work qualified a man to comment on the defining features of species and varieties and on the mutability, or lack thereof, of the former. To Hooker's dismay, Charles took the comments personally, responding, "How painfully (to me) true is your remark that no one has hardly a right to examine the question of species who has not minutely described many."[14]

By the fall of 1846, Charles had a plan to earn his spurs as a comparative zoologist. Beginning with an interesting specimen collected during the *Beagle*'s time in the Chonos Archipelago, he would make a study of those "lower marine animals" the barnacles. The plan was simple at first: it was a project that would last "some months, perhaps a year." But once begun, Charles's work on the cirripedes took on a life of its own, expanded into an exhaustive analysis of both living and fossil barnacles, and continued for eight long years, 1846 to 1854.[15]

As her house filled up with barnacles, Emma found herself pregnant yet again. Not only did she not have "the luck to escape having another [baby] soon," she was, had she only known it, just half done with her childbearing. The Darwins' fourth baby girl, Elizabeth, was born on July 8, 1847. Lizzy (later called Bessy) was an unusual child from the beginning. She had a "fit" of some sort at about ten months of age, later developed a lifelong habit of twiddling her fingers when concentrating (in this peculiarity, Lizzy resembled her father), and grew into a woman who "could not have managed her own life without a little help and direction now and then." As discussed in chapter 10, it seems possible that Lizzy had a mild neurological disorder.[16] After Lizzy would come four more little Darwins: Francis, the third son, born on August 16, 1848; Leonard on January 15, 1850; Horace on May 13, 1851; and Charles Waring, born on December 6, 1856, when Emma was forty-eight years old.[17]

The children brought a lively and jolly, if somewhat chaotic, atmosphere to the household. Neither Emma nor Charles was a heavy-handed parent. So much did the children have the complete run of Down House that it was said "the only place where you might be sure of not meeting a child was the nursery."[18] They raced around the house, swung on a rope attached to the ceiling of an upstairs hallway, "butt[ed] like young bulls at every chair & sofa," and generally enjoyed themselves. The resulting household clutter bothered Susan Darwin, who could not abide a mess, but not Emma, whose attitude was to let the untidiness "accumulate till the room becomes unbearable, and then call [a maid] in to do it." And although usually respectful of their elders, including the servants, the Darwin children could be cheeky at times. Once, catching Lenny breaking the rules by hopping about on the drawing room sofa, Charles told him he didn't like what he saw, or words to that effect. To which young Lenny replied, "Well then I advise you to go out of the room." And then there was the time when Lenny reprimanded one of the maids, saying, "Janey, a maid oughtn't to speak like that to a child."[19]

Despite these cases of childish freshness, the kids were normally small versions of their parents: kind, well behaved, and civilized. When a child balked at instructions from an adult, Emma's first reaction was to resort to bribery. She had the "habit of enforcing the law in insignificant matters by small brides and sometimes in the oddest circumstances," remembered her grandson Bernard Darwin many years later. Bernard recounted the time when, as a boy, he had had "a temporary passion for landscape [and] would sit out on a little knoll at the end of the lawn, sketching the house for hours, and was ultimately bribed to come in lest [he] should get sunstroke."[20] But even Emma could be pushed beyond her easygoing limits. Once, when about four years old, George drew a sharp slap from his mother for collapsing onto the floor and throwing a temper tantrum. Significantly, this sort of physical punishment was so rare at Down House that George turned the episode into a badge of superiority, boasting to his siblings, "Mama always spanks me when I am naughty."[21]

Both Charles and Emma like to play with the children, although Charles's play bouts were more frequent and physical. He loved to "opera dance" his daughters on his knees and to roughhouse gently with both the boys and girls. When the children ran their hands up under his shirt, Charles would growl like the hairy bear they imagined they were feeling. Not surprisingly, Emma's main contribution to boisterous play involved music. In the evenings, the drawing room furniture would be pushed back and she would play "the galloping tune" on the piano. This spirited piece, her own composition, was designed exclusively to let the children leap and caper about the room, working off steam before bedtime.[22] Less vigorous games among the daughters included dressing up in Emma's clothes, lace "fallals," and jewelry, and peacocking about her bedroom. Despite the fact that these were her good clothes and best jewelry, the girls played with "pearls and all," remembered Etty. Emma was always an indulgent accomplice.[23]

Emma read to the children regularly and, at least for the first five, Willy to Lizzy, she was instrumental in teaching them to read. She used the old Maer reading book for their instruction, with its little moral tales "The Plumb Pie" and "The Little Foal," and after 1852 she used her brother Harry's child's tale of the Orient, *The Bird Talisman*. This story of a kindly hermit, a magic ring, talking beasts, and a princess in peril was destined to become such a favorite that Emma would have it privately published in 1887 for distribution to the extended family. One of Etty's personal favorites was a book titled *Little Servant Maids* because it "described in the most delightful way all the activities of the little maids, their sins & the sins of their mistresses." George, very much the bluff little boy, wanted to hear "Jack the Giant Killer" over and over. As we shall see, after 1848 a series of governesses was hired to help educate the girls and younger boys, and Emma played less of a role in their instruction.[24]

Not surprisingly, the Darwin children developed distinctly different personalities as each carved out his or her unique niche within the family. William grew into a classic firstborn, helpful and obedient. Henrietta remembered him as "a delightful elder brother" who was sometimes pressed into service to coax her to put on her "night gown when nurses had failed." This was a reflection of Etty's "framsy" (unmanageable, irritable) side, a part of her nature that made her finicky about clothes and food as a child, and about almost everything as an adult. Etty came out of her framsy self most often when playing with the animals at Down House; she was devoted to the cows, chickens, pigeons, donkeys, and above all cats, among whom a "rather fierce" tabby named Bullzig was a great favorite. Annie was a sweet and cuddly child, very neat and eager to please; Lizzie was quiet, self-contained, and unusual; and George was a boy's boy whose main interest was playing at being a soldier.[25]

On Sundays, after everyone was properly cleaned and dressed, Emma led the family—eventually just the children, with some of the boys going unwillingly—down the winding lane to the village church. As they trooped toward the front door of St. Mary the Virgin, they passed the grave of baby Mary Eleanor, a grave that would hold many other Darwins as the years passed. Once inside, they took their places in the family pew and listened to a service that featured chanted canticles, songs by the choir (Parslow the butler sang tenor), and a sermon. Coming from a thoroughly mixed Anglican and Unitarian background, Emma was comfortable with the service at St. Mary's except for the practice of turning to face the altar during the Creed. At this point, she led her family in expressing their nonconformist side by steadfastly facing the front of the church, which left them "sternly look[ing] into the eyes of the other churchgoers," as one son remembered years later. For the children, church was generally more of a trial than a treat, and the same son recalled leaving services "cold and hungry." Thank goodness there were a few things to catch a child's interest, such as Sir John Lubbock's magnificent beaver hat, and silverfish darting in and out of the prayer books and cushions.[26]

Most of the sermons the family heard at St. Mary the Virgin were delivered by the Reverend John Innes, who assumed the post of perpetual curate of Downe in 1846 after the untimely death of his predecessor John Wilmott. As a High Church Tory, Innes held very different liturgical and political views from the Anglican/Unitarian and Whiggish Darwins, and, of course, his Bible-based creationism clashed strongly with Charles's evolutionism. Nevertheless, thanks to gentility and forbearance on both sides, Charles and Innes found that not only could they work together on parish affairs but they actually liked each other. For her part, Emma wasn't so sure about Innes, at least not at first. She was positively disgusted whenever he blasted dissenters from his bully pulpit and she disliked his Anglo-Catholic leanings. "Having so bigoted a Puseyite makes me desperately vicious against the church," she wrote to her aunt Jessie in 1848. "High Church mummery" was not for Emma; her Wedgwood Unitarianism simply wouldn't allow it. The cozying up to Rome advocated by Edward Bouverie Pusey and his fellow Oxford "Tracterians"—a cozying up that some feared was but one step from idolatry and two steps from popery—did not find favor with the mistress of Down House.[27]

Charles's health nose-dived in 1847–48, probably worsened by a combination of overwork and worry about his aging father. The old symptoms of a bad stomach, boils, and exhaustion returned to plague him early in 1847 and continued almost nonstop throughout the year. In April he wrote to Hooker that he had "been almost continually unwell, & at present I am suffering from four boils and & swellings, one of which hardly allows me the use of my right arm & has stopped all my work & damped all my spirits." He made it to the BAAS meetings in Oxford in June, but only after considerable effort to find accommodations where he could be ill in private.[28]

The barnacle work was picking up speed and, in addition, Charles was disturbed by new studies of the "parallel roads" of Glen Roy that challenged his sea-beach theory. Furthermore, Hooker seemed dead set on making a lengthy botanical expedition to India, an excursion that would temporarily deprive Charles of his favorite scientific confidant. But there were happy developments as well, and in July Darwin was all smiles and congratulations over Hooker's engagement to Frances, the eldest daughter of the J. S. Henslows: "Long may you live, & much happiness may you enjoy with your charming & excellent choice."[29] No sooner were the young folks engaged, however, than everything was put on hold. Hooker had obtained government funding for the longed-for expedition and sailed to India on November 11.[30]

Charles visited Shrewsbury in May 1848 and found his father alternately comfortable and "wretched," but on the whole definitely declining; "His health [is] rapidly breaking up," he reported to Emma. Dr. Darwin periodically had trouble breathing and sensations of dying, but still thought he might live for some time "with care." Ten days of this stress was about all Charles could stand, and on May 27 he wrote to Emma complaining of a breakdown in his own health. He headed for home and the security of her care on June first.[31]

That summer Charles's health hit absolute rock bottom. His ever-worsening symptoms included depression, trembling, dizziness, nausea and vomiting, "fainting feelings," and "black spots before his eyes." His father was now very near the end, Hooker was far away, Emma was once again approaching a confinement, always a worrisome time, and the scientific workload was crushing. It was a combination of stresses that would have made anyone sick.[32]

Dr. Robert's last illness came in mid-November. Charles had made a two-week visit to Shrewsbury in October and did not try to return for the deathwatch. The doctor's devoted spinster daughters, Catherine and Susan, and his married daughter Marianne Parker and her husband bore the brunt of the final hours, which were marked by great pain and labored breathing. (At over 335 pounds, the doctor's bulk no doubt compounded his breathing problems.)[33] When at last it was over, Cath sent Charles the sad news.

[November 13, 1848] My dearest Charles.

You will, I trust be prepared for what I must tell you—Our dear Father died this morning about half past 8—his last end was as little suffering as could be hoped with his complaint—I will tell you all I can since yesterday—He . . . failed rapidly about 5 or 6, in the evening; it was evident that it was drawing to a close.—He went to bed before 8—and mercifully lay down (tho' with exhaustion at first,) and continued lying down till about ½ past 12, or sooner, when his breathing compelled him to get up, and he was wheeled into his own room, the effort making him unconscious for a short time. . . . [About] 3 o'clock he was wheeled into the morning room (we were all up) and had a period of great suffering—but mercifully fell into a kind of slumber between 6 and 7 which ended without any return of consciousness. . . .

Susan sat close to him the whole time. . . . [Father's doctor] came but nothing could be done—The most painful part was the extreme difficulty of understanding him—from his breath being so gone—it was most painful;— [The doctor] called it a very peaceful end. . . . We must all give thanks to God that he was spared a very suffering termination of all, which he dreaded so much.

The Funeral will be on Saturday—which will give you time to come. . . . God comfort you my dearest Charles. You were so beloved by him.[34]

Although anything but unexpected, the death hit Charles like a body blow, and he immediately took to his own sickbed. This caused him to be late traveling to the funeral and he ended up missing the service, staying instead at The Mount with Marianne, who was also too ill to go. Ras Darwin too was struck ill by the news of his father's death, but he did manage to attend the funeral. At the church, the coffin was followed down the aisle by Marianne's four sons, Caroline and Joe Wedgwood (Caroline feeling very low because she had missed seeing her father at the very end), Henry Parker, Catherine, Susan, and Ras.[35]

The doctor's body was interred at the small country church of St. Chad's, Montford, five miles west of Shrewsbury and the larger St. Chad's Church that had been the scene of Darwin baptisms and Sunday worship. In 1817 Susannah Darwin had been buried in the chancel at Montford and now, thirty-one years later, she was reunited in death with her husband. After the service, all the Darwins went back to The Mount and were sick.[36]

Dr. Darwin had long since distributed most of his considerable fortune to his various children in the form of land bequests, trust funds, and other secure investments. Nonetheless, at his father's death Charles came into a second farm, this one at Sutterton Fen in Leicestershire. Additionally, he inherited one-quarter of the doctor's residual estate, including some choice mortgage holdings. The total value of Charles's inheritance was just over £51,000 (about $4.25 million today). Ras also received a quarter of the estate and, in a genderized division typical of the time, the four daughters each received an eighth. The Mount and its contents went to Susan and Catherine for as long as they remained unmarried.[37]

And so the old order had nearly all slipped away. Susannah had died in 1817, Jos in 1843, Bessy in 1846, and Dr. Robert in 1848. Of the generation immediately preceding Charles and Emma's, only four aged aunts remained alive: Sarah Wedgwood at Petleys in Downe and the three Allen sisters, Emma and Fanny and Jessie Sismondi, all living together at Tenby.[38] It was discouraging and depressing, this loss of the parental generation that had always been there to give support and guidance and, in the case of Dr. Darwin, to provide a never-ending stream of medical advice. Although the doctor was sometimes overbearing to the point of being dictatorial and "had the art of making every one obey him to the letter," Charles's main memory of him would be as "the wisest man I ever knew."[39]

Small wonder, then, that Charles's symptoms not only continued but actually worsened after his father's death. In early 1849, desperate after a fruitless consultation with Henry Holland—who suggested that he might have inherited a "suppressed" form of Dr. Robert's gout—Charles considered trying the "water cure" at the resort town of Malvern. Encouraged by positive comments from W. D. Fox, he uprooted the entire family in March and relocated to Malvern for a course of treatments with Dr. James Manby Gully.[40]

One of the travelers to Malvern that March was the Darwins' new governess, Catherine Thorley. She had been hired the previous summer, at nineteen years of age, after it had become obvious that Emma could not both teach her existing children and produce a new baby every eighteen months. The hire was a happy one for many reasons: Emma gained some relief, Miss Thorley got a much-needed job in the aftermath of her father's death (he had left a widow and five children, of whom Catherine was the eldest), and Emma's old childhood friends the Tollets were gratified, since the deceased Mr. Thorley had been their family solicitor. For the "neither generous nor miserly" salary of £50 per year, Miss Thorley became part of the Down House staff. Annie Darwin took to her immediately; Etty had little use for her at all.[41]

Once in Malvern, the Darwin contingent settled into a large hillside house called The Lodge just off the Worcester Road. It was "a very comfortable house," Charles reported to W. D. Fox, "with a little field & wood opening on to the mountain, capital for the children to play in." Happily, it was also relatively close to the Malvern Priory and to shopping in the village. After moving in, Charles placed himself in Dr. Gully's hands for what he hoped would be a life-changing treatment.[42]

Gully's hydropathic treatments involved both internal and external applications of the famously pure Malvern spring waters. Gully believed that most patients with Charles's symptoms were suffering from either "nervous dyspepsia" or "mucous dyspepsia" or both. The first complaint was thought to stem from "chronic inflammation of the nerves of the stomach," while the second was caused by an underactive stomach that was somehow obstructed. To treat nervous dyspepsia, patients were given daily "sitz baths, foot baths, wet sheet packing, and rubbing with a dripping sheet"—all with cold water—treatments designed to comfort the stomach by establishing a counteracting irritation in other bodily regions. Mucous dyspepsia was treated with cold showers, baths, and wet packing, and with regimes to increase the patient's tolerance of food and exercise.[43]

Following Dr. Gully's directions, Charles started each day at 6:45 with a cold water scrub-down that made him look "very like a lobster." Then he drank a tumbler of water, took a twenty-minute walk, and was wrapped in cold wet linen topped by a rubber garment called a "mackintosh" to protect his clothes. This "Neptune girdle"—which left him "moist as a frog" in a "suit of wet swaddling clothes"—was worn all day. "Lamp baths" were also prescribed, and these involved Charles sitting blanket-wrapped on a chair over a lighted alcohol lamp. This was designed to produce profuse sweating, which was then relieved by an attendant who provided sips of cold water. The lamp bath could go wrong, however, and no doubt Charles heard rumors about the patient whose blanket caught on fire and "was so scorched in the nether regions as to be laid up for some weeks."[44] Although modern readers may find it amazing, Charles responded well to this treatment regime and in a month's time wrote to Fox that he had shown an "increase in weight," had "escaped sickness for 30 days," and was walking up to seven miles in a day. Whether it was the water treatments, the simplified diet (he was not allowed sugar, butter, spices, tea, bacon, "or anything good"), simply being away from home and work, or a combination of all those things, *something* had given Charles a new lease on life. And in a not unrelated development, Emma too was feeling new life: midway through their Malvern stay, she had conceived once again.[45]

Malvern may have been an ordeal for their father, but for the Darwin children it was a great adventure. They played in the field and woods behind The Lodge, shopped with their parents—purchasing, among other things, a toy crank-organ for George and little china mugs for Etty—and watched the invalid patients riding donkeys up and down the hills from one spring to another. Henrietta later recalled that her first memory of a beautiful sunset came from those days as a five-year-old at Malvern. All the children took dancing classes, which eight-year-old Annie especially enjoyed, and they all got daily lessons from Miss Thorley. Willy, who at ten was nearing the age for public school, also received lessons from a specially hired tutor. Even baby Francis managed to do something special in Malvern: he was baptized at the Priory Church during the family's stay.[46]

By the end of June, Dr. Gully and his patient agreed that Charles was ready to return home. The Darwins had stayed in Malvern for sixteen weeks instead of the six they had originally planned, but clearly it had been worth the prolonged dislocation because the improvement in Charles's health was nothing short of miraculous. He wrote to his cousin Fox that he "consider[ed] the sickness as absolutely cured," although noting that he intended to follow Gully's orders and do some small-scale hydropathy at home for a year. Accordingly, a hut equipped with a cold shower was built in the backyard of Down House and, with Parslow's help as bathman and scrubber, Charles pressed on with his treatment. Every morning he would enter the hut, undress, and pull a string that released 640 gallons of icy water slowly over his head. The children would gather round outside listening to their father's groans and then, when he finally emerged "half running & half frozen," they would go with him around the Sandwalk.[47]

While Darwin was taking cold showers and trying to recover some semblance of good health, his young friend Joseph Hooker was making the botanical expedition of a lifetime in Sikkim (now a northeastern state of India) near the Tibetan border. Early in May, Hooker and his party proceeded up the Teesta River toward the Tibetan passes, collecting plants, especially rhododendrons, on the way. Everything went relatively smoothly until November 7, 1849, when representatives of the rajah of Sikkim made prisoners of Hooker and his traveling companion Archibald Campbell, the British political agent to the region. The rajah was angry over what he considered to be the Englishmen's high-handed exploration of the frontier and Hooker's entry into Tibet without permission. Additionally, by holding the two men, the rajah and his dewan (chief minister) hoped to gain political leverage for Sikkim vis-à-vis British India, and also to influence the location of the Sikkim-Nepal border and secure the rajah's right of possession over fugitive slaves. Campbell was mildly tortured when the rajah's men tried to force his compliance with the scheme, but Hooker, although detained, was not badly treated.[48]

The Hooker-Campbell arrest continued for a month. But after learning that the British were not amused—indeed, that they were so unamused that they were considering a military invasion to rescue the captives and punish their captors—the rajah capitulated, blaming the whole thing on his dewan, who in turn blamed lesser court officials. Hooker and Campbell rode back into British-controlled Darjeeling on December 23.[49]

The Darwins had first learned of Hooker's detention when Charles read about it in the newspaper. Understandably, they were quite concerned for their friend's safety until Sir William Hooker reassured them that things were not so bad as they appeared. Still, completely forgetting all the risks he himself had run while on the *Beagle* and all the worries his own family and friends had borne, Charles wrote to Joseph in February 1850 that he hoped after the close call "Sir William & Lady Hooker will insist on your coming home." They didn't. Joseph continued his explorations, pushing on into Assam before returning to England in early 1851.[50]

9. A Dear and Good Child

THE FALL OF 1849 began happily enough, but then went abruptly downhill. In September Charles felt sufficiently well to travel to Birmingham for the annual BAAS meetings, and after arranging for Elizabeth to supervise the household in her stead, Emma went with him. October brought visits to Down House by Mary Lyell and her newly knighted husband, Sir Charles, and later by Caroline and Joe Wedgwood. Even W. D. Fox managed to extract himself from his familial and parish duties in Cheshire long enough to come for a short stay in early November. Undoubtedly this was an especially sweet visit for Charles, as he saw so little of this favorite cousin; indeed, it had been six years since Fox's only other visit to Downe.[1]

Illness struck swiftly in mid-November, however, with Annie showing signs of scarlet fever on the twelfth. This was a painful, highly infectious, and dreaded disease that could carry away a child as easily as not and for which there was no effective treatment. Parents sometimes lost most or all of their children from a single, terrible sweep of scarlet fever through the family, and there was nothing they could do but look on in anguish. A particularly poignant example was the case of the Reverend Archibald Tait, then dean of Carlisle and later archbishop of Canterbury, and his wife. In 1856, five of the seven Tait children were killed by scarlet fever in a matter of weeks. The Darwins were justifiably alarmed, and Charles wrote to Henslow on November 20, 1849: "We have scarlet fever amongst our children & are anxious."[2]

One common medical recommendation to protect uninfected children was to quarantine diseased individuals as soon as they were diagnosed. Following this wisdom, the Darwins sent Annie to recuperate at Petleys under Aunt Sarah's supervision. The move failed to prevent the spread of the disease, however, and by November 19 both Etty and Lizzy were running fevers. Judging from entries in the Darwin family Bible, none of the boys came down with the disease, and so the two little girls were probably quarantined as well. In the end, the three girls recovered completely, although they had given their parents quite a scare. The angel of death had circled Down House, but then flown on.[3]

Early in January 1850, Elizabeth checked into Down House for the familiar work of nursing her sister through another confinement, and in due course, on January 15, Emma gave birth to her seventh child and fourth son, Leonard Darwin. Happily, this time she was spared the agony of delivery, because Charles put her under with the recently discovered anesthetic agent chloroform.[4]

The obstetrical possibilities of chloroform had been known since 1847, when Dr. James Simpson published a paper reporting the compound's use in painless childbirth. Although such use was initially branded "unnatural" by some traditionalists, chloroform gained widespread acceptance in Britain after Queen Victoria used it for the birth of Prince Leopold in 1853. Darwin had been aware of the obstetrical use of chloroform at least since the spring of 1848, and there is some reason to think that Emma may have been given the compound in August of that year for Francis's birth. If that is true, Charles must not have been the one who administered it, because he clearly thought he was performing a very daring act when he did so in 1850. He wrote to W. D. Fox:

> The day before yesterday Emma was confined of a little Boy. Her pains came on so rapidly & severe, that I cd not withstand her entreaties for Chloroform & administered it myself which was nervous work not knowing from eyesight anything about it or midwifery. The Doctor got here only 10 minutes before the Birth.—I thought at the time I was only soothing the pains—but, it seems, she remembers nothing from the first pain till she heard that the child was born.—Is this not grand?[5]

A letter to Henslow continued in the same vein and included information about how long Emma was unconscious. Charles wrote:

> I was so bold during my wifes confinement which are always rapid, as to administer Chloroform, before the Dr. came & I kept her in a state of insensibility of 1 & ½ hours & she knew nothing from the first pain till she heard that the child was born.—It is the grandest & most blessed of discoveries.[6]

Emma may have been extremely lucky in her brush with Charles's amateur administration of chloroform. Use of the compound certainly has its risks, including toxemia and cardiac arrhythmia, and an overdose can be lethal.[7] In the event, she not only survived the experience but also rejoiced in having found a pain-free way to bring babies into this world. It was an experience she would have twice more.

Baby Lenny had no sooner raised the number of resident little Darwins to seven than his big brother Willy left for school, restoring the complement to six. At ten years of age, Willy was ready for something more than home schooling by Emma and assorted governesses. Entrusted to the tutelage of the Reverend H. J. Wharton, vicar of Mitcham, Surrey, about ten miles from Downe, the first fledgling to leave the Darwin nest was boarded comfortably close to home. The plan was for Mr. Wharton to drill enough Latin grammar into Willy to ensure his acceptance by a proper public school. To Charles's dismay, Wharton didn't come cheap, and Willy's lessons cost £150 per year ($12,500 today). It was one of many reminders the Darwins would have over the years that children, and especially sons, cost money.[8]

Willy was duly drilled in Latin grammar throughout the spring. It's probably also fair to say that he was "dully" drilled, since years later he claimed to remember nothing of Mr. Wharton's school other than the boys playing with the stag beetles that were common locally. He came home for a few days each month and enjoyed a three-week holiday at Easter.[9]

By the fall of 1850, however, Charles and Emma were having second thoughts about their choice of tutors. In September, after consulting W. D. Fox for his views on education for boys, they visited the Bruce Castle School near Tottenham. Bruce Castle had the important advantage of being about half the cost of Mr. Wharton's school, but the disadvantage of being twice as far from home. Furthermore, Bruce Castle emphasized modern languages and science rather than classical studies, and while Charles despised the latter, both he and Emma were nervous about the benefits of the more modern curriculum. At nearly eleven, Willy was "backward for his age; though sensible & observant" in their view. What to do? After further consideration the Darwins' educational traditionalism apparently won out, dooming Willy to another year of Latin lessons before entering Rugby School in early 1852.[10]

The angel of death returned to Down House in the summer of 1850, this time intent on finding a victim. In late June, during a visit by five of her Wedgwood cousins, Annie Darwin's health broke down. In her diary notes for June 27, Emma made this entry retrospectively: "Annie first failed about this time."[11] Although the child seemed to recover almost completely—enough to make August excursions to Knole and Leith Hill, and to play with her Wedgwood cousins on the second occasion—Annie had come out of her illness delicate and clingy; in Emma's words, she was "never easy without being with one of us."[12]

This delicate, marginally ill state continued into the fall. In October it was decided to try a change of air and some saltwater bathing, following the Victorian notion that there was "physic in the sea." Accordingly, on October 3 Miss Thorley took Annie and Etty to the mild climate of Ramsgate on the Strait of Dover.[13] Willy Darwin was home on school vacation at the time, and Emma and Charles stayed on at Down House for a few days enjoying their oldest son's company and supervising his Latin exercises. They joined the older girls at Ramsgate on October 18 but had an unexpectedly short stay. Annie developed a fever three days after her parents' arrival, and it was thought best to send Etty and Miss Thorley back to Downe, with Charles as escort. Emma and Annie stayed at Ramsgate until October 24, then they returned home as well.[14] The sea had failed to answer.

In early November and again in December, Emma took Annie to London for examinations by Dr. Henry Holland. He apparently had little to suggest, and the child's health continued to seesaw. One nasty new symptom, a barking cough, appeared in mid-December.[15] Finally, near their wits' end for an effective treatment, the Darwins decided to give Annie an at-home version of the water cure. Following instructions from Dr. Gully, the unfortunate little girl was put through a daily regime of wet sheet wraps, spinal rubs with a wet towel, and cold baths of her feet and hands. Through it all, Annie was courageous and patient, although she whimpered at the application of the cold sheets and had occasional crying spells. She continued to have a combination of good and bad days throughout the winter.[16]

Annie turned ten on March 2, 1851, and she personally recorded the event in her mother's diary ("Annies birthday") in a large and shaky scrawl. By all accounts it was a good day, with presents and cavorting on the Sandwalk. Within a few days, however, Annie and almost everyone else at Down House had come down with the flu and, to make matters worse, Annie's cough was back. In an attempt to halt her continuing decline, it was decided that she should go immediately to Malvern and be placed under Dr. Gully's personal care. Thus on March 24 Charles and nurse Brodie accompanied Annie and Etty (who was taken along as a playmate for her sister) to Malvern. The girls' governess, Miss Thorley, followed four days later.[17]

Charles installed the little group in Montreal House, a large villa on one of Malvern's main roads. He stayed with them for a couple of days and then, leaving the girls in the care of Dr. Gully and the two women, he returned home to his work and his once again heavily pregnant wife. In Malvern, Gully began his hydropathic treatments with Annie, and for a while they seemed to be beneficial. On April 7, however, she had a setback: an attack of vomiting followed by a fever. A week later she was "very weak," and on April 16 Gully was sufficiently alarmed to send for Charles.[18]

There began a series of agonized letters between husband and wife, he at Annie's bedside and she at home unable to come to her desperately sick child. Charles's letters reported the daily swings in their daughter's condition and Dr. Gully's fluctuating prognosis; Emma responded with words of love and encouragement and, additionally, either on the actual date or later, recorded pertinent details about Annie in her diary. Letters and responses usually took a day or less thanks to the mail trains, and especially pressing news could always be telegraphed from Malvern to Erasmus in London and then carried by carriage to Downe. On April 17 Aunt Fanny Allen arrived at Down House to support Emma, and two days later, at Emma's request, Fanny Hensleigh went to Malvern to provide sickroom help. As it became ominously clear that Annie was gravely ill, Etty was sent to be with her Wedgwood cousins at Leith Hill Place. Poignant excerpts from letters between Malvern and Downe describe Annie's desperate fight for life.

April 17: Charles to Emma
I am assured that Annie is several degrees better. . . . Dr Gully is most confident there is strong hope. . . . My own dearest support yourself—on no account for the sake of our other children; I implore you, do not think of coming here.

April 17: Emma's diary
dreadful day   A[nnie] dosed all day   asked to have hands & face washed knew Ch   bad pulse in evening

April 18: Charles to Emma

Dr. Gully slept here last night & is most kind. . . . he did not think she wd last out the night. Today, he says she is no worse. . . . She does not suffer thank God.—It is much bitterer & harder to bear than I expected—Your note made me cry much. . . . She . . . vomited badly at 6 A.M . . . [and in the afternoon] vomited a large quantity of bright green fluid. . . . We must hope against hope.

April 18: Emma's diary

[vomited] 4 times   pulse better   gruel & brandy every ½ hour   rallied & slept well

April 19: Charles to Emma

She keeps just the same. . . . You would not in the least recognize her with her poor hard, sharp pinched features; I could only bear to look at her by forgetting our former dear Annie. . . . [She is] in same tranquil, too tranquil state.

April 19: Emma's diary

slight sickness   spoke more   good night

April 20 (Easter): Charles to Emma

It is a relief to me to tell you [all] . . . for whilst writing to you, I can cry; tranquilly. . . . We . . . had to get the Surgeon to draw her water off; this was done well & did not hurt her. . . . She has . . . taken less gruel this night & is fearfully prostrated. Yet when Brodie sponged her face, she asked to have her hands done and then thanked Brodie. & put her arms round her neck, my poor child & kissed her. . . . Your two heart-moving notes have come. My dear dear wife.—I do not sit all the while, with her, but am constantly up & down; I *cannot* sit still. . . . These alterations of no hope & hope sicken one's soul. . . . I never saw anything so pathetic as her patience & thankfulness; when I gave her some water, she said "I quite thank you."

April 20: Emma's diary

sick 3 or 4 times & took brandy once

April 21: Charles to Emma

In the night she rambled for two hours. . . . [Also,] her bladder acted of itself . . . & so have her bowels. . . . I was in wonderful spirits about all this . . . [but Dr. Gully has a] strong dislike to her bowels having acted loosely. . . . Fanny is devoting herself too much sadly, but I cannot stop her; she sat up till 4 this morning. . . . [Annie] asked for orange this morning, the first time she has asked for anything except water. . . . If diarrhea will but not come on, I trust in God we are nearly safe. . . . She is certainly now going on very well.

April 21: Emma's diary
much better

April 22: Fanny (Mrs. Hensleigh) Wedgwood to Emma
My Dearest Emma
I grieve to write you a worse report this evening there has been a change today & signs of sinking. . . . her night was not disturbed . . . but the effort of the fever throwing itself off from the bowels is more than her strength seems able to bear & she has lost strength every time—we are now giving brandy & Ammonia every qr of an hour. . . . Dr. Gully . . . thinks her in imminent danger & not having gained ground—Oh that I should have to send you such sad sad news—

April 22: Emma's diary
Diarrhea came on

April 23: Charles to Emma
My dear dearest Emma
I pray God Fanny's note may have prepared you. She went to her final sleep most tranquilly, most sweetly at 12 o'clock today. Our poor dear dear child has had a very short life but I trust happy, & God only knows what miseries might have been in store for her. She expired without a sigh. How desolate it makes one to think of her frank cordial manners. I am so thankful for the daguerreotype. I cannot remember ever seeing the dear child naughty. God bless her. We must be more & more to each other my dear wife—Do what you can to bear up & think how invariably kind & tender you have been to her.—I am in bed not very well with my stomach. When I shall return I cannot yet say. My own poor dear dear wife.

April 23: Emma's diary
12 o'clock[19]

Emma received the final news at home surrounded by her other children, minus Etty, and also Fanny Allen and sister Elizabeth. Her response to Charles reflected both her numbing sorrow at Annie's death and her fears for her grieving husband.

My dearest

I [knew] too well what receiving no message yesterday [meant]. Till 4 o'clock I sometimes had a thought of hope, but when I went to bed I felt as if it had all happened long ago. Don't think it made any difference my being so hopeful the last day. When the blow comes it wipes out all that preceded it & I don't think it makes it any worse to bear. . . . My feeling of longing after our lost treasure makes me feel painfully indifferent to the other children but I shall get right in my feelings to them before long. You must remember that you are my prime treasure (& always have been) my only hope of consolation is to have you safe home to weep together. . . . What a blank it is. . . . We shall be much less miserable together.

yours my dearest

Poor Willy sends his love. He takes it & cried quietly & sweetly.[20]

Charles's letters and Emma's responses are still heartrending to read a century and a half after Annie's death. The loss of any child is hard, but Annie was clearly a very special little girl in many ways, and undoubtedly the apple of her father's eye. In the swirl of this wrenching illness and death, it is worth noting how much Charles's letters read like one long prayer beseeching God to cure his darling child. In the letters of April 17–23 he referred to God fully a dozen times, as in "Thank God she does not suffer at all," "God Help us," "I trust in God we are nearly safe," and "I pray God Fanny's note may have prepared you." In contrast, the devout Emma mentioned God only twice in her responses. Although dismissive of orthodox Christianity, Charles was still no "foxhole atheist."[21]

Annie's death was officially certified by Dr. Gully as due to "bilious fever with typhoid character." In the medical language of the time, this simply identified the fatal fever as associated with vomiting (perhaps especially the green bile on April 18) and delirium (Annie's "excited wandering" in her sleep). The latter symptom particularly made the illness "typhoid," or typhuslike. Vague diagnoses such as this were common in the nineteenth century, and they reflected the state of medical knowledge at the time. Today we can do better, and recently Annie's great-grandnephew Randal Keynes asked several modern physicians to look over her symptoms and give retrospective diagnoses. The consensus was that Annie Darwin probably died from tuberculosis. The disease may have manifested itself at the end as tuberculous peritonitis or as a blood infection that led to vomiting and coma.[22]

This diagnosis immediately leads to the question whether other members of the family might also have been tubercular and possibly the source(s) of Annie's infection. There are no clear answers to either part of this question. Baby brother George was often ill as a child and grew into a sickly adult, but there is no proof that his symptoms were due to tuberculosis. There was consumption in the Langton family, and Annie's uncle-by-marriage Charles Langton may have had the disease. Additionally, cousin Allen Wedgwood and even uncle Ras Darwin may have suffered from consumption. These are only surmises, however, and the tuberculosis bacillus can be picked up in other ways than through human contact, such as from infected milk, so we will never really know how or whether Annie may have contracted the disease.[23]

One week after Annie's death, Charles wrote a short memorial of his and Emma's lost child, hoping that in their old age "the impressions now put down will recall more vividly her chief characteristics." After describing Annie's personality and appearance, and a selection of his favorite memories of her, Charles closed with these words, doubtless accompanied by tears:

> We have lost the joy of the Household, and the solace of our old age:—she must have known how we loved her; oh that she could now know how deeply, how tenderly we do still & shall ever love her dear joyous face. Blessings on her.[24]

Charles's grief ran so deep that he simply could not dwell upon his loss, and he rarely referred to Annie in the years that followed. Indeed, more than sixty years later Henrietta remembered: "My father could not bear to reopen his sorrow, and he never, to my knowledge, spoke of her."[25] This is not quite an accurate statement. There are a few instances of Darwin mentioning Annie, at least in writing. For example, in October 1856 he thanked W. D. Fox, who was in Malvern for a course of the water cure, for a report on Annie's grave: "Thank you for telling me about our poor dear child's grave. The thought of that time is yet most painful to me. Poor dear happy little thing. I will show your letter tonight to Emma." Four years later in September 1860, in a letter of condolence to T. H. Huxley following the death of Huxley's son Noel, Charles again referred to Annie: "I know well how intolerable is the bitterness of such grief. . . . To this day, though so many years have passed away, I cannot think of one child without tears rising in my eyes; but the grief is become tenderer."[26] And in 1876, a full quarter century after Annie's death, Charles wrote this passage in his private autobiography:

We have suffered only one very severe grief in the death of Annie at Malvern on April [23], 1851, when she was just over ten years old. She was a most sweet and affectionate child, and I feel sure would have grown into a delightful woman. . . . Tears still sometimes come into my eyes, when I think of her sweet ways.[27]

Back home in Downe during the spring of 1851, Charles threw himself into his barnacle work. "Blessed work" was the only sure distraction from grief, illness, and worry.[28] Emma too suffered dreadfully after Annie's death. Henrietta remembered that her "mother never really recovered from this grief. She very rarely spoke of Annie, but when she did the sense of loss was always there unhealed."[29] In her sorrow, Emma alternated between being indifferent to the other children and then solicitous and gentle. She also felt a good deal of bitterness, an unusual—or at least rarely admitted—emotion in Victorian culture, where mothers often claimed to find quiet consolation in the Christian belief that they would be reunited with their lost children in heaven.[30]

One big difference between Charles and Emma in the aftermath of Annie's death was that Emma had to deal much more directly with the other children's reactions. Willy had sobbed quietly at the news of his sister's death, but, showing the resiliency of an eleven-year-old, within two weeks he was sufficiently recovered to return to Mr. Wharton's school. George (five years old), Lizzy (three), Franky (two), and Lenny (one) were all too young to be much affected. It was spring, after all, and there were games to be played and mischief to be gotten into, despite their parents' obvious grief. Of all the children, Etty showed the strongest and longest-lasting reaction to Annie's death. The seven-and-a-half-year-old had gone to Malvern as her sister's playmate, but then, "never dream[ing] of danger to Annie," she had been shipped off to stay with Aunt Caroline and Uncle Joe at Leith Hill when Annie's condition plummeted. It was there that she learned that her sister had died and that Annie had asked for her near the end, and it was there that, along with cousin Effie Wedgwood, Etty shed her first tears for Annie.[31]

Etty reacted to Annie's death with a mixture of grief and fear. She had loved and idolized her older sister, but at some level she must have resented her as well. After all, Annie had so much talent, beauty, and charm. Hadn't the maids at Down House repeatedly told Etty that Annie exceeded her "in all ways but especially in sweetness of disposition"?[32] Annie had been so good, so much better than Etty, but even all that goodness hadn't saved her, and now she was gone. But *where* had she gone, that was the question: to heaven or hell? Emma's conversations with Etty during the summer of 1851 record the child's sadness, guilt, and fear of eternal punishment. Etty's first question came on an undated August evening:

"But Mamma where do the women go to, for all the angels are men." She burst into tears when I asked her if she had been thinking of Annie, but said she had not.

Aug. 20. She came to me looking very much distressed in the afternoon E. Mamma what can I do to be a good girl? I told her several things openness &c said she had better pray to God to help her to be good. E. Shall I pray to God now? She then said a little prayer after me.

Aug. 24. At bed time. E. Will you help me to be good? I told her that Annie was a good child & that I did not think she would find it difficult to be as good as she was. I asked her what made her so unhappy when she thought of being good. E. I am afraid of going to hell. I told her I thought Annie was safe in Heaven. M[e]. Come to me & I will try to help you as much as I can. E. But you are always with somebody.

Aug. 25 bedtime. E. (whispering) do you think I have done any thing wrong today? M. No I don't think you have. We consulted a little over her prayers. I repeated "Suffer little children" &c. It did not seem to be Pilgrims Progress as I had suspected which had alarmed her. E. Do you think you shall come to Heaven with me? M. Yes I hope so & we shall have Annie. E. And Georgy too I hope.

The next day she seemed trying to be good all day, & ended at night looking very sweet & happy, & I hope her fears are passed.[33]

By February 1852 Etty had made good progress dealing with her grief and fears. She even asked her mother to put some of Annie's hair in her locket. Nonetheless, Emma's notes on their conversations reveal some continuing turmoil.

[Two] nights ago she said "Mamma I think of Annie when I am in bed."

Last night. ["]Mamma when I see any thing belonging to Annie it makes me think of her. Sometimes I make believe (but I know it is not true) that she is not quite dead, but will come back again sometime.["] Some time ago she cried in great distress & said ["]Mamma I used to be a very naughty girl when Annie was alive. Do you think God will forgive me? I used to be very unkind to Annie.["]

Last night "Mamma I want you to put something in my prayers about not being proud, as well as not being selfish.["][34]

A second major preoccupation for Emma in the immediate aftermath of Annie's death was her own approaching confinement. As usual, Elizabeth was on hand for the delivery, having arrived early at Downe, on April 22, in light of the situation in Malvern. Emma wrote to Charles that same day that she planned to ask her sister "to get up chloroform," although she didn't "expect to want it till the right time." And although Emma dreaded the delivery itself—"my troubles," she called it in a letter to Fanny Hensleigh—she looked forward to the "soothing occupation [of] looking after a young baby."[35]

On May 13, 1851, exactly three weeks after losing one child, Emma brought another into the world. Horace, the fifth Darwin son, was hale and hearty, but the combination of Annie's death, repeated pregnancies and births, and advancing age was beginning to tell on his mother. Emma was two weeks past her forty-third birthday when Horace was born, and he was her ninth baby in twelve years of marriage. Turning most of the care of the newcomer over to his nanny and wet nurse, Emma took her time recovering from the delivery. She did not come downstairs and fully rejoin family activities until the fifteenth of June.[36]

10. The Great Exhibition, War in the Balkans, and the Last of the Barnacles

BY EARLY SUMMER 1851, Emma was feeling well enough to once again open her home to guests. She began to host small dinner parties, including one for the local curate, John Innes, and his wife. House-guests included Susan Darwin for a short stay in late June and then, in July, the Hensleigh Wedgwoods for a week. It was Emma and Charles's first glimpse of Fanny and Hensleigh since Annie's death, and no doubt there were tears aplenty as they recounted "that sad & last work of laying [the] dear child in her earthly resting place."[1]

The Great Exhibition of 1851 had opened in London in May, and the Darwins traveled up to town on July 30 to see what all the excitement was about. Some two years earlier, Prince Albert had proposed an international exhibition of the "works of Industry and Art" to the Royal Society of Arts. The idea of such a display—international, to be sure, but highlighting the works of British industry and artisans—quickly caught on and, under the guiding hands of Prince Albert and Henry Cole, the civil servant in charge, funds were raised and a panel of governing commissioners (including Sir Charles Lyell) was formed. Joseph Paxton, an architect with a long history of designing glass conservatories, won the contract for the exhibition hall to be constructed in Hyde Park.[2]

The hall, dubbed the Crystal Palace by *Punch*, was huge, with an area exceeding 75,000 square feet and a central transept 108 feet high. Its arched roof soared more than three stories above the floor-level exhibits, and an elevated viewing gallery circled the building's interior. More than three thousand cast-iron columns and a complex system of iron and wood beams supported the 900,000 square feet of glass panels that gave the building its name.[3] Many visitors, like the American Horace Greeley, were greatly impressed by the structure: "The Crystal Palace . . . is really a fairy wonder, and is a work of inestimable value as a suggestion for future architecture." Others, such as the English architect August Welby Pugin, were unimpressed. When Joseph Paxton asked Pugin what he thought of the building, Pugin replied: "Think! Why, that you had better keep to building greenhouses, and I will keep to my churches and cathedrals."[4]

Despite differing opinions about the hall, everyone who could make it turned out for the exhibition, which was opened on May first by the queen and Prince Albert in a great show of pomp. By any measure it was a massive display, with 13,937 exhibitors from the United Kingdom and thirty foreign countries, and 100,000 objects on exhibit. Among the British exhibits, which collectively took up about half of the hall, was crockery manufactured by Wedgwood & Brown. This afforded Frank and Hensleigh Wedgwood and their respective Fannys special invitations to the opening, but disappointingly the queen walked right past the Wedgwood & Brown display during her selective tour of the exhibits.[5]

Among the objects on display were machines of many kinds. There were steam hammers, steam cranes, steam riveters, and steam printing presses; water pumps; carding and spinning machines; looms; a sewing machine capable of an amazing 600 stitches per minute; a gas cooking range (one of the first); and a prototype submarine that had traveled underwater from Calais to Dover on its way to the exhibition. There were fancy and utilitarian textiles; precious stones including the Kohinoor diamond; British-made metal stoves, grates, and fenders; and exotic plants (young Joseph Hooker was a juror in the botanical section). There were fox skins, beaver skins, and maple sugar from Canada; silk palanquins and jeweled thrones from India; and a revolver collection on loan from the American gunsmith Samuel Colt. In Commissioner Charles Lyell's geological section, there were iron, lead, copper, and gold ores from Canada; marble from India; fossils from the United States; and malachite from Russia.[6] Lyell's hope was that the exhibition would have an educating effect on its visitors, who would be able, without foreign travel, to see "the result of the highest civilization[s]."[7]

Of course, there were also art and craft objects of all sizes including an ornate candelabra made by British silversmiths; a colossal wooden buffet with elaborate carvings (the Kenilworth Buffet); various "ladies' needleworks"; Sèvres porcelain from France and Minton porcelain from England; an inlaid-mosaic table from Spain; and a multitude of sculpted pieces.[8] Among the most admired sculptures was *The Greek Slave* by American artist Hiram Powers. This life-size female nude was described by reviewers as "one of the most exquisite objects" in the exhibition and always at the "centre of a bevy of admiring spectators." (Interestingly, Americans had been much more prudish in their reception of *The Greek Slave* during an earlier tour of the United States. To get American viewers beyond the shock of the figure's nudity, it was pointed out that she "was nude *against her will*" and that prominent clergymen considered her "clothed with spiritual innocence.")[9]

Finally, there were the inevitable novelty pieces. There was a cast iron coal stove modeled as a suit of armor; a scale model of the Liverpool docks; a "stuffed buck-eyed squirrel" from America; a "bedstead adjusted mechanically to turn the occupier out of bed at any hour"; and the Anhydrohepseterion, a device for stewing a potato in its own liquid.[10] Most likely, it was novelty items such as these that were the exhibits of greatest interest to children, including the young Darwins. Of course, children and adults alike would have flocked to the various refreshment stalls that featured "sandwiches, pastries, patties, hot beverages and soft drinks ... cocoa, spruce beer, bread and butter, and cheese," offering welcome relief from the seemingly endless displays.[11]

Charles, Emma, Willy, Etty, and George stayed with Uncle Ras for twelve days while they saw the big show. Ras apparently paid for cabs to transport his guests back and forth—a gesture that must have set him back a pretty penny, since cabs and omnibuses were price-gouging terribly as thousands of people vied for rides to Hyde Park. Emma and Charles made four visits to the exhibition, clear testimony that they enjoyed themselves. It was less fun for the children, at least for some of them. Etty went once and then decided "not to go again, but to stay at home [Uncle Ras's] and scrub the back-stairs, as being better fun." Much better than the exhibition in the children's view were other London treats. They talked the adults into taking them twice to the Zoological Gardens—which had a new hippopotamus, Obaysch—and twice to the Royal Polytechnic Institute. The Royal Polytechnic was good fun because one never knew when demonstrations of new technologies might be accompanied by the odd explosion, and because of its spectacular magic lantern shows. For her part, Emma kept up her social contacts in London by calling on Fanny Hensleigh's half-sister Mary Rich, who reciprocated the call a few days later. It was all good fun but exhausting, and after a frantic week of sightseeing, first Emma and then Etty came down with fevers. Everyone had returned to Downe, tired but happy, by August tenth.[12]

Emma and Charles recovered from Annie's death in characteristically different ways. True to form, Charles threw himself into his work. He completed two volumes on the stalked barnacles before the end of 1851 and then began a detailed analysis of the sessile species. Except for the excursion to the Great Exhibition, Charles stayed at home. Emma, always more gregarious than her husband and more interested in cultural events, resumed a schedule of regular trips to London for social calls, shopping, plays, and concerts at the Philharmonic. For the first time since her marriage, she was being spared another pregnancy for a longish period of time—almost three years—and she took advantage of her unencumbered condition.[13]

Despite their tragedy in the spring, life for the Darwins had nearly returned to normal by the end of the year. Willy was back at Mr. Wharton's school, where he was working (or so his parents hoped) on developing pleasant manners: "try to please *everybody* you come near," they advised, "your schoolfellows, servants & everyone." The little children were as healthy as little children ever are, and six-year-old George was showing the first signs of what would become a near obsession with all things military. He spent his days "drawing ships or soldiers, more especially drummers, whom he [would] talk about as long as anyone [would] listen to him."[14] Between their bank accounts and investment portfolios, the Darwins were millionaires several times over in today's currency, and although Charles fretted over professions for the boys, life was good.[15]

In November, Charles's old shipmate from the *Beagle*, Bartholomew James Sulivan, came for a short visit accompanied by his wife. Since Darwin had last set eyes on him, Sulivan had married, fathered six children, been promoted to captain, and tried his hand at horse and cattle ranching in the Falkland Islands. He was full of tales of nautical adventures, including lots of pirate stories, much to the delight of young George. Emma invited three local couples, including the Reverend Mr. and Mrs. Innes, to meet the Sulivans and round out a jolly dinner party of ten.[16]

Undoubtedly, one of the topics discussed around the dinner table that night was the unstable political situation in France where Louis Napoleon, the nephew of Napoleon Bonaparte and president of the French Republic since 1848, was busy consolidating his political power. Despite the fact that he had been given refuge in England in the 1830s and 1840s, Louis Napoleon's political and territorial ambitions could certainly be construed as threatening to Britain, and Sulivan, for one, feared an invasion.[17]

Such fears were sharply increased on December 2, 1851, when Louis Napoleon seized absolute power in a coup d'état—a move that so delighted the French people that they immediately extended his presidency for ten years. (The title of president proved insufficient for Louis, however, and he assumed the title Emperor Napoleon III a year later.) Aunt Jessie Sismondi was greatly alarmed and wrote to Emma from Wales: "I write again to accuse myself of being a duped fool to my last hope for France, and to ask your pity. . . . The Beast [Louis] has taken the wrong turn. . . . Now I think everything may be possible, even an invasion." With his home and family situated not too far from the coast, the political situation in France added yet another worry to Charles's ever-growing list: "The French coming by the Westerham & Sevenoaks roads, & therefore enclosing Down."[18]

Also in 1851, a major scientific friendship was begun between Charles and Thomas Henry Huxley, a young biologist who was destined to become one of Darwin's fiercest scientific allies. Huxley was back in England after completing his own voyage of discovery on HMS *Rattlesnake* to Australia. During the trip he had become engaged to Miss Henrietta Heathorn of Sydney, and in 1851 he was in search of a job, or jobs, that would pay enough so he could marry his Nettie. One of Charles's first connections with Huxley was writing a letter of recommendation supporting Huxley's application for a teaching post at the University of Toronto. The application was not successful, however, and as later chapters will show, Huxley stayed in England, married his Nettie and raised a large family, and became a frequent visitor at Down House. Over the years, Emma and Nettie Huxley would find that they had much in common and would become staunch friends.[19]

In February 1852, twelve-year-old Willy Darwin was enrolled as a boarding pupil at Rugby School in Warwickshire, where his thirteen-year-old cousin Ernest Hensleigh "Erny" Wedgwood was already a student. Rugby School was organized into six "forms" or grades, with boys in the first four forms making up the Lower School, while the fifth and sixth forms constituted the Upper School. Upper Schoolers lived at the top of a well-organized pecking order: fifth- and sixth-form students had the power to make Lower School boys "fag" for them by running errands and cleaning their rooms. Furthermore, in a system first introduced by headmaster Thomas Arnold in the 1820s, sixth formers were designated as prefects or "praepostors" and given considerable disciplinary authority over the younger boys. Lest their authority be abused, however, prefects were also expected to set the moral tone for their young charges.[20]

Charles Darwin was on record as deploring traditional systems of "old stereotyped stupid classical education," but in fact Rugby was quite modern in comparison to some other public schools. During his period as headmaster (1828–42), Arnold had extensively overhauled and updated the curriculum, adding among other things "mathematics, modern history and modern languages." When Willy entered Rugby, ten years after Arnold's death, this modernized curriculum was in full swing under the direction of headmaster E. M. Goulburn.[21]

It is worth noting that Willy's entrance at Rugby marked a significant change in Emma's letter writing, a fact that has considerable importance for this book. In contrast to the Reverend Mr. Wharton's school at nearby Mitcham, Rugby was a hundred miles away from Downe. Willy could no longer easily come home for quick visits, and to compensate, his mother began to write to him regularly and at length. This habit of regular correspondence was then naturally extended to the other sons as they grew up and went off to school, and to Henrietta when she began her adult travels and later married (Lizzy remained a homebound spinster). Detailed and gossipy, Emma's letters and the children's responses provide a wealth of information about family affairs.

In March 1852, Emma wrote this response to what was probably Willy's first letter home from Rugby.

> My dear Willy,
>   Papa and I were delighted with your tremendous long letter and I don't wonder it made your fingers ache. It told us just what we wanted to know. . . . I shall not be able to write you such a long one, for we have gone on so quietly there is little to tell you. . . . Georgy is more crazy about drawing than ever and makes little picture books for Franky and Lizzy which I buy from him to give them, but he draws such a number that he does not take pains and so does not improve. . . . It was lucky you had that large trunk as it will be more handy to keep your clothes in than a portmanteau would have been. . . . When you write to Mr Wharton do not write a very short letter as that does not seem friendly, but tell him about your study and being with Erny &c and send your love or kind remembrances to Mrs Wharton.[22]

Charles also wrote at about the same time, commiserating with Willy on the "tremendous, awful, stunning, dreadful, terrible, bothering steeple-chase" that the latter had run soon after arriving at school—perhaps a "hare and hounds" run, as described in *Tom Brown's School-Days*. Charles also commented on how "Georgy draws every day many Horse-guards; and Lizzie shivers & makes as many extraordinary grimaces as ever, & Lenny is as fat as ever."[23]

These comments by Charles beg some explanation, especially those concerning Lizzy. We characterized Lizzy Darwin earlier as a quiet, self-contained, and unusual child. A devoted niece described her adult Aunt Bessy (as Lizzy was then called) as "nervous . . . apt to fumble her fingers when agitated . . . not good at practical things" and a woman who "could not have managed her own life without a little help and direction now and then."[24] This description is amplified somewhat by Emma's notes on Lizzy's behavior as a young child.

> Jan. 1852 Lizzy 4½ years old. She has always had the oddest pronunciation possible. When first she began to speak she added an s to the end of every word . . . afterwards all the ws were turned into b's. . . . When telling her a story or if she is observing any thing she has the most curious way of playing with any dangling thing she can get hold of sometimes twiddling her fingers as Charles used to do. Aug. This has grown into a great habit of abstraction going by herself & talking to herself for an hour. She does not like to be interrupted.

Her speech abnormalities were still present in early 1853:

> Lizzy 5½. I —get what the —ginning is —splain it to me. How —licious that orange is —gin at the —ginning. that story about —lina & —phia or else —ladin.

By about age six, the various speech issues had corrected themselves and Lizzy was also beginning to gain some self-confidence. In August 1853 she was heard to mutter indignantly when leaving the drawing room: "I'm so dull. There is only horrid beastly boys in the drawing room." And not too many months later she became quite pert with Miss Thorley. When the governess asked if she wouldn't like "a bit of bread with your egg," Lizzy replied, "I've told you 100 times that I don't want any thing with my egg." Then when Miss Thorley asked, "Shall I cut up your meat?" Lizzy responded, "I don't care whether you do or not."[25]

Identifying the etiology of Lizzy's slow development and odd behavior is challenging, as are all retrospective diagnoses. There seems to be some basis for a diagnosis of mild cerebral palsy, however, with certain symptoms supporting such a case: Lizzy's "fit" or seizure at about ten months of age;

"shivers" (tremors) and "extraordinary grimaces" as a child; linguistic delays compared to her siblings; and adult clumsiness of limbs and extremities, including difficulty with precise movements ("Aunt Bessy's" fingers "had always been very clumsy indeed").[26] But even if this diagnosis is accurate, it should be emphasized that Lizzy Darwin's affliction was relatively mild. As we shall see, she grew into an adult who was functional both mentally and socially, but who also knew she was just a little different and who suffered when others treated her that way.

In mid-March 1852 Emma wrote to Willy again, catching him up on family travel plans and the misbehavior of his siblings: "Franky was brought down in disgrace a few days ago from scratching Lizzy. He crumpled himself up on Papa's lap and became so gumflustigated we were obliged to put him to bed at once." Later that month, Emma headed to London for society and culture. She dined with Ras, drank tea with Jane and Thomas Carlyle, and heard Beethoven's *Eroica* at the Philharmonic. Then she traveled with Charles and Etty to Rugby School, where they saw Willy's rooms and took him and Erny Wedgwood out to dinner.[27]

April was a month of balls and visitors. Down House filled up with Wedgwood kinfolks and assorted friends including J. D. Hooker and his new wife Frances, and there were two balls one week apart at High Elms, the large country house just down the road. (This impressive estate befitted a successful banker like John William Lubbock, 3rd Baronet. The oldest Lubbock son, just plain John until he became 4th Baronet and later 1st Baron Avebury, was a novice biologist whose studies of crustaceans were being encouraged by Darwin in 1852. The younger Lubbock would later gain considerable fame as an archaeologist.) On April 23, one year to the day after Annie's death, Emma wrote again to Willy. After saying regretfully, "I have left you a long time without a letter," and telling him they were all enjoying riding their new donkey, she alluded to a neighbor's cruel usage of his horses. Her comments reflect her lifelong concern, shared by Charles, about the humane treatment of animals:

> Papa is in hopes that Mr Ainslie will be punished for working his horses with sore places on their necks. An officer of the Society for preventing cruelty to animals was sent for by your father to see what state his horses were in and he is going to have him up before a magistrate and his ploughman also. . . . Mr Appleton [the publisher] sent a box of maple sugar from America for all of you children. It looks exactly like pieces of Brown sweet soap. . . . We gave

Georgy a piece of it on his birth day calling it Brown soap and it puzzled him very much. I gave him a kite and Etty gave him sixpence. It made me very melancholy to think of our dear Annie's last birth day and putting her book by her plate at breakfast. . . . The holidays will soon be here.

Your affectionate mother[28]

May was another musical month, with Emma returning to London for a choral symphony at the Philharmonic and, together with Charles, joining a Lubbock dinner party that included the musician Sir Frederick Ouseley (two baronets at the same table!). In mid-June, as summer was beginning, Willy came home from Rugby for his long vacation.[29]

The rest of 1852 passed nearly without incident. Willy made adequate progress at Rugby, although not without failing a subject or two and getting the occasional caning. Charles pressed on with his barnacles, but after six years of work the subject had lost its allure. He complained to his cousin Fox: "I hate a Barnacle as no man ever did before, not even a Sailor in a slow-moving ship." And in the larger world, there was a major passing when the Duke of Wellington died in September. The Iron Duke was given a grand send-off by his grateful nation. The state funeral was preceded by several days of lying in state—the wait to see the body sometimes exceeded five hours—and then an elaborate procession to the service at St. Paul's Cathedral. An estimated 1.5 million people watched the duke's funeral coach pass by, including some of Sarah Wedgwood's servants from Petleys in Downe.[30]

The new year began just as the old one had ended, with a death. For Emma, this one was much closer to home: Jessie Sismondi passed away in Tenby on March 3, 1853, after a week's illness. Less than a month before she was stricken, Aunt Jessie wrote one of her usual lively letters to Emma discussing the continuing political turmoil in France and expressing approval of Napoleon III's recent "romantic marriage" to the Spanish countess Eugénie de Montijo. Napoleon III was turning out to be much more clever, and less threatening, than Jessie had expected. Now if the French would only learn "what is new . . . even to the best of their politicians, [namely] the necessity of a high morality in politics." Jessie died with her sisters Fanny and Emma at her bedside, and in good Victorian style her last words were uplifting for the loved ones left behind. "Sismondi, I'm coming," she called out just before death claimed her.[31]

In July, Emma and Charles and the children (plus supporting servants) packed their bags for a three-week seaside vacation in Eastbourne, Sussex. Charles was worn out from his barnacle work, Willy was home on summer vacation, and everyone was in the mood for a change of scenery. Unfortunately, the weather failed to cooperate, at least initially. The day they arrived and checked into Sea House #13 it was windy and stormy, and it stayed that way for three days. Charles remarked in a letter to W. D. Fox that the children had a case of foul-weather ennui. After this poor start they had a mixture of good and bad days, and on the good ones they took walks along the coast near Beachy Head or drives to nearby sights such as the martello tower at Pevensey. The little Darwins all got sick for a day or two midway through the vacation, and Emma suffered throughout from a sore thumb. All in all, it wasn't one of their most successful holidays.[32]

Sore thumbs and sick tummies paled in comparison to the tragedy that was playing itself out among the W. D. Foxes. Scarlet fever had entered that household and had killed two young boys residing with the family and also the Foxes' two-year-old daughter Louisa Mary. For the Darwins, this brought flooding back all of the grief of Annie's death, and Charles wrote feelingly to his cousin:

> Your letter affected me much. We both most truly sympathise with you & Mrs. Fox. We too lost, as you may remember, not so very long ago, a most dear child, of whom, I can hardly yet bear to think tranquilly; yet . . . time softens & deadens, in a manner truly wonderful, one's feelings & regrets. At first it is indeed bitter.[33]

In August the Darwins made a brief family visit to the Harry Wedgwoods at The Hermitage near Woking in Surrey. To the delight of Charles and the children (at least the boys), they were able to watch military maneuvers at nearby Chobham Camp. No doubt the maneuvers were especially intensive because of continuing concern about the political situation in France and because Britain was slowly but surely drifting toward war with Russia over events in Turkey. Tsar Nicholas I was actively trying to take control of portions of the old Ottoman state with the flimsy excuse that Russia had a duty to protect Orthodox Christians living under Turkish rule. (France claimed a similar duty to protect Roman Catholic Christians in Turkey, and France and Russia squabbled over who should have control over such holy places as the church at Bethlehem, supposedly built on the site of Jesus's birth.) The tsar's land grab began in July 1853 when Russian troops moved into the Balkan principalities of Moldavia and Wallachia (roughly, modern Romania). This move was of grave concern to the British, partly because, like the French, they wanted to constrain Russian influence in the region, but more especially because they knew the tsar had his eye on Constantinople and feared Russian control of that city would threaten British trade with India. To try to keep a lid on things, Britain and France sent a joint naval force to the straits below Constantinople in September 1853. The stage was set for the Crimean War.[34]

It didn't take long for that war to unfold. Emboldened by the show of support from Britain and France, Turkey demanded that Russia remove its forces from the occupied provinces. When the tsar predictably refused, Turkey declared war. British sympathy was strongly aroused when "poor little Turkey" suffered an annihilating naval defeat at Sinop on November 30, 1853. Four months later, pushed along by strong anti-Russian public opinion and a desire to keep the land-hungry tsar in check, Britain and France joined forces with Turkey and also declared war on Russia. By April 1854, Allied troops—eventually amounting to 27,000 soldiers from Britain and 28,000 from France, adding to some 7,000 Turkish troops—had begun to arrive at the Dardanelles. Their objectives were first to protect Constantinople and second to bloody the Russian bear's nose by destroying the military base at Sebastopol.[35]

At Down House the Darwins perused each day's newspapers for political developments, and there was general opposition to the impending war. In a letter written back in October 1853 to Syms Covington in Australia, Charles had noted: "We are all much afraid of war with Russia, which pray God, may be prevented." The Darwins' antiwar sentiments were out of step with the feelings of most of their countrymen, however, and war was either unavoidable or simply not avoided. At least on the fateful day of the battle of Sinop, Darwin was happily preoccupied with science, not politics. On that day he stood before the Royal Society in London and received its Royal Medal for Natural Science. The award was based partly on Charles's geological studies, but more especially on his stalked-barnacle volumes. He received official notification of his selection from Edward Sabine, then vice president of the Society. In the same post was a letter from Joseph Hooker, who was clearly thrilled for his friend:

> My dear Darwin
> I hope that this may be acceptable news to one who is so high above working for a reward. The R.S. have voted you the Royal Medal for Natural Science—*All along of the Barnacles*!!! I am intensely delighted.[36]

Charles was delighted too, although more, he claimed, by Hooker's warm words than by the medal itself. He wrote back that they "made me glow with pleasure till my very heart throbbed. Believe me I shall not soon forget the pleasure of your letter. Such hearty affectionate sympathy is worth more than all the medals that were or will be coined." Nonetheless, the importance of the medal should not be underestimated, since it marked Darwin's arrival among the doyens of British science and can be viewed as the scientific equivalent of a knighthood.[37] Emma must have been thrilled for her "science knight," but, typically, her reaction was muted. Her only diary comment regarding the award ceremony was made on November 28: "C. went to London."[38]

The year 1854 began uneventfully enough, at least at Down House. In February ten-year-old Etty was taken to London to have four teeth removed. Mr. James Robinson, who was not only the Darwins' dentist but also Prince Albert's, did the extractions. In the early summer Emma missed her monthly period and realized that at the age of forty-six she was pregnant once again. She began ticking off the weeks in her diary: July 9, "7th week"; July 23, "9th week." This little Darwin was not destined to come into the world, however. The weekly count stopped abruptly in early October, presumably when Emma miscarried. Her diary is silent on the actual event.[39]

Also in the early summer, Charles and Emma, accompanied by Etty at least, attended the opening of the relocated Crystal Palace at Sydenham, a mere ten miles from home. "We are going to act . . . in a very profligate manner [and] have just taken a pair of Season-tickets to see the Queen open the Crystal Palace," Darwin joked to Hooker. At the opening the famous soprano Clara Novello sang "God Save the Queen," and the scene, the personages, and the music moved Emma so profoundly that, most uncharacteristically, she broke down in public. Years later, Henrietta commented that her mother

> was calm over music, deeply as she enjoyed it. But one of the very few times in my life that I saw her lose her self-control was when Clara Novello sang the solo verse of *God Save the Queen* at the opening of the Crystal Palace. My mother broke down then and sobbed audibly. The scene was extraordinarily impressive—the standing crowd, the Queen and Prince Albert present, and the wonderful volume of the rich soprano voice, sustained and round and full, filling the enormous building.[40]

A year later the Darwins were back in Sydenham, this time with Elizabeth Wedgwood, watching as the queen toured the grounds with Napoleon III and his wife. On that occasion it was Elizabeth who was overcome, swooning in the heat of the day. "[I]t was very frightening & disagreeable," Charles wrote to Willy; "we had to lay her flat on the ground."[41]

In contrast to the relatively peaceful flow of life in Downe, events in the Balkans both heated up and deteriorated as 1854 progressed. In the late spring the British army passed through the Dardanelles and landed at Scutari on the east side of the Bosporus opposite the French, who were already settled in Constantinople on the west shore. Before long the British forces were moved to Varna on the Black Sea in search of a healthier campsite. Unfortunately, despite the best intentions of the high command, Varna proved to be a pest-hole, and soon cholera—which was probably endemic in the local seawater, but was further spread by the army's lack of sanitary procedures—was sweeping through the British troops. Before they had fired a single shot in battle, the British forces found themselves severely diminished by disease.[42]

Then the tsar did something unpredictable: he removed his troops from the occupied territories, apparently opening the way for a diplomatic solution to the entire crisis. Battle fever back home had been raised beyond diplomacy, however, and the decision was made in London and Paris to teach the Russians a lesson by attacking their naval base at Sebastopol. The Allied troops were put in motion, and in mid-September approximately 50,000 British, French, and Turkish troops were landed on the beach of Calamita Bay, thirty-five miles north of the Russian base. Moving south, they engaged the Russians on the heights above the Alma River. Advancing up steep slopes directly into Russian artillery fire, the Allies lost about 3,300 men killed or wounded, yet won the day. From the Alma, the Allied armies continued south, but instead of actually attacking Sebastopol—when the time was ripe, the British and French commanders could not agree on how this should be done—they simply laid siege to the city.[43]

In late October the Russians attempted to break the siege and drive their enemies into the sea by attacking near the British supply port of Balaclava. This effort was unsuccessful, but the Allies' "victory" was costly. Nearly four hundred men were killed or wounded at Balaclava, and the Light Brigade of the British cavalry was demolished. The loss of this splendid brigade, immortalized by Alfred, Lord Tennyson, was probably the result of garbled orders given to Lord Cardigan, the brigade's commander, causing him to charge directly into Russian artillery fire. The first two stanzas of Tennyson's poem capture the tragedy of the event:

Half a league, half a league,
Half a league onward,
All in the valley of Death
Rode the six hundred.
'Forward the Light Brigade!
Charge for the guns!' he said:

Into the valley of Death
Rode the six hundred.

'Forward the Light Brigade!'
Was there a man dismay'd?
Not tho' the soldier knew
Some one had blunder'd:
Theirs not to make reply,
Theirs not to reason why,
Theirs but to do and die:
Into the valley of Death
Rode the six hundred.[44]

In 1855 Tennyson had copies of the poem made and sent to the soldiers in the Crimea. He wrote in a preface:

> Having heard that the brave soldiers before Sebastopol, whom I am proud to call my countrymen, have a liking for my ballad on the charge of the Light Brigade at Balaclava, I have ordered a thousand copies of it to be printed for them. No writing of mine can add to the glory they have acquired in the Crimea; but if what I have heard be true they will not be displeased to receive these copies from me, and to know that those who sit at home love and honour them.[45]

Balaclava was followed on November 5 by another pitched battle at Inkerman, just east of Sebastopol. Once again the Russian intent was to drive the Allies from the peninsula and relieve the city, but for the second time they were defeated, this time at a cost of more than 10,000 Russians killed, wounded, or taken prisoner. The Allies' losses were lower but still significant: more than 2,400 killed or wounded for the British and almost 900 for the French. Nine days later the peninsula was hit by an icy gale that marked the beginning of a deadly Crimean winter. Now the sorry state of the logistical support for the British forces became all too clear. "There was no food for the horses and little for the men, no shelter, no medicine and no order." The "muddled organization" of the British forces—with no unified command, a commissariat that reported not to the army but to the treasury, and a semi-autonomous medical department that reported directly to the secretary of war—began to be more lethal than Russian bullets and bayonets. Although unvanquished in battle, by early 1855 the British army "was dying on its feet" from wounds, disease, malnourishment, and exposure.[46]

British sick and wounded were sent back to Scutari for treatment and convalescence at two facilities provided by the Turks: the General and Barrack Hospitals. The two hospitals were overcrowded and unsanitary, and medical treatment was both inadequate and uneven in its application (officers first!). The inevitable result was a high mortality rate. If a man didn't die in the field, he was quite likely to do so in the hospital. It was to address some of these issues that Florence Nightingale, along with a group of nurses she had recruited, was sent to Scutari by Sidney Herbert, secretary of war, in October 1854. Nightingale was given the title of "Superintendent of the female nursing establishment in the English General Military Hospitals in Turkey." The story of Nightingale's success at Scutari is well known and marks the beginning of the modern era in nursing.[47]

Florence Nightingale's adventures were being followed closely at Down House and throughout the extended Darwin-Wedgwood-Allen family. After all, the Nightingales—William Edward, the father; Fanny, née Smith, the mother; and Parthenope and Florence, the daughters—were old acquaintances of the Wedgwood circle. Among other connections, the Nightingales were cousins of the Tollets of Betley Hall, childhood friends of Emma Wedgwood and the other Maerites. Additionally, Fanny Nightingale and the Allen sisters, especially Fanny Allen, were longtime friends. Thus it was quite natural for Aunt Fanny Allen to take a special interest in Florence's accomplishments in Turkey, and she wrote to Elizabeth Wedgwood in December 1854:

> Have you heard that [Florence] astonishes all the surgeons by her skill and presence of mind? After amputating a limb, they pass on to another, leaving her to take up the artery and do all that is necessary. . . . We are very busy here in Tenby in sending out clothing and necessaries to the Crimea and Scutari. My stock goes to the latter place, Emma[Allen]'s is for the fighting part.[48]

Whether Emma Darwin followed her aunts' example and sent supplies to the troops at the front is unknown.

Charles's comprehensive analysis of the world's barnacles came to an end in the fall of 1854. He noted in his diary: "On Oct. 1st it will be 8 years since I began! but then I have lost 1 or 2 years by illness." No more boxes of barnacles coming and going in the mail; no more barnacles in spirits to be dissected; no more barnacle shells to be soaked and analyzed. De-barnaclizing Down House must have been gratifying to both Charles and Emma. Charles immediately returned to work on his beloved species theory. Emma directed her attention to family health issues.[49]

11. For Better or Worse, in Sickness and in Health

WHILE FLORENCE NIGHTINGALE was struggling with sick soldiers in Scutari, Emma Darwin was struggling with sickness at home. In addition to Emma's likely miscarriage in October 1854, Etty was ill for a short period that same month, George was unwell for most of September and October, and Franky ended the year with a "fit" of some sort that kept him in bed for ten days.[1]

Sickness continued to dog the Darwins during a monthlong stay in London that overlapped January and February 1855. The weather was cold and snowy, and Emma in particular was unwell much of the time. Nonetheless, they managed to squeeze in two trips to the dentist, a half dozen dinner parties, and two concerts, one of them featuring Luigi Cherubini's Choral Piece in C. (The Cherubini concert was a charity event. The *Times* advertisement noted that all proceeds would go to aid the Asylum for Idiots.)[2]

The Darwins had barely returned to Downe before the whooping cough hit in March. All of the children except Willy, who was away at school, came down with it, making the house "terribly noisy," according to Charles. Willy was not to escape his own bout of sickness; in May he contracted scarlet fever while at Rugby. Given the Foxes' tragic loss the previous year, this turn of events terrified Charles and Emma, and she flew to Willy's bedside for a week of mother's loving care.[3]

In the fall of 1855, Emma accompanied Charles to Glasgow for the annual

BAAS meeting. While he went to the various sessions and enjoyed the scientific papers, Emma, true to form, preferred to shop and socialize. On the day of the closing dinner, an event that should have proved interesting to both of the Darwins, Emma was unwell with a head cold and Charles had to attend alone. At the end of the weeklong meeting, they traveled home together as far as Shrewsbury, whence Charles proceeded to Downe, while Emma made a brief visit to Barlaston to see the Frank Wedgwoods and then to Rugby to check on Willy.[4]

Charles was now heavily into work on the "species question." How should species be defined and recognized? How much variation could they contain? How did new species come into being? And how did any given species come to have wide geographic distribution? He had learned from his barnacle studies that well-accepted cirripede species could show considerable trait variation, and now he wished to extend that type of analysis to other organisms. His first step was to mobilize, by post, a small army of informants and collaborators near and far. He wrote to Hooker in London, Henslow in Hitcham, Asa Gray in America, and other botanists asking for plant specimens, as well as their opinions on the question of acceptable levels of intraspecific variation. He begged animal specimens from W. D. Fox, William Tegetmeier in London, Edward Blyth in Calcutta, and numerous others. At Down House, seeds were soaked in salt water to see how long they could float on ocean currents and still be viable. Animal specimens were measured and weighed, and carcasses were reduced to skeletons. The whole process had its ghastly aspects. Charles wrote to Fox:

> The Box was hardly strong enough in which you sent the Duckling, for it had been compressed, & the intestines had been forced out, but not much injured, which I am very glad of, for I intend to measure length of intestines in tame & wild old Ducks, & if there be, (as I should not be surprised) any considerable difference, I should wish *particularly* to look at the intestines of the young.

The seed-soaking, skeletonizing, and intestine-measuring projects had their odorous drawbacks. Cress seeds especially "smelt very badly" after a week's soaking, Charles admitted to Hooker. Emma's reaction to this new line of Charles's work went unrecorded, but one guesses that she was responsible for much of it being relegated to the outdoors or the Down House cellar. A hothouse would have been just the thing for the seed-soaking and subsequent sprouting, but it would be the early 1860s before Charles had one built in the backyard.[5]

While Charles was doing the spadework that would lead to his "species book," another member of the extended family was about to try her authorial wings with a very different sort of publication. Fanny and Hensleigh's oldest daughter Snow spent October and November 1855 in Manchester as a guest of the writer Elizabeth Gaskell. Famous for such novels as *Mary Barton*, *Ruth*, *Cranford*, and *North and South*, Mrs. Gaskell was a second cousin of Emma and her Wedgwood siblings, and she and Fanny Hensleigh were particularly good friends. Through their mothers, Snow had become friendly years before with the oldest Gaskell daughters, Marianne and Meta. The autumn of 1855 found Mrs. Gaskell busy with a solemn literary duty: preparing a biography of her fellow novelist and friend Charlotte Brontë, who had died the previous March. During her visit with the Gaskells, Snow made herself useful by joining Marianne and Meta in copying Charlotte's letters as they were sent by the Brontë family.[6]

This literary work for Mrs. Gaskell came at a good time for Snow. Twenty-two years old, highly intelligent and equally highly principled, Snow nonetheless lacked direction in her life. Suffering from a significant degree of deafness, she was intimidated by social gatherings lest she embarrass herself by responding inappropriately while conversing. Furthermore, perhaps as part of an elaborate set of defense mechanisms, she had developed a "mistrust of marriage" and thus appeared to be on track for a lifelong spinsterhood. (It may be significant that two of Snow's primary role models, Florence Nightingale and Harriet Martineau, were also spinsters.) Despite her physical handicap and social unease, however, Snow "had a mystical belief in her own destiny." She wished to make a name for herself, and working for Mrs. Gaskell inspired Snow to try her own hand at writing a novel.[7]

Accordingly, Snow sat down in late 1855 and began work on a moralistic tale titled *Framleigh Hall*. From the start, she was anxious about how the family would respond to her literary efforts. "I shd be miserable ever after if any of our people don't like it," she wrote to her sister Effie (Euphemia) just before *Framleigh Hall* was published in 1858. "I was rather depressed by the way you spoke about it, though you are such a rabid novel reader, & if you did not like it, how much more Mack [Bro] and all our people who are so dreadfully critical—Oh dear! I have given myself up to be made a pincushion!" Snow tried to shield herself a little by publishing the book anonymously, despite encouragement to the contrary from Meta Gaskell and her aunt Emma and uncle Charles Darwin. And, sure enough, her worst fears came true: her parents labeled it "foolishly sentimental" and "boring." These criticisms cut deep and were especially galling since established authors such as Harriet Martineau and Mrs. Gaskell liked the book. Whatever its strengths and weaknesses, a contemporary reviewer was probably near the mark when he blamed its flaws on the author's inexperience, saying that *Framleigh Hall*

> is evidently the production of a lady, and of a young lady, who has read and thought more than she has seen or felt; but of whose powers, when they have been developed and enriched by the experience of life and a more wide and varied knowledge of the world, we are inclined to augur very highly.[8]

The new year began on a dismal note with the death of a brother-in-law on the Darwin side of the family. Henry Parker, the husband of Charles's oldest sister Marianne and a physician in Shrewsbury, passed away in January at sixty-seven years of age. The sorrow at his passing was muted by the fact that the Parkers had married when Charles was only fifteen, and they and their five children had always lived at the edge of his and Emma's lives, though they had unsurprisingly maintained closer relations with fellow Shrewsburyites Susan and Catherine Darwin. It seems likely that Dr. Parker had been ill for some time before his death, since Charles mentioned his "release" in a note to W. D. Fox. True to habit in his avoidance of funerals, Charles made no attempt to attend Henry's.[9]

For Emma, 1856 brought that old familiar feeling of being pregnant. At nearly forty-eight years of age, she must have dreaded the symptoms despite knowing from her regular monthly cycles that she was still at risk for childbearing. By April she was ticking off the weeks in her pocket diary: April 13, "6th w[eek] "; April 20, "7th." It wasn't until mid-April, however, that she began to feel real discomfort from the pregnancy, and before that happened she had squeezed in two short trips into London to hear the renowned soprano Jenny Lind. On March 11 Lind performed at Exeter Hall, singing Mendelssohn's hymn "Hear My Prayer, O God," as well as several other pieces. Jenny's husband, Otto Goldschmidt, accompanied her on the pianoforte. After the concert, word spread that Goldschmidt and Lind, who was called the Swedish Nightingale, had donated all of the proceeds—more than £1,800, or $150,000 today—to the Nightingale Fund, an act of generosity that must have pleased Emma enormously. The fund had been established in November 1855 in the wake of extraordinary public acclaim for Florence's efforts at Scutari and in the Crimea, and its purpose was to support the professional training of English nurses. In a clear indication that the Nightingale Fund enjoyed backing at the very highest levels, its kickoff meeting was chaired by Queen Victoria's cousin the Duke of Cambridge, a Crimea veteran and the British army's commander-in-chief.[10]

One week after the first concert, Emma was back at Exeter Hall for a second Jenny Lind performance. This time Madame Goldschmidt sang selections from Handel's oratorio *Messiah*. Emma wrote to Willy at Rugby that she had heard "Jenny Lind at last" and it "was very beautiful."[11]

Emma came home from the Lind concerts to a flurry of houseguests and entertaining. Frank Wedgwood and the Hensleigh Wedgwoods, the latter accompanied by Meta Gaskell, arrived in Downe on March twentieth. Harry Wedgwood drifted in a week later. The Lubbocks hosted everyone to a fancy ball on the twenty-fifth and, in turn, three days later they were part of a large dinner party at Down House. In mid-April, Sir Charles and Lady Lyell came for a four-day stay that included another dinner party. During lulls in the socializing the two Charleses squeezed in some science, of course, including Darwin giving Lyell for the first time a full explanation of natural selection.[12]

Shortly after the Lyells' departure, the unpleasant side effects of Emma's pregnancy settled in. She confided to her diary on April 17: "I began to be bad." Then followed about ten weeks of nearly constant sickness. Entries of "very bad," "very sick," "headache," and "worse than ever" were interspersed with the occasional "better" or "tolerable." She got through this sick spell by self-medicating with "blue pills," a mixture of glycerin, honey, and mercury. These were taken on at least three occasions in May and June, between the tenth and sixteenth weeks as Emma reckoned her pregnancy.[13]

As Emma sank into a state of discomfort and "general oppression" (as her husband wrote to J. D. Hooker in July), Charles found himself being urged by both Lyell and Hooker to publish a preliminary sketch of his evolution theory. But such a sketch would have involved presenting the theory without details and supporting evidence, and this Charles was reluctant to do. He did allow himself to be convinced that the time was ripe for the full publication of his species theory, however, and on May 14 he commenced writing "by Lyells advice."[14]

George turned eleven in July 1856, and the next month he became the second Darwin son to go away to boarding school. On August 14 Charles traveled up to London with George and enrolled him at the private Clapham Grammar School. The founder and headmaster at Clapham, the Reverend Charles Pritchard, "had a special gift for teaching mathematics," which in George's case was good, since he entered school deficient in that subject. Furthermore, unlike Rugby, Clapham placed much more emphasis on science than on classical studies. This suited both Charles and George, the latter having an "entire ignorance of Greek" when he was enrolled. Educational niceties aside, for Emma and Charles one of the main advantages of Clapham School was its nearness: George would be able to come home one Sunday each month and for short holidays at Easter and Michaelmas.[15]

George had been away barely two weeks before his great-aunt Sarah Wedgwood fell at her home in Downe and broke her hip. She was "utterly crippled," as Charles reported to Fox, a fate "far worse than death."[16] As it turned out, Aunt Sarah didn't have to suffer invalidism for very long. She died two months after the fall, and Charles reported the details of her funeral—one of the few he hadn't been able to avoid—to Willy and George:

> [November 13, 1856] I have thought that you would like to hear about poor Aunt Sarah's funeral. Aunt Elizabeth, & Uncles Jos, Harry, Frank, Hensleigh, & Allen all attended, so that we had the house quite full. The Funeral was at 3 o'clock, & Mr. Lewis managed it all. We walked down to Petleys & there all put on black Cloaks & crape to our hats, & followed the Hearse, which was carried by six men; another six men changing half way.—At the Church Door Mr. Innes came out to meet the Hearse. Then it was carried into the Church & a short service was read. Then we all went out, & stood uncovered round the grave whilst the Coffin was lowered, & then Mr. Innes finished the service, but he did not read this very impressive service well. [Aunt Sarah's servants] attended & seemed to cry a good deal.—Then we all marched back to the House, Mr. Lewis & his two sons carrying a sort of black standard before us; & we then went into the House & read Aunt Sarah's will aloud. She desired her Funeral to be as quiet as possible, & that no tablet should be erected to her. She has left a great deal of money to very many Charities.[17]

In compliance with Aunt Sarah's last wishes, hers was a very simple Victorian funeral. Nonetheless, the proper mourning customs had to be followed, even by great-nephews away at school. Thus, a few days after his first note, Charles wrote to Willy a second time: "First in regard to your clothes you had better get a warm waist-coat & Trowsers, black & white,—something that will do for half mourning & yet will do afterwards."[18]

The death at seventy-eight years of age of this "double aunt"—Emma's through her father and Charles's through his mother—marked the end of the children of Josiah I. A tall, thin old lady who at the end had looked a half century behind the times, Aunt Sarah was fastidious in her manners—she had kept special black gloves for handling coal and shaking hands with children—and reserved in her displays of affection. That aloofness, a trait that Sarah shared with Josiah II, prevented her from social intimacy even with kin. Thus Henrietta Darwin could remark many years later that Emma had been "beautifully faithful to her, but . . . the rigidity of her aunt Sarah's character prevented ease of intercourse and therefore strong affection on [Emma's] part."[19]

Two weeks after Aunt Sarah's funeral, Elizabeth arrived at Down House to provide her usual help during Emma's confinement. The baby, a sixth son, was born (with the aid of chloroform) on December 6, 1856, and named after his father and his paternal grandfather: Charles Waring Darwin. From High Elms, Lady Lubbock generously sent an invitation to have the older boys, Franky, Leonard, and Horace, come to stay with them while Emma was recuperating, but the offer was declined. In fact Emma bounced back fairly quickly, coming downstairs for meals less than three weeks after her delivery.[20]

Although Charles Waring was pronounced "beautiful" by his father and congratulations came pouring in ("I must congratulate you on the addition of another [male] to your vivarium. . . . Vivat Darwinianus masculus sextus," wrote the entomologist T. V. Wollaston), it soon became clear that he was not quite normal. "He was . . . [delayed] in walking & talking . . . [had] a remarkably sweet, placid & joyful disposition; but had not high spirits . . . [and] often made strange grimaces & shivered, when excited."[21] Retrospective diagnoses of the baby's condition have ranged from Down syndrome to retardation due to prenatal exposure to mercury. The Down syndrome hypothesis is supported by Emma's age, then forty-eight, since the risk increases with maternal age. The hypothesis of mercury poisoning is supported by Emma's use of blue pills early in her pregnancy, since two to three blue pills, a typical daily dose in Victorian times, contained many times the amount of mercury now considered safe to ingest in a day.[22]

Whatever the etiology of Charles Waring's condition, it is certain that the baby "was born without its full share of intelligence," as Henrietta remarked years later. He was baptized at the village church in Downe in May 1857 (Emma entered "baby Xned" in her diary), with representatives of the Wedgwood and Darwin families gathered round, but Charles Waring was clearly a fragile child.[23]

A change of governesses took place early in 1857. Catherine Thorley, who had served the family for half a decade and was at Annie's bedside in Malvern in 1851, left the Darwins' employ and was replaced by Miss Pugh. Miss Pugh turned out to be less stable psychologically than her predecessor—"neurotic & semi-mad," thought Etty—but at least she made the lessons interesting.

Apparently suffering from a bad case of unrequited love, Miss Pugh occasionally sat "at meals with tears quietly pouring down her cheeks."[24]

Willy and George were both doing well at school. At Rugby, Willy was in the sixth form and had been added to the rota of lectors for chapel services. His father wrote to him saying, "Mamma desires that you will read the Chapters *very well*; & the dear old Mammy must be obeyed." Charles and Emma were toying with the idea of guiding Willy into a legal career, believing that he had the "gift of gab" that Uncle Harry Wedgwood said was a prerequisite for that field. At Clapham, George was off to an adequate start and "not nearly so low in the school as . . . anticipated."[25] Clearly, George had room for improvement.

Charles worked steadily on his evolution book, which, it was now clear, would be a very long one. As he labored, and as the work wore on his health, the flow of scientific visitors to Down House slowed significantly, although scientific correspondence continued apace. In the course of 1857 Charles wrote or received about 150 scientific letters, nearly one-quarter of them communications with Hooker. He pumped information out of Hooker, Huxley, Lyell, Henslow, Wollaston, and others in Britain, and also American scientists including Asa Gray and J. D. Dana. Significantly, Charles also extracted information from Alfred Russel Wallace, a young scientist who was eking out a living as a specimen collector in Malaysia, apparently never suspecting that Wallace was also zeroing in on the mystery of how species originate. By the end of 1857, Charles was well into the ninth chapter of his big book, having completed the crucial chapters on variation, competition, and natural selection.[26]

Family, friends, and the occasional scientist continued to drop in at Down House, of course, and in February 1857 Admiral and Mrs. Robert FitzRoy came for lunch. FitzRoy, who had only recently been promoted to rear admiral, was chief of the Board of Trade's meteorological department, and in that position he was leading Britain into the modern age of weather forecasting. His wife Maria was the second Mrs. FitzRoy, the first having died in 1852, and she seems to have been somewhat reserved.[27] Emma judged the luncheon less than a huge success, which is understandable when one remembers the stock she put in lively conversation. In a letter to Willy, she poked fun at both Mrs. FitzRoy and Charles:

On Monday Ad. and Mrs Fitz Roy and their son a pale boy of 18 who has been 4 years in the navy . . . came to luncheon in their way from Sevenoaks. Papa was much awestruck with the honour, and the Ad. was very gracious and friendly. Mrs Fitz Roy is a cold dry stick and I cd not find a word to say to her. Papa says she is a *remarkably* nice woman (because she laughed at his jokes I say).[28]

Besides having to struggle to pry a conversation out of Mrs. FitzRoy, Emma may not have enjoyed this luncheon for another reason: she was still recovering from facial surgery and may not have looked or felt her best. On February 13 she had seen James Paget at St. Bartholomew's Hospital in London and had her "lip done." It is unclear whether this was cosmetic surgery or Emma had somehow injured her lip, but either way, Charles wrote to Willy on the seventeenth that his mother's lip was still "plaistered up, so we cannot tell yet how she will look."[29]

There were more urgent health problems on the horizon. Charles's work was making him sick, and Emma pressed him to return to Malvern for another water cure session with Dr. Gully. This was sage advice, he knew, but the mere thought of the place plunged his soul into agony. Returning to Malvern would cause "old thoughts" of Annie's death to "revive so vividly" that he wasn't sure he could bear it. Of course, at some level, this was simply an excuse to keep working, since there were other water cure clinics, like the one run by Dr. Edward Lane at Moor Park in Surrey. Darwin was stubbornly delaying taking a break, and he paid for it as winter wore on into spring. While he dithered about changing hydropathists, he made do by self-medicating his stomach with "mineral acids," probably a mixture of hydrochloric and nitric acids.[30]

Considerably more worrying than Charles's complaints, thirteen-year-old Etty seemed to be experiencing a general breakdown in health. The first signs had come the previous summer, at which point Charles had taken her to London to see Dr. Benjamin Brodie. Dr. Brodie's advice led to little if any improvement, and by March 1857 Etty's deterioration had picked up speed. "Etty very poorly since Sunday," wrote Emma in her diary on March 24. Finally it was decided that Emma would take her to Hastings in hopes that sea air and a change of scenery might perk her up. Leaving the other children at home with Charles and Miss Pugh, Emma and Etty took the train to Hastings on April 9. As it happened, the Hookers were there too, and Joseph wrote back to Darwin that "Etty is thin & pale, but not looking worn or anxious." Mother and daughter took walks and drives by the sea, although some days were too bitterly cold to do much out of doors.[31]

At home, Charles had suffered enough by mid-April that he was ready to go to Moor Park. Accordingly, Emma swapped places for a few days with Miss Pugh and Lizzy so she could pack her dyspeptic husband off to the water spa. Now caught between an ailing daughter and an ailing husband, Emma called for backup. Miss Thorley was brought out of "retirement" to watch over Etty in Hastings, and Emma went to Moor Park to watch over Charles, who, true to form, was able to "walk & eat like a hearty Christian" soon after leaving the pressures of his work.[32]

Charles came home on May sixth and Etty on the twelfth, allowing Miss Thorley to go back to her home. Neither patient was particularly well, however, and the rest of the year was spent shuttling one or the other of the "sickies" between Downe and Moor Park. Emma checked Etty into the clinic for a course of the water cure at the end of May. The little girl was Dr. Lane's patient until August seventh, came home for two weeks only to relapse, and returned to the clinic until the end of October. September twenty-fifth must have been a dismal fourteenth birthday for Henrietta, but at least her mother came to be with her. Charles was at Dr. Lane's establishment for the second half of June and again for a week from November 5. All in all, it was quite a year, stressful for the whole family but clearly formative for Henrietta, who in many ways never recovered from her breakdown of 1857. Henceforth throughout a long life, Etty was always delicate and prone to real or imagined ill health. Sickness, hers and others', became "her profession and absorbing interest." As part of her slide into hypochondria, she never again came down to the breakfast table, but instead had her morning meal in bed for the rest of her life. (It is worth noting that her mother, and perhaps her father as well, may have unintentionally enabled Etty's developing invalidism. Writing many years later, Gwen Darwin Raverat looked back at Down House and remembered a "cult of ill health" fostered especially by overly solicitous behavior on her grandmother Emma's part. Raverat felt that a firmer maternal hand might have prevented Etty from becoming obsessed with sickness in the first place.)[33]

As 1857 ended, Charles was plugging away at his chapter on hybridism. Significantly, he had let another person in on his evolutionary secret. In July he wrote to Asa Gray at Harvard: "I have come to the heterodox conclusion that there are no such things as independently created species—that species are only strongly defined varieties." This was followed up in September by sending Gray a short, but fairly detailed, abstract of his ideas on natural selection and species formation. (This document would play a key part in the public announcement of natural selection the next year.) Gray thus joined Hooker and Lyell as full confidants in Charles's evolution work, with Huxley, Wollaston, and several others being aware of bits and pieces of his thinking.[34]

There was also formal recognition that fall that they were outgrowing Down House. By 1857 Emma and Charles had eight children and employed a staff of about ten servants. The extended Darwin-Wedgwood circle totaled some seventeen adults and thirty-six children. At times, particularly around major holidays, Down House groaned from the crowd of resident family, staff, and visitors. There simply was no escaping the need to enlarge the house, as Charles explained to W. D. Fox in November: "We have . . . been recreating ourselves with building a new Dining room & large bedroom over it; for we found our party, when we had cousins had quite outgrown our old room."[35]

The two-story expansion extended Down House to the northwest. Originally planned as a dining room, the first-floor space was actually used as the main drawing room once completed. Here the family gathered in the evening for conversation, games (backgammon was a nightly pastime for Emma and Charles), music, and reading amidst framed watercolors and various objets d'art. Emma went to London in search of suitable wallpaper, but brought back samples in earth tones that failed to impress her family. Charles wrote to Willy: "Mamma went up yesterday & brought down two such patterns, of the exact colour of mud, streaked with rancid oil, that we have all exclaimed against them; & I have agreed to take anything in preference & we have settled on a crimson flock-paper with golden stars, though unseen by me." With its velvety texture and bold colors, the latter paper would have made for a striking drawing room, albeit one somewhat reminiscent of Macaw Cottage. Indeed, one modern biographer reflecting on this little episode has suggested that Emma's taste in interior decoration was spoiled by those years on Upper Gower Street. But this hardly seems fair, since Charles and the children were the ones who preferred crimson over brown. Still, one wonders how the crimson wallpaper looked as a background for Emma's favorite lilac dress.[36]

As he wrote his evolution opus, Charles continued to solicit vast amounts of scientific information from his global network of correspondents. Besides data, their replies often included interesting comments on political events in the world beyond Downe. By 1858 the Crimean War was just an ugly memory (the Treaty of Paris was signed in March 1856) and Florence Nightingale had returned home. After a bout of post-traumatic stress, Florence had begun work, at the queen's invitation, on a study of "the state of the army," work that would eventually lead to widespread military reform.[37] But no sooner had peace returned to the Crimea than war broke out in India. In May 1857, native troops in the Bengal Indian army mutinied, killed their officers and many Europeans, captured Delhi, and laid siege to Lucknow. Britons at home and abroad were horrified and outraged. In January 1858, after Lucknow had been relieved and its European residents rescued, Edward Blyth wrote to Charles from his headquarters in Calcutta:

> As I write, a royal salute is firing in honour of the arrival of the glorious garrison of Lucknow, i.e., the wounded officers, & the ladies and children. How amazingly the force of character of our countrymen & countrywomen has been evinced in the course of this terrible struggle! The wonderful superiority of the European to the Asiatic, from the days of Xenophon and Alexander even unto now! Against such overwhelming odds, nobody ever conceived the possibility of the insurrection proving successful,—this grand struggle of barbarism against a higher civilization ennobled by the application of all the sciences.[38]

To a modern reader, these comments are offensively racist, but to a Victorian Englishman they simply reflected the realities of the world. Almost certainly, the Darwins were not offended by Blyth's racial comparisons. Although utterly opposed to slavery, Charles and Emma were comfortable with the notion of a hierarchy of human races, a hierarchy capped by civilized, intelligent Europeans.[39] It goes without saying, of course, that they shared the general horror at the murder of Britons by the mutineers.

Speaking of intelligent Europeans, one young member of that set—namely, William Erasmus Darwin—was now being actively groomed for university matriculation. William, who at eighteen was now addressed as an adult, had left Rugby at Christmas 1857 and two months later started private tutoring with the Reverend William Greive Wilson in Norfolk. Before enrolling at Cambridge, William urgently needed help with mathematics and the Latin and Greek classics. As for the other older sons, George was still at Clapham School, and Franky was about to follow in George's footsteps and receive private tutoring from the Reverend Mr. Reed in Hayes.[40]

Happily, these three sons, plus Lizzy and Horace, were in good health as the new year dawned, but the same could not be said for the other children. Baby Charles Waring continued to be delicate and backward, eight-year-old Lenny was sick on and off throughout the winter and spring with symptoms that included a "badly intermittent pulse," and fourteen-year-old Henrietta was now having dental problems. Etty's teeth urgently needed to be realigned, and to that end her London dentist, Thomas Bell, crafted a "gold plate [to be] put in her mouth . . . to try to get her teeth in better shape." Unfortunately, the plate made the poor girl lisp and otherwise speak unclearly. Additionally, Etty apparently had several cavities that needed Mr. Bell's attention and at least one tooth that required extraction. (It is interesting to speculate that the rich diet favored at Down House might have contributed to the family's chronic dental problems.) Finally, as if Etty didn't have enough on her plate, she reached menarche in the spring of 1858 and began monthly menstrual cycles. For a while Emma, who had yet to go through menopause, marked both her own and Etty's periods in her pocket diary.[41]

Despite having to deal with family health worries—a "daily & nightly bug-bear," as Charles put it—Emma managed to find a little time for recreation, as usual. After all, trips to see Mr. Bell could double as opportunities for concertgoing, and accordingly in February she and Charles attended a program of Mendelssohn and Mozart at St. Martin's Hall. A few days later Emma heard Mendelssohn's *Elijah* at the same venue. On another visit to Mr. Bell in May, she got in some London shopping and took in an exhibit of modern French paintings. The French exhibition may have been an early birthday present to herself: the next day, Emma turned fifty.[42]

By April, Charles's stomach was in such bad shape that he checked himself into Moor Park for more water treatments. As usual, getting away from the daily grind of his scientific work did him good, both physically and mentally. He wrote to Hooker that once again, "Hydropathy has made a man of me for a short time." At the clinic, Darwin amused himself by reading novels, chatting with the other patients, and sharpening up his billiard game. Out of doors, he observed the behavior of ants. That Moor Park had restored his joie de vivre is obvious from this poetic passage written to Emma:

> The weather is quite delicious. Yesterday after writing to you I strolled a little beyond the glade for an hour & half & enjoyed myself—the fresh yet dark green of the grand Scotch Firs, the brown of the catkins of the old Birches with their white stems & a fringe of distant green from the larches, made an excessively pretty view.—At last I fell fast asleep on the grass & awoke with a chorus of birds singing around me, & squirrels running up the trees & some Woodpeckers laughing, & it was as pleasant a rural scene as ever I saw, & I did not care one penny how any of the beasts or birds had been formed.[43]

It is a lovely letter and must have been a pick-me-up for Emma. She would not have been fooled by the last sentence, however. She knew all too well that her Charles cared *deeply* how the beasts and birds had been formed and would soon be back working obsessively on that very mystery.

Professionally and emotionally, the summer of 1858 was a nightmare. Dealing with the scientific issues first, on June 18, just as he was finishing a chapter titled "Divergence" and starting the next one on variation in pigeons, Charles received a short manuscript from A. R. Wallace in Malaysia. In his paper, Wallace demonstrated beyond a shadow of a doubt that he too had discovered the speciation process Darwin was calling "natural selection." Two years earlier, Lyell had urged Darwin to publish his evolutionary ideas before someone beat him to the punch, and now Charles wrote to Lyell saying, "Your words have come true with a vengeance that I shd be forestalled. . . . if Wallace had my M.S. sketch written out in 1842 he could not have made a better short abstract!" In his cover letter accompanying the manuscript, Wallace asked only that Darwin read the paper and, if he thought it had merit, to show it to Lyell. There was no mention of submitting it for publication, but Charles knew all too well that it had to go to a journal.[44]

What to do? Darwin hated the thought of losing priority for the discovery of natural selection, but ignoring Wallace's paper would be behaving dishonorably. He could prove, after all, that he had been working on the species question since the 1840s, but wouldn't it look rather shabby to rush an abstract of his views into print in obvious response to Wallace's codiscovery of the mechanisms of evolution? Charles's emotions and motivations were complex, his agony of indecision was real, and, as we shall see, it was all made worse by life-threatening illness among the children. In the end, in letters to Hooker and Lyell, Darwin floated the idea of presenting Wallace's paper along with evidence from his own 1844 essay and from letters to Asa Gray showing that he, Charles, had been working on the solution to the species question for many years—and in this way preserving his priority. His friends agreed that this was both justified and morally acceptable, and it was decided that a meeting of the Linnean Society would serve as the venue for a joint Darwin-Wallace presentation. Accordingly, acting on behalf of the two evolutionists, Hooker and Lyell submitted a packet of papers labeled "Laws which affect the Production of Varieties, Races, and Species" to the secretary of the Linnean Society. These were duly read to the Society on July 1, 1858. The evolutionary cat was finally out of the bag.[45]

These concerns over scientific priority and paltry behavior were exhausting for Charles, both mentally and physically. And his and Emma's troubles that summer were far from over. In an awful coincidence, on precisely the same day that Wallace's paper arrived, Etty's health broke down once again. Emma's diary entry for June 18 reads, "Etty taken ill." The child's throat had swelled painfully and was producing a copious discharge, rendering her unable to swallow or speak. At first they thought she had tonsillitis, but later the diagnosis was changed to diphtheria.[46]

A week later and "after much suffering," Etty was clearly on the mend, but then a second child, in many ways the most vulnerable of them all, fell ill. The baby, Charles Waring, came down with a high fever and one of the maids with a sore throat. These were truly terrifying developments, because scarlet fever was just then raging in Downe village and three local children had already died. In agony Charles wrote to W. D. Fox, his cousin who had lost a daughter to scarlet fever five years before, to say that "our Baby has become suddenly most ill.—It is Scarlet Fever, & the Doctor can only say there is yet some hope." Sadly, the doctor had been overly optimistic, and on June 28, 1858, Charles Waring Darwin died at only eighteen months of age. Emma's diary entries tell the tale of a brief final illness: June 23, "Baby taken ill"; June 27, "Baby worse"; June 28, "death." Backward but lovable, the baby had never learned to walk or talk, but nonetheless had captured his parents' hearts with his "sweet, placid & joyful disposition . . . little bubbling noises . . . [and] wicked little smile." Charles wrote a short memorial that, among other things, described the baby's joy at standing on his father's hands and being tossed lightly into the air. Fifty years later, Henrietta remembered that after their initial grief had passed, her parents were thankful the poor impaired child had lived no longer than he did. That first grief, however, went deep.[47]

The day after the baby died, Elizabeth came over from Sussex, gathered up all of the remaining children except Etty, who was too weak to move, and took them to her fever-free home in Hartfield. A few days later, Emma and Charles and Etty traveled first to Hartfield and then on to the Isle of Wight, where it was hoped sea air and sea bathing would hasten the young girl's recovery. They could not shake death off their trail, however. No sooner had they settled into the King's Head Hotel in Sandown than word came from Shrewsbury that Marianne Parker had succumbed to a long and painful illness. Marianne's children were all grown—the youngest was twenty-two— but nonetheless they were adopted by their aunts Catherine and Susan Darwin and went to live at The Mount. Charles added Marianne's to the long list of family funerals that he had missed.[48]

All of the other Darwin children had arrived on the Isle of Wight by mid-July, and for the next month the family enjoyed life at the seashore as much as recent events and the weather allowed. They drove out to see the local sights, took a boat ride to picturesque Luccombe Village, and bathed in the salt water. Happily, the Isle had the longed-for therapeutic effects. By the time they headed home in August everyone felt better, even Etty and Charles—the latter despite the fact that, at Hooker's and Lyell's insistence, he had begun working on an "abstract" of his evolution theory. Originally envisioned as a journal piece of about thirty pages, the "abstract" would eventually grow into a 490-page book Darwin would name *On the Origin of Species*.[49]

In October 1858, William Darwin ended his studies with the Reverend Mr. Wilson and matriculated at Cambridge University for the Michaelmas term. Following his parents' wishes, he moved into rooms in Christ's College, which Emma then helped furnish with items purchased at estate sales. Charles did his part by fretting over money. He wrote to William, "Remember to let me know in good time before you run short of money & do, I earnestly beg you, keep accounts *carefully*." As the year ended, the nascent *Origin* was about two-thirds completed, but the writing was having its predictable effect on Charles, and he retreated once again to Moor Park for a week's soak and douche.[50]

12. Midwiving the *Origin*

EMMA'S DIARIES ARE OFTEN maddeningly silent just when one hopes they will yield insights into their author's personality and thinking. The entries are almost always terse and emotionless, and significant events are sometimes ignored entirely or marked with only the briefest of comments (on the day baby Charles Waring died, "death"). Among the apparently significant omissions, 1858 was an important birthday year for Emma—her fiftieth!—but she made no mention of the event in her diary. Similarly, on January 29, 1859, she and Charles celebrated their twentieth wedding anniversary, and two weeks later he turned fifty, but neither of these occasions merited diary entries. One wonders whether these omissions reflect a general downplaying of birthdays and anniversaries at Down House or whether Emma simply felt these particular ones needed no commemorative notation. Or are we asking too much of what was, after all, only a pocket calendar and not a true journal?[1]

As we attempt to understand what sort of woman Emma Darwin was in 1859—spiritually, philosophically, and in her everyday behavior—it might be enlightening to take her twentieth wedding anniversary as a milestone and to tally the major positive and negative events of her married life to date. On the positive, happy side, she loved and was loved by a man with whom she shared a small fortune, a lovely country home, and a comfortably elevated position in society. Furthermore, her husband was an established star of British science, a man who had not only published several books but also won the Royal Society's Royal Medal for Natural Science. Together they had produced ten children, who had already brought their parents much joy and promised to bring much more. On the negative, sad side, by 1859 Emma had already buried three of her children. Her parents and parents-in-law were all dead, and her ancestral home at Maer Hall had been broken up and sold out of the family. She had some relatively minor but nagging health issues personally, but worried more about the chronic bad health of her husband and certain of the children. And finally, although Emma had long ago learned to coexist with her husband's evolutionary beliefs, she still found his views to be contrary to Scripture and therefore threatening in their implications about the fate of his soul.

All of these points are well established, but they provide frustratingly little substance as regards Emma's persona at middle age. Clearly she was tireless in her solicitude toward Charles and the children, a patient nurse for anyone who was ailing, and the family's spiritual bedrock. As shown by her diaries' lists of visits, visitors, and dinner parties, Emma was extroverted and social, but hardly bubbly (and never boisterous) in her interactions. She liked a good joke, but rarely told them (leaving that to Charles), and preferred a steady stream of serious talk at dinner parties to mere frivolous banter. Years later, Henrietta remembered her mother as "serene but somewhat grave" at middle age, suggesting that the years had dulled the high spirits that had characterized Little Miss Slip-Slop. Perhaps this was simply the Wedgwood heritage of gravity finally coming to the surface, but it could be intimidating, and "people were sometimes afraid of her" until they came to know the warmth behind Emma's severity. Nonetheless, some caution was advisable around Emma, since she did not suffer fools readily, "was easily wearied with tediousness in people," and "had no sympathy with any sentimentality or over-exuberance of expression." Combine these traits with a distinct tendency to speak her mind—sometimes before examining a question from all sides—and one can understand why some people might have ranked Emma somewhere between prickly and dour.[2]

As 1859 got under way, Emma once again had an overworked and sickly husband on her hands, as well as a delicate elder daughter. She also had to deal with a governess, Miss Pugh, who was showing distinct signs of mental breakdown (something she later accomplished). At the end of January, it was arranged that Miss Pugh would leave the Darwins' service and be replaced by Mrs. Grut, a German lady fluent both in that language and in French. But it soon became apparent that the Darwins had gone from bad to worse in their governesses. Mrs. Grut was domineering and tyrannical toward the children, and unresponsive to directions from Emma. Barely three weeks into the new governess's tenure, Emma wrote to William at Cambridge:

> I thought [while visiting] at Hartfield that I should have come to a regular blow up with the G., but I wrote her a note "stern but just" (as she talks so much she never listens to a word I say) & that brought her to reason & we have gone on quite smooth since. How long it will last I know not. She used to keep poor Skimp [seven-year-old Horace] stupefying over a lesson for 2 hours & then told him he should have no breakfast till he said it. Fancy the consternation of Frank & Lizzy. They came solemnly to tell me, & then she scolded them for telling tales, & then I scolded her & said they always were to tell every thing & then she scolded me & said they were such naughty children behind my back I could not judge any thing about them. But we are the best of friends now, but I feel there is a volcano beneath the surface.[3]

There was indeed a volcano rumbling just below ground, and Etty, who judged Mrs. Grut to be utterly incompetent and who had a controlling personality equal to that of her governess, knew just how to trigger an eruption. At fifteen, Etty was now a fully operational iron-willed teenage know-it-all.[4] One fine morning in March she deliberately precipitated the fatal showdown by publicly challenging Mrs. Grut on a point of language. Etty reported her triumph to William:

> Solemn events have happened. Mrs. Grut is gone for ever. this is how it came about. On Monday at breakfast Mama said very civilly that she wanted some alteration in Horace's lessons. Mrs. Grut was evidently miffed at that, & then I said that I thought s'eloigner wasn't to ramble very mildly & that miffed her again & she made me some rude speech or other 'Oh very well if I knew better than the dictionary.' I quite lost that speech then, Ma repeated it afterwards. Nothing more came of it then, & all went smooth till I went up to my German lesson in the evening. When I came in I saw there was the devil in her face, well she scolded the children a bit & then sat down by me, when I showed her my lesson (a bit of very bad french) she said, if I knew better than she did it was no use her teaching me & so & so on, till it came to a crisis, & she worked herself into a regular rage. [']Oh you've no feelings, but I have. I feel these things['] & so on. This all referred to my saying I thought s'eloigner wasn't to ramble, she had been brooding over it all day & then when she had got me all to herself it burst forth. I left the room then, &

went down stairs to tell my injuries. When Papa & Mama heard all about it they settled she shd go at once, so Papa wrote a letter telling her she should have her 33£ & nothing more. Mama went upstairs to watch till the children had done, they all came out crying. After [Mrs. Grut] cdn't scold me she fell upon them I suppose, [then] Papa was to go upstairs & deliver the letter. The very first thing she said was '*I* don't care for your legal notice to quit' & tossed the letter to one side. 'Mrs. Darwin engaged me for six months & you'll have to keep me.['] the line of conduct they had settled upon was not tell her why she was sent away so that if there was a law suit it might only rest upon whether we had the right to dismiss her without paying her board & lodging. Papa got *such* a torrent, telling him he was no gentleman, & white with passion all the time. Wanting to know what she had done, what he had to accuse her of—telling him he was in a passion—she wd give him time to think. . . . We had a very flustered tea, & all evening we sat preparing for the worst, what we shd do if she refused to go out of the house etc. However she did turn out much milder & sent us a letter to say she wd go on Wednesday.[5]

Mrs. Grut duly took her leave of Down House on March 16, probably very happy at the thought of never, ever seeing Etty again. Left without any governess, Emma took over the little children's lessons and Etty lent a hand—doubtless confirming in her own mind the high state of her knowledge. The entire unpleasant Grut episode may have contributed materially to Henrietta's adult belief that her mother "apparently did not try to get the best possible teaching" for the Darwin children. This notion hardly squares, however, with Emma's lifelong concern about education or, for that matter, with Mrs. Grut being hired in the first place because of her supposed linguistic skills. For some time the Darwins watched the mail for a "lawyers letter from the Grut," but it never came.[6]

Three days after "the Grut" departed, Charles noted in his private journal that he had finished the last chapter of his evolution manuscript and started revising the earlier chapters. He had also just won another medal, the Geological Society's Wollaston Medal, in recognition of his barnacle studies and various geological works. This was a nice plump-up for his vanity, but physically he was working himself to the bone and paying the price for it. He had already done two weeks at the Moor Park water cure back in February, having spent his fiftieth birthday there, and before the year was out and *Origin of Species* finally published, he would visit water cure clinics three more times. Charles's daily recreations from his labors included making regular laps around the Sandwalk and shooting billiards on his newly purchased table. Each evening there were backgammon games with Emma, followed by reading aloud (in May from Dickens's *Pickwick Papers*; Emma and Lizzy found the descriptions of "constant drinking" to be "a great blemish" on the book).[7]

The two sons away at school continued to work reasonably hard. George was still under the tutelage of Charles Pritchard at Clapham, while William—now occupying his father's old rooms at Christ's College, Cambridge—finished his first year of study and, after winning a competitive scholarship, proceeded into his second. Undergraduates being the same then as now, William had also found a variety of extracurricular activities to fill the odd hour. He joined in "dissipations" with friends and visiting cousins, attended the occasional opera, and, in an athletic vein, tried his hand at rowing on the Cam. (The last item prompted a gentle warning from his mother to remember "it is possible to damage one's inside by over exertion in rowing.") William also attended church, at least occasionally. Whether this was the result of personal conviction or strictly in order to please his mother is hard to tell, although the latter explanation seems more likely. Emma reinforced his churchgoing by writing: "It was very nice of you going to Church on Sunday in the midst of your bustle, because you saw I wished it, but I should be very sorry if you got to consider going to Church on Sunday as only a decent form (which may be put aside for a small reason) & not a real duty."[8]

Charles's *Origin of Species* was now in its final stages. In April the firm of John Murray had agreed to publish the book, and Emma's old friend Georgina Tollet was reading through the manuscript making last-minute corrections and stylistic suggestions. (Georgina now lived in London, the ancestral Tollet home at Betley Hall in Staffordshire having gone out of the family after the death of her father.)[9] By May, Charles and Emma were working side by side reading printers' proof sheets—a task that was completed on October first, but not before it had triggered in Charles a health breakdown that required two short visits to Moor Park for hydropathy. The day after sending off his final proof sheet, Charles traveled to yet another water cure establishment, Ilkley Wells House in Yorkshire, hoping against hope to regain some of his health. He was at Ilkley Wells when the *Origin* was released to the public on November 24, 1859.[10]

To Charles's surprise, the book was an instant success. At a trade sale two days before the actual publication date, Murray took orders for 1,500 copies, 250 more than had been printed. Many of these copies were ordered by Mudie's Select Library, a subscription lending library based in London, thus ensuring that the book would be widely available to the public at large. Charles sent out numerous presentation copies—to Hooker and Lyell, of course, but also to Huxley, Wallace, Henslow, Asa Gray, Adam Sedgwick, and many others including his brother Ras—and he got back several gratifying (and some not so gratifying) responses. Huxley wrote saying Charles had "earned the lasting gratitude of all thoughtful men" and that he was "sharpening up [his] claws & beak in readiness" to defend Darwin's doctrines. Hooker declared that he "would rather be [the] author of [the *Origin*] than of any other [book] in Nat. Hist. Science." Asa Gray liked the *Origin* so much that he offered to negotiate with publishers on his side of the Atlantic for an American edition. And in a flurry of fraternal support, Ras Darwin judged the *Origin* to be "the most interesting book [he] ever read" and declared that Charles's "a priori reasoning [was] so entirely satisfactory . . . that if the facts won't fit in, why so much the worse for the facts." It was all so splendid that Charles confided to Emma that he would "never think small beer of himself again" and that, just between the two of them, he thought the book was "very well written."[11]

Of course, there were also negative reactions, including one from cousin Sir Henry Holland. (The doctor had been made a baronet in 1853.) Holland wrote expressing doubt that natural selection, or any mechanism based on chance, could ever account for such anatomical complexities as "the *chain of little bones* within the tympanum of the Ear." Surely a "final cause"—that is, a divine Creator—was affirmed by such cases, insisted Sir Henry. Richard Owen, the anatomist, was civil and apparently encouraging in his thank-you note after receiving a presentation copy of the *Origin*, but then anonymously blasted the book in a published review a few months later. And Adam Sedgwick, still going strong at seventy-three as Woodwardian Professor of Geology and vice-master of Trinity College, Cambridge, sent such a strongly negative "thank you" note that Emma wouldn't allow the children to read it. Sedgwick wrote:

My dear Darwin

I write to thank you for your work on the origin of Species . . . [but] I have read your book with more pain than pleasure. Parts of it I admired greatly; parts I laughed at till my sides were almost sore; other parts I read with absolute sorrow; because I think them utterly false & grievously mischievous— You have *deserted* . . . the true method of induction—& started up a machinery as wild I think as Bishop Wilkin's locomotive that was to sail with us to the Moon. . . . As to your grand principle—*natural selection*— . . . [God] acts by laws which we can study & comprehend—Acting by law, & under what is called final cause, comprehends, I think, your whole principle. . . . There is a moral or metaphysical part of nature as well as a physical. A man who denies this is deep in the mire of folly. Tis the crown & glory of organic science that it *does* thro' *final cause*, link material to moral. . . . You have ignored this link; &, if I do not mistake your meaning, you have done your best in one or two pregnant cases to break it. Were it possible (which thank God it is not) to break it, humanity in my mind, would suffer a damage that might brutalize it—& sink the human race into a lower grade of degradation than any into which it has fallen since its written records tell us of its history.[12]

Little wonder that Emma didn't want the children to read about their father being "deep in the mire of folly" and the author of a theory that threatened to "brutalize . . . & sink the human race." In his theological zeal, Sedgwick had crossed the line of gentlemanly propriety. And then, of course, there was the additional issue that some portion of the blame for the *Origin* could legitimately be directed at Emma herself. She was by no means responsible for the book's ideas, but she had, after all, failed over the years to really press her objections to Charles's evolutionary work; edited and actually agreed to help publish the essay back in 1844; and at the end, helped her husband read the *Origin*'s final proof sheets. In many ways large and small, she was guilty-as-charged of being the *Origin*'s midwife. And it didn't help one bit that Sedgwick had ended his letter on a humorous and friendly note, calling himself a "son of a monkey & [Charles's] old friend." He had then gone on to touch on Emma's worst fear—the eternal fate of her husband's soul—by saying that he and Charles would meet in Heaven *if* they both accepted "God's revelation of himself both in His works & in His word" and did their "best to act in conformity with that knowledge." No, the children most certainly *would not* be allowed to read Professor Sedgwick's letter.[13]

Actually, Sedgwick's fears were getting well ahead of Charles's prose. Humans were hardly mentioned at all in the *Origin*, but nobody missed the implication that humans too must be the serendipitous result of a naturalistic process, not the product of divine creation in God's image. Even Lyell, friend and supporter of Darwin though he was, had a real problem with the question of human origins and therefore, to Darwin's dismay, found it hard to embrace evolution fully: "the case of Man & his Races & of other animals & that of plants is one & the same," Lyell wrote to Darwin, and "if a 'vera causa'"—in this case, evolution by natural selection—"be admitted for one instead of a purely unknown & imaginary one such as the word 'Creation' all the consequences must follow." Perhaps so, but for some people—Jane Carlyle, for example—it was all just a tempest in a teapot. She wrote to a friend:

But even when Darwin, in a book that all the scientific world is in ecstasy over, proved the other day that we are all come from shell-fish, it didn't move me to the slightest curiosity whether we are or not. I did not feel that the slightest light would be thrown on my practical life for me, by having it ever so logically made out that my first ancestor, millions of millions of ages back, had been, or even had not been, an oyster. It remained a plain fact that I was no oyster, nor had any grandfather an oyster within my knowledge; and for the rest, there was nothing to be gained, for this world, or the next, by going into the oyster-question, till all more pressing questions were exhausted![14]

After all was said and done, however, and despite shielding the children from scathing attacks like Sedgwick's, Emma was actually fairly comfortable with the *Origin* once it was a reality. She had changed a good deal in twenty years of marriage to Charles. True, his evolution theory was something she could live without, but the man himself was not. Willing to take the bitter with the sweet, she even managed to exult a bit over the first edition's sales. To William at Cambridge she wrote: "It is a wonderful thing the whole edition selling off at once & Mudie taking 500 copies."[15] Still, was that "wonderful" as in *astonishing* or as in *terrific*?

The old year ended and the new began with a flurry of positive reviews of the *Origin*. Huxley gave it a strongly favorable airing in the *Times* on the day after Christmas, as well as reviewing it for *Macmillan's Magazine*. Richard Chambers, the old evolutionist and closet author of *Vestiges*, recommended it in the December 1859 number of *Chambers's Journal*, and Hooker chipped in with a brief review in the *Gardeners' Chronicle*. William Benjamin Carpenter, the physiologist, added enthusiastic support in the pages of the *National Review* in January, prompting a note from Charles that his review would "do great good" for the evolutionary cause and congratulating Carpenter on how well he "turn[ed] the flanks of theological opposers." And in America, Asa Gray praised the *Origin* in the March 1860 issue of the *American Journal of Science and the Arts*.[16]

Reinforcing the notion that Emma was now positively invested in the *Origin* and its fate, she joined Charles in rejoicing over good reviews and repudiating bad ones. Richard Owen authored one particularly negative review published anonymously in the April 1860 issue of the *Edinburgh Review*. In the words of modern Darwin biographer Janet Browne, Owen was "malevolent . . . scornful, condescending, [and] rude" as he went about the task of "slicing up Darwin like any carcass on an anatomist's dissecting table"; the critic, said Browne, "doubted Darwin's competence . . . ridiculed [his] literary style . . . [and] sneered at Darwin's friends," among other things calling Hooker a "short-sighted disciple." Little wonder, then, that when an anonymous rejoinder was printed the next month in the *Saturday Review* (fondly known by its readers as the "Saturday Slasher"), Emma crowed to William at Cambridge that the *SR* writer "[cut] up Owen's review." Charles too had had enough of Owen. How could "a friend of 25 years duration" write such a mean-spirited review? Owen could, after all, "have been just as severe without being so spiteful." Charles wished the "Slasher" writer "had slapped Owen a little bit harder."[17]

Crowing or groaning over reviews became a regular event at Down House during the year that followed the *Origin*'s appearance, as a total of forty-four such items rolled through the presses. In May 1860, Darwin claimed to Fox that he had grown "case-hardened" with regard to negative reviews. No doubt this was equal parts truth and bravado, but certainly the public support of Hooker, Huxley, Gray, and other reputable scientists—and the private support of Emma and the family—helped buffer Charles against the unrelenting attacks of Owen and his ilk.[18]

Alongside the heightened scientific activity caused by the *Origin*'s publication—reading reviews, preparing a new edition, corresponding with colleagues and well-wishers—that old Darwin bugbear of ill health was once again a major concern in the winter of 1860. First there were the children: Lenny came down with measles the first week of January and, true to Charles's prediction that it was "sure to run like wild-fire through the house," ten days later Lizzy and Franky had also broken out and Etty was "very languid." After the measles passed, the children were relatively well from February through April, though Etty of course continued delicate. But then it was Charles's turn. He suffered a sharp attack of fever and pleurisy in February, and by March his stomach had driven him to try a new doctor, Edward Headland, who was headquartered in London.[19]

Charles was well enough to help host a series of visitors to Down House in March and April: the Lyells, Hookers, and Huxleys all came for short stays. But no sooner had these "scientifics" headed home than Etty began what eventually became another serious breakdown in her health. On April 28 Emma recorded "Etty poorly." The next day it was "Etty headache in bed." And her entry for May 8, 1860, suggested that the girl's "remittent Fever," as

Charles called it, was going to be a stubborn thing to cure: "Etty fever every day since the 1st."[20]

By the second week in May, the local doctor had decided that Etty was suffering either from typhus fever or typhoid fever (the two diseases overlap in their symptoms), and starting on May 12 and continuing throughout the year, Emma kept a careful record of her daughter's symptoms, pulse rate, medications, and visits by doctors. Additionally, Emma noted which foods triggered bad reactions and should be avoided ("sick from coffee"), days when Etty was more active than usual ("sat up 3 h. in evg."), and often, simply whether her daughter had had a good, very good, or bad day.[21]

In early June, Henry Holland came down from London to examine Etty and to add his diagnosis to those of the local physicians. She was in no immediate danger of dying, Holland reassured her parents, but "her recovery would be very slow." Happily, not long after Sir Henry's visit some combination of the various treatments began to help, and Etty showed marked improvement throughout June and into July. Unhappily, as his daughter's condition was improving, Charles's was going in the opposite direction. He wrote to Hooker on June 26 that his stomach had "utterly failed" and that he had given up all plans to attend the upcoming BAAS meeting in Oxford. On June 28 Charles admitted himself for a week of treatment at Dr. Edward Lane's new water cure facility at Sudbrook Park, Surrey.[22]

Etty was well enough in early July to accompany the family to The Ridge in Hartfield, where Aunt Elizabeth joined in her care. All was well until the twenty-first, when the patient relapsed with a night and day of severe vomiting. Sir Henry was sent for again and duly arrived at The Ridge on the twenty-sixth. Once again he spoke optimistically of a slow recovery, but now he was troubled at the possibility that the fever had done permanent organic mischief. He prescribed a course of "grey powder," a preparation of mercury mixed with chalk, and Etty took this medication nine times in the subsequent three weeks, including a double dose on the first day. About halfway through this course of medication, Emma began to check her daughter's pulse once or twice a day, with alarming results. Etty's heart was racing at around 90 beats per minute, with occasional bounces to over 100 bpm and a high reading of 112. These readings were "sadly too high," Darwin told Lyell, and indeed they were at the high end of the range now considered normal for adults (60–100 bpm for resting pulse). It was all very worrisome.[23]

Eventually the grey powder treatment seems to have perked Etty up a bit—or at least it didn't make her noticeably worse—and by mid-August she was back at home, sitting out in the garden and going for occasional drives in the carriage. From mid-August to mid-September, the invalid improved slowly but surely, her resting pulse dropping into the low 80s and apparently stabilizing there. Plans were being finalized for a seaside vacation to speed Etty's recovery when devastating news came from the Huxleys. Their oldest child, Noel, then nearly four years old, had died from scarlet fever on September 15. For Emma and Charles, it brought back all of the old pain of their lost children, especially Annie, and doubled their fears for Etty. Despite knowing it was impossible to truly console his friend, Charles wrote to Huxley:

> I know well how intolerable is the bitterness of such grief. Yet believe me, that time, & time alone, acts wonderfully. To this day, though so many years have passed away, I cannot think of one child without tears rising in my eyes; but the grief is become tenderer & I can even call up the smile of our lost darling, with something like pleasure. My wife & self deeply sympathise with Mrs. Huxley & yourself. Reflect that your poor little fellow cannot have had much suffering. God bless you.[24]

On September 21—four days after packing George and Frank off to Clapham School, where their mother was happy Frank had his older brother as a "great protection"—Emma and Etty traveled to Eastbourne and settled into a seaside house on Marine Parade. Charles, Lizzy, and the little boys joined them the next day. At first the stay was satisfactory, with enough good weather that they could sit or walk on the parade and take sightseeing drives. But then on October 21–22, Etty suffered a terrifying setback with twenty-four hours of agonizing stomach pain and vomiting. Over the next week, things got worse. The pain spread to her back and the vomiting continued unabated. Elizabeth came to her niece's bedside on the twenty-fourth and Henry Holland came for a third time on the twenty-ninth. For Charles, it was a déjà vu of Malvern in 1851. Once again a daughter's life hung in the balance. Worn to the bone—as was Emma—he wrote to Huxley on November first, just after Etty had begun to rally:

> I am exhausted & not well so write briefly; for we have had 9 days of as much misery as man can endure. My poor daughter has suffered pitiably, & night & day required three persons to support her. The crisis of extreme danger is over & she is rallying surprisingly, but the Doctors are yet doubtful of [the] ultimate issue. But the suffering was so pitiable I almost got to wish to see her die. She is easy now. When she will be fit to travel home we know not.[25]

Etty was given that old standby calomel during her Eastbourne rally, and after the family had returned home, Etty in a bed-carriage, she continued to take this medication, consuming fifteen or sixteen doses before the year's end. Therefore, between calomel and grey powder, Etty took approximately twenty-five doses of mercury-based medicine in a five-month period, perhaps enough to have been a contributing factor in her subsequent lifelong infertility. Such a speculation is impossible to prove retrospectively, of course, and an alternative hypothesis is that Henrietta, William, and Leonard Darwin all inherited a fertility-destroying recessive gene whose homozygous pairing was facilitated by their parents' first-cousin marriage. Setting aside possible reproductive effects, it is clear that while the mercury medications may have provided temporary relief of Etty's stomach problems, they did not produce a lasting cure. As 1860 came to a close, she was still having "pain in [the] night" and Emma was once again making daily notations about her daughter's pulse.[26]

A handful of other events and milestones from 1860 bear mentioning. Some were scientific and involved raised voices and public displays, while others were quieter, family affairs. In the first category, Charles's evolution theories were discussed and, from some quarters, intensely criticized at the June meeting of the BAAS. At one scientific session, Samuel "Soapy Sam" Wilberforce, the bishop of Oxford, took the floor and blasted evolution generally and the *Origin* in particular. Thoroughly primed by that vicious antievolutionist Richard Owen, the bishop laced his address with sneers: "Is it credible that a turnip strives to become a man?" (Jane Carlyle would have substituted "oyster" for Wilberforce's turnip.) And did Professor Huxley claim to be descended from the apes through his grandfather or through his grandmother? Both Huxley and Hooker were at the session and rose to rebut the bishop's remarks, resulting in an exchange so hot and angry that at least one woman fainted. In a letter to Darwin written two days later, Hooker claimed that he had smitten "that Amalekite Sam hip & thigh" and demonstrated to everyone that the bishop "could never have read your book & . . . was absolutely ignorant of the rudiments of Bot[anical] Science." After four hours of verbal battle, reported Hooker, Wilberforce "was shut up" and Darwin was left as the "master of the field."[27]

From Sudbrook Park, Charles happily acknowledged Hooker's and Huxley's separate reports on the boisterous events at Oxford and thanked both of them warmly for their efforts on his and evolution's behalf. To Huxley he kidded: "But how durst you attack a live Bishop in that fashion? I am quite ashamed of you! Have you no reverence for fine lawn sleeves?" The rallying around of Charles's friends no doubt pleased Emma too, but the public alignment of his theories in opposition to the beliefs of the Church must have confirmed some of her worst fears. In any event, her reactions to Oxford apparently went unrecorded and it seems entirely possible that she was too involved that summer nursing Etty to pay much attention to scientific brouhahas.[28]

And, no doubt to the displeasure of Richard Owen and Bishop Wilberforce, all the controversy over the *Origin* didn't hurt its sales one bit. By April 1861, John Murray's firm had printed 6,250 copies and brought the book into its third edition, while across the Atlantic the New York publisher D. Appleton and Company had brought out an American edition. (There was also a German edition out by then which, to Charles's dismay, had been heavily modified by its translator.) Late that spring, when Charles totted up his combined British and American royalties, they came to a gratifying £1,219—more than $100,000 today. People were buying and reading his species book![29]

In the second category, family affairs, in 1860 William Darwin was well into his third year at Christ's College, Cambridge, and with his parents' approval he was preparing for a career as a lawyer. He was also drilling regularly with the University Volunteers, a semiofficial military unit that, like many others across Britain, had been formed in anticipation of an imminent invasion by the French. While fifteen-year-old George and twelve-year-old Frank were now both away at Clapham School, back home Leonard was nearing his eleventh birthday and starting regular tutoring sessions with the Reverend G. V. Reed at Hayes. Charles feared that Leonard was "rather slow & backward" and hoped studying with Reed would brace him up academically.[30]

Emma too passed a milestone in 1860, in her case a physiological one. Her diary records show that she went through menopause that year, having her very last periods in August and September. She had been either pregnant or nursing a new baby for a good half of her twenty-one years of marriage, but now pregnancies and painful deliveries were behind her. Any woman would have breathed a sign of relief, and almost certainly Emma did just that. Of course, menopause had its potential downsides. A woman could feel devalued after losing her reproductive function, and perhaps see herself as less sexually attractive to her husband. Hand in glove with these concerns, Victorian medical wisdom suggested that postmenopausal women had "a predisposition towards depression, melancholia, and hysteria." Although Emma, with her calm, matter-of-fact approach to life, seems unlikely to have worried much about mood changes or loss of sexual attractiveness, we will never know for sure, because her diaries and letters are silent on these points. A woman who rarely put private thoughts on paper—perhaps especially thoughts on such delicate topics—she seems to have kept her "change of life" and any ripple effects to herself. One wonders, however: Might she not have used it as a "teachable moment" for her thirteen- and seventeen-year-old daughters?[31]

13. A Banker in the Family

To EVERYONE'S SURPRISE AND DELIGHT, Henrietta's health actually perked up a bit as 1861 got under way. January found the seventeen-year-old still taking calomel and being visited periodically by Edward Williams, a physician from nearby Bromley, but she began the year having mostly "good" or "very good" days. On January eighth Emma had the pleasure of noting in her diary that Etty "came down in evg." and joined the family circle.[1]

It was simply a lull in her chronic ill health, however, and on January twenty-first Etty took another one of those alarming turns for the worse. Pain and vomiting set in at 2:00 A.M. and she was immediately given calomel. Between 3:00 A.M. and 9:45 P.M., she was sick nineteen times, vomiting at approximately hourly intervals, sometimes more frequently. Four more vomiting sessions occurred during the night despite a dose of calomel, and an exhausted Emma made an unusually emotional entry in her diary: "very distressing day." The nausea continued almost unabated on the twenty-second and twenty-third—nine bouts of vomiting on one day followed by five the next. The poor girl was given "gigantic doses of Calomel," Charles wrote to William, in an attempt to break the cycle of sickness, and by the twenty-fourth the treatments seem to have worked. On January 26 Etty's pulse was down to 73 and she was comfortably eating bread and butter, with chicken on the menu for the next day.[2]

Then it was George's turn. His complaint was dental, not digestive. On January 28, leaving Etty and Emma worn out at home, Charles took George to London to see Mr. Woodhouse in Hanover Square. The dentist's report was not good, as Charles told Hooker: "Poor George has literally every tooth in his head, except a few lower incisors decayed: they have all gone suddenly together & been stopped & drawn by Mr. Woodhouse."[3] Some of the extractions proved difficult, and George was under chloroform for quite some time. Emma reported to William that

the chloroform was a baddish job. The teeth were so difficult to get out that they had to give it to him twice & at last they could not get out all the fangs, however, he did not feel any thing but he was a very long time coming to himself & you may imagine that your daddy was in something of a fidget.

George came home "very pale & poorly" the next day, but he was soon back to normal.[4]

The dental miseries at Down House didn't stop with George. Lizzy had "2 teeth stopped by Mr. Robinson" in March, a procedure that she "bore . . . very tolerably," despite being understandably nervous. Robinson noted at the time that the thirteen-year-old had three other teeth that were bad enough to warrant extraction, procedures that appear to have been done in August and/or December. Etty, who was feeling much better by the late spring, went to Woodhouse for dental work in May, and even Emma had a tooth removed by the local Downe surgeon, S. P. Engleheart, in November.[5] What, one wonders, caused all of these rotten teeth? Was it genetics, an extremely rich diet, or some other, unknown factor(s)? Whatever the cause, clearly toothaches and gappy smiles were very common in the Darwin household.

Returning briefly to Henrietta's health, February 1861 was immeasurably better than January, although she continued on and off with calomel, and prolonged illness had left her underweight and weak. To aid in her convalescence, Hooker recommended that Emma rub Etty each day with cod liver oil. Believed to help correct various maladies and to stimulate the appetite, cod liver oil was widely used on the Continent. External applications were adopted in Etty's case because she had trouble taking the oil orally. Concluding, undoubtedly correctly, that "it would be a rather nasty proceeding for Etty to be thus basted," Charles applied to Hooker for information about the oil's efficacy. Apparently reassured, Emma began "basting" her daughter in mid-February and continued to do so at least through September.[6]

In March the Darwins invited the T. H. Huxleys into their fish-oily, toothachy, and dyspeptic household for a few weeks of rest and recuperation.

Nettie Huxley was still in a deeply despondent state over the death of their son Noel the previous September. She had just given birth to another son, Leonard—so named because Leonard, read backwards, "held [their] lost boy's name" inside it—and the exertions of childbirth had further sapped her strength.[7] Charles had first learned of Nettie's sad condition during a London trip on February 21, and the next day he sent this invitation on behalf of himself and Emma.

> My dear Huxley
>   On my journey home, a scheme occurred to me, which I think is worth your thinking about.—Do you not think a little change would be the best thing for Mrs. Huxley, if she could be induced to try it? I have been talking with my wife & she joins heartily in asking whether Mrs. Huxley would not come here for a fortnight & bring all the children & nurse. But I must make it clear that this House is dreadfully dull & melancholy. My wife lives upstairs with my girl & she would see little of Mrs. Huxley, except at meal times, & my stomach is so habitually bad that I never spend the whole evening even with our nearest relatives. If Mrs. Huxley could be induced to come, she must look at this house, just as if it were a country inn, to which she went for a change of air.[8]

Not exactly an altogether attractive prospect, to come spend time in a "dreadfully dull & melancholy" house, and Nettie's initial response was to say "no thanks." She wrote to Emma that she was "too weak and ill to be out of [her] home" and besides, she did "not get downstairs till 1 o'clock." Unfazed, Emma wrote back that not coming down until one o'clock was "the usual state of the family at Down," and that Nettie "should just be following suit." With this encouragement, Nettie accepted the invitation and the visit was on.[9]

As the Darwins had hoped, a stay at Downe was just what Nettie needed. Rest and recuperation were interspersed with pleasant socializing. J. D. Hooker came for a day's visit, as did W. B. Carpenter. Both were good company, but undoubtedly their science talk was of more interest to Darwin and Huxley than to either Emma or Nettie. On the more feminine side of things, one of the neighbors from High Elms, either Lady Lubbock or her daughter-in-law Ellen, stopped in one day for a bit of singing. The Huxleys' fortnight-long visit to Down House cemented the friendship between Emma and Nettie. Henceforth Nettie would have "a sort of nestling feeling" toward Emma. She said she found Emma more comforting than any woman she had ever known. It was a feeling all the Darwins knew well.[10]

Henrietta's health gained ground throughout April 1861, although it was still deemed necessary for her to take regular doses of grey powder. By early May she was well enough to go to London with her mother and Lizzy for her visit to the dentist and then to have some fun in the metropolis. Lodging with the Hensleigh Wedgwoods for ten days, the Darwin women made social calls on Georgina Tollet and others, and ventured out to operas, plays, and art exhibitions. Emma reported to William at Cambridge that the male singers in *Don Giovanni* were excellent "but the women unpleasant," and that she had seen several pictures at the Royal Academy that she "should not object to having." Emma and her daughters were still in London on May 16 when John Stevens Henslow died at the age of sixty-five at his home in Hitcham. Although Charles would miss his old mentor—"a better man never walked this earth," he wrote to Henslow's son-in-law, Hooker—predictably he skipped the funeral, opting to guard his health by staying at home.[11]

Despite indifferent results in the past, the Darwins still had considerable faith in the power of sea air and saltwater bathing to improve one's health, and so in late May plans were made to move the entire family to Torquay for a month or more for the benefit of the two main "sickies," Henrietta and her father. Charles was "extra dyspeptic & fit for utter extermination," he wrote to Hooker on May 22.[12] Although the Darwins had thought to make the move the first week in June, their schedule was derailed when John Lubbock (the younger) contacted Charles to see whether William might not be interested in a career in banking. Thanks to a long history of involvement in financial services, the Lubbock family had personal connections with bankers all across Britain, and one of these men, George Atherley, had passed the word that a new junior partner was needed at the Southampton and Hampshire Bank. Charles and Emma were excited about the opportunity on William's behalf, even though it would delay his graduation from Cambridge and possibly also end his plans to enter the law. Investigating the details of the position and making the necessary arrangements took time, however, especially once lawyers at both ends got involved. William himself quickly agreed to take a shot at the job, but it was mid-August before the arrangements were finalized. On October 2 Emma noted in her diary, "Wm went to Southampton." Eager to please and hungry for success, the Darwins' eldest son took rooms in a local boardinghouse and began what would turn out to be a forty-year career as a banker.[13]

Long before William's fall relocation to Southampton, the Torquay scheme, although delayed, had been put into action. On July first the Darwins and their entourage, totaling "16 souls & ¾ tun of luggage," as Charles wrote to W. D. Fox, departed from Downe for lodgings on Hesketh Crescent in Torquay. The seaside location of their house provided lovely views and easy access to the beach for walking. Charles alternated scientific work on adaptations in orchids with recreational excursions. Emma accompanied the children on walks and carriage drives, and watched as they bathed in the sea. At first Henrietta did very little walking, instead being wheeled about in a "bath chair." But eventually, thanks to some combination of a change of scenery, sea air, exercise, cod liver oil, grey powder, and calomel, she gained strength and was able to participate more fully in the beach walking, boating, and touring. On August eighth a delighted Emma noted that Etty was "very well all this week."[14]

Predictably, Henrietta's spirits rose along with her strength. Years later, she remembered the vacation as the time when she "began to get well." One of her favorite Torquay memories was the "little trip around Dartmoor" that she made with her mother and her cousin Hope Wedgwood. On August 26 the Darwin party loaded up their three-quarters of a ton of luggage and headed back to Downe. On the way, they toured Salisbury Cathedral.[15]

Back at home, Henrietta continued to gain strength as summer turned into autumn. She began taking longer walks, went riding on the family pony, and was a regular player in croquet tournaments on the back lawn. Croquet, first introduced into England in 1851, had become quite popular by the 1860s and was claimed to be good (but not, thank heaven, sweaty) physical exercise, as well as a mental stimulant. One player enthused: "Its rules are so varied, so rational, that the intellect is constantly kept on the alert,—never summoned to a painful stretch, and never allowed to subside into an equally painful inaction." Certainly the game was flourishing at Down House in the fall of 1861 and Henrietta was in the thick of it. There is no evidence, however, that Henrietta, now eighteen and marriageable, had begun using the game for another of its popular purposes, namely, as an opportunity for a bit of outdoor courting.[16]

Among Emma's diary entries during the Torquay vacation are several that read "Etty went to church." It seems likely that on many, if not all, of these occasions, Emma accompanied her daughter to divine services, as she often did back in Downe. On no occasion is Charles mentioned as a churchgoer (nor are the sons, for that matter), which is not surprising since formal religion had not been a part of Darwin's life for some time. Additionally, he had not had a good winter and spring, describing himself to Huxley in May as "fit for utter extermination," and so even if he had been inclined to go to church, illness might have prevented it. Whatever Charles's reasons for continuing to turn his back on God, his lack of faith still bothered his wife, particularly when he was unwell. Accordingly, in June 1861 Emma expressed herself in writing for the second time on the subject. It had been twenty-two years since her first appeal to her then new husband on religion.[17] Much had transpired over the years, but still she was far from easy about the state of his soul.

> I cannot tell you the compassion I have felt for all your sufferings for these weeks past that you have had so many drawbacks. Nor the gratitude I have felt for the cheerful & affectionate looks you have given me when I know you have been miserably uncomfortable.
>
> My heart has often been too full to speak or take any notice. I am sure you know I love you well enough to believe that I mind your sufferings nearly as much as I should my own & I find the only relief to my own mind is to take it as from God's hand, & to try to believe that all suffering & illness is meant to help us to exalt our minds & to look forward with hope to a future state. When I see your patience, deep compassion for others[,] self command & above all gratitude for the smallest thing done to help you I cannot help longing that these precious feelings should be offered to Heaven for the sake of your daily happiness. But I find it difficult enough in my own case. I often think of the words "Thou shalt keep him in perfect peace whose mind is stayed on thee." It is feeling & not reasoning that drives one to prayer. I feel presumptuous in writing thus to you.
>
> I feel in my inmost heart your admirable qualities & feelings & all I would hope is that you might direct them upwards, as well as to one who values them above every thing in the world. I shall keep this by me till I feel cheerful & comfortable again about you but it has passed through my mind often lately so I thought I would write it partly to relieve my own mind.[18]

At the bottom of the letter, Charles penned a little note: "God Bless you. C.D. / June 1861." Coming from a man who, judging from Emma's letter, never or only rarely prayed, this blessing might be viewed either as pure hypocrisy or as the mindless repetition of a stock phrase. Alternatively, however, like his invocations from Annie's bedside, it can be interpreted as stemming from a deep-seated vestigial theism that had no effect on Charles's science, had very little effect on his daily life, and virtually never nudged him into attending church. Confronted with the letter from his beloved Emma, Charles may briefly have turned his mind to God and called down blessings on her, but with little or no expectation that his prayer would be answered. Then, just as quickly, he returned to his everyday religion-free life.

And if his wife was prodding Darwin about his personal faith, others were testing his patience with suggested connections between God and evolution. Harvard professor Asa Gray, for example, argued that variations in nature might be beneficially designed by the Almighty. After all, couldn't "God . . . create favorable variations and thereby still oversee the evolutionary process from a distance"? Charles Lyell rather agreed with Gray that variations might be divinely designed, and even Snow Wedgwood mooted the idea of divine design in nature in a piece she wrote for *Macmillan's Magazine*.[19] Darwin would have none of it. He wrote back to Lyell:

> If you say that God *ordained* that at some time & place a dozen slight variations should arise, & that one of them alone should be preserved in the struggle for life, & that the other eleven should perish in the first, or few first, generations; then the saying seems to me mere verbiage.—it comes to merely saying that everything that is, is ordained.

And besides, he added self-derisively, "Will you honestly tell me . . . whether you believe that the shape of my nose (eheu) was 'ordained & guided by an intelligent cause'?"[20]

The weather in the southeast of England was exceptionally beautiful in late September and early October 1861, perfect for day trips to country estates or, if you were a young man starting off in a new career, perfect for moving house. On October third Emma and Henrietta did the former, touring the house and grounds at Knole near Sevenoaks, while William did the latter, traveling from Downe toward Southampton to begin work at the Southampton and Hampshire Bank. Frank and George were back at Clapham, Charles was happily putting the finishing touches on a book about orchids, and, except for the fact that her sister Charlotte Langton was gravely ill, the world must have looked pretty good to Emma. Among its most gratifying aspects was the fact that Henrietta was feeling so much better.[21]

After securing lodgings in Mrs. William Pratt's boardinghouse, "extra superb" lodgings in his father's view, William pitched into his new job and new environs. Charles wrote several letters of introduction for his son, including one to Henry Bonham-Carter seeking an invitation to the W. E. Nightingales in Embley Park.[22] Bonham-Carter was Florence Nightingale's cousin and the fiancé of Sibella Norman of Bromley; the Normans and Darwins had long been friendly.[23] Eager beaver that he was, William made short work of his training at the bank, and by mid-November he was knowledgeable enough to oversee the running of the place for short periods. His banker's hours, roughly 10:00 to 4:30, gave him plenty of time for long walks around Southampton after work. (George and Frank, inspired by tales of violent crimes in London, inquired whether William's new residence was a "very dangerous place for garroting.") In the evenings, William often did a bit of mathematics in anticipation of his university exams scheduled for the next spring. Although he had completed the Cambridge residency requirement, William still had to pass the dreaded tripos exams before he could take his degree.[24]

Everyone sent news from home to the novice banker. Charles kept him informed about the doings of the Farnborough Rifle Volunteer Corps, of which William had been an officer, and commented on financial matters when necessary ("Your [rent] is an awful sum"). Emma sent along lots of family gossip and also the details of trips she and others had made. On November 10, for example, she caught William up on a recent trip to St. Leonard's-on-Sea near Hastings, where his aunt Charlotte Langton had gone for her health.

> I came home yesterday from St. Leonards after a sad enough visit. Aunt Charlotte is very much weaker & I don't think there are any hopes of her getting any more strength except for a day or so. . . . Uncle Charles [Langton] was very low & unhappy the first two days but Charlotte revived a little after having some good nights & he was in better spirits. . . . [Elizabeth] & I went one evening to hear Dickens read the *Christmas Carol* & the Trial scene in *Pickwick* which last was very good fun. . . . Dickens himself is very horrid looking with a light coloured ragged beard which waggles up & down. He looks ruined & a roué which I don't believe he is however. . . . Papa is quite poorly today. . . . His . . . orchises have all gone wrong just lately.[25]

And a week later, after another long, newsy letter, she ended with this affectionate closing: "Goodbye my dear old man. It seems an age since we saw you. Are you grown bald or grey headed or fat?"[26]

Even ten-year-old Horace or "Skimp" got in on the correspondence. Shortly after William moved to Southampton, he received this atrociously spelled letter from his youngest brother:

Dear William

We are reading Byron narrative we lick it very well. It has raned nearly all morning. Henryetta went up to London today. . . . We have not got any horses except hired ones. Henrietta has got a killer of corse. We are going to send Gorgs and Franks letter. I am going to make a neel holder for Henrietta.

    Goodby William

    I am skimp[27]

To everyone's delight, William was able to get time off to come to Downe for Christmas. He got home late on the twenty-fourth, probably delayed because as the junior partner he couldn't leave the bank until the very last minute. In his three-month absence, he had grown neither bald (that would come soon, however) nor gray-haired nor fat; photos from the time show a tall and slender young man with a nose that was much finer than his father's. He arrived home just as the entire household was coming down with the flu.[28]

As the Darwins were celebrating Christmas 1861, events unfolding on the international stage had their close attention. In the United States the Civil War had begun, and it looked like Britain might be pulled into the fray.[29] Early in the year, following Abraham Lincoln's election as president after a strong North-South split in the vote, seven southern states had seceded from the Union and banded together as the Confederate States of America. These states "feared they could no longer trust the federal government to safeguard states' rights and southern institutions, especially slavery." Actual hostilities between the North and South commenced on April 12, 1861, when rebel forces bombarded Fort Sumter, a federal base in Charleston harbor. Following that brief contest, four more southern states seceded, and Lincoln declared a blockade of the southern ports. In July 1861 the first major battle of the war, First Bull Run, was fought in northern Virginia. To the chagrin of the more populous and industrialized North, the battle ended with a chaotic rout of the federal troops. Both sides prepared for a prolonged struggle.

    As part of its preparations, the Confederacy sought to secure the support of key European allies. To that end, Confederate president Jefferson Davis sent James Mason and John Slidell as emissaries to Britain and France, respectively. Having successfully eluded the federal naval blockade and reached Havana, Mason and Slidell boarded the British mail steamer *Trent* for the transatlantic voyage. Their crossing was interrupted on November 8, when the USS *San Jacinto* intercepted the *Trent* on the high seas and forcibly removed the two emissaries. Britons, including the Darwins, were understandably outraged, and in fact the two nations nearly went to war over it. Charles wrote to Asa Gray on December 11:

What a thing it is, that when you receive this we may be at war, & we two be bound, as good patriots, to hate each other, though I shall find this hating you very hard work. . . . I fear there is no shadow of doubt we shall fight, if the two Southern rogues are not given up. And what a wretched thing it will be, if we fight on side of slavery.[30]

Gray responded a few weeks later:

We should indeed find it hard to hate each other pro amore patriae. Of all my English correspondents you are the only one touching upon our relations with the South & with England whose views and sentiments are perfectly satisfactory to me. And my wife—as is natural to her sex—takes a stronger line, and bids me send her *love* to Mr. Darwin, & say that his is the only Englishman whose letters do not give her a shock to read.[31]

In the end, Lincoln and his cabinet gave in to British demands that Mason and Slidell be released, and both men completed their missions, albeit unsuccessfully. At Downe, the Darwins tried to make sense of a bewildering mix of feelings and circumstances: personal friendships with Americans like Gray; their strong opposition to slavery, and perhaps an equally strong aversion to war; the anger they felt at U.S. high-handedness on the seas; and the dangers that an American war would pose for the British economy: generally, a depression in overseas trade, and specifically, a devastating shortage of cotton for the Lancashire textile mills.[32] The year ended under a cloud of uneasiness.

Charlotte Langton died on the afternoon of January 2, 1862, but not before her little sister had seen her one last time. Two days after Christmas, Emma slipped away from the crowd at Down House—which included all of the young Darwins, a couple of Wedgwood nieces, and a friend of one of the nieces—for a quick trip to St. Leonard's-on-Sea. She returned home on New Year's Eve, and just two days later Charlotte breathed her last. It had been thirty years since Emma had lost a sibling (Fanny in 1832), and she would miss the "gentle and strong" Charlotte very much. Emma's grief paled, however, compared to that of her surviving sister Elizabeth. For more than a decade Elizabeth had lived a quarter mile from the Langtons, and now her primary tie to Hartfield was broken. Although Charles Langton, the grieving widower, lived on for a time at Hartfield Grove, by mid-1864 Elizabeth had relocated to 4 Chester Place, London, to be near Fanny and Hensleigh.[33]

Emma came home from St. Leonard's-on-Sea to a house full of the flu.

First Horace and Frank came down with it, which prompted Miss Ludwig (the governess), the two Wedgwood nieces, and the friend to flee the house. Next to become feverish were Charles and William, then Henrietta, and finally Lizzy and Emma herself. At times there were six Darwins bedridden simultaneously and, all told, sixteen people in Down House were stricken. By January 13, however, Emma was able to record "all mending" and to note that Miss Ludwig had returned to the household. Remarkably, despite having just gotten out of a sickbed, William managed to get himself up to Cambridge to take his mathematics tripos. His diligent practice in Southampton served him well, and he earned twelfth place among the *junior optimes*—the lowest of the honors classes, but still well above the lowly "pass candidates" or hoi polloi. He was awarded his B.A. degree that year, and would apply for and receive an M.A. in 1889.[34]

But now a health threat much more serious that the flu arose. In early February 1862, ten-year-old Horace began a long and worrying illness marked by the "oddest attacks, many times a day, of shuddering & gasping & hysterical sobbing, semi-convulsive movements, with much distress of feeling . . . [though no] loss of consciousness." Charles's London physician, Edward Headland, suspected that the Horace's problems could be traced to a concussion suffered in a fall from a cart. In contrast, Mr. Engleheart, the village surgeon, thought Horace simply had some sort of alimentary irritation, while Sir Henry Holland wondered if he didn't have roundworms and prescribed salt and/or castor oil enemas![35]

Emma and Miss Ludwig—who was devoted to Horace and vice versa—hovered around the suffering child. Occurrences and times of his attacks were carefully recorded in his mother's diary. Numerous medications were tried, including doses of castor oil and, for dyspepsia, the digestive enzyme pepsin. On two occasions "blisters" were applied, apparently in an attempt to substitute a specific pain for Horace's generalized affliction. (Mrs. Beeton's just-published manual *Household Management* recommended applying blisters to the nape of the neck to treat cases of "weak fits.")[36]

February stretched into March with little lasting improvement in Horace's condition. Charles suspected guiltily that the boy had inherited his father's "poor constitution" and worried that Horace might "become insane" as a result of his convulsive attacks. But then the youngster began to perk up. March 23 saw the last two attacks; notations of "good" and "very good" days started to appear in Emma's diary. By April 14 Horace was well enough to go "out in [the] sand walk" and the illness was over. Emma, Charles, and Miss

Ludwig were all thrilled with the child's recovery, and everyone's life might have returned to normal except that Mr. Engleheart and Emma had concluded that Horace's problems stemmed at least partially from an unhealthy devotion to his governess. In order to sever this supposedly debilitating connection, in early June Miss Ludwig was put on extended paid leave and sent back to her family in Germany. She never again returned to Down House as governess—but then, at eleven, Horace was near the age when other forms of education were more appropriate. In October 1862 he would follow in his brothers' footsteps and begin tutoring sessions with Mr. Reed.[37]

On May 1, 1862, a second International Exhibition of art and industry opened in London. It had been scheduled to mark the decade that had elapsed since the Great Exhibition, but war on the Continent had forced a one-year delay. Housed in a newly built glass and iron structure on Cromwell Road in South Kensington, the International Exhibition drew huge crowds to see machines billed variously as luxuries or necessities for modern life. Among the machines on display was Platt Brothers' "mule," a cotton processing and spinning machine. Significantly, in the newspaper illustration of the "mule," the cotton being spun was from Surat, India. By 1862 a "cotton famine" caused by the American Civil War had forced the closure of numerous Lancashire mills.[38]

Charles viewed the exhibition in early May while he was in London for scientific discussions with Lyell and others. He was having a bad health day, however, and was not impressed by the displays, writing to Hooker later that he "had only a glance . . . was not well . . . saw nothing, & was dispirited." Later in May, Emma and Lizzy braved the crowds at the big show, and then it was Miss Ludwig's turn to go. For Miss Ludwig this amounted to a going-away present, since she was to be put on leave and sent back to Germany just a few weeks later. Emma, at least, was sufficiently impressed by the exhibition to make a second visit in October accompanied by William. Henrietta too may have visited the "Internat," but here the record is unclear. She went to London with her aunt Elizabeth and cousin Amy Wedgwood on May 21, but given her reaction to the Great Exhibition of 1851—when she opted to stay at Uncle Ras's place and scrub the back stairs—Henrietta may have given this one a miss.[39]

Unlike the day-tripping Darwins, J. D. Hooker was spending untold hours at the exhibition in his capacity as juror for "Vegetable substances used in manufactures, etc." and one other section. His mind was elsewhere, how-

ever, as his house had just been burgled "by a nice young man who introduced himself to [the] maids" and in that way gained entry. Altogether, some
eighty pieces of silver were stolen, including all of the spoons and forks, and
the Hookers were furious with their staff and with themselves. They decided
to fire both the cook and the governess and to hire replacements "beyond the
age of flirtation." Did Emma know of anyone suitable, especially for the cook's
job? No, said Charles. They knew of one "trustworthy oldish cook," but she
was about to marry. Too bad, he continued, that "Nat. Selection had [not]
produced 'neuters' [to hire as servants], who would not flirt or marry."[40]

Anxious to see William's digs and also to distract Horace from the pain of
Miss Ludwig's departure, Emma gathered up her youngest son and traveled
down to Southampton in early June. The visit was brief but generally satisfactory. Emma got a look at William's lodgings with Mrs. Pratt, and she met
and lunched with the wife of William's partner and boss George Atherley.
The two Darwin brothers, one twenty-two and the other eleven, took walks
around Southampton together, in hopes that the sea air would do Horace
good. But the sea air was up to its old disappointing tricks, and at the end of
the visit Horace was still "not brisk."[41]

Unfortunately, the "not brisk" Horace was about to look blooming in
comparison to twelve-year-old Leonard. Lenny, who had been attending
Clapham Grammar School since January, was sent home on June 12 with
the first signs of scarlet fever. He was only mildly symptomatic until the first
week in July, but then his "neck swelled" and he had "bad symptoms of [the]
kidney" as well as fever fits and vomiting. A week later Lenny seemed to be
on the road to recovery, only to relapse with "a rare case of second rash &
sore throat," a relapse that scared his parents greatly. Charles told Asa Gray
that they had all "despaired of his life," and Henrietta remembered years later
that her brother had "hung between life and death for weeks." Aunt Elizabeth came down from London to help at Lenny's sickbed, and various foods
were tried to boost his strength. ("Port-wine every ¾ of an hour day & night"
seemed to do best.) By July 21 Emma was able to write "decidedly mending"
in her diary.[42] She reported the good news to William:

> Lenny keeps on getting stronger & eating a little more. . . . His poor face is so
> little & grave & his nose so sharp. The chief interest in life he has is thinking
> of things to eat, not the most wholesome or easy to get however, viz raccoons
> & trifle. . . . He ate chicken yesterday however, & strawberries & cream sev-
> eral times.[43]

One interesting possibility that has become part of Darwin lore is whether Lenny's illness might have prevented a meeting between his father and the botanist and geneticist Gregor Mendel. By 1862 Mendel had been investigating the mechanisms of inheritance in peas and other plants for several years, but he was still three years away from publishing his results. Mendel had heard of Darwin's evolution theory, possibly as early as 1861 (although Darwin had no reason to be aware of Mendel's work at this point), and he knew that his own hybridization experiments could make an important contribution to the evolution debate. In late July 1862, Mendel and several companions set off on a trip that took them from Moravia to Paris and ultimately to London, where they visited the International Exhibition, returning home around mid-August. While in London, Mendel was within fifteen miles of Downe, but whether he tried to see Darwin, or even considered doing so, is unclear. Nonetheless, the possibility that such a visit was thwarted by Lenny's scarlet fever was mooted years later by his niece Margaret Darwin Keynes. She wrote that Leonard's "illness may have had momentous consequences if it prevented—as is possible—a meeting taking place between his father and the Abbé Mendel!" Leonard himself, always the cutup, joked eighty years after the event that if he had prevented such a meeting of the titans, perhaps he should "be hung, drawn, and quartered" even in old age. Today, the possible missed meeting between Darwin and Mendel persists as one of those intriguing what-ifs. The two men went to their respective graves having never made contact.[44]

Emma was the last one to be ill. Advised by their doctors to take Lenny back to the seaside, Charles and Emma sent the other children on ahead to Bournemouth and set out themselves with Lenny on August 12, stopping to see William on the way. Emma had no sooner reached Southampton than she began to show unmistakable signs of scarlet fever. A week later Charles wrote to Asa Gray that his "poor dear wife [had] sickened with Scarlet-fever & . . . had it pretty sharply, but [was] recovering well." They completed the Southampton-to-Bournemouth leg of the journey two weeks behind schedule on September first and were "very glad to be once more a reunited family."[45]

They had hoped "to engage the best house for a month at 10£," but were fearful that they might have to settle for "the sea view house with no sea view at 6½." Once in Bournemouth, however, they found their party was so large they needed two houses, and the fact that one of them was called Cliff Cottage suggests they got their view.[46] The month at Bournemouth was filled with drives, walks, and boating and, to Charles's delight, a flash of evolutionary thinking on Horace's part. He wrote to Gray,

> Horace said to me, 'there are a terrible number of adders here; but if everyone killed as many as they could, they would sting less.'—I answered 'of course they would be fewer.' Horace [replied] 'Of course, but I did not mean that; what I meant was, that the more timid adders, which run away & do not sting would be saved, & after a time none of the adders would sting.'

"Progress of Education" and "Natural selection!!" wrote the proud father. "A chip of the old block," replied Gray.[47]

Back at home, the fall proceeded more or less uneventfully. Henrietta started voice lessons with her friend Elinor Bonham-Carter at Ravensbourne, that family's home in nearby Keston, but the biggest news by far was fifteen-year-old Lizzy's desire to go to boarding school. Although undoubtedly with some trepidation, Emma and Charles decided to let Lizzy try her wings and made arrangements to enroll her at Miss Buob's school in Kensington, London, starting in January 1863. That November, between trips to concerts, Emma made the rounds of the London shops assembling Lizzy's school "trousseau." Lizzy, reported Emma to William, was "full of zeal" about going to Miss Buob's and was "learning to mend stockings & do her hair etc in preparation for it."[48] Lizzy may have been an odd girl, but she was quite normal in her desire to grow up and make her own way in the world—just as her older and cleverer sister Henrietta was now able to do.

14. Lives Lived, Lives Lost, and Closure at Malvern

WRITING IN THE EARLY TWENTIETH CENTURY, two decades after her mother's death, Henrietta remembered her as "serene but somewhat grave," a woman who rarely laughed and almost never told jokes.[1] Written with love by a devoted daughter, these words no doubt capture much of Emma's temperament and demeanor. Nonetheless, there are a few bits and pieces of evidence that challenge this image of Emma Darwin as humorless. One such is a scrap of paper in Emma's handwriting that was pocketed inside her 1863 diary and contains three riddles.

> *If a man's wife fell overboard what letter of the alphabet would he call out?*
> [Answer] *Letter B.*
>
> *What did a blind man take at breakfast and recovered his sight?*
> [Answer] *He took a cup & saucer (saw sir).*
>
> *Why may not a man marry the second cousin of his widow?*
> [No answer given, but the man would clearly be dead.][2]

These little jokes—in all probability jotted down as a memory aid before they were sent to the boys at Clapham School, and maybe even to William in Southampton—suggest that, contrary to Henrietta's recollection, Emma did have a sense of humor and enjoyed sharing it with her children. In fact, Henrietta seems to have been the one with a decidedly less-than-light heart, not so much her mother.[3]

If further proof of Emma's wit is needed, it is found in a joke note that she sent to Leo in the fall of 1863.[4] On a slip of paper just a few inches square, Emma drew a little picture of a mustachioed man encircled by the words "I HOPE YOU ARE WELL E. D." Then she addressed it to "Leonard Darwin Esq, The Rev. A. Wrigley, Grammar School, Clapham S.," and wrote:

> *My dear Lenny*
> *You cannot write so small as this I know. It is done with your crow quill. Your last letter was not interesting but very well spelt which I care more about. We have a new horse on trial very spirited & pleasant & nice looking but I am afraid too cheap. Papa is much better than when Frank was here. Hen. came home today. We have some stamps for you: one Horace says is new Am. 5 cent.*
> *yours my dear old man*
> *E. D.*
> *begin your Jerseys*

Emma may not have been a comedian, but she had her moments. More important, she knew that her cutup son Leonard wasn't really all that keen on boarding school,[5] and a little laugh would help his day go by. A mother's love comes in many forms.

The stamps Emma mentioned in her novelty letter most likely came from Asa Gray in Massachusetts. Still corresponding with Charles despite their differing views on America's ongoing Civil War, Gray often sent gifts of stamps for the family's thirteen-year-old philatelist, Leonard.[6] In their letters, Darwin and Gray exchanged scientific information on plants and discussed the spread of Darwinian views on both sides of the Atlantic. Additionally, Charles commented cautiously on the progress of the war and its effects in Britain. By 1863 the "cotton famine" had caused widespread unemployment in the northern county of Lancashire and a Cotton Districts Relief Fund had been organized. The Darwins contributed £32 (close to $2,700 today) toward cotton district relief in 1862.[7] Anxious for a speedy end to the war's horrific bloodshed and dire economic effects, while also wishing with every fiber of their beings for the abolition of slavery, Emma and Charles followed the American conflict with rapt attention. Along with Hooker, they were unhappy that President Abraham Lincoln's "Emancipation Proclamation" called simply for the *curtailment* of slavery in America, not its complete abolition. Using his power as commander-in-chief in a time of war, on January 1, 1863, Lincoln proclaimed freedom for slaves held in "any State or designated part of a State . . . in rebellion against the United States." Of great significance to Hooker and the Darwins, however, the Emancipation Proclamation did not free slaves held in Union states such as Maryland: there abolition would have required legislative action.[8]

January and February 1863 saw a lot of traffic between Down House and London. To the delight of the younger members of the Darwin-Wedgwood circle—the "juvenile world," as Uncle Ras put it—there was a ball at the Hensleigh Wedgwoods on January 22. Anxious to be part of the preliminaries, Henrietta went to town a day early with her cousins Lucy and Clement Wedgwood and Edmund Langton. Leaving Charles at home, since balls were definitely *not* his thing, Emma too came to town, most likely accompanied by Lizzy, who was scheduled to begin school with Miss Buob two days later.[9]

In early February Emma was back in the city for a ten-day stay at Ras's house, along with Charles, Henrietta, and Horace, whose health continued to be marginal. While Charles visited with his scientific cronies, Emma went to luncheons, teas, and a play with the children, including Lizzy, who took time off from her studies. To Emma's delight, they were able to catch a performance of *The Duke's Motto* starring Charles Fechter and one of her very favorite actresses, Kate Terry (best known today as the grandmother of the late Sir John Gielgud).[10] Charles's health was passable while in London, but a bombshell of a book was waiting at home that would bring him lower than he had been in months.

On February 9, 1863, the publisher John Murray released Sir Charles Lyell's latest book, *The Geological Evidences of the Antiquity of Man with Remarks on Theories of the Origin of Species by Variation* (usually shortened to *The Antiquity of Man*). Darwin received an advance copy on February 4 but had little time to read it before going to London. It was a book he had been anxiously awaiting. It contained, he hoped, Lyell's complete endorsement of evolution by natural selection. Such a prominent scientist nailing his colors to the Darwinian mast would have great effect on the theory's visibility and viability. But such was not to be the case. Lyell was way too tame, at least in Darwin's view, regarding an evolutionary origin for humans. Indeed, his book was absolutely theistic in places, or at least sympathetic with the possibility of divine involvement in the appearance of humans. In a passage that made Darwin groan, Lyell wrote at the very end of his book that even if, in conformity with the theory of progression [i.e., evolution], we believe mankind to have risen slowly from a rude and humble starting point . . . leaps [in intelligence] may have successively introduced not only higher and higher forms and grades of intellect [among the living human races], but at a much remoter period may have cleared at one bound the space which separated the highest stage of the unprogressive intelligence of the inferior animals from the first and lowest form of improvable reason manifested by man.[11]

Accepting the possibility of "progressive jumps" in human evolution departed strongly from Darwin's insistence in the *Origin* that *natura non facit saltum* (nature makes no leap) and opened the way for a belief in miraculous intervention by God.[12] In fact, Lyell made his own views on the matter crystal clear:

> There is no tendency in the doctrine of Variation and Natural Selection to weaken the foundations of Natural Theology; for, consistently with the derivative hypothesis of species, we may hold any of the popular views respecting the manner in which the changes of the natural world are brought about. We may imagine[, paraphrasing Asa Gray,] "that events and operations in general go on in virtue simply of forces communicated at the first, and without any subsequent interference, or we may hold that now and then, and only now and then, there is a direct interposition of the Deity; or, lastly, we may suppose that all the changes are carried on by the immediate orderly and constant, however infinitely diversified, action of the intelligent, efficient Cause." They who maintain that the origin of an individual, as well as the origin of a species or a genus, can be explained only by the direct action of the creative cause, may retain their favourite theory compatibly with the doctrine of transmutation.[13]

Comments like these, plus Lyell's irritating habit of referring to Darwin's theory as "a modification of Lamarck's doctrine," literally turned Charles's stomach. Not only would Lyell's book fail to draw converts into the Darwinian fold, it would, in the words of one reviewer, "leave the Public in a fog." Charles was vomiting so badly as he worked his way through *The Antiquity of Man* that Emma suggested it was time for a return to Malvern and the water cure.[14]

Lyell defended himself to Darwin, saying, "I have spoken out to the utmost extent of my tether, so far as my reason goes, and farther than my imagination and sentiment can follow." He even stood fast behind the connection he had drawn between Lamarckism and Darwinism. And with regard to humans, despite trying his best, he could not "go the whole orang" and accept human evolution as simply the result of "secondary causes" such as natural selection. "I feel that Darwin and Huxley deify secondary causes too much," he complained to Hooker, who was caught in the crossfire of complaint and countercomplaint flying between Darwin and Lyell. Besides, said Lyell, his book would probably "bring hundreds [of people] towards [Darwinian views], who if [he had] treated the matter more dogmatically would have rebelled."[15]

Fortunately, another book—this one much more to Darwin's liking—arrived at Down House exactly two weeks after Lyell's supremely disappointing volume. Huxley had gathered his "Lectures to the Working Men" into a small volume titled *Evidence as to Man's Place in Nature*. In this little "Monkey Book," as Darwin called it, Huxley reviewed the anatomical similarities between humans and the manlike apes (gorillas, chimpanzees, orangutans, and gibbons), as well as those between manlike apes and "lower apes" (monkeys and prosimians, like lemurs). After presenting considerable anatomical information, Huxley concluded that the evidence seemed to show "no rational ground for doubting that man might have originated, in the one case, by the gradual modification of a man-like ape; or, in the other case, as a ramification of the same primitive stock as those apes." There was "no absolute structural line of demarcation, wider than that between the animals which immediately succeed us in the scale [of nature that] can be drawn between the animal world and ourselves," declared Huxley, adding that he believed "the attempt to draw a psychical distinction" between humans and other animals was "equally futile." He provisionally accepted Darwin's natural selection as the mechanism of evolution, although he noted that more proof was needed. "Hurrah the Monkey Book has come," exclaimed Darwin.[16] At least Huxley could be counted on, if not Lyell.

With her husband being pulled back and forth between Lyell's and Huxley's books—an emotional and scientific tug-of-war that was sure to do his digestion no good—Emma argued strongly in early March for another round of the water cure.[17] For first one reason and then another, however, they repeatedly delayed going to a hydropathic establishment. In late March, mid-April, and possibly May, Charles suffered through bouts of eczema on his face, a condition that made the cold water treatments intolerable. Further complicating things—though nothing new for the sickly Darwins—Horace was still far from well, and he and his father paralleled one another in ill health for much of the spring and summer.[18]

That summer found Down House having its usual flow of visitors. There was a big dinner-and-dancing party at a neighbor's house in July; needless to say, Charles didn't go. And there was a lawn party at the Darwins' for thirty children from the Bromley workhouse, one of the many small acts of charity regularly done by Charles and Emma, very much in the roles of the local squire and his wife.[19] There was one bit of hot news, however, and it involved summer love of a rather surprising sort. After a year and a half of being a widower, Charles Langton had proposed to Catherine Darwin and she had accepted! This was all very shocking to the children of the extended family, as Henrietta remembered years later: "It seemed to us incredible that anyone over fifty should think of such a thing as marrying. Catherine was 53, and had neither good health nor good spirits, and both she and Charles Langton [who was sixty] had strong wills."[20] Henrietta recalled that her parents thought the marriage had little chance of success, but her recollection is belied by Darwin's comment to Lyell just months before the wedding: "I believe the marriage will answer well to both." In his new role as a banker, William Darwin was appointed a trustee for his aunt Catherine—one of many financial chores for the family that William would handle over the years. It was "not a thing one could decline," Emma told her son, and anyway it would be "but little trouble as the settlements [were] chiefly aim[ed] at the unusual object of neither husband or wife having any thing to do with the others money." The wedding, scheduled for August, had to be postponed when Catherine came down with a life-threatening case of scarlet fever, but she and Langton finally managed to celebrate their nuptials in early October, although without the presence of the senior Darwins.[21] They were in Malvern, where both Charles and Horace were enjoying the pleasures of the water cure.[22]

It had been obvious since late August 1863 that Charles could avoid the water cure no longer. Thus on September first Emma, Horace, and a few of the servants traveled to Malvern to find a house big enough to hold their party. Unable to find suitable lodgings in Great Malvern, they rented Villa Nuova just down the road in Malvern Wells. Charles, Henrietta, and the rest of the servants arrived on the third, and Charles immediately began cold water douching and bathing under the direction of Dr. James Ayerst. Horace began his own version of the water cure on September fifteenth.[23]

While their men were undergoing hydropathy, Emma and Henrietta attended the *Messiah* and other concerts and explored Malvern. One of their main objectives was to find Annie's grave in the Priory churchyard, but a first try failed, leaving them fearful that the stone had been stolen. Luckily W. D.

Fox, who had been in Malvern seven years before for his own round of water treatment, had located Annie's grave at that time and was able to direct Emma to the overgrown site. She wrote back:

I am glad to say that by the help of your directions & the lady at whose house our poor Annie lodged we have found the tomb stone. It is very much covered with trees & looks so green & old I am sure I looked at it many times thinking it quite out of the question that should be it. Also the iron palisades are gone, at least both the sexton & lady thought there had been rails round it, but that does not signify. This has been a great relief.[24]

At least one scholar has concluded that Darwin never saw Annie's grave,[25] but we agree with Randal Keynes that Charles probably visited the grave once Emma and Henrietta had determined its whereabouts.[26] Sick though he was, surely Charles made the short trip to the Priory graveyard to share in his wife's "great relief." Emma's words suggest elements of closure and healing.

But if the Darwins were experiencing the calm of emotional healing, Hooker and his wife were in hell. On September 28th, perhaps the very same day Annie's grave was located, Hooker wrote an agonized note to Charles:

Dear dear friend
My darling little 2nd daughter died here an hour ago, & I think of you more in my grief, than of any other friend. Some obstruction of the bowels carried her off after a few hours *alarming* illness—with all the symptoms of strangulated Hernia.[27]

Maria Elizabeth Hooker was only six years old when she died, and the loss broke her parents' hearts. Fanny Hooker, in delicate health since the death of her father J. S. Henslow two years earlier, immediately took to her sickbed. Her husband, however, committed his grief to paper, writing to Darwin that "it will be long before I cease to hear her voice in my ears—or feel her little hand stealing into mine, by the fire side & in the Garden.—wherever I go she is there."[28]

Charles, so sick himself at the moment Hooker's news arrived that he was living on little more than brandy, knew all too well that he could give no real comfort to his friend. "Trust to me that time will do wonders, & without causing forgetfulness of your darling" was about the best advice he could offer. The Darwins stayed at Malvern until October 14 and then returned to Downe, with neither Charles nor Horace having gained much from the water cure.[29]

Back at home, Charles quickly plunged into such extreme ill health that his correspondence had to be largely taken over by Emma and Henrietta. A new doctor, William Brinton of St. Thomas's Hospital in London, was consulted in November and prescribed mineral acid—probably prussic acid, a weak form of hydrocyanic acid that was used by the Victorians to treat ailments as diverse as chronic coughs, neuralgia, stomach complaints, and (applied externally) skin diseases. To everyone's disappointment, neither prussic acid nor any other medications had much effect and Charles continued to be very ill and weak for some months.[30]

Among the memorable publications of 1863, two have already been mentioned: Lyell's *Antiquity of Man* and Huxley's *Man's Place in Nature*. For the purposes of this biography, however, there was a third. In July of that year a pamphlet was published that protested the use of steel vermin traps with their mangling toothed jaws. This pamphet was coauthored by Emma and Charles, who had long shared an abhorrence of cruelty to animals, even including vermin caught in unattended traps. The Darwins' "Appeal" was first privately printed, and Emma sent hundreds of copies to influential "Squires, Ladies & MPs," as well as to relatives such as W. D. Fox and scientific friends such as Hooker. Additionally, versions were published in the Darwins' local newspaper, the *Bromley Record*, and in a popular journal, the *Gardeners' Chronicle*. By December Emma was busy organizing subscriptions toward a prize for the best design for a humane trap to replace the toothed steel model. Administered by the Royal Society for the Prevention of Cruelty to Animals, this competition produced several new designs and awarded a few small prizes, but none of the new traps was fully successful in combining portability, low cost, and effectiveness. Although the Darwins' "Appeal" was part of a growing humane movement toward wild animals, old attitudes proved hard to change, and years later Henrietta sadly judged her parents' efforts to have done "little direct good."[31]

Meanwhile, across the Atlantic in the United States, the issue of cruelty revolved not around mistreating wild animals but rather around holding humans as slaves. In the summer of 1863 the American Civil War, for which slavery had been a primary flashpoint, was slowly grinding toward its end and victory by the Union. The month of July was a major turning point. On July fourth the city of Vicksburg, Mississippi, surrendered to besieging forces commanded by General Ulysses S. Grant, and five days later Port Hudson, Louisiana, followed suit. The fall of these two Confederate ports gave the North control of the entire Mississippi River, effectively splitting the Confederacy in two. And at precisely the same time, on July 1–3, Robert E. Lee's invading Army of Northern Virginia engaged George Meade's defending Army of the Potomac at Gettysburg, Pennsylvania. After fierce fighting that cost a combined total of 50,000 lives, Lee was defeated and retreated southwards. Of particular significance to the Southern cause, the defeat at Gettysburg essentially ended the Confederacy's hopes of formal recognition by foreign governments—including Great Britain.[32]

As always, Emma and Charles followed events in America closely, mainly through articles and editorials in the *Times*. They were growing impatient with the anti-Union sentiments of that newspaper, however, as Emma wrote to J. D. Hooker in December 1863:

> About America I think the slaves are gradually getting freed & that is what I chiefly care for. The Times evidently thinks that is to be deplored, but I think all England has to read up Olmsted's works again & get up its Uncle Tom again.[33]

The second reference is obviously to Harriet Beecher Stowe's novel *Uncle Tom's Cabin*, while the first is to Frederick Law Olmsted's series of books reporting on his travels in America's "cotton kingdom." By October 1864 Emma had become so put out with the *Times* that she canceled the family's subscription (rather against Charles's wishes) and substituted the *Daily News*, a paper with a somewhat more liberal bent.[34]

Darwin's terrible ill health continued unabated into 1864. In the never-ending search for a cure for his dyspepsia, Charles consulted Dr. William Jenner, physician-in-ordinary to the queen and a member of the staff of University College Hospital, London. Jenner visited Downe several times in the spring and prescribed a "combination of antacids that included lime-water, chalk, and carbonate of magnesia," as well as the purgative podophyllin, an extract of the mayapple plant. These medications seem to have helped somewhat, but the patient continued to seesaw throughout the year.[35]

While Charles was struggling with his health, George Darwin was struggling to win a scholarship to Cambridge. By 1863 George had done seven years of tutoring with the Reverend G. V. Reed, and he aspired to move on to university in the status of a Scholar, even though his parents would have had no difficulty paying his entire tuition. An entrance scholarship proved elusive, however, and George competed unsuccessfully for financial assistance at St. John's College in 1863 and at Trinity College in 1864. Feeling he could wait no longer, he entered Trinity as a paying student, a Pensioner, in the fall of 1864 and began to read mathematics. Happily, George turned out to be a rather gifted mathematician, and within two years of his matriculation he had obtained the long sought scholarship.[36]

Frank and Leonard, and Horace when he was feeling up to it, continued to study with Mr. Reed. Knowing Lenny's love of riddles, Emma sent this one to him at boarding school in 1864:

> What is the difference between killing a man & pig sticking? (Do you give it up?)
> [Answer] Because one is assault with intent to kill & the other is killing with intent to salt.[37]

With Charles consistently ill and Horace consistently delicate, Emma stayed close to home throughout 1864. Family and other guests came and went, but apart from occasional brief forays to London, Emma spent the year at Down House preoccupied with bedside duties. Still, her lot in life looked good when compared with that of Fanny and Hensleigh Wedgwood. Their thirty-year-old son James Mackintosh (Bro) had developed incurable cancer, and in a last desperate attempt to save her son, Fanny took him to the warmth of Italy. It was a futile gesture, however, and by late June Bro was gone. Now the dear sister-in-law who had deputized for Emma at Annie's deathbed knew firsthand the agony of losing a child. Emma sent a poignant request to Henrietta, who was visiting in London, to "buy me an elegant mourning cap that wd do for the evening."[38]

Compounding the extended family's sadness, there was double reason to wear mourning clothes that June. Twenty days before Mack's passing, Emma Allen had died in her eighty-fourth year. The death left her spinster sister Fanny Allen as the sole representative of the generation that immediately preceded Emma and Charles's. Although probably more devoted to her late aunt Jessie Sismondi than to either of her other Allen aunts, Emma Darwin nonetheless treasured them all and mourned each loss. The aunt who forty-five years earlier had described little Emma Wedgwood as "the happiest being that ever was looked on" would be greatly missed.[39]

The winter of 1865 was marked by heavy snow in Great Britain. Most of it fell in the last week in January, leaving drifts almost fifteen feet high in places. South Wales had seen nothing like it in forty years.[40] Gaining some relief from the frozen dreariness, Henrietta and George Darwin attended a mid-winter ball hosted by the James Fry family at their home in Hayes, just the other side of Keston.[41] Other than the occasional local party, however, there wasn't much going on in 1865 for either the junior or senior Darwins. Horace felt much better and had regained so much of his strength that walking the four miles to study with Mr. Reed in Hayes was no longer beyond his capacity. On the other hand, Charles was distinctly ill early in the year and experienced such a vigorous downturn in April that the blue pills came into action. He improved slowly thereafter, albeit with many ups and downs, and by the fall Emma was noting numerous "good" and "very good" days in her daily record of her husband's health.[42]

On the education scene, Frank was about ready to move from Clapham to Cambridge. In December Charles wrote to the bursar of Trinity College entering Frank's name for the fall 1866 term and putting down a deposit. Meanwhile George had passed the dreaded Little Go examination—the first major hurdle for a B.A. degree—in October 1865. George's talents at mathematics were rapidly becoming evident, but, like undergraduates of any era, he often "took his studies lightly so that they did not interfere with his enjoyment of other things." As for the Darwin daughters, Lizzy continued her studies in London with Miss Buob, and twenty-two-year-old Henrietta was, in a phrase, "out and about." Judging from her mother's diary, Henrietta was away from home more than 20 percent of the time in 1865, including a lengthy stay in Barlaston in March and a three-week trip to Wales in June.[43] From Wales she sent a note to her "Dearest Mamy" urging her not to "let Papa's stingyness" curtail the treatments recommended by his latest doctor.[44]

Perhaps more than anything else, 1865 was a year of endings, both small and large. Among the large endings, the American Civil War essentially came to a close on April ninth when Lee surrendered to Grant at Appomattox. After four years, 630,000 deaths, and more than a million combatants wounded, the North had prevailed, as Asa Gray had always said it would. The Union's victory abolished slavery in the South, and eight months later, on December 6, 1865, the ratification of the Thirteenth Amendment to the Constitution outlawed the practice across the length and breadth of the United States. The final outcome was extremely gratifying to the Darwins. The abomination of slavery had been dealt a severe blow. Still, Gray went a bit too far for Emma when he expressed the hope that Jefferson Davis, erstwhile president of the Confederacy, would be hanged for his crimes. Emma wrote to Henrietta in Wales (after hoping she would eat "a great deal of Welsh mutton to fatten you up") that she was "shocked at [Asa Gray] about Jefferson D."[45]

Among the smaller endings of 1865—though large to those persons intimately involved—were the deaths of Sir William Jackson Hooker, J. D. Hooker's father, in August and of Admiral Robert FitzRoy in May. Sir William's death occurred after a short illness beginning with a "septic throat" that was making the rounds among the staff at Kew. Although eighty, he had been active right to the end and had escorted the queen of the Sandwich Islands around the gardens just two days before falling ill. Joseph Hooker was devastated by his father's death, and his pain was only exacerbated by the fact that a severe attack of rheumatic fever prevented him from attending the funeral. Darwin wrote a brief note of condolence to his "best of old friends."[46]

Robert FitzRoy's death came at the comparatively young age of sixty and ended years of professional and personal agitation. Given the vagaries of predicting the weather, his work at the Meteorological Office had often been held up to ridicule, and the *Times* went so far as canceling the daily forecasts in 1864. FitzRoy took each hurtful remark personally. On the Sunday morning of April thirtieth, it all came to a head. Nervous, depressed, and worn out, FitzRoy left his wife in their bedroom and walked calmly to the nursery, where he kissed their seven-year-old daughter. He then went into his dressing room and, in an act that is gruesome to envision, slit his throat with a razor— a death that mirrored precisely that of his uncle Lord Castlereagh in 1822. Darwin was shocked when he heard the news, but not really surprised when he thought back to the man whose "mind was quite out of balance once during [the *Beagle*'s] voyage." He sent a check for £100 to the Testimonial Fund that was established to support FitzRoy's husbandless and fatherless family but, of course, did not attend the funeral.[47]

The winter of 1866 tried its best to match the weather excesses of the previous year. A severe storm in early January blanketed southern England with several inches of snow, and additional storms swept through in February and March ("deep snow," noted Emma on March 21). At Down House there was the usual series of weeklong visitors, including the Joe Wedgwoods and the Hensleigh Wedgwoods at different times, and also social calls by the Lubbocks from next door. The socialite part of Emma enjoyed all the company, but still it was hard work, and by the spring she was putting all of her kin on notice that for visits "5 days suit better than 7."[48]

Henrietta spent much of the winter in a state of keen anticipation of her first trip to the Continent. Accompanied by Elinor Bonham-Carter (at twenty-nine, six years older than Henrietta) and Elinor's spinster "Aunt Ju" (Julia Smith, aged sixty-seven), she embarked in mid-March for a leisurely trip to the south of France. "It seems so odd that *I* should be in Paris," she wrote back to her mother just after the crossing. "It *is* more cheerful [and sunnier] than dear old London." In the Bois de Boulogne, Henrietta delighted in the "children all so fairly dressed, the bright booths & whirligigs & goat carriages, & the funny little 2 horse cabs." Less delightful was the discovery that often those same "cabs tho' empty won't look at you tho' you wave your parasol ever so vehemently."[49] Some things never change.

The band of travelers made their way to Arles, Marseille, and finally Cannes. In Cannes they put down roots for several weeks, and despite Aunt Ju catching a bad cold and, at least in Henrietta's opinion, being a general drag on the younger travelers, they had a good time seeing the local sights and sampling the French cuisine. "You'll be glad to hear," Henrietta reported to her mother, "I am growing fat & have to unbutton my gown of an evening."[50]

Emma wrote back with news of home, including her visit to see poor, mad Miss Pugh in her asylum home in London. Miss Pugh was in a terrible state, "miserable & irritable" and prone to interact with her fellow patients in such "rude & intolerable" ways that she had to be separated from them. Visiting the former governess had become a "horrid job," reported Emma sadly. Much better news was that, at nineteen, Lizzy was making good progress in her social graces and confidence. Lizzy had "got thro'" a social call on the Bonham-Carters "very well," and on another occasion she had successfully conversed for some time with Sir Charles Lyell—which would have been a challenge for even the best conversationalist, since Lyell, it will be remembered, tended to speak in an inaudible whisper. "[A] little more society would make her manners quite nice," thought Emma.[51]

In the middle of Henrietta's excursion on the Continent, Charles felt strong enough to accompany his remaining two ladies to London for a few days. While there, he attended a soirée at the Royal Society where, to Charles's amusement, his new beard made him initially unrecognizable to several of his old friends. At one point the Society president presented Charles to the Prince of Wales. Prince and scientist considered each other briefly and then the prince "muttered some little civility which [Charles] cd not hear." Too embarrassed to ask for a repeat, Charles "made the profoundest bow he could" and took his leave of HRH Albert Edward. Despite that little glitch in the proceedings, Darwin had a grand time, and Emma, who did not go to the soirée herself but made sure "Papa dressed up quite tidy in his dress suit," wrote to Henrietta: "It was quite cheering to see him go."[52]

For her part, Emma enjoyed London in her usual "profligate" ways. One evening she and Lizzy accompanied the Harry Wedgwoods to see Charles Fechter's famous interpretation of *Hamlet*. A few days later, after some mind-numbing shopping for picture frames, Emma and Lizzy joined Elizabeth and Carry Wedgwood (Harry and Jessie's unmarried daughter Caroline) at the Philharmonic. They heard a program that included one of Mozart's symphonies in G minor and an aria from *Don Giovanni*. Emma liked the former but hated the latter: "Mlle Sincio sang *Vedrai Carino* as slow as a Psalm tune and as loud as she could." Holding nothing back, Emma rated Sincio's singing "hideous."[53]

Henrietta's trip stretched through April and into May. From Cannes the travelers moved to the area around Nice, at Cimiez and St. Jean, but Elinor had developed a bad back, and this hampered all sightseeing activities. For a time she considered going to a German spa for therapy, but in the end she stayed in Nice with her companions, all of them hemming and hawing about when they should head back to England. By the end of the month it was clearly time for Henrietta to return home, because she was broke. "Dearest Mamy. Please I want some money," she wrote on May 30. Whether or not her mother complied is unclear, but in any event the trip came to its conclusion within a week and William met his sister in Paris on June 5 to escort her home.[54] Henrietta's example had given her siblings a severe case of wanderlust, however, and no sooner was she back than everyone else hit the road. Lizzy traveled with Wedgwood kin to Ireland for the month of June, Frank and Horace went to Wales for ten days in July, and George and Frank went on a tour of Norway in August.[55]

In the fall Lizzy was put to a test of faith when Emma pressed her, gently, to be confirmed in the Church of England. Emma wrote to Henrietta—who, having found travel to her liking, was once again away from home:

> My dearest Hen.
> There is to be a confirmation in Nov. & I want you to try to remember the sort of exam Mr S. [T. S. Stephens, the curate of Downe] gave you, & especially how much Cat[echism]? Lizzy says she shd feel hypocritical to have any thing to do with the Cat & that as she does not believe in the Trinity or in Baptism she does not feel much heart for it. The per contra is that I think it would give her a zest in searching in the Bible (I remember thinking it was good for you) & though the doctrine wd most likely slip over her mind without any impression I think the ceremony itself is impressive & simple. Otherwise I have no doubt Mr S. wd give her the Sacrament without enquiry. Please write soon. She half wishes it herself if she cd get rid of the Cat.[56]

This is one of the clearest examples of Emma's increasingly laissez-faire attitude toward her children's religious lives. Comfortable with her own faith, even though it was becoming more liberal and less dogmatic the longer she lived with Charles, she guided her children toward the Church with gentle nudges, not stern directives. The occasion also tells us a bit more about Lizzy.

Her thinking may have been a bit slower than average, but it was not necessarily less deep. She obviously had qualms about confirmation and was able to state them in doctrinal terms. A "fumbler" perhaps, but Lizzy was growing up to be her own person, and Emma respected that. Whether Elizabeth Darwin's confirmation actually took place that November is unclear. If so, it did not rate an entry in her mother's diary.[57]

The ranks of the senior Darwins were thinned significantly in 1866 with the deaths of Catherine Darwin Langton in February and Susan Darwin in October. In neither case was death sudden or painless. In early January 1866, Cath realized that her time was near and wrote to Down House:

> Dearest Emma & Charles
>
> I am so rapidly weaker I can lose no time in sending you all & Elizabeth my dearest farewell. It is grievous to think I shall never see any of your dear faces. On New Year's day I knew this, and what a different world it seems to me. . . . [P]oor Susan feels my loss so cruelly. . . . I am grieved indeed at [her] loneliness, but there seems no help. . . . My dearest husband will feel my loss too; *what a nurse he is*, if he was not deaf— . . . Every body's love & goodness to me are past speech— . . . May God bless you all & may we meet hereafter.[58]

Cath died on February 2 at fifty-five years of age, having never reached her third wedding anniversary and leaving Charles Langton a widower for the second time in four years. She was buried alongside her father and near her mother at St. Chad's Church in Montford, on the outskirts of Shrewsbury. The family was relieved, of course, that Catherine had been spared "prolonged & greater suffering."[59] Nonetheless, there was some feeling, at least on the part of Aunt Fanny Allen, that Cath's life had been an "abortive one." She wrote to Elizabeth that Dr. Darwin "used to joke about [Cath's] 'great soul'; what he spoke in jest she had in earnest, but somehow it failed to work out her capabilities either for her own happiness or that of others (perhaps), but this I speak with uncertainty."[60]

Eight months later, on October 3, Susan followed her sister into death and to the Darwin burial plot at St. Chad's, Montford. Sixty-three years of age and never married, Susan was still living at The Mount along with the youngest son and daughter of her deceased sister Marianne Parker. Immediately after Susan's death, her executor-nephews Henry and Frank Parker, with help from Ras Darwin—who, unlike his brother, had come to Shrewsbury for the funeral—began the dispersal of her estate. William Darwin inherited a farm at Claythorpe in Lincolnshire that had originally been purchased by his grandfather Darwin and was worth some £13,500. William's siblings received considerably smaller bequests of £100 each and, in addition, George got an ornamental set of "Indian Chessmen," Henrietta a silver tea urn and scissors, and Lizzy a smelling-salts bottle. Charles inherited a picture of his father, as well as portraits of Emma and Ras that had been painted years earlier by the artist George Richmond.[61]

Dr. Robert's surviving children, Caroline, Erasmus, and Charles, agreed that The Mount should be emptied of its contents and put on the market, thus forcing the two young Parkers—actually thirty and thirty-five years of age—to relocate. The furniture was sold at auction, with proceeds going to the Parkers, and, after a year of being rented, the house and grounds were sold in 1867 for £3,450.[62] With Susan's passing, the Darwin presence in Shrewsbury, which had peaked during Dr. Robert's days as the town's most prominent physician, had run its course at last.

FIGURE 1. Maer Hall, from the yard of St. Peter's Church. (Photograph property of the authors)

FIGURE 2. Josiah Wedgwood II. (Reproduced with permission from John van Wyhe, ed., The Complete Work of Charles Darwin Online, http://darwin-online.org.uk/; henceforth "Courtesy John van Wyhe, Darwin Online")

FIGURE 3. Elizabeth "Bessy" Wedgwood, wife of Josiah II and mother of Emma Wedgwood among others. (Courtesy John van Wyhe, Darwin Online)

FIGURE 4. A portrait of Emma Darwin painted by George Richmond soon after her marriage. (Courtesy John van Wyhe, Darwin Online)

FIGURE 5. George Richmond's painting of Charles Darwin, done at about the same time as Emma's portrait. (© English Heritage Photo Library)

FIGURE 6. The front of Down House as it is today. Charles and Emma moved here in 1842 to escape life in the city. (Photograph property of the authors)

FIGURE 7. The old study at Down House where Darwin did his thinking and writing. (Darwin Archives, by permission of the Syndics of Cambridge University Library; henceforth "Darwin Archives, courtesy CUL Syndics")

FIGURE 8. The drawing room at Down House as it was in the early 1880s.
(Darwin Archives, courtesy CUL Syndics)

FIGURE 9. Annie
Darwin in 1849, two
years before her death.
(© English Heritage
Photo Library)

FIGURE 10. A careworn Emma, then forty-five years of age, and her young son Leonard, two years after Annie's death. (Darwin Archives, courtesy CUL Syndics)

FIGURE 11. A clean-shaven and dapper Charles Darwin, photographed in the mid-1850s. (Darwin Archives, courtesy CUL Syndics)

FIGURE 12. Erasmus Alvey Darwin and several of his nephews in the mid-1870s. *From left to right:* Horace Darwin, Leonard Darwin, E. A. Darwin, Frank Darwin, and William Darwin. Note that we disagree with others about the identification of Horace and Frank in this photograph. Our comparisons with other family photos have convinced us that the above order is the correct one. (Darwin Archives, courtesy CUL Syndics)

FIGURE 13. George Darwin as a young man. (Darwin Archives, courtesy CUL Syndics)

FIGURE 14. Henrietta
Darwin as a young woman.
(Darwin Archives, courtesy
CUL Syndics)

FIGURE 15. Elizabeth "Bessy"
Darwin as a young woman.
(Darwin Archives, courtesy CUL
Syndics)

FIGURE 16. Bernard "Dubba" Darwin as a young boy, around 1878. His presence brightened a traumatized Down House. (Darwin Archives, courtesy CUL Syndics)

FIGURE 17. Charles Darwin at about seventy years old, with the white beard that marked his old age. (Darwin Archives, courtesy CUL Syndics)

FIGURE 18. Emma Darwin in 1881, a year before her husband's death. (Courtesy John van Wyhe, Darwin Online)

FIGURE 19. The Grove, Cambridge, the winter residence of Emma and Bessy after Charles's death. (Photograph property of the authors)

FIGURE 20. Emma at the age of eighty-eight years, sitting in the Down House drawing room and holding her "peggywork" frame for making woolen strips to be stitched into rugs. (Courtesy John van Wyhe, Darwin Online)

15. A Book about Man, and Henrietta Takes a Husband

B Y THE MID-1860s Charles had become quite a famous man. He had gathered in the Royal and Copley Medals awarded by the Royal Society, as well as the Geological Society's Wollaston Medal. He had published a dozen books, the most famous being *On the Origin of Species*, which alone had gone through four editions by 1866 and had been translated into French, German, Dutch, Italian, and Russian.[1] As a result of Charles's growing reputation and international network of scientific correspondents, a steady stream of notable visitors, most of them scientific and many of them foreign, began to make the pilgrimage to Down House.

Among the most memorable of these visitors was Ernst Haeckel, director of the Zoological Institute at the University of Jena, who arrived on the Darwins' doorstep on October 21, 1866. On his way from Germany to Madeira and Tenerife to do zoological research, Haeckel had made a special side trip to London just to meet his evolutionary hero.[2] Henrietta reported on the occasion to George:

> On Sunday we had a gt visitation. One of Papa's most thorough going disciples, a Jena professor came to England on his way to Madeira & asked to come down to see Papa. . . . He came quite early on Sunday & when first

he entered he was so agitated he forgot all the little English he knew & he & Papa shook hands repeatedly. Papa reiterated remarking that he was very glad to see him & Haeckel receiving it in dead silence. However, afterwards it turned out that he could stumble on very decently.[3]

Charles sent Haeckel on his way with a note of introduction to Hooker, remarking to the latter a few days later that he had found the German to be "a very nice fellow & a first-rate zoologist but [a person who] talks atrocious English."[4]

Eighteen sixty-seven was marked mainly by Charles's completion of yet another book, *The Variation of Animals and Plants Under Domestication*. The material in this book had been selected to provide conclusive proof for natural selection, and Darwin regarded the volume as an essential sequel to the *Origin*. Henrietta helped read the galley proofs during a brief trip to Cornwall. Her father wrote back that Hen's comments and corrections were "excellent, excellent, excellent."[5]

Emma, of course, continued to help out as Darwin's amanuensis, editor, and sounding board, and while she was not an active proselytizer for evolution, when the need arose she was quick to defend Charles and his work. Such a case occurred in January 1867 when George Campbell, Duke of Argyll, published a book titled *The Reign of Law* in which he challenged certain of Darwin's evolutionary ideas. Circling the wagons, Emma declared flatly that the problem was "the Duke did not understand" the *Origin*.[6]

The next month, another foreigner came unexpectedly into the Darwins' lives. Vladimir Kovalevsky, a young Russian paleontologist and admirer of Darwin's works, asked if he might translate *Variation Under Domestication* into Russian. Always anxious to have his scientific work disseminated as widely as possible, Charles agreed, and the collaboration began. The delighted Kovalevsky gave Darwin as a thank-you gift a rug made from a "fine big black Russian bear" that he had personally killed. It was duly laid out in the drawing room, but only over the children's protests. Writing to a cousin, Henrietta complained that the rug had "an enormous head to tumble over & 4 large paws with sharp slightly upturned nails which tear yr gown & scratch yr legs." To Hen, the bearskin merely served to "endanger life & limb" and give "the boys frequent opportunities of swearing."[7]

As for the children's education, by the fall of 1867 twenty-year-old Lizzy had long since finished at Miss Buob's school and soon would have no home instruction either. (Darwin's household accounts ledger eliminated "governess" as a line item at the end of 1868.) The family involvement with Clapham

Grammar School was also winding down. George, Frank, Leonard, and Horace had all been pupils there for varying periods, but in September Charles wrote to the headmaster, Alfred Wrigley, that pending the outcome of his entrance exam, Leonard would soon be leaving Clapham for the Royal Military Academy at Woolwich, and that Horace was going to be sent to a private tutor.[8] To his father's happy surprise, Leonard did quite well on the Woolwich exam ("Who would ever have thought that poor dear Lenny would have got so magnificent a place?" remarked Charles), and by the next fall Cadet Darwin was looking "quite grand in his uniform."[9]

At Cambridge, Frank was well into his second year and George was prepping for his tripos exam in mathematics, scheduled for the period between Michaelmas and Lent terms. Thanks to a combination of innate talent and hard work, George thrilled the family (and himself) by acing the exam and coming in Second Wrangler—that is, second within the highest honors class. "My dear old fellow," wrote his father. "I never expected such brilliant results as this. Again and again I congratulate you. But you have made my hand tremble so I can hardly write." Emma reported further details to Henrietta in London:

> George's success made a tremendous stir at Clapham. Wrigley [George's former math instructor] had never been seen in such a state. He gave the fact out from the platform as if he was going to cry & gave a half holiday & sent [the students] to the C[rystal] P[alace].... When the boys heard about G. in the 1st Class room they had a regular saturnalia & played at football for some time to the great danger of the windows and pictures.[10]

George took his B.A. degree in January 1868 and then, with one success following another, he was elected a fellow of Trinity College in the autumn.[11]

Emma, Charles, Hen, and Lizzy spent almost all of March 1868 visiting with Elizabeth in London. Among the highlights of their stay in the metropolis was attending a performance of Schubert's Octet in F, and they made a number of new acquaintances, including the social activist and author Frances Power Cobbe and Thomas Henry Farrer and his wife, another Frances. Emma found Mr. Farrer "very genial and agreeable" at their first meeting, not knowing that he would annoy her greatly a few years later when he balked at the thought of his daughter marrying Horace Darwin. Miss Cobbe, a woman destined to gain fame particularly for her campaign against vivisection, was described as "very agreeable" by Emma, perhaps not least because she knew and liked Charles's scientific work.[12]

The Darwins returned home on April first, and two weeks later Elizabeth

Wedgwood made her final change of residence, moving into Tromer Lodge in Downe. Now the two sisters, always close emotionally despite an age difference of fifteen years, were also close geographically. Elizabeth's new house was rather close to the noise of the village school, Emma remarked to Fanny Allen, but at least the children's voices would not be "uncheerful." Still feisty at seventy-five, Elizabeth soon worked out a shortcut from her garden straight to Down House and became a regular drop-in visitor. Indeed, she made such frequent calls that Parslow, the Darwins' butler, gave up announcing her every arrival. "Where is Emma?" Elizabeth would call out as she tottered in, causing Parslow and the children to "hop to" and produce the desired person.[13]

In July and August 1868 the Darwins made a lengthy vacation trip to Freshwater at the west end of the Isle of Wight. They rented a house called Dumbola Lodge from the well-known photographer Julia Cameron, but Henrietta at least was not impressed. She wrote to George that they were situated in a "mean little valley [amidst] half a dozen sordid red brick houses." Although they had a croquet ground (a good point) and were only a quarter mile from the sea (another good point), there was "no beach—[only] gt big chalk cliffs." Chalk cliffs are fine if one likes them, observed Hen, but "I don't."[14]

Despite any real or imagined topographical drawbacks, Freshwater certainly abounded with interesting people, among them Alfred (later Lord) Tennyson and his wife. The Darwins socialized with the Tennysons on several occasions, but whether or not they got on with them depends on which informant one believes. Emma wrote a vacation note to Fanny Allen saying that "Mrs Tennyson is . . . very pleasing and gracious" and that "one likes" Tennyson himself. Charles had "spent a very pleasant hour" with him, she added. Henrietta's recollection, however, was that Tennyson "did not greatly charm" either of her parents. Concerning his poetry, Emma wrote years later that she had "never really care[d] for anything . . . but some bits of *In Memoriam*." For his part, Tennyson seemed to be mainly concerned during their Freshwater talks in finding out how Darwin's theories fit with religion. "Your theory of Evolution does not make against Christianity[?]" he asked Charles. "No, certainly not," replied Darwin, who impressed Mrs. Tennyson as being "very kindly, unworldly, and agreeable."[15]

There were poets galore in Freshwater that summer. Besides Tennyson, Emma and Charles met the American bard Henry Wadsworth Longfellow. A member-by-marriage of the Darwins' family circle (Longfellow was the brother-in-law of Fanny Hensleigh's American sister-in-law, Mary Mackintosh), Longfellow was a widower of seven years' standing and was traveling with his late wife's brother, Tom Appleton, yet another poet. Charles and Henry had a common interest in Harvard University, Darwin because of his friendship with Asa Gray and Longfellow because he too was a professor there. Thus much of their talk involved the merits of that university.[16]

And finally, of course, there was the owner of their rental house, Julia Cameron herself. Clearly a remarkable woman, Cameron had been taking and showing her photographs for only a few years, but already was making quite a name for herself. She favored pictures made in subdued lighting, a style that necessitated exposures of several minutes and prolonged and absolute stillness on the part of the sitter. Mrs. Cameron was able to obtain her subjects' compliance through sheer force of personality, as reflected by Tennyson's remark when he dropped Longfellow off at her studio: "Longfellow, you will have to do whatever she tells you. I shall return soon and see what is left of you." Eminent men were perhaps her very favorite subjects, and at Freshwater she took three photos of Darwin, as well as one each of the less eminent Ras and seventeen-year-old Horace. Cameron refused, however, to do a photograph of Emma, maintaining that "no woman [should] be photographed between the ages of 18 and 70."[17]

The Darwins were back at Down House by late August and soon found that some new and interesting people had moved, at least temporarily, into the neighborhood. The American literary editor and Dante scholar Charles Eliot Norton had leased the rectory in nearby Keston for a period of quiet recuperation. Accompanied by several members of his family, including his wife Susan and her unmarried sister Sara Ashburner Sedgwick, Norton had chosen Keston as his retreat largely because of its rural location. He wrote back to America about the beautiful English countryside with its "upland common[s] . . . covered with heather and gorse . . . hills and dales [with] sweetness and tenderness of curves and slopes . . . [and] picturesque farm houses and farm yards." But he was not fleeing human society entirely, and a second factor in Norton's choice was having easy access to London and the company of artistic and literary friends such as John Ruskin and Charles Dickens. Of course, living so close to the famous English evolutionist, Norton was also interested in meeting Darwin.[18]

An excursion to Knole was organized for the first Saturday in September, with the party consisting of the Nortons, the Darwins, Alice Bonham-Carter, and one or two others. Lizzy reported on the jaunt in a note to Henrietta, who was traveling in Switzerland:

> Yesterday the expedition to Knole took place—it went off very well and the boys liked it very much although they went rather with the spirit of a martyr. . . . [Driving over] Mrs Norton talked unceasingly the whole time and could scarcely be got to look about her at all. . . . Of cours we had to go and see the house first, and I hope I may never have to see it again. Those old pictures are so tiresome. . . . We then sat down and eat our lunch . . . [which] cheered us up wonderfully. . . . Mr and Mrs Norton . . . are coming to lunch today. . . .
>
> Goodbye dear Henrietta. I hope you will have a good time which you are sure to have. I envy you awfully.[19]

The closing here is telling. Now twenty-one years of age, Lizzy was really starting to chafe at being different—and being *treated* differently—from her siblings. She longed to travel independently on the Continent, as Henrietta was now allowed to do, but if that wasn't possible, she at least wanted to be included in *local* excursions and social events. Lizzy's vexation at being left out is shown in a note fired off to Hen a few days after the Knole trip:

> Yesterday George and Frank went to dine at the [Bonham-] Carters. I must say I think they might have asked me. I should have liked very much to have gone. Not that I think I should have cared for the dinner itself much, but I should like to be asked. Alice has proposed to George and Frank to go with her and the Nortons down The Thems. I dare say it will never take place. I should like to go very much if it does take place and if they ask me.[20]

To her credit, Lizzy didn't wallow in self-pity about being different; she worked hard not to be. That same autumn, her mother noticed a marked "improvement in animation & talk & . . . enjoy[ment] being somebody." Nonetheless and quite understandably, Lizzy's sensitivity about social slights could flash into outright indignation if she was actually ridiculed. She told Hen of a recent dinner guest at Down House, a man she didn't "think much of," who "asked me in a patronizing way whether I played [an instrument]—whether I sang and whether I drew, and when I said no to all, then he said—then what *do* you do."[21]

Aware as she was of her little oddities—and the fact that they were obvious to others—one wonders how Lizzy saw the rest of her life playing itself out. Did she entertain hopes of marriage and children? Disappointingly, snippets from her letters provide only limited insights into her hopes and dreams.

The Nortons, after the visit to Knole together, enjoyed a flurry of social inter-actions with the Darwins, including lunches and dinners and a joint visit to the Lubbocks' home at High Elms. Whether William Darwin was present at any of these events is unclear from his mother's diary. William was at Down House for a visit on November 28, but he may have just missed meeting the Nortons, since they relocated to London at about that time. Perhaps it was not until the spring of 1869, or even later, that William met his future wife, Sue Norton's sister Sara Sedgwick.[22]

Certainly, at twenty-nine, William was primed for love and marriage. In early March 1869 he wrote to his mother asking her advice on finding a wife:

> I have been trying to clear up my ideas on marriage for some little time past & find it a difficult job. . . . the cons appear to me to about balance the pros, therefore I am in a position to consider it on general principles without prej-udice. . . . How is a man to get to know what a girl really is from meeting her at balls & parties? One sees nothing but society manners, society giggles, & society ideas. Entirely artificial, and made up to look well. Therefore Ques-tion 1 is, is a man to go in like at Blindman's buff, & take the first that comes uppermost with about as much to guide him? Again granting one does in time get to know a girl to some extent, they all or a great majority of them turn out insipid with hardly any interests but in the most ordinary things, & none of them with any music, which would make up for a great pile of sins. Question 2 is, is a man to go in just for an amicable sociable person and not much else, or to wait till he comes across something approaching his ideal? Judging from my experience it comes to this, is a man wise in making the best choice he has the chance of, or is it better to remain unmarried sooner than marry any one but an exceptional person? . . . I should like to know what your ideas are on these points.[23]

Ouch! Modern readers may well shudder at this bald expression of male superiority, but it should be remembered that it was part of a private letter from a son to his mother written 140 years ago. Emma responded by offering to send William his father's 1838 list of marital pros and cons, and then con-tinued with her own bit of advice:

> In the first place do not marry for marrying sake (look at Uncle Frank as a warning). What you say about the difficulty of knowing society girls is v[ery] true. One knows a little what girls are from knowing what their parents are, that is to say if you liked what you saw, you would venture more safely than if you did not know the family. F[ather] says marry a healthy wife & I say

marry a wise one, which you will say is all v fine talking. Don't feel in any hurry, you are quite young enough. My opinion you know well enough that men are m[uch] better & happier when young for being married, & that an old bachelor's later life is generally desolate. Even Uncle Ras who is almost as fond of Hope & Effie as if they were his own feels desolate & melancholy. When you do see any body that rather hits your taste like the nice Scotch girl follow up the acquaintances.[24]

Whoever the Scotch girl was, in the long run she lost out. William eventually met and wooed Sara Sedgwick, although they did not marry until 1877.

William's nascent love life has taken us far, however, from other important events in 1868 that deserve notice. For one thing, in February of that year Margaret Wedgwood, Joe and Caroline's middle daughter, married the Reverend Arthur Vaughan Williams. Although the wedding was a happy occasion for the parents on both sides, by September Caroline was missing her daughter so terribly that she sank into a deep and worrying depression. Emma wrote to Hen:

> Poor At. C. does look so ill & so depressed. . . . Her health is so bad & she feels so desponding about her life & feels so utterly unable to reconcile herself to the loss of Margaret (no doubt owing to her health). She is grown immensely lar[ge] & feels so great a figure she can hardly bear to go any where.

Margaret's union would produce three children, including the composer Ralph Vaughan Williams, about whom more later.[25]

Second, Professor and Mrs. Asa Gray made their first visit to Down House in October 1868 and were enchanted with the place and their hosts. Mrs. Gray was especially taken with Charles, whom she described as "entirely fascinating . . . tall & thin, though broad-framed . . . [with] the sweetest smile, the sweetest voice, the merriest laugh! and so quick, so keen!"[26] Darwin, the old flirt, was clearly at the top of his game during the Grays' visit and had won another female heart.

And finally, there was a bit of juicy scandal in Downe village having to do with the current curate, the Reverend John Robinson. Robinson was the latest in a string of ministers left in nominal charge of the parish when the incumbent vicar, John Innes, retired in 1862 to his newly inherited Scottish estate (adding Brodie as his middle name on the occasion) without resigning his ecclesiastical living. A close friend of the Darwins despite vast theological differences with Charles, Innes stayed in regular correspondence with them after he relocated to the North. Unfortunately for all concerned, the curates that Innes selected to minister to the people of Downe were, almost to a man, unsatisfactory in one way or another. Samuel Horsman, who immediately preceded Robinson, "ran up a string of bills and made off with the [National School's] money after Darwin had mistakenly shared treasurer's duties with him." Horsman left the village under a cloud and was replaced in August 1868 by Robinson, who Innes initially thought was "little less than a saint." The saintly Mr. Robinson, however, not only proved prone to absent himself from his duties for weeks at a time but also had a habit of "walking with girls at night," an offense that hardly seems scandalous today but was strongly censured in Victorian times. Darwin wrote to Innes that

> rumours are very common in our village about Mr. Robinson walking with girls at night.—I did not mention this before, because I had not even moderately good authority; but my wife found Mrs. Allen very indignant about Mr. R's conduct with one of her maids. I do not believe that there is any evidence of actual criminality. As I repeat only second hand my name must not be mentioned.—Our maids tell my wife that they do not believe that hardly anyone will go to church now.[27]

It should be noted that the "Mrs. Allen" mentioned here was a villager, not one of the Allens of Cresselly and thus not a kinswoman of Emma's. In any event, Robinson's nightly strolls were too much for the local morals, and by early 1869 he had been replaced by the Reverend Henry Powell. Powell did better than a curacy, however: Innes had finally resigned the Downe living, and Powell was installed as the vicar of St. Mary the Virgin.[28]

The family vacation in 1869 was to Wales. Setting up headquarters in Merioneth County, the Darwin party toured the surrounding countryside, visiting Caerdeon and Barmouth locally, as well as other points farther afield. One day in July they drove over to Pantlludw and were guests in the home of the Lawrence Rucks. The two families had known each other for some time, thanks to friendships formed between their sons at Clapham School. The sons had visited back and forth, but this was probably the first time the senior Darwins had visited Pantlludw. The visit went well, and before the Darwins returned to Downe, they had gotten together with the Rucks a total of three times, a good indication that the parents too were compatible. This was fortunate, since five years later, when Frank Darwin married their beautiful raven-haired daughter Amy, Lawrence and Mary Ann Ruck would become part of Emma and Charles's extended family.[29]

It was 1870 and Charles Darwin was busy writing another book. That in itself wasn't unusual, of course; for years he had been constantly at work on one book or another. Most recently, the two volumes of his *Variation of Animals and Plants under Domestication* (1868) had been followed by a fifth edition of the *Origin* (1869). No, the distinction was that this time Darwin was writing a "man book." Ultimately named rather cumbrously *The Descent of Man, and Selection in Relation to Sex*, it would finally present his ideas on the course and causes of our own evolution. Barely mooted in the *Origin*, by the 1870s human evolution had been addressed by Haeckel in his *Natürliche Schöpfungsgeschichte* (1868) as well as by Huxley in *Man's Place in Nature* (1863). It was now possible to discuss the question without being immediately vilified, and everyone wanted to know what the famous Darwin had to say on the subject. Even Emma thought the "man book" would "be very interesting, but"—and here was her old concern—she feared she would "dislike it very much as again putting God further off."[30]

It was fortunate that a relaxation of public reprobation made it relatively safe for Charles to address the question of human evolution, for in 1870 there were strong reasons not to wait any longer. Certain scientists he had formerly considered to be thoroughgoing supporters were starting to openly challenge the theory of natural selection and using the human case to do so. One of these was St. George Jackson Mivart. A zoological disciple of Huxley's despite being an unwavering Catholic, Mivart was a primate anatomist whose works Darwin had found useful and with whom Darwin had begun a correspondence in 1867. Initially a convert to Darwinism, by the late 1860s Mivart had begun to distance himself from that camp and its belief in purely naturalistic evolutionary processes. As part of his shift of theoretical position, Mivart published several papers in the Catholic magazine *The Month* that were critical of natural selection and that argued instead for "an element of design" in the history of life. These articles enraged Huxley, of course, but worse was to come. Unbeknownst to either Huxley or Darwin, Mivart was also busy writing a book-length anti-Darwinian diatribe that he sneeringly titled *The Genesis of Species*. In this book, which was published just before *The Descent of Man* in 1871, Mivart pounded on the Darwinians, noting among other things that the "remarkable simplicity" of the theory of natural selection made it appealing to "half-educated men and shallow thinkers," and charging "not a few" Darwinians with virulent *odium antitheologicum* (undoubtedly he was thinking of Huxley here). Charles described Mivart's book as an exercise in pettifoggery, yet he took its criticisms seriously enough to add a rebuttal chapter to the *Origin*'s sixth edition some years later.[31]

But Mivart wasn't the worst of it. A second waffler on natural selection was much more surprising and distressing to Darwin. In April 1869, in an article in the *Quarterly Review*, Alfred Russel Wallace had opined that "natural selection could not account for the mental attributes of modern humans." Modern-day savages, Wallace argued, have brains far too large and highly developed for their simple needs, which is puzzling since "natural selection . . . can only build structures immediately useful to animals possessing them." Thus it seemed to Wallace that some other force—some supernatural force—must also have contributed to the evolution of the human brain. After this "Overruling Intelligence" took charge, he argued, the human mind developed independently of our ape-descended bodies, and "human societies emerged, cultural imperatives took over, a mental and moral nature became significant, and civilization took shape." Predictably, Darwin was horrified at this theistic backsliding on the part of natural selection's codiscoverer. "I hope you have not murdered too completely your own & my child," he wrote to Wallace.[32] Clearly it was time for Charles to publish his own, strictly scientific explanation of human evolution.

Accordingly, again with editorial and other support from Emma and Henrietta, Charles swung into action on his "man book." He methodically ground out the chapters and passed them along to his wife and daughter. Emma's main roles in the production seem to have been watching Charles for signs of overwork (in which case she immediately began lobbying for a break), directing sections of the manuscript to Henrietta (who was traveling in Europe most of the winter), and excising the occasional passage (Charles, Emma wrote to Hen, "is putting Polly"—the family dog and a great favorite of Charles's—"into his man book but I doubt whether I shall let it stand, a fond grandfather is not to be trusted"). Henrietta was much more of a general editor for the nascent book, a demanding task that she performed well, to her father's great appreciation. "[Y]our corrections and suggestions are *excellent*," Charles wrote to his daughter. "I have adopted the greater number, and I am sure that they are very great improvements. . . . You have done me real service."[33]

Much of Hen's editorial work was done on the road. She left Downe on January 12, 1870, for a lengthy tour of France and Italy that didn't bring her home until the end of April. For her Continental romp, Hen partnered up with four cousins: Godfrey and Amy Wedgwood, and Edmund Langton and his wife Lena. Writing from home, her sister Bessy (who at twenty-two had graduated from the little-girl "Lizzy") expressed the opinion that Hen was lucky in having the Wedgwoods along, "as the Langtons are such lazys."[34]

Between letters from Bessy and her parents, Henrietta was kept well abreast of events back home. Shortly after her departure, Hen was told, a crowd of scientists had descended on Down House for a two-day stay. There was Alfred Newton, professor of zoology at Magdalene College, Cambridge, with whom Frank Darwin had become friendly; Albert Günther, staff zoologist at the British Museum; and Robert Swinhoe, former diplomat and ornithologist. Rounding out the group, J. D. Hooker had joined the three men for their second day at the Darwins'. Emma reported that Günther was "most agreeable" company despite a thick German accent that had him "Grumbling his shirt" and working on "a broplematical question." Bessy was quite taken with Swinhoe, whom she described as "so very handsome," but whose tales of his consular days in Japan left her thinking it "a very unpleasant place to live in." According to Swinhoe, wrote Bessy, "there are a certain set of men who walk around with two swords, and they make bets how many dogs heads they will cut off, and if they meet a European they sometimes count him as a dog too and off goes his head, so that it is rather ticklish work passing them."[35]

In addition to tales of visiting scientists, Henrietta learned that St. Mary's new priest Mr. Powell, thankfully not a man who "walked with women" at night, had been a luncheon guest at Down House, and also that the village Penny Readings—musical and theatrical evenings organized and priced for the working classes—were drawing good crowds despite the occasional bad act. "The 1d Reading was v[ery] successful tho' we had that nasty scene of Mr. Brumble & Mrs. Corney out of Oliver Twist," reported Emma. At one performance, Bessy complained, there were "two irish stories about a gridiron which was rather too much of a good thing, and one man had such a voice that it nearly cracked our heads in two." Perhaps the biggest bit of home news concerned a keenly anticipated ball given for the Darwins' servants. On the bitterly cold evening of February 9, forty-five servants and guests crowded into Down House. Beginning with a gala meal in the formal dining room, in two sittings, they then progressed to dancing in the kitchen. Although Emma and Charles steered clear of the party—"Parslow wanted us to come & look at the guests, but we were too shy & they wd not have known what to say or do any more than we should," Emma noted—they could hear the dance music, which consisted mainly of polkas and waltzes played by two "not v. good" fiddlers. Still, it appears that a good time was had by all.[36]

On the national scene, in late February there was a spectacular divorce trial that made headlines in the *Times*. Sir Charles Mordaunt, MP, sued for divorce from his wife, Harriet Moncrieffe Mordaunt, on grounds of adultery.

Lady Mordaunt freely confessed to conceiving a child with Viscount Cole while her husband was traveling abroad, but because there was some question as to whether she was sane enough to aid in her own defense, it was unclear whether the divorce would be granted, bastard child or not. Adding to the trial's erotically charged atmosphere, several men besides Cole were mooted as Lady Mordaunt's lovers, including Albert Edward, Prince of Wales. Emma wrote almost in a whisper to Henrietta:

> We have all been full of the "Warwickshire scandal" which is almost too indecent to mention. It is satisfactory that the P. of W.'s letters to Lady M. are so extremely dull & common place that I think he must be innocent. I quite believe her to be insane now whatever she has been, & also that she is guilty. What women there are in this world, many of them forced their way in to hear this horrible trial. I suppose from the decision of the jury that she is insane that Sir C. M. will not be able to go on w[ith] the divorce.

It was as nice a bit of upper-class scandal as one could wish for, and while Emma would never have been among the women jostling for a courtroom seat, she clearly relished the juicy details in the *Times*. As she anticipated, the jury eventually found Lady Mordaunt to have been insane both when originally charged and at the time of the trial. When the Prince of Wales gave testimony in the case, it was revealed that he had visited Lady Mordaunt at times when her husband was away. But this behavior was judged to be merely indiscreet, not demonstrably adulterous, and so Albert Edward got away with only a bit of public embarrassment.[37]

Not all of the news sent to Henrietta was gossipy and good. A family tragedy occurred in early March when Harry Wedgwood and his son John had a boating accident and thirty-year-old John was drowned. Everyone took the death hard, of course, but Harry was very nearly inconsolable. Despite his advanced age (seventy-one), he was haunted by the "gnawing feeling that he mt have made more efforts to save his beloved son." John's death made Emma nervous for her traveling daughter.[38]

Actually, even without the case of nerves brought on by their nephew's death, both Charles and Emma were ready for Hen to wrap up her trip and come home. For one thing, between staying in first-class hotels and adding side trips to her itinerary, it was turning out to be a very expensive excursion. "F. is resigned" to the costs, wrote Emma, who then added her own private worry: "I only hope you may not turn into a regular travelling old maid living abroad." Perhaps stung a little by this image, Henrietta turned her head toward Downe and was home at the end of April. By the time she rejoined the family, Frank had succeeding in passing the tripos exam and earning his B.A. at Cambridge, and was beginning work toward a medical degree. At Woolwich, Lenny had survived a close call when student mischief got out of control and a few pupils were locked temporarily in the gym and a cannon was pushed into a ditch. Cadets thought to know anything about these high jinks were expelled when they refused to turn informer. "One of the officers proposed expelling [Lenny and one of his classmates] by way of putting pressure on the others to tell the truth." Happily, this never came to pass.[39]

Henrietta had not been home for long before the Continent was rent by war. Two old antagonists, France and Prussia, were once again struggling for dominance in Europe, and after a series of relatively minor diplomatic incidents, France declared war on July 19, 1870. Almost immediately the French, who were outnumbered two to one, began to get the worse of the fighting. By late August the French forces were split, with one army besieged in the town of Metz and a second attempting to relieve it. Unfortunately for the French, on September first the relief force itself was defeated at the battle of Sedan and its commander, the comte de MacMahon, badly wounded. The next day, Napoleon III and 83,000 of his troops surrendered to a combined German army from Prussia and several south German states.[40]

Emma had been against the European war from the start, commenting acidly just before its beginning that it was "incredible that France shd be so wicked & mad" as to attack Prussia. That she had not changed her mind by the time of the French defeat at Sedan is reflected in these comments to Henrietta:

> I wonder when you heard yesterday's wonderful news of the Emperor giving himself up; & when Aunt Eliz. was coming back from New Cross she heard that he was dead which wd be better still poor wretch. I think McMahon had better die of his wound too.[41]

The outcome of the struggle was inevitable. German forces moved ever deeper into France, and on January 28, 1871, Paris formally capitulated to the newly unified Germany headed by Kaiser Wilhelm I. In the settlement that ended the war, large parts of the provinces of Alsace and Lorraine were ceded to the Germans, whose star was clearly on the rise in Europe. The Treaty of Frankfurt, signed in May 1871, made it possible for travelers—including honeymooners, Henrietta among them—to safely return to the Continent.[42]

Yes, to everyone's enormous satisfaction, Emma's fears about Hen proved groundless: she was not destined to be a globe-trotting old maid after all. Her spinsterhood came to an end in August 1871 when she married a barrister and civil servant, Richard Buckley Litchfield. Far from finding the stereotypical modern heartthrob, a man who is tall, dark, and handsome, Hen fell in love with a man who was short, egg-shaped (at least in his later years), and bearded. Much more important than his build, however, was Litchfield's contented submissiveness when given direct orders by his wife, a trait that contributed substantially to the long-term success of their marriage.[43]

Henrietta and Richard had met in London in the spring of 1871, apparently through Uncle Ras and the Hensleigh Wedgwoods. It quickly became apparent that the two were a good match, with many interests in common including liberal politics, music, and London society. They also shared high moral principles and unorthodox views on religion: both tended to be agnostic on the question of God's existence. (Clearly, in the ten years since her churchgoing days in Torquay, Henrietta's theology had moved away from her mother's views and toward her father's. Perhaps it was all that travel on the Continent.) In June, after a whirlwind courtship, Hen shared the news of her engagement with George and Frank:

My dear George

Please prepare your mind for the most tremendous piece of news concerning myself I could tell you. *The* supreme crisis of my life.

I am going to be married to Mr. Litchfield. You will say that I don't know him, that was true a fortnight ago when he asked me but since then I do, & he has made me believe that he does care for me, as I have dreamt of being loved, but never expected that supreme happiness to fall to my lot.

I am sure he is no relation to the pastry cook, however like their beards are. His father was a retired Indian officer. He is a Cambridge man, 2nd class classic & just escaped being a high enough wrangler to get a Trinity Fellowship which enraged his Father, but as he was even then profoundly unorthodox was a relief to him. He is a clerk in the Ecclesiastical Commission.... He enraged his Father also by giving up law for which he was educated, but he felt no desire for either nothing or too much to do, & has never repented his unambitious choice especially as he has enough money. I think he said abt £1000 a year. . . . He seems to be friends with all our sort of people. . . . The only other fact is that he is 39 years old.

I write this letter to Frank as well as to you. Tell him not to hate the "cool beast" if he can help it. We all like that name & Uncle Ras especially. By the way it is to be announced to you boys only just for a day or two, to get our courage up to tell the world.

Sympathise with me in my happiness my own dear boys. You must try to like him for my sake for I couldn't bear anything to come between our most precious friendship. There are very few sisters in the world who have received more happiness than I have from all of you.[44]

Besides working at the Ecclesiastical Commission, Richard Litchfield was one of the founders of the Working Men's College, along with fellow social reformers Frederick Denison Maurice, Thomas Hughes, and others. After that institution began operation in 1854, men from London's working classes could take advantage of affordable instruction in music (Litchfield's specialty), languages, English grammar, mathematics, drawing, humanities, and the physical sciences. Among some of the more famous instructors at the College were the founders themselves (Maurice was a prolific author of theological and philosophical works, and Hughes wrote the now classic novel *Tom Brown's School-Days*), artists Ford Madox Brown and Dante Gabriel Rossetti, and art critic John Ruskin.[45]

Litchfield, it appears, was particularly dedicated to his work at the WMC, and his decision to leave the law and take a civil service position was at least partially motivated by a desire to have afternoons and evenings free for College activities. His £1,000 annual income (today some $83,000) was not a lot, relatively speaking, but Henrietta was not put off either by this or by the fact that Richard was her senior by some twelve years. Although Litchfield was not the kind of ardent swain who would "sweep her up in his arms," Hen was thoroughly smitten.[46]

Compared to Henrietta, Richard was less emotional in his account of the engagement and more candid in describing his fiancée. He wrote to Jane Mowatt Lushington, wife of Vernon Lushington—barrister, fellow WMC teacher, and one of the folks Henrietta had in mind by "our sort of people":

> Something has happened to me today that will interest you. I am engaged to be married. The lady is known to you by *name* as her father is a great man— Darwin the Savant. She is Henrietta Darwin, his eldest daughter. Having much to do I will only tell you further that she is (all but) 28—very wise & good, not particularly beautiful, perhaps not beautiful at all. You are sure to like her when you know her. All the minor incidents are just what one wd wish. The family are all delightful—Darwin is a quiet country gentleman of

moderate but ample fortune & her nearest relations are old friends of mine. I am extremely happy. There seems to be no reason why we should not be married by September.[47]

In fairness to Litchfield, his description of Henrietta as "not particularly beautiful" was a private remark to a close friend and never meant to be repeated. On the other hand, while not particularly complimentary, it was essentially accurate. A male contemporary of the couple described Henrietta's face as a "feminine and tender" version of her father's, and no one ever accused Charles of being overly handsome. (A comparison of childhood photographs suggests that Annie Darwin would have been the most beautiful of the three sisters, had she survived to adulthood.) In any event, modest salaries and plain faces notwithstanding, Hen and Richard were well contented with one another, and after hosting Litchfield at Down House several times during July and being reassured by Ras that he was not a "gold-hunter," Emma and Charles gave the marriage their approval. Charles proposed a marriage settlement of £5,000 in stocks and an annual allowance for Henrietta of around £350–£400, giving the Litchfields' yearly household budget a substantial boost. The wedding was set for the end of August.[48]

J. D. Hooker once remarked that he "would rather go to two burials than one marriage, any day," reflecting the view that weddings, and the run-up to them, are never easy things. Henrietta's was no exception, and although she tried to keep it small and simple, it almost killed her father. Perhaps to please Emma—certainly neither the bride nor the groom was particularly religious—the ceremony was held at St. Mary the Virgin in the village center, and Charles had to conquer his churning stomach long enough to give Henrietta away. It was intended that only immediate family be in attendance, but at the last minute a few WMC friends of Richard's invited themselves and trained down from London. And so, on August 31, 1871, in front of a small gathering, R. B. Litchfield, Bachelor, married Henrietta Emma Darwin, Spinster. William and Leonard Darwin signed the register as witnesses, and everyone went back to Down House for a sit-down (or lie-down in Charles's case) and a quiet piece of wedding cake.[49]

The newlyweds departed almost immediately for Switzerland and Italy, but not before the WMC faculty threw them a party that made up for the lack of one at Downe. Emma wrote to her honeymooning daughter that the wedding announcement had "looked very nice in the Daily News," that

Charles was once again "pretty well & at work," and that Horace, who was now at Trinity College, Cambridge, was studying hard for his Little Go.[50] Henrietta reciprocated with news about their travels and (being a Darwin) their health. Both she and Richard had been ill for part of the trip, wrote Hen, but "we feel very married each lying sick in our beds as if we'd been at it 30 years like Father and you." Emma's response was telling: "Nothing marries one so completely as sickness."[51]

16. Two Weddings, Four Funerals, and the Fiendish Mr. Ffinden

EIGHTEEN SEVENTY-ONE ENDED ON A distinctly high note. At Cambridge, Horace passed the classics-heavy Little Go and was now free to study the technical subjects that actually interested him. His proud father sent a congratulatory note, saying that everyone at home "rejoiced . . . that you are all right and safe through the accursed" exam. "You have passed this Charybdis," wrote Darwin with a mythological reference, "and now you can follow the bent of your talents and work as hard at Mathematics and Science as your health will permit." The last words reflect Charles and Emma's lingering concern about the son who had been so sickly as a child.[1]

Darwin himself was happily following the bent of his talents with the second phase of his study of human evolution: this time teasing out the evolutionary origins of our emotions. His analysis compared the emotional displays of a variety of human subjects—infants, including some of the little Darwins, normal adults of different races, and patients in lunatic asylums—with those of selected animal species, and focused strongly on the involvement of the muscles and features of the face in expressing emotional state. Combined with *The Descent of Man*, this new book would neatly wrap up Charles's evolutionary analyses of our own species. Family members and friends supplied observations on one another and on their babies; a questionnaire was circulated to observers overseas soliciting information about the behavior of local people (sample: "Is extreme fear expressed in the same general manner as with Europeans?"); and comparisons were made between humans and the primates at the London Zoo, where "Mr. Sutton, the intelligent keeper," made observations for Darwin revealing that when chimpanzees and orangs "are made angry, as by being teased, their hair becomes erect." Even Richard Litchfield, the Darwins' new son-in-law, helped out by offering "thoughts on the origins of music and singing." For her part, Emma—to whom the notion of human evolution was now thoroughly old hat, though not necessarily something with which she agreed—was happy with the thought that Charles's latest book was unlikely to "affront anybody" and might even "be generally interesting."[2]

Work on *The Expression of the Emotions in Man and Animals* continued throughout the winter and spring of 1872, with a break in February when Emma hauled her workaholic husband to London for a five-week rest. While in the city she attended concerts, visited the waxworks, and shopped for a sewing machine. In the evenings they dined with London-based friends and family. By late March, however, the call of the proof sheets was too strong for Darwin to resist, and they returned to Downe. Gratifyingly, all of the work paid off handsomely when *The Expression of the Emotions* was published in November: it sold 5,267 copies on the day of its release and some 9,000 copies in the first four months. Human evolution, far from being the shocking notion of 1859, was now viewed as good fun, and Charles found himself caricatured as often as he was lambasted. *Fun* magazine, for example, portrayed him as a monkeylike figure taking the pulse of a well-dressed young woman. "Really, Mr. Darwin," she scolds, "say what you like about Man; but I wish you would leave *my* emotions alone!"[3]

As spring turned to summer and the weather grew warmer, the flow of people in and out of Down House picked up speed. Henrietta and Richard came down from town every couple of weeks, sons and all manner of distant kin came and went, and scientific and nonscientific friends were always filling up the guest bedrooms. Among the scientific acquaintances who came for a visit was the anthropologist Edward Burnett Tylor, who had become very interested in Darwin's work. Departures from Downe for overseas travel included Horace to Ireland and George to Switzerland; Bessy stayed closer to home, but did manage a trip to Wales. The Litchfields headed back to the Continent, and they were there when Georgina Tollet died in early September. This death of a woman exactly her age and a friend since childhood must have been especially sad for Emma. Of the eight Tollet siblings, now only Ellen was left. With the certain knowledge that her Staffordshire connections were coming to an end, Emma simply noted in her diary, "Georgina died."[4]

While the Litchfields were still abroad, Richard scored some points with Emma by writing to her on the occasion of their first wedding anniversary. Although she had been somewhat taken aback by the brevity of Hen and Richard's engagement, Emma was warming rapidly to this attentive son-in-law. She responded:

My dear Richard

It was very nice of you to write to me. Although we Wedgwoods are so bad about anniversaries I shd have thought of the 31st. . . . I think it must have been second sight that made you two know so well how you wd suit. It cd not have been knowing each other in the common acceptation. There are so many sad things to think of that I often feel, Well there are 2 belonging to me whose happiness it is a comfort to think of. . . .

I am glad you are reading Plato, as you will be able to tell me whether I cd endure any of it; as I have always had some curiosity to know something about the ancients.[5]

Directly on the heels of Georgina Tollet's death came another piece of sadness. Jessie Wedgwood, Harry's wife and Emma and Charles's sister-in-law/cousin, was wasting away. Despite the attentions of a team of doctors, illness had reduced sixty-eight-year-old Jessie to a "very hopeless" condition, leaving the family miserable and fearing (along with certain of Jessie's physicians) that she might linger "for a considerable time." Slow deaths such as this were especially abhorrent to Emma, who wrote to Henrietta that "Uncle Harry's letters are very pathetic." Jessie's firm religious faith made Emma hope that she was comforted in her decline by the thought of a "future life." To Harry, the vision of his wife in heaven was not much comfort. Mercifully, the prediction of a drawn-out ending was wrong, and Jessie died before the year was out.[6]

Switching from human evolution to botany, Charles was in high gear with studies of insectivorous and climbing plants in early 1873. Among his new favorite pastimes was watching the movements of the telegraph plant, *Desmodium gyrans*. Fascinated by the twitching leaflets of this Asian shrub, Darwin once got up in the middle of the night to check it for nocturnal activity. He found the plant "dead asleep," Emma reported to Aunt Fanny Allen, "all but its little ears, which were having most lively games, such as he never saw in the day-time."[7]

January was highlighted by the usual ball at High Elms. That same month, the Darwins were visited for the first time by Moncure Conway, an American minister whose unorthodox Methodist beliefs had long since morphed into liberal Unitarianism. Conway had been an admirer of Charles's ever since reading *On the Origin of Species* years before and, unlike some other theologians, he had never seen Darwinism as a serious, or intentional, threat to organized religion. Conway was fascinated with scientific men and collected them as acquaintances. "It has been my privilege to know the leading scientific men in America and Europe," he wrote in his autobiography. Charles was a prime specimen. Besides, Conway shared with the Darwins an intense abhorrence of slavery. The conversations during his visit were lively.[8]

In March Emma dragged Darwin away from his plants and brought him to town for their now routine winter-spring vacation. They stayed in rented lodgings for a month—rather too long for Charles but, Emma wrote to Aunt Fanny, he "knows his place and submits." Uncharacteristically, Emma attended neither concerts nor exhibitions on this trip. Instead she devoted her time to socializing with a long list of family and friends, including Fanny Frank, Ellen Tollet, the Vernon Lushingtons, the Huxleys, the Thackerays, Francis Galton, the Hookers, Meta Gaskell, Mary Anne Ruck, and Mary Lyell. Sadly, this was the last time she would see Lady Lyell, whose "constant supply of talk" had been the salvation of Emma's first "scientific dinner party." On April 24 a "feverish cold" carried off Mary Lyell with stunning suddenness. Her husband was understandably devastated: nearly twelve years his wife's senior, he had never anticipated outliving her. The Darwins felt the shock as well since, as Emma wrote to Horace: "Some how [Lady Lyell] was a person whose death seemed out of the question." An obituary in a Boston newspaper remembered Lady Lyell's "strength and sweetness" and opined that "her friends must feel . . . something of the light of life" had been lost. Hooker reported to Darwin that Mary Lyell had looked "calm and beautiful" in her coffin. She was sixty-five when she died, a fact that was not lost on Emma, since it matched her own age precisely.[9]

In May 1873 a happier event occurred: Fanny and Hensleigh's middle daughter, Katherine Euphemia "Effie" Wedgwood, married the widower Thomas Henry Farrer. Actually, the wedding can be considered only "sort of" happy, because that seems to have been the mood of many members of the Wedgwood family, including the bride! Not too long before she accepted Farrer, Effie had received a proposal from her cousin Godfrey, Fanny and Frank's oldest son. For a variety of complicated reasons—although certainly not because of any reservation among the Wedgwoods about marrying first cousins—Effie declined Godfrey's offer. Then when Farrer popped the question six months later, she turned him down too, raising the possibility that, at the age of thirty-four, Effie had opted for a lifetime of spinsterhood. Farrer was not to be denied, however, and he pressed his case, telling everyone who would listen how desperately unhappy Effie had made him. His strategy worked: for reasons fully known only to Effie, she finally gave in and agreed to marry Farrer, saying that "she couldn't bear his looking so miserable and going around telling everyone that *she* was the cause."[10]

The marriage between Effie and "Theta" Farrer took place on May 30, 1873. Bessy Darwin reported to Horace at Cambridge that the ceremony went off smoothly "except that Effy nearly fainted." Directly after the service, the newlyweds drove to Farrer's country home, Abinger Hall in Surrey, where Effie had arranged for the loan of a "kitten for a fortnight" to "help her to bear things better." In the early summer the Farrers visited Down House on two occasions, and in August the Darwins made a reciprocal visit to Abinger. They arrived to hear the grisly tale of the death of Samuel Wilberforce, most recently the bishop of Winchester and the very cleric who had argued so vigorously against the *Origin* at the 1860 BAAS meeting. As it happened, on July 19 Wilberforce, accompanied by the foreign secretary, Earl Granville, had been traveling past Abinger when the bishop fell from his horse and died. (Whether death caused the fall or the fall caused death was never determined.) The body was brought to Abinger Hall and laid out in Effie and Theta's drawing room while an inquest was held and a parade of dignitaries, including Prime Minister W. E. Gladstone, came to pay their respects. It all made a good tale for the Darwins' visit, and certainly no one present was vindictive enough to take pleasure at the death. Not quite the same can be said for T. H. Huxley. If not actually pleased by Wilberforce's death, Huxley at least would not miss him. He wrote to a colleague: "Poor dear Sammy! His end has been all too tragic for his life. For once, reality & his brains came into contact & the result was fatal."[11]

Huxley's own life, if not near its end, was more than a little sad that winter and spring of 1873. Exhausted, dyspeptic, overworked, short of money, and probably drinking too much, Huxley was in rocky shape when his scientific friends decided to club together and collect enough money to send him, as his doctor had advised, on a recuperative holiday. Everyone chipped in—Charles and Emma gave £300 and Ras Darwin added another £100—and in the end eighteen donors had put together the rather magnificent sum of £2,100, more than two years' salary for Huxley. Now the problem was getting their proud friend to accept the gift. Darwin was elected to tell Huxley about it, and in late April Emma wrote to Henrietta that the offer had been made: "F. sent off the awful letter to H. & I hope we may hear tomorrow. It will be v. awful."[12]

Happily for all concerned, it turned out not to be awful at all. Somewhat to the donors' surprise, Huxley graciously wrote to Darwin:

> I accept the splendid gift. . . . I have for months been without energy & without hope & haunted by the constant presence of hypochondriacal apprehensions which my reason told me were absurd but which I cd not get rid of—for I was breaking down. . . . I have poured out all this Jeremiad that you may understand what your . . . great gift will do for me. . . . I shall keep [your letter] for my children that their children may know what manner of man their father's friend was & why he loved him.

Accompanied by Hooker, Huxley set out in early July for a walking holiday in the Alps.[13]

Throughout 1873 the junior Darwins' adult lives continued to come into focus. William, steady as always, plugged away at the Southampton and Hampshire Bank in Southampton. Whether or not he was still pining for a certain Scotch girl is unknown. Henrietta and Richard were now happily settled at 4 Bryanston Square in Marylebone, an easy walk to Regent's Park and Hyde Park, as well as to Emma and Charles's old neighborhood of Upper Gower Street. (The Litchfields' house quickly became a second "safe haven" in London for the dyspeptic Darwin to visit, Ras's place being the original. "Very pleasant," noted Darwin in his personal journal after his first stay with Hen and Richard. Emma, of course, immediately voiced her preference for Bryanston Square because staying there gave her maximum visiting time with Henrietta.) Bessy Darwin was still living at home in 1873 and would do so until her parents were both gone, and Leonard was well into his army career, having joined the Royal Engineers in 1870 after finishing at Woolwich.[14]

Only George, Frank, and Horace remained unsure about their futures. Since taking his B.A. in 1868, George had found it difficult to make a final career decision. Between 1869 and 1873 he read law with a variety of tutors in preparation for a career as a barrister. Poor health, as well as a growing realization that he was more interested in science, slowed his progress, however. A chip off the old Darwin block, George was a "highly-strung nervous man, easily upset and worried, a bad sleeper and very thin." After a sharp decline in health in 1871–72, George sought relief first at Malvern and later in the sun and sea air of Cannes, but with little lasting benefit from either place. In the spring of 1873, his continuing digestive troubles and general discomfort drove George to consult Huxley's London physician, Andrew Clark. It was a good move. Under Clark's care, George's health began to improve—positive results that almost certainly led Emma to call for Clark when Darwin himself had a sort of "fit" that August that resulted in a temporary loss of memory. The episode was distinctly frightening for all concerned. "I would far sooner die than lose my mind," Charles told Hooker. Happily, he bounced back quickly, and Clark was sure that no permanent brain damage had been done. Bessy expressed the wish that Dr. Clark had told her father to work less, but Clark was a workaholic himself. He prescribed a new diet for Darwin and then tried to leave without accepting a fee. Knowing that if Clark were not paid, Charles would be reluctant to consult him again, the family finally prevailed on the doctor to accept payment for services rendered.[15]

Returning to George, by the fall of 1873 he had definitely decided in favor of a scientific and academic life, and accordingly took rooms in Trinity College, Cambridge, where he was a fellow. At about this time he began to try his hand at writing for publication, producing among other things a lighthearted piece for *Macmillan's Magazine* on the evolution of dress. A later essay on the evolutionary origins of morals was much less humorous and more controversial. Both Charles and Henrietta urged George to reconsider the paper before sending it off to a journal, and since the essay exists today only in manuscript form, its author may have had second thoughts himself. Hen also sent a long list of editorial suggestions, which may have dampened George's enthusiasm for revising the morals paper. "[C]riticising style to me is like the trumpet to a warhorse," she warned her brother. Her father already knew this.[16]

The middle son, Frank, was still studying medicine at Cambridge in 1873, but as with George, basic science—in this case botany—exerted a stronger pull. After finally earning his M.B. degree, by 1875 Frank would be back in Downe doing research with his father. Horace, the youngest, was still at Cambridge working steadily toward a mathematics degree and would receive his B.A. in 1874. His health remained somewhat delicate, but this in no way dampened Horace's zeal for mechanics and experimentation. He was also beginning to show the genius for invention that would distinguish his career and ultimately earn him a knighthood.[17]

In Downe village's ecclesiastical affairs, 1873 marked the beginning of open feuding between the Darwins and the Reverend George Sketchley Ffinden, vicar of St. Mary's. Two years earlier Brodie Innes, acting now in the capacity of patron of the Downe living, had formally approved Ffinden's appointment, but even then his private appraisal of the new vicar had been distinctly mixed: "Though I heard all good of Mr. Ffinden's moral character," Innes wrote to Darwin, "his clerical ability was not stated as very high." In retrospect, these words were a portent of hard times in the parish, though whether the troubles were due more to flawed "clerical abilities" or to Ffinden's oversized ego is hard to determine from the record.[18]

Ffinden was a High Church Tory cut in the mold of Samuel Wilberforce, who in fact had ordained him back in 1861. Despite differing strongly on liturgical styles—the Darwins were distinctly Low Church Anglicans—Emma and Charles made an honest effort to welcome the new vicar and his wife. The Ffindens appear to have been invited to tea at Down House just weeks after their arrival in the village, and then were dinner guests on two occasions, in January and September 1872; if these meals were ever reciprocated, Emma's diary does not show it. Emma also called on Mrs. Ffinden at home in November 1872. These social niceties were very much in keeping with the Darwins' position as one of the prominent families in Downe, and with Charles's membership on the supervisory committee for the local National (nondenominational) day school. Emma, and possibly Bessy, continued to attend church throughout 1872, and the Darwins made a handsome contribution to the church coffers of £50 (more than $4,000 today), but trouble was brewing.[19]

By early 1873 Mr. Ffinden was being referred to in private Darwin family letters as "the Ffiend," and around the village a good number of parishioners were voicing complaints about their "wretched clergyman." People were also slashing their contributions to the church budget left and right: the Darwins dropped from £50 in 1872 to £10 a year later, and in absentia Innes himself dropped from £60 to £25. One parishioner, Mr. Wallis Nash, complained that Ffinden was "so tremendously *high* about the Sacrament that he [Nash] meant to appeal to the Arch[bishop]." Such an appeal up the Church hierarchy was not for Emma, despite her increasing displeasure with Ffinden. When asked to sign a petition to the archbishop of Canterbury, she declined, explaining in a letter to Horace: "I should have a bad life of it if I memorialised the Arch[bishop] every time I disagreed w. a sermon. If a man is High Church he must preach according & [Ffinden preaches] just the sort of sermon we used to have constantly from Mr Innes & we were none the worse."[20]

It's unclear whether Nash's outrage was ever expressed to the archbishop, and some parishioners like Mrs. Evans, the Darwins' cook, were simply amused by the vicar's antics. But for some reason—falling attendance and contributions, perhaps?—by the autumn of 1873 Ffinden had backed off his High Church style a bit. As Emma apprised Hen,

> some of the servants report that Mr. Ff. has softened off matters, has left off intoning, so that the only change is singing the Psalms & his kneeling in the aisle w. his back to us [while] saying the Litany. I am sure the village will feel quite flat at his having subsided so soon—indeed Mrs. Evans said as much e.g. that she was going to church but was afraid she was too late to see the fun.[21]

The vicar may have been willing to tone down Sunday services a bit to keep his congregation happy, but he dug in his heels over the village day school. Long before Ffinden's arrival, a National school had been established in Downe for the education of the poor children of the parish. Administered by a small committee of village dignitaries that included John Lubbock and Darwin and was chaired by the current parish priest, the school was largely nondenominational and operated under a "conscience clause" that protected dissenters from Anglican indoctrination. Ffinden set out to change all that, and he began by adding High Church teachings and the daily recitation of the Thirty-nine Articles to the curriculum. As the chairman of the school committee and the local champion of revealed religion, Ffinden was determined to flex his muscles.[22]

Darwin stuck it out on the school committee for a while despite the vicar's high-handedness, but in late 1873 Ffinden took a stand that triggered a showdown between the two men. The Darwins, Lubbocks, and several others had petitioned the school committee to continue using the classroom as an evening Reading Room for villagers. As in the past, they proposed to provide a "respectable newspaper & a few books," with "a respectable householder . . . there every evening to maintain decorum" and a "woman . . . employed every morning to air & clean the room & put it in order before school opened." These provisions notwithstanding, Ffinden and his allies objected to the plan, arguing that past Reading Room patrons had used the space mainly as a venue for low habits like gambling, drinking, and smoking. Since "the effects of tobacco smoke & spitting" were all too evident when the children came to school next day, Ffinden claimed, it was a clear "perversion of the building." Nonsense, grumbled the petitioners; most of "the children must be . . . well accustomed" to tobacco smoke at home. Eventually Darwin went over Ffinden's head and wrote privately to the Education inspectorate in London asking for approval of the Reading Room. Ffinden was predictably outraged—and doubly outraged when the Education Department gave its permission. Left with no choice in the matter, the vicar wrote a curt note to Emma, grudgingly notifying her that the Reading Room would be allowed, but indicating his extreme annoyance at Charles's action: "As I am the only recognized correspondent of the School, according to rule 15, Code 1871, I deem such a proceeding quite quite out of order." The Darwins had won, but at a cost. There were bad feelings on both sides, and when Ffinden became publicly rude, cutting the Darwins dead when he passed them in the street, Charles resigned from the school committee and Emma moved her church-going to nearby Keston.[23]

Thank goodness there were other things, happier things, going on at Down House that fall. Everyone was excited because there was soon to be another family wedding. To the delight of the entire family, Frank Darwin had proposed to Amy Ruck and been accepted. Frank's new plan—besides taking a wife—was to live in Downe and work as his father's scientific assistant and secretary. Being relatively far along in his medical studies, he intended to complete his M.B. degree, but like his uncle Ras, Frank had no real desire to practice medicine. The Darwins were thrilled at the thought of having Frank nearby; Charles certainly knew he could use his son's help. The Rucks, for their part, were split on the issue. Amy's mother worried about what it might mean for her daughter's future lifestyle. Lawrence Ruck, however, understood that Frank was better suited for a laboratory than a surgery, and so he approved of the plan. A hasty trip by Frank to Pantlludw apparently reassured his prospective mother-in-law.[24]

The engaged couple scoured the village and found, to their surprise, that a perfectly acceptable house, Down Lodge, was available just up the road from the senior Darwins. The owner, Mr. Allen, was asking an annual rent of £160, but there were two cottages and twenty-three acres of pasture on the property to be sublet, and this would reduce Frank and Amy's outlay by some £40 per annum. Mrs. Ruck took a look at the house and liked what she saw, and although Mr. Allen was none too pleased that the young couple didn't want to buy the Lodge furniture as part of a package deal, this didn't stop the rental from going through. A country girl, soft-spoken and slender (although too thin to suit Emma), Amy was quite happy at the thought of living in Downe rather than London. Emma reported to Horace, with an almost audible sigh of relief, "I quite believe she likes to be near us, which is not the case w. all daughters in law."[25]

On July 23, 1874, Amy and Frank were married in London. The venue was All Souls Church, Langham, a location convenient for friends and relations on both sides, and a choice that thumbed its nose at that "ffiend" Ffinden. Characteristically, Charles didn't make it to the ceremony, but the other three parents were there along with a host of lesser kinfolks. Emma described the big day to Leonard, who was on an army assignment in New Zealand:

> I hope no body will have told you about the wedding. Bessy & I started at 8 a.m. on a lovely mg. Poor old G[eorge] did not feel up to going, which was a disappt to him. We got first to [Ras's] & found Frank in his workaday clothes & rushing about full of care, but what he was doing we did not know. Wm was there all prepared in his wedding trowsers. . . . Ten minutes to the time we walked across to Langham church & just caught a glimpse of Amy running up the steps in her cloak over her gown. They were lodging at Cav[endish] St close by, so she & Mrs R walked over. She looked m. shaken & agitated before the wedding; but after it was over as calm & comf. as poss. eating her own wedding cake, when we assembled at the lodging. She was in a white muslin & bonnet w. some of our Stephanotis in it. . . . We had a cheerful assembly at the lodging chiefly occupied in looking at Amy's beautiful jewelry, which wd rival Lady L[ubbock's] if she put it on all at once in Lady L's fashion. . . . The clergy[man] did the service nice & short.[26]

After eating their share of wedding cake, the newlyweds left for a honeymoon on the Continent, not returning until early September. Not surprisingly, the trip agreed with them both and Amy gained a little weight, which pleased her mother-in-law. Once back in Downe, they immediately began redecorating Down Lodge to their taste, among other things changing the drawing room wallpaper to a new pattern purchased from William Morris in London. Always one to worry about money and still reeling from wedding costs exceeding £1,100 ($92,000), Darwin had to be shielded from the fact that Amy and Frank had made their wallpaper selection "without asking the price." He was going to have to get used to having another daughter, perhaps one who had expensive tastes. And how did one treat a daughter-in-law, anyway? Following Bessy's and Emma's advice, Charles welcomed Amy back from the honeymoon with a kiss, but being a good Victorian, he was horrified "at taking such a liberty."[27]

Lieutenant Leonard Darwin was among the few family members who missed Frank and Amy's wedding. His absence was unavoidable, since he was sailing to New Zealand on official business when the wedding bells rang out at All Souls. Detached from his regular army duties to photograph an upcoming astronomical event, the transit of Venus, Lenny was headed to a site near Christchurch to join a team headed by Major Henry Spencer Palmer, a brother officer in the Royal Engineers. Clear photographs of the transit from several geographic locations were needed to calculate the earth-sun distance and, ultimately, the size of the solar system (done by combining the phenomenon of parallax with the laws of planetary motion and a bit of trigonometry). Lenny hoped to shoot as many as 190 photos with a photoheliograph during the approximately six-hour passage of Venus across the face of the sun.[28]

Of all the Darwin children, Lenny was by far the most engaging and amusing correspondent, a fortunate happenstance since he also turned out to be the greatest globe-trotter. His letters from New Zealand to his mother (who wrote back that she missed his "whistle . . . about the house") contain several memorable comments:

[August 1874, on board the emigrant ship *Merope*] It is of no use putting a heading of any sort as I have no notion where this will be posted. . . . As it had been raining all Friday, I got my first and last view of Plymouth Harbour at the same time . . . [then] I went down to my cabin, and spent an hour in making all snug for the first few days of expected misery. . . . [Happily,] my own stomach . . . never came to an actual crisis but it makes me very bilious and uncomfortable. I think I ought to be very contented with my state in comparison with the wretchedness of the others. . . . Many of the passengers cant sleep at night when it has been rolling but I have managed it as yet by turning up the mattress on each side and pushing in between it and the sides of the bunk two rugs and about four complete suits of clothes. This leaves only just room for me to lie so that I can't move about at all, and I wake up in the morning feeling rather stiff and uncomfortable.

[October 2–13, Burnham, NZ] I think I brought my last letter up to our first Sunday at Christchurch. Since then we have been flying all over the country seeing places for our observatory. . . . We decided to go to Burnham a place 18 miles from Christchurch on a line of Railway leading to the south. The place consists of two or three cottages, an accommodation house or small public [house], and a reformatory, of which the government has given us a wing to live in, so that we shall be able to make ourselves very comfortable. . . . Your letter about the marriage has come, but I had heard some of the details before, including a bit of cake from Retta, which arrived safely—a little flat but quite as good as new. . . . All most every one here is a sheep farmer except for a few clergymen, and the talk is awfully sheepy at times, though I should think as a set they were greatly in advance of the country gentlemen class in England.

[November 10, Burnham, NZ] We have been sticking to work pretty hard since last mail, I dont think I have even been into Christchurch. . . . I feel a little more easy about the photography as we have already had some good photos, but what I am afraid of is the weather. It is either cloudy or else blowing very hard with a clear sky—the wind coming right in the direction which we want to look at the sun, and it is almost sure to shake the instruments. We have all got horses as the only decent means of getting exercise; at least I have only tried one or two horses and can't get one yet that suits. The one I am trying now is said to be given to "pig leaping" which I believe means a mild sort of buck jumping; I don't think he is likely to suit as I am sure a "pig jump" would finish me.[29]

As he had feared, Lenny's hard work was negated by foul weather on December 9, the day of the transit. Clouds and rain obscured the observers' visibility for major portions of the event, rendering it impossible to make many useful measurements or photographs. A disappointed Lenny wrote home to his mother: "I managed to get about a dozen weak photographs; they were very poor as the light was so bad. . . . it was next day that I felt most aggravated by our bad luck, as it was a glorious day."[30]

After all of the transit-tracking equipment had been packed for shipment and the Burnham team officially disbanded, Lenny headed home via Hawaii and the United States, thus becoming the second Darwin to make a complete trip around the globe. Emma wrote ahead to the Eliot Nortons in Boston alerting them to the date when Lenny would be passing through and thus ensuring that he had a friendly face in at least one foreign port.[31]

While Lenny was busy trying to photograph the transit, family activities continued in various pleasant ways back in Downe. Frank and Amy carried on through the fall of 1874 redecorating Down Lodge; "they *say* they have not yet impinged on their fourth hundred [pounds]," Emma wrote to Lenny. And in October, William and Horace made a brief hunting trip to Scotland with the Balfour family. Arthur Balfour, who would later be prime minister and was then a member of Parliament from Hertford, "took us out deer stalking," reported William; "it is most exciting work, & by riding ponies to & from the forest not very hard work."[32]

There was trouble brewing, however, and St. George Jackson Mivart was once again about to intrude on the tranquility of Down House in a most annoying way. The preceding summer, George Darwin had published a short essay titled "On Beneficial Restrictions to Liberty of Marriage." In this paper George had argued that society would benefit from certain reforms to the laws governing marriage and divorce. These reforms included allowing spouses to divorce without prejudice if either showed evidence of "certain diseases," especially insanity; the establishment of medical examinations for these same diseases; and the requirement that engaged couples produce "untainted [health] pedigree[s]" before they were allowed to marry. No sooner had George's paper been published than Mivart blasted it and its author in an anonymous piece in the *Quarterly Review*. "Mr. George Darwin" was part of a "constant attack" on the institution of marriage and advocated views that justified "unrestrained licentiousness," Mivart charged. "There is no hideous sexual criminality of Pagan days that might not be defended on the principles advocated by the school to which this writer belongs," Mivart wrote in disgust. Understandably, the Darwins and their friends were infuriated by these slurs. George wrote a letter to the next issue of the *Quarterly* denying the charges, Charles considered a lawsuit, and Huxley promptly severed all remaining connections with Mivart and helped blackball his bid to join the Athenaeum.[33]

It is worth noting in passing that Mivart also published a second anti-Darwinian volume in 1874 titled *Man and Apes*. In this slim volume he argued that, despite considerable anatomical similarities, the living apes were not connected to humans by any process of natural evolution. This was shown, according to Mivart, by the fact that humans possess an "informing rational soul" and apes do not. All of this was old hat, of course, very much along the lines of *On the Genesis of Species,* and hardly raised an eyebrow at Down House. The slurs against George, however, were a very different matter.[34]

To square with the title of this chapter, a fourth death needs to be mentioned. In March 1874, while Frank and Amy were still in the planning stages of their happy marriage, a most unhappy one ended with the horrific death of Fanny Frank. During a holiday on the Channel Island of Guernsey, Fanny fell while carrying a lighted candle down an inn's dark corridor and set her dress on fire. She suffered severe burns on her legs and torso, and died after eight days of agony. Frank Wedgwood, never a particularly attentive husband even at the best of times, "refused to believe that her condition was critical" and didn't bother to summon the family. Some of their six children might have made it to Fanny's deathbed, but none had the chance.[35]

Fanny Frank had long been a soul in torment and her marriage a disaster. In the forty-two years since her wedding to Frank, Fanny had become "lonely, fat, embittered and bored," and regularly sought escape through drink. By

1859 her torment had reached such a peak that she suffered a nervous break-down—an illness that was utterly denied by Frank—and a decade later, hus-band and wife were living "virtually separate lives," with Frank being suffi-ciently bitter to denigrate Fanny to their son Godfrey with these words:

> Your mother has come back persuaded by her new doctor (or perhaps more likely having persuaded him) that she is too weak to take her walking exercise so she is to take carriage (exercise!) and drink plenty of wine.[36]

Even Emma thought Fanny Frank had become "unbearable" in the years just before her death. In her view, Frank and Fanny's impulsive marriage had been a mistake from the start: "Look at Uncle Frank as a warning," she had told William. And now it was over. Fanny Frank had been released from her troubles in a most terrible way. The extent to which this poor drunken sister-in-law had become estranged from the family circle is shown by the fact that Emma made no mention of the death in her daily diary.[37]

17. An Irreparable Loss

BRITAIN WAS AT OR NEAR its peak as a colonial and trading power as it entered the last quarter of the nineteenth century. In 1875 the sun really did not set on Victoria's empire, and British exports of manufactured goods accounted for more than one-third of the world's total. The rate of industrial growth in Britain had been declining slowly for years, but the United Kingdom's power and influence were still enormous.[1] In the thirty-eighth year of her reign, Queen Victoria was a mature monarch but a lonely one, still dressing in mourning for her beloved Albert, dead fourteen years before. Benjamin Disraeli was in his second term as prime minister, having once again "climbed to the top of the greasy [political] pole" in 1874. This suited the queen, who strongly preferred Disraeli to his Liberal predecessor, W. E. Gladstone. Militarily speaking, there was not much going on. The brief Ashanti War had been successfully wrapped up in 1874 by General Garnet Wolseley, whose grateful nation awarded him £25,000 and knighted him twice over. That victory set the stage for a half decade of relatively small-scale "punitive excursions, field forces and . . . expeditions" overseas. And at home the prosperous times were marked by the successful opening of the first operetta by William Gilbert and Arthur Sullivan, *Trial by Jury*, and the founding of the Regent Street retail outlet Liberty of London.[2]

At Down House, Charles and Emma were both sitting for the painter

Walter Ouless. Charles's portrait was turning out to be melancholy and Emma thought hers showed "a most morose old lady," but they both found Mr. Ouless a pleasant fellow, so they put up with the process. Charles's health, always subject to ups and downs, was generally up—as it was for most of the last decade of his life—and he was still working away on insectivorous and climbing plants. At neighboring Down Lodge, Amy and Frank were billing and cooing, and she would be pregnant before the end of the year. Frank was working out satisfactorily as his father's assistant, although Charles did wish that Frank could somehow go faster with his scientific research. He rarely seemed to make much real progress, but still he did work "like a Turk," and that was something.[3]

Sadly, the year picked up where 1874 had left off, with three deaths of family members or friends before mid-May. On February 9, 1875, Arthur Vaughan Williams died after a brief but violent illness. The death left Margaret, née Wedgwood, a widow at thirty-two and her three young children fatherless; Ralph Vaughan Williams was only twenty-eight months old when his father died. Margaret very sensibly gathered up the children and moved in with her parents, Caroline and Joe, at Leith Hill Place. Not long afterwards, Emma visited Leith Hill and, willing herself to see beauty at even the worst of times, thought Margaret looked "very pretty in her widow's cap."[4]

Two weeks after Arthur Vaughan Williams's death, a bigger fish, at least in the eyes of the world, passed away: Sir Charles Lyell died at the age of seventy-seven "without m. suffering," Emma reported to Leonard. Lyell's own family had been dwindling for years: he lost one brother in 1871, a second just two weeks before his own death, and Mary, his wife of forty years, in 1873. They had no children. "Life was done" for the poor old man, wrote Emma, "& one cd not wish him to live." Although Lyell had been failing for some time and his death was not unexpected, an overly officious coroner insisted on an inquest, apparently to determine whether death had been hastened by a fall down stairs a few weeks earlier. "As nobody knocked [Sir Charles] down it was most meddling," remarked Emma, expressing the general feeling of indignation. Hooker especially was affected by the death. He wrote to Darwin: "I feel Lyell's loss most keenly, he was father and brother to me; and except yourself, no one took that lively, generous, hearty, deep, and warm interest in my welfare that he did." Lyell was laid to rest in the nave of Westminster Abbey, with Bessy, Frank, and Amy representing the Darwin family. Charles was asked to be one of the pallbearers, but he declined, saying it was likely he would become giddy and "fail in the midst of the ceremony." As usual, Darwin was at home when his old friend was laid to rest. Lyell's tomb was marked by a stone praising his efforts at "deciphering the fragmentary records of the earth's history . . . [and] enlarging the boundaries of knowledge."[5]

The third death was that of Emma's beloved aunt Fanny Allen on May 6. At ninety-four years of age, Aunt Fanny was ready to go to her rest and she wanted to do it privately. Thus, when she was stricken by illness around May Day, she simply holed up and told no one except a trusted neighbor, whom she swore to secrecy. Emma understood this readiness to die and honored it, saying her aunt would "have been dreadfully disappointed if she had recovered." In notes received posthumously, Fanny Allen sent the family her love and begged them not to grieve too much in light of her great longevity. With Aunt Fanny's passing, the entire generation that preceded Emma and Charles's had now vanished.[6]

Halfway around the world, Leonard Darwin was quite alive and enjoying himself exploring New Zealand before starting his homeward voyage. On the North Island, Leo (as Emma now addressed him) got a good look at New Zealand's native people, the Maoris. He judged them to be "curious looking . . . savages" but, interestingly, savages who "dressed in European fashion." One group of Maoris out horseback riding included a man judged by Leo to be "the chief" who dressed in "top boots, a tall hat and dark coat," and also brightly dressed women smoking "short black [pipes] in their bright blue lips." Leo thought the tattooed lips and pipes rather spoiled the effect of the women's costumes, and he was taken aback by their scant "sense of decency" when they casually walked too near—that is, near enough to embarrass Leo—while the Englishmen were bathing in public.[7]

From Auckland, Leo sailed for San Francisco aboard the *Mikaro*. The ship was overcrowded, and Leo had to "sleep on the seats round the saloon," but he reassured his mother that this arrangement was not too bad, since the saloon was "cool and well ventilated." Measles among the passengers kept the ship from calling at Honolulu, which disappointingly prevented Leo from meeting the local king, a man reported to be a great admirer of Darwin's books. On April 11 the *Mikaro* docked in San Francisco, disembarking Leo—"fatter and balder than ever," he confessed to Horace, and sporting "a scrubby brown beard 3.1415962 inches long or there abouts"—into a city that he found filled with people obsessed with "the almighty dollar." Emma answered her son's San Francisco letters with a bit of home news: His cousin Rowland Wedgwood, Harry and Jessie's youngest son, had been charged with breach of promise and come close to a trial. At the last minute Rowland had settled out of court for £800 (some $67,000 today), an amount that Emma thought was well worth it "to avoid publicity." Rowland's jilted lover offered to shake hands and promised she would give the money to hospitals, but Harry allowed that he would "not give much chance" of her philanthropy.[8]

Leo found the railroad trip across the United States agreeable in all particulars with the exception of the "imperfect" American sleeping car system. "Twice I had to sleep in the berth above a lady . . . [which] I do not think is a nice idea," he told his mother. But adopting a when-in-Rome attitude, Leo put up with this indelicate arrangement, noting that, "as there was really nothing unpleasant about it and as the ladies in question did not mind, it did not affect me." After stops in Washington, Philadelphia, and New York, Leo arrived in Boston, where he visited briefly with the Asa Grays and then was feted thoroughly by the C. E. Nortons. Then it was back to New York for a June 9 departure on the Cunard ship *Abyssinia* for the Atlantic crossing. He rejoined the family on June 20 at Abinger, where the Darwins were enjoying a month's vacation courtesy of the Farrers. After a year away and a trip around the world, Lieutenant Darwin was back on English soil.[9]

He wasn't there long. In early September the Royal Engineers assigned Leo to the garrison on Malta. His job, he wrote home, was basic engineering duty beginning with "district work," that is, "looking after . . . little repairs [and] alterations . . . in the fortifications." It was a quiet peacetime assignment in an out-of-the-way post. Leo shared a spacious rental house with three other RE lieutenants and, when not on duty, enjoyed sea bathing and lounging around the Officers' Club. True, he did have to go to church occasionally—each Sunday's duty officer had to march the men to church—but *only* occasionally, he was "thankful to say." And Leo did see some "military action" while on Malta, if one doesn't mind stretching the definition a bit. One day while "leading a file of men down a narrow high-walled lane," Lieutenant Darwin found himself face to face with an infuriated cow. Thinking quickly, he gave the order to about-face and retreat.[10]

Emma was thrilled that Leo was no longer "at the Antipodes" and kept him fully informed on all family news. Horace, she wrote, had been sent to "work at the pumping engines [being erected] at Brighton" as part of his apprenticeship with the engineering firm of Easton and Anderson. Horace had almost no real part in the construction, but he enjoyed being a paid observer and riding his "gigantic bicycle" between his lodgings and the work site. (This was probably a "penny-farthing bicycle" with an enormous wheel in front and a small one in the back. Later, Horace enjoyed telling the story of a fall he took over the bike's high front wheel, saying it "was a remarkable sensation" to have so much time in the air "in which to realize that a smash was inevitable.") Even at this early date, Horace's genius at invention was becoming clear, and he was justifiably pleased when Mr. Anderson put in an order for several of his "self adjusting nipper[s] for screwing nuts."[11]

In November 1875 Emma reported to Leo that his father had been called to testify in front of the Vivisection Commission. The pros and cons of vivisection were very much in the news in the mid-1870s, and strong feelings existed on both sides of the question. On the one hand there was the problem of cruelty to animals, on the other the medical and scientific benefits to be gained from experiments on living creatures. Both of the senior Darwins were strongly opposed to any sort of cruelty, of course, as shown by their campaign years earlier to eliminate steel traps. Thus they were much in favor of ensuring that experiments on animals be done only after the subject had been rendered "insensible" by anesthesia. Henrietta favored a harder line, and supported the efforts of Frances Power Cobbe to get Parliament to pass laws severely restricting experimentation on animals. But when Hen approached her father in January 1875 and asked him to sign Miss Cobbe's petition, Darwin refused, arguing that to do so would cause the study of physiology to "languish or quite cease" in England, an outcome that would hamper scientific progress.[12]

Despite the misgivings of Darwin and other scientists, Miss Cobbe and her supporters were able to bring forward an antivivisection bill for Parliament's consideration. In response, the pro-vivisectionists introduced their own blocking bill into the legislative pipeline. The upshot was the formation of a royal commission, headed by Viscount Cardwell and including Huxley as a commissioner, to thoroughly investigate the issue.[13] It was before this commission that Charles was called to testify. Emma described the event to Leo:

> F. went to the Vivi[section] Commission at 2. Lord Cardwell came to the door to receive him & he was treated like a Duke. They only wanted him to repeat what he had said in his letter (a sort of confession of faith about the claims of physiology & the duty of humanity) & he had hardly a word more to add, so that it was over in 10 m[inutes]. Lord C. coming to the door again & thanking him. It was a great compliment to his opinion wanting to have it put upon the minutes.[14]

In early December Emma sent Leo the sad news that his cousin Edmund Langton, the only child of Charlotte and Charles Langton, had died at the age of thirty-four, leaving his wife Lena with four children. The death was no surprise, but still it was devastating for his father, who had lost his Christian faith years before and thus found no solace in religion, and for his devoted aunt Elizabeth Wedgwood. The same letter also contained some happy news, namely that Darwin had been elected "a foreign associate of the Royal Academy of Sciences at Rome"—actually, the Accademia Nazionale Reale dei Lincei, the Royal National Academy of Lynxes (or the Lynx-Eyed), founded in 1603, revived by Pope Pius IX in 1847, and boasting Galileo as an early member. Charles's selection had been done right "under [Pius IX's] very nose." Emma, reflecting her long-standing negativity toward all things papist, noted mischievously, "Only think of the Pope's feelings."[15]

In January of 1876, George traveled to Malta for a visit with his brother. He arrived suffering the aftereffects of seasickness, but well enough to join Leo in the Maltese version of Mardi Gras, complete with a "fancy dress ball at the Palace" and street parades with costumed marchers throwing sugarplums. In March, Leo got a fortnight's leave and the brothers traveled to Sicily (more seasickness for George), where they got a good look at then-peaceful Mount Etna before going on to Naples. Their reports of foul weather in Naples reminded Emma of her own Neapolitan explorations fifty years before. "I remember I quite disliked the dull grey promontory of Pausilipo like a slug crawling into the sea," she wrote. From Naples, Leo traveled back to Malta. George headed for home, one suspects by rail.[16]

Shortly after George's return to England there was a dramatic, if largely symbolic, change of titles for the queen. Victoria took advantage of Disraeli's incumbency as prime minister to press her desire, which had been growing for some time, to be named empress of India. How would it look, argued the queen, if her daughter Vicky—married to Frederick, crown prince of Germany, and thus in line to become an empress herself when her father-in-law the emperor (Kaiser) Wilhelm gave up his throne—gained titular precedence over her own mother? Would it not diminish the dignity of the British Crown? Although much less concerned about such questions than the queen, Disraeli listened with a sympathetic ear because he saw considerable value in an act of "imperialism of [a] grand stroke designed to impress politicians and public alike." After all, the Russians were flexing their muscles in the regions northwest of India, and perhaps it was a good time to "emphasize and consolidate the British dominance of the [Indian] subcontinent" by bestowing an imperial title.[17]

Whether to please his queen or to cause ripples on the international stage (or both), Disraeli brought the Royal Titles Act before Parliament in the spring of 1876. But because he arrogantly made no attempt to reach a deal with the opposition party, Disraeli found it rough work getting the bill through. There could be no "more grand title than Queen of England," the critics argued. Gladstone so strongly opposed the act that he got carried away with "the violence of [his] reaction" and probably harmed rather than helped his cause. "Unprincipled maniac," muttered Disraeli.[18] At Down House, Emma's main reaction to the Titles Act and the behavior of her queen and the politicians was shoulder-shrugging amusement, albeit with a Liberal pro-Gladstone tilt. She wrote to Leo: "Every body seems in a fury with the Queen doing so snobbish a thing as taking the title of Empress. Some of Dizzy's speeches on the subject are so indiscreet & silly that I think he must have lowered himself very much."[19]

Disraeli's silly speeches and Gladstone's offensively violent opposition notwithstanding, the Royal Titles Act passed into law, and in April the queen issued her royal proclamation:

> Victoria, R.
> Whereas an Act has been passed in the present Session of Parliament . . . [enabling] an Addition to the Royal Style and Titles . . . [in] recognition . . . of the transfer of the government of India . . . we have thought fit, by and with the advice of our Privy Council to appoint and declare and we do hereby, by and with the said advice, appoint and declare that henceforth, so far as conveniently may be, on all occasions and in all instruments wherein our style and titles are used . . . the following addition shall be made to the style and titles at present appertaining to the Imperial Crown of the United Kingdom and its Dependencies: that is to say, in the Latin tongue in these words: "Indiae Imperatrix," and in the English tongue in these words: "Empress of India."
>
> . . .
>
> Given at our Court, at Windsor, the 28th day of April, 1876, in the 39th year of our reign.
> God save the Queen.[20]

The next January, a grand durbar was held in Delhi in honor of India's new empress. Lord Lytton, the viceroy of India, stood in for Victoria, who was celebrating at home by wearing "masses" of Indian jewelry, including the fabulous Star of India sapphire, to a New Year's dinner party. It is said that at the durbar a representative of the Poona Sarvajanik Sabha, a provincial political association, read a polite statement begging the empress "to grant to India the same political and social status as is enjoyed by her British subjects." Although hardly recognized as such at the time, it was an early step on the road to India's independence.[21]

On April 28, 1876, the day when it pleased the queen to become empress of India, Amy Ruck Darwin was just over halfway through her first pregnancy. The baby she was carrying was large, and Amy was quite visibly "with child," a fact that had not escaped her sister-in-law Henrietta, still childless after nearly five years of marriage. During a visit to Down House in March, Hen and Richard had joined the Frank Darwins and Mrs. Ruck for a dinner party. On returning to Bryanston Square, Hen wrote a moving thank-you note to her mother, touching lightly on the subject of her probable barrenness:

> Good bye dear Mother. We have both enjoyed our stay so much at Down— & it is such a delight to me that you like R[ichard] & make him so tame there. It is such a happiness to me to have two homes—& I feel as long as I have Father & you it does instead of our having children & makes our lives quite full, for you are the dearest Father & Mother that ever anyone had.

Whether or not Henrietta's childlessness was related to the mercury-based medications of her youth, as we have suggested, must remain speculation. But she would go on to become a most memorable aunt, as described years later by her devoted niece Gwen Raverat.[22]

By late August "Amy's size [was] something portentous" and everyone was anxiously awaiting "news of the Event." Floating suggestions for the baby's name became a favorite family activity, and Henrietta wrote to George saying, "I want it to be christened Erasmus or Susan as the case may be. I'm so sick of Mauds & Ethels & Ediths etc. A good old name like Susan wd be v. refreshing."[23] One hopes that George had forgotten this letter by the time he married Maud Du Puy some years later.

Amy's labor began on September sixth. Emma described the entire affair to Hen in a letter written the next day:

> I had forgotten what a horrid thing confining was. Yesterday morning at 8 we heard that Dr. Willey had been sent for. I went over about 10.30 to see what progress, & found Amy walking about & coming down to breakfast. She looked shaken & ill poor soul, but ready to talk about other things. Dr. W. came about 11.30 & said it wd be a long affair but that every thing was quite right—so it went on all day. I backwards & forwards. Poor Dr. W. made an

attempt to go away & come again, but the nurse took a high hand & wd not hear of it. I was going over for the 4th time about 8 when I met Frank coming about chloroform, of which they gave her little whiff, to her immense comfort. She suffered most stoically & never made a sound. I came away at 10 & we went to bed having left orders to be informed when it happened. F[ather] & I woke about 12.30 & began to get more & more uneasy at not hearing. . . . [At half past three, William came] to say it was over & a boy but what gave us a fright was to hear that he had fetched Mr. Hughes.

I went over early this mg. & found Mrs. Ruck writing telegrams as fresh as possible. She told me she thought every thing was q[uite] right till 11, when Dr. W. said he wanted to send for his instruments; that there was no progress making & they should have to resort to it at last when she was more exhausted. Mrs. R. came over to our kitchen where Wm was sitting up & sent him off & was charmed w. his willingness & activity.

Every thing quite prosperous.

Mr. Hughes came too, & I am so sorry they did not have him instead, Mrs. R. says he was such a support & was a man of power, & Dr. W. is only nice & gentle (to be sure he is Welch & they talked Welch together). He agreed w. Dr. Ws opinion & the child was soon brought into the world with a great cry.

The child is enormous so I am not surprized. Amy was not at all frightened, having read that it is the fashion now to use instruments in America when every thing is quite right only by way of hastening the labour. When it was all over Mrs. R. & Fr. indulged in a good cry—and he went to bed utterly done up. He had been giving chloro. for 6 or 7 hours—Amy finding it an immense comfort but never insensible. Mrs. R. comes out in the best light, so calm & cheerful & self forgetful. I saw Amy for a minute owing to the nurse telling me she wd be sure not to wake & I was a fool to believe her. She looked bright & happy & wanted to talk so I came straight away. She has been sleeping peacefully ever since. They say it is never likely to be necessary again.[24]

Most of this is self-explanatory. Between Willey, Hughes, Frank Darwin, and the unnamed nurse, Amy had a roomful of obstetrical helpers, as well as her mother in watchful attendance. Emma's comment "it is never likely to be necessary again" probably refers to a reduced need for forceps in subsequent births because of cervical and other tissue changes.[25]

Twenty-four hours after delivery, both mother and child seemed to be doing well. "Every thing quite right nursing & all," reported Emma to Hen, adding somewhat unkindly, "the baby . . . is uglier than usual, as I was sure a Ruck baby wd be." But then everything went terribly, horribly wrong. Within days, Amy developed a feverish postpartum infection and slipped into a coma. At the end, Frank sat beside his dying wife "supporting her poor insensible head," but neither he nor the other medical men could do anything to save her. Amy Ruck Darwin died on September 11, 1876, at the age of twenty-six. Her spirit had returned to her beloved Wales, to the old homeplace at Pant-lludw "where magical things could happen."[26]

Amy's death left an infant son, a shattered husband, and two families numb with grief. Frank was inconsolable. He found some small relief in tears and in the support of his family, but his heart was broken. In fact, everyone's heart was broken including Charles's; Amy had "loved you like a daughter," Frank sobbed to his father. For Emma, the death was nearly unbearable. It "had a very deep effect on my mother," Henrietta remembered years later, and made Emma "more fearful and anxious" than she had been previously. Writing to William, Charles declared it "the most dreadful thing which has ever happened, worse than poor Annie's death, though not so grievous to me." He continued, "God knows what will become of poor Frank, his life will be a miserable wreck."[27]

Next to Frank, perhaps the most grief-stricken of all was Bessy Darwin. For her, the loss was truly irreparable. Quiet, withdrawn, and a little uncomfortable in society, Bessy had connected on many levels with her charming Welsh sister-in-law. She told Emma that "she could express her affection to Amy & to no other creature," but then added, "I *do* love you but I can never shew it." ("However she has shewn it now," Emma wrote feelingly to Hen.) In the immediate aftermath of Amy's death, Bessy sank into a period of mourning during which she thought only of her lost friend, obsessing on things she regretted saying or doing and "short comings on her own part" (these last were "imaginary I fully believe," remarked Emma). Family support and changes of scenery seemed to help a little as Bessy struggled with her depression. Cousin Rose Wedgwood provided sympathetic companionship at Down House right after Amy's death and then took Bessy back to Barlaston for a few days. From Barlaston, Bessy went on to London for a stay with Hen and Richard. Henrietta found her sister bearing up bravely, though still grappling with a loss that "seems to darken her whole life."[28]

Frank and the Rucks took Amy's body back to Wales for burial. Horace went along to provide fraternal support, but all of the other Darwins remained grieving at home. At the last minute, Frank found that he lacked the strength to go to the actual funeral, and so he stayed away, comforted by Mrs.

Ruck. Amy's father, her brothers Arthur and Dickie, Horace Darwin, and just a few others were in attendance when she was laid to rest.[29] It was a sad, sad business.

Frank rested and grieved in Pantlludw for almost a month, glad to be away from Downe and the scene of Amy's death. In his absence, Emma and Charles brought their infant grandson, Bernard Richard Meirion Darwin, to live at Down House until more definite plans could be made for the future. A wet nurse named Harriet was found without too much effort, and by early October Emma was able to write to Leo in Malta, "The baby is thriving." Indeed, little Bernard was doing so well that Emma and Charles felt comfortable going to Leith Hill Place for a few days while Hen and Richard took over as babysitters. Henrietta took to the task with maternal relish and soon was devoted to her "Babsy" (a.k.a. Dubba or Dubsy), even though a bout of dyspepsia in the baby gave her the "wibber jibbers" the first week on the job. "We think he is a little Darwin," Hen crowed to George, obviously meaning it as a compliment. Aunt Henrietta, at least, was not buying into her mother's first impression that Bernard was an "ugly Ruck baby."[30]

Frank came home in late October and immediately moved from Down Lodge to Down House, getting as much distance as he could from the deathbed memories. The old billiard room was converted into his sitting room, and he threw himself full time into botanical research. By focusing on work, Frank could achieve a level of "tolerable cheerfulness," and slowly he began to take pleasure in parenting his infant son. By the end of the year, everyone at Down House was coming under Babsy's spell. Emma wrote to Leo that the "baby has quite got a little soul by this time, & likes people's faces, & is amused at things & sounds, especially Fr. whistling." Bessy Darwin, who had needed a little practice before being comfortable holding the baby, was thrilled at being rewarded with "real smiles" for her efforts; Charles and Emma had predictably become adoring grandparents, the latter now allowing that Bernard might someday "become handsome, though far from it now"; and Henrietta was totally besotted. Despite seeing the baby only occasionally, Hen had taken so enthusiastically to surrogate mothering that Emma "wish[ed] there was a natural reason for her to adopt one." But adoption was not to be entered into lightly and Emma thought it "too dangerous to do unless you have a good reason." (One wonders what better reasons there could have been than Hen's barrenness coupled with her obvious love of children.) At year's end, little Bernard was "quite a prize article in point of fat & healthiness." His doting grandmother declared, "We think he . . . is a sort of Grand Lama, he is so solemn."[31]

In the world beyond Down House, 1876 saw other events of note. On the wedding front, Frank Wedgwood's oldest son, Godfrey, married his cousin Hope, Fanny and Hensleigh's youngest daughter, in October. Godfrey had been a widower since 1863, but this second marriage was complicated for a variety of reasons. For one thing, Godfrey probably loved Hope's sister Effie Farrer more than he did his bride, leading Fanny Hensleigh to worry that a Hope-Godfrey union would cause dissention between her daughters. Besides, all four of Godfrey's sisters and several other members of the extended family disapproved of the marriage on principle and/or because a civil ceremony was planned rather than a church wedding. The whole situation was "dreadfully flat," remarked Emma. Nonetheless, it was a marriage that Frank Wedgwood favored, and it came off on schedule.[32]

That August another widower, J. D. Hooker, had married as his second wife Hyacinth (née Symonds) Jardine, who was a quarter century his junior. The Darwins hosted the couple for the first time in December, and Emma reported to Leo that the new "Mrs H is very gracious & discreet & soft in her manners & Dr H very jolly & happy. She did not look free from cares & I don't believe that adopting 2 grown up step-sons & one grown up daughter is altogether a pleasant affair. We have heard that [the children] do not like it."[33]

On the literary side, during the spring and summer of 1876 Charles wrote a short autobiography for the enjoyment of his children and grandchildren. In it he reviewed his childhood, university years, voyage around the world, and scientific career to date, and also made some personal comments on such subjects as religion and marriage. Addressing his children, Charles wrote this about his beloved Emma:

> You all know well your Mother, and what a good Mother she has ever been to all of you. She has been my greatest blessing, and I can declare that in my whole life I have never heard her utter one word which I had rather have been unsaid. She has never failed in the kindest sympathy towards me, and has borne with the utmost patience my frequent complaints from ill-health and discomfort. I do not believe she has ever missed an opportunity of doing a kind action to anyone near her. I marvel at my good fortune that she, so infinitely my superior in every single moral quality, consented to be my wife.

She has been my wise adviser and cheerful comforter throughout life, which without her would have been during a very long period a miserable one from ill-health. She has earned the love and admiration of every soul near her.[34]

In the geopolitical realm, trouble was brewing (not for the first or last time) in the Balkans. For some while, there had been pockets of insurrection against Ottoman rule in Herzegovina and Bosnia, and in 1876 the unrest spread to Bulgaria. The Turks put down the Bulgarian uprising with a heavy hand, killing 12,000 people in the process. Gladstone was horrified at what he judged to be atrocities, and he made his outrage known in pamphlet form. Disraeli tended to downplay the killings, thus earning the reputation of being pro-Turkish, while vigorously saber rattling to prevent Russia from entering the conflict and perhaps making another grab at Constantinople.[35] In an up-braiding letter written to Leo in December 1876, Emma weighed in on the so-called Eastern Question:

> I am afraid your politics are rather corrupted. I send you a few words on Dizzy's conduct at the Mansion House feast. It can only be accounted for on the belief that he really wishes for war. It was almost insulting to the Czar & he shewed that he took it as an insult. I don't think Gladstone did misrepresent the feeling of England some months ago, tho' I am afraid it is gone to sleep now.[36]

From these comments, it is obvious that Emma was pro-Gladstone and anti-Turk in her views on the Balkan situation. And while his actual words have not been preserved, it appears that Leo—perhaps with the natural pugnacity of a young soldier—had expressed a rather different view.

In the event, Britain did not go to war with Russia over the Balkans, but it was a near thing. Russia and Turkey came to blows in 1877–78 and, although the victories swung back and forth, finally the Turks were forced to sue for peace. When the tsar moved to strengthen Russia's presence on the east side of the Black Sea, international pressure—including more intense saber rattling by Britain—brought all parties to the negotiating table at the 1878 Congress of Berlin. At that congress, Russian influence in the Balkans was throttled back a notch and Cyprus was transferred from Turkey to Britain for use as a military outpost in the eastern Mediterranean.[37]

In Southampton, William Darwin began 1877 with a brush with one of Britain's most remarkable military men, albeit not one involved with the Balkan situation. Colonel Charles George Gordon was in Southampton on a family visit, and somehow William made his acquaintance. "My dear Mother," William wrote home, "I have just done what few people would not envy, dined alone with Col. Gordon & his sister . . . [who] tells me that Gordon says I just suit him which I am delighted to hear."[38]

Gordon had just completed a stint as governor-general of the province of Equatoria in the Sudan. Working under the authority of the khedive Ismail (khedive being the title granted by the sultan of Turkey to his viceroy in Egypt), Gordon had spent nearly three years in the Sudan trying to reduce the slave trade and to open the upper White Nile for commerce. Over dinner with William in Southampton, Gordon delighted the young banker by giving him a few African trinkets from Gondokoro (near modern Juba). William's impression of the globe-trotting soldier, who was not quite seven years his senior, was relayed to Emma:

> There is a sort of sublime modesty about him that is quite astonishing, and he seems to be utterly above all worldly & selfish notions of all kinds, and is very sensitive to the feelings of others. . . . We had a long talk about his going back [to the Sudan] again, [and] he evidently dreads it very much. . . . the Khedive treating him shamefully never answering his letters and evidently shamming as to any real wish as to putting down the slave trade, and he said it was so disheartening to feel that directly he left all would be oppression & misery.[39]

And a few days later:

> I have had another very long talk with Col. Gordon about his religious opinions which are striking; he seems to me to have escaped from Calvinism into the opposite extreme that everyone is saved & that there is no free will (though he agrees with me that at the present moment it is just the same as if one had free will) without losing faith in Christianity; it was very striking the gleam of content that came over his face when he said how perfectly happy his religion made him; but it is sad to see how indifferent he is to life. I feel sure it is absolutely the same to him whether he is dead or alive, which, whether owing to his religion or constitution is unnatural and somewhat chilling.
>
> He has compelled me to write today to Leonard . . . to tell him to write to his [commanding officer] a polite note and ask him to plump it when peace is declared [in the Balkans], and we have to lend engineers to open up roads in Bulgaria that Leo may be appointed. [Gordon] says it is extremely likely to happen, and that . . . it would be a fine opportunity [for Leo, with] good pay,

a charming country, and he could come home every winter. I was surprised by Gordon shewing he had so much of the serpent in him as when he told me he had got most of his good appointments by that sort of haphazard foresight.[40]

Whether Leo wrote such a note is unknown, but when he left Malta in 1877 it was not to build roads in Bulgaria but to become an instructor at the military school at Chatham. And as is well known, Gordon did return to the Sudan, where he died in 1885 at the hands of rebel fighters loyal to the Islamic holy man Muhammad Ahmad ibn Abdullah, called the Mahdi.[41]

As the spring of 1877 turned into summer, baby Bernard Darwin was coming into his own and enchanting everyone who came near him. Between pulling faces and making funny noises, he managed to keep the Down House troops constantly amused. "Baby is turning into a little Hottentot," Emma wrote to William in May, "& has learnt the cleverest way of clicking w. his tongue which he feels to be v. clever." A month later, she reported to Hen that "Babsy had his 1st night w.out Harriet & so now I consider that job is done." Although it hard to tell if Bernard actually went off breast milk "cold turkey" at eight months of age, his grandmother's comment certainly sounds like it.[42]

In June a family excursion to Stonehenge was organized. Emma worried that the trip would "½ kill" Charles, but he was anxious to see whether worm activity at the site had altered the elevation of the stones. The first stage of the trip was a train ride to Salisbury, where George met them with a carriage. Then it was off to Stonehenge over a road that was both "striking & ugly." As Emma related to Hen, at the ruins they

> loitered about & had a gt deal of talk w. an agreeable old soldier placed there by Sir Ed. Anthrobus (owner) who was keeping guard & reading a devout book w. specs. on. He was q. agreeable to any amount of digging; but sometimes visitors came who were troublesome & once a man came w. a sledge hammer who was v. difficult to manage. 'That was English all over' said he. Prince Leopold had been there. 'I wish he wd come again, he gave me a yellow boy' [a gold guinea], [said the guard]. They did not find much gold about the worms, who seem to be very idle out there. . . . The next time we are here we mean to come to Salisbury & see that & the Cathedral. I was not so tired as I expected & F. was wonderful as he did a gt deal of waiting out in the sun. Today I am only dead.[43]

Darwin's observations on worm activity at Stonehenge would ultimately be combined with other data, mostly from other English sites such as Leith Hill

Place and Abinger, and published in 1881 in his last book, *The Formation of Vegetable Mould, Through the Action of Worms, with Observations on Their Habits*. Darwin himself would judge it to be "a curious little book," and he would be right.[44]

But worms, although curious and interesting, were small potatoes compared to the affair of the heart that was playing itself out in Southampton that summer. William Darwin was in love, and the object of his affections was C. E. Norton's sister-in-law Sara Sedgwick from Cambridge, Massachusetts. On July 23 the smitten young banker shared his secret—and his doubts about being accepted—in a letter marked "Private" in very large letters across the top:

> Dearest Mother,
>
> . . . I believe my mind is made up, and after a week's change of scene & ideas that I shall come back to Down determined to see her again. I feel she would make me happy & I think I could her, though I should dread the dullness here of the society for her. . . . Her health is poor, but I don't feel it much use in discussing that. It is odd I have often in former times had, when her name was mentioned, gleams of what a charming wife she would make. . . . Please keep secret as it is probably all moonshine & waste of resolution.[45]

The courtship continued through August and into September, with William showing a lack of self-confidence that his mother disliked ("I should feel sure almost that [Sara] wd consent if Wm wd be more headlong," Emma wrote to Hen).[46] And then William's prayers were answered. On September 27 he told his mother the great news:

> I return my darling's sweet & touching note. My happiness & good fortune are past words. I keep saying to myself how can I have deserved such a woman, & I have up & downs of dread that she is too superior to me to be happy with me. . . . I know it will be a real delight to Henrietta to have Sara as a sister. I forgot to tell Bessy how very warmly Sara spoke of her liking for her. . . . [Sara] was very much pleased at having a line from Frank, please thank him.[47]

In another letter, this time to Henrietta, William was a bit more effusive with words, albeit stingy with commas:

> All is right the darling Sara has accepted me. I feel too blessed for words when I think of her trust the tremendous sacrifice she is making and her loving ways & great happiness I am quite overwhelmed. Nothing I can do in this life can ever repay her. . . . The angel has done more for me. She felt if she

now went home she would break down and she is going to stay & marry me now. Write to her . . . but do not mention about her not going back as it is a terrible strain for her, and she does not yet know what they will say at home. My own are so happy here and she is so glad to feel they like [the match]. Father I hear has written a letter to her that only he could write, and I must ask her to show it me. . . . it all seems a dream.[48]

Charles's letter was, indeed, a gem. He began by assuring Sara of his great esteem for her, continued with a testimony to William's good character, and ended by thanking her "from the bottom of my heart for having accepted" his son's proposal. The letter reflected the general delight the Darwins felt that William was about to climb "out of the pit of bachelorhood" with its solitary lifestyle. There was some concern, of course, about the extreme contrast between William's happy prospects and Frank's tragedy of the year before. As the great day approached, Emma tried to shield Frank from some of the wedding "effusions," a motherly gesture that was probably unnecessary. Frank was genuinely happy for his brother and behaved in a "charmingly feeling & cordial" manner throughout.[49]

William was getting a wife who would suit him well. He was famous in the family for being "clean and wholesome"—so tidy that "you could eat a mutton chop off [his] face," Frank once remarked. His neat and orderly habits matched both his banker's profession and his bride's tastes. Sara too was tidy—"painfully tidy," remembered a niece years later, and a woman who liked her home to be "perfect in [its] organization"—but this "psychological" need for order was combined with intelligence, a strong awareness of duty, and a lively sense of humor. In some important ways, she and William counterbalanced one another: Sara was very religious and William less so; Sara was prone to ill health, especially depression, while William was "the only one of the five [Darwin] sons entirely free from hypochondria."[50] They would have no difficulty creating a happy life together.

They were married on November 29, 1877, when Sara was thirty-eight and William just a month shy of the same age. Sara's sister Maria Theodora came over from America to lend familial support at the wedding (their parents had died many years before). At a mere twenty-six, Theo was "fond of all sorts of gaiety" and entered into the social whirl with considerable spirit. Bets were made that, before it was all over, the lively Theo would be snatched up by some English suitor and "never . . . see the wilds of Massachusetts again." Emma and Charles made a wedding gift of £300 to the newlyweds, part of which William immediately earmarked to buy "a small close carriage" for Sara's use. It was a "splendid present," wrote William in thanks, adding, "No man in the world ever had a more loving father & mother than me or a happier home." The newlyweds settled down to married life at Ridgemount, William's estate in the Southampton suburb of Bassett.[51]

One other event made the fall of 1877 happily memorable. Two weeks before they watched their oldest son take a bride, Charles and Emma made a brief trip to Cambridge for Charles to receive an honorary Doctor of Laws (LL.D.) degree. It was his first honorary doctorate from an English university, although Breslau, Bonn, and Leyden had all given him honorary M.D. degrees years earlier, and Oxford had offered the title Hon. Doctor of Civil Law in 1870 only to be turned down owing to ill health. This one was doubly sweet coming from his alma mater. Emma was not at all sure that Charles was up to the rigors of the ceremony and the accompanying socializing, but he was flattered and excited by the honor and eager to make the trip.[52]

As the journal *Nature* reported a few days after the event, the "occasion was in many ways remarkable . . . [since to] appoint a special congregation of the [university's] senate for the transaction of no other business but the conferment of a solitary degree, although it be *honoris causâ*, is only resorted to in exceptional and important cases."[53] It was also remarkable because of the happy, boisterous spirit of the gathering. University officials, fellows, undergraduates, and guests filled the Senate House to overflowing, all eager to get a glimpse at the reclusive evolutionist and, in the case of the undergraduates, eager to have a little fun. Emma reported the action to William back in Downe:

> It was a great disappt yr not coming yesterday to witness the honours to F & so I will tell you all about it. Bessy & I & the 2 youngest brothers went first to the Senate Hall & got in by a side door, & a most striking sight it was. The gallery crammed to overflowing w. Undergraduates, & the floor crammed too w. Undergs climbing on the statues & standing up in the windows. There seemed to be periodic cheering in answers to jokes which sounded deafening; but when F came in in his red cloak ushered in by some authorities, it was perfectly deafening for some minutes. I thought he wd be overcome but he was quite stout & smiling & sat for a considerable time waiting for the Vice Chancellor. The time was filled up with shouts & jokes & groans for an unpopular Proctor Mr Humphrey which were quite awful & he looked up at them with a stern angry face wh was v bad policy. We had been watching some cords stretched across from one gallery to another wondering what was

to happen; but were not surprised to see a monkey dangling down, which caused shouts & jokes about our ancestors etc. A proctor was foolish enough to go up to capture it & at last it disappeared I don't know how. Then came a sort of ring tied with ribbons wh we conjectured to be the "Missing Link." At last the Vice Ch. appeared more bowing & hand shaking & then F was marched down the aisle behind 2 men w. silver maces & the unfortunate public orator came & stood by him & got thro' his very tedious harangue as he cd, constantly interrupted by the most unmannerly shouts & jeers & when he had continued what seems an enormous time some one called out in a cheerful tone "Thank you kindly." At last [the orator] got to the end w. admirable nerve & temper & then they all marched back to the Vice Ch. in scarlet & white fur & F joined his hands & did not kneel but the Vice Ch. put his hands outside [Father's] & said a few Latin words & then it was over & every body came up & shook hands.

Of all days in the year I had a baddish headache but by dint of opium managed to go & enjoyed it all. I shd have been most sorry to miss it. F has been to Newton's Museum today & seen many people—also a brilliant luncheon at G[eorge's]. H[enry] Sidgwick . . . [and his nice wife, Eleanor] & Miss [Helen] Gladstone also v. pleasant. J. W. Clarke [the zoologist] not pleasant; but he did me a good turn as I followed his lead in tasting Gallantine which is v. superior.

Sidgwick's stammer is so rapid that it sounds like some small machine whirring but he does not mind it himself & is agreeable & entertaining. Now we are expecting F[rancis] Galton & [Henry] Fawcett for an evening call & we mean to wind up by Trinity Chapel—which I can't believe F will be up to. F has been thoroughly pleased by the cordiality of every one. . . . I felt very grand walking about [with] my L.L.D. in his silk gown.[54]

And so a good time was had by all, even Charles. By nightfall he had had enough, however, and he skipped the gala dinner sponsored by the Cambridge Philosophical Society. T. H. Huxley, Charles's reliable old "bulldog," was there, and he responded to the various toasts in Darwin's stead. Then, quite in character, Huxley scolded the university for being so long in honoring his friend's achievements. "Mr. Darwin [was] the foremost among men of science, with one exception, since the days of Aristotle," proclaimed Huxley. Presumably the exception was Isaac Newton.[55]

The last two years of the 1870s were marked by prosperity and relative good health at Down House and throughout the extended family. Except for occasional giddy spells, Charles was feeling pretty fit. He and Emma took several short vacations each year, including a trip to the Lake District in 1879. When they were at home, there was the usual steady stream of visitors. Among the regulars was the recently knighted Sir Joseph Hooker, K.C.S.I. (Knight Commander of the Order of the Star of India, awarded 1877). Hooker had been proposed for knighthoods before, but had always declined the honor for one reason or another. This one suited him to a tee, however, as he confided to Darwin:

> I had always regarded the Star of India as the most honourable of all such distinctions—it is very limited (to 60 K.C.S.I.'s)—is never, like K.C.B. [Knight Commander of the Order of the Bath], given by favor or on personal considerations, and it has a flavor of hard work under difficulties, of obstacles overcome, and of brilliant deeds that is very attractive. Assuredly I would rather go down to posterity as one of the 'Star of India' than as of any other dignity whatever that the Crown can offer. . . . Is this not a jolly strain of self-gratulation and glorification?[56]

In Cambridge, George was living in college at Trinity and working away at various research projects that were always strongly mathematical and increasingly astrophysical. He published two important papers between 1877 and 1879, and in the latter year, to Darwin's delight, was made a fellow of the Royal Society. Thanks to their shared scientific interests, George had made the acquaintance of Sir William Thomson, later 1st Baron Kelvin, and soon a friendship had developed between the two men that would last until Kelvin's death in 1907. Horace, also living in Cambridge, was spending his time doing freelance instrument design work, and Leo was still teaching at Chatham, although in 1878 he came close to being reassigned to Bulgaria to help settle boundaries in the region.[57]

At Downe, Frank continued to serve as his father's secretary and botanical assistant—Charles was still deep into studies of the power of movement in plants—as well as having at least nominal charge of Bernard's upbringing. Dubba was now a toddler and on the go, and Emma had gone back to her old trick of bribery, using lumps of sugar in this case, to obtain good behavior. Not caring much for the practice, Frank asked his mother to abandon it, and she agreed. "I will not yield to the temptation in any way," promised Emma, "as you do not approve of that method of education." Bernard was also having his share of childhood medical issues, some typical and some not. Predictably, cutting teeth dulled his appetite and made him cross. Unexpectedly, Dr.

Moore diagnosed the little boy as "slightly rickety" and prescribed more milk and regular doses of cod liver oil, which luckily he didn't balk at taking.[58]

The William Darwins began 1878 with a visit by the American novelist Henry James, whom Sara had known in Massachusetts before her marriage. James's impressions of Ridgemount, his hosts, and the British people in general are interesting, although not always flattering. In a letter back to the States, James wrote:

> The visit was very pleasant, although it poured with rain from the moment of my arrival. Sara seems utterly unchanged by matrimony—neither exhilarated nor depressed: very sweet, soft, gentle and without initiative. She is in a densely English milieu and has a densely English husband. Both, however, are excellent in their way. [William] Darwin is a gentle, kindly, reasonable, liberal, bald-headed, dull-eyed, British-featured, sandy-haired little insulaire, who will to a certainty never fail of goodness and carefulness towards his wife and who must have merit, and a good deal of it, to have appreciated merit so retiring, appealing and delicate as Sara's.... [Their] house is a very pretty roomy villa, with charming grounds and views, completely in the country, though in the midst of a very agreeable residential suburb of Southampton. [Sara] is surrounded by plenty of solid British comfort, and judged by American habits would appear to be mistress of an opulent home. She had on Saturday a couple of genteel people (very pleasant ones) to dinner and apparently may have as much as she desires of the society of the "upper middle class": the more so as she keeps a very pretty brougham! Altogether, [Sara] struck me as very happy and comfortable, and I should have great confidence in [her husband] and his prosaic virtues.[59]

If this sounds a bit hard on poor William, in another letter James noted approvingly that the two men found common ground in conversation, books, and etchings, and declared William "wholly free from any of those noxious affectations which at times seem . . . rather the rule than the exception among English people." Given some of these attitudes, one wonders what prompted James's 1876 immigration from America to England in the first place.[60]

To his credit, when William had a chance to see Americans in situ in the fall of 1878, he was much kinder to them than James had been to the British. William and Sara sailed for America on September 14, arriving in New York harbor eleven days later. Sara's brother Arthur Sedgwick met them at the pier and "after a lunch at the great Delmonico's" the trio caught the train to Boston, where the rest of Sara's family awaited them. William was charmed by his first views of New England, telling Emma that "where it was not a town it was a panorama on both sides of the train of comfortable little wooden villas each with their patch of [Indian] corn; it was also very pretty in many parts as we here & there had glimpses of the sea." He was quite amused by the "very easy & gentlemanlike manners of the conductor."[61]

Sara's family was delighted to meet William, and even Aunt Anne, although "a little silent and restrained at first," finally came around. The Sedgwicks' house was such a busy place, full of people coming and going and doors constantly banging, that William imagined Sara found their quiet married life at Ridgemount like going from "Bedlam to a desert island." Cambridge, Massachusetts, at least the area near Harvard, was a pretty place, he reported to his mother, filled with "wooden [houses] with comfortable verandahs." He and Sara made an exhausting number of social calls, including visits with the Charles Eliot Nortons, the Alexander Agassizes, the Asa Grays, and Frederick Law Olmsted, the famous landscape architect. Olmsted and William then traveled together for two days in Newport, Rhode Island, where Olmsted had created a number of landscape designs. The day-trippers had the good luck of beautiful October weather, and their tour was a complete success, at least as far as William was concerned. "Newport," he reported to his mother, "is the most charming pleasant place, but it is also a most fashionable place & more like Torquay than any other place in England.... The brilliant sky & blue sea was most delicious and if there was any place in America where one could settle down to an idle life, it would be Newport."[62]

William proved to be an energetic tourist as well as a good observer, and during his short stay in America he managed to cover a good bit of ground. A few days after the Newport jaunt, Theo Sedgwick took him to Stockbridge to see the "old country home" and to meet the cousins still living at the west end of Massachusetts. Fearful of getting overtired from the five-hour train trip and intensive family visiting, Sara stayed in Cambridge. Besides, she hadn't lived in Stockbridge for more than twenty years, and her last memory of the place was not a good one, namely, nursing her parents through their final illnesses. William admired the old Sedgwick home place, set high on a hill above the Housatonic River, and thought Lake Makheenac (the Stockbridge Bowl) to be rather similar to England's Lake District. And finally, in early November he squeezed in one last side trip, this time to Gardiner, Maine, on the Kennebec River. Seemingly always in the company of the rich and famous, William returned to Cambridge "in the charge of a Miss Howe . . . the daughter of a certain Mrs Julia Ward Howe, who is a celebrated Woman's Rights [campaigner]." They shared lunch, William told his mother, "and as [Miss Howe] was handsome & pleasant I enjoyed the journey."[63]

Tired but happy, the William Darwins returned to England in mid-November. The trip had been an unqualified success. His American in-laws had met William and grown to love him (the children were already calling him Uncle Darwin and wheedling him for bonbons). Sara wrote to Emma that her family could now "feel & understand his great worth & attraction, & cannot wonder that I should have abandoned them all & my country for his sake!" These were words to warm the cockles of any mother's heart, to be sure, as was Sara's closing: "Ever y[our] most affec daughter. Sara D."[64]

On the Lake District getaway in August 1879, the main vacationers were Emma, Charles, Bessy, three-year-old Bernard, and the Litchfields (as well as the requisite maids and nurses, of course). Later arrivals during the month's stay at Lake Coniston included Frank, George, and Leo. They made the Waterhead Hotel their headquarters, and day-tripping was facilitated by the kind loan of a carriage by the hotel's owner. Excursions to Yewdale, Tilberthwaite Farm, Skelwith Bridge, Old Coniston Hall, and Grasmere were enjoyed by all, with Charles being particularly struck by the view of "a fine rugged mountain . . . seen over a flat field, with an old farm-house with fine sycamores on the left-hand" and also by the area around Rydal Water. "The scenery gave me more pleasure than I thought my soul, or whatever remains of it, was capable of feeling," he remarked later.[65]

On two occasions they socialized with John Ruskin, whose home, Brantwood, was on the shore of Lake Coniston. Richard Litchfield knew Ruskin well, of course, thanks to their mutual involvement with the Working Men's College, and he was delighted to see him again. Unfortunately, Ruskin had recently "been seriously ill with brain trouble," and his thinking was confused ("his brain was becoming clouded," Henrietta wrote later). Ruskin "knighted [Darwin] in his imagination" and addressed him as "Sir Charles" throughout their conversations. The two men apparently enjoyed each other, however, even though Ruskin thought that Darwin's "views on evolution [were] pernicious nonsense" and that "if Mr Darwin would get different kinds of air & bottle them, & examine them when bottled, he would do much more useful work than he does in the contemplation of the hinder parts of monkeys"—a reference to Charles's comments on monkeys' sexual signals in *The Descent of Man*. For his part, Charles found little to appreciate in the watercolors by J. M. W. Turner that Ruskin displayed so proudly at Brantwood. It was a meeting of two colossuses that ended in an amicable draw. Emma's diary entry recorded the event, but as usual was short on both detail and emotion, reading simply "Lunch at Ruskins."[66]

Still, Ruskin did well in Emma's diary compared to another famous writer who crossed paths with the Darwins in the Lake District. On August 19 they met and conversed briefly with Samuel Clemens, a.k.a. Mark Twain. Both Charles and Emma liked Twain's books, although one guesses that Charles, much more of a jokester than his wife, got the greater enjoyment. After Twain had been pointed out to Darwin and vice versa, they met and "had a pleasant talk." Mark Twain's "manner is oddly like that of Carlyle," noted Emma, presumably as a compliment since she had always found Thomas Carlyle "pleasant to talk to" and "very natural" in his interactions. Nonetheless, she was not moved to record the meeting with Twain in her daily diary. "Drove by Hawks' head road [and] Marshalls' grounds" is all one finds for August 19. Twain did a little better by Charles: "Talked with the great Darwin," he jotted in his travel journal.[67]

It was good that the Lake District vacation was so successful and so relaxing, because the fall of 1879 was marked by intrafamilial bickering within the Darwin-Wedgwood circle. Ironically, the cause of the unhappiness was a love affair: Horace had fallen in love with Emma Cecilia "Ida" Farrer and she returned the feeling. The problem was that Ida's father, T. H. "Theta" Farrer, objected strenuously to the thought of his only daughter marrying the sickly Horace, who he declared was "too damned hypochondriac." Theta also suspected that Horace had such limited professional and financial prospects that he would never be able to support any wife properly, and certainly not Ida. The Darwins quite naturally took umbrage at T. H.'s attitude, and the normally good relations between Down House and Abinger grew testy.[68]

For a while, communications between the Darwins and Farrers ceased altogether; nobody wanted to make the situation worse by sending a letter that might actually increase the bad feelings on the other side. Emma hoped T. H. would invite Charles, herself, and Horace to Abinger so the matter could be talked out, but as September wore on, that didn't happen. For her part, Ida continued to be devoted to Horace and determined that the wedding would take place. She wrote to her "Aunt" Emma on September 13:

I am overflowing w. every sort of feeling about yr dear letter w[hich] Horace forwarded to me yesterday. . . . I feel such a longing to tell you somehow— altho' you do know it perfectly—of the happiness w[hich] comes over me whenever I think of you in the light of a mother to me. I think becoming your & Uncle C's daughter has had quite as m. to do w. "it" as the principal person himself.[69]

Finally, apparently near the end of September, Farrer gave his grudging consent to the marriage. Charles was then free to respond with some specifics about Horace's financial status and prospects:

My dear Farrer

I am delighted for Horace's sake to hear that the marriage will take place early in the ensuing year. He tells me that you would like to hear about his future and present income prospects. William estimated carefully a few years ago the amount of my property (including some which I know to have been bequeathed to me) and from this it follows that after my death and Emma's, Horace will receive about £40,000 a little more or less. At present, I allow him £300 annually, and I have made over to him property producing annually rather above £100. For the future I intend to divide annually the overplus of our income, amongst my children; and on an average from the last ten years, this amounts annually to £2728. This will give to Horace at least £400; so that his annual income will be at least £800—always assuming that my income does not fall off, and none of my investments are speculative.

With respect to a marriage settlement, I think it would be the best plan, as I am not a man of business, for my Solicitor [Mr. Hacon] to call on your brother; and I understand that you concur in this. . . . Your suggestion about Horace possibly becoming a partner in some business, seems to me a very wise one, which had not occurred to me, and which I will pass on to Mr. Hacon, as it bears on the amount advisable to be settled. . . . I shall always consider Horace as one of the most fortunate of men.[70]

One assumes that Farrer was considerably reassured by the knowledge that, without lifting a finger, Horace was worth around $67,000 per year in modern terms, with the prospect of inheriting $3.3 million when his parents died. In any event, Theta no longer tried to prevent the union, and the wedding was scheduled for January 1880.[71] The Darwins, at least, were thrilled.

18. "Our Secure Happiness . . . Shattered"

IDA AND HORACE'S WEDDING TOOK place without incident on January 3, 1880. If the father of the bride was grumbling to himself, at least it didn't spoil the occasion. The only bit of confusion—for the observers, not the wedding party—was the fact that several people mistakenly thought George was the groom because he ended up kneeling nearer the center of the altar than did Horace and his bride. (Bessy wrote afterwards to Ida that the couple "had put yourselves so much to one side that George was the central figure which he felt acutely." And then came a clear offer to bond with this new sister-in-law: "I hope you will write to me some time.") After the service was over and the wedding cake ceremoniously consumed, the newly-weds took their leave for a honeymoon at Penzance. Given the nerve-wracking run-up to the wedding, Horace and Ida were quite happy to drop out of sight for a while. "Mr & Mrs Horace do not fatigue themselves with writing," Emma commented to William on January 19, adding, "but I think they are still at Penzance."[1]

The happy couple resurfaced toward the end of the month and stopped by Downe on their way back to Cambridge, where they would make their home during their entire married life. Their visit to see old William Brooks, long retired from his position as gardener at Down House, elicited a compliment that tickled Emma: "Well," remarked Brooks to Horace, "you have got a nice little wife." Emma thought so too. She wrote to Sara, "F and I often reflect how well off we are in daughters-in-law and how easily our sons might have married very nice wives that would not have suited us old folks, and above all that would not really have adopted us so affectionately as you have done. I never think without a pang of the third that is gone."[2] The last sentence is telling. Amy's death and Frank's long depression still haunted Emma's soul.

It was good that Emma had pleasant children and children-in-law to occupy her thoughts, because the atmosphere at Down House turned distinctly sour at the end of January 1880. The cause was a letter by Samuel Butler published in the *Athenaeum* accusing Darwin of fostering plagiarism and deceptively condemning Butler's views on evolution. The sequence of events that led to these charges went as follows.

In February 1879 an article by Ernst Krause about the life and works of Dr. Erasmus Darwin was published in the German journal *Kosmos*.[3] Charles was intrigued by the article and, with Ras's encouragement, decided to arrange for it to be published in English, accompanied by a "preliminary notice" about their grandfather that Charles would write. Krause was pleased at the idea of an English version of his work, and accordingly Charles contacted W. S. Dallas, who agreed to do the translation for a nominal fee. By June it had been arranged that Charles's regular publisher, John Murray, would bring out the translation.

A month earlier, while all of the dealings with Krause, Dallas, and Murray were in the works, Samuel Butler—coincidentally the grandson of Charles's old master at the Shrewsbury School—brought out a book titled *Evolution, Old and New; or, The Theories of Buffon, Dr Erasmus Darwin, and Lamarck, as Compared with That of Mr Charles Darwin*. Charles didn't think much of Butler's book, since it argued against natural selection and in favor of more orthogenetic views, but nonetheless he notified Krause about the volume, and the German author ordered a copy. Then, as Krause was revising and shortening his *Kosmos* article to Murray's specifications, he inserted a few bits and pieces from Butler's book, as well as adding a curt dismissal of modern thinkers foolish enough to champion Dr. Erasmus's antiquated views. To wit:

> Erasmus Darwin's system was in itself a most significant first step in the path of knowledge which his grandson has opened up for us, but to wish to revive it at the present day, as has been seriously attempted, shows a weakness of thought and a mental anachronism which no one can envy.

Finally, to cap off the whole bad business, in the rush to publish the English version, which appeared in November 1879 and was called simply *The Life of Erasmus Darwin*, both Charles and Krause failed to mention that the original *Kosmos* article had been revised and added to. Thus the above critical comments, instantly obvious to Butler as referring to him, seemed to anticipate, rather than follow, the publication of *Evolution, Old and New*.

Butler was outraged. He wrote to the *Athenaeum* charging that although *Erasmus Darwin* was passed off as an accurate translation of Krause's original work, it actually was a revision that included passages lifted unacknowledged from *Evolution, Old and New*, as well as a deceptively dated attack on Butler himself.[4]

Now it was Charles's turn to be outraged. He felt that Butler had accused him "of lying, duplicity, and God knows what," and his first inclination was to answer the charges with a countering letter to the *Athenaeum*. Although the publication of *Erasmus Darwin* had clearly been botched, Charles was insulted and longed to strike back. He wrote out draft letters of rebuttal, which were circulated among the family and a few scientific friends for advice. Some of the sons thought a response was needed, but after discussion cooler heads prevailed. Henrietta and Richard argued strongly in favor of ignoring Butler's charges and simply letting the controversy fade away. Litchfield's legal opinion was especially valuable. A rebuttal would bring about "exactly the result [Butler] most wants," Richard argued: "a 'Butler-Darwin affaire.'" Surprisingly, even Huxley agreed that ignoring Butler was the best course of action. Clearly, said Huxley, Butler had a bad case of "Darwinophobia," adding, "It's a horrid disease and I would kill any son of a [bitch] I found running loose with it." Still, in this case perhaps an aloof silence was preferable to murder. It galled Charles to comply, but he remained silent.[5]

On March first, with the Butler unpleasantness now behind them, Emma and Bessy went to London for a week of shopping and concerts. They bought candlesticks and an inkstand at the Baker Street bazaar, apparently for a servant who was getting married, and they attended a concert featuring Joseph Joachim on the violin and Natalie Janotha on the piano. Unfortunately, by the end of the evening Emma could give only a mixed review. Beethoven's "Razumovsky 3" string quartet in C major had been beautiful except for the last movement, but then Joachim's performance had fallen below par. "[W]hat trash [Joachim] played by himself," Emma reported to Hen, "w such a thumping stupid man to accomp. him on that harsh P. Something of Paganini." Janotha's performance had been little better as she "played a son[ata] of Schumann generally hideous w sweet bits in it & she thumped enough to split one's head; but I think it is chiefly the Piano. We were in the front row too close . . . but I prefer it to being too far." Clearly, this particular concert failed to please.[6]

As she approached her seventy-second birthday, Emma was one of the healthiest members of her generation and retained a lively interest not only in music but in literature and politics as well. Unfortunately, her eighty-five-year-old brother Joe was breathing his last at Leith Hill Place even as Emma and Bessy did their London shopping. And Joe's end was not easy. The days before his death on March 11 were marked by delirium and repeated "suffering attacks," sometimes as many as nine in a single day. Joe's wife, Caroline, had "always had . . . a dread of the suffering of death," perhaps because she had been old enough at the time to remember her mother's painful passing, and thus the deathwatch was especially hard for her. When at last Josiah III passed from this world, Emma wrote to Henrietta: "It felt an immense relief to think that the suffering at [Leith Hill Place] was over. . . . It is a very painful aggravation to the grief not to have any alleviation of the distress at the very last, & I think it must be very rare." Although neither Emma nor Elizabeth Wedgwood tried to go to the funeral, all three surviving brothers—Harry, Frank, and Hensleigh—managed to get to Leith Hill Place to bury Joe and console Caroline.[7]

William Darwin was the executor for his uncle Joe's estate, and he was the perfect man for the job. He dealt gently and consolingly with Aunt Caroline and his spinster cousin Sophy. A grateful Caroline wrote to Emma that "Sophy found [William] such a pleasant person to do business with—explaining so clearly what she did not understand & so kind in his manner—he has always been a special favourite of mine." Thanks to the provisions of the will, William's job was an easy one: everything passed smoothly to the widow with the exception of a £5,000 bequest to Sophy, a gift that matched the marriage settlements of the two other daughters, Margaret Vaughan Williams and Lucy Harrison, and thus equalized the financial affairs among the sisters.[8]

Mercifully, the family circle was distracted almost immediately from the sadness of Joe's death by love affairs involving Frank Wedgwood's youngest daughters. Twenty-eight-year-old Mabel became engaged to Arthur Parson, and her older sister Rose, now approaching thirty-four, accepted a marriage proposal from Hermann Franke, a German geologist and musician who was also the organizer of conductor Hans Richter's newly debuted London concerts.[9] Parson easily passed muster with Mabel's aunt Emma, but she had serious doubts about Rose's choice. Hermann Franke had "a feeble look" and was a "quiet mouse of a man," was Emma's first impression. She thought better of him after another visit or two, and was able to remark to Hen: "I am come to think that if he had not so long a neck, I shd think him good looking."[10]

The political landscape in Britain changed fairly dramatically in the spring of 1880 and, as always, the Darwins followed the various developments attentively. Abroad, Disraeli's government had presided over a couple of serious military blunders. First, in South Africa the Zulu War had started off in January 1879 with a stunning defeat for the British at Isandhlwana. The causes of the war were complex, but as usual they involved imperial expansion and the flexing of British muscle. In December 1878, ostensibly to protect the European settlers in the newly annexed Transvaal from their well-armed Zulu neighbors, the British administration headed by Sir Bartle Frere had made a series of demands designed to sharply curtail Zulu power. Among these demands were that the Zulus disband their substantial army, alter their traditional marriage rules, and allow a good deal of British involvement in their internal affairs. A deadline was set for Zulu compliance, and on January 11, 1879, when it was not met, British forces commanded by Lord Chelmsford entered Zululand. Eleven days later, as Chelmsford's army was advancing to confront King Cetshwayo at Ulundi, a momentary splitting of the invading forces resulted in 1,800 British troops and loyal natives coming under attack by 20,000 Zulu warriors. The result was horrendous—some 1,500 of Chelmsford's men died at Isandhlwana, including 900 European soldiers. It was a major black eye for the Disraeli administration.[11]

It wasn't long before the second Tory eye was also blackened. In the spring of 1879, British-Indian troops invaded Afghanistan in order to establish a resident mission in Kabul—the aim being to reverse a buildup of Russian influence in the region. Although the invasion was successful, a few months later a mutiny within the Afghan army resulted in the new station's complete massacre. The arrival of a second British-Indian force quieted the region once again, but the earlier slaughter went down badly with the British public. The Tories' handling of foreign affairs was not going well.[12]

At home, the situation was not much better. A depression was creeping across the commercial and industrial sectors, and both bankruptcies and unemployment were up. In addition, between poor harvests and declining market prices for local produce, there was widespread distress in rural districts. British farmers demanded government assistance and a return to protective tariffs. Disraeli's Tory government found itself caught between a rock and a hard place: while low prices threatened the farmers and landowners, urban industrial communities benefited from cheaper food. The agricultural problems were especially severe in Ireland, where they led to increased evictions of smallholders and the inevitable subsequent violence. In the shadow of the increasing unrest in Ireland, the Home Rule Party had acquired a new and strongly nationalistic leader in 1877, Charles Stewart Parnell (in whose antics Emma Darwin would take much interest over the next few years). Thus several factors, both local and international, played against the Conservatives in the general election of 1880. The result was a landslide victory for Gladstone's Liberal Party and, despite distinct misgivings on the part of the queen, the Grand Old Man once again assumed the office of prime minister that April.[13]

At Down House, Emma and Charles celebrated the Liberal victory, even though they increasingly found themselves on the opposite side of the political fence from certain of their grown children. Emma wrote to Hen on April 4, 1880, as the election results were still coming in:

> F & I are just beginning to find out whether we are on our heads or our heels (politically) but [as I] am 100 times more pleased than you can poss. be sorry, I think you ought to give up being sorry at all. Our mental Champagne has had v little sympathy except from A[unt] Eliz. as Frank hardly cares & George cares a little the wrong way; tho' he says now that he hopes the Lib[erals] may be as strong as poss. so as not to have to truckle. Seriously I shall be very glad if my opinions & yours gradually converge as I have felt it r[ather?] painful to have them so diametrically opposite to each other. Leo. says that he is reckoned the most outrageous Liberal at Chatham, & that he has about five companions in Liberalism. . . . A European war is George's bugbear in the matter.[14]

In late May, Emma and Charles spent a few days at Bassett with William and Sara. As was her wont, the delicate Sara spent little time with her guests. Emma reported to Hen that much of her time at Bassett had been devoted to "listening to the parrot who is evidently possessed with the spirit of brawling women of the lowest class; but stops dead if ever he perceives he is listened to." In July, back at Downe, the Darwins were inundated by "scientifics" in small and large groups. On one particular afternoon, some fifty scientific gentlemen and their wives descended on Down House (the men came walking and the women in carriages) and were entertained with cookies and lemonade. Unfortunately, the group included an "objectionable" German or two, prompting Emma and Frank to conclude that "a vulgar German was much horrider than a ditto English[man]." Charles rose to the occasion and, quite out of character, gave the group an impromptu lecture, on *Drosera*.[15]

Emma and Charles were once again on the road in August, this time to Cambridge to see Horace and Ida, as well as George. While there, they enjoyed excursions to Jesus College, Trinity Chapel, King's College Chapel, and the Botanic Garden. They also spent a pleasant afternoon chatting with Miss Helen Gladstone, the prime minister's youngest daughter, who had just taken an administrative position at Newnham College, one of Cambridge's two residential colleges for women. Miss Gladstone, reported Emma, "is ev[idently] v fond of H & Ida & v nice & cordial & with humour & merriment." One troubling incident during the Cambridge stay was Emma experiencing a bout of cardiac discomfort and needing to be examined by Dr. Andrew Clark. She bounced back quickly, however, and was not particularly worried by her symptoms. "Dr C saw me at once," she reassured Henrietta, but "thought there was little amiss that my heart was weak & yr doctoring of strychnine v good, but I am to take Nux Vom[ica] instead & leave off tea for a time as that does affect the heart." (Derived from the Southeast Asian strychnine tree, nux vomica contains the alkaloids strychnine and brucine. Prescribed by Victorian physicians as a tonic and stimulant, nux vomica is still used in herbal medicine to treat a variety of maladies including certain heart diseases and circulatory problems.)[16]

They returned home to a blazing hot September. Down the road at Tromer Lodge, Elizabeth Wedgwood was "utterly done up by the heat, w. her breath v short & too languid to do anything." Just a few months shy of eighty-seven, Emma's dear Elizabeth was having the predictable health problems of old age, exacerbated by progressive blindness. She self-medicated with coffee laced with brandy. Emma dreaded the thought that years of suffering might be in store for her sister.[17]

In Elizabeth's case, fate was kind and she was spared a prolonged decline. Her health gave way rapidly that fall and she passed away on November 7, 1880. For the second time that year, the extended family gathered to lay a beloved senior member in the grave. Ras Darwin and the Hensleigh Wedgwoods came down from London and Frank Wedgwood came from Barlaston. When his son Godfrey offered to go in his place, Frank said, "I mean to go. I could not let her be buried & me not there." The bent little figure "leaning on her stick, and followed by her dog, Tony," would never again walk up from Tromer Lodge and into the drawing room at Down House. Emma had lost the older sister who had always been there for her, first throughout childhood and later as her strong right arm during all those confinements. Her grief at Elizabeth's passing went deep, but it was mixed with relief. "[When] I think what her life might have been this winter even with something like a recovery I feel nothing but joy," Emma wrote to Hen.[18]

After the funeral, Emma turned to the tasks of answering the many letters of condolence and helping Godfrey, who was his aunt Elizabeth's executor, deal with the estate. A "little seal" that had originally come into the family as a gift to Jessie Sismondi from a "Grand Duchess" (possibly Albertine, duchesse de Broglie, the daughter of Madame de Staël) was earmarked for Henrietta, while other items were offered to the Tromer Lodge servants or evaluated for liquidation. On one trip to the Lodge, Emma noted her sister's parasol in its familiar place by the door: a "most pathetic" sight, she wrote to Hen. Another pathetic sight was Elizabeth's dog Tony, who sank into a silent depression after his mistress's death. Elizabeth had been extremely generous to her devoted servants—indeed, overly generous to some of them, at least in Emma's and Hensleigh's opinion—and there was talk of establishing annuities for them rather than simply making cash bequests. After discussion within the family, the annuity scheme was abandoned and the maids were "more than satisfied with their [cash] legacies." Emma persevered with her responses to condolences, and by the end of the month she was down to "tiresome letters to people I don't care for," including the Reverend Brodie Innes![19]

Charles ended up 1880 with two achievements, one scientific and one altruistic. On the scientific side, he published his biggest botanical book to date, *The Power of Movement in Plants*. Bragging a bit in his personal journal, Darwin noted on November 6: "1500 copies of Power of Movement sold at Murray's sale." Now he could turn his attention to that "curious" little book on earthworms he had long planned to write.[20]

On the personal side, in December 1880 Darwin mobilized several other scientific luminaries and a few key political friends to secure a Crown pension for Alfred Russel Wallace. Unlike Darwin and Hooker but rather like Huxley, Wallace had not been born into wealth. Despite having published several noteworthy books that brought him scientific fame—he won the Royal Society's Royal Medal in 1868—Wallace was perpetually short of money. At the age of fifty-seven, he was becoming a little desperate for a steady source of income, "some employment less precarious than writing books etc. which are wretched pay." Alerted to Wallace's financial troubles by Charles Lyell's former secretary, Arabella Buckley, Darwin began drumming up support for a petition to be sent to Prime Minister Gladstone on Wallace's behalf. After a bit of campaigning, the petition carried a dozen famous signatures including those of Huxley, Hooker, and the presidents of the Royal, Linnean, and Zoological Societies. The Duke of Argyll also joined the list of Wallace's supporters, and by the first week in January 1881, Prime Minister Gladstone had given his approval for a civil list pension of £200 per year, backdated six months. Darwin was delighted, and Wallace was graceful in his acceptance of the fruits of his colleagues' efforts. "It will relieve me from a great deal of the anxieties under which I have laboured for several years," he wrote in thanks.[21]

In late 1880 and early 1881, Gladstone had much more on his plate than Wallace's pension, and as always the Darwins enjoyed kibitzing the political scene. At the top of the list for the second-term prime minister was the situation in Ireland. Agricultural depression in the late 1870s had led to increased evictions of tenant farmers for nonpayment of rent, and this in turn gave rise to a sharp jump in rural crime. In 1880 alone there were more than 2,500 rural "outrages" ranging from maiming cattle to the murder of land agents. (The Irish nationalist Parnell and his Land League colleagues encouraged much of this agitation.) Hoping to gain new insights into the Irish situation, in the summer of 1880 Gladstone appointed a study group headed by the 6th Earl of Bessborough. Working quickly, the Bessborough Commission submitted its findings and recommendations in January of the following year. Those recommendations included granting the "three F's" to Irish smallholders: Fair Rents, Fixed Tenancies (making eviction possible only for nonpayment of rent), and Free Sale of a tenant's lease to his successor. The Bessborough report became the basis for Gladstone's Land Act of 1881.[22]

While the Bessborough recommendations met the general approval of Irish smallholders—and made enough sense to both houses of Parliament that the 1881 Land Act was passed into law—the report predictably drew fire from the landlords, who saw it as a serious threat to their property and power. In a letter to the *Times*, the Marquess of Lansdowne (who was also the Earl of Kerry and a thus an Irish landlord himself) warned that "an Act of Parliament founded upon the [Bessborough] recommendations . . . would, unless accompanied by large compensatory provisions [to the landlords], effect a confiscation of property the like of which has not been attempted within the memory of living men . . . [and] drive out of the country or convert into idle annuitants the only persons who have made intelligent or effectual efforts to raise the standard of Irish agriculture." At Down House, the Darwins—absentee landlords themselves, although with no property in Ireland—sided more with their Irish counterparts than with the tenant farmers. Emma wrote to Hen: "I read Lord Lansdowne's letter about Land to F & we both thought it very sensible & moderate & that most of what he said is unanswerable." For the Darwins, and perhaps especially for the fiscally conservative Charles, this was a time to apply the dictum of "all things in moderation," in this case moderation in liberal sentiments about "equal justice between man and man," as the Bessborough report had put it.[23]

A second thing on the prime minister's mind was the small-scale war going on in South Africa. Gladstone hadn't been any too keen on Disraeli's annexation of the Transvaal and its Boer inhabitants in 1877, and he did not move quickly to improve conditions there once he was back in office. The result was an armed rebellion by the Boers in December 1880, an uprising that Gladstone felt required a "vigorous response." Unfortunately, two factors weighed against the success of that response: first, the British had fewer than 2,000 troops in the Transvaal to bring order to 40,000 rebellious Boers, and second, the courage, determination, and military effectiveness of the Boers was grossly underestimated.[24]

The tragic result of being overconfident and undermanned was a very brief war (only three months in duration) that cost many British lives. Among the defeats suffered by the British, perhaps the best known is the battle of Majuba Hill where, on February 27, 1881, a small force of Boer sharpshooters routed 554 British troops out of a seemingly impregnable position and in the process killed their commander, Sir George Colley. Writing to her son George, Emma called Majuba Hill "a horrid affair" and wondered if Colley hadn't acted rashly. Richard Litchfield was so downcast that he thought the disasters in the Transvaal were "the beginning of the end & that it [was] all up with England," and Leo, still in the army, reported that his brother officers felt considerable uneasiness about the African situation. In the end, the British saved what face they could by suing for peace and signing a rather humiliating agreement that recognized "the 'independence' of the Transvaal subject to British 'suzerainty,'" whatever that meant. It was not the empire's finest hour.[25]

As the winter of 1881 turned into spring, the residents of Down House, now down to the senior Darwins plus Bessy, Frank, and Dubba, were joined by a regular flow of relatives and friends who provided entertainment for the home folks when the political news went flat. In February, Margaret Shaen came for a week's stay. A family friend since the early 1870s, Margaret may have met the Darwins through the Litchfields, since her father, William Shaen, was a solicitor and educator whose connection to London's Bedford College must have brought him into contact with Richard at the Working Men's College. Or the Gaskells, close friends of the Shaens, may have provided the link. However she was initially introduced to Emma, Margaret soon became the older woman's close friend and would visit Emma frequently over the years. Following hard on Margaret Shaen's heels, Laura Forster, a neighbor of the Farrers in Abinger and a lifelong friend of Henrietta's, arrived in March for a stay of eleven days. The married children and their spouses were in and out, of course, as were the unmarried sons. In April, Horace and Ida came for a week, bringing a full report of their recent—and disastrous—stay at Abinger. "The visit [was] an utter failure," Emma wrote to George, adding that "tho' Effie was civil . . . Mr F did not seem as if he cared about seeing any thing of Ida." Clearly, Theta Farrer was still brooding about Ida's choice of a husband, and his annoyance threatened to alienate father from daughter. Horace and Ida "will not try [an Abinger visit] again," reported Emma.[26]

Later that spring a special musical guest visited Down House. Accompanied by the Hermann Frankes, Hans Richter dropped by for lunch on May 20. For one accustomed mainly to entertaining scientific outsiders, it must have been a real treat for Emma to host someone from the music world. The talk probably centered on Richter's London concerts and the music of Richard Wagner, with whom Richter had long been associated. Henrietta was there too, having popped down from London for the day to round out the luncheon group. Besides meeting Richter and seeing her cousin Rose, Hen was no doubt interested in finalizing the details of that year's summer vacation, which was to be a return to the Lake District.[27]

The trip took the Darwin party to Patterdale near Ullswater, where they rented Glenridding House for the month of June. Most of the grown children, along with Mary Anne Ruck, managed to join the group for at least a few days, and they all passed their time boating, walking along the lake, or making day trips to local sites such as Borrowdale near Derwent Water, Kirkstone Pass, and Troutbeck. It was a lovely and relaxing time; Emma found the area "prettier than Coniston & [the] house . . . comfortable & luxurious." Glenridding House came complete with "a little rocky shore of [its] own," and nearly-five-year-old Dubba had a "delightful spit of shingle & mud to play on."[28]

The only cloud in the Darwins' sky that summer was the downturn in Ras's health. Truly never strong and compounded by hypochondria, "by the winter of 1880, Ras's chronic invalidism had become a real and serious stomach disorder which caused him constant pain and left him in a weakened condition." The extended family began to have genuine fears that this could be the start of a fatal decline, but at the same time they worried that a stream of concerned visitors might exacerbate rather than improve Ras's condition. Back from vacation, Emma wrote to William in August:

> We have been very uneasy about Eras who has been v unwell, or ill indeed for about a week, & has been troubled for several days & nights with a constant hiccup. . . . Aunt Caroline was so alarmed she came up for a few days which was very bad for her, & I am afraid not good for him. She is so nervous that she gets overwhelmed with alarm & must make a bad nurse. Aunt Fanny is up there now, & then I hope Hen will look after him, & I believe she suits him the best, as she has good courage & knows when to persuade him into doing things.[29]

In fact, nothing much could help. As his health continued mediocre at best and his personal circle of friends to decline, Ras had grown "weary of life." Most recently, his dear friend Thomas Carlyle had died in February 1881 (Jane Carlyle, whom Ras had loved to transport about London, had been dead for a full fifteen years), and not too many months earlier another literary friend, George Eliot (Marian Evans), had passed away. With 1880 having also claimed two first cousins, Elizabeth and Joe Wedgwood, and with neither of Ras's remaining siblings, Caroline and Charles, in particularly good health. Ras's world was closing down.[30]

Charles and Emma's last brief visit with Erasmus was August 3–5, and they found him "comfortable & cheerful" for at least part of that time. Similarly, Caroline and her daughter Margaret Vaughan Williams also found Ras relatively lively and talkative on August 20. These good days were deceptive, however. Ras's final sickness began on Sunday, August 21, showed slight abatement at midweek—at which point Caroline returned home, thinking her brother was out of the woods—but then turned fatal on the twenty-sixth. At the end there was no time to gather the far-flung members of the family, and when death came to Ras Darwin late on that Friday night, only a few London-based kin, including Fanny Hensleigh and Henrietta, were at his bedside. Of these two, Fanny was doubtless the more comforting. Long the true love of Ras's life, it was entirely fitting that she was there to hold his hand as he passed from this world.[31]

On September 1, 1881, an unusually bitter day with a dusting of snow, priest and cousin Allen Wedgwood committed his kinsman Erasmus Alvey Darwin to the cold ground of Saint Mary the Virgin's churchyard in Downe. "One of the sincerest, truest, and most modest of men," the mourners were told. Uncharacteristically, one of those mourners was Charles, who, deluding himself that Ras would stage a last-minute recovery, had been greatly shocked by the news of his brother's death. The old boyhood team of amateur experimenters, Ras and "Gas," was now broken up. The brother to whom Charles had always turned for mathematical help, the med school roommate, the staunch supporter who had labeled the *Origin* "the most interesting book I ever read," was no more. Erasmus's death left a huge hole in Charles's life.[32]

Between Ras's death and funeral, Emma wrote to William:

> I think there never was an old person who was so lamented by the young as Eras. All of you sons must feel that you valued him & went to see him whenever you could. It was the most cheerful part of his solitary life, except the habitual visits of Hen & Effie to both of whom he will be a loss daily felt. One can hardly define what his charm consisted in.[33]

William knew exactly what his mother was trying to say. He had long considered Ras to be "much more than an uncle" and to have "a charm in his manner . . . never [seen] in anybody else."[34] Emma too knew that charm; she had basked in it as a girl and young woman, but nonetheless had found it inadequate grounds for marriage. One wonders whether in the end she felt any responsibility for Ras's "solitary life." If so, the thought went unrecorded.

Immediately after the funeral, the family set to work settling Ras's estate and putting his house on the market. George was in charge of arranging the estate sale, but first everyone was given an opportunity to claim mementos from Ras's life. Emma made the trip to Queen Anne Street and "marked a good many things," and the Litchfields did likewise. Content with just her memories, Fanny Hensleigh asked only for a "little low what-not" and Ras's pocket edition of Milton. Most of Ras's other books ended up at Down House—so many, in fact, that they had to "lower the bookshelf" to accommodate them all. The Queen Anne Street house itself sold almost immediately.[35]

After everything had been liquidated, Charles and Caroline, as Ras's remaining siblings, split the proceeds between them. The inheritance brought Darwin's personal fortune above £250,000, nearly $21 million in today's currency. Despite the unhappy circumstances of this windfall, the Darwins couldn't help but be a little excited. Emma jokingly described their financial status as "enormously rich" and "disgustingly rich" in letters to Hen and Sara, respectively. Everyone came up with a different plan for a frivolous spending spree: Leo urged the purchase of an adjacent piece of land and the construction of a tennis court—a scheme that was subsequently carried out—while Bessy and Emma "ran riot" thinking of new bulbs and flowers for the

Down House gardens. Even Charles, normally the epitome of fiscal caution, entertained visions of "reckless extravagance in the matter of Chutnee & Bananas."[36]

In addition to the inheritance from Ras, the Darwins' fortune was enhanced that fall by the royalties from Charles's "curious" little worm book. *The Formation of Vegetable Mould, Through the Action of Worms* was published on October 10, 1881, and its popularity surprised everyone, including Darwin and John Murray the publisher. Two thousand copies sold immediately, and a second print run was ordered. By December there were 5,000 copies in print. Soon, to his amazement and then exasperation, Charles was "driven almost frantic" by an avalanche of letters from worm book readers full of all manner of odd facts and questions about the little creatures. One writer asked whether she should refrain from killing snails, fearful that they, like Darwin's worms, might be useful in the garden. Even Hooker got in his two cents' worth with a punning thank-you for his gift copy:

> I take shame to myself for not having earlier thanked you for the Diet of Worms, which I have read through with great interest. I must own I had always looked on worms as amongst the most helpless and unintelligent members of the creation; and am amazed to find that they have a domestic life and public duties! I shall now respect them, even in our Garden pots; and regard them as something better than food for fishes.[37]

One of the worm book's greatest fans was George John Romanes, a young biologist and enthusiastic disciple of Darwinism since the mid-1870s. As it happened, it fell to Romanes to review the book for the journal *Nature* and, not surprisingly, his review was glowing in its praise. Charles wrote on October 14 to thank Romanes for "the splendid review," and mentioned in passing how worn out he felt, but said he was nonetheless looking forward to discussing Romanes's research when they met later in the autumn.[38]

That conversation almost took place on Thursday, December 15, while the Darwins were in London on a pre-Christmas visit to Henrietta and Richard. Charles called unannounced at Romanes's house, hoping to find the biologist at home. He was disappointed in that respect, but while talking with the butler he was staggered by the onset of sharp chest pains. Realizing that the pale and gasping Darwin was in distress, the butler asked if he didn't want to step inside for a rest. Charles declined the invitation and turned to make his way back to Bryanston Street, but hadn't gone far before he reeled and had to clutch at some nearby railings to keep from going down. Still watching, the

Romanes's butler rushed to his aid and then called a cab to take Darwin to the Litchfields'.[39]

The next day Emma went to see Dr. Andrew Clark, who told her he suspected a "derangement of the heart." On Saturday, however, after actually examining the patient, Clark revised his diagnosis, saying that Charles's heart was "perfectly sound" and that he probably had "some internal eczema" that should respond to a change of diet. But medicine was even more of an inexact science in 1881 than it is today, and Clark's first hunch turned out to be the better one. It had been a heart attack after all, and Charles at least knew it. Not long after the episode, he told a geological friend that he had "received his warning."[40]

By the end of their London stay, Charles was feeling "quite comf." Back at Down House in January and the first part of February 1882, he continued in relatively good health, taking quinine for a nagging cough and as an appetite stimulant. Like everyone else in the family, he was full of excitement about the safe arrival of the second grandchild, a son born to Ida and Horace on December 7, 1881, and named Erasmus after his great-great-grandfather and his late great-uncle. (With her usual understatement, Emma described little Erasmus as "a placid satisfac[tory] baby but not pretty.") By late February, however, the chest pains were back, and Charles had to restrict his laps around the Sandwalk to keep his discomfort under control. He was feeling badly enough by March 10 that Emma sent for Dr. Clark, who now reversed himself and identified the heart as the seat of Charles's troubles.[41]

Clark's latest diagnosis was, understandably, distressing for the whole family and "excessively depress[ing]" for the patient. Not only that, but Clark, busy man that he was, still had the annoying habit of making very brief visits and then refusing to take a fee. Desiring a second opinion—and longer consultations—Emma brought in Dr. Norman Moore, who, no doubt to her satisfaction, gave the opinion that although Charles's "heart was weak" there were "no signs of its being organically wrong." Caught between two conflicting diagnoses, Charles struggled on from day to day with a good appetite, but so "oddly feeble" that in the evening he had to be carried upstairs by Jackson the butler. In retrospect, this lack of strength was clearly the result of cardiac insufficiency.[42]

Thus, as the winter of 1882 wore on toward spring, the mood at Down House was somber. For those with eyes to see, Charles was clearly in decline, and Emma anxiously watched as her beloved husband struggled with his symptoms. Still, there were a few pleasant diversions, the new grandchild for one and five-year-old Bernard for another. Additionally, in late March, Leonard wrote to tell his parents that he was engaged to Miss Elizabeth Fraser, the sister of a fellow officer. Miss Fraser went by the name of Bessie, but Leo renamed her "Bee" to avoid confusion with his sister (not that the Darwins ever had problems dealing with multiple Fannys!). Bee was three years older than Leo, not particularly healthy—her doctor had diagnosed "exhausted nerve tissue, and an unusually sensitive and highly strung temperament"— and very religious. One wonders if the last item didn't remind Emma of her own difference with Charles. But of course, when one is in love, small things like age, health, and religion can be overlooked, and Leo and Bee hoped to marry in the summer, just as soon as Bee returned from a restorative sea voyage to South Africa and Leo got past his Staff College exam.[43] A delighted Emma responded to Leo:

> Your letter was no great surprize but a great joy to us. We have felt for some time that it was such a waste you should not be married, you would make a woman so entirely happy & you would be so happy yourself. . . .
>
> You may be sure we will be most careful to avoid saying any thing to annoy her or shock her, but in these days I do think there is a marked difference in the way people feel the religious opinions of others. Your father is in favor of her going this voyage because of doing her good & I am quite against it, so you will not find much help from us. I think an entire change & the beginning of a happy life might do as well. But then you must be married soon, as a *long* engagement is oddly wearing. . . .
>
> Here is my scheme—persuade her to give up the voyage now, be married as soon as possible & take her with you to Australia which would be quite as good for her health. . . . One of my objections to her going [on the African voyage] is the losing of 3 months of happiness . . . & the other is that if you go together to Australia you will be drowned together but in this case she will be drowned by herself.[44]

The last sentence was humor of the blackest sort, of course, but Leo knew his mother, and the joke no doubt made him smile. The Australian comments refer to a trip to Brisbane that Leo was scheduled to make in the fall. Once there and working as part of a three-man Royal Engineers team, he would try once again to observe a transit of Venus. It is also interesting to note that in her response Emma made no attempt to identify with Bee's religious fervor. Rather, she aligned herself unequivocally with the religious skepticism/heterodoxy of the other Darwins. This was an important point, and she made her position on religion—remarkably different in 1882 from the one she had held as a young woman—crystal clear in a follow-up note to Leo: "I have no doubt of our being fond of [Bee]—& I *trust* she will like us—& get to feel a confidence that we do sympathize in & entirely respect her deepest feelings tho' we may differ in opinions." And then there was the matter of the name. "Bee" was probably a little too pert for Emma's taste, just as "Harriet" had been rejected as a nickname for Henrietta years before, and she tried for a change. "What do you think of Betty," she asked Leo. "It is so old fashioned as to have lost all vulgarity." It was a good try, but it didn't work. "Bee" was Leo's choice, and "Bee" stuck.[45]

Dr. Moore's opinion that Charles's heart was weak but not diseased was comforting, but only temporarily so. On April fourth his chest pains were back with a vengeance, and they continued, although fluctuating in intensity, over the next several days. To alleviate his distress, Charles took the newly introduced antispasmodic amyl nitrate, which had been prescribed by Dr. Clark. On April fifteenth he fainted while moving from the dinner table to the sofa. Some brandy helped him come around fairly quickly, and no doctor was sent for. April sixteenth and seventeenth were good days, marked by very little discomfort and no need for amyl nitrate, but on the eighteenth the pain was back, and at midnight he woke Emma, saying, "I have got the pain & I shall feel better or bear it better if you are awake."[46]

At 2 A.M. they sent for Mr. Charles Allfrey, a surgeon in nearby Chislehurst. He stayed overnight at Down House and was "a great support" to Emma. Charles was asleep when Allfrey left at 8:00 A.M. on the nineteenth, but not long after that he awoke with violent vomiting and retching in addition to his chest pains. Emma, Henrietta, Bessy, and Frank were in attendance on the patient, but there was little they could do. Throughout the morning Darwin tossed and groaned in his suffering, saying several times, "If I could but die!" Mr. Allfrey and another physician, Dr. Walter Moxon, were sent for and arrived at the house in the early afternoon, but by then Charles was unconscious. By four o'clock his labored breathing had ceased.[47]

In his last agony Charles murmured words of thanks and love to his wife and children. To Emma he said, "I am not the least afraid of death," and "Remember what a good wife you have been to me." To Henrietta and Frank, watching at his bedside while Emma rested, he said, "You two dears are the best of nurses." To all the children he sent words of love. After her beloved husband had breathed his last, Emma—no doubt numb from exhaustion—was "very calm but . . . cried a little."[48] Her "own dearest Charley" was gone, and nothing would ever be the same.

19. Life at a Lower Pitch

EMMA AWOKE ON APRIL 20, 1882, and began her first full day of widowhood. Charles was gone, taking with him so many of the worries, duties, and joys that she had known. They had been husband and wife for forty-three years, during which she had seen him through endless illnesses and he had seen her through (seemingly) endless pregnancies and births. Their daily lives had become inextricably intertwined; the rituals of eating, sleeping, working, relaxing, entertaining guests, and sharing private intimacies had been fine-tuned through the years. Now all of that had changed at a stroke. Her daily existence would need much restructuring.

Looking back, Emma must have marveled that she had had Charles for as long as she did. The man who at age thirty-five had committed his nascent species theory to her keeping because he feared his "sudden death" had lived almost four more decades, dying at the respectable age of seventy-three. Together they had experienced the joys of parenthood and grandparenthood, the triumphs of Charles's scientific achievements, and the devastating sorrows of deaths—Annie's and Amy's chief among them. As the remaining sons and their wives joined the Litchfields and Frank and Bessy at Down House on that April Thursday, one can picture Emma greeting them in something of a mental fog as she tried to get a handle on her loss and altered circumstances.[1]

As the day progressed, William arrived from Southampton, George and Horace from Cambridge, and Leo from Chatham. All were stunned by the loss of their father, but Leo, usually so jolly and full of fun, was particularly deeply grieved and his anguish brought tears to his mother's eyes. The wheels were already in motion to have the funeral at St. Mary's Church in the village, followed by burial in the churchyard where so many Darwins—now including Ras—already resided. These arrangements were announced on April 21 in the *Times* in a lengthy obituary that also compared the impact of Darwin's death with that of Benjamin Disraeli exactly one year earlier to the day.[2]

But then Darwin's scientific colleagues stepped in. Spearheaded by Francis Galton (a grandson of Erasmus Darwin and his second wife, thus a half-cousin), T. H. Huxley, John Lubbock (MP and president of the Linnean Society), and William Spottiswoode (president of the Royal Society), plans were hatched to petition the dean of Westminster for permission to bury Darwin in the Abbey. It was "the will of the intelligence of the nation," declared Huxley in his eulogy in *Nature*. Lubbock canvassed his colleagues in the Commons, and twenty influential individuals including the speaker and deputy speaker, as well as several Royal Society Fellows, readily signed the petition. The document was then sent to the dean, who happened to be abroad but nonetheless promptly telegraphed back his assent.[3]

Now the scientists had only to convince the family. Predictably, Emma and the children were initially doubtful about abandoning the long-established plans for a Downe burial. After all, Darwin was already laid out in the rough wood coffin ordered from John Lewis, the local joiner, and besides that, he had loved the village and the Kentish countryside for more than forty years. Surely the most appropriate thing would be to lay his bones in St. Mary's churchyard. William Darwin, however, thought burial in the Abbey was a good idea, and when the scheme became public knowledge, the family was inundated with letters and newspaper appeals urging them to acquiesce. The *Times* in an editorial declared that Darwin's mortal remains

would have rested not inharmoniously under the tall elms in the quiet churchyard of Down. They could rest nowhere so fitly as among the brotherhood of English worthies at Westminster. By every title which can claim a corner in that sacred earth, the body of Charles Darwin should be there. Conquerors lie there who have added rich and vast territories to their native empire. Charles Darwin has, perhaps, borne the flag of science farther, certainly he has planted its standard more deeply, than any Englishman since Newton. He has done more than extend the boundaries of science; he has established new centres whence annexations of fresh and fruitful truths are sure continually to be made. The Abbey has its orators and Ministers who have convinced reluctant senates and swayed nations. Not one of them all has wielded a power over men and their intelligences more complete than that which for the last twenty-three years has emanated from a simple country house in Kent.[4]

In the end, the family gave in to the general clamor for a Westminster burial. Writing to Fanny and Hensleigh, Emma confided: "It gave us all a pang not to have him rest quietly here by Eras-; but William felt strongly, & on reflection I did also, that his gracious & grateful nature wd have wished to accept the acknowledgement of what he has done. Wm. & Geo. went to Brasted after the Tel. from Mr. Spottiswoode saying what he & the R. S. wished. The only stipulation they made was that we would not consent in the face of any opposition or discussion." Emma went on to say she doubted that either Fanny or Hensleigh would want to go to the funeral service because "it will be long & agitating & prob. cold & a considerable risk."[5]

And so Darwin, who in Huxley's words had been "ignored in life by the official representatives of the kingdom," was immortalized in death. The *Times* devoted a column and a half to its description of the funeral. Among the dignitaries in attendance were peers and politicians including Earl Spencer, president of the queen's Privy Council, four European ambassadors, and of course innumerable "scientifics." Among the many academics who made the trip to the Abbey were the master of Christ's College, Cambridge, and the headmaster of the Shrewsbury Grammar School. Charles's coffin, covered with a black velvet pall and topped with white flowers, was borne by ten pallbearers: the Dukes of Devonshire and Argyll, the Earl of Derby, American ambassador James Russell Lowell, Westminster canon Frederic Farrar, and Darwin's closest scientific friends, Spottiswoode, Hooker, Huxley, Wallace, and Lubbock. Emma did not try to attend the service, but the family was well represented by all of the Darwin children and their spouses except for Ida, who was at home with baby Erasmus, as well as an impressive array of nieces, nephews, and cousins from the Darwin, Wedgwood, and Allen families. Mrs. Ruck was there, and so was Hensleigh, despite Emma's warning about catching a cold. Caroline, Charles's only surviving sibling, was not well enough to attend, but her daughters Sophy and Margaret came in from Leith Hill Place. The Darwins' current butler, William Jackson, and their devoted retired butler, Joseph Parslow, represented the Down House staff. Side by side with the write-up of the funeral, the *Times* printed a letter to the editor from John Lort Stokes, one of the *Beagle*'s former officers and now an admiral. Stokes's letter was a brief tribute to Darwin and a remembrance of their time as ship-mates back when Charles was called "Philos" and before he achieved fame as the author of the *Origin*. Here were memories from Darwin's scientific begin-ning, and they paired nicely with the funeral's demarcation of his scientific and earthly endings.[6]

In the days before and after the funeral, Emma was kept busy writing to friends and relations, first notifying them of Charles's death and later thank-ing them for their letters of condolence. She wrote to Joseph Hooker immedi-ately after the death, sending such "a touching letter" that Hooker told Hux-ley, it "quite upset me." She poured out her heart to Fanny and Hensleigh, saying that she had not been unprepared for Charles's death, but had felt for "2 months (& before that in the winter—tho' that fear passed away) that our secure happiness (& oh what happiness, but I have appreciated it all along it seems now) was all shattered." She then alluded to Fanny's presence in Mal-vern in 1851 when Annie died:

> I hardly know how I shall get thro' my days so empty & desolate; but I do feel life worth having & that my children want me—my dear Bessy especially who is with me night & day. How often [Charles] has mentioned with emo-tion your going to him in his deep sorrow in 51 & what a support you were.[7]

By mid-May "the great blank" left by Darwin's death (as Henrietta de-scribed it to George) was settling in, but despite the predictable emotional ups and downs, with the help of the children Emma found herself coping. She wrote to William, who was struggling mightily with his own grief over his father's death, that she had gone "in the Bath chair to the sand walk to see the bluebells and it was all so pretty and bright it gave me the saddest mixture of feelings, and I felt a sort of self reproach that I could in a measure enjoy it." To Leo she said much the same: "I feel a sort of wonder that I can in a measure enjoy the beauty of spring. I am trying to get some fixed things to do at certain times, Bernard's lessons are a gt help to me; & some read-ing with Bessy; but oh how I miss my daily fixed occupation, always received when I went to [your father] with some sweet word of welcome." And most intimately of all, she confided in Hen.

> I am trying to make stages in the day of something special to do. It often comes over me with a wave of desolate feeling that there is nothing I need to do & I think of your true words 'poor mother you have time enough now.' The regularity of my life was such an element of happiness, & to be received

every time I joined him by some word of welcome, & to feel that he was happier that very minute for my being with him. Some regrets will still come on but I don't encourage them. I . . . feel it such a comfort to write & tell you every thing.

It was an intimacy that Henrietta welcomed with her whole heart. She wrote back to her mother: "It is such a blessed feeling to me that you do care for my love & that you will lean upon it. I think you hardly know how precious you are to us. I sometimes feel such a passionate wish to cherish & comfort you—almost as if you were my child as well as my dearest Mother." By June, in a letter written from Leith Hill Place during a visit that enabled widow and sister to have a long memory-fest about Charles, Emma was able to reassure Hen that she did not find life "flat . . . only all at a lower pitch."[8]

Politics, as always, were diverting, even in the midst of personal grief. In Ireland, agrarian agitation continued in 1882 despite the passage of the Land Act the year before. Establishing fair rents was proving difficult, especially for tenants already in arrears, and Irish juries had become increasingly reluctant to convict defendants in cases with land and/or nationalistic overtones. In response to a situation that, from their perspective, was steadily worsening, the British authorities passed ever stronger coercion legislation—laws that the chief secretary for Ireland, W. E. Forster, would direct primarily at militant nationalist groups. When Charles Stewart Parnell was imprisoned in October 1881 after making an inflammatory speech, his Land League was promptly declared dangerous and illegal. Parnell was not in jail long, however. He was released in May 1882 as part of a behind-the-scenes deal with Gladstone. Strongly opposed to Parnell's release, Forster resigned his post as the Irish secretary.[9]

Lord Frederick Cavendish, Gladstone's nephew by marriage, was selected to replace Forster. Cavendish arrived in Dublin on May fifth, and by the evening of the sixth he was dead, assassinated along with the permanent undersecretary, Thomas Burke, as they strolled in Phoenix Park. It was a brutal and horrifying crime: Cavendish and Burke were slashed repeatedly with surgical knives before their throats were cut. Outrage swept Britain, and Parliament promptly passed a bill authorizing even greater coercive action. This, of course, led to increased opposition by the nationalists, and so the situation spiraled even further out of control.[10] Emma commented on the Irish situation to William four days after the murders: "I never remember being so horror struck with any public event—(What a beautiful speech Forster made about Mr Burke—) I believe some good may come out of it in spurring on Gladstone to take some decisive step such as martial law or abolishing juries along with measures about arrears."[11]

To Henrietta, Emma voiced agreement with the view that a strengthened Coercion Bill was necessary because, as W. E. Forster had argued in the Commons, although force was "not in itself a remedy for the evils of Ireland . . . there must be nothing to anticipate or take the place of stopping murder or terrorism; this must be done before anything else." "Yesterday I was gloating over the Irish bill & enjoying the rage of the Irish in a truly Carlylian fashion," Emma wrote to Hen. When it came to assassins, she was all for using a heavy hand.[12]

A second diversion for Emma—unlike Irish politics, a happy one—was Leo and Bee's upcoming marriage. After weighing all of their options, Bee had canceled her trip to South Africa and she and Leo had set July 11 as their wedding day. By then the newly promoted Captain Darwin would be past his Staff College examination, which was scheduled for June, and the newlyweds would honeymoon en route to Australia and a second go at the transit of Venus. Emma was still dragging her heels about Leo's choice of nicknames for Miss Fraser—to Hen, Emma grumbled that "the best plan is to call Bee Bessy & when there is any ambiguity to say Bessy Leonard"—but she was delighted that the wedding was going forward and that Bee and Charles had had a chance to know one another, albeit ever so slightly.[13]

As exam time approached, Leo crammed like mad, boning up especially on military history, reputed to be the most difficult of the various subtopics. His hard work paid off. To everyone's surprise, Leo not only passed the exam but actually took a "first." "Isn't it splendid abt Pouts," wrote Henrietta to George, using Leo's childhood nickname. "I never doubted much as to his passing but I never hoped for first." Leo himself did not learn of his success until early October while en route to Australia with Bee. He wrote back to his mother: "I must say I was very pleased. . . . My reason told me that I ought to have been beaten, and I had with difficulty almost made myself expect to get the news of a failure; so that it came as a pleasant surprise, or almost surprise, because in the bottom corner of my heart I always thought I had done well."[14]

The Fraser-Darwin wedding came off on schedule on July 11—unfortunately, one of those "cold & dismal" English summer days—and as it was not performed in Downe, one assumes it took place in Bee's home parish. In any event, Emma did not attend, although most of the rest of the family did. "They all started this mg before I was up," she wrote to Hen. Six weeks later, after a little prevoyage honeymooning, the newlyweds found themselves headed south aboard the SS *Liguria*. Unfortunately, they didn't even make it out of the English Channel before they were both seasick. This malady proved to be temporary for Bee but, taking after his father, a more chronic complaint for Leo. A month into the voyage, he was still unable to "sit out dinner" and wrote to his mother, "My stomach is perfectly consistent; from the first day to the last it says, 'I am not going to make much of a fuss about it, but I don't like it, and no amount of banging about will alter my opinion.'" Just after rounding the Cape of Good Hope, the *Liguria* was hit by a heavy storm that "swamped the steerage passengers," washed a couple of pigs overboard, and caused the ship to roll "so heavily that the [life]boats on the davitts touched the water sometimes." Emma's joke about Leo and Bee drowning together had very nearly come true.[15]

By early October they had reached Australia. Disembarking at Melbourne, "a disappointing town," Leo and Bee made their way overland to Sydney. Sydney was much more to their taste, with a harbor that was "quite worthy of its reputation" and, in the middle of town, impressive "Botanical gardens, Governors House and grounds." Sydney would "in time be a wonderful city," enthused Leo. They didn't have long to enjoy Sydney's wonders, however, because another steamship ride soon brought them to Brisbane, and from there they traveled 150 miles inland to the tiny settlement of Jimbour, where the transit team planned to make its observations. Befitting their married status, Captain and Mrs. Darwin rented their own house, and after a discouraging search for servants—"there are only 2 cooks to be had," reported Leo, "one of whom I know is a drunkard; so I have taken the other on chance"—they settled in for a two months' stay.[16]

There was plenty of testing of equipment and practicing to be done before the transit date of December 7—"the fatal 7th," said Leo, already worried about bad weather. Nonetheless, there was time for a bit of local sightseeing, including a trip into the bush to an Aboriginal camp. Leo's report to his mother about this excursion is revealing. Startlingly racist to a modern reader, Leo's disinterested comments about the Aboriginals and their probable fate remind one of his father's equally unemotional forecast of genocide in *The Descent of Man*, where he predicted: "At some future period . . . the civilized races of man will almost certainly exterminate and replace throughout the world the savage races." Leo wrote:

> The natives never stick in one place long, and only make the roughest huts of bark, supported by stakes, and quite open at one side. . . . I believe this tribe is

going to fight another before long. The English never interfere in these fights and I fancy are only too glad if they kill each other. I expect they have been abominably treated, but it is a good thing that the poor wretches are dying out as quickly as possible. They are very cruel, & treacherous; a story is told, and I believe a true one, how they attacked one English family, and killed everyone except one lad; when this man grew up he devoted himself to killing the blacks, and is said to have disposed of over three hundred himself.[17]

Leo simply was not fated to photograph a transit, and on the "fatal 7th" the day was so cloudy at Jimbour that no observations could be made. "It feels much flatter and duller than I expected it would," he told his mother. The team had "nothing to show for these weeks of work; there are few people who have been twice round the world to see a thing without seeing it." Now the plan was for the Darwins to proceed to Singapore, where Leo would use telegraphic exchanges to help "determine the difference of longitude between that station and Port Darwin," Australia, a town named years earlier for his famous father. Shortly after New Year's 1883, they were steaming their way north around the coast of Queensland.[18]

Meanwhile back in England, a plan for Emma and Bessy to split the year between Down House in the summer and Cambridge in the winter had been proposed. George and Horace (plus Ida and Erasmus) already lived in Cambridge, and Frank had decided to relocate there as well. Having lost his job as scientific assistant when his father died, Frank now felt a need for salaried employment. He had started on a life-and-letters volume commemorating his father, but he also hoped to land a research or teaching position at Cambridge. The prospect of having three sons and both of her grandchildren in Cambridge tipped the balance for Emma, and she and Bessy began the search for a winter home.[19]

It did not take long for them to settle on The Grove, a charming house on the Huntingdon Road that took its name from its numerous wych elms. Just about a mile from the center of town, The Grove also had lovely gardens with plenty of "nooks & corners for shelter & seats." It was "the very place for an old person," declared Emma. A minor drawback was that it needed some alterations before they could move in, but an arrangement was made with Caroline Jebb, the American wife of R. C. Jebb, then professor of Greek at the University of Glasgow, to rent the Jebbs' Cambridge home, called Springfield, from November 1882 through the following April. The deal was brokered by George Darwin, who had been a friend of the Jebbs for several years.[20]

Before beginning her split-year schedule, Emma took two short vacation trips. In August, accompanied by Bessy and Bernard, she spent ten days in Southampton with William and Sara. In most ways the visit was unremarkable, but Sara's "care-worn" and joyless demeanor depressed Emma enough to prompt a comment to Henrietta that "the mistress of the house bringing so little cheerfulness makes one feel that it is a great want." Sara's low spirits didn't affect William personally, but they certainly dampened the general atmosphere at Bassett. Interestingly, new evidence suggests that her mood swings, from easy laughter to cheerlessness, might have had a medical explanation. It is now known that a strong strain of manic depression ran—and still runs—through the Sedgwick family. This malady would lead her brother Arthur, whom William Darwin had enjoyed meeting in America, to commit suicide many years later.[21]

Emma's second excursion took place in September, when she and Bessy met the Litchfields for ten seaside days in Eastbourne. She enjoyed listening to the waves "clapping like guns" and watching the children run up and down the beach. It was all "much superior to Hastings," she told George. But then it was back to Downe to get ready for the change of houses, a move that was accomplished during the first week in November. On November 22 Emma wrote to Leo and Bee:

> We are all well & have been settled in this pretty & cheerful house [Springfield] about a fortnight. We find the life here cheerful especially for Bessy, what with lectures, calls, A[mateur] D[ramatic] C[lub] & Greek plays. The Horaces come in very often which alas! we shall miss at the Grove, which however I think partic. nice & snug, & the building going on tol[erably] fast. . . . Rasmus almost walking. Bernard v jolly & learning to bowl a hoop. Frank busy preparing for his spring lectures & without m time for the Life [and Letters]. I think this place will suit him well.[22]

Frank had, in fact, found quite a satisfactory job in the university's Botany Department teaching and doing research on the physiology of plants. And, unbeknownst to him, one of the instructors Bessy had approached about auditing lectures was Miss Ellen Crofts, lecturer in English Literature and fellow of Newnham College, who within a year would be the second Mrs. Francis Darwin.[23]

Wintering in Cambridge turned out to suit everyone quite well. Frank had his work, Bessy her pastimes, and Emma her grandchildren. Erasmus was now a toddler referred to by his doting grandmother as "sweet little Razimoffsky." Little Ras would soon have competition for his parents' and grandmother's attention: by the end of 1882, Ida was pregnant once again. For his part, Bernard was a normal, lively six-year-old, into everything and quite used to ruling the roost at his grandmother's house. One of his first reactions to life in Cambridge was to complain about the increased flow of friends coming to lunch with Emma and Bessy. "Grand mamma," asked Bernard, "do you like these people coming always to the house—I hate it—I hate shaking hands with them." On a trip in February to check on renovations at The Grove, Bernard managed to have "a souse in the ditch . . . in a velvet suit." Despite being cold and wet, Bernard rather enjoyed the dunking, since he hated the velvet outfit and had been looking for a way to spoil it. A few days later he had his first riding lesson on a "fidgetty screw" that Emma judged to be not quite safe. Never a particularly brave little boy, Bernard pleased Emma when he took to riding and made rapid progress, being able to go "without a leading rein" by early April. He was growing up.[24]

It was soon decided that Horace and Ida would build a house for themselves near The Grove. This would put them closer to Emma, Bessy, Frank, and Bernard, and also get Horace a bit further away from his work at the Cambridge Scientific Instrument Company on St. Tibb's Row. From its plans, the house looked "enormous" to Emma and carried an impressive cost of £2,500. Horace and Ida had to struggle with the architect, who wanted to make the design more ornate than they wished.[25] The house, which was named The Orchard, would ultimately be part of a three-family Darwin compound on Cambridge's Huntingdon Road.

At the university, George Darwin began 1883 by putting his hat in the ring for the position of Plumian Professor of Astronomy and Experimental Philosophy. The previous holder of the position, the astronomer James Challis, had died in 1882 after forty-six years in the Plumian Chair. Luckily for George, who was a good mathematician but no astronomer, the job actually carried no practical astronomical duties, despite its title. His main competitor turned out to be George's old undergraduate mathematics coach, E. J. Routh, a man that Emma, showing unvarnished maternal bias, characterized to Leo as "the stupidest man in private that ever was." When the election was held in January, George won by the slimmest of margins, five to four. This close call notwithstanding, the victory pleased him greatly, "the pleasantest part," said his mother, being "the warm sympathy of his friends." With this lifetime appointment in his pocket, George's academic future was assured.

Now if he could only attract a few more students into his advanced math classes—he usually got just a handful, and some of these would occasionally doze off—and if he could only find a wife.[26]

In fact, George had been searching for a wife for some time. His first proposal, dating perhaps to the late 1870s or very early 1880s, was apparently made to Miss Eleanor Butcher, the youngest daughter of the bishop of Meath. Unfortunately for George, the gaunt and sad-eyed Eleanor loved another, and she rejected the offer. Then in 1882 another possibility arose. In April of that year, eighteen-year-old Nellie Du Puy came over from Philadelphia to visit her aunt Caroline Jebb in Glasgow. Cara, who freely admitted that she was an "inveterate match-maker," immediately began introducing Nellie to a series of eligible men, first in Glasgow and then during the summer in Cambridge. At the top of the list of bachelors were the brothers Gerald and Frank Balfour, aged twenty-nine and thirty, and thirty-seven-year-old George Darwin, all Trinity graduates and longtime friends. Besides arranging all manner of social interactions between Nellie and these marriageable males, Mrs. Jebb instructed Nellie on proper dress and behavior while in Britain. "I want greatly to try to teach her to carry herself more gracefully . . . [and giggle] less," Cara wrote to Nellie's mother in America. Despite her best efforts, however, Mrs. Jebb's matchmaking proved unsuccessful. Gerald Balfour showed some interest in the young American, but Nellie thought him "the most conceited man she ever met." Frank Balfour was more charming, but he came to a tragic end while mountain climbing in the Alps that July, leaving all his friends in England devastated. According to Mrs. Jebb, a brokenhearted George Darwin commented that "he could have spared better any of his own brothers." (One assumes that if this quote is accurate, it could only have been hyperbole born of grief. All indications are that George was devoted to every one of his brothers.) George continued to haunt the Jebb household throughout August 1882, being so much in evidence that Nellie nicknamed him the Constant One, and he proposed to Nellie in the early fall. But constancy was not enough for Miss Du Puy, who may have been put off somewhat by George's being nineteen years her senior. Whatever her reasons, Nellie rejected George's proposal—and, in fact, remained a spinster for the rest of her life. Two years later, her sister Maud would make a different decision.[27]

As 1883 began in the Antipodes, Leo and Bee were rounding the north coast of Australia en route to Singapore on their way home. Having recovered from the disappointment of his second failed transit of Venus, Leo was enjoying the return trip and so was his bride. Shopping was high on Bee's list of favorite pastimes, and Leo joined right in, helping her make memento purchases at each port of call. In Rockhampton, Bee bought "a bit of Queensland opal"; on Thursday Island, just off Cape York, she shopped for pearls but had to settle for "two bird of paradise tails . . . at 10 [shillings] each" ("quite high enough price," grumbled Leo); and in Singapore she picked up a nice collection of Japanese items from pawnshops, besides buying several colorful sarongs.[28]

After Leo had completed his longitude work in Singapore, he and Bee went on to Sri Lanka, where they visited the ancient royal capital of Anuradhapura, dating to 380 B.C. At the next stop, Cairo, they stayed a fortnight. They enjoyed seeing Bee's brother, Tom Fraser, a staff officer serving under Sir Evelyn Wood as part of the new British military presence in Egypt. They also devoted a day to visiting the Pyramids, but were disappointed, finding the gigantic structures "rather a delusion and a snare, as they are so exactly like their pictures." And of course, true to form, they went shopping in the Cairo bazaars. Keen to take home an Oriental rug, Leo and Bee spent some little time bargaining with a dealer, only to come away empty-handed when he refused to meet their demand for a 60 percent reduction in price. To Emma's enormous pleasure, "the Leonards" were back on English soil by the end of April, with Bee looking "better & younger" and Leo "a good deal fatter." In fact, Emma confided to William, she hoped that once at Staff College, Leo would start a regime of daily horseback riding and shed a few pounds.[29]

Emma's diary entry for February 24, 1883, included the notation "Miss Crofts dined." This was the same Miss Ellen Crofts whose literature course Bessy had hoped to audit and who now had caught Frank Darwin's eye. A twenty-seven-year-old Newnham College bluestocking, Ellen was, in Emma's words, "nice & merry & natural . . . almost pretty [with] black hair & dark eyes & a bright smile." A thoroughly modern woman, she cut her hair short, smoked cigarettes, and preferred Robert Louis Stevenson's novels to Dickens's. Along with her merry and "chattering" side, however, Ellen had a reserved and melancholy streak that could render her moody and unhappy even when she had no apparent reason to be. Perhaps it was this very aspect of Ellen's persona that appealed to Frank, who could be depressed and moody himself, especially since Amy's death. Whatever the attraction, throughout the spring of 1883 Frank and Ellen proceeded to fall in love, and by June they were engaged. The prospect of Frank's life being "turned [once again] into wholesome happiness" was delightful to his mother, although she worried a little that neither Frank nor Ellen had much sense about money. If there was a single dark cloud on the horizon, it was the prospect of Bernard going to live in a new home with his father and stepmother. "Poor Bessy can think of little else but losing Bernard," Emma confided to William. Dubba would always be Bessy's "special nephew." She had helped raise him in Amy's stead, and he had become very much the child she would never have.[30]

In London, the Litchfields were preparing to move from Bryanston Square in Marylebone to a larger house in the tony neighborhood of Kensington Square. Hen and Richard were busy making decisions about wallpaper and paint for their new home, and since Emma was doing likewise for The Grove, mother and daughter probably conferred about decorating schemes when Emma visited London in early March. Additionally, the one-year anniversary of Charles's death was fast approaching, and she took this opportunity to view his grave for the first time, probably with Hen by her side. Ever thrifty expressing her feelings, Emma simply noted in her diary on the day of the visit: "Westminster Abbey."[31] After the anniversary, she opened up a little more in a letter to Henrietta, saying, "It seems to me that the actual anniversary does not bring so much to one's mind as the time before it. Sometimes it feels to me nearer than it did six months ago." Nonetheless, with the help of her children and friends, she was steadily making the adjustment to widowhood, and the success of that transition surprised her a little. Emma confided to Henrietta that she felt "astonished at myself that I can make out a cheerful life after losing him."[32]

Emma, Bessy, Frank, and Bernard returned to Downe in early June. It was wonderful to be back in the dear old place, of course, and Emma reveled in "the quiet & greenness, & freshness." The country air was invigorating and strengthening as she walked through the familiar fields and "loitered about the haystack," and she especially enjoyed the freshly picked strawberries (although she was a little taken aback at the cost of cream to go with them). Bernard too was happy to be back at Down House with its spacious lawns and fields. At nearly seven, he was now playing cricket and hijacked Jackson the butler as a playmate for hours at a time. Frank and Bessy were not in Downe long, however, before they were off to Switzerland to join Ellen, who was already there. Despite the fact that Ellen was twenty-seven and Frank nearly thirty-five, the etiquette of the age necessitated the presence of a chaperone, in this case Bessy. Frank was considering applying for a job at Oxford, a prospect that his mother dreaded and his academic friends discouraged. After more thought, he gave it up, particularly after William, in his ongoing capacity as the family accountant, informed Frank that his annual income was already a comfortable £1,250 (some $104,000 today) and would be more if only he took more care with his investments.[33]

By the end of the summer, Frank and Ellen were engaged. The family was delighted: Ida thought Ellen had "great depth" and Richard Litchfield found her charming. Emma and William were both of the opinion that she needed some fattening up, but there would be plenty of time for that. The only thing that bothered Emma was that Frank, "that tiresome boy," was procrastinating about telling Bernard of the engagement; "my back is a little up on the subject," she told George, but "Frank is obstinate." In the end the delay didn't matter: Bernard accepted his new stepmother, although they were never close. The wedding took place on September 13, 1883, and as it was not in Downe, Emma stayed home, just as she had for Leo and Bee's nuptials. Henrietta and Richard weren't there either; they were traveling on the Continent that September. Hen did watch the *Times* for a wedding announcement and was greatly perplexed when none was forthcoming. From Austria she wrote her mother, "I want to know whether Frank is married for it seems to me so odd it isn't in the Times. Of all marriages a second one shd be put in." Two days later she still wondered: "Why didn't he put it in the Times? Economy or radicalism (not that *he* is one)?" The wording here is interesting and suggests that Henrietta, ever the Victorian lady, suspected her new sister-in-law was a bit too modern in some ways.[34]

In October Emma moved not only back to Cambridge but also—along with Bessy, Frank, Ellen, and Bernard—into the refurbished Grove for the first time. William helped out by making sure the buildings and contents at his mother's two properties were adequately insured. Emma's first big dinner party at The Grove was given on December first and featured a list of scientific guests: T. H. and Nettie Huxley, the physiologist Michael Foster and Mrs. Foster, and the zoologist Alfred Newton. Charles's lively presence must have been greatly missed.[35]

It wasn't long before Frank and Ellen were drawing up plans for their own house, to be named Wychfield after a huge elm tree on the building site, next door to The Grove on the northwest side. Building here had the advantage of keeping them close to Emma and Bessy, and since the Horace Darwins had already built on the other side of The Grove, Wychfield would create a little Darwin compound on the Huntingdon Road. Bernard would have cousins nearby for playmates, and Emma and Bessy would not lose the company of their dear Dubba. Besides sports, Bernard was now displaying an interest in writing, an enterprise that would prove to be his life's work. His first childish attempts were stories "about gosts & robers fiting with all their mite." Unfortunately, not all of Dubba's early writing was done on paper. When he developed "a habit of scribbling on the China inkstand" at The Grove, his grandmother fined him a halfpenny for each offense. Bernard's reaction was to bury all of his remaining money in the garden, and Frank had to break the bad news that this would "not save him from paying his ½ᵈ if he had to do it."[36]

The last bachelor among the Darwin brothers took the marital plunge in 1884. George's courtship of Maud Du Puy, Nellie's older sister, had begun a year earlier while Maud was visiting in Cambridge with her aunt Cara Jebb. Nearly twenty-two when she arrived from Philadelphia, Maud was "pretty, affectionate, self-willed, and sociable," and her matchmaking aunt immediately set out to find her a suitor. As it happened, Cambridge was in the midst of a matrimonial frenzy following a relaxing of the rules against fellows of a college marrying. Within just months of coming to England, Maud found herself being courted simultaneously by two Trinity fellows: Harry Goodhart, a Latin specialist, and Henry Taylor, a lawyer. Goodhart dropped out of the competition after only a short period, but Taylor actually worked himself up to a proposal in the fall, only to be turned down flat. (To his credit, Taylor did not take no for an answer readily, possibly because he had already gone to the expense of buying a house to share with Maud. It took two letters of refusal to cool his ardor.) For his part, George Darwin hung back from the scrum of wooers that initially developed around Maud, instead developing a "brotherly intimacy" with her that even included offering advice about dealing with her other pursuers.[37]

In October 1883, Maud left England for a winter of Continental touring with yet another American aunt. Early in the new year George too was traveling, going first to Paris and then on to Tunis for some weeks. Encouraged by Mrs. Jebb, he wrote to Maud from Tunis and arranged to rendezvous with her in Italy. Thus in February 1884 their paths crossed in Castellammare di Stabia, a small town near Salerno, and it was soon clear that George's "brotherly intimacy" had developed into love and that his affection was reciprocated. He did not propose right away, however, but rather held off until they reached Florence. This delay prompted a volley of advice to Maud from Aunt Cara about what was and was not proper behavior vis-à-vis George:

Until you *are* engaged, do not go out with him at all without a chaperone. You can sit and talk to him in the hotel drawing-room, at his [invitation], of course. . . . You know even in Philadelphia you would use judgment in giving a man your society, and you would take care not to be seen so much with him as to make people talk. In Florence you must be very particular. Besides, a man thinks none the worse of a girl for being a little particular. . . . I wish he would let me choose the engagement ring, or you when you come to London. I fancy those things are frightfully dear in Florence. Still, of course, in things of this kind you must let him take the initiative.[38]

The travelers hadn't been in Florence very long before the city worked its romantic magic and George popped the question. Maud made him a happy man by accepting, even though he was just a tad too short for her taste. (Maud apparently had a horror of marrying a short man. In fact, at five foot ten, George Darwin was two or three inches taller than she was.) George's letter announcing the engagement made everyone at The Grove "very happy," and Emma wrote back that they had received "a flock of congratulations" from well-wishers, especially from the extended family. "A[unt] C[aroline] wd not quite approve of a second American d-in-law," but otherwise will "sympathise . . . heartily," she noted. The betrothed couple, plus Maud's aunt, traveled on to Paris, where George selected an engagement ring and Maud picked out a wedding dress. Emma wrote to George there, in the process misspelling her future daughter-in-law's name slightly: "I want you to buy something pretty for Maude from me, now you are together, any bit of jewelry (to the amount of about £40). I should expect you would find good jewelry there, as you succeeded in the ring." A few days later, Emma's input to George's shopping list had gone from engagement gift to whimsy: "When you are loafing about looking at the shop windows in Paris, do buy some charming little hairy dogs if you see them about an inch high."[39]

Unlike William's wife Sara, who had wanted to be married promptly lest she go back to Boston and lose her nerve, Maud wanted to be wed back home in Pennsylvania. Accordingly, Maud and George sailed for America, albeit separately since George had to finish May Term before he could leave Cambridge. The Jebbs made the trip too, partly to attend the wedding and partly because Richard Jebb had agreed to lecture at Harvard. After some rearranging of the date, the wedding took place on July 22, 1884, in Erie, Pennsylvania, at the home of Maud's sister Mary Spencer. Cara Jebb wrote a full report back to Emma:

Maud looked really beautiful; her colour brilliant, her eyes shining, her figure shrouded in a veil, tall and graceful. She is much prettier this summer than you have ever seen her. It does not suit her to be fat, and the whole stone and more of weight she has lost, is a great improvement.

Directly the ceremony was over, and oh, dear, it takes one's breath away to think how much destiny for two lives can be fixed in that short eight minutes, George went about talking to the people and in the interests of conversation, entirely forgot, I suspect, the interesting position he occupied. Never in my life saw I a bridegroom act with such an absence of self-consciousness. He whispered to me that being married made a man ravenously hungry, when did I think they would have supper? He watched the door with perfect singleness of mind, and picked up Maud and marched her in with an expression of interest quite independent of the occasion.

They started for Buffalo [and Niagara Falls] at eight-thirty, the ceremony had been at six. . . . George is not as delighted with the habits and customs of the people and climate as I should like to see him. He doesn't like what they give him to eat, he thinks the sun is hot, the railway carriages different from the English, the arrangements in general much inferior to those of his dear native land. He will only be thoroughly and entirely happy when he can bring his bride back to you at Down.[40]

And so now all of the children were married—except for Bessy, of course, who would live out her life a spinster. "Now there are 5 Mrs D's besides myself," Emma commented to George. Maud and George were back in England by late September, and they soon made arrangements with the Jebbs to rent Springfield for the winter while they sought more permanent housing. Emma urged them to consider living close to the center of Cambridge, perhaps in the suburb of Newnham, rather than joining the family cluster along the Huntingdon Road. Although it would be pleasant to have them right next door, Emma thought "Maude wd find her life much more sociable & pleasant if more near the centre of things." By December, George and Maud had decided to buy a large house abutting Silver Street Bridge and the university. The property, which they named Newnham Grange, was bounded at the back by the River Cam. The deal was struck for £4,600, and renovations started in February 1885. It was all very exciting.[41]

Fate is fickle about dealing out happiness, however, and while George and Maud were busy with the relatively pleasant task of house hunting, Frank Darwin suffered through the agony of nearly losing Ellen just as he had lost Amy seven years earlier. Although the details are sketchy, it appears that

Ellen conceived fairly soon after their marriage and was well into her first pregnancy in November 1884 when she experienced difficulties. A nurse and a doctor (the first of three) were called to The Grove on November sixth, and for a time it seemed possible that Ellen had successfully given birth: Emma's diary entry for the seventh reads "birth of child to Ellen?" But Ellen either miscarried or had a stillbirth, and then to everyone's horror her temperature skyrocketed, signaling an infection. The flashback to Amy's sickness and death was excruciating, especially for poor Frank. For forty-eight hours Ellen's fever raged, driving "all hope . . . out of" the watchers at her bedside. Frank was so utterly undone that he couldn't even talk with the doctors and had to depend on Henrietta as a go-between. But then on the third day "came the blessed news of the temp[erature] lowering 2 [degrees]" and they were done with "living over again that horrid time." By November tenth Ellen was clearly on the mend: her voice was strong, she was eating satisfactorily, and she had only a low-grade fever. And a week later she was well enough to be carried downstairs, where her solicitous mother-in-law read to her and played the piano for her enjoyment. By a happy coincidence, Wychfield was nearing completion and Ellen was able to celebrate her full recovery by moving into her own "very pretty & nice" new home in time for the holidays. At only twenty-eight, Ellen had plenty of time to have other babies; now it was time to celebrate a very special Christmas.[42]

20. *The Life and Letters*

THE YEAR OF OUR LORD 1885 was not a good one for Major General Charles Gordon. The man who eight years before had so impressed William Darwin in Southampton was now in serious trouble in the Sudan, besieged in Khartoum by the forces of the rebel leader Muhammad Ahmad, the self-proclaimed messiah or Mahdi. Thanks in no small part to his own actions, Gordon found himself at the eye of a storm that pitted Europeans against Africans, Muslims against Christians, and, within the British Parliament, Liberals against Conservatives.[1]

The British had been in charge in Egypt since 1882, when they reacted to an internal coup d'état by sending an expeditionary force. Then, as British and Egyptian officials were trying to gain control over affairs in Egypt proper, the Mahdi made his appearance in the southern territory of the Sudan, a vast land also nominally under Egyptian control. The Mahdi had soon attracted a huge body of followers, called dervishes by the British, and in November 1883 they annihilated an Egyptian force under William Hicks, a retired British colonel who had been hired to command the Egyptian forces in the Sudan. Other battles followed, but the upshot was that by early 1884 most of the Sudan was controlled by the Mahdi, and the Gladstone government in London decided to abandon the territory after evacuating all remaining Egyptian garrisons and officials.[2]

In January 1884, General Charles Gordon was sent to the Sudan to organize and carry out the evacuation. Nicknamed "Chinese" Gordon because of his exploits during the Taiping Rebellion in the 1860s, and known as a skillful soldier with little regard for personal safety, he was a popular choice with the public and was swept into the job amidst much clamor. Nonetheless, Gordon's tendency to be mercurial and uncontrollable—not to mention seeing himself "as the hand of God's purpose" on earth—made many politicians and some military men uneasy about his appointment to the Sudan. E. W. Hamilton, one of Gladstone's close advisors, described Gordon as a "half cracked fatalist." Cabinet member Charles Dilke, although initially in agreement with Gordon's appointment, was soon describing the general as "a wild man [who was] quite mad." Also, Gordon's Sudan assignment was at odds with his professed belief that a better solution was to crush the Mahdi once and for all and then stabilize the government there with a new constitution. To his credit, Gordon did manage initially to evacuate a few hundred Egyptians, but it was soon clear that he was not moving aggressively to complete this task, but rather was wasting time scheming how to decisively defeat his opponent. Between his own delays and further military gains by the Mahdi's army, by March 1884 Gordon found himself besieged in Khartoum.[3]

Back in England, there was a public clamor for a relief force to rescue Gordon. The queen's views on the matter were clear: "Gordon is in danger: you are bound to try to save him," she wrote to the secretary for war. At The Grove, Emma Darwin was worried along with everyone else: "I got Gordon on the brain last night and he bothered me very much," she wrote to Hen in April. The politicians were not to be hurried, however, and they dithered throughout the summer, not approving a relief force until September. By the time it got to Khartoum on January 28, 1885, Gordon was dead and the Mahdi's forces were in control of the city.[4]

Emma had predicted back in February 1884 that although "Gen. Gordon will not m. mind being killed . . . if he is, Gladstone will go." In a very real sense, she was right. "After the Gordon debacle . . . [it] was mainly a question of how long [Gladstone] could keep afloat." All of England was plunged into despair at the news of Gordon's death and the fall of Khartoum. Gladstone's nickname GOM, or Grand Old Man, was reversed into MOG: Murderer of Gordon. A horrified Queen Victoria added to the uproar by shooting off a blistering telegram to her prime minister: "These news from Khartoum are frightful and to think that all this might have been prevented and many precious lives saved by earlier action is too fearful." In Parliament, the opposition brought forward a motion of censure that was defeated by a mere fourteen votes. Lost in the hubbub were opinions like that of Colonel Tom Fraser that

Gordon himself might have been partly to blame since he "never gave a hint of wanting military support until . . . it was too late for English soldiers to bear the heat." As things turned out, Gladstone and the Liberals were able to survive in office for several months after Gordon's death, only to finally lose power over a question of taxation.[5]

Compared to General Gordon's plight, the start of 1885 was a breeze for the Darwin family. By January Ellen was feeling well enough after her obstetrical close call of November to accompany Frank to Eastbourne for a month by the sea. During his parents' absence, Bernard was left at The Grove with his grandmother and Aunt Bessy, and he amused everyone there with his latest hobby, "painting the signs of all the public houses he [could] remember." Since Dubba had recently gone through a period of "Pantomime fervour," Emma, for one, was happy about the switch to the more sedate activity of painting. The eight-year-old also seemed to have grown out of the previous year's disturbing tendency to throw temper tantrums whenever something displeased him. These rages coincided roughly with the period after Frank and Ellen's wedding and may reflect the difficulty of that transition for Bernard. As we have noted, Ellen and Bernard did not enjoy a particularly close mother-child relationship.[6]

Most significantly for young Bernard, he had just been introduced to golf, a sport that would become both obsession and occupation for him in adulthood. Beginning in 1884, he regularly tagged along with his father to the new course at Felixstowe. Dressed for the occasion "in a flannel shirt, brown holland knickerbockers, and [with] bare legs burned to a painful redness by the sun," Bernard would spend the day playing the course alone, "dodging in and out between grown-up couples." All of this solitary practice was rewarded in the evening, when Frank joined his son for one last round. "We played one ball between us, a foursome against nobody," Bernard remembered fondly some forty years later.[7]

The George Darwins were happily overseeing the renovations at Newnham Grange in 1885, although Maud's enthusiasm was probably dulled a bit by morning sickness, since she had conceived in December. Bessy Darwin was well, and so were William and Sara. In fact, Sara struck Emma as "much better & cheerfuller" than she had seen her in years. Leo and Bee were starting the year anticipating Leo's new job in the Intelligence Division of the War Office. It would require moving into London, but it would also ensure that Leo was not sent into the Egyptian debacle. In Cambridge, Horace and Ida were becoming prominent community activists, Ida as a member of the Association for the Care of Girls, and Horace as a founder of the Association for the Protection of Public Morals. In their first year of operation, the Public Moralists succeeded in shutting down no fewer than eight brothels. And finally, those longtime London dwellers Henrietta and Richard Litchfield were cozily ensconced at 31 Kensington Square.[8]

The happy lives of her children and grandchildren were great comforts to Emma as she approached her seventy-seventh birthday. She had long since made the adjustment to her split-year living arrangements, taking full advantage of all Cambridge had to offer during the winter and the country delights of Downe in the summer. In both locations Emma continued to receive visitors and entertain at a pace that would exhaust most modern people, and if she ran short of energy, she simply "gave up coming in to dinner" or made a discreet withdrawal from her company just as Charles used to do. Of course, the downside of a constant flow of visitors is that a hostess has to put up with the occasional dud. Emma was not immune to this sort of thing, despite the generally elevated nature of her guests, and Bernard remembered years later hearing his grandmother complain before one garden party that she expected to have only "the humble and the dull" as guests that day.[9]

Energy and strength were, in fact, becoming increasingly challenging for Emma. Rather than walking, she was now often drawn in her wheeled bath chair when she moved around Cambridge or Downe, in the latter location often going to favorite spots she had shared with Charles. In a note marking William's forty-fifth birthday in December 1884, Emma wrote: "Yesterday was your birthday & I am beginning to feel old enough (in my legs at least & my ears) to have a son [your age]." Her progressive loss of hearing was perhaps more annoying than her declining physical strength, since the deafness hampered conversation. After a spring garden party she confided to Hen, "there was plenty of talk. If it were not for the bother of talking, and still more of listening, I should like it very well." She occasionally had her ears lavaged by her doctor in Cambridge, but with little improvement.[10]

Besides family and socializing, reading and politics continued to be keen interests even as Emma slowed down physically. The amount of reading she did was staggering—she often went through a volume in a single day—and included materials of virtually all genres: newspapers (several), periodicals, and books including fiction, nonfiction, biography, and poetry. Reading kept Emma abreast of the times and "made her company refreshing and even exhilarating," observed Henrietta, who also remembered her mother having a wonderfully "original way of looking at [books]." She certainly knew what she liked and, at least in her letters to Hen, pulled no punches when she disliked a book. On George Eliot's *Adam Bede*: "I am driven by stress of weather to read Adam Bede, but it is more pain than pleasure." On Justin McCarty's *Maid of Athens*: "Nobody need trouble to read the Maid of Athens, unless they like descriptions, I like descriptions neat & not watered with a rubbishy story." On Anthony Trollope's *Is He Popenjoy?*: "I have been reading one of Trollope's worst 'Is he Popenjoy'—& a more contemptible vulgar book cd not be written." On the other hand, Emma could be lavish with her praise for books that struck her fancy. She found Mark Twain's *Huckleberry Finn* "a work of genius—you are kept in the company of the most utter scamps & villains & through it all there is a sort of innate goodness in Huck himself (who is the most tremendous [of] liars) which makes the book bearable. It is also very entertaining."[11]

On June 9, 1885, a memorial statue of Charles was unveiled in the Central Hall of the Natural History Museum in South Kensington. The life-size marble replica was the work of Sir Joseph Edgar Boehm and depicted Darwin seated in a meditative pose with clasped hands and his coat draped over his knees. The unveiling was a gala event. The Prince of Wales was there, as was T. H. Huxley, then president of the Royal Society, numerous other scientists, and many of the museum's trustees. Among other luminaries in attendance was Admiral B. J. Sulivan from the *Beagle* days. Huxley opened the official part of the program with a flattering presentation speech, after which the prince accepted the statue on behalf of the trustees. In his dedication, Huxley noted that the donors were not asking the museum to "preserve the statue in its cynosural position in [the] entrance-hall . . . as evidence that Mr Darwin's views have received . . . official sanction." Science, he continued, "does not recognize such sanctions, and commits suicide when it adopts a creed." (With regard to the statue's position, Huxley's remarks proved prescient. Since 1971 the statue has been located in the North Hall of the museum, under the Central Hall's grand staircase. Darwin sits there side by side with a remarkably similar statue of Huxley himself, the place of honor in the Central Hall having long since been given over to a bronze likeness of Richard Owen.)[12]

Emma was sorely tempted to travel up to London for the unveiling, but finally decided to stay away, thus "avoiding all greetings & acquaintance" that the affair would involve. Standing and chatting were now quite tiring for her, especially when she found herself in a noisy crowd and had to struggle to follow the conversation. Better to skip the thing altogether. She spent the day of the unveiling at The Grove with Henrietta and Richard. The Darwin family was well represented, nonetheless: William was there and probably Leo too, as well as old Joseph Parslow and some of the other Down House servants. Parslow, especially, had a wonderful time. He told Emma that "he should never forget the scene as long as he lived" and was especially gratified at being recognized by Admiral Sulivan. After the dedication, Leo and Bee hosted a "Port & Sherry" reception that was "delightful" to Parslow's tastes.[13]

Boehm's statue was the second public memorial to Darwin, his funeral and grave at Westminster being the first. A third memorial was also well under way in 1885, namely Frank's combination biographic-scientific remembrance of his father, which was to be called *The Life and Letters of Charles Darwin*. As part of *The Life and Letters*, Frank planned to include the short autobiography that Charles had written, originally as a vacation diversion, back in 1876. As he began working with his father's manuscript, however, it became clear that some members of the family had problems with its unaltered publication. Darwin had, after all, composed his life story for a strictly familial readership, and he had written baldly in places, including casual comments about old friends as well as potentially offensive views on Christianity. Emma in particular wanted Frank to edit out certain portions of the section on religion. In virtually all cases Frank acquiesced to his mother's requests, which are revealing. The main expurgated passages from Charles's original manuscript are shown below with the deletions in italics. Emma's comments, where those are known, follow.

[Original] But I had gradually come, by this time, to see that the Old Testament *from its manifestly false history of the world, with the Tower of Babel, the rainbow as a sign, etc., etc., and from its attributing to God the feelings of a revengeful tyrant,* was no more to be trusted than the sacred books of the Hindoos, *or the beliefs of any barbarian.*[14]

[Emma] The first opening sentence about the God of the Old Testament appearing as a revengeful tyrant (I quite agree w [Charles] that it does so) would raise a storm of indignation especially as he omits the higher & more sublime views of God in Isaiah & some of the Psalms—and that sort of passage makes me feel that his view was narrow & wanted study. There is also a passage about the supposed intuitive idea of God, which I think inconclusive & narrow, & not worthy of his mind. . . . I hope I am not biassed by feeling how very painful the attacks upon his opinions would be to me. A smaller objection I have omitted, viz. How great a pity I shd think it if the book was ill looked upon for the young—owing to that part. But that is perhaps a feeling carried on from my youth.[15]

For my self I quite agree with these opinions, but it would give such a violent revulsion & shock to most believers that . . . I should feel it wrong [to publish them] without a very strong motive to do so.[16]

[Original] *Beautiful as is the morality of the New Testament, it can hardly be denied that its perfection depends in part on the interpretation which we now put on metaphors and allegories.*[17]

[Original] Thus disbelief crept over me at a very slow rate, but was at last complete. The rate was so slow that I felt no distress, *and have never since doubted even for a single second that my conclusion was correct. I can indeed hardly see how anyone ought to wish Christianity to be true; for if so the plain language of the text seems to show that men who do not believe, and this would include my Father, Brother and almost all my best friends, will be everlastingly punished. And this is a damnable doctrine.*[18]

[Emma] I should also like to omit (& Henrietta feels this strongly too) the short passage . . . ending "& have never doubted for a single second that my conclusion *was correct.*" This sounds presumptuous & I don't think it was what your father meant to express; but [rather] that he never for a single second altered his opinion on this part of the subject (viz. the evidences of Christianity). To say that one's conclusion is *correct* on such an immense subject as religion does strike me as dogmatic.[19]

I should dislike [this] passage . . . to be published. It seems to me raw. Nothing can be said too severe upon the doctrine of everlasting punishment for disbelief—but very few now wd call that "Christianity," (tho' the words are there).[20]

[Original] That there is much suffering in the world no one disputes. Some have attempted to explain this in reference to man by imagining that it serves for his moral improvement. But the number of men in the world is as nothing compared with that of all other sentient beings, and these often suffer greatly without any moral improvement. *A being so powerful and so full of knowledge as a God who could create the universe, is to our finite minds omnipotent and omniscient, and it revolts our understanding to suppose that his benevolence is not unbounded, for what advantage can there be in the sufferings of millions of the lower animals throughout almost endless time?*[21]

[Original] Another source of conviction in the existence of God, connected with the reason and not with the feelings, impresses me as having much more weight. This follows from the extreme difficulty or rather impossibility of conceiving this immense and wonderful universe, including man with his capacity of looking far backwards and far into futurity, as the result of blind chance or necessity. When thus reflecting, I feel compelled to look to a First Cause having an intelligent mind in some degree analogous to that of man; and I deserve to be called a Theist.

This conclusion was strong in my mind about the time, as far as I can remember, when I wrote the Origin of Species; and it is since that time that it has very gradually with many fluctuations become weaker. But then arises the doubt—can the mind of man, which has, as I fully believe, been developed from a mind as low as that possessed by the lowest animal, be trusted when it draws such grand conclusions? *May not these be the result of the connection between cause and effect which strikes us as a necessary one, but probably depends merely on inherited experience? Nor must we overlook the probability of the constant inculcation in a belief in God on the minds of children producing so strong and perhaps an inherited effect on their brains not yet fully developed, that it would be as difficult for them to throw off their belief in God, as for a monkey to throw off its instinctive fear and hatred of a snake.*[22]

[Emma] My dear Frank, There is one sentence in the Autobiography which I very much wish to omit, no doubt partly because your father's opinion that *all* morality has grown up by evolution is painful to me; but also because where this sentence comes in, it gives one a sort of shock—and would give an opening to say, however unjustly, that he considered all spiritual beliefs no higher than hereditary aversions or likings, such as the fear of monkeys towards snakes. . . . I should wish if possible to avoid giving pain to your father's religious friends who are deeply attached to him, and I picture to myself the way that sentence would strike them, even those so liberal as Ellen Tollett and Laura [Forster], much more Admiral Sullivan, Aunt Caroline, &c., and even the old servants.[23]

From her remarks, it is clear that Emma had a variety of motives for editing Charles's comments on religion. First, some of his views were personally painful since they conflicted sharply with the broader and deeper beliefs that she had long held. The notion that human morality was entirely the result of blind evolution, rather than a gift bestowed by the Almighty to order and refine human affairs, was repugnant to Emma. So too was the comparison of a child's inculcated or inherited belief in God with a monkey's instinctive fear of a snake. These comments did not strike her as reflecting well on her beloved Charles; they cheapened him and were "not worthy of his mind." Second, she dreaded the possibility of her husband's religious views being offensive to his surviving family and friends. Wouldn't Caroline, Charles's only living sibling, be shocked by talk about monkeys and snakes, and by her brother's portrait of God as a vengeful tyrant? (Ras Darwin, of course, had he been alive, would simply have nodded in agreement about the monkeys and so on. After all, he had abandoned religion long before Charles did and much more thoroughly.) And what about friends such as Ellen Tollet, Laura Forster, and B. J. Sulivan? Surely their memories of Darwin would be sullied unnecessarily by including these offensive passages in *The Life and Letters*. Finally, of course, there was the general public. Emma could well imagine the outpouring of bile that would result if Charles's private views on religion were published. Wouldn't it be advisable, she wondered, to cut out the questionable comments about religion or, better yet, to delete that section of the autobiography entirely and let Frank summarize his father's religious views as part of editing the volume?[24]

Clearly, all of these concerns contributed to Emma's desire to sanitize Charles's admittedly heterodox religious views. Nonetheless, it must also be kept in mind that her own beliefs had become less orthodox and "vivid" (Henrietta's word) over the course of their married life. As a prime example, abandoning the traditional notion that nonbelievers were destined for hell was a huge change from Emma's early fear that she and Charles might be separated for all eternity, she in heaven and he in the netherworld. After forty-three years of marriage, she knew just how good a person her Charles had been, regardless of his stand on matters of faith. Surely a merciful God would not damn such a soul to hellfire. No, the possibility was too terrible to contemplate and therefore could be renounced. Still, one wonders whether the claim that "very few now" would call belief in eternal punishment Christianity wasn't more Emma reassuring herself about her altered views than an accurate statement of fact.[25]

In the end, Emma got her way. When Frank finally published *The Life and Letters* in 1887, the offending passages were gone. It was not until the middle of the twentieth century that a Darwin granddaughter, Nora Barlow, published an unabridged and nonsanitized version of Charles's autobiography. By then, of course, all of those sensitive Victorians who might have been put off by the bluntness and agnosticism of Darwin's views were long gone.[26]

Three new grandchildren entered Emma's life in 1885–86, bringing the total count to six. After their marriage in 1884, George and Maud had wasted no time before starting a family. By January of the following year, Maud was supervising the renovation of Newnham Grange while "feeling sick all day."

Aunt Cara Jebb "guessed instantly" that her niece was pregnant and, given Mrs. Jebb's powers as a gossip, the news probably spread quickly. In consultation with her sister-in-law Ida, Maud began lining up doctors and nursemaids in anticipation of her first confinement.[27]

On August 26 Maud gave birth to an eight-pound baby girl. Ida was there, along with George, who spent most of his time pacing and smoking, and also Maud's visiting cousin Ella Du Puy. A nervous first-time father, George "looked at the baby . . . but from a distance." Only after Maud gave her husband direct "orders to hold [the baby] and kiss it" did he finally summon up the courage to touch his child. Even then, George showed "great horror when [the baby] cried." A telegram was immediately dispatched to Emma at Down House announcing that Gwendolen Mary Darwin had arrived: "Girl—quite well & not long." Emma got her first glimpse of the baby in early October when the "GHDs" plus cousin Ella made the trek to Downe. At one point during the visit, possibly after she had let Gwen howl for a while, Maud made the mistake of soliciting Emma's views on dealing with crying babies. Should one check on them promptly or wait and see if they cried themselves to sleep? Unwittingly Maud had touched a nerve among the Down House women. "I shd always consider it a first object to stop a baby's crying," replied Emma bluntly. Bessy then weighed in and "spoke hotly" on the subject, presumably backing up her mother's views. Although Bessy later regretted the heat of her words, all was "taken good humouredly" by the new parents. Maud was still getting the measure of her in-laws.[28]

Another granddaughter, named Emma Nora in honor of her Darwin grandmother (a combination of names that Henrietta found "dreadful"), was born at The Orchard on December 22, 1885. This brought Horace and Ida's brood to three, with four-year-old Erasmus and two-year-old Ruth. And then three months later, on March 30, 1886, Ellen and Frank did their bit with the birth of her first and his second child, a daughter named Frances Crofts Darwin.[29] The relief at Wychfield at the safe birth of the baby was almost palpable. Memories of Amy's death and Ellen's near tragedy with her first pregnancy made this confinement frightening for everyone, especially Frank. A delighted Emma wrote to Bee:

> But here is my great piece of news. Yesterday mg Ellen's troubles began (no nurse in the house, but she was tel. for & arrived by one o'clock) & the baby (a girl to Bernard's great disgust) was born about 7—every thing quite smooth. [Ellen] had engaged the nurse for the 16th thinking that quite soon enough, so she must alter her ways of reckoning [her pregnancies].[30]

It took baby Frances several weeks to begin to thrive. In early May Emma wrote to Hen that the baby looked and acted delayed for a one-month-old. "It is languid," she wrote, "& makes no approach to a smile wh it ought to do at 3 weeks." Nicknamed "the Piggamy," Frances had escaped inheriting the Darwin nose, to Emma's great relief, but was born with a misaligned eye and a drooping eyelid, a combination that made it hard to "know whether she is looking at you." Ellen apparently had difficulty nursing her baby, and they tried Frances first on cow's milk and then on ass's milk. Whatever her mother's problem, soon there was nothing wrong with Frances's appetite and she was kicking up "a rage when her bottle [was] not ready." And as it turned out, Ellen Darwin did not need to "alter her ways of reckoning" her pregnancies: baby Frances was the only child she would bear during her twenty-year marriage to Frank.[31]

The 1885 summer migration to Downe occurred on June 26. Emma and Bessy were accompanied on the trip by the entire George Darwin family, still supplemented by cousin Ella. To the delight of all the children and not a few of the adults, the list of Down House residents had recently been bumped up by the addition of Dickey, a small fox terrier that Margaret Vaughan Williams gave to her aunt Emma. Although disobedient and prone to roam—a tendency that Emma cured by carrying partridge bone treats when she and Dickey went on excursions—the dog soon charmed his way into his mistress's heart.[32]

Almost immediately after settling in for the summer, Emma made plans to have some of the old "scientifics" come for a visit. The Huxleys were invited, and so were the Hookers, with Sir Joseph and Lady Hooker bringing their new baby for the group's inspection and admiration. It promised to be an enjoyable gathering with lots of reminiscing. Nonetheless, there was one dark cloud on the horizon: at the Hermitage in Surrey, Harry Wedgwood was gravely ill. With her characteristic lack of sentimentality, Emma wrote to Hen on the subject in early July:

Poor Uncle Harry's illness puzzles me about the Huxleys visit. If his death shd take place before Sat. I conclude that I must put them off for a few days; but as we ask nobody to meet them & nothing is known about his illness I should be sorry to do so for any degree of anxiety about him. I do not wish for his recovery, indeed if he seemed to recover now I should expect that it would only be for a time.[33]

Uncle Harry hung in there, however, and the scientifics were able to come on schedule. "The Hookers arrived very prosperous," Emma reported to Hen. "Lady H. looks so big & handsome w her very pretty baby wh she still nurses entirely. . . . Sir J. and Mr. H. had a long talk yesterday & they were very merry over the whist & also playing their best. I believe Mr H's deafness accounts for part of his silence & apparent want of spirits. He was quite in his old way at times when Leo and H[orace] were here. He & Mrs H. have taken long walks every day. . . . She tells me Mr H. says [the visit] has done him great good."[34]

In September, Harry Wedgwood actually gathered enough strength to do a little corresponding, including sending a letter to his sister. It must have been a rambling affair, however, that reflected its writer's recent stroke. "I have actually had a letter from poor Uncle Harry," Emma told Henrietta. "He seems to be aware that his brain was affected wh is a pity; but I will send it to you." By October 3 the news from the Hermitage was bad. "A wretched acc[ount] of poor U. Harry, sometimes not sleeping at all—& not being persuaded to take his sleeping draught." Now it was only a matter of time, and not much time at that. Henry Allen Wedgwood passed away on October 7, 1885. Frank Darwin drew the short straw and was sent to represent his branch of the family at Harry's funeral. Emma told Hen that "Frank was the one to go as Horace is but poorly. George's lectures came in the way & he also has a bad cold. Frank disliked going v m—but it was not any feeling about a funeral. We cd not make out what. He went late yesterday & wd sleep at Oxford." As mentioned earlier, in tribute to her late brother Emma commissioned the printing of two hundred copies of his little book *The Bird Talisman* for distribution to the family.[35]

A second death in the older generation involved a person more at the fringes of the family than Harry. In late August 1886, Charles Langton became gravely ill while on the Continent. The eighty-five-year-old Langton had been Emma's brother-in-law twice, having married Charlotte Wedgwood in 1832 and Catherine Darwin in 1863. Accompanied by his third wife, Langton was in Germany when he was stricken. "Husband ill—strange state—come at once if only for a few hours," read the telegram received by William Darwin. In response to this summons, William set out immediately for Frankfurt, as did Langton's English doctor. The precise nature of the illness was unclear, but since Langton was described as in a "strange state" and "difficult or impossible to manage," Emma was of the opinion that he had gone insane.[36]

When William arrived at Langton's sickbed on August 26, he found his uncle "looking not uncomf. [but rather] . . . pleased at some favorable symptom," and anxious that William should see something of Frankfurt during his visit. This was the peak before the final decline, however, and when William was called back to the sickroom in midafternoon, Langton "was sinking so gradually that they hardly knew when his death took place." Poor Mrs. Langton was in a terrible state, distressed not only at having lost her husband after only three years of marriage but also at his possibly fatal refusal to follow doctor's orders at the end.[37]

Acting in the capacity of his uncle's executor, William helped the grieving widow bring the body back to England for burial. On September 4 the Reverend Charles Langton, who long ago had lost his faith and given up his ministry, was lowered into the ground in Bournemouth. William was there, along with Clement Wedgwood, Langton's daughter-in-law Emily Caroline "Lena" Langton, and his grandson Stephen Langton. William reported to his mother that he and Lena's father, Charles Massingberd, "had to support [the widow] over the grave. We feared she wd fall in." For her part, Emma feared that the third Mrs. Charles Langton would not be very well off in her widowhood. Langton had apparently left several financial obligations that threatened his estate.[38]

As always, politics kept Emma riveted to the newspapers in the mid-1880s, and this time it was the antics of her old favorite Gladstone that drew most of her ire. To set the stage, the Liberals' ouster from power in the summer of 1885 was followed by a very brief Conservative government under Robert Arthur Gascoyne-Cecil, Lord Salisbury. By February 1886, however, Gladstone was back in power and quickly showed that he was a very different Grand Old Man. Since his last spell as prime minister, he had become convinced that the solution to the continuing unrest in Ireland lay in Parliament providing some degree of Home Rule. Gladstone's "conversion" into a Home Ruler obviously delighted the Irish leader, Charles Stewart Parnell, whose nationalist followers held a swing block of votes in both Salisbury's and Gladstone's governments. But Gladstone and Parnell had different ideas about precisely what form Home Rule should take, with Gladstone wishing to see Ireland assume the same type of dominion status that Canada enjoyed.[39]

Unfortunately for the GOM, many members of his own Liberal Party were vigorously opposed to Home Rule, as were most of the Salisbury Conservatives. So was Emma, who solidly favored continuing coercive policies in Ireland rather than dissolving the Union by granting Home Rule. She wrote to Bee in January 1886, just after Salisbury had resigned, "I am hoping that Gladstone will not be able to form a Govt. But I believe my chief motive is hatred & vengeance against the Irish—which perhaps would not be the best way of managing a nation." After Gladstone had, in fact, been successful at putting together a cabinet and introducing his Home Rule Bill, Emma turned her guns on the debate. To Henrietta, she wrote:

> I was absorbed in the debate yesterday, Gladstone['s] was a very fine speech with all the obstacles to the scheme slurred over, and with a very unworthy comparison about intimidation in England. I am glad he spoke so highly of Albert D[icey]'s book. Trevelyan's speech was grand, and Parnell's a mere personal attack and squabble, and very bad even for him.

It is worth noting that although Gladstone apparently found some parts of A. V. Dicey's book *Law of the Constitution* congenial, Dicey was actually an outspoken opponent of Home Rule. Dicey was also a close friend of the Litchfields, and it seems likely that his political views influenced Henrietta's opinions and possibly her mother's.[40]

Despite speeches that slurred over the obstacles, Gladstone's Home Rule Bill was in trouble. In June, after a prolonged and spirited debate following its second reading, it was decisively rejected. More than one hundred Liberals deserted Gladstone on the issue, and it soon became clear that by pushing Home Rule the Grand Old Man had split his party. Emma was elated over the vote. She wrote to Bee: "Home Rule is dished at present I am glad to think." To William, she confided her fear that Gladstone might be experiencing "some deterioration of his mind as there is said to be in an Eastern Despot." Emma had grown increasingly conservative with age, and she now took her stand within the Liberal Unionist branch of the old Liberal Party. In 1892 she would be thrilled to watch as her son Leonard was elected a Liberal Unionist MP representing Lichfield.[41]

A pair of delicious public scandals also held Emma's attention in 1885–86, the first of them centering on a newspaperman named W. T. Stead. In 1885 Stead, the crusading editor of the *Pall Mall Gazette* and such "a puritan fascinated by sex" that he was nicknamed "Bed-Stead," was promoting a parliamentary bill to raise the age of consent from twelve to sixteen, thus making it more difficult to recruit and/or abduct young girls into prostitution. To show how easily English girls could be trapped into a life of crime and vice, Stead staged the sham purchase and exportation of thirteen-year-old Eliza Armstrong. Although never actually sexually used, Eliza was put through some of the same degrading experiences as real child prostitutes before she was taken to France and left in the care of the Salvation Army. Stead then published the details of the squalid affair in the *Pall Mall Gazette*.[42]

Stead's efforts at promoting the age of consent bill were successful, but they backfired personally in a most painful fashion. Hauled into court and charged with a technical offense in the purchase and transportation of young Eliza, Stead was found guilty in November 1885 and sentenced to three months in prison. Among the fascinated public who followed the news of the Armstrong case was Emma Darwin. She wrote to Hen saying, "I am intensely interested in the Armstrong trial. I don't wonder that [the authorities] tried not to send back Eliza to such a home—a drunken father & mother & 5 brothers all in one room. . . . I cannot make up my mind whether this trial is a benefit or not to the *Pall Mall* in the object they aim at, but I feel it is a blunder as to hushing up the horrid part of the subject."[43]

Stead emerged from prison just in time to be a bit player in a second sensational case then entering the courts: the divorce suit *Crawford v. Crawford and Dilke*. In this case, sex was mixed in a most shocking way with the behavior of the rich and famous. The apparent facts were these: On July 19, 1885, Sir Charles Dilke, forty-one-year-old baronet and former cabinet minister under Gladstone, learned that Virginia Crawford, a sister-in-law of Dilke's late brother, had confessed to her husband that she and Dilke were lovers. Donald Crawford had been prompted to question his wife's fidelity by an anonymous warning that he was being "vilely deceived" sexually. "Virginia, is it true that you have defiled my bed?" Crawford asked his wife. "Yes, it is true," replied Mrs. Crawford, adding, "The man who ruined me was Charles Dilke." Based on this allegation, Donald Crawford sued for divorce, naming Dilke as corespondent.[44]

The case came to trial on February 12, 1886. Ten days earlier Gladstone had resumed the office of prime minister, and this time he had no cabinet opening for Dilke. It was a smart move by Gladstone to abandon his former colleague; the ensuing trial included descriptions of wonderfully salacious goings-on. Donald Crawford testified that his wife admitted to becoming Dilke's mistress just months after their marriage, and that the "liaison continued . . . for two and a half years." And if that wasn't sufficient grounds for divorce, the aggrieved husband had other bombshells. Dilke, he claimed, had told Virginia that he had previously been her mother's lover, saying it was "her likeness to her mother" that had first attracted him. Also, Dilke had talked Virginia into occasionally forming a threesome with himself and a servant girl. Dilke "taught me every French vice," Mrs. Crawford reportedly said, with typical Victorian disdain for all things Gallic.[45]

Legally, the case against Dilke was very weak. Two former servants of the Crawford family were called to testify, but each could provide only inconclusive evidence of the alleged adultery. After hearing both sides, the presiding judge, Mr. Justice Butt, had no choice but to throw the case out. "I cannot see any case whatever against Sir Charles Dilke," he remarked.[46] Here Justice Butt and Mrs. Darwin parted ways: despite the flimsy evidence, Emma believed Dilke was guilty as charged and that both Virginia Crawford and her mother were loose women. The whole thing was "a story wicked enough for the middle ages," she commented to Henrietta.[47]

Like Emma, many other Britons suspected that Dilke was actually guilty, and regardless of the outcome of the divorce suit, his reputation took a beating in the court of public opinion. W. T. Stead contributed to this character assassination, motivated at least partly by a need to boost the *Pall Mall Gazette*'s sagging circulation. Dilke was a survivor, though, and eventually he was able to resume his parliamentary career and even help found the modern Labour Party. And he may actually have been innocent in the Crawford case. One modern biographer has concluded that he was "the victim not of his own actions but of an elaborate conspiracy," the details of which remain "shrouded in mystery."[48]

While Charles Dilke was having his day in court, Frank Darwin was in the last stages of preparing his father's *Life and Letters* for publication. As part of the wrapping-up process, Frank was dealing with the somewhat delicate matter of a letter that his father had sent Charles Lyell back in 1845 rebuking Lyell for his casual attitude toward human slavery. The question was whether to publish the letter and risk offending Lyell's surviving sister-in-law and biographer, Katherine Lyell, or to suppress it. Interestingly, Emma, who had shown no hesitation about suppressing potentially embarrassing remarks made by her husband, apparently felt less protective of Charles Lyell's reputation. She and her Charles had always held strong views on the subject of slavery, and it was important to her that the record be crystal clear on this matter. She wrote to Hen:

> [Frank] came across a letter of F's to Sir C. Lyell shewing such disapproval of Sir C's lukewarm feeling about slavery. [Frank] is for publishing it, & so am I, tho' it will vex Mrs Lyell. In these days there is very little feeling about slavery. The letter ends "Now I will leave this odious subject wh has kept me awake for some hours."

When *The Life and Letters* appeared the next year, the letter was included. Katherine Lyell's reaction is not recorded.[49]

For Leonard Darwin the summer of 1886 brought yet another astronomical adventure. Although still assigned to the Intelligence Division at the War Office, Leo was seconded in July to be part of a Royal Society expedition to the West Indies to photograph an eclipse of the sun. He and Bee, with the other observers, departed England for Grenada on July 29, arriving there on August 12. After a few days together in St. George's, the group split into four teams of observers, each working from a different vantage point. Leo was assigned to the station at Prickly Point, along with the physicist Arthur Schuster.[50] Leo's letter to his mother provides the best description of the expedition.

> Captain Maling, who had offered to put us up during our stay at Grenada, came off to meet us on the steamer, and made the landing comfortable and easy. The Malings did all they could for us, and were wonderfully kind: we stayed with them for four days, and then, rather to our relief, moved away to the site of the observatory some six miles away. Of Captain Maling it might be said what I heard one of Bee's relatives say of another—'He has only one fault—he is an ass.' But they did a wonderful lot for us.

The time for the eclipse approached. As Leo explained, his

> instrument was kept pointing on the sun by means of clock work, and nearly the whole success depended on its not stopping. I had taken much pains to regulate it, and up to Saturday afternoon it had behaved well but then it showed signs of jibbing. On the Sunday morning it seemed going all right but at about 15 minutes before the eclipse it slowed gradually and then stopped. The moment was a pretty nasty one, but more by good luck than anything else, I hit on an alteration of the weights which made it go. As soon as I saw it steadily going on, I gave vent to my feeling in whistling. This was about 10 minutes before the time, and some one asked in Schuster's hut— "Who is that calm man whistling?" On which one of the sailors replied "Oh it is only Capt. Darwin—there is something wrong with his clock"—as if the two went together naturally enough.
>
> Of course, I could not see very much of the eclipse myself, but nevertheless it was most striking. The light got steadily less and less, and a huge and curious cloud could be seen forming right under the sun, causing us a good deal of apprehension. The popular notion of complete darkness during a

total eclipse is quite false, and the light is more like a late twylight than anything else. But the excitement, the stillness all round, and the sudden way in which the darkness fell on us at the moment when the last spec of sunlight was extinguished, produced an effect which none of us could ever forget.[51]

A proud Emma wrote to Hen on September 2: "Did you see the little [paragraph] in the *Times* 'Good photos of the Eclipse taken by &c & good photos of the Corona of the sun by Capt. Darwin &c.'"[52]

21. Banting, Books, and the Queen's Jubilee

I N 1862, WILLIAM BANTING WAS AN overweight undertaker at the
end of his rope. Desperate to lose weight, Banting tried exercise, starva-
tion diets, tonics, Turkish baths, and seaside vacations, all to no avail.
Then, on the advice of his new physician, he tried a low-carbohydrate
diet that prohibited, among other things, milk, sugar, pastries, potatoes,
beer, and toast. To Banting's great delight, the pounds began to melt away.
He described his experience in an 1863 booklet titled *Letter on Corpulence
Addressed to the Public*. The Banting Diet soon became all the rage among
the svelteness-challenged, and the mortician's name entered the language as a
verb for slimming.[1]

As it happened, Bessy Darwin was one of the overfed readers of Banting's
booklet, and as 1887 commenced, she was busy applying the good undertaker's diet to her ever-expanding waistline. Like many women in her comfortable level of English society, Bessy had little to do. Her niece Gwen Raverat,
writing many years later, said that Aunt Bessy "seemed only to sit about on
the veranda with the other ladies, reading and talking." When not socializing on the veranda, Bessy "read a good deal . . . went for little walks, and
wrote letters." Not a particularly active lifestyle, even counting Bessy's regular
trips to the Cambridge workhouse to read to the female inmates, and at forty
years of age she was working toward the "cumbrous body" her niece would
remember.[2]

Bessy's mother, who loved rich foods and once postscripted a letter to Henrietta that it was "only chocolate on the envelope," was supportive but skeptical about Bessy's odds for success, suspecting that her daughter's Darwin heritage would be her undoing. "Bessy continues her Banting virtuously," Emma confided to Hen, "but I am much discouraged by thinking how constantly Dr Darwin increased in weight until he was very old, & yet he certainly did not eat half as much as most men."[3]

Predictably, Bessy had about as much success with dieting as the rest of us do. At her first weighing in January 1887, as recorded in her mother's diary, Bessy tipped the scales at thirteen stone six pounds (188 pounds) while wearing a "winter dress." One month later she had lost five pounds, and by April 19 another five pounds had disappeared. These were gratifying results if they could be maintained. Emma confirmed the successful slimming in a note to Hen: "B's last weighing shewed her to have again lost 5 lb in about 6 or 8 weeks."[4] In May she reached her lowest weight of twelve stone seven (175 pounds), a level that she maintained until September despite a three-week trip to the Continent and its tempting food. By autumn, however, the weight was slowly creeping back on: 177 pounds in October in a light wool dress, 179 in January 1888 in a "winter dress after lunch," and 180 pounds by the following April. Thereafter no more weights are recorded in the diaries. But Gwen Raverat's adult memory of her aunt's cumbrousness leaves little doubt about the further adventures of Bessy's waistline.[5]

Bessy was at least physically well enough to embark upon a regimen of banting, which made her unusual among the Darwin women in January 1887. Emma was under the weather ("I go on very *slow*," she wrote to Hen in January, "tongue & appetite better, cough decidedly better, perspiration less"); in Southampton, Sara was "poorly & feeling depressed" (true to her Sedgwick heritage); and in London, that consummate "sickie" Henrietta was recovering from a some malady she had contracted while on one of her many trips ("being sick away from home is so horrid," sympathized her mother).[6]

Despite feeling peaky, Emma continued to receive guests and to enjoy sitting in The Grove's greenhouse watching the bulbs come up. Two zoologists dropped by one day in late January. Alexander Agassiz, the son of the glaciologist Louis Agassiz, who had been a fierce anti-Darwinian in his time, was visiting England from America and was brought round by Cambridge professor Alfred Newton to pay his respects to Mrs. Darwin. Frank Darwin joined them to help with any scientific aspects of the conversation, and Emma found it all "very agreeable." Another day Helen Gladstone, still on the staff of Newnham College on the opposite side of town from The Grove, came by for a chat with Emma. "I felt that my politics prevented my having my former sympathy with her account of her father's visit," Emma reported to Hen, adding that, "as I had to 'favour the delusion' a little, I was glad to have done with it."[7]

Emma's comment alludes to the presence of the Grand Old Man himself in the Cambridge area that winter. Out of the prime minister's office since mid-1886, he now had time for a bit of traveling and family visiting. Helen Gladstone took advantage of her father's visit to introduce him to several local friends, including some of the younger Darwins. Emma described Horace and Ida's encounter with the GOM: "Horace disliked the tea drinking to meet Gladstone to an absurd degree. They were just going to slip away, when Miss G. caught Ida & brought her up to him. . . . Then Horace was brought up looking very wretched (I can't think why he minded) & Miss. G. said a few words about 3 brothers Darwin & after a shake hand H made off."[8]

For his part, Frank Darwin literally dodged the Gladstone issue entirely, turning down an invitation to mingle with the erstwhile PM at a tree-planting ceremony at Newnham. While Emma thought this sort of avoidance a bit "absurd," she herself was so displeased with Gladstone's Liberal Party that she stopped her annual £1 contribution to the local association, "which I hope they will feel," she grumbled.[9]

And finally, in late February 1887 the master of Trinity College, Henry Montagu Butler—a sort of relation by marriage: he was the brother-in-law of Charles's half-cousin Francis Galton—came calling at The Grove. Butler also had an academic connection with the Darwin family, since George held a Trinity Fellowship. With her tongue firmly in her cheek, Emma reported to Hen:

> Only think of my honour & glory the "Master" coming to call on me. I hardly knew how to bow down low enough. He was very civil (too civil, as it prevents one being at ease). After a time George came in & [the Master] talked pleasantly, cheerfully about his daughter at Davos. One is surprised to see Mrs Galton's brother such a "pretty" man. 'Was there no chance of his persuading me [to join them] &c &c when the Galton's were w. him?' [10]

Although it seems likely that Emma was referring here to Montagu Butler's pretty manners, she may actually have been making a frank comparison between his looks and those of his sister. One biographer of Francis Galton bluntly described his wife Louisa Jane as "plain," and commented that Galton was "more handsome as a man than [Louisa Jane was] beautiful as a woman."[11]

Also in February, Emma acquiesced to her children's wishes that she sit for an oil portrait, and in due course Charles Fairfax Murray came to The Grove to make preliminary sketches. A sort of "second generation Pre-Raphaelite," Murray had profited from the friendship of John Ruskin, who sent him to Italy to copy frescoes in the Sistine Chapel, and from training by Edward Burne-Jones. Additionally, he had worked as a glass painter and manuscript illuminator for William Morris and as a copyist for Dante Gabriel Rossetti. Emma rather liked Murray—"He is a harmless simple mannered man," she wrote to Leo—but was doubtful that he would ever make much of a success of his art. "Mr Murray . . . is very nervous & distrustful of his own powers," she told Hen. One wonders whether Emma would have been quite so sympathetic to her portraitist had she known that he was a de facto bigamist, with a long-term mistress in England and a wife and children in Italy. In all, wife and mistress would eventually bear him a dozen children. Perhaps it was his secret life, not his art, that made Charles Fairfax Murray nervous.[12]

In any event, sensitive to the frailty of his nearly seventy-nine-year-old subject, the artist asked only for short sittings, during which he made quick sketches in chalk to be taken away and used as models for the finished product in oil. Work on the portrait continued throughout the summer, requiring Murray to make one trip to Downe, and it was completed in the fall. Although William (and others?) had had misgivings at the beginning, the family generally deemed the final portrait a success when it was hung at Newnham Grange in December. Emma wrote to William: "I went to the Grange on Monday, to see myself hanging up. It was too dark . . . however I managed just to make out that I looked dignified & George is highly pleased with it." Certainly the likeness was good enough for baby Frances to recognize her grandmother, as "the Pigamy at once said Ganama to it," Emma reported to Hen. Today the portrait, showing an "impressive but not beautiful" elderly woman with "grey eyes, firm chin and high forehead," hangs in Darwin College in Cambridge.[13]

In April Emma observed the fifth anniversary of Charles's death in her characteristic low-key manner. By now she was well accustomed to widowhood, her solitude cushioned by family, friends, and numerous interests. She was no calendar watcher but was well attuned to the seasons, remarking to Hen, "I do not find that the day of the month makes the anniversary with me, but the look out of doors, the flowers & the sort of weather. Yesterday we had the S.W. wind & I suppose the flowers will now make a little progress." As she approached eighty, Emma found so much going on around her that it was easy to live in the present. Indeed, she made a joke of her disregard for anniversaries, telling Hen on May first, "To-morrow is my birthday, which is the one anniversary that is solemn to me."[14]

There was, of course, one other anniversary that Emma was tracking that spring, although its solemnity for her is debatable. Along with most other Britons, Emma was looking forward to Queen Victoria's Golden Jubilee. The eighteen-year-old girl who had acceded to the throne in 1837 was now a rather stout widow and great-grandmother. Her fifty years as sovereign were to be celebrated with kingdomwide festivities starting months before the actual anniversary of her ascension on June 20. Innumerable "soirées, symposia, balls, garden parties, commemoration services, presentations of testimonials, royal progresses, dinners with interminable toasts and droning addresses, dedications of buildings and statues, naval reviews, [and] openings of exhibitions" would mark the queen's half century in power, with congratulations and gifts pouring in from all around the empire and the world. Even little Downe village was getting ready to celebrate the queen's longevity and everyone's good fortune at being British. Emma, who loved a party, did her bit to subsidize the local festivities and even made promises on her children's behalf. She wrote to Henrietta in May: "I have ventured to assume that you will add 10/ to the Down Jubilee Fund for a feast for old & young & fire works. This with the same from the 3 brothers makes our contingent £10—£5 from me & £3 from Bessy."[15]

As Jubilee Day approached, the queen crisscrossed the kingdom attending one preliminary event after another. The demanding schedule was wearing for the sixty-eight-year-old monarch, who embarrassed herself by dozing off after tea at one palace reception, and by the eve of the grand public celebration, set for June 21, she was dreading the sore knees and swollen ankles the next several days' ceremonies would inevitably bring on. Jubilee Day began with a glorious procession from Windsor Castle to Westminster Abbey. Escorted by Indian cavalry and accompanied by numerous royal relatives and guests, the queen rode in an open landau drawn by six cream-colored horses. The procession marched past ten miles of wooden bleachers holding huge crowds of spectators before arriving at the Abbey, where admission was strictly limited.[16] One lucky ticket holder, Lady Monkswell, wrote that after waiting inside the Abbey for some time,

> we heard a flourish of trumpets which meant that the Queen had arrived. . . . We were all standing up, I on the extreme of my toes and on the seat, when, escorted by the Lord Chamberlain, she came in. It was too far off to see

the expression of her face, but I could see that she was flushed, but not the least flurried. She bowed twice, I think to our side, and took her seat on the throne. Then all the princes and princesses (there were thirty or thirty-five of them) filed round in front of her, bowed, and passed on to take their seats. She was dressed in black with the blue ribbon of the Garter over her shoulder, she had a white lace bonnet and strings, and I could see jewels sparkling round the front when she moved her head. The service itself lasted about forty minutes. The *Te Deum* set to music by Prince Albert, an anthem and some prayers. . . . The Queen stood up bravely for a good part of the *Te Deum*, and joined in all the service. When it was over . . . [we] walked back across the road to the House of Lords . . . where we had a picnic lunch [in the Chief Clerk's room]. . . . We got home about three.[17]

Emma's personal participation in Jubilee celebrations is not recorded. She did not leave The Grove for her summer stay at Downe until June 23, two days after the main festivities had wrapped up in London, so she was still in Cambridge on June 20 when Dr. A. H. Mann led a festival service in King's College Chapel in honor of the queen. Despite being a lifelong music lover, however, it seems doubtful that Emma attended this service, since at the time she was burdened with houseguests—the Asa Grays and J. D. Hookers—and had already spent several hours that particular day at the university's Senate House watching Gray and others receive honorary doctorates. During the presentation to Gray "there was some mention of the Origin of Species & your father's name," Emma reported to Leo. In sum, it seems likely that the only Jubilee celebration Emma actually witnessed was some fireworks, and even those at a distance. Shortly after the summer move to Downe, there was a belated fireworks display at Holwood House in Keston. Emma reported to Hen on June 29 that "at 9 o'clock last night Maud & the 2 B's [Bessy and Bernard] drove to Holwood to see the Jubilee fireworks. G & I saw them from here & the rockets were fine."[18] God save the Queen!

The summer and early fall of 1887 passed relatively uneventfully, but November was marked by the long-awaited publication of *The Life and Letters of Charles Darwin*. The three-volume work's appearance came none too soon for its editor: Frank Darwin was exhausted from dealing with last-minute details, and he was quite glad when the task was over. So was his normally reserved wife: "I have never seen Ellen so merry as she is now," observed Emma to Hen.[19] Frank's mother had also been "in a state of tension & anxiety," worrying that the book would be too long, too personal, and, in places, frankly offensive to some readers, including her sister-in-law Caroline. Still, Emma knew that if Charles's life "was to be written at all" and a true picture given of "his delightful nature," it could not be done without providing "a good deal of detail."[20]

Thus it was with a huge sense of relief that Emma watched as the newly minted book was warmly received by both the family and the general public. Lovingly she read through her copy of *The Life and Letters*, finding in almost every letter "some characteristic bit which charms one." Some of those bits touched her deeply. There was "a little mention of me in a note," she told Frank, that "sent me to bed with a glow about my heart coming on it unexpectedly." Frank Wedgwood wrote to Emma with words of "the highest praise," saying reading the book was "like hearing Charles's voice & seeing the expression of his face." Albert Dicey, Oxford professor and a close friend of the Litchfields, told Henrietta that Frank had done a superb job with the volume, showing "great literary power & charm" in some of his original passages. "Altogether I am sure you must be delighted at what people feel about it," added Hen when she relayed Dicey's praise to her brother.[21]

The published reviews too were good. Professor Alfred Newton wrote a complimentary piece for the *Quarterly Review,* and Bessy wrote to Hen that the *St. James Gazette* and *Leeds Mercury* had also published favorable comments. "I think Mother is not at all sensative about [the book] now & does not mind it at all," Bessy told her sister. But it was perhaps the full-page-plus review in the *Times* that left Emma most "delighted."[22] The *Times* review fairly glowed with praise for Frank's work as editor:

> Mr. Francis Darwin has performed his part with a reticent and judicious hand; he has not sought to go over the ground already so thoroughly traversed by his father, [but rather] . . . contents himself with simply introducing a few necessary connecting links [between letters and episodes in the elder Darwin's career], and with some 50 pages of most interesting reminiscences of his father's every-day life. . . . The all-round humanity of [Charles Darwin], the complete sanity of his nature, and his wonderful lovableness are, perhaps, the characteristics that will come out most conspicuously in these volumes to those who had not the rare privilege and honour of his personal acquaintance. . . . [*The Life and Letters of Charles Darwin*] must take its place among the very, very few biographies of the first rank. In unreserved candour, in [its] earnest endeavour to be perfectly truthful and fair, the [book is] unequalled.[23]

High praise indeed, and enough to make any mother's heart swell with love and pride. Emma immediately sat down and drew up her personal list of people to be sent gift copies, including former governesses Catherine Thorley and Mrs. Camilla Patrick, lifelong friend Ellen Tollet, old servants Joseph Parslow and Henry Lettington, Charles Lyell's former secretary Mrs. Arabella Fisher, and friend and political informant Lady Derby (Lady Mary Catherine Stanley, née Sackville-West, later to become the great-aunt of Vita Sackville-West).[24]

Among the very few sour responses to *The Life and Letters* was a review in the *Spectator* in December 1887. This review was "a curious and unsatisfactory performance," Leo wrote to his mother, partly because it took a swipe at evolution (and thus indirectly at Charles) for the theory's potentially "destructive effect" on faith and morality, and partly because it had all the earmarks of being written by a traitor in the familial ranks, namely Snow Wedgwood. Leo continued to Emma:

I have just been reading the Spectator review [and] . . . I guess by the manner that [it was written by Snow]. I have a strong feeling after reading it that the writer has never read the book, perhaps glancing at one chapter. It is so odd that she quotes recollected passages of conversations to hang her remarks on when the Book would show I think that the impression left on her mind was not an accurate one. It almost looks as if she had only seen review extracts. At least that was my feeling. . . .

Then again it is curious to complain of the destructive effect of modern thought and to write such a non-constructive article. I think one can see that she disbelieves in the Old Testament and in eternal punishment and on the other hand it is only possible to perceive that she believes in a God and a hereafter—that is the only two beliefs one can see she has are the two Father was careful in [*Origin of Species*] never to deny though he did not affirm. She is rejoiced to be delivered from the "ghastly fear" of eternal punishment—at least that is what I suppose she means—and yet sees no advantages in the trains of thought that led to this deliverance.

I presume from one sentence that she believes in Evolution. If so would she have held this truth back for the sake of the possible side effects of its publication? If it is true, she must see that it was certain to come to light before very long, and from her standpoint it ought to be an inestimable advantage to have this new truth with all its effects connected with the name of a man of such high moral fame. It might and probably would have been connected with a man who made it a direct attack on religious beliefs. I suppose she would say that evolution may be truth but it has dragged some untruths along with it. I suppose that that is the case with every new revolution in thought, and it is the main conservative doctrine which has made all of them hard to introduce. But I for one feel sure if ever we are to know what the truth of these things is, it can only be done by pushing boldly for truth in all directions. So long as evolution is true it must be a step towards finding out the final truths of the world, even if it has dragged some errors with it; for 'truth comes sooner out of error than out of confusion' and evolution has certainly helped to make confusion of thought less on many subjects.

As long as modern science goes its course numbers of men for a long time to come will have to go through the stages of doubting and disbelieving. And this utterly and entirely independent of Father's influence. But his will be books much read at such a period. A man at such a period often fears that his moral sense will go along with his faith, and I for one firmly believe that the full publication of Father's life will have a wonderfully reviving and strengthening influence on such men; it will show them that the change may take place and leave behind it an unshaken moral faith as bright and clear as any they will read of in all history.

P.S. Possibly I have misunderstood the article in some respects as it is difficult to follow. If I am right in my wild shot that Snow wrote the article without reading the book, one can imagine that after doing so she would feel it a little awkward meeting Frank.[25]

Leo was right in his suspicion that Frank would be annoyed by Snow's caviling comments. Emma wrote to Henrietta: "I will send you Leo's disquisition on Snow. . . . There is a gt assumption of superiority in [her review] wh sets Frank's back up tremendously."[26] Luckily, the two cousins crossed paths rarely, or there might have been scowls, if not sharp words, between them.

After all the worries about how Caroline Wedgwood would react to *The Life and Letters*, she turned out to be only a little unhappy with the book. She wrote to Emma on November 19 that Charles had been mistaken in his belief that their father, Dr. Robert Darwin, "did not understand or know what ability and power of mind he had." Said Caroline, "I long to strike a pen through that mistaken sentence of my Father's estimation of Charles."[27]

But this minor annoyance would not weigh long on Caroline's mind, because less than two months after Frank's book appeared she was dead. Her eighty-seven years of life, the last of which had been plagued with illness, ended on January 5, 1888. The funeral was at Leith Hill Place, but Emma didn't go, sending instead Bessy, Horace, Ida, and Richard Litchfield. Emma did truly mourn the passing of the last of Charles's siblings, however, and said so in a feeling note to Henrietta on January 8:

> I feel that I have lost the only real link with old times. I do not count my [remaining] brothers, as I think most men, & they especially, do not like remembering. I keep almost the last letter [from Caroline] which speaks so warmly of caring for my letters & I am glad that I wrote more often than usual lately. Hers was a very wonderful nature in the power of her affections & interests conquering such discomfort as she constantly had. She even spoke warmly of having enjoyed my last visit & I believe she did at times.[28]

Writing to William, Emma contrasted her feelings for Caroline with those for her sole remaining sister-in-law, Fanny Hensleigh, very much to the latter's disadvantage: "I find the loss of Aunt C leaves a large blank in my life. . . . When with her she always cared for my affairs & liked hearing every thing. I never had the same feeling with Aunt F who has no real interest outside her own belongings."[29]

As she was all too aware, Emma's generation was nearly gone. Caroline had been the last of Dr. Robert's children, while the offspring of Josiah II, that lively group of "Maerites," had now dwindled to Frank, Hensleigh, and Emma, none of whose health was particularly good, although Emma's was probably the best. Frank Wedgwood had been too fragile with winter chills to attend Caroline's funeral. "I should have liked to be at the funeral as I was at Elizabeth's and Joe's and Harry's," Frank told his son Godfrey, "but it was out of the question." And in July 1888, during a visit to Abinger, Emma gloomily wrote to Hen about the "waning" lives of both Hensleigh and Fanny. Her brother, she said, was "v feeble" and "A[unt] F has taken a considerable downward step since last year; she does not feel up to be moved outside her door to hear the singing."[30]

As it turned out, Hensleigh and Fanny weren't quite ready to go, but Frank Wedgwood did not live to see the end of 1888. He passed away on October first in what Emma, always a believer in dying quickly, described to Henrietta as "a blessed death." That last day, "Uncle Frank was quite well & cheerful & Amy with him, when he got up to reach something & fell down & was dead instantly," she told Hen. Frank Wedgwood, who had been on the cantankerous side as a young man, had mellowed with age to the family's satisfaction. "I think his was the happiest old age I ever knew," Emma continued. "He was entirely without the faults of old age, & wiser & gentler than when he was young. . . . How differently I shd have felt Frank's death even 3 or 4 years ago," she confided, but now she merely felt "strangely callous" although "utterly knocked up."[31]

In large families, deaths and births sometimes seem to counterbalance. Back-tracking just a bit from Caroline's death in January 1888, one can see that it was offset precisely by Maud giving birth to a baby boy just days before. "G & Maud dined with us yesterday," Emma wrote to Hen on December 19, 1887, "she comf. & well, & this mg is telephoned the arrival of little master X. It is a relief to me that there is only one. Bessy will go & learn more presently. Certainly one thought from [Maud's] appearance that it must be close at hand. I am glad it is a boy, as they both wished it much."[32]

Emma now had seven grandchildren ranging from eleven-year-old Bernard to the new infant, Charles Galton Darwin, and they were fairly evenly split by sex with three boys and four girls. Bernard, growing rapidly toward maturity, was equally at home in Cambridge, at Downe, or with his Ruck relatives in Wales. A sweet-natured youngster, he was utterly devoted to both of his grandmothers. For her part, Mrs. Ruck continued to exert a strong hand in Bernard's upbringing. "Now Frank," she said to the boy's father during a visit to Cambridge in 1887, "Bernard has to go to church in preparation for school, & Bessy has only 3 Sundays more to take him & so you must tell him to go with her next Sunday." When Frank replied, "I will think about it," Mrs. Ruck laid down the law: "No you must not think about it but do it."[33]

In general, Emma was pleased with these and other little bits of religious education for her grandchildren, but out of respect for her sons' lack of faith, she didn't push the matter. To Hen, she wrote: "I am glad to find that Ras say[s] a little prayer—some of it what he chooses. He says them now to Horace." On the other hand, Emma didn't want the children taught a faith that was revoltingly sentimental. She also observed to Hen: "I am sorry to hear that Maud teaches Gwen a little hymn & especially that most mawkish 'Gentle Jesus.'" To her grandmother's satisfaction, "Gwen declined saying it & said she wd say 'Yankee Doodle.'"[34]

Young Erasmus Darwin was not only trying his hand at praying—including asking God's help in resisting temper tantrums: "Help me to do what I am told & not be so furious"—but also at using adult language, something for which he was firmly upbraided by Ida. "Horace was dressing w Ras in bed," Emma reported to Leo, "& said 'Dash it all.'" Ras then said, "'Mumma does not like those words. Do you ever say beastly & mucky? She does not like those words [either].'"[35]

Like her slightly older cousin, three-year-old Gwen was starting to display an independent spirit and to challenge adults' attempts to mold her to what she considered peculiar norms of behavior. In October 1888 Emma wrote to Henrietta: "I am afraid the Swiss maid is not good for Gwen's temper. She steadily refuses every thing Louise wants her to do, & G told me there was an awful scene in the road when she was going a message w L[ouise], refusing to go the right way lying down in the mud & roaring." One wonders if this was the same nursery maid that Gwen once bit—a flash of temper that resulted in the little girl having her mouth washed out with soap and water.[36]

The eldest, Bernard, in a sure sign of approaching adulthood, had a growing fixation on his clothes. In March 1888 Emma described this new "phase" to William:

> We have had Bernard for the last week, till F[rank] & Ellen return. He amuses himself v well with writing imaginary articles in the *Field*, & takes ½ an hour to dress for dinner & comes down in polished shoes & a carnation in his button hole & a new necktie made under his partic. orders by Agnes. He considers all life under the view of neckties & looked at the photos of Lyell etc in the study, saying "What a horrid necktie." He is happy at school & has not a word of complaint. His manners are improved & he is affectionate. I am pleased at this "necktie" phase as that will tend to good manners.[37]

In fact, judging from family photographs, Bernard's "necktie phase" rather stuck, and he remained a natty dresser throughout life.[38]

Eighteen eighty-eight found both Leo and Frank making, or at least contemplating, job changes. In February Leo was jockeying for a promotion to section head within the army's intelligence service, but he hit a snag. He reported to his mother:

> At the beginning of the week I heard definitely that I was not to get the section at the Intelligence Dept. It was not any surprise to me, but it made me feel a little flat all the same. . . . After recommending me, Brackenbury went on to say that a certain Capt. Lake had better be appointed if I was not considered available. Lord Wolseley then wrote that under the circumstances he thought I had better get it. But H.R.H [the Duke of Cambridge, commander-in-chief of the army] decided that there are too many R[oyal] E[ngineers] in the place, and that Lake is to have it. It gives me a nice little grievance, but I don't suppose I shall have a chance of airing it to advantage. A grievance to be useful must be kept well bottled till the right moment, and then uncorked with great care. Since I have been at the Intelligence I

have been twice applied for other work—Engineer appointments—one of which I should have liked. Therefore I have been refused R.E. appointments because I am in the Intelligence Department, and I have been refused Intelligence Department appointments because I am in the R.E. I don't really much mind. I have been gradually making up my mind to leave the army in three years time, and under those [circumstances] it makes little odds whether I get this or not.[39]

Captain Darwin's mother and oldest brother were not quite as cavalier about the professional slight as Leo. "William is very indignant at your grievances," Emma wrote to her soldier son, "& I heartily hang H.R.H. for going against such powerful opinions."[40]

As for Frank, in November he succeeded Dr. S. H. Vines as Reader in Botany at Cambridge, and in December 1888 he was elected to a fellowship at Christ's College. These developments not only bolstered Frank's income substantially, they also dismissed once and for all any lingering doubts about not applying for an opening at Oxford years earlier. The promotion of course thrilled Emma, because it guaranteed that for the foreseeable future she would continue to have three sons living close by. "Now Frank will feel really belonging to Cam[bridge]," she rejoiced to Henrietta. Still, from Frank's perspective, the increase in duties was a downside, as he always had been rather slow at his tasks. To William, Emma wrote: "Frank has got his readership . . . & m more work, wh Ellen says rather oppresses him. F[ather] used to wonder long ago how little work [Frank] cd get thro! I think it is his diffidence and indecision."[41]

Yet another family accomplishment, this one on the Wedgwood side of the ledger, occurred in the summer of 1888 when Snow published her latest book, *The Moral Ideal*. In her dedication, Snow described the book as "a History of Human Aspiration" or a "review of human thought . . . starting from an attempt to follow the development of the Aryan race in its early branches." In fact, it consisted of a rather loosely connected "series of separate studies on important types of moral aspiration, found in civilizations so diverse as those of Egypt, India, Persia, Greece and Rome."[42] Although one reviewer called it "an able and a delightful book," *The Moral Ideal* was rather hard going for most readers, owing to Snow's turgid writing style. Even her aunt Emma, avid reader that she was, had a difficult time with Snow's tangled prose. Emma wrote to Hen: "I have tried [one] page wh I found so hopeless that I shall try it again as feeling it *too* odd that I can't form a guess what she means." By dint of sheer effort, Emma managed to penetrate the volume by the fall, at which point she bragged to Henrietta that she had "read 100 p[ages] of Snow's but it [is] almost too fatiguing." Snow "irritates me," she complained, "by concluding that her readers are all good historians & classics" and thus need little clarification of her text.[43]

Interestingly, Snow stated in her chapter on Rome that she had once tried to interest her uncle Charles in a passage from Lucretius that she saw as pregnant with pre-evolutionary meaning: "Accident . . . originated all kinds of varieties of structure . . . and those only were preserved which were fitted to the condition of things in which they found themselves." When she "showed [this] passage to Mr. Darwin," wrote Snow, "the dialect was too unscientific for him, and I do not think he recognized it as the anticipation of his own views." Darwin may be excused. At least one biological authority, the late Ernst Mayr of Harvard University, declared that Snow's reading of Lucretius as a potential evolutionist was in error.[44]

If *The Moral Ideal* was low on Emma's reading list for 1888, the following year brought an abundance of books that likewise failed to measure up to her standards. At eighty-one, her take-no-prisoners book reviews to Hen took on a harder edge than ever. Here are some examples:[45]

[February 25] The Tom Poole book [*Thomas Poole and His Friends*] is pleasant except that every word of Coleridges letters revolts me, they are a mixture of gush & mawkish egotism & what seems like humbug. . . . I can't imagine how my father ever liked & admired Coleridge. I believe Dr Darwin wd have been more acute.

[June 3] Don't read *A London Life* by Henry James. It is nothing but disagreeable, or *Roumania* by Mrs Walker [which contains] only the description of one convent after another.

[July 23] We found *Greifenstein* too tedious to read aloud, & all the exag[gerated] horror of Grief. on discovering that he was illegitimate, after quite getting over the trifling discovery that his father had murdered his mother, is too absurd.

[August 13] Don't read Principal Shairp's Life [*Principal Shairp and His Friends*]. It is entirely composed of other people's acc[ount]s & opinions of him, w hardly any thing of his own writing. How few people know how to write a life. Bessy is reading a Life of Garrick, quite intol[erable] from the old trick of never letting a man speak for himself without an introduction.

[October 25] We have such a stupid set of Mudie books. Garibaldi Auto 3 vols [*Memorie autobiografiche*] quite unreadable. The Italians think nothing too commonplace to say.

There were, of course, a few books that suited Emma's taste, among them Amy Levy's *Reuben Sachs* ("sharp & incisive [but] I wonder whether she does not generalize absurdly about Jewish peculiarities—e.g. that the men have all bad figures"); Richard Jefferies's *Wild Life in a Southern County* ("The descriptions of country & birds are excellent & if one is patient & willing to loiter & watch [with] him it gives one nice images"); *Fanny Burney and Her Friends* ("So well done & short that I find it pleasant reading"); and the *Wise, Witty, and Tender Sayings . . . of George Eliot*. On this last, Emma's comments provide some insight into her own religious beliefs as an octogenarian: George Eliot "suits me exactly sometimes, e.g. 'that the idea of God, so far as it has been a high spirited influence, is the ideal of a goodness entirely human (i.e. an exaltation of the human).'"[46]

These words show clearly just how far Emma had moved away from her early, orthodox Christianity toward a more humanistic stance. Her shift in philosophy—as well as the fact that she never suffered fools gladly—was further illustrated in a September 21, 1889, letter to Hen: "An idiot writes to me that as he hears I am proud of my husband's discoveries I shall be glad to hear that he can quite confirm the 'descent of man' from scripture: therefore I may make myself quite easy that they will not die out &c."[47] Whereas earlier in her marriage she would have been relieved to have Charles's theories reconciled with Scripture, by 1889 a stranger making the attempt was deemed "an idiot."

Of course, Emma rarely had much use for religious extremists of any sort, be they zealots or doubters, and this attitude was simply strengthened by old age. She weighed in against zealots in a letter to Henrietta in June 1889: "How the Evan[gelical]s can imagine they feel shame or repentance for an inherent sinful nature which all share, I can't imagine. I think all those opinions have been so modified. I remember the infant school at Kingscote shouting out jollily 'There is none that doeth good. *No not one*[!]'" And among outspoken doubters, T. H. Huxley drew her fire. Huxley wrote several pieces for the *Nineteenth Century* magazine in the late 1880s that explored the differences, as Huxley saw them, between religion and science. Emma, for one, rather disliked his sneering tone. To Hen, she wrote: "Huxley gets more & more unpleasant in the agnostic controversy. He likes being insolent—carefully calling them demonatized pigs—instead of the common name of the miracle," the Gadarene Swine.[48]

Rather sadly, as part of the dulling of her faith, Emma experienced a steady decline in the comfort and beauty she found in the Bible. In her mid-eighties, she wrote to Hen: "I am reading the psalms & I cannot conceive how they have satisfied the devotional feelings of the world for such centuries. I am at the 35th and about 3 or 4 I have found beautiful & satisfac. the rest are almost all calling for protection against enemies or for vengeance."[49]

Besides books good and bad, 1889 was marked by a couple of juicy scandals, and the Huxleys featured in one of them. Marian "Mady" Huxley, T. H. and Nettie's second-oldest daughter, had married the artist John Collier in 1879. Five years later, following the birth of her one and only child, Mady began to show "melancholia of the most intractable kind." A nurse and two special maids were hired to provide home care, but by the fall of 1887 it was clear that Mady was developing a crippling combination of somatic and mental illness. In November a desperate Collier took his wife, who now was blind and unable to speak, to Paris to consult the noted neurologist and hypnotist Jean-Martin Charcot. But the famed "Napoleon of the neuroses" had little chance to effect a cure, because Mady lasted only a week at his Salpêtrière Hospital before succumbing to pneumonia. The grieving Huxley wrote to a friend: "Rationally we must admit it is best so—but then . . . man is not a rational animal—especially in his parental capacity."[50]

In the dark aftermath of Mady's death, her younger sister Ethel stepped into the breach and assumed the role of mother to Mady and John's toddler, Joyce. Inevitably, perhaps, Ethel and John grew increasingly fond of each other, and by early 1889 they had become engaged. The senior Huxleys were not displeased with the arrangement, which ought have been the happy end to a family tragedy. The problem—and scandal—was that it was then illegal under English law for a widower to marry his dead wife's sister. The betrothed couple pinned their hopes on a bill then working its way through Parliament that would remove the sanction against their union. Unfortunately, this Deceased Wife's Sister Bill met opposition in the House of Lords, where the bishops argued it was contrary to certain sexual prohibitions set forth in Leviticus.[51] Ethel and John found themselves separated by social convention and the law, although not by the wishes of their families.

Emma was none too sure herself about the wisdom and propriety of the union. In a letter to Henrietta, she exclaimed: "Ethel Huxley is engaged to J. Collier! I am sorry—you shall see Mrs. H. She is r[eally?] too joyful about it." And in another note Emma described the planned nuptials as Ethel's "so called marriage to her brother in law." While admitting that Collier had been and would "be an excellent son" to the senior Huxleys, Emma was clearly bothered by Ethel and John's determination to fly in the face of convention.[52]

Ethel and John finally decided to do an end run around a law that J. D. Hooker called "an ageing iniquity." In March 1889 the couple sailed to Norway, where marriages such as theirs were allowed, and in Christiania (now Olso) they said their vows. The bride's father accompanied them, but Nettie Huxley was too frail to make the trip. Emma, still unpersuaded about the legitimacy of the whole thing, sent the couple a "cheap wedding present," as did Frank.[53]

A second bit of scandal was played out at the national level and involved the Irish nationalist Charles Stewart Parnell, never one of Emma's favorite people. Back in May 1882, one will recall, the English diplomats Lord Frederick Cavendish and T. H. Burke were brutally murdered in Dublin's Phoenix Park. Five years later, in March 1887, the *Times* published letters purported to be by Parnell that condoned the murders. "Burke got no more than he deserved," he was alleged to have written. Parnell immediately denied authorship of the letters, calling them a "felonious and bare faced forgery." Reading the back-and-forth of charges and denials in her morning paper, Emma was intrigued but cautious about the allegations against her old political foe. "I am afraid the Times has been rash about Parnell's letter, however genuine it may be," she wrote to Henrietta in April. "It all depends on the signature. If it had been manufactured to damage P[arnell] I think it wd have been less moderate & more brutal."[54]

She was right to be cautious. Parnell requested that a parliamentary committee be formed to investigate the *Times*'s charges, and although it took more than a year and a good deal of political squabbling to accomplish, by September 1888 a special commission headed by a trio of judges had begun to consider the case. The investigative body sat for just over four months, and Emma hung on every word of its published proceedings, writing to Hen in February 1889: "How interesting the Commission is!" (Actually, both interesting and healthy. The diversion of reading the proceedings helped her cut down on between-meal snacks, something her doctor had advised.) As Emma wrote those words, things were about to become even more interesting. On February 28, 1889, the *Times* published a blockbuster confession by Richard Piggott, the anti-Parnell journalist who had "obtained" the contested letters in the first place and then sold them to the newspaper for a tidy sum. Piggott wrote to the commission from his refuge in Paris that he had "fabricated them, using genuine letters of [Mr.] Parnell . . . in copying certain words, phrases, and general character of the handwriting." Following a reading of Piggott's confession before the commission, the embarrassed chief counsel for the *Times* rose and expressed "sincere regret" on behalf of his employers "that these [faked] letters were published." At a stroke Parnell was vindicated and, to crown his triumph, a later libel action against the paper brought a £5,000 settlement. Piggott did not fare nearly so well. From Paris he fled to Madrid, where he put a revolver to his brain just as the police arrived to take him into custody.[55]

On May 30, 1889, Fanny Hensleigh died. She had been ill, and at the end bedridden, for such a long time that even her husband could only say "Thank God" when told that the end had come. Emma too must have breathed a sign of relief for her sister-in-law, the woman who had supported Charles at Annie's deathbed so many years earlier. But these deaths among her contemporaries had become so commonplace for Emma—and, far from being depressing, so *blessed*, given her views about lingering on when old and ill—that Fanny's passing was not even marked by a diary entry. (As evidence of her impatience with lingering deaths, Emma once remarked about three sick villagers in Downe: "I wish [Mary Elliot] & her poor old mother could be asphyziated—& James Osborne in the same batch, as I hear he is going blind.")[56] With Fanny gone, Hensleigh and Emma were the sole surviving members of their generation.

Not long after Fanny's death, the spring move to Down House took place and a delightful summer began. True, the local flower show in August was a washout with no one but the exhibitors and the fife and drum corps venturing out in a violent southwest gale, but after that the weather turned pretty and the gardens came into their own. Emma wrote to Hen describing the flower beds as a "brilliant mass" of color, with the "Gladiolus Phlox & Jap[anese] Anemone" being especially pretty. In late August and early September the place was alive with children: Maud and George had come from Newnham Grange with their two, and Ida and Horace from The Orchard with three more. Emma wrote to Hen on the twenty-eighth and thirtieth:

This is the 4th fine day. . . . The children were out the whole of the day. There is always perfect peace. Ras form of sport is v harmless rushing about w an opaque butterfly net, & never catching any thing.

The weather comes sweeter & sweeter like L[eo]'s kisses. We were sitting under the lime trees yesterday. Ida came on Wed. & had a nice lazy day, w the chicks [children] about. Ras caught a butterfly—he looks at them & lets them go. . . . Ida & I & some chicks went into the field & admired the valley. I suppose one does admire ones own view absurdly.[57]

Just before the summer crowd broke up in late September, the village band dropped by to serenade Mrs. Darwin and her guests. The performance was spirited, but somewhat lacking in variety. "The Down band came to play on Sat. ev round by the d. room," Emma reported to Hen. "They played one polka certainly 20 times over. It was ludicrous. Then a waltz & another polka, all rubbish. The head man (& teacher) played softly & well. Frank went out & was civil also gave 10 [shillings] & I £1. What it goes for I don't know. I hope not drink."[58]

At the end of that beautiful summer, Emma and Bessy went back to their winter home at The Grove and the rest of the family to their respective homes in Cambridge or London. All but one, that is. Thirteen-year-old Bernard went straight from Downe to Eton College, just up the road from Windsor Castle in Berkshire. There, as a new Colleger (a resident, as opposed to an Oppidan, who lived off campus), Bernard began a five-year stint of preuniversity education that he would remember fondly for the rest of his days. His devoted aunt Henrietta, to whom Bernard would always be the closest thing to her own child, was worried lest he be homesick. Hen wrote to her mother: "You must *mind* & tell me about dear old Dubbins first letter & what account he gives of himself & his first night. I hope going with boys he knows will prevent his feeling very desolate." Aunt Hen's fears were groundless, however, and the tone of Bernard's first letter from Eton, sent to his Grandmother Ruck, was "jolly." The new boys "had had great fun at night, as they were allowed on the first day to make as much noise as they liked."[59]

22. The Leos Abroad, and the Last Maerite Left Standing

THE HIGHLIGHT OF 1890, at least in the family's view, was Leo Darwin's change of careers. After twenty years of service and reaching the rank of major, Leo had finally decided to resign his commission in the Royal Engineers, partly for health reasons and partly because, as we have seen, he was both frustrated and bored in his assignment at the Intelligence Division of the War Office. For a time it looked as if he might take a position with the Board of Trade, but that came to naught. In June he testified before a parliamentary committee investigating the organization of the Royal Engineers and their contribution to the coastal defenses of Great Britain, and by midsummer he was out of the army for good.[1]

July found Leo and Bee in Malvern taking the water cure. Following her doctor's orders, Bee took a full treatment, while Leo, who at the time was in better health than his wife, was good sport enough to try a mild version of hydropathy. As always, Leo's letters to his mother were full of fun:

[July 14] In the morning [Bee] has a hot electro-brine bath at 11.45, sitting in hot salt water for about half an hour, which does not seem to make her feel wrung out in the way that sitting in fresh hot water would do. In the afternoon she is rubbed for half an hour, and then rests for half an hour. Thus till four in the afternoon her day is quite taken up with rubbing, tubbing, dressing and undressing. After four we drive out with our Etna [portable stove], and make tea by the roadside. . . . The first day the Doctor told Bee to eat her food slowly, and said that she had better give me the same advice. Now I feel a doctor's eye on me every meal I think I am not bolting my victuals quite so much. Then Bee said that as I had such faith in the water cure, I ought to show my faith by practice. The result is I go and have a very hot shower bath followed by an awfully cold ditto, which I really like, at all events when it is over.[2]

As a matter of fact, the couple's afternoon outings-plus-tea weren't quite as innocent as Leo made them seem. It appears that he and Bee were tucking into a nice little snack each day as they sat and enjoyed the Malvern countryside. When Bee's doctor got wind of what was going on, he put his foot down:

[July 21] The wretched doctor has issued a decree that there is to be nothing to eat with our tea which we take out with us. This has cut us off from the most fascinating large light milk rolls which we used to buy, but without consulting the doctor we have made a bye law that if we buy plenty of cream, taking strawberries and cream is drinking, not eating.[3]

Despite all the Malvern rubbing and tubbing, Bee's health remained borderline, and her doctor recommended overseas travel as a treatment. Accordingly, she and Leo sketched out a half-year circumnavigation of the globe that would take them to New York, across North America, to Japan and China, and finally home via Egypt. It would be a long and complicated trip, and among the first decisions to be made was whether to take personal attendants or simply travel as a couple. After some discussion, Bee declared heroically that she had enough "energy to go without a maid," and so on August 27 just the two of them boarded the SS *Chicago* bound for New York.[4]

Once on the road, Leo rose to the occasion and sent home an engaging series of letters full of details about the sights they saw and the people they met. High on the list of their adventures in Japan was attending the Chrysanthemum Party at the Imperial Palace in Tokyo and catching a glimpse of the emperor and empress.[5] On another occasion Leo was asked to address, through an interpreter, a Japanese audience on the subject of Darwinism. The language barrier made it all a bit tense and confusing, as Leo reported to his mother.

[October 31] [At] 7.30 p.m. I went out to—I will give you ten thousand guesses—to address a Japanese audience on Darwinism. The night before soon after I arrived I had been asked to do this, and I did not see how I could refuse. All I tried to do was to tell them a little bit about Father's life, what his work was in the very fewest words, and what was the state of belief on these questions amongst scientific men in Europe now. I was shown into a room holding perhaps 200 people . . . [and introduced] in Japanese, which made it a little awkward as I did not know in the least what he said. Then I stood up, with a slim little Japanese interpreter beside me, and fired away in short sentences. Bee says I got through it pretty well, but I was glad when it was over. They were exceedingly attentive, but very little demonstrative which made it difficult to guess how things were going.[6]

Such was frequently the fate of a Darwin son or daughter when traveling abroad. There simply was no escaping Father's fame.

Also while in Japan, Leo had an opportunity to tour the Yoshiwara, Tokyo's red light district. Even a casual drive-through of this part of the city was too risqué for a proper Victorian lady, of course, and so Bee stayed at their hotel. The tour was also a bit tricky to describe to one's mother, even a mother with Emma's wide latitude for scandalous information. Thus Leo marked the outside of his notes on the Yoshiwara *Private* and warned her that the contents were sensitive.

Perhaps you will think this sheet is not suitable for reading out, or for general circulation.

One evening at Tokio I went to see the quarter of the city which is inhabited by what we should call the women of no character. Whether this is a just description of these girls is another matter, as they often lead this life for the sake of getting their parents out of debt, and such conduct is considered highly meritorious on their part, although a sort of disgrace, perhaps more social [than] moral, is attached to the life. In Japan such subjects as these are so much on the surface that they cannot be overlooked.

I go to this quarter, called the Yoshiwara, about 7 o'clock in the evening, and found few people about at that time because it was so early. The streets were wide and somewhat brightly lighted up. The houses had wide fronts composed of wooden uprights some few inches apart, behind which could clearly be seen the brightly lighted room, and the beautiful gold screens at the back. In each house there were sitting in a row some twenty or thirty girls, all most richly and beautifully dressed, each house having a kind of uniform, or pattern of dress peculiar to itself. The girls took no notice of anyone outside and were simply chatting amongst themselves, some few drinking tea. Generally speaking they had nice quiet faces, with nothing unusual about them. The owner of the house advances a considerable sum to the girl or her parents on joining the house, and (until recently) she could not leave till she had repaid the sum in full, which generally meant that she sold herself for life. Now they can leave after three years, debt or no debt, but during the three years it is in fact imprisonment, as they are not allowed out of that quarter of the city without a police permit. It was one of the most curious sights I ever saw in my life, and if one had known nothing about it, quite a pretty sight.[7]

These observations show that Leo would have made a pretty good anthropologist; certainly he had no qualms about applying the principle of cultural relativity to behaviors different from those of his native England. Old postcards from Yoshiwara match very closely his descriptions of Tokyo's "Good Luck Meadow" licensed quarter.[8] For her part, as Leo had rather expected, Emma was unperturbed by his cultural explorations. "Your account of that establishment for immorality is most striking," she wrote back, "that so civilized a community should have no blame for 'immorality' in that sense. Were not the Greeks of the same opinion?" Overall, Leo's letters home left his mother feeling that the Japanese were "a curious mixture . . . of coarseness . . . indecency & refinement."[9]

As was her wont, Bee spent much of her time shopping as she and Leo made their way around the world. "Another letter from Leo," reported Emma to Hen. "They are both now raging among the shops. . . . Bee assures him it is the strictest economy that makes her buy so many pieces of brocade." And then teasingly to Leo, Emma wrote: "I shall enjoy seeing the brocade & the china, the fruits of your & Bee's economy." Young Gwen Darwin did not share her grandmother's sanguine take on the bounty of Oriental items. Years later she wrote that "Aunt Bee seemed to have furnished [her house] entirely out of the purchases she had made on a tour round the world: carved Oriental furniture, all of it quite black, except a few brass trays. It *was* a dark and dismal house. . . . Once . . . I went to a dinner-party . . . and . . . it was the dullest I ever endured, but I am sure it was chiefly the fault of the furniture. Nobody could possibly have sparkled in that somber setting."[10]

Emma had hoped the travelers might "see a bit of India," but as it happened, they steamed directly from China to Egypt and thence home. They walked through the front door of The Grove on April 1, 1891, after an absence of seven months. "We enjoyed the sight of Leo & B v m," Emma reported a few days later to George. "They had a gt deal fresh to tell. . . . They are both v thin & brown & Leo does not look well." So much for the health benefits of foreign travel.[11]

On the home front in 1890, there was one significant death, Ellen Tollet's on January 20. Ellen was the sole surviving child of George Tollet of Betley, Staffordshire, and her passing cost Emma her last childhood girlfriend. The sad diary entry read simply: "Ellen T. death." But on the positive side of the ledger, in the early spring Maud gave birth to her third child at Newnham Grange. Little Margaret Darwin was born on March 22, with Maud enjoying the blessed effects of chloroform during the delivery. When the baby's two-year-old brother Charles Galton ("Boy" to the family) was introduced to his little sister, he immediately declared that she looked just like a monkey. Far from being offended, "Maud was delighted at this answer coming from a Darwin," chuckled Emma to Hen.[12]

In another family matter, concern was building, at least in the imagination of certain of the Darwins, about the musical future of eighteen-year-old Ralph Vaughan Williams, Emma's great-nephew on the Wedgwood side. During the Litchfields' visit to Leith Hill Place in August there was an interesting, and in retrospect quite laughable, exchange of letters between Henrietta and her mother. Hen wrote first, reporting that Ralph, who was about to matriculate at the Royal College of Music, "wdn't play anything" for the assembled houseguests and, indeed, "said he couldn't," which made her wonder, "Don't you think that hopeless after 4 or 5 hours practice per diem?" Emma responded with discouraging words about Ralph's prospects, saying she feared that he might "undergo m mortification" in the future. But to Hen's way of thinking, a little mortification was precisely what Ralph needed: "He's awfully cocky about his music & I am sure it will be a very good thing for him to go amongst other musical people." Besides, said Hen, getting personal in her gossip, she and Richard suspected "there is something funny in Ralph & that he won't come to anything." He was "a feeble youth," she thought, with "a very weak tho' amiable face & the same fat cheeks & (excuse the coarseness) a rump somewhere up in the middle of his back." Happily, wherever Ralph Vaughan Williams's rump was—and family pictures suggest it was in the usual place—it had no effect whatsoever on his ultimate musical success. The fat-cheeked young fellow went on to become an internationally celebrated composer and conductor, and in recognition of his accomplishments was awarded the Order of Merit by King George V in 1935.[13] By then neither Emma nor Henrietta was alive to see how comically wrong their dire predictions had been.

Books read in 1890 may have been somewhat more attuned to Emma's tastes than in recent years, but only marginally so. *Troublesome Daughters* by Lucy Walford was pleasant, but Walter Besant's *Captain Cook* was "a stupid life—telling o." Her greatest fire was reserved for Henry Morton Stanley's brand-new book *In Darkest Africa*:

> Mrs Ruck has read *all* Stanley. Thank goodness I have nearly finished, & it must be the most tiresome book in the world—so confused & diffuse w immense long conversations verbatim that lead to nothing. His contempt for [Equatorial Province governor] Emin [Pasha]'s taste for Nat. Hist. is very comical—& certainly [Stanley] does not fall into that mistake himself. He observed nothing.[14]

In politics, Charles Stewart Parnell was back in the news in 1890—not that he had ever really gone away. This time, unlike the *Times* letters case, the scandal he was involved in was not fabricated. On Christmas Eve 1889, Captain William O'Shea filed a petition for divorce from his estranged wife Katherine and cited Parnell as corespondent. It took almost a year for the case to come to trial, but when it did, the facts were relatively straightforward. Parnell and Mrs. O'Shea had been lovers since 1880 and, in fact, they had three children together. Captain O'Shea had been aware of the lovers' relationship but had not previously sought a divorce, apparently because he hoped to cash in on an inheritance that his wife was expecting. Parnell did not contest the allegations of adultery, and on November 17, 1890, O'Shea was granted his divorce with all court costs charged to Parnell. Two days later Emma wrote to Hen comparing Parnell's predicament to Charles Dilke's scandal four years earlier: "So Parnell's reputation is nearly as low as Sir C. Dilke, but not quite, as the disgusting details of the latter's trial made such an impression, & the youth of [Mrs. Crawford]. I shall be curious to see what line W.E.G. takes."[15]

The last comment referred to the political ramifications of the O'Shea divorce case. Gladstone's shift of position on Irish Home Rule back in 1885 had brought him into partnership with Parnell on many points while simultaneously splitting the GOM's Liberal Party. If he now abandoned the disgraced Parnell, it could have further seismic effects in both Ireland and England. But could Gladstone do otherwise than repudiate his adulterous colleague? In the end, for a variety of political reasons and not a few personal ones, the Grand Old Man severed their connection by stating that Parnell's continuance as head of the Irish Party "would render my retention of the leadership of the Liberal party, based as it has been mainly upon the prosecution of the Irish cause, almost a nullity." Parnell was having no part of it. His refusal to relinquish power, combined with Gladstone's abandonment, led to the formation of rival Parnellite and anti-Parnellite Irish factions. The struggle between men and factions was still going on when Parnell died unexpectedly in October 1891 from a heart attack. He had made an honest woman of Mrs. O'Shea, however, marrying her just four months before.[16]

Emma's reaction to Parnell's death was guarded. She wasn't really sorry to see him go, but she fretted that in the aftermath of his death the remaining Irish nationalists might reunify. She wrote to Hen: "I think his death is a misfortune on the whole, tho' no doubt he did some mischief by stirring up passion,"[17] and "I am afraid it may enable the Nationals to be one party again. Only they might set him up as a martyr hounded out of life, so he may still be a power."[18]

Parnell's death may have made news at the national level, but another 1891 passing was of much greater concern to the Wedgwood-Darwin circle. On June first Hensleigh's feebleness finally reached its inevitable conclusion and he died at eighty-eight, leaving Emma as the sole survivor of her generation. Her brother had died "peacefully," she reported to George the next day, adding that an upcoming dinner party at the Grange need not be postponed, but that "Maud must wear a black dress . . . even if she does not go into regular mourning afterwards (about which I am quite indifferent)."[19] In reply to George's return note of condolence, Emma wrote:

> Your affectionate note was a great pleasure to me. My feeling on this occasion is almost entirely for the ones closely connected. The possession of my dear children has carried me through the great loss of my life & makes my happiness now. Hen. came yesterday which was very nice. The funeral is to be on Friday if possible. Horace & Ida will go & no doubt Leonard, so that will be quite enough—possibly also William. I shall like to have you & Maud today very much.[20]

William's "possibly" turned into a no-show, and he felt badly about it. His mother reassured him in a note on June 8, writing, "You may feel quite easy about the funeral as the relations who came . . . were quite enough." And then reflecting on Hensleigh, his marriage to Fanny Mackintosh, and the past, she continued:

> It seems strange to me that you should all (Hen felt the same till she was grown up) have felt afraid of him when you were children. He was so especially open & natural; but he had no taste for children. It was the misfortune of his life to have married a person of such a complex nature that he never understood her. I remember when I was a girl what a pleasure it was when he came home from school or college & how comfortable we felt his society to be.[21]

With Hensleigh's death an era came to within one person of ending. He was the penultimate survivor, after all, of that happy, reading, conversing, and intellectually curious group of Maerites that Josiah II and Bessy Wedgwood had raised. Now they were all gone—save for Emma—as well as generation-mates on the Darwin side of the family. Now only memories connected the youngest Doveley to the past.

Not that the present and its challenges weren't quite sufficient to keep one occupied, as Emma was reminded three months after Hensleigh's passing. The occasion was a near tragedy during Henrietta and Richard's trip to Scotland and the North of England. Richard wrote to his mother-in-law from Durham on September 14 describing the hair-raising event:

> Dear Mrs. Darwin,
> You will have heard today that we are kept here. The fact is Henrietta, just as she was getting up, took by mistake a small dose of liniment instead of a bro-mide draught. Luckily she knew it at once & doctors were immediately sent for. They gave strong emetics & did all the regular things & though she had a bad day she is now (9 pm) only suffering from weakness, and they speak quite confidently of her being much better tomorrow.[22]

In fact, Henrietta had poisoned herself quite effectively and come perilously close to dying. Her arms were paralyzed for a period and, adding insult to injury, hot water bottles applied to her numb feet burned them so badly that they blistered. There was little that Emma could do except worry about her daughter and write comforting notes. Could she send any of Hen's favorite foods? she wondered. "Grapes? I always used to find them the first things I could endure to eat & they are most satisfying." Or how about "a bit of salt beef wh is partic. tender & well cured" or "mutton broth . . . chicken panada . . . [or] a little gruel powder [to be mixed with] water & a little cream"?[23]

Emma was desperate for Henrietta to come and recuperate under her watchful eye either at Down House or at The Grove. But Hen, like most folks, just wanted to get home—to *her* home, not someone else's, not even her dear mother's. It was some weeks before this could be accomplished, what with the weakness and the dreadful condition of Henrietta's heels. The right heel was "discharging still," Richard wrote on October 12, though the doctor had been able to remove some dead skin without too much pain to the patient. It wasn't until November second that Hen was well enough to be transported back to London. No doubt Kensington Square had never looked better.[24]

After he and Bee returned to England from their global circumnavigation, Leo cast about for some new occupation. He tried his hand at writing pieces for the *Dictionary of National Biography* but found the pay was "not much of an attraction" and his subjects were mostly "dull men." For his mother he described one assigned subject, a British general of the previous century, in these waggish words: "After serving a few years in the army, during which time he served in the America War of Independence, being taken prisoner by the Americans in Bargoyne's Campaign, he went up in a balloon, and fell into the sea, and was not drowned, and died a few years later, having exhibited no other signs of genius, at a good old age."[25]

By January 1892, Leo was preparing to take a fling at politics. He wrote to Emma on the thirty-first:

> I think it is now certain that I shall stand for the London County Council of West Islington, a part of London I have hardly ever seen. It begins at Kings Cross Station, and goes northward to Highgate. . . . I go in as a "Moderate," and hope to get the support of Conservatives and Liberal Unionists, though the latter seem to be an uncertain element. . . . I am rather in a funk about speechifying.[26]

His campaign addresses must not have been too bad, however, and Leo was successful in his first try at public office. He won a seat on the LCC and began a short period of service at the local level. The experience merely served to whet his appetite, and within months he had his sights set on a higher position: a seat in Parliament. By May Leo had been accepted as a Liberal Unionist candidate from Lichfield—where the Darwin name had long been known, thanks to old Dr. Erasmus's residence there—and he and Bee were soon making the rounds stumping for votes. Back at The Grove, Emma followed the campaign news closely in the *Lichfield Mercury*, paying particular attention to the dreaded "speechifying," to which Leo settled down after some practice. She also contributed a substantial sum to her son's efforts, writing to Hen: "I am quite for giving money for the election."[27]

The general election of 1892 found Liberal Unionists, Gladstonian Liberals, Parnellites, anti-Parnellites, and Conservatives locked in a struggle for parliamentary control. After six years of uncontroversial Conservative government under Lord Salisbury, many voters were in the mood for change, and Gladstone's Liberals made sure the question of Irish Home Rule would be a campaign flashpoint when they included it it their platform. Certainly the Irish question was controversial in Lichfield. Early in his campaigning there,

Leo was told that "an unpleasant affair had occurred in the neighbourhood" when a local man was discovered to be a Gladstonian.[28]

Faced with a mixed electorate of "Mine Managers . . . coal owners . . . clergy . . . and shopkeepers," among others, Leo and Bee got down to the hard work of campaigning. Unexpectedly, Bee proved to be an excellent and energetic campaigner, willing to cover lots of ground and put in long hours for the cause. "I am rather alarmed at the great amount of fatigue [Leo and Bee] go through," worried Emma to Hen, adding, "Bee [drove] 30 m[iles] one day." Not only was she tireless, but Bee actually seemed to enjoy bellicose rallies, which was a good thing, since coal miners made up a substantial part of the Lichfield constituency and they tended come in one variety: rough-and-rowdy. (During the actual election, the miners went so far as to attack a wagon full of Darwin supporters on their way to vote, knocking the men down and then kicking them.) Bee was undaunted and, after one particularly stormy meeting, famously declared: "I'm afraid of a cow, I confess, but I'm not afraid of a miner!"[29]

When the election finally took place in July, both Leo and Gladstone came up winners. Leo's win was by the narrowest of margins, a mere four votes, and the seat's incumbent, Sir John Swinburne, promptly challenged the results. A recount verified Leo's victory, and his mother was triumphant. To the new MP and his wife, she wrote: "I must tell you how your two delightful letters warmed my heart. We shall have a happy meeting on Friday & I have asked G & F to rush over for a day. They will not have a brother elected to Parlt every day in the week. Wm laments that he cannot come—also Horace. . . . I always feel—how your father would have enjoyed it." Privately she did worry a little, as she confided to George: "It is all very delightful & the more I think about it the more I enjoy it. I feel sure that Leonard's steadfast morality & good sense will make its mark in the House & that he will get to know all the best men. My only fear is for his health. It will also be excellent for Bee."[30]

After all the results were in, Gladstone found himself with only a four-seat majority in the House: 272 Liberals versus the Conservatives' 268, with Liberal Unionists holding 46 seats, Leo's among them, and Irish Home Rulers 81. Clearly, both major parties were dependent on their allies—the Home Rulers in Gladstone's case and the Liberal Unionists for the Conservatives—if they hoped to advance any important legislation. Emma was not particularly sympathetic with Gladstone's predicament, noting to Henrietta: "My theory is that W.E.G. will come in & die of the excitement & incapacity to frame a Home Rule bill or carry on the Govt. I think he is in a sort of passionate dotage."[31]

Dotage or not, Gladstone was persistent in his pursuit of a Home Rule Bill. A fresh attempt at such legislation was drawn up by the new government soon after it took office and introduced in Parliament in February 1893. Despite his misgivings about "speechifying," Leo found himself drawn into the debate, as he told his mother:

> I expect you were rather astonished to see my name appearing in the debates. I was asked on Friday night by one of the Whips whether I would speak, because they wanted to keep the debate going; no Gladstonians would speak, and the leaders on our side did not wish to take part in the debate till they had had time to consider Gladstone's exposition of the Bill. Hence the lesser fry were called on. I was very doubtful at first whether I should do so, but plucked up courage, and worked all Saturday and Sunday at it. I did not know till about six on Monday whether I should speak. Then I was kept on in uncertainty as what time I should probably come on—for such a debate is more or less arranged when there are not a lot wanting to get up. At last at about 9.20 my turn came. The man before me came to a rather sudden end, and I sprang to my feet with a horrible sensation in my stomach. However, after a few sentences, I got calm and went on all right for some 30 to 40 minutes. . . . It is the most unpleasant place to speak in that one can imagine; no sort of desk or table for notes; rows of mens backs in front of one—inattentive backs near one, and inattentive faces further off. Then, except when leaders are speaking, there is nearly always a slight buzz of talk. Also a scattered audience is not very encouraging. I got through all right with one or two spasms of nervousness, and with the sensation that I had better sit down for fear of interrupting the general conversation. Bee, who luckily managed to get a place, said I did well. I think I was a little too commonplace to be effective, as what the House likes—as Bee says—is a commonplace thought expressed in an epigram. . . . Gladstone's voice was feeble, but his mind perfectly clear. Parts of his speech were excellent, but the part about the retention of the Irish Members most unsatisfactory.[32]

Seven months after introducing his Home Rule Bill, Gladstone saw it successfully passed out of the House of Commons on September 1, 1893. "This is a great step. Thanks be to God," he wrote in his diary. His triumph was short-lived, however, since one week later the Lords thoroughly squashed the bill by a vote of 419 to 41. Emma's comment to Leo was full of satisfaction at the outcome: "I think England at least has felt nothing but relief at the downfall of Home Rule." The Grand Old Man managed to stagger on as prime minister for another six months and then resigned from public office for the last time in March 1894. First Parnell and now Gladstone: Emma was losing all of her old political foes either to death or to political senescence.[33]

While the prime minister was getting his lumps in 1893–94, first-term MP Leo Darwin was having a tolerably enjoyable—or at least interesting—time of it, and Emma followed her son's adventures closely. True, a strike by the coal miners made the summer of 1893 a turbulent one in the Midlands and elsewhere. Mine owners argued that, with coal profits falling, they needed both to halt production for a period, during which they would stockpile their coal in hopes of selling it at a higher price in the future, and also to cut hourly wages by 10 percent once production resumed. The miners responded that such action, coming on top of earlier reductions in the number of workdays per week, would make it impossible for them to earn a living wage. Stoppages at the coal pits brought terrible hardship for the strikers and their families, including many residents of the Cannock Chase community in Leo's district. Leo and Bee, who had taken up temporary residence in the area, found themselves deluged with personal applications for help. "We get a good many coming to the door," Leo reported to his mother, "and we give them bread and cheese for which they seem very grateful. . . . I believe they like the feeling that I have come to live amongst them in their trouble." Bee worked in a soup kitchen feeding hungry children, visited people in their homes to check on their well-being, and taught geography in the local school.[34]

The miners' strike spread across the Midlands, Yorkshire, and Lancashire, and had a few violent episodes, the most serious of which occurred at Featherstone in West Yorkshire, well away from Leo's district. On September 7, 1893, locked-out miners caused a disturbance at one of the coal pits. Troops were summoned to the scene and the Riot Act read. The crowd was unruly, and when it did not disperse immediately on being told to do so, shots were fired and two persons were killed. This so-called Featherstone Massacre contributed—along with skyrocketing coal prices in London—to the government's decision to intervene in the strike in November.[35]

It wasn't long before Leo was hobnobbing with seriously prominent politicians, including Liberal Unionist Party leader Joseph Chamberlain, anti–Home Ruler Sir Henry James, future prime minister A. J. Balfour, and Spencer Cavendish, 8th Duke of Devonshire. Her son's new and illustrious company pleased Emma and, as she said to Hen, it showed that Leo was getting "to be somebody" in Parliament. Just as gratifying was a verbal attack on Leo by Irish Home Ruler T. P. O'Conner, who was reported to have said that Charles Darwin "left the most portentous bore in the H[ouse] of C[ommons] in the person of his son." In Emma's view, if the Irish nationalists were mad at Leo, he must be doing something right.[36]

Emma's health was not particularly good in 1893, so it was just as well that she had politics to take her mind off her symptoms. Her doctor prescribed mercury-based Pil Hydrargyrum tablets, and they brought some relief. Writing to Henrietta in April, she referred to this medication as "that blessed Pil Hydrarg." Notes in her daily diary show that Emma also took blue pills, castor oil, and cascara sagrada on occasion. To help her sleep, she took doses of bromide and other sleeping draughts. For her part, Hen had lots of food recommendations for her peaky mother. "It's delightful . . . to hear of your appetite coming back. I was astonished to hear of Champ[agne] but that is no such treat to you as to me. For thickening soups the Groutts farines are the nicest & if you are not the least gouty I suppose you might have chestnut (Groutts farine de Chataigne) wh is extremely good. Don't run Benger['s Food] too hard & get tired of it, but remember baked flour, barley flour, arrowroot, Savoy & Moore's infant food to make little messes of & A.B.C. oats." By late autumn, some combination of medications and diet had achieved the desired results and Emma was regularly recording days that were "excellent" or "very comfortable."[37]

As always, whether comfortable or uncomfortable, books helped her get through the day. Throughout 1893 and 1894, she continued to read at a furious pace and to send regular literary reviews to Hen:[38]

[July 16, 1893] Don't attempt . . . *Bob Martin's Little Girl*—it is detestable.

[July 18, 1893] I have just finished *The Sorceress* by Mrs O[liphant]. She is grown very cynical, & without any real value for her heroes & heroines. Her cleverness carries you on, but you end with a hearty contempt of herself.

[April 22, 1894] *What Necessity Knows* is tedious beyond expression & the 2 heroines are quite odious, but yet one is interested. . . . I shd like to pay some one to write a stinging review. I think it so impertinent of a young author to print such stuff.

[May 11, 1894] We find Mrs Besant['s *Autobiography*] very lively & interesting, tho' one dislikes her heartily. . . . Mrs B is full of vanity & always posing.

[May 24, 1894] I am m interested in Selous['s *Travel and Adventure in South-East Africa*] & rejoice in the death of every lion & hyena.

Finally, in August 1894, Emma read and commented on Snow Wedgwood's latest book, *The Message of Israel in the Light of Modern Criticism*. Responding to an inquiry by Henrietta, Emma wrote: "You asked me about The Message of Israel. I believe no books now affect me any more than by a transient interest. It did draw my attention to some sublime bits in the prophets & Psalms & I enjoyed her abuse of Esther."[39] Lukewarm praise at best, but then Emma almost always found Snow's writing convoluted and tiresome to read. Still, Aunt Emma's review might have been the most positive one forthcoming from the family, and she always managed to encourage Snow's literary efforts, tiresome or not, and enjoyed her company and conversation. (That said, there seems to be no evidence that Snow was a special favorite of Emma's, as has been asserted by the authors of *The Wedgwood Circle*. In particular, the claim that Emma "enjoyed the companionship of Snow far more than that of her daughter and son-in-law," Henrietta and Richard Litchfield, seems preposterous.)[40]

At the age of eighty-six, Emma continued to be delighted with her grandchildren, who now ranged in age from young adulthood to infancy. By 1894 Bernard's time at Eton had come to a close, and in October of that year he matriculated at Trinity College, Cambridge. By his own admission, Bernard had been rather lazy while at Eton, a trait that once earned him such a dressing-down from Frank that, despite being nearly seventeen at the time, Dubba was reduced to tears. "[I] played above my form in the Scholarship examination" for Eton, Bernard wrote years later. But after starting out highly placed, he "sank ever afterwards lower" in his class through idleness. Being punctual in the completion of assignments was simply part of his façade—"a superficially virtuous manner," in his words—and the resulting work tended to be slipshod. Bernard even cheated a bit in mathematics, having worked out "a discreditable arrangement" with a classmate for "a sight of his 'problem paper.'" Without doubt, Dubba's fondest memories of Eton were of sports and friendships, and especially those "ecstatic moments . . . spent on that muddiest of little golf courses." Luckily golf, not mathematics, would prove to be his mainstay in life.[41]

Emma's last grandchild, William Robert "Billy" Darwin, was born at the Grange on August 22, 1894, rounding out George and Maud's brood at four. Combined with Frank's two children and Horace's three, that brought the grandchild total to nine lively souls. For one reason and another, there would be no more. William and Sara never reproduced—which Gwen Raverat felt was a good thing, since her aunt Sara was "painfully tidy [and] psychologically clean"—nor did Leo and Bee, perhaps because, as everyone understood, Bee did not "care for children." Bessy Darwin, still unmarried and living with her mother, had no children, of course, and neither did her sister, Henrietta. In Hen's case, it would seem that childlessness was not by choice but was rather a cruel card that fate dealt to her and Richard. Henrietta's last chance at motherhood slipped quietly away in the early 1890s when she passed through menopause. In March 1893 Emma remarked to her nearly fifty-year-old daughter: "I fully expect your irregularity is a sign of the end."[42]

Lastly, the elevation to the peerage of Thomas Henry Farrer deserves mention. In recognition of many years of "distinguished public service," especially as permanent secretary to the Board of Trade, Queen Victoria named him Baron Farrer, and Emma duly began to refer to him as "Lord F" in her letters to the children. Cranky old Theta (who, after thirteen years, was finally showing signs of accepting Horace Darwin as his son-in-law) took his oath of allegiance and a seat in the House of Lords in June 1893, and immediately began to complain about Gladstone's government.[43]

One of the sequels to Farrer's elevation was an obligatory appearance at Court by the new nobleman and his wife. Effie Farrer invited her stepdaughter Ida Darwin to go with her to meet the queen, and Ida agreed, after arranging with Maud for the loan of a train. The big event took place in late February 1894 and, judging from Ida's report to Emma, it must have been comical to watch. Decked out "in her grandeur" of fancy gown, borrowed train, and beautiful nosegay, Ida unwisely chose vanity over vision at the last minute and took her glasses off. Thus, at the critical moment, she found herself "advancing blindly towards the Q without her specs," with a Court attendant "telling her sternly 'closer, closer.'" The terrifying audience lasted only an instant, of course, and then Ida "put on her specs & enjoyed herself, & saw many beauties."[44]

23. The Last Wind of the Watch

As was often the case, Emma began 1895 worried about sickness. This time, however, her own health was not at issue, nor was she focused on her children or grandchildren. Rather, in January 1895 the sufferers were a parrot and the son of her pensioner butler, Joseph Parslow.

To deal with the human patient first, Parslow's grown son Arthur was critically ill as the New Year began. Emma wrote to Hen on January 16:

> Poor Arthur P has had a very bad turn again. I think as he has been ill for 5 weeks that they must want some money. What do you think of my writing to Parslow, & asking if he will join me in a present or an allowance? He has just had his annuity [from me].[1]

A week later Arthur was no better, and old Parslow, who was going on eighty-six and becoming forgetful, had given Emma no reply regarding pooling their money to help the son. Sounding somewhat exasperated, Emma mentioned the subject again to Henrietta on January 24:

> I wrote to Parslow a v mild note on Sat. saying I was as anxious that Arthur shd have every comfort as I shd have felt in his (Parslow's) case if he had been ill & saying I wd add the same sum to whatever he wd give to assist Arthur. I have not heard from him & I dare say he has forgotten my letter; but on

looking into his necessary expenses I find he has very little money to share (to my surprize)—so I will send £2 or 3 at once. If the illness goes on m longer I think we shall have to make a regular allowance.[2]

While a gift of two or three pounds may not sound very generous, three pounds was the equivalent of $250 today and thus not insubstantial. It is interesting, however, that Emma was surprised at the discovery that Parslow had almost no excess money to help Arthur in his illness. Was the old butler's £50 annuity from the Darwins truly inadequate to cover his basic expenses, or was he simply a poor budgeter? Whatever the case, William Darwin had soon been brought in to help Parslow manage his income, a move that no doubt made the money go further.[3]

As it happened, no "regular allowance" was ever needed, because Arthur Parslow wasn't long for this world. When he died in early February, Emma noted in her diary that a letter of condolence had been sent to the grieving father. "Did poor Arthur ever regain consciousness?" wondered Henrietta when notified of the death.[4]

Closer to home, Emma and Bessy's parrot Jacko was literally on his last legs in early 1895. A relative newcomer to The Grove's menagerie, which was headed by Emma's beloved dog Dickey, Jacko was at first lively, entertaining, and the picture of health. "I . . . joined Jacko in the bow room," Emma wrote to Hen on September 10, 1894; "he preened himself vigorously for ½ an hour & then took to vigorous gymnastics & squeals. He is certainly in good health."[5] Yet it soon became apparent that the bird didn't have anywhere near ten-year-old Dickey's staying power. In January Emma wrote to Hen that Jacko was off his food and spent most of his time dozing. Anticipating a fatal seizure, they put him in the smaller of his two cages so he wouldn't fall so far from his perch when death came. By February second they could no longer stand to watch the poor bird's decline and decided to euthanize him. Leo was up from London and helped do the deed, as Emma described:

> Poor Jacko was so miserable yesterday that we decided to chloroform him. He seemed to be able to keep on his perch only by putting his beak into his pan, & he was in constant movement. Horace was in London & Leonard undertook it. . . . Leo put a quantity of chlorof on a handkerchief & [one of the maids] took poor J. & popped him on the handk. under a bell glass & he v soon fainted. Then they put him in water for fear of his reviving.[6]

This Rasputin-like treatment was indeed the end of Jacko, whose body was then tucked into a biscuit box while Henrietta decided whether she wanted a postmortem. "I am sorry for his loss," Emma wrote to Hen; "he was a gentle creature, but I don't think I shall ever venture on another." Never say never, however, and by April a new Jacko was roaming freely about The Grove, eating the primroses, learning to whistle, and talking "like a vulgar old woman."[7]

March 24, 1895, was a rather terrifying day at The Grove and, indeed, all across the United Kingdom. A strong gale swept in from the southwest and caused considerable damage in several counties. Emma made a full report to Henrietta on the morning after:

> I wonder whether you had yesterday's storm. It increased in violence all mg—& was at its height about 2. Carry [Wedgwood] was just saying she shd be afraid of being blown over if she went out, & I looked out to see the trees swaying, & remarked on the big wych elm. I looked away for a minute & then looked again & saw it was down. Then came a great noise as if of a great weight falling & we saw part of a chimney down near the n[orth] corner. Frank & Bernard soon came in to see if we were frightened. They said some trees were down across the road. Then came another great bang & we settled to go down to the drawing room. Eventually 2 stacks of 3 chimneys each were blown down. We shut the 3 w[est] windows & felt more quiet there, not that I was frightened. . . . Your room & the study were full of soot & smoke. Carry's escaped tho' I believe her chimney was down. At the Orchard the beaut pear tree near the division is gone & the ugly tree in the gravel walk, which was blown against the house, without damage. G & M & the children came in. They had taken no harm at the Grange. Price [the butler] chiefly lamented a moderate sized walnut tree. . . . It is not a handsome tree however—but bears the best nuts. I hope it was a partial storm. It wd have been v disagreeable in the night to hear all those tremendous bangs. It is so bright & calm I hope I shall go out & see the damage esp. the big tree.[8]

The gale had blown out into the North Sea, and no one was hurt. But with six chimneys down at The Grove and the house smoky and sooty, it must have been a nerve-wracking experience, despite Emma's claim of being unafraid. Elsewhere in Cambridge, there was structural damage at Christ's College and at Magdalene, and numerous trees were blown down at Jesus College, but miraculously the town suffered no loss of life. London was not so fortunate. In Whitechapel a partially demolished wall came down, killing a man and two children, and on the Thames three boats of the St. James's Rowing Club were swamped and one rower drowned. Church spires and pinnacles were blown down all over Britain, ships were blown ashore at the Isle of Wight and in the Yarmouth Roads, and in Emma's old home county of Staffordshire, falling chimneys crashed through the roofs of two wards at the Walsall Hospital, severely injuring several patients. All across the kingdom, people agreed that nothing like the gale of 1895 had been seen for a quarter century.[9]

Among the family residences, the Litchfields' London house seems to have survived unscathed, but Godfrey and Hope Wedgwood's Staffordshire home, Idlerocks, suffered serious damage. The Frank Darwins and the Horace Darwins, whose Cambridge homes flanked their mother's, both lost trees to the storm—"6 old fruit trees" including the "beautiful pear tree" came down at The Orchard, Emma noted. Only a week later, however, Emma was able to refer to the big storm and its damage as "an old story" and to report to William that the damage to The Grove was "almost repaired."[10]

As we know from his grandmother's letter, Bernard Darwin was visiting his father and stepmother next door at Wychfield when the great storm hit. Halfway through his first year at Trinity College, Cambridge, Bernard was much more interested in making the university golf team than in studying, but nonetheless he was dutifully slogging along toward the classics tripos. Classics turned out to be only a passing fancy for Bernard, who had little idea what career he wanted to pursue after graduation—"whatever was the least horrid," he supposed—and it wasn't long before he switched to reading law, ultimately scoring a "decent second class" on the tripos in that field.[11]

Attending Cambridge rather than some other university was both a blessing and a curse for Bernard, as he wrote many years later:

> To go to Cambridge when your home is there is, I think, to miss something of the romance and excitement of the place. Its social life may be new to you, but not its beauties or its buildings, and though you live in College you have yet something of the feeling of a day boy. I had not only my own parents, but one grandmother and two uncles living in Cambridge. It was very pleasant to visit them, but there was a slight feeling as of one dwelling in Utah in the days of Brigham Young, with the all-seeing wide-open Mormon eye painted on every rock.[12]

Not surprisingly, Bernard thought having a relative around every corner cramped his style. Not that he had much of a style, as he later admitted. He was too shy to ask his friends to put him up for membership in "the Pitt," an exclusive, male-only club devoted to "conviviality," and that same shyness also kept him from joining Trinity's Magpie and Stump debating and humor society. He came away from his university years wishing he had made more friends and also regretting that he hadn't started smoking sooner, since in his view the latter facilitated the former: "There is nothing so friendly as tobacco ... and nowhere is this more so than at the University, where you can on the spur of the moment ask a man to come up and smoke a pipe in your rooms; the pipe will fill up any gaps in the conversation, or even dispense with the need for it altogether, whereas you cannot sit and look at each other and do nothing."[13] Happily for Bernard, he found camaraderie on the Cambridge golf team.

The year's move to Down House took place on June 11, and not quite three weeks later Emma received the news that the ranks of evolution's Old Guard had been thinned by a significant death—T. H. Huxley's on June 29, 1895. The seventy-year-old Huxley had been battling the flu and its sequelae since midwinter, and Emma had written a series of concerned notes to Nettie. After giving the family several "terrible scares," it looked by mid-June like he was turning the corner. But sadly—at least for Huxley's family and friends, although to the hardly concealed satisfaction of conservative Christians who deplored his views on revealed religion—recovery was not in the cards for the original agonistic, and on Saturday the twenty-ninth a heart attack carried him off.[14]

The obituary in the *Times* called Huxley a scientist whose work stood out "as among the most substantial confirmations and illustrations of the doctrine of evolution as propounded by Darwin." Such words undoubtedly pleased Emma and the children. J. D. Hooker, whose birthday came one day after Huxley's death, remembered them being "fast friends for 42 years" and enjoying a "brotherly love . . . shared by none in its depth and strength." A love of science had bound the two men together, along with a shared devotion to Darwin and Darwinism, and the historical fact that both "began life as Assistant Surgeons, R.N."[15]

There would be no Westminster funeral for Huxley, despite the fact that he was only slightly more skeptical about organized religion than Darwin, whose remains were already safely interred inside the Abbey's walls. Following his own wishes, Huxley's body was committed to the earth at St. Marylebone Cemetery, Finchley, alongside his son Noel and his brother George. Although no invitations were sent, the scientific community turned out in force for the burial, producing what has been called "the last and greatest constellation of Victorian scientists ever to gather on one spot." Among the scientists gathered at Finchley on that July afternoon was George Darwin, accompanied by his banker brother, William. And throughout a long and foggy day back at Down House, Emma's thoughts must have turned many times to Nettie Huxley and her children, and the end of "Darwin's bulldog."[16]

In 1895 Leo Darwin was puttering his way through his third year in Parliament. The use of the word "puttering" is not intended as a slur on Leo, for that was what the entire Parliament had been doing since Gladstone's resignation in 1894. The Grand Old Man had been replaced as prime minister by Archibald Primrose, Earl of Rosebery, Queen Victoria's personal choice for the office. But Lord Rosebery's premiership was destined to be "short and inglorious." Rosebery was more interested in "good food, good drink, good tobacco, witty conversation" and his horses' chances in the annual Epsom Derby than he was in public service. To make matters worse, this halfhearted PM quickly found himself faced with serious infighting within his cabinet and with an emboldened House of Lords eager to dismantle the Liberal government's legislative program.[17]

Rosebery lasted only until June 1895, when he led his government's resignation after a relatively minor defeat in the House of Commons; clearly, the premiership had become an "uncongenial situation" for Rosebery. The Marquess of Salisbury now became prime minister once again, this time leading a coalition of Conservatives and Liberal Unionists, with Leo Darwin among the latter. In the general election that followed the change of governments, the coalition's strength was increased significantly by gains in both factions. Leo, unfortunately, was an exception: he lost his seat from Lichfield.[18]

Leo had run against Mr. H. C. Fulford, a wealthy brewer and Gladstonian Liberal, and he had lost by 44 votes. Not long after the election, it was alleged that Fulford and his supporters had cheated in a variety of ways, including bringing in carriageloads of fraudulent voters from nearby Birmingham, and also by buying local votes with "treats" at the pub or securing them through intimidation. Leo, who was bone tired from the campaign, initially did not favor launching a challenge. Ultimately such a petition was filed, and many months later—after testimony had been taken from dozens of witnesses and after one pub owner had been badly beaten by strong-arm Liberals—the election was declared null. This mollified Emma, who had earlier described herself "nearly as vicious as Bee in hoping for Fulford's downfall," but it merely left Leo facing a second campaign.[19]

This time his opponent was Mr. T. C. T. Warner, another Liberal. In a moment of confidence Leo described Warner to his mother as "a feeble politician," but his optimism was misplaced, and when the election dust cleared in February 1896, Warner had scored an easier victory than Fulford, beating Leo by 528 votes. A now doubly exhausted Leo concluded that he had been voted out of office by a strange combination of political allies: "drunkards who were discomfited by the petition. . . . temperance people who [had originally] voted for him against a brewer, [but] now voted against him. . . . [and] miners . . . angry at the defeat of the man [Fulford] who subscribed £250 for the strike." Despite having steeled herself for just this sort of result, Emma admitted to Henrietta that she had an awful feeling of "flatness on receiving the [news]." Maybe it was all for the best, however, since Leo and Bee had now decided that Lichfield was "a very troublesome & fatiguing place," which they would just as soon leave to its own devices. And at the party level, Liberal Unionist leader Joseph Chamberlain, who liked Leo personally but knew he would never rise to the political heights, wrote a note of sympathy and farewell that echoed Prince Henry's tribute to the apparently dead Falstaff: "We could have better spared a better man," wrote Chamberlain.[20]

Backtracking a few months from the election, the summer of 1895 at Downe was a pleasant one for Emma, full of visits by family and friends, and marked by general good health. Emma was feeling so good, in fact, that she remarked on it in a note to Sara in May: "I think it is a surprizing thing that at 87 I should feel stronger & better in every way than I did at 85." She enjoyed social calls by former servants—including Lettington, the old gardener at Down House, and Mary Anne Parslow, Bernard's old nurse—and neighbors including the Lubbocks. Lady Derby stopped by within days of Emma's move back to Down House and then returned eight more times over the course of the summer. Widowed for the second time when the 15th Earl of Derby died in 1893, Lady Derby had relocated from the Stanley family seat at Knowsley Hall, Lancashire, to Holwood Park, Keston. This put her close to Knole and her brother Lionel, Lord Sackville, and also within easy visiting distance of Down House. When together, Emma and Lady Derby usually gave themselves over entirely to politics, a shared interest of many years' standing. Other nonfamily visitors that summer included Emma's friend Margaret Shaen for several days in August, and in September Sir Joseph and Lady Hooker for a long weekend.[21]

Not long after the Hookers' visit, Emma and Bessy were back in their winter quarters in Cambridge. In November Emma had a brief period of rheumatism combined with a head cold, but otherwise she sailed smoothly through fall and early winter. December was highlighted by several dinner parties at The Grove, including a "youthful [and] v jolly" party on the third and a Christmas Eve gathering of the entire family—and also by the publication of Frank's latest book, *The Elements of Botany*. Although he is best remembered as the first editor of his father's letters, Frank was an accomplished botanist in his own right, and this book would be his greatest original contribution to science. With his characteristic self-deprecation and moody pessimism, Frank accompanied his mother's copy of the book with the comment that he feared she wouldn't be able to understand much of it.[22]

In January 1896 another book arrived at The Grove, one that Emma knew she *would* be able to read but, unlike Frank's *Botany*, fully expected to dislike. "Fr has got Romane's Life," she reported to Hen. "The life of a foolish man (tho' a clever one) by a foolish woman is rather sure to be objectionable." The book in question was *The Life and Letters of George John Romanes*, edited by his wife, Ethel Romanes, and it is not exactly clear why Emma was initially so negative. Admittedly, Romanes's adulation of Charles Darwin had always been a bit over the top, and so were Ethel's gushy descriptions of her husband's devotion to Darwin:

> Perhaps no hero-worship was ever more unselfish, more utterly loyal, or more fully rewarded. As time went on, and intimacy increased, and restraint wore off, Mr. Romanes found that the great master was as much to be admired for his personal character as for his wonderful gifts, and to the youth who never, in the darkest days of utter skepticism, parted with the love for goodness, for beauty of character, this was an overwhelming joy.

Pretty syrupy stuff, but perhaps forgivable when written by a widow about her lost husband, and certainly flattering toward Darwin. It may have been only a visceral reaction against flatterers that caused Emma to cringe when Frank brought home the Romanes book. In any event, she surprised herself by liking the book once she got into it, and by February she was telling Henrietta, "Romane's Life . . . seems to me well done."[23]

Besides fretting about national politics—that is, Leo's exasperating petition against Fulford—Emma was quite concerned that winter about the ongoing massacres of Armenians in the Middle East. Between 1894 and 1896, Ottoman forces commanded by the last sultan, Abdul Hamid II, killed thousands of Armenians. Now known as the Hamidian Massacres (to distinguish them from similar atrocities in 1915), these pogroms may have resulted in 100,000–300,00 deaths and thousands of refugees. In March 1896 Emma contributed £8 to an Armenian relief fund. She hoped the money would go to help the starving refugees "at Van," she told Hen, "where we have a consul & so can get at them." Later she railed against "the wickedness of all the European papers" that prevented effective international reaction to the massacres. She cut the French some slack in this regard, however, noting that France was at least "helping the poor creatures to emigrate."[24]

The other international theater that drew Emma's attention was Egypt, or more precisely the Sudan. In the decade since the failed attempt to rescue Gordon at Khartoum, the Sudan had been left under the control first of the Mahdi and then of his successor the Khalifa. In 1895, however, as British, French, and Belgian territorial interests converged in East Africa and the question of who would control the upper Nile became a pressing issue, Britain decided to send Major General H. H. Kitchener on an expedition to reconquer the Sudan for Egypt and the United Kingdom. The 25,000-man Anglo-Egyptian Nile Expeditionary Force advanced south from its headquarters at Wadi Halfa in March 1896, and Emma registered her uneasiness in several comments to Henrietta:

[March 18] I am v uneasy about the Egyptian exped[ition]. It may turn out [to be] some tremendous undertaking.

[March 19] I wish this Egyptian affair may not be the small beginning of a torrent.

[March 24] Leo is a good deal alarmed about Egypt, & he thinks that Govt. must have some stronger reason [for going in] than they avow.[25]

These comments reflect Emma's lifelong aversion to war, although she was perfectly ready to use coercion against the perpetually unruly Irish and she accepted the necessity of armed conflict in some cases, such as freeing the slaves in America. As fate would have it, Britain's involvement in Egypt would not concern her for long. By the third week of September 1896, Kitchener's forces had moved south of the Nile's third cataract and won the battle of Dunqulah, although it would be two more years before he truly broke the Khalifa's strength at Omdurman. But Mrs. Darwin wouldn't make it that far. Death was due to end her personal war-watch eleven days after the British forces triumphantly entered Dunqulah.[26]

Spring 1896 found Emma planning for the upcoming summer at Downe and worrying about her beloved fox terrier, Dickey. Down House needed painting both inside and out, but with a shortage of workers anticipated during the busy summer season, it was decided to split the job, doing the inside work immediately and postponing the exteriors of the house, stables, and outbuildings until the fall. Emma also wanted George to put an end to the distribution of bread tickets to beggars at Down House. This small charity, which Emma herself had started some fifty years before, had now grown to be something of a burden, particularly when the yard filled up with "hearty Irish men refusing to go away, till [someone] sent for the policeman." Besides, she was none too sure that the tickets didn't actually *encourage* begging. In any event, she did not want Mary Anne Parslow, who took charge of the house during the winter months, to have to deal with a constant stream of tramps. To ease the cessation of bread tickets, Mary Anne's "allowance" was increased slightly so she could help out in cases of exceptional need, should she choose to do so.[27]

As regards Dickey, the unfortunate animal had "met with an accident and had to go to the [veterinarian] for some time." Since dog and owner were inseparable as a rule—their days began with Dickey joining Emma for her breakfast in bed—Emma missed him very much during his hospitalization. With Dickey being in his mid-teens and thus an old dog, it took a few weeks for him to heal, a process that may or may not have been facilitated by Emma regularly sending him treats of "spunge" cake via Bessy or one of the maids.[28]

By June 9 they were back in Downe, and it was the beginning of what everyone later agreed was a delightful summer. Emma made the change of houses with minimal fatigue and started in immediately seeing old friends and servants in the village. As usual, Lady Derby was among the earliest drop-in visitors at Down House, making her first of several calls on June 17. She was followed closely by Mrs. Ffinden, who was typically invited for tea at least once each year despite two decades of bad blood toward her husband. Happily, even those old bad feelings had mellowed over the years, with the two parties now being reconciled enough so that Emma felt inclined to make small contributions toward Ffinden's work at St. Mary's. (In 1895, for example, she gave £1 to a church-run clothing fund and 10 shillings toward Sunday School prizes.) Nonetheless, there was a note of genuine surprise in Emma's report to Henrietta about the friendliness of her most recent interaction with Mr. Ffinden in September 1896: "On Friday . . . I went up the Luxted road & had quite a gay time, meeting Mr. Ff[inden] so debonnaire & friendly & following an elegant goat carriage w baby and nursemaid."[29]

In the course of the summer, all of the grown Darwin children and their spouses, with the possible exception of Frank and Ellen, made it to Down House at least once. William and Leo even bicycled down from London on one occasion (Bee came by train). The weather was generally good—at least until September, when it rained almost every day—and the flowers were breathtaking, particularly the roses and phloxes. There were mushroom hunts in the fields near the house, carriage rides to Holwood Park, hikes for the younger folks to the "Orchis bank," where in bygone days Emma and Charles marveled at the wild orchids, and rides for Emma in her bath chair to view the fields bordering the Sandwalk. She took special pleasure in sitting out in the cool summer air, chatting with family and friends, and watching the grandchildren playing on the lawn. In the evenings she played the piano for everyone's enjoyment, no doubt including the "galloping song" so the little ones could tear around the drawing room.[30]

In July, Nettie Huxley came for a five-day visit. She and Emma had not seen each other in years; even more important, this was their first meeting since the death of T. H. Huxley thirteen months before. Coming to Down House also brought Nettie back to the place that she had found so restful and restorative in the sad days after Noel's death in 1860.[31] Emma described the visit to Henrietta:

> Mrs. H came at 3.30 [on the 22nd] & sat w me before her tea, & then went w B[essy] round the sand walk. She looks very haggard since I saw her about 6 or 7 years ago—& was cheerful & ready to tell me every thing; B tells me that she quite broke down talking to her in the evening & cried very much. I am surprized at her strength, as she is subject to terribly painful attacks, of which the cause is unknown. . . . Mrs. H was confined to her bed w influenza during Mr. H's last illness, & has now the usual regrets that more might have been done &c—or that some carelessness had some bad effects.[32]

And two days later:

> Mrs. Huxley reads a good deal & sits out of doors, but she is rather lame at present & does not walk. She returns to Eastbourne tomorrow & [her daughter] Jessie joins her the next day. [Among] her chief darlings [are her daughters-in-law]—next to them & their husbands come Ethel & Jessie; but she is well off in all; tho' I do not think they are aware that having the [grand]children is too much of a care for her.[33]

During Nettie Huxley's stay, Emma and Bessy hosted the local Band of Hope for a day's outing at Down House. Never a fan of strong drink, Emma hoped this temperance organization would help keep working-class children on the straight and narrow path. Teetotalism was a tough sell, however, particularly as the children grew up, and she was disappointed to "see not one big boy" in her yard full of youngsters. One boy "might have been 13 possibly," she told Hen. "He look[ed] quite young & handsome & [played on the swing] for hours. He joined Bessy & Miss Meek (a governess who helps) for tea in the veranda, wh he took so leisurely that it lasted an hour. . . . [The children played] till past 8 all in peace & good behaviour."[34]

Just a couple of days later, still in the role of charity hostesses, Emma and Bessy welcomed "Mr. Steane [and] his 60 cripples" from Bermondsey in central London for yet another lawn party. Emma described the event to Henrietta:

> They arrived at 3 having been on the road since soon after 11. However they did not seem tired, & as they could very few of them play about, the drive seemed to be the principal treat. We furnished jam & gooseberries, wh last were considered too precious to be eaten at once; but were put into bags & given to each to eat on the way [home]—& no doubt they helped to pass the time. They had their tea on the grass out of the wind on the N side & looked well dressed. Some few played & swung a little. They set off again at 5.30 & were quite eager to be put into the vans before the horses were in. . . . The poor cripples could cheer very well & the vans stopped opposite my windows for that purpose.[35]

On August 29, Henrietta and Richard left Down House for a trip to the Continent with cousin Mildred Massingberd, a granddaughter of Charlotte and Charles Langton. They were delayed in Dover by illness, however, and Emma's September letters were sent to her ailing eldest daughter in that seaside town:[36]

> [September 9] I hate your being sick away from home. I believe your Dover Dr is more cautious than your London Dr wd have been, who has seen you thro' so many of these. What a comfort Mildred has been—to R as well as to you. . . .

> [September 16] I hope R will soon be better. . . . Have you been out in a Bath chair yet?

> [September 18] On Wed. we drove that new way up the [Holwood] Park to the Ponds, but it is not nearly so pretty as the other ways & a much steeper hill; but the mare tugged cheerfully up as if I was a load of coals & [everyone else] (including Carry) walked. Trees always seem to know when they are in a lordly Domain. I am sure the beeches & Spanish chestnuts by the ponds do. . . . [Carry's] reading is more comical than ever. When Dickey is not there to be talked to, she takes off her spectacles & rubs them, or alters her shawl

or looks on a few pages, but as I am always knitting I am not impatient & her voice is clear & pleasant & I hear every word, & keep her at it longer than I shd without these pauses. . . . Your card & Mildred's cheerful & comfort. letter are just come in, to begin my day so brightly. I used to abuse & dislike Dover, when I came w Wm & poor Annie to take you back from Aunt Charlotte & they took to crying & being miserable & the shore was unwalkable—but I shd now like sitting on the shingle w Mildred.[37]

In so many ways, it had been a remarkable summer. Despite being well into her eighty-ninth year, Emma had lost neither her mental sharpness nor her zest for life, and physically she seemed "younger & more vigorous" than she had in years. She "was quite wonderfully strong" in 1896, remembered Henrietta, reflecting on the steady flow of visitors through Down House that summer and how much Emma had enjoyed them. Nonetheless, at eighty-eight Emma's physical fragility was just below the surface, and—although no one recognized it at the time—when she took to her bed on Sunday, September 27, with shoulder pains and digestive problems, it was actually the beginning of the end. Monday saw her bounce back a little, only to sink again the next day. Dr. Norman Moore, who had attended Charles in his last illness, was called down from London, and a local nurse was found.[38]

Unaware that Emma's illness needed to be taken seriously, Henrietta and Richard went directly home to London from their own sickbeds in Dover. Hen wrote to her mother from Kensington Square on September 30, sending little bits of health and family news, and also a wish that Emma might soon be well enough for the move back to Cambridge. By the next day, however, Henrietta had learned that her mother was gravely ill and, leaving her still-recuperating husband, she rushed to Down House. Hen's own words tell the rest of the story:

I arrived about 6 o'clock & she was asleep. I did not go in to her that night. If I had I could have read to her & she wd have liked to listen but it was thought too late & that it might upset her I was in the house. The next day the discomfort & pain returned. Dr Scott was sent for & arrived about 10 o'clock. I had seen her then, but she was too uncomf. to speak more than a word. She asked after Richard. She sent for me to put on my liniment my way which I did & then she said she was very weary of the pain. Her last words to me were 'Dont stay in the room Body [an old nickname]; I'll send for you when I am better.' This was between 4 & 5. Dr Moore & Dr Scott arrived between 5 & 6. They saw her & the account made us feel of course that she was very ill. Dr Scott had gone & Dr Moore had just sat down to his tea, when an urgent message came for him to come up immediately. She had been preparing for the night & had asked [the maid] in her usual voice to wind up her watch when she fell back unconscious with no struggle or sign of distress & a few fluttering breaths & all was over. We were all in the room. After a little consideration I decided it was best for me to return that night to Richard. I went back with Dr Moore. But before going I went in to see the beautiful pale solemn sweet face composed for its last rest.[39]

And so, with "a few fluttering breaths," the mainstay of the Darwin family was gone. Although hardly consoling to the grief-stricken family, it was precisely the sort of exit that Emma would have scripted for herself, or for anyone else for that matter. A brief illness and gentle death surrounded by loved ones was such a blessing compared to the long, slow declines suffered by her parents and father-in-law. Now she was free of worldly cares, able at last to find out whether she and Charles would be together for all eternity. Emma had loved her scientific maverick of a husband for more than forty years, had given birth to their ten children, and had provided a moral compass for their lives together. She had conscientiously lived out her Christian faith, albeit with a few doctrinal modifications along with way, and had generally managed to "love her neighbors" and "do unto others"—although the fiendish Ffinden had put her good will to the test. She had enjoyed her world and all of its pleasures, particularly its music, art, literature, gardens, and politics, and she had attracted a devoted circle of friends and admirers. Although not a scientist—indeed, a woman bored by science—she had contributed to Charles's work not a little, mainly by tolerating his heresies, of course, but also by serving as a sounding board for ideas, editing and proofing manuscripts, and helping with correspondence. Although not a cutup, she had had a ready laugh for the jokes of others. And although undemonstrative with her emotions, she had been a font of unqualified and unending love for her husband first and foremost—"as good as twice refined gold," he had described her[40]—and later for her children and grandchildren. Now that font was gone. The last of her generation and of the lively Maerites, in turn "Little Miss Slip-Slop," Charles's "Dearest Emma" and "own poor dear, dear wife," "Mama," "Mother," "Grandmamma," and more, Emma would be mourned in the village of Downe, among her many friends and acquaintances at all levels of society and around the world, and, most of all, across the breadth of her own family circle. The death of a matriarch leaves an enormous void.

The obituary in the *Times* was short and to the point, announcing the death "at the age of 88, of Mrs. Darwin, widow of the late Charles Darwin, the illustrious naturalist." Emma's similarly illustrious Wedgwood father and grandfather were also identified, as were a few of her surviving children. True to the custom of the age, only the three most accomplished sons were named: George ("F.R.S., Plumian Professor of Astronomy at Cambridge"), Frank ("F. R.S., University Reader in Botany at Cambridge"), and Leonard ("late member for the Lichfield Division of Staffordshire"). William the banker, Horace the mechanic and inventor, and (of course) both surviving daughters, Henrietta and Bessy, went unmentioned.[41]

The burial took place on October 7 in the yard of St. Mary the Virgin Church in Downe. George Ffinden officiated, a point that could no longer trouble Emma but possibly annoyed some of the children. Her body was lowered into a grave that already held the remains of her brother-in-law Erasmus and would have held Charles's had it not been for the switch to Westminster Abbey. But even without Charles, Emma joined an extensive group of Darwins and Wedgwoods in St. Mary's yard. Across the way lay the graves of her two lost babies, Mary Eleanor and Charles Waring, as well as those of her beloved sister Elizabeth and her aunt Sarah Elizabeth. And before the Darwin burying was through in the 1960s, the churchyard would also contain Bessy, Henrietta, and Bernard.[42]

Three days after the funeral, Henrietta wrote to George as she tried to pick up the threads of all their lives:

> Now our centre is gone we must write more to each other. I, at any rate, kept the run of all your lives from Mother. I am so glad the children are old enough to remember her. All but [two-year-old] Billy, and he can be told what pleasure he gave her last few months of life. Dear old George your constant faithfulness gave her such pleasure & she was always so glad that you loved Down in a way the others did not. If it is possible I should like to pay my last visit to Down when you are there if I can. The dear chicks wd make it less sad & I should feel Maud's calm presence a help.[43]

Truly, the center was gone. Charles had brought fame to the family and, of course, had loved his children dearly. But it seems fair to say that Emma had provided more of the emotional core of the family and, by virtue of outliving her husband, had done so for a longer period of time. Regrouping after the center is lost is never easy, but predictably the Darwin children did so, and in ways that would have made their parents proud. Brief descriptions of the later lives of the seven "little Ds" are thus fitting.

William continued in banking for his entire career, retiring shortly after Sara died in 1902. He relocated to London and spent the years until his own death in 1914 being, in the words of his niece Gwen Raverat, "a really first-class uncle."[44]

George served as president of the Royal Astronomical Society in 1899 and of the British Association in 1905. Knighted in 1905 for his scientific accomplishments, he lived only another seven years, dying of cancer in 1912. Maud lived on through both world wars, dying in her eighty-sixth year in 1947.[45]

Frank lost his second wife, Ellen, in 1903, but married for the third time "when he was quite old" in the view of his niece Gwen Raverat; actually, Frank was sixty-five. This time his wife was "the strange and beautiful widow of Professor F. W. Maitland, the historian," which made Frank the stepfather of the two strangely and beautifully named Maitland daughters, Ermengard and Fredegond. For his biographic and scientific efforts, Frank was knighted in 1913, and he lived until 1925.[46]

Elizabeth "Bee" Darwin, the veteran of all those election confrontations with Lichfield miners, died in 1898, leaving Leonard a widower. He married again in 1900, this time to his cousin Mildred Massingberd. From 1908 to 1911, Leo served as president of the Royal Geographical Society, and then in 1911 he succeeded his cousin, Sir Francis Galton, as president of the Eugenics Society. In the latter position, he advocated negative eugenics—encouraging, and possibly enforcing, "conception control" among people deemed unfit, such as criminals and persons with "some grievous mental or bodily defect"—a controversial, if not positively offensive, position today. Leo was the longest-lived of the Darwin children, dying in 1943 at the ripe old age of ninety-three.[47]

Horace continued to run the Cambridge Scientific Instrument Company until his death in 1928. In 1897 he served a term as mayor of Cambridge, an honor his mother would surely have enjoyed witnessing. During World War I, Horace made important contributions to the Air Ministry's exploration of the use of aircraft in war and to the Munitions Ministry's Inventions Department. For his various "services in connection with the War," Horace was awarded a knighthood in 1918. Ida Darwin survived Horace by eighteen years.[48]

Henrietta was widowed in 1903, then moved from London to a country house called Burrows Hill in Surrey. By far the strongest character of all the Darwin children, "Aunt Etty" was immortalized by her adoring niece Gwen Raverat in *Period Piece: A Cambridge Childhood*. In 1904 Henrietta privately published a heavily edited collection of excerpts from her mother's letters.

This was followed in 1915 by a public edition of the same material titled *Emma Darwin: A Century of Family Letters*. We have drawn extensively from Henrietta's two-volume memorial to her mother.[49]

Finally, there is Bessy Darwin. Surely this spinster daughter—her mother's "dear Bessy"—must have felt Emma's death in ways deeply different from her siblings. Bessy was forty-nine when her mother died, and she had lived with Emma since birth. But despite her oddities and limitations, Bessy was able to rebound and fashion a busy and productive life. From her mother, Bessy had inherited a charitable streak, and this manifested itself in such activities as reading aloud at the Cambridge Association for the Blind and, for more than forty years, visiting the pauper women living out their lives in the Cambridge Workhouse. After Emma's death, Bessy relocated from The Grove to a more manageable house on West Road in Cambridge. When she passed away in 1926, she was remembered fondly not only by her many nieces and nephews but by the entire city of Cambridge.[50]

This narrative of Emma Darwin's long and involved life is now at an end, but despite all of the details of growing up and aging, tastes and travels, family and friends, happiness and sorrow that have filled these pages, we cannot help but feel that she has somewhat eluded our grasp. Knowledge of a person's life history can never really replace the sound of a voice, the twinkle of an eye, the emotion of deeply felt opinions. Quite ordinary physically, Emma was extraordinary in her quiet but powerful personality—her "calm strength," in Henrietta's words.[51] But besides being the wife of a famous scientist, what specifically, we have been asked, is Emma Darwin's "claim to fame"? We can only respond that we make no such claim for her, nor would she have made one on her own behalf during life. Nonetheless, we find her story both fascinating and inspirational. From her girlhood at Maer to her adulthood in Charles's shadow, Emma's was quite simply a long and beautiful life lived *positively*: without complaints, self-pity, overweening pride, or regrets; marked by caring more for others than for self; and filled with acts both small and large that made her world a better place. Surely these things count for just as much as some single "claim to fame," and surely there is much to be learned from a life such as hers. The world would be a better place with more "wise advisers and cheerful comforters."[52]

Acknowledgments

We gratefully acknowledge the late Stephen Jay Gould as the muse for this book. While attending one of Gould's Harvard classes in the mid-1990s, James D. Loy heard him remark that a full-length biography of Emma Darwin had yet to be written—in contrast to the numerous biographies of Charles—and that hers was a life well worth exploring. We took these words to heart and soon thereafter began to make plans to write Emma's story. Ultimately, this project would last for more than a decade and would involve three trips to England, including a six-month sabbatical in Cambridge, and hundreds of hours reading family letters at the Cambridge University Library (CUL, Darwin Archives) and at Keele University (Wedgwood Archives). Now our work is concluded, and although we had hoped to publish the book in 2008, the year that marked Emma's 200th birthday, we are pleased that its debut will come hot on the heels of Charles Darwin's 200th birthday celebrations, as well as the 150th anniversary of the publication of *On the Origin of Species*.

Not surprisingly, the international nature of our research and the length of our project have resulted in a long list of people on both sides of the Atlantic to whom we owe our thanks. In the acknowledgments that follow, we have grouped our main benefactors first by location and then alphabetically. We hope that we have not forgotten anyone. Following the individuals, institutional acknowledgments are given.

Our deepest thanks go to these people in England:

* Helen Burton, archivist at Keele University Library and keeper of the Wedgwood papers. Helen's warm welcome and expert assistance made our forays into the Wedgwood collections both pleasurable and productive.

* Bernard and Susan Campbell, who have become our close friends since text-book collaboration brought Bernard and JDL together some years ago. The Campbells not only gave us constant encouragement throughout the Emma Darwin project, regularly inquiring about the state of "the book," but also found and vetted our sabbatical rental. Additionally, they helped us maintain a semblance of work-life balance by providing opportunities for recreational getaways as only dear friends can do.

* William Huxley Darwin, who as Charles and Emma Darwin's great-great-grandson and the copyright holder of their unpublished writings, graciously gave us permission to quote from these materials.

* Richard Darwin Keynes, professor emeritus of physiology, Cambridge, who gave us unlimited access to the diaries kept by his great-grandmother Emma Darwin, as well as permission to quote from the same. We further thank Professor Keynes and his wife, Ann, for the hospitality and friendship they extended to two Americans who dropped unexpectedly into their lives.

* Adam Perkins, Curator of Scientific Manuscripts, Cambridge University Library, friend and colleague who has been our CUL mainstay since the beginning of the project. Without his expert guidance, we might easily have been overwhelmed by the enormous, and enormously complex, Darwin Archives. In addition to assisting us in Cambridge, Adam patiently answered questions and solved problems via international e-mail and, of vital importance, directed us to members of the Darwin and Keynes families whose permission we needed to quote from private and unpublished material.

* Gaye Blake Roberts, director of the Wedgwood Museum, who supported our research by giving us access to archival material at Keele University and who also helped us obtain the museum trustees' permission to quote from the Wedgwood papers.

* Godfrey Waller, archive librarian, Cambridge University Library, who not only put up with our endless requests for Darwin materials but also alerted us to the delights of the CUL tearoom.

* And finally, among those people who helped in smaller but still important ways in England, we are grateful to P. C. Lee, Biological Anthropology, Cambridge, for helping James Loy obtain visiting scholar status during our sabbatical visit; Ruth Long and Don Manning of the Cambridge University Library for assistance purchasing Darwin images; James Ryder of CUL for tracking down Darwin file numbers; Kees Rookmaaker and John van Wyhe

for assistance with images from Darwin Online (http://darwin-online.org.uk/); and Richard Tremaine for loaning us a copy of *Horace Darwin's Shop*.

We also extend our sincere thanks to these benefactors in the United States:

* Winifred Brownell, dean of arts and sciences, University of Rhode Island, a valued colleague and friend who has been consistently encouraging as our project has gone from data collection to writing to publication.

* Helen Mederer, friend and departmental colleague, who has been an enthusiastic supporter of our project from the beginning. Helen's feedback on portions of the manuscript was both valuable and encouraging.

* C. B. Peters, another friend and University of Rhode Island colleague, whose humor has helped break the stress of many a long writing session and who, as James Loy's self-styled "research assistant," has helped us keep abreast of Darwin-related material.

* Karen Ramsay, formerly a senior librarian at the University of Rhode Island, who helped us track down several nineteenth-century medical terms. Given the Darwins' many ailments and medications, this was a great help with our research.

* And finally, the people who fall into the category of "solicitous friends" who listened to more about the Darwins than they ever wanted to hear, regularly inquired about our progress, cheered when things were going well, and gave us a pat on the back when they weren't: Bob Bullock, Barbara Costello, Laurie and Stan Cobb, Carol and Charlie Cox, Bette Erickson, Margaret Olsen, and Glen Ramsay.

We also extend our thanks to the institutions and organizations that have granted permission to publish portions of their holdings or have provided monetary support to our project:

* The Syndics of Cambridge University Library have kindly given permission to publish portions of the Darwin family collections held at that facility.

* By courtesy of the Trustees of the Wedgwood Museum, Barlaston, Staffordshire, we have kindly been given permission to publish portions of the Wedgwood Archives.

* The University of Rhode Island graciously awarded James Loy a one-semester sabbatical leave for research in England during the spring of 2000.

* The University of Rhode Island Foundation provided $1,000 to help defray our sabbatical expenses. Additionally, the foundation approved a grant of $2,000 to help pay for illustrations for Emma Darwin's biography.

* The University of Rhode Island Center for the Humanities provided $1,500 for the purchase of a laptop computer to aid in our research.

It remains only to express our gratitude to John Byram and Jacqueline Kinghorn Brown at the University Press of Florida, for having confidence in our book and for overall editorial guidance, and to Ann Marlowe, our copy editor, for help getting the manuscript into final form.

Notes

Abbreviations Used

Beagle   *HMS* Beagle: *The Story of Darwin's Ship*, by Keith Stewart Thomson (New York: W. W. Norton, 1995)

CCD   *The Correspondence of Charles Darwin*, vols. 1–16 (1821–68), edited by Frederick Burkhardt, Sydney Smith, et al. (Cambridge: Cambridge University Press, 1985–2008)

Companion   *Charles Darwin: A Companion*, by R. B. Freeman (Folkestone, Kent: Dawson; Hamden, Conn.: Archon, 1978)

DAR   Darwin Papers, Cambridge University Library

DNB   *Dictionary of National Biography*

ED   *Emma Darwin: The Inspirational Wife of a Genius*, by Edna Healey (London: Headline, 2001)

ED-CFL   *Emma Darwin: A Century of Family Letters, 1792–1896,* edited by Henrietta Litchfield, 2 vols. (New York: Appleton, 1915)

Power   *The Power of Place*, vol. 2 of *Charles Darwin*, by Janet Browne (New York: Knopf, 2002)

Tormented   *Darwin: The Life of a Tormented Evolutionist*, by Adrian Desmond and James Moore (New York: Warner, 1991)

Voyaging   *Voyaging*, vol. 1 of *Charles Darwin*, by Janet Browne (New York: Knopf, 1995)

WC   *The Wedgwood Circle, 1730–1897*, by Barbara Wedgwood and Hensleigh Wedgwood (Westfield, N.J.: Eastview, 1980)

W/M   Wedgwood-Mosley Collection of Wedgwood Correspondence, Keele University Library

For the epigraph, see Barlow, 96–97.

CHAPTER 1. The Family Circle

1. *ED-CFL*, 1:51; Harrison and Wild, 7, 25.
2. *ED-CFL*, 1:xxxii–xxxiii, 7 ("dangerous . . ."); Perkin, 68–69; *WC*, 136.
3. Magnusson, 521; McCord, 78.
4. Mowat, 569–79; Sweet.
5. *WC*, 105. Trying to make sense of nineteenth-century monetary values in terms of modern-day wealth is a tricky business. We follow Roy Jenkins in *Gladstone*, 4, in applying the "fifty factor." That is, all nineteenth-century values will be multiplied by fifty to produce approximate modern equivalents in British pounds. A further multiplication by 1.67 produces the rough United States dollar equivalent in November 2009.
6. *WC*, 102–5.
7. *WC*, 105–7.
8. *WC*, 123.
9. Magnusson, 329–30, 394–95, 1582–83; *WC*, 101–10.
10. *WC*, 116–17, 123–30.
11. *WC*, 117.
12. Colp, *To Be an Invalid*, 3; *WC*, 132.
13. *ED-CFL*, 1:xxviii–xxix, 2.
14. *ED-CFL*, 1:xxviii–xxix, 2–4; Magnusson, 943, 1364; Pearson, 172; *WC*, 106–7, 128, 140.
15. *ED*, facing 117; *ED-CFL*, 1:4–5 ("half-formed . . .").
16. *WC*, 133–34 ("A coach . . ."), 138.
17. *ED-CFL*, 1:27, 29 ("We . . ."); *WC*, 119, 132–34.

CHAPTER 2. The Two Dovelies

1. *ED*, 63 ("Since . . ."); *ED-CFL*, 1:61, 2:189 ("sheltered . . .").
2. *ED-CFL*, 1:61.
3. *WC*, 138–39, 145–46, 155.
4. *WC*, 144, 148–49.
5. *WC*, 147.
6. *ED-CFL*, 1:30, 54 ("Mamma . . ."), 134; *WC*, 156–58.
7. *ED-CFL*, 1:7.
8. *ED-CFL*, 1:7 ("Wedgwood's . . ."); Magnusson, 1364.
9. *ED-CFL*, 1:7.
10. *ED-CFL*, 1:14–15.
11. *ED-CFL*, 1:59–60.
12. *ED*, 68; *ED-CFL*, 1:58, 61; *WC*, 166.
13. Magnusson, 1065–66; Mowat, 587–91.
14. *ED-CFL*, 1:71–72.

15. *ED*, facing 117 and 174; *ED-CFL*, 1:77–98, 128; Magnusson, 1355, 1383.

16. *WC*, 166, 173–79, 184.

17. *ED-CFL*, 1:xxviii, 120; *WC*, 182.

18. *Voyaging*, 18–19 ("The Dr . . ."); *WC*, 181.

19. *Voyaging*, 19; *WC*, 181.

20. *CCD*, 2:439 ("I recollect . . ."); F. Darwin, *Autobiography of Charles Darwin*, 5–6 ("It is . . .").

21. Magnusson, 1223.

22. *ED*, 69; *ED-CFL*, 1:113–16; *WC*, 183.

23. *ED-CFL*, 1:117.

24. *ED-CFL*, 1:119.

25. *ED-CFL*, 1:121.

26. *ED-CFL*, 1:134–35.

27. Heyck, 203.

28. *ED*, 74; *ED-CFL*, 1:141; Magnusson, 1371; W/M 158.

29. Dolan, 262.

30. Burke, 528.

31. W/M 158.

32. Munson, 330, 338–39.

33. *ED-CFL*, 1:141–42.

34. *ED-CFL*, 1:141–42.

35. DAR 219.11:2.

36. DAR 219.11:2.

37. W/M 1151 (diary for 1823).

38. *ED-CFL*, 1:155 ("If . . ."), 170.

39. DAR 242 (Emma's diaries; henceforth each reference to DAR 242 will give a diary year, here 1824). Emma also used the inside front and back covers to record all manner of things including shopping lists, musical pieces, plants, addresses, poems, and recipes both for foods and medicines. The small pockets inside the covers of the diaries were used to hold stamps, fabric samples, train schedules, tickets to various events, etc.

40. DAR 242 (1824).

41. *ED-CFL*, 1:220.

42. DAR 242 (1824).

43. *ED-CFL*, 1:160–61.

44. DAR 242 (1824).

45. *ED-CFL*, 1:161–62.

46. *ED-CFL*, 1:162.

47. We disagree with the claim that Charles Darwin also attended these postconfirmation revels (*Tormented*, 19). In DAR 242 (1824) Emma records neither his arrival nor his departure.

48. Barlow, 55–56.

49. Barlow, 28 ("You . . ."); *Tormented*, 17–20.

50. *CCD*, 1:15; *Tormented*, 22.

51. *ED-CFL*, 1:177.

CHAPTER 3. A Woman of the World

1. *WC*, 197.
2. *WC*, 192.
3. *ED-CFL*, 1:170.
4. *WC*, 194.
5. *ED*, 81–82; *ED-CFL*, 1:166; *WC*, 197.
6. *ED*, 76; *ED-CFL*, 1:166.
7. W/M 178.
8. *ED*, 83–84; W/M 178 ("not…").
9. W/M 178 ("making…"); *ED*, 84.
10. W/M 178.
11. Temperley, 172–91.
12. *DNB*, s.v. "Peel, Sir Robert."
13. McCord, 32; *Times* (London), 2–3 March 1825.
14. *ED-CFL*, 1:175–76.
15. *ED*, 85–86.
16. *ED*, 86; *ED-CFL*, 1:172, 175–76 ("the filthy…").
17. *ED-CFL*, 1:174–75.
18. *Companion*, 54; *ED*, 90–97; *ED-CFL*, 1:177; Magnusson, 847.
19. *ED-CFL*, 1:177–80.
20. *ED-CFL*, 1:180–81; *WC*, 198.
21. *ED-CFL*, 1:181 ("We …"); Desmond and Moore, *Darwin's Sacred Cause*, 13–16, 59–63.
22. *ED-CFL*, 1:255; McCord, 139.
23. *ED*, 100; W/M 158 ("I thank…").
24. *ED*, 100–102; Jalland, 306–7.
25. *ED-CFL*, 1:187 ("The first…"); Magnusson, 842.
26. *ED-CFL*, 1:188–92 ("I am …," 188; "anxious-looking …," 190; "disposition …," 192).
27. *ED-CFL*, 1:187–88.
28. *ED*, 121.
29. *ED*, 144–45; *ED-CFL*, 1:286; Hedley; Magnusson, 1292.
30. *ED*, 103–5; *ED-CFL*, 1:201.
31. W/M 1151 (travel journal 1827).
32. Ibid.; *ED*, 106.
33. *ED-CFL*, 1:208.
34. *ED-CFL*, 1:206; McCord, 37–38; *WC*, 200–201.
35. *WC*, 199–202.
36. Barlow, 48 ("I…"); *CCD*, 1:16; *Tormented*, 26–43.
37. *Companion*, 99; *CCD*, 1:46–49 ("shootables," 47); *Tormented*, 46–47.
38. *Companion*, 99; *Tormented*, 47–49.
39. *ED-CFL*, 1:214–16.
40. *ED*, 115.
41. *ED*, 114–15; *ED-CFL*, 1:217.
42. *ED-CFL*, 1:229; *WC*, 201–7 ("I have …," 203).

43. W/M 1151 (diary for 1830).

44. *ED-CFL*, 1:224; *WC*, 205.

45. Colp, *To Be an Invalid*, 261; Weintraub, 65; "George IV (1820–30 AD)," www.britannia.com/history/monarchs/mon56.html.

46. Holmes, 11.

47. Greville, 2:1–2; Magnusson, 627.

48. Greville, 2:3–5 ("as merry..." and "This..."); Magnusson, 762; Weintraub, 70; Ziegler, 151 ("an easy...").

49. Greville, 2:2; McCord, 43–44.

50. McCord, 40–41; Magnusson, 1139.

51. McCord, 43–44, 129–31.

52. *ED-CFL*, 1:231, 237; McCord, 129–31; *WC*, 210.

53. *WC*, 212.

54. Mosley, 2:2767; *WC*, 212 ("My principles...").

55. *ED-CFL*, 1:237–38.

56. McCord, 131–33.

57. McCord, 133–37; *WC*, 219.

58. *ED-CFL*, 1:253–54.

CHAPTER 4. A Traveling Cousin, a Doveley's Death,
and the Abolition of Slavery

1. Richard Keynes, *Charles Darwin's* Beagle *Diary*, 17.

2. *Tormented*, 88.

3. *CCD*, 1:128–29.

4. *CCD*, 1:128–29; McCord, 4; *Tormented*, 104; *Voyaging*, 146; *Beagle*, 88.

5. *CCD*, 1:131–33 ("wild...," 133); *Tormented*, 102.

6. *CCD*, 1:133–34.

7. Barlow, 72; *CCD*, 1:135, 143n1; *Voyaging*, 160–61.

8. Barlow, 58–71; *CCD*, 1:129 ("a finished..."); *Voyaging*, 118–43.

9. W/M 1151 (diary for 1832).

10. *Companion*, 197; *WC*, 204–9.

11. *CCD*, 2:64; *WC*, 211–12.

12. *WC*, 216–17.

13. W/M 1151 (diary for 1832).

14. *WC*, 216–18.

15. *Companion*, 185; *ED-CFL*, 1:243; *WC*, 217; W/M 1151 (diary for 1832; "the happiest...").

16. W/M 1151 (diary for 1832).

17. W/M 1151 (diary for 1832, "February 13..."); *CCD*, 1:216 ("Franks Miss..."), 208 ("very...").

18. *Companion*, 209; *WC*, 217; W/M 1151 (diary for 1832).

19. *CCD*, 1:219.

20. *CCD*, 1:72.

21. *CCD*, 1:61, 325.

22. *CCD*, 1:220 ("I don't . . ."), 614.

23. *CCD*, 1:213–14 ("that no . . ."), 220.

24. W/M 1151 (diary for 1832).

25. *ED-CFL*, 1:244; Greville, 2:240 ("News . . ."); Porter, 260.

26. *ED-CFL*, 1:244–46 ("become . . . ," 245; "extravagance . . . ," 246); Magnusson, 761.

27. McCord, 134; W/M 1151 (diary for 1832).

28. Mackintosh, 2:483–90 ("I said . . . ," 489–90). Note that *WC*, 218, appears to be in error when it gives the date of the chicken bone incident as May 2, 1832.

29. *ED*, 127; Mackintosh, 2:490; Pearson, 171 ("He . . ."); *WC*, 218–19; *CCD*, 1:235 ("retrench . . .").

30. W/M 1151 (diary for 1832).

31. W/M 1151 (diary for 1832).

32. Crowl, 668; *ED-CFL*, 1:251; Morris, 11; Newsome, 84.

33. Bowlby, 196.

34. Pierce and Mondal, 209–20.

35. *ED*, 129–30 ("On Monday . . ."); *ED-CFL*, 1:250.

36. *ED-CFL*, 1:250.

37. DAR 219.11:41.

38. W/M 1151 (diary for 1832).

39. *CCD*, 1:269.

40. *ED-CFL*, 1:250–51.

41. *ED-CFL*, 1:251.

42. *CCD*, 1:272 ("taken . . ."); *ED-CFL*, 1:215; Jalland, 122–23.

43. *ED-CFL*, 1:251.

44. *ED-CFL*, 1:254.

45. Pine, *Burke's Peerage*, 2190; *WC*, 1.

46. DAR 242 (1833).

47. DAR 242 (1833); *ED-CFL*, 1:255 ("quite . . ." and "half . . ."); Gilbert; Venn.

48. Arbuckle, xvi; DAR 242 (1833); Magnusson, 980; Porter, 130 ("a main . . .").

49. *CCD*, 1:274 ("and Mrs . . ."); *ED*, 135; Magnusson, 263; *WC*, 223.

50. Chapple, 444; *CCD*, 1:302 ("Erasmus . . ."), 318 ("I . . .").

51. DAR 242 (1833).

52. *ED*, 136; *Voyaging*, 356 ("marriage . . .").

53. *CCD*, 2:172–73.

54. Arbuckle; *ED-CFL*, 1:257 ("happy . . .").

55. Richard Keynes, *Charles Darwin's* Beagle *Diary*, 153.

56. DAR 242 (1833); *ED-CFL*, 1:255.

57. *ED-CFL*, 1:255.

58. DAR 242 (1833).

59. *CCD*, 1:357.

60. *CCD*, 1:360.

61. *ED-CFL*, 2:101.

62. Desmond and Moore, *Darwin's Sacred Cause*, 59–61; Finer and Savage, 309, 311; Uglow, *The Lunar Men*, 411–13.

63. Finer and Savage, 311.

64. Uglow, *The Lunar Men*, 412.

65. Magnusson, 409; Molesworth, 1:255–56 ("religious").

66. DAR 242 (1833); *Times* (London), 31 May and 1 June 1833.

67. Desmond and Moore, *Darwin's Sacred Cause*, 116; Molesworth, 1:258–59; *Times* (London), 29 August 1833.

68. Molesworth, 1:259.

69. *CCD*, 1:336–38 ("You will . . . ," 337–38).

70. Desmond and Moore, *Darwin's Sacred Cause*, 74–116; Richard Keynes, *Charles Darwin's* Beagle *Diary*, 195–96; *Voyaging*, 221.

CHAPTER 5. The Return of the *Beagle* and "The days of days!"

1. DAR 242 (1834).

2. Magnusson, 430.

3. *Times* (London), 29 April 1834.

4. DAR 242 (1834).

5. Arbuckle, 1–2; DAR 242 (1834); Martineau, 1:260–70; McCord, 190–96.

6. DAR 242 (1833); *DNB*, s.v. "Martineau, Harriet"; Weinreb and Hibbert, 62.

7. DAR 242 (1835); *ED*, 139.

8. *WC*, 225–26 ("going . . ."); *ED-CFL*, 1:xxviii–xxix, 269–70 ("We were . . .").

9. *WC*, 226.

10. *CCD*, 1:488; *ED-CFL*, 1:xxxii–xxxvi.

11. *CCD*, 1:364–65, 424, 487–88, 627, 634; *Companion*, 145.

12. *CCD*, 1:425.

13. *CCD*, 1:429–30.

14. *CCD*, 1:420–21; DAR 242 (1834).

15. *WC*, 226.

16. *CCD*, 1:469–70 ("keep . . ."), 474 ("a nice . . ." and "whatever . . ."), 494.

17. McCord, 190–93 ("aged . . . ," 191).

18. Molesworth, 1:313–16 ("loading . . . ," 315); Newsome, 18–19; Perkin, 179.

19. *Times* (London), 2 July 1834; *CCD*, 1:309 ("strong . . .").

20. *Times* (London), 24 June 1833.

21. McCord, 140; Molesworth, 1:286–90.

22. Molesworth, 1:294–99; Magnusson, 1096; McCord, 140–41.

23. *CCD*, 1:425; Greville, 3:143–44; Magnusson, 1276; McCord, 141–43; Ziegler, 255–62.

24. A. Desmond, *The Politics of Evolution*, 105–6; *Times* (London), 23 May 1834; "Taxes on Knowledge," www.spartacus.schoolnet.co.uk/PRknowledge.htm.

25. *Times* (London), 19 August 1833, 19 April 1834.

26. *WC*, 220.

27. *CCD*, 1:367, 413, 421–22, 425, 469–70, 494; Molesworth, 1:329.

28. *CCD*, 1:372.

29. *CCD*, 1:469.

30. *Companion*, 99–100; C. Darwin, *Voyage of the* Beagle, throughout; Richard Keynes, *Fossils, Finches and Fuegians*, throughout; *Voyaging*, throughout.

31. As examples of familial concern, see *CCD*, 1:268, 424–25.

32. *Beagle*, 147, 186–88; Richard Keynes, *Fossils, Finches and Fuegians*, 250–54; *CCD*, 1:418 ("Hurra . . .").

33. C. Darwin, *Voyage of the* Beagle, 312; Richard Keynes, *Fossils, Finches and Fuegians*, 269–75.

34. Richard Keynes, *Charles Darwin's* Beagle *Diary*, 315.

35. Ibid.

36. *CCD*, 1:466.

37. Richard Keynes, *Fossils, Finches and Fuegians*, 307–30, 374.

38. *CCD*, 1:469.

39. *ED-CFL*, 1:274.

40. *CCD*, 1:473, 645; *Voyaging*, 338, 348–49.

41. *Voyaging*, 344–45.

42. *Tormented*, 200.

43. *CCD*, 1:613, 630, 636, 654; *Companion*, 309.

44. *Voyaging*, 348.

45. *Tormented*, 206 ("dirty . . ."), 210; *Voyaging*, 344.

46. *CCD*, 1:616, 643; *Companion*, 100; *Voyaging*, 353–55; Magnusson, 1378.

47. Barrett et al., 6–8; *Tormented*, 220–21; *Voyaging*, 359–63.

48. Barrett et al., 6–20.

49. Barrett et al., 213 ("If . . ."), 228–29 ("the soul . . ."), 549–50 ("the mind . . .").

50. *Companion*, 100; Greville, 3:410 ("with . . ."); Plowden, 164; Weintraub, 40, 96–99, 112–13; L. Wilson, 505 ("had . . ."); Sanders et al., 10:114 ("Crowds . . ."); Ziegler, 289.

51. *CCD*, 2:64; *WC*, 229–31.

52. *CCD*, 2:29.

53. *WC*, 228.

54. *CCD*, 1:509, 627, 644; *ED-CFL*, 1:xx–xxi.

55. *CCD*, 1:518–19.

56. *CCD*, 2:80.

57. *CCD*, 1:524.

58. CCD, 2:80 ("a wonderful . . ."); ED-*CFL*, 1:284; *Tormented*, 217; *Voyaging*, 356.

59. *CCD*, 1:47.

60. *CCD*, 2:36; *Companion*, 166.

61. *CCD*, 1:277.

62. *CCD*, 2:443.

63. *CCD*, 2:444.

64. *CCD*, 2:444–45 ("Marry . . ."); Desmond and Moore, *Darwin's Sacred Cause*, throughout.

65. *CCD*, 2:5 ("much . . ."); *ED-CFL*, 1:275–76.

66. *ED-CFL*, 1:283–84.

67. *ED-CFL*, 1:287, 2:5 ("the week . . .").

68. *CCD*, 2:94–95 ("fat . . ."), 432; *ED-CFL*, 2:5.

69. *CCD*, 2:432.

70. *ED-CFL*, 2:5–7.

71. *ED-CFL*, 2:7.

72. *ED-CFL*, 2:9–10.

73. *CCD*, 2:116 ("I give . . ."); *ED-CFL*, 2:3.

74. *ED-CFL*, 2:11–12.

75. *ED-CFL*, 2:2–3.

76. *ED-CFL*, 2:2.

77. *CCD*, 2:119. While most authorities agree that Dr. Darwin was having a little joke at Martineau's expense, Arbuckle (xviii) concluded that this was a comment acknowledging her "as a woman of consequence." Among the few other recorded examples of Dr. Darwin's sense of humor is the pre-*Beagle* story told in CD's *Autobiography*: "I had been rather extravagant at Cambridge and to console my father said . . . I should be deuced clever to spend more than my allowance whilst on board the *Beagle*. . . . [To which] he answered with a smile, 'But they all tell me you are very clever'" (Barlow, 72).

78. *CCD*, 2:119; Shanley, 8–9; *Voyaging*, 393; W/M 17978–23, 17980–23.

CHAPTER 6. Bride, Mother, Nurse

1. *CCD*, 2:432.

2. *CCD*, 2:115–16 ("My dear . . ." and "How . . .").

3. *CCD*, 2:118.

4. *CCD*, 1:277.

5. Richard Keynes, *Charles Darwin's* Beagle *Diary*, 349–50.

6. Barrett et al., 574 ("Sexual . . ."), 577–78 ("Blushing . . ." [Notebook N]).

7. Barlow, 95; *CCD*, 2:432; Herbert and Barrett, 517–19.

8. Barlow, 95.

9. *CCD*, 2:122–23.

10. *CCD*, 2:120, 126, 127 ("nice ones").

11. *CCD*, 2:135.

12. *CCD*, 2:133.

13. Richardson, 262.

14. *CCD*, 2:147 ("not . . ."), 149; Randal Keynes, 6; *Voyaging*, 401.

15. *CCD*, 2:151, 157 ("I . . ."), 159 ("scolding . . ."; italics added in Emma's letter, underlining in CD's original).

16. *CCD*, 2:150; *ED-CFL*, 2:17 ("bought . . .").

17. *CCD*, 2:144 ("Ten . . ."), 160; DAR 242 (1839); Humble, 16.

18. *CCD*, 2:170–71.

19. Harrison and Wild, 21.

20. *ED-CFL*, 2:26–27 ("My dear . . ."), 28; *Tormented*, 279.

21. W/M 178.

22. *CCD*, 2:172, 263; DAR 242 (1839); *ED-CFL*, 2:26, 30; Trewin, 154.

23. *ED-CFL*, 2:40–41.

24. *CCD*, 2:171–72.

25. *CCD*, 2:172.

26. Gillespie, 138.

27. *ED-CFL*, 2:42 ("not . . ."); DAR 242 (1839 ["half . . ."]); *CCD*, 2:236 ("poorly . . .").

28. *CCD*, 2:198; DAR 242 (1839); *Companion*, 78; *Tormented*, 285; *Voyaging*, 417, 422.

29. *ED*, 174; *ED-CFL*, 2:44; *CCD*, 2:255 ("little . . .").

30. *CCD*, 2:262.

31. DAR 242 (1840); *ED-CFL*, 2:50 ("Now . . . "); *Voyaging*, 424.

32. McCord, 146; Symons, 259–94 ("That . . . ," 291; "Not . . . ," 284).

33. *ED-CFL*, 2:52.

34. *ED-CFL*, 2:274.

35. *CCD*, 2:263; DAR 242 (1840); *ED-CFL*, 2:51; Sadie, 197–98.

36. Colp, *To Be an Invalid*, 20–21; *ED-CFL*, 2:51 ("without . . ."); *Voyaging*, 426.

37. *CCD*, 2:262.

38. *CCD*, 2:263; DAR 242 (1840).

39. *Companion*, 228; DAR 242 (1840); *ED-CFL*, 2:54–55 ("the most . . .").

40. DAR 242 (1840).

41. DAR 242 (1840)

42. Smith, "Charles Darwin's Health Problems"; Smith, "Charles Darwin's Ill Health."

43. Bowlby, throughout.

44. *Tormented*, throughout; Sheehan et al., 205–9.

45. Colp, *Darwin's Illness*, 167–70; Orrego and Quintana, 23–29.

46. Richard Keynes, *Charles Darwin's* Beagle *Diary*, 315.

47. Adler, 1102–3; Colp, "*To Be an Invalid*, Redux"; Colp, *Darwin's Illness*, 182–83 ("injuring . . .") et passim.

48. *CCD*, 2:149–50.

49. *ED-CFL*, 2:51.

50. *Voyaging*, 429.

51. *CCD*, 2:279; D. Fauvell and I. Simpson, "The History of British Winters," www.netweather.tv/index.cgi?action=other;type=winthist;sess=.

52. *CCD*, 2:279–80 ("a noble . . ."); Randal Keynes, 12.

53. Agassiz, throughout; *CCD*, 2:279, 284–85, 288; *Companion*, 149; Herbert, 272–73.

54. DAR 242 (1841); Randal Keynes, 12–13.

55. DAR 242 (1841). Randal Keynes, 14, states that Annie was baptized along with Sophy Wedgwood, daughter of Caroline and Joe. That appears to be incorrect, however, since that couple's first surviving child, Katherine Elizabeth Sophy, was not born until February 1842 (*ED-CFL*, 2:xx).

56. DAR 242 (1841).

57. *CCD*, 2:296.

58. *CCD*, 2:293–94 ("very . . .").

59. Atkins, 17; *CCD*, 2:296, 304–5 ("great . . ."), 324, 350; DAR 242 (1841, 1842).

60. Randal Keynes, 56–58 ("goat . . .," 58), 72; *CCD*, 2:312 ("go . . ."), 318; DAR 242 (1841, 1842 ["languid . . ."]).

61. *ED-CFL*, 2:62; *WC*, 238; A. N. Wilson, *God's Funeral*, throughout.

62. *CCD*, 2:303 ("believing . . ."), 305.

63. *CCD*, 2:315–16.

64. *CCD*, 2:312–13 ("quite . . ."); *ED-CFL*, 2:62.

65. Barlow, 120; *Companion*, 101; F. Darwin, *Foundations*, xix, 1–53 ("omniscient . . .," 52); *Voyaging*, 436–39.

66. "History of Punch," www.punch.co.uk/historyofpunch.html.

Chapter 7. Narrow Lanes and High Hedges

1. Atkins, 20–21; *CCD*, 2:324–25 ("We . . ."), 352; *CCD*, 3:132; Raverat, 152. The official spelling of the village's name was changed from Down to Downe in the mid-nineteenth century, and that spelling is used throughout this book. The name of the Darwins' home, Down House, retained the old village spelling (*Tormented*, 395).

2. *CCD*, 2:325.

3. *ED-CFL*, 2:73.

4. DAR 242 (1842); Randal Keynes, 64–65.

5. *CCD*, 2:325–26.

6. Keith, 35; *WC*, 246.

7. *CCD*, 2:332–33, 335–36 ("country . . ." and "Down- . . ."); DAR 242 (1842); Randal Keynes, 65.

8. *WC*, 240.

9. *CCD*, 2:333–34.

10. *WC*, 240.

11. *Tormented*, 303 ("fairly . . ."); *CCD*, 2:335; DAR 242 (1842); *ED-CFL*, 2:78 ("Thank you . . .").

12. McCord, 212.

13. *Tormented*, 12 ("Everybody . . ."); DAR 242 (1842); *ED-CFL*, 2:45–48 ("abounding . . .," 45; "was never . . .," 48).

14. Atkins, 23; *CCD*, 2:360–61 ("truly . . ." and "a cool . . .").

15. Bridgeman and Drury, 114; *CCD*, 2:414 ("very bad"); DAR 242 (1843 ["play . . ."]); Loeb, 169; Trewin, 191; Vries, 115.

16. DAR 242 (1843).

17. *CCD*, 2:435; DAR 242 (1843); *ED-CFL*, 2:82–83 ("My dearest . . .").

18. *CCD*, 3:345; DAR 242 (1843); Nichols, 254–60.

19. *CCD*, 2:409 ("has never . . ."), 414.

20. *CCD*, 2:408–13 ("curious . . ." 408).

21. *CCD*, 3:2.

22. *CCD*, 3:7.

23. *CCD*, 3:395–96; F. Darwin, *Foundations*, xxv; *Companion*, 142–43.

24. *CCD*, 3:43–45 ("My Dear . . ."); *Voyaging*, 446–47.

25. DAR 262.11.1.

26. *CCD*, 2:122–23 ("a painful . . ."), 171–72 ("not . . .").

27. *CCD*, 2:123 ("honest . . ."); F. Darwin, *Foundations*, 55–255.

28. F. Darwin, *Foundations*, 128.

29. *Tormented*, 319.

30. *Tormented*, 320–21.

31. Millhauser, throughout; Secord, throughout.

32. [Chambers], 260.

33. *Tormented*, 321; *Voyaging*, 468.

34. Secord, 242.

35. *Voyaging*, 464.

36. *Voyaging*, 462.

37. Secord, 140.

38. *CCD*, 3:103.

39. [Chambers], 133–37.

40. *CCD*, 3:108.

41. *Tormented*, 359.

42. *ED-CFL*, 2:98; W/M 193 ("I find . . .").

43. Cook, 46.

44. *ED*, 196–97.

45. Cook, 88; Randal Keynes, 10.

46. Companion, 145; *ED-CFL*, 2:xx–xxv; Walters and Stow, 262.

47. *CCD*, 3:90–94; DAR 242 (1845); K. M. Lyell, 2:83.

CHAPTER 8. The Old Order Changeth

1. W/M 193.

2. Meteorology @ West Moors, "1800–1849," www.booty.org.uk/booty.weather/climate/1800_1849.htm.

3. Royal Horticultural Society, "Gardening Advice: Potato Blight," www.rhs.org.uk/advice/profiles0701/potato_blight.asp.

4. Kinealy, 31; McCord, 165.

5. McCord, 165, 190–96; Walters and Stow, 197.

6. *CCD*, 3:157, 256.

7. *CCD*, 3:228, 260; Walters and Stow, 209–10.

8. *Tormented*, 333.

9. *CCD*, 3:248, 260 ("a pretty . . ."), 4:337; Walters and Stow, 212.

10. Atkins, 23, 34; *CCD*, 3:248, 276–77.

11. *WC*, 246.

12. *ED-CFL*, 2:98, 101 ("Lord . . ." and "purest . . ."), 103 ("was almost . . .").

13. Atkins, 11; *ED-CFL*, 2:102–3; *WC*, 246.

14. *CCD*, 3:250–55 ("a specific . . .," 250; "a distorter . . .," 254; "How . . .," 253).

15. *CCD*, 3:346–47 ("lower . . ."); Stott, throughout.

16. W/M 193 ("the luck . . ."); *CCD*, 4:147; *ED-CFL*, 2:105; Raverat, 146 ("could not . . ."); *Tormented*, 402; *Voyaging*, 534.

17. *ED-CFL*, 2:119, 126, 140, 162.

18. Randal Keynes, 86.

19. F. Darwin, *Springtime*, 61; *CCD*, 3:132 ("butt[ed] . . ."), 4:430 ("Well . . ."); *ED-CFL*, 2:99 ("accumulate . . ."); DAR 246, 7 ("Janey . . .").

20. B. Darwin, *Life Is Sweet, Brother*, 22.

21. DAR 246, 8–9.

22. Randal Keynes, 84 ("opera dance"), 87 ("the galloping . . .").

23. *ED-CFL*, 2:122.

24. *Companion*, 36; DAR 246, 2–3 ("described . . ."); Randal Keynes, 81, 97, 104; H. A. Wedgwood.

25. *CCD*, 3:134, 5:540–42; DAR 246, 6–7 ("a delightful . . .") and 9–12 ("rather fierce"); Stott, 228.

26. Moore, "Darwin of Down," 467, 480; F. Darwin, *Springtime*, 52–53 ("sternly . . ." and "cold . . .").

27. *ED*, 115; Magnusson, 1200; Moore, "Darwin of Down," 468–69, 477; A. N. Wilson, *The Victorians*, 141; W/M 193 ("Having . . ."); Young, 89. For information on E. B. Pusey, see the Catholic Encyclopedia, "Pusey and Puseyism," www.newadvent. org/cathen/12582a.htm.

28. *CCD*, 4:xx, 29 ("been . . ."), 44, 50–51.

29. *CCD*, 4:xv, 55.

30. *CCD*, 4:86–87.

31. *CCD*, 4:142–43 ("with care"), 145 ("His . . ."), 384.

32. Colp, *To Be an Invalid*, 38–39.

33. Barlow, 29; *CCD*, 4:180–83.

34. *CCD*, 4:182–83.

35. *CCD*, 4:183; *WC*, 249–50.

36. Lerwill, 9–10; *WC*, 250.

37. *CCD*, 4:151; *Voyaging*, 490.

38. *Companion*, 21; *ED-CFL*, 2:xvi–xxi.

39. F. Darwin, *Life and Letters*, 1:18 ("had . . ."), 10 ("the wisest . . .").

40. *CCD*, 4:209–10, 224–25.

41. DAR 246, 30–31; Randal Keynes, 104–5 ("neither . . .").

42. *CCD*, 4:226 ("a very . . ."); Weaver, *Darwin and Evelyn Waugh*, inside front cover.

43. Colp, *To Be an Invalid*, 39–40 ("nervous . . ." and "sitz . . ."); Weaver, *Spa Town*, 1–7.

44. *CCD*, 4:224–27 ("very like . . . ," 224); Weaver, *Spa Town*, 6 ("Neptune girdle"), 11 ("Lamp . . ." and "was so . . .").

45. *CCD*, 4:234–35 ("increase . . ."), 224 ("or anything . . ."); DAR 242 (1849).

46. DAR 246, 17–18; Randal Keynes, 140–42; Moore, "Darwin of Down," 479; *Tormented*, 365.

47. *CCD*, 4:246 ("consider[ed] . . ."); DAR 246, 18–20 ("half . . ."); *Tormented*, 366.

48. R. Desmond, 108, 141–59.

49. R. Desmond, 159.

50. *CCD*, 4:294–95, 310–11 ("Sir . . ."); R. Desmond, 161–66.

1. *CCD*, 2:409, 517, 4:651; DAR 242 (1849).
2. *CCD*, 4:282 ("We..."); DAR 242 (1849); Jalland, 119–42.
3. DAR 242 (1849); Randal Keynes, 148.
4. Colp, *To Be an Invalid*, 168; DAR 242 (1850).
5. *CCD*, 4:140, 302–3 ("The day..."); Colp, *To Be an Invalid*, 167–68.
6. *CCD*, 4:303.
7. BLTC Research, "Chloroform," www.general-anaesthesia.com/images/chloroform.htm.
8. *CCD*, 4:362–63; DAR 242 (1850); Randal Keynes, 147.
9. DAR 242 (1850); Randal Keynes, 147.
10. *CCD*, 4:354–55, 362–63 ("backward..."); DAR 242 (1850).
11. DAR 242 (1850).
12. Randal Keynes, 149.
13. DAR 242 (1850); Randal Keynes, 151; Walton, 66 ("physic...").
14. *CCD*, 4:386; DAR 242 (1850).
15. DAR 242 (1850); Randal Keynes, 154–56.
16. DAR 242 (1850); Randal Keynes, 156–59; Stott, 157–59.
17. DAR 242 (1851); Randal Keynes, 160.
18. DAR 242 (1851 ["very weak"]); Randal Keynes, 162–67.
19. *CCD*, 5:13–24 ("I am...," 13; "Dr...," 14; "She...," 16; "It...," 18; "In the...," 19; "My Dearest...," 23–24; "My dear dearest...," 24); DAR 242 (1851).
20. *CCD*, 5:24–25.
21. *CCD*, 5:13–24 ("Thank...," 13; "God...," 14; "I trust...," 20; "I pray...," 24); Gillespie, 134–37; for a contrary interpretation, see Jalland, 347.
22. Randal Keynes, 199–200.
23. Randal Keynes, 200, 206; MicrobiologyBytes, "Mycobacterium tuberculosis," www.microbiologybytes.com/video/Mtuberculosis.html.
24. *CCD*, 5:540–42.
25. *ED-CFL*, 2:137.
26. *CCD*, 6:238 ("Thank..."), 8:365–66 ("I...").
27. Barlow, 97–98.
28. Stott, 172.
29. *ED-CFL*, 2:137.
30. *CCD*, 5:24–27; Jalland, 349.
31. *CCD*, 5:16 ("never..."), 21, 25, 31.
32. DAR 246, 22–23.
33. *CCD*, 5:542–43.
34. *CCD*, 5:543.
35. *CCD*, 5:22 ("to get..."), 33 ("my troubles..."); DAR 242 (1851).
36. DAR 242 (1851); Randal Keynes, 212.

CHAPTER 10. The Great Exhibition, War in the Balkans, and the Last of the Barnacles

1. *CCD*, 5:29 ("that . . ."); DAR 242 (1851).

2. DAR 242 (1851); Ffrench, 22 ("works . . ."), 37, 96; Magnusson, 329; Richardson, 272–73.

3. Ffrench, 103–5; Millar, 42–43; Richardson, 273.

4. Ffrench, 201–2.

5. Ffrench, 181–98, 213, 276; Richardson, 273; *WC*, 250–51.

6. Ffrench, 213–48; L. Huxley, 1:364.

7. K. M. Lyell, 2:174.

8. Ffrench, 228–48.

9. "The Greek Slave," www.victorianweb.org/sculpture/usa/powers2.html ("one . . ."); Gerdts, 183 ("was . . .").

10. Ffrench, 238–39 ("stuffed . . ."), 249–50 ("bedstead . . ."), 262; George P. Landow, "Victorian Design and the Medieval Revival," www.victorianweb.org/art/design/armor.html.

11. Ffrench, 264.

12. DAR 242 (1851); *ED-CFL*, 2:142 ("not . . ."); Ritvo, 228; *Voyaging*, 504–5; Richardson, 272; University of Westminister, "Timeline for the History of the University of Westminster: 1838–1881, Royal Polytechnic Institution," www.wmin.ac.uk/page-9781.

13. *CCD*, 5:536; DAR 242 (1851, 1852).

14. *CCD*, 5:xv, 63 ("try . . ." and "drawing . . ."), 535–36.

15. *Tormented*, 396–97.

16. DAR 242 (1851); *Companion*, 268; Stott, 200–202.

17. Magnusson, 1066; Stott, 202–3; *Tormented*, 399.

18. *ED-CFL*, 2:144 ("I write . . ."); *CCD*, 5:83–84 ("The French . . ."); Magnusson, 1066.

19. *CCD*, 5:64; A. Desmond, *Huxley*, throughout; J. Huxley, throughout.

20. Bradby, 426, 428; *CCD*, 5:81; Magnusson, 66; Rugby School, www.rugby school.net.

21. Bradby, 442; *CCD*, 5:83 ("old . . ."); Magnusson, 66; Rugby School, www.rugby school.net.

22. DAR 219.1:3.

23. *CCD*, 5:81 ("tremendous . . ."); Bradby, 166–78.

24. Raverat, 146.

25. *CCD*, 4:425–27.

26. *CCD*, 4:147, 425, 5:81 ("extraordinary . . ."); National Institute of Neurological Disorders and Stroke, "Cerebral Palsy Information Page," www.ninds.nih.gov/disorders/cerebral_palsy/cerebral_palsy.htm; Healthcommunities.com, "Cerebral Palsy," www.neurologychannel.com/cerebralpalsy/symptoms.shtml#signs; Raverat, 146–49 ("Aunt . . .," 148); *Voyaging*, 534.

27. DAR 219.1:3 ("Franky . . ."); DAR 242 (1852).

28. DAR 219.1:4 ("I have . . ."); DAR 242 (1852).

29. DAR 242 (1852).

30. *CCD*, 5:100 ("I hate . . ."); DAR 219.1:6; Jalland, 196; Richardson, 277.

31. *ED-CFL*, 2:151–52 ("romantic marriage" and "Sismondi . . ."); Jalland, 33; Magnusson, 1066.

32. *CCD*, 5:147; DAR 242 (1853).

33. *CCD*, 5:151–52.

34. DAR 242 (1853); *ED-CFL*, 2:154; Hoppen, 167–69; McCord, 245–47; Mowat, 769–70; Tim Pickford-Jones, "Crimean War," www.timmonet.co.uk/html/body_crimean_war.htm.

35. Hoppen, 170–77; McCord, 245–47.

36. *CCD*, 5:163–65.

37. *CCD*, 5:165–66 ("made me . . ."); *Tormented*, 408, 713.

38. DAR 242 (1853).

39. *CCD*, 7:255, 618; DAR 242 (1854).

40. *CCD*, 5:194–95 ("We . . ."); *ED-CFL*, 1:271 ("was calm . . .").

41. *CCD*, 5:321–22.

42. Gill, 303–5.

43. Battery B, 4th U.S. Light Artillery, "Calamita Bay to the Battle of Alma," www.batteryb.com/Crimean_War/crimea_part1.html; Gill, 305–9.

44. Battery B, "Balaclava to Inkerman," www.batteryb.com/Crimean_War/crimea_part2.html; Gill, 309–10; BritishBattles.com, "The Battle of Balaclava," www.britishbattles.com/crimean-war/balaclava.htm.

45. Tennyson, 1:386.

46. "Balaclava to Inkerman" (see n. 44); Farwell, 70–71; Gill, 340; Harris, 238–39 ("There . . .").

47. Gill, 315–52.

48. *ED-CFL*, 2:156 ("Have you . . ."); Gill, 474; Uglow, *Elizabeth Gaskell*, 359.

49. *CCD*, 5:537.

CHAPTER 11. For Better or Worse, in Sickness and in Health

1. DAR 242 (1854).

2. DAR 242 (1855); *Times* (London), 13 February 1855.

3. *CCD*, 5:289 ("terribly noisy"); DAR 242 (1855).

4. *CCD*, 5:538; DAR 242 (1855).

5. Atkins, 29–30; *CCD*, 5:xv–xix, 305 ("smelt . . ."), 308, 331–34, 352 ("The box . . ."), and throughout; *Tormented*, 427.

6. Uglow, *Elizabeth Gaskell*, 219, 389, 396, 617–18; *WC*, 258.

7. *WC*, 253–59 ("mistrust . . ." and "had . . . ," 258).

8. *WC*, 259–60 ("I shd . . ." and "foolishly . . ."); Greg, 106 ("is . . .").

9. *CCD*, 6:58–59 ("release"), 523; DAR 242 (1856).

10. DAR 242 (1856); Gill, 401; Knowledgerush, "Prince George, Duke of Cambridge," knowledgerush.com/kr/encyclopedia/Prince_George,_Duke_of_Cambridge; *Times* (London), 11 and 19 March 1856.

11. DAR 219.1:9 ("Jenny . . ."); DAR 242 (1856); *Times* (London), 11 March 1856.

12. *CCD*, 6:xix; DAR 242 (1856).

13. DAR 242 (1856); Pool, 272.

14. *CCD*, 6:xix, 89–90, 109, 191 ("general . . ."), 522 ("by Lyells . . .").

15. *CCD*, 6:249 ("entire . . ."), 346, 476, 523; DAR 242 (1856); M. Keynes, *House by the River*, 34 ("had . . ."); Moore, "Darwin's Sons," 53.

16. *CCD*, 6:238 ("utterly crippled"); DAR 242 (1856).

17. *CCD*, 6:268.

18. *CCD*, 6:285 ("First . . ."); Jalland, 194–203.

19. *ED-CFL*, 2:105, 161 ("beautifully . . .").

20. *CCD*, 6:301, 334; DAR 242 (1856).

21. *CCD*, 6:303 ("beautiful"), 305–6 ("I . . ."), 7:521 ("He . . .").

22. Colp, *Darwin's Illness*, 42; "Blue Mass," www.everything2.com/index.pl?node =Blue%20mass; Randal Keynes, 225–26; Mayo Clinic, "Down Syndrome," www. mayoclinic.com/health/down-syndrome/DS00182/DSECTION=risk-factors; Medical News Today, "Prenatal Exposure to Mercury Can Impair Child's Brain Function," www.medicalnewstoday.com/articles/5803.php; Smith, "Charles Darwin's Health Problems," 292.

23. *ED-CFL*, 2:162 ("was . . ."); DAR 242 (1857); Moore, "Darwin of Down," 479.

24. DAR 242 (1857); DAR 246, 36 ("neurotic . . ." and "at meals . . .").

25. *CCD*, 6:343 ("Mamma . . ."), 218 ("not . . .").

26. Burkhardt, Smith, et al., *Calendar*, 101–8; *CCD*, 6:523; Raby, 117–34.

27. *CCD*, 6:345, 596; Magnusson, 521; Nichols, 284–89.

28. *CCD*, 6:345; DAR 219.1:12 ("On Monday . . .").

29. DAR 242 (1857 ["lip done"]); *CCD*, 6:343 ("plaistered . . ."), 615.

30. *CCD*, 6:238–39 ("old . . ."), 335–36, 346; Colp, *To Be an Invalid*, 57.

31. DAR 242 (1856, 1857 ["Etty very . . ."]); *CCD*, 6:369 ("Etty is . . ."), 523; *ED-CFL*, 2:163.

32. *CCD*, 6:384 ("walk . . ."); DAR 242 (1857).

33. *CCD*, 6:524; DAR 242 (1857); Raverat, 121–23 ("her . . ." and "cult . . .").

34. *CCD*, 6:431–33 ("I have . . .," 432), 445–50.

35. *CCD*, 6:477 ("We have . . ."), 7:215.

36. Brent, 348; Bridgeman and Drury, 312; *CCD*, 7:318 ("Mamma . . ."); *ED*, 237; *ED-CFL*, 2:164; Morris and Wilson, inside back cover.

37. Gill, 414–22 ("the state . . .," 416); Tim Pickford-Jones, "Crimean War," www. timmonet.co.uk/html/crimean_war.htm.

38. *CCD*, 7:3–4 ("As I . . ."); Farwell, 84–133.

39. Bowler, *Charles Darwin*; Desmond and Moore, *Darwin's Sacred Cause*, throughout.

40. *CCD*, 7:21–22; F. Darwin, *Springtime*, 62–63; Moore, "Darwin's Sons," 52.

41. *CCD*, 7:9 ("badly . . ."), 586; DAR 214 (Emma Darwin's recipe book); DAR 219.1:19 ("gold . . ."); DAR 242 (1858); Smith, "Charles Darwin's Health Problems," 298.

42. *CCD*, 7:9 ("daily . . ."); DAR 242 (1858); *Times* (London), 16 and 24 February and 1 May 1858.

43. *CCD*, 7:80, 84 ("The weather . . ."), 87, 89 ("Hydropathy . . ."), 504.

44. *CCD*, 6:106, 7:107–8 ("Your . . .").

45. *CCD*, 7:107, 117–19, 121–24. See also the descriptions of these events in *Power*, 14–42; *Tormented*, 466–70; Wright, 301–10.

46. *CCD*, 7:113, 115–16; DAR 242 (1858).

47. *CCD*, 5:151, 7:116 ("after . . ."), 120–21 ("our . . ."), 521 ("sweet . . ."); DAR 242 (1858); *ED-CFL*, 2:162.

48. *CCD*, 7:136–39, 504; DAR 242 (1858); *ED-CFL*, 2:xxiv; *Companion*, 116.

49. *CCD*, 7:122–24, 130; C. Darwin, *On the Origin of Species*; DAR 242 (1858).

50. *CCD*, 7:163–64, 170–71 ("Remember . . ."), 503–4; DAR 210.6:30; DAR 242 (1858).

CHAPTER 12. Midwiving the *Origin*

1. DAR 242 (1858, 1859).

2. Barlow, 96; *ED-CFL*, 1:7, 2:44–49 ("serene . . . ," 45; "people . . . ," 46; "was . . . ," 46; "had . . . ," 47).

3. DAR 210.6:36 ("I thought . . ."); DAR 242 (1859).

4. DAR 246, 38; Raverat, 121.

5. *CCD*, 7:264; DAR 210.6:41 ("Solemn . . .").

6. DAR 210.6:42 ("lawyers . . ."); DAR 242 (1859); *ED*, 244; *ED-CFL*, 2:172 ("apparently . . .").

7. *CCD*, 7:237, 246, 251–52, 269, 504–5; DAR 210.6:44 ("constant . . .").

8. *CCD*, 7:247, 319; DAR 210.6:39 ("it is . . ."), 44 ("It was . . ."); Moore, "Darwin's Sons," 53.

9. *CCD*, 7:275, 278; Speake, 109–10.

10. *CCD*, 7:269, 299, 365, 505; DAR 242 (1859); *ED-CFL*, 2:172.

11. *CCD*, 7:xxiii, 390–91 ("earned . . ." and "the most . . ."), 395, 426 ("would . . ."), 440; DAR 210.6:52 ("never . . .").

12. *CCD*, 7:419 ("the *chain* . . ."), 325, 373–74, 396–98 ("My dear . . ."); *ED-CFL*, 2:172.

13. *CCD*, 7:278–79, 396–98 ("son . . .").

14. *CCD*, 7:340 ("the case . . ."); Froude, 2:119–20 ("But . . .").

15. DAR 210.6:52.

16. *CCD*, 8:21 ("do . . ."), 599; *Power*, 101.

17. *Power*, 101, 110–11 ("malevolent . . ."); DAR 219.1:27 ("[cut] . . ."); *CCD*, 8:166 ("a friend . . ."), 193 ("had . . ."), 600.

18. *CCD*, 8:216 ("case-hardened"), 599–602.

19. *CCD*, 8:8 ("sure . . ."), 45, 115; DAR 242 (1860 ["very languid"]).

20. *CCD*, 8:192; DAR 242 (1860); *ED-CFL*, 2:176.

21. *CCD*, 8:205; DAR 242 (1860).

22. *CCD*, 8:232–33, 238 ("her . . ."), 268 ("utterly failed"); DAR 242 (1860).

23. *CCD*, 8:306, 319 ("sadly . . ."); DAR 242 (1860); Wood, 287; WebMD, "Pulse Measurement," www.webmd.com/heart-disease/pulse-measurement.

24. *CCD*, 8:365–66 ("I know . . ."); DAR 242 (1860).

25. *ED-CFL*, 2:177 ("great protection"); *CCD*, 8:377, 458 ("I am exhausted . . ."); F. Darwin, *Springtime*, 63; DAR 242 (1860).

26. *CCD*, 8:466; DAR 242 (1860 ["pain . . ."]); Golubovsky, 1237–38; Injury-Board, "Infertility Linked to High Amounts of Mercury in Seafood," www.injuryboard.com/national-news/infertility-linked-to.aspx?googleid=27294.

27. *Power*, 118–25 ("Is it . . . ," 121); *CCD*, 8:270–72 ("that Amalekite . . .").

28. *CCD*, 8:272–73, 280 ("But how . . .").

29. *CCD*, 8:551; Peckham, 24; *Power*, 133, 141–42.

30. *CCD*, 8:118–19, 358–59 ("rather . . ."), 472–73; F. Darwin, *Springtime*, 63.

31. DAR 242 (1860, 1861); Perkin, 148 ("a predisposition . . .").

CHAPTER 13. A Banker in the Family

1. *CCD*, 9:559; DAR 242 (1861).

2. *CCD*, 9:14 ("gigantic . . ."); DAR 242 (1861).

3. *CCD*, 9:20 ("Poor . . ."), 560; DAR 242 (1861).

4. DAR 219.1:36.

5. *CCD*, 9:329–30; DAR 219.1:40 ("2 teeth . . ."), 43; DAR 242 (1861).

6. *CCD*, 9:25–26 ("it would . . ."), 277; DAR 242 (1861).

7. Clark, 376–77; A. Desmond, *Huxley*, 289–91 ("held . . .").

8. *CCD*, 9:33–34.

9. CCD, 9:34; *ED-CFL*, 2:186 ("too weak . . ." and "the usual . . .").

10. *CCD*, 9:538, 560; DAR 242 (1861); *ED-CFL*, 2:186 ("a sort . . .").

11. *CCD*, 9:133 ("a better . . ."), 391; DAR 219.1:44 ("but . . ."); DAR 242 (1861).

12. *CCD*, 9:134.

13. *CCD*, 9:134, 140–41, 143–45, 166–68, 199–200, 203–4, 219–20, 229, 231–32, 306–7; DAR 242 (1861); *Companion*, 119.

14. *CCD*, 9:195–96 ("16 souls . . ."), 213–16, 220–21; DAR 242 (1861).

15. DAR 242 (1861); *ED-CFL*, 2:178 ("began . . .").

16. *CCD*, 9:303; DAR 242 (1861); Haley, 135 ("Its . . ."); Houston Croquet Association, "The History of Croquet," www.houstoncroquet.com/history.htm; Perkin, 52.

17. DAR 242 (1861); *CCD*, 2:171–72, 9:9, 32, 81, 126, 134 ("fit . . .").

18. *CCD*, 9:155–56.

19. *CCD*, 9:156, 200–201, 238; *Power*, 156 ("God . . .").

20. *CCD*, 9:238.

21. DAR 210.6:76; DAR 242 (1861).

22. *CCD*, 9:306–7.

23. Gill, x–xi; Pine, *Burke's Landed Gentry*, 1895–1896.

24. *CCD*, 9:313 ("very . . ."), 341–44.

25. *CCD*, 9:312–13, 322 ("Your . . ."), 340–41; DAR 210.6:88 ("I came . . .").

26. DAR 210.6:90.

27. DAR 210.6:72.

28. *CCD*, photograph facing 9:125; DAR 242 (1861).

29. Background information on the American Civil War comes primarily from two sources: Joanne Freeman, "Time Line of the Civil War, 1861," memory.loc.gov/ammem/cwphtml/tl1861.html; Henry William Elson, "Timeline for the Civil War and Our Own Times," www.usahistory.info/timeline/civil-war.html.

30. U.S. Department of State, "The Trent Affair, 1861," www.state.gov/r/pa/ho/time/cw/92452.htm; *CCD*, 9:xx–xxi, 368 ("What…").

31. *CCD*, 9:383.

32. "The Trent Affair, 1861" (see n. 30); A. N. Wilson, *The Victorians*, 253.

33. *CCD*, 12:493; DAR 242 (1861, 1862); *ED-CFL*, 2:106, 178 ("gentle…"); *WC*, 287.

34. *CCD*, 10:25, 45, 81; DAR 242 (1861, 1862); Peile, 2:555; Stubbings, 115.

35. *CCD*, 10:80–81 ("oddest…"), 123, 134.

36. Colp, *To Be an Invalid*, 210; DAR 242 (1862); Humble, 536.

37. *CCD*, 10:92 ("poor…"), 135 ("become…"), 301, 491, 11:35; DAR 242 (1862).

38. Richardson, 286; Science and Society Picture Library, "International Exhibition of 1862," www.scienceandsociety.co.uk/results.asp?txtkeys1=International+Exhibition+1862; A. N. Wilson, *The Victorians*, 253.

39. *CCD*, 10:185, 245–46 ("had…"), 481, 666; DAR 242 (1862).

40. *CCD*, 10:181 ("by…"), 224, 237–38 ("beyond…"), 245 ("trustworthy…").

41. *CCD*, 10:245; DAR 242 (1862 ["not brisk"]).

42. DAR 242 (1862 ["neck…"]); *CCD*, 10:170, 309, 330 ("a rare…" and "Port-wine…"); *ED-CFL*, 2:178 ("hung…").

43. DAR 219.1:58. Precisely what "raccoons" were in the Darwin household is not clear. Possibly this was Lenny's mispronunciation of macaroons.

44. Burkhardt, Smith, et al., *Calendar*, throughout; Iltis, 108, 206; M. Keynes, *Leonard Darwin*, 2 ("illness…" and "be hung…"); V. Orel, 1, 83–84, 191–92.

45. *CCD*, 10:373 ("poor…"); DAR 242 (1862); *ED-CFL*, 2:178 ("very…").

46. *CCD*, 10:389; DAR 219.9:3 ("to engage…").

47. *CCD*, 10:390–91 ("Horace said…"), 428.

48. *CCD*, 10:491, 799; DAR 219.1:63 ("full…"), 65, 68; DAR 242 (1862).

CHAPTER 14. Lives Lived, Lives Lost, and Closure at Malvern

1. *ED-CFL*, 2:45–48.

2. DAR 242 (1863).

3. Raverat, 119–38.

4. DAR 258:663.

5. M. Keynes, *Leonard Darwin*, 3.

6. *CCD*, 11:1, 3.

7. *CCD*, 11:2, 4.

8. *CCD*, 10:274–75, 331, 11:75, 582, 584; National Archives and Records Administration, "The Emancipation Proclamation," www.archives.gov/exhibits/featured_documents/emancipation_proclamation/transcript.html ("any…").

9. *CCD*, 11:63 ("juvenile world"); DAR 242 (1863).

10. *CCD*, 11:714; DAR 242 (1863); *ED-CFL*, 2:180; Hartnoll, 258; Alfrida Lee, "The Adelphi Theatre 1806–1900: The 1866–1867 Season," www.emich.edu/public/english/adelphi_calendar/hst1866.htm.

11. *CCD*, 11:xv–xvii, 114, 209; *Power*, 217–19; *Tormented*, 515–16; C. Lyell, 504–6 ("in conformity . . .").

12. C. Darwin, *On the Origin of Species*, 460 and elsewhere.

13. C. Lyell, 505–6. Lyell refers to Gray, 130.

14. Bowlby, 371; *CCD*, 11:207 ("leave . . ."), 222–23 ("a modification . . ."); *Tormented*, 516.

15. *CCD*, 11:218, 230–31 ("I have . . ."); K. M. Lyell, 2:361 ("I feel . . .").

16. T. H. Huxley, xv, 97–143, 146–47 ("no rational . . ."), 152 ("no absolute . . ."); *CCD*, 11:148 ("Hurrah").

17. *CCD*, 11:200.

18. *CCD*, 11:255, 293, 328, 438; DAR 242 (1863).

19. *CCD*, 11:561–62; DAR 242 (1863); *ED-CFL*, 2:164–65; Moore, "Darwin of Down," 471.

20. *ED-CFL*, 2:180.

21. *CCD*, 11:590 ("I believe . . ."), 600; DAR 219.1:75 ("not . . ."); *ED-CFL*, 2:180.

22. *CCD*, 11:714; DAR 242 (1863).

23. *CCD*, 11:599, 616, 620; DAR 242 (1863).

24. *CCD*, 6:238, 11:620, 624–25, 642–43 ("I am . . ."); DAR 242 (1863).

25. Jalland, 348.

26. Randal Keynes, 245.

27. *CCD*, 11:640.

28. *CCD*, 11:45, 645 ("it will . . .").

29. *CCD*, 11:646 ("Trust . . ."), 691; DAR 242 (1863).

30. *CCD*, 11:650, 660 (for examples of Henrietta and Emma acting as Charles's amanuensis), 691–92; Colp, *To Be an Invalid*, 266; DAR 242 (1863).

31. *CCD*, 11:776–81; *ED*, 265–68; *ED-CFL*, 2:179.

32. National Park Service, "CWSAC Battle Summaries," www.nps.gov/history/hps/abpp/battles/bystate.htm; Joanne Freeman, "Time Line of the Civil War, 1863," memory.loc.gov/ammem/cwphtml/tl1863.html.

33. *CCD*, 11:695.

34. *CCD*, 11:167, 695, 12:387–88.

35. *CCD*, 12:104, 135–36 ("combination . . ."), 563; DAR 242 (1864); *Oxford English Dictionary*, s.v. "podophyllin."

36. F. Darwin, "Sir George," iv; Stubbings, 26, 102.

37. DAR 239.23:1.8 ("*What is* . . ."); Moore, "Darwin's Sons," 59–60.

38. DAR 242 (1864); *WC*, 274–75, 279; DAR 219.9:11 ("buy . . .").

39. DAR 242 (1864); *ED-CFL*, 1:135 ("the happiest . . .").

40. Meteorology @ West Moors, "1850–1899," www.booty.org.uk/booty.weather/climate/1850_1899.htm.

41. *CCD*, 11:820; DAR 242 (1865).

42. *CCD*, 13:xvi–xvii, 17; DAR 242 (1865).

43. *CCD*, 13:xxiv, 285, 316–17; DAR 242 (1865); M. Keynes, *House by the River*, 34 ("took . . .").

44. DAR 245:27.

45. *CCD*, 13:27, 125–26, 144–46; DAR 219.9:31 ("a great ..."); National Park Service, "Appomattox Court House, Virginia: The Surrender, April 9, 1865," www.nps.gov/archive/apco/surrend.htm; U.S. Constitution Online, "Amendment 13," www.usconstitution.net/const.html#Am13.

46. L. Huxley, 2:68–69 ("septic throat"); *CCD*, 13:xv, 224–25 ("best ...").

47. *CCD*, 13:xxiii, 135–38 ("mind ..."), 258–59, 524; DAR 242 (1865); Nichols, 319–23; *Power*, 264–65; *Tormented*, 104.

48. DAR 242 (1866); Meteorology @ West Moors, "1850–1899" (see n. 40); DAR 219.9:39 ("5 days ...").

49. *CCD*, 14:222; DAR 219.10:2 ("It seems ..."); DAR 242 (1866); Gill, x–xi.

50. DAR 219.10:2–6 ("You'll ...," 4); DAR 242 (1866).

51. DAR 219.9:41 ("got ..."), 42 ("miserable ..." and "[A] little ..."); *ED-CFL*, 2:40.

52. *CCD*, 14:179; DAR 219.9:42 ("muttered ..."); *ED-CFL*, 2:184–85.

53. DAR 242 (1866); *ED-CFL*, 2:185 ("Mlle ..."); Hartnoll, 258; Magnusson, 505; Robert Glaubitz, "The Aria Database: Vedrai, carino—No. 18," www.aria-database.com/cgi-bin/aria-search.pl?83a.

54. DAR 219.10:8–9, 11, 17 ("Dearest ..."), 19; DAR 242 (1866).

55. *CCD*, 14:221, 301; DAR 242 (1866).

56. DAR 219.9:47 ("My ..."); Moore, "Darwin of Down," 477.

57. DAR 242 (1866).

58. *CCD*, 14:xxiv, 5 ("Dearest ...").

59. *CCD*, 11:589, 14:46 ("prolonged ..."); *Companion*, 74; DAR 242 (1866); Lerwill, 9–10.

60. *ED-CFL*, 2:184.

61. *CCD*, 14:340, 342, 345–46, 381, 15:232; DAR 242 (1866); *ED-CFL*, 2:184; Lerwill, 10.

62. *CCD*, 14:xxxviii, 340, 395–96, 15:70, 326.

CHAPTER 15. A Book about Man, and Henrietta Takes a Husband

1. *CCD*, 14:151–52, 481.

2. *CCD*, 14:473, 514; DAR 242 (1866).

3. DAR 245:269.

4. *CCD*, 14:358, 367 ("a very ...").

5. *CCD*, 15:330 ("excellent ..."), 521; *Companion*, 79; *Power*, 200–201.

6. *CCD*, 15:xxiii, 181 ("the Duke ...").

7. *CCD*, 15:144, 235, 568; DAR 219.10:25 ("fine ...").

8. *CCD*, 11:655, 15:362–63; DAR 262.11.1.

9. DAR 219.9:60; M. Keynes, *Leonard Darwin*, 4 ("Who ...").

10. *ED-CFL*, 2:187–88 ("My ..."); *CCD*, 15:598; DAR 219.9:56 ("George's ..."); M. Keynes, *House by the River*, 35; Stubbings, 113–15.

11. F. Darwin, "Sir George," v.

12. *Companion*, 103; DAR 242 (1868); *ED-CFL*, 2:188–89 ("very ..."); *Power*, 296–97.

13. DAR 242 (1868); *ED-CFL*, 2:xx, 189–90 ("uncheerful . . ."); *Power*, 298 ("Where . . .").

14. *CCD*, 16 (part II):975; DAR 242 (1868); *ED*, 276–77 ("mean . . .").

15. DAR 242 (1868); *ED-CFL*, 2:190–91 ("Mrs . . ." and "did . . ."), 286 ("never . . ."); Tennyson, 2:57 (Your . . .").

16. DAR 242 (1868); *ED-CFL*, 2:190; *Power*, 299; *WC*, inside front cover.

17. "Cameron, Julia Margaret," in Robert Leggat, "A History of Photography," www.rleggat.com/photohistory/history/cameron.htm ("Longfellow . . ."); *ED*, 278; *ED-CFL*, 2:190 ("no . . ."); *Power*, 300–303.

18. DAR 242 (1868); NNDB, "Charles Eliot Norton," www.nndb.com/people /514/000115169/; Norton and Howe, 1:304–6 ("upland . . . ," 306); Turner, 217–25.

19. DAR 219.8:8 ("Yesterday . . ."); DAR 242 (1868).

20. DAR 219.8:9.

21. DAR 219.8:9 ("think . . ."), 9:61 ("improvement . . .").

22. DAR 242 (1868, 1869); Turner, 225.

23. DAR 210.5:4.

24. *CCD*, 2:444–45; DAR 219.1:85 ("In . . ."); *WC*, 263.

25. DAR 219.9:61 ("Poor . . ."); Vaughan Williams, 6–7.

26. DAR 242 (1868); *Power*, 309 ("entirely . . .").

27. Moore, "Darwin of Down," 469–70 ("ran . . ."), 477; Stecher, 224 ("little . . ."), 226 ("rumours . . .").

28. *Companion*, 19; Moore, "Darwin of Down," 477.

29. *Companion*, 248; DAR 242 (1869); B. Darwin, *The World That Fred Made*, 53.

30. Bowler, *Theories of Human Evolution*, 67; *Companion*, 77–79; *ED-CFL*, 2:196 ("be very . . ."); T. H. Huxley, 1–209; *Tormented*, 567.

31. Barlow, 126; *CCD*, 15:469; Mivart, *Genesis of Species*, 11–12 ("remarkable . . .") et passim; Peckham, 56; *Power*, 329–30 ("an element . . ."); *Tormented*, 577.

32. *Power*, 317–18 ("natural selection could . . . ," "human . . . ," and "I hope . . ."); Gould, 38 ("natural selection . . . can . . ."); Raby, 203 ("Overruling Intelligence").

33. DAR 219.9:72 ("is putting . . ."), 78, 80; DAR 242 (1870); DAR 248/1; *ED-CFL*, 2:196 ("[Y]our . . .").

34. DAR 242 (1870); DAR 248/1; DAR 219.8:16 ("as . . .").

35. *Companion*, 216; DAR 219.8:16 ("so very . . ."), 9:70 ("Grumbling . . ."); DAR 242 (1870); DAR 248/1; F. Darwin, *Springtime*, 64–65; Magnusson, 641, 1424.

36. "About Penny Readings," in Lee Jackson, comp., "The Victorian Dictionary," www.victorianlondon.org/publications/habits-10.htm; DAR 219.8:16, 18 ("two . . ."); DAR 219.9:71, 73 ("Parslow . . ."), 76 ("The 1d . . ."); Moore, "Darwin of Down," 477.

37. Weintraub, 359–60; Darryl Lundy, "Lowry Egerton Cole, 4th Earl of Enniskillen," www.thepeerage.com/p1079.htm#i10790; DAR 219.9:76 ("We . . ."); *Times* (London), 25 February 1870.

38. DAR 219.9:78, 79 ("gnawing . . .").

39. DAR 219.8:15; DAR 219.9:73 ("F. is . . ."), 86 ("One . . ."); DAR 242 (1870); Peile, 2:746.

40. World History International, "The Franco-Prussian War," history-world.org/ franco_prussian_war.htm.

41. DAR 219.9:90 ("incredible . . ."), 92 ("I wonder . . .").

42. DAR 242 (1871); "The Franco-Prussian War" (see n. 40).

43. DAR 248/1; *Power*, 356–57; Raverat, 121.

44. DAR 245:298 ("My dear . . ."); DAR 247; Harrison, 34; *Power*, 356–57.

45. Harrison, vii–66; Magnusson, 213, 744, 991, 1265, 1275.

46. DAR 245:298; Harrison, 42; *Power*, 357 ("sweep . . .").

47. *Companion*, 193; DAR 245:512 ("Something . . ."); Harrison, 45.

48. DAR 242 (1871); *Power*, 356–57 ("feminine . . ." and "gold-hunter").

49. DAR 245:500; Downe Parish Records, Bromley, P123/1/13; L. Huxley, 2:128 ("would . . ."); *Power*, 358.

50. Cattermole and Wolfe, 5; DAR 219.9:93 ("looked . . ." and "pretty . . ."), 95; DAR 242 (1871); DAR 245:252.

51. *Power*, 358 ("we . . ."); DAR 219.9:95 ("Nothing . . .").

CHAPTER 16. Two Weddings, Four Funerals,
and the Fiendish Mr. Ffinden

1. *ED-CFL*, 2:207.

2. C. Darwin, *Emotions*, 12–16 ("Is . . . ," 16), 95 ("Mr . . ."), and throughout; Loy, 53–60; *Power*, 360–61 ("thoughts . . ."), 368 ("affront anybody").

3. DAR 158, 50; DAR 242 (1872); *ED-CFL*, 2:209; *Power*, 368–69 ("Really . . . ," emphasis added).

4. DAR 242 (1872); Speake, 94.

5. *CCD*, 14:497; DAR 219.9:99 ("My dear . . ."); DAR 242 (1872); *Power*, 356.

6. DAR 219.9:98 ("very hopeless" and "Uncle . . ."); DAR 242 (1872); *ED-CFL*, 2:xx.

7. DAR 158, 51; *ED-CFL*, 2:216 ("dead . . .").

8. DAR 242 (1873); Magnusson, 341; *Power*, 191, 386–87 (It . . .").

9. DAR 242 (1873); *ED-CFL*, 2:41 ("constant . . ."), 212 ("knows . . ."); K. M. Lyell, 2:451 ("feverish cold"), 467–69 ("strength . . ."); DAR 258:574 ("Some . . ."); L. Huxley, 2:188 ("calm . . .").

10. DAR 242 (1873); *ED-CFL*, 2:xxi; *WC*, 302–3 ("she . . .").

11. DAR 242 (1873); DAR 258:559 ("except . . ." and "kitten . . ."); A. Desmond, *Huxley*, 431 ("Poor . . ."); *ED-CFL*, 2:213; Jenkins, *Gladstone*, 372–73; Meacham, 306–7; *Tormented*, 600–601.

12. DAR 219.9:101 ("F. sent . . ."); A. Desmond, *Huxley*, 425–30; *Tormented*, 598.

13. A. Desmond, *Huxley*, 430 ("I . . ."); *Power*, 395–96.

14. *Companion*, 116; DAR 158, 52 ("Very pleasant"); DAR 219.9:106.

15. DAR 219.9:105; DAR 242 (1873); DAR 258:560; F. Darwin, "Sir George," vi–vii; *ED-CFL*, 2:214–15; M. Keynes, *House by the River*, 36–37 ("highly-strung . . ."); *Power*, 400 ("I would . . ."); *Tormented*, 601.

16. F. Darwin, "Sir George," vi–vii; M. Keynes, *House by the River*, 36–37; DAR 245:300 ("[C]riticising . . .").

17. Cattermole and Wolfe, 6–7, 129; DAR 210.2:25; DAR 219.11:18; DNB, s.v. "Darwin, Sir Horace."

18. Stecher, 237.

19. DAR 242 (1871, 1872); Downe Parish Records, Bromley, P123/3/7; Moore, "Darwin of Down," 470–71; *Power*, 454.

20. DAR 258:574 ("the Ffiend"), 575 ("so . . ."); *Companion*, 213; DAR 219.9:100 ("wretched clergyman"); Downe Parish Records, Bromley, P123/3/7.

21. *Companion*, 137; DAR 219.9:108 ("some . . .").

22. Downe Parish Records, Bromley, P123/25/3; Moore, "Darwin of Down," 470–71; *Power*, 454–55; *Tormented*, 600.

23. Downe Parish Records, Bromley, P123/25/3 ("respectable . . . ," "the children . . . ," and "As I . . ."); *Power*, 455–56; *Tormented*, 605–6 ("the effects . . .").

24. DAR 258:583.

25. DAR 219.9:112, 115; DAR 258:583 ("I . . ."), 585.

26. DAR 158, 53; DAR 239.23:1.20 ("I hope . . ."); DAR 242 (1874).

27. DAR 219.9:115 ("at taking . . ."), 117 ("without . . ."); DAR 239.23:1.20; DAR 242 (1874); DAR 262.11.1.

28. DAR 239.1:2.5; DAR 242 (1874); Royalengineers.ca, "Lieutenant Henry Spencer Palmer," www.royalengineers.ca/Palmer.html; NASA, "Predictions for the 2004 Transit of Venus," eclipse.gsfc.nasa.gov/transit/TV2004.html; NASA, "Sun-Earth Day 2004 Venus Transit," sunearth.gsfc.nasa.gov/sunearthday/2004/vt_vtstory_2004.htm.

29. DAR 239.23:1.19 ("whistle . . ."); DAR 239.1:2.1–3 ("It is . . ." and "I think . . .").

30. DAR 239.1:2.5.

31. DAR 239.23:1.23; M. Keynes, *Leonard Darwin*, 7.

32. Bigham, 334; DAR 210.5:7 ("took . . ."); DAR 239.23:1.22, 23 ("They . . .").

33. G. Darwin, "Beneficial Restrictions" ("certain diseases"); Mivart, "Primitive Man," 70 ("Mr . . ."); DAR 239.23:1.21; G. Darwin, "Note"; *Power*, 355.

34. Mivart, *Man and Apes*, 191 et passim.

35. *WC*, 304.

36. *WC*, 217, 263 ("lonely . . ."), 267, 291 ("virtually . . ." and "Your . . .").

37. DAR 219.1:85 ("Look . . ."), 9:96; DAR 242 (1874).

CHAPTER 17. An Irreparable Loss

1. Hoppen, 275–84, 293.

2. Bigham, 293 ("climbed . . ."); Farwell, 190–201 ("punitive . . . ," 200); Jalland, 320; Richardson, 299; Weintraub, 409.

3. DAR 239.23:1.28 ("a most . . ."); Colp, *To Be an Invalid*, 90; *Companion*, 222; DAR 219.9:123 ("like . . .").

4. Vaughan Williams, 7, 9–10 ("very . . .").

5. DAR 239.23:1.28 ("without . . ." and "Life . . ."), 30; DAR 242 (1875); L. Huxley, 2:199 ("I feel . . ."); F. Darwin, *Life and Letters*, 2:375 ("fail . . ."); K. M. Lyell, 2:462 ("deciphering . . ."); Pine, *Burke's Peerage*, 1338.

6. DAR 239.23:1.31 ("have . . ."); DAR 242 (1875); *ED-CFL*, 1:xxviii–xxix, xxxii–xxxiii.

7. DAR 239.1:2.8.

8. DAR 239.1:2.8 ("sleep . . ."), 10 ("fatter . . ."), 23:1.31 ("to avoid . . ."); *WC*, inside front cover.

9. DAR 239.1:2.11–14 ("Twice . . . ," 11), 23:1.31; DAR 242 (1875).

10. DAR 239.1:3.1–3 ("looking . . ."), 5 ("thankful . . ."); Raverat, 196 ("leading . . .").

11. DAR 239.23:1.33, 35 ("at . . ."); Cattermole and Wolfe, 6 ("was . . ."); DAR 219.9:127 ("self . . ."); Mary Bellis, "Bicycle History," inventors.about.com/library/inventors/blbicycle.htm.

12. *ED-CFL*, 2:219–20 ("languish . . ."); *Power*, 418–23; Richards, 130–31.

13. F. Darwin, *Life and Letters*, 2:377–79; A. Desmond, *Huxley*, 457–59; *Power*, 422–23.

14. DAR 239.23:1.36.

15. Scholarly Societies Project, "Accademia dei Lincei," www.scholarly-societies.org/history/1603al.html; DAR 239.23:1.38 (" a foreign . . ."), 23:1.39; F. Darwin, *Life and Letters*, 2:547; Pine, *Burke's Peerage*, 1727; Catholic Encyclopedia, "Pope Pius IX," www.newadvent.org/cathen/12134b.htm.

16. DAR 239.1:3.12, 1:4.1–6 ("fancy . . . ," 5), 23:1.41 ("I remember . . .").

17. Hoppen, 628–29 ("imperialism . . ."); McCord, 274–75 ("emphasize . . ."); Weintraub, 413–19, 488.

18. McCord, 274–75; Weintraub, 418 ("more . . ."); Hoppen, 629–30 ("the violence . . ." and "Unprincipled . . .").

19. DAR 239.23:1.41.

20. Victoria R, "Proclamation, respecting the Alteration of Her Majesty's Style and Titles . . . April 28, 1876," www.heraldica.org/topics/britain/britstyles.htm#1876.

21. Brendon, 237–38; Weintraub, 423 ("masses"); Ryan Thompson, "The Star of India," famousdiamonds.tripod.com/starofindia.html; Dimdima.com, "The Delhi Durbar," dimdima.com/knowledge/freedom.asp?tit=The+Delhi+Durbar ("to grant . . ."); Field Marshal Lord Roberts, "When Queen Victoria Became Empress of India, 1877," www.fordham.edu/halsall/india/1877empressvictoria.html.

22. DAR 219.9:139; DAR 242 (1876); DAR 245:55 ("Good bye . . ."); Raverat, 119–38.

23. DAR 219.9:138 ("Amy's . . ."); DAR 245:307 ("I . . .").

24. DAR 219.9:139.

25. Suzanne Stipe Persaud, "Giving Birth Again?" www.parenting.com/article/Pregnancy/Health/Giving-Birth-Again.

26. DAR 219.9:140 ("Every . . ." and "supporting . . ."); DAR 239.23:1.50; *ED*, 297 ("where . . ."); Pine, *Burke's Landed Gentry*, 610.

27. DAR 239.23:1.49 ("loved . . ."); *ED-CFL*, 2:225 ("had . . ."), 255; *Power*, 437 ("the most . . .").

28. DAR 239.23:1.49 ("she . . . ," "However . . . ," and "short . . ."); DAR 242 (1876); DAR 245:308–9 ("seems . . .").

29. DAR 239.23:1.49.

30. *Companion*, 70–71; DAR 219.9:140; DAR 239.23:1.51 ("The baby . . ."); DAR 242 (1876); DAR 245:308 ("We . . .").

31. DAR 219.9:141; DAR 239.23:1.52 ("baby . . ."), 23:1.56 ("tolerable cheerfulness,"

"become . . . ," and "quite . . ."), 23:1.57 ("wish[ed] . . ."); *ED-CFL*, 2:225 ("We . . ."); *Power*, 438.

32. Pine, *Burke's Peerage*, 2190; DAR 219.9:141 ("dreadfully . . ."); *WC*, 310–11.

33. *Companion*, 160; DAR 239.23:1.54 ("Mrs . . ."); L. Huxley, 2:202.

34. Barlow, 96–97 ("You . . ."), 145.

35. Hoppen, 620–24; Newsome, 136; McCord, 275–77.

36. DAR 239.23:1.56.

37. McCord, 276–77.

38. DAR 210.5:8.

39. *Encyclopaedia Britannica*, 15th ed., s.v. "Gordon, Charles George"; Chenevix Trench, 13, 68–121; DAR 210.5:8 ("There . . .").

40. DAR 210.5:9.

41. Chenevix Trench, 187, 290–91; M. Keynes, *Leonard Darwin*, 7.

42. DAR 219.1:92 ("Baby . . ."), 9:145, 147 ("Babsy . . .").

43. C. Darwin, *Mould*, 154–56; Jackson, 331; DAR 219.9:149 ("½ kill"), 153 ("striking . . ." and "loitered . . .").

44. C. Darwin, *Mould*, 137–56, 165–72, 178–92, et passim; F. Darwin, *Life and Letters*, 2:394 ("a curious . . .").

45. DAR 210.5:16 ("Dearest . . .").

46. DAR 219.9:157, 159–161 ("I should . . .").

47. DAR 210.5:19.

48. DAR 219.8:32.

49. *ED-CFL*, 2:228–29 ("from . . ." and "out . . ."); DAR 219.9:162 ("charmingly . . ."), 164.

50. Raverat, 176–80 ("clean . . ." and "the only . . . ," 176; "painfully . . . ," 177); DAR 219.9:167.

51. *Companion*, 29; DAR 219.9:166 ("fond . . ." and "never . . ."); DAR 242 (1877); DAR 210.5:21 ("a small . . ." and "splendid . . ."), 29; *ED-CFL*, 2:xxv.

52. *Companion*, 224; DAR 242 (1877); F. Darwin, *Life and Letters*, 2:544; *Power*, 449–50.

53. "Mr. Darwin at Cambridge," 64.

54. *Companion*, 56; DAR 219.1:98 ("It . . ."); Magnusson, 1346.

55. "Mr. Darwin at Cambridge," 64.

56. Colp, *To Be an Invalid*, 88–92; DAR 158, 56–58; DAR 242 (1878, 1879); L. Huxley, 2:145–51 ("I had . . . ", 150–51).

57. DAR 219.9:180; F. Darwin, "Sir George," vii–viii; M. Keynes, *House by the River*, 38–39; M. Keynes, *Leonard Darwin*, 7; Magnusson, 817; Today in Science History, "Lord Kelvin (William Thomson)," www.todayinsci.com/K/Kelvin_Lord/Kelvin_Lord.htm.

58. *ED-CFL*, 2:237 ("I will . . ."); DAR 158, 56–58; DAR 219.9:169 ("slightly . . ."), 171, 178.

59. Kirkland, 91–92.

60. Kirkland, 92 ("wholly . . ."); Magnusson, 773.

61. DAR 242 (1878); DAR 210.5:25 ("after . . .").

62. DAR 210.5:25 ("a little . . ."), 26 ("Newport . . ."); Kay Davis, "Class and Leisure at America's First Resort: Biographies: Frederick Law Olmsted," xroads.virginia. edu/~MA01/Davis/newport/biographies/olmsted.html.

63. DAR 210.5:28–30.

64. DAR 210.5:28 ("feel . . ."), 30.

65. DAR 242 (1879); *ED*, 301–3 ("a fine . . ."); *ED-CFL*, 2:238; *Power*, 476–77 ("The scenery . . .").

66. *Power*, 476–77; *ED*, 302–6 ("been . . ." and "knighted . . . ," 304); *ED-CFL*, 2:238 ("his brain . . ."); C. Darwin, *The Descent of Man*, 2:293–94; DAR 242 (1879).

67. *ED-CFL*, 2:52; *ED*, 303 ("manner . . ." and "pleasant . . ."); Anderson et al., 339 ("Talked . . ."); DAR 242 (1879).

68. *ED*, 307 ("too . . ."); *Power*, 475–76; *WC*, 314.

69. DAR 219.9:203–8; DAR 258:1050 ("I am . . .").

70. DAR 185/19 ("My dear . . ."); DAR 219.9:209.

71. *ED*, 307.

CHAPTER 18. "Our Secure Happiness . . . Shattered"

1. DAR 242 (1880); DAR 258:564 ("had . . ." and "I hope . . ."); DAR 219.1:131 ("Mr . . ."), 9:219.

2. DAR 219.9:221 ("Well . . ."); *ED*, 307 ("F and . . ."); *Power*, 457–58.

3. Barlow, 167–82 ("Erasmus . . . ," 178); Burkhardt, Smith, et al., *Calendar*, 504–10; Power, 475; Willey, 74–80.

4. Barlow, 180–82.

5. Barlow, 182–88 ("of lying . . . ," 186); DAR 219.1:133–34; *Power*, 473–75; *Tormented*, 641 ("exactly . . ." and "Darwinophobia . . .").

6. DAR 219.9:223 ("[W]hat . . ."); DAR 242 (1880); Magnusson, 782; *Allmusic*, "Natalia Janotha," www.allmusic.com/cg/amg.dll?p=amg&sql=41:64092~T1.

7. DAR 219.9:224–27 ("suffering attacks," 224; "always . . . ," 225–26; "It felt . . . ," 227); DAR 242 (1880); *WC*, 314.

8. DAR 219.9:229; *ED-CFL*, 2:xx.

9. *Companion*, 145; *WC*, 314; Magnusson, 1240; Allmusic, "Hans Richter," allmusic.com/cg/amg.dll?p=amg&sql=41:69091.

10. DAR 219.9:233 ("a feeble . . ."), 236 ("I am . . .").

11. Barthorp, 1–14, 45–69; Farwell, 223–27; McCord, 278–79.

12. McCord, 278.

13. Hoppen, 632–37; Jenkins, *Gladstone*, 433–39; McCord, 279–82; Number10.gov.uk, "William Ewart Gladstone," www.number10.gov.uk/history-and-tour /prime-ministers-in-history/william-ewart-gladstone.

14. DAR 219.9:229.

15. DAR 219.9:238 ("listening . . .") 242 ("a vulgar . . ."); DAR 242 (1880).

16. Colp, *To Be an Invalid*, 230; DAR 219.9:244 ("is ev[idently] . . ."), 245 ("Dr C . . ."); DAR 242 (1880); Newnham College, "Helen Gladstone," www.newn.cam. ac.uk/about-newnham/college-history/biographies/content/helen-gladstone;

American Cancer Society, "Strychnos Nux-Vomica," www.cancer.org/docroot/ETO/content/ETO_5_3X_Strychnos_Nux-vomica.asp?sitearea+ETO.

17. Pine, *Burke's Peerage*, 2190; DAR 219.9:247 ("utterly . . ."), 251; *ED*, 310.

18. *WC*, 314 ("I mean . . ."); DAR 219.9:251 ("[When] I . . ."); *ED*, 310–11 ("leaning . . .").

19. DAR 219.9:251–253 ("little seal," 252; "most . . . ," 251; "more . . . ," 253); *ED-CFL*, 1:97; *Encyclopaedia Britannica*, 15th ed., s.v. "Broglie, (Achille-Charles-Léonce) Victor, 3ᵉ duc de."

20. DAR 158, 58 ("1500 copies . . ."); *Tormented*, 644.

21. *Power*, 482–83; Raby, 220–26 ("some . . . ," 221; "It will . . . ," 226); *Tormented*, 646–48.

22. A Web of English History, "Gladstone and Ireland 1880–1886," www.history home.co.uk/peel/ireland/gladire2.htm; Jenkins, *Gladstone*, 475; McCord, 371–72.

23. Pine, *Burke's Peerage*, 1223; *Times* (London), 16 March 1881, letter to the editor from the 5th Marquess of Lansdowne; DAR 219.9:259 ("I read . . .").

24. Farwell, 241–44; Hoppen, 657 ("vigorous response").

25. DAR 210.3:5 ("a horrid . . ." and "the beginning . . ."); Farwell, 241–52; Hoppen, 657–58.

26. *Companion*, 144; DAR 210.3:3 ("The visit . . ." and "will not . . ."); DAR 242 (1881).

27. DAR 242 (1881); "Hans Richter" (see n. 9).

28. DAR 158, 60; DAR 210.3:14 ("prettier . . ."); DAR 242 (1881).

29. DAR 210.3:7; *WC*, 315 ("by . . ."); DAR 219.1:145 ("We . . .").

30. *ED-CFL*, 2:247 ("weary . . ."); Magnusson, 263, 472; *WC*, 315.

31. DAR 219.1:146 ("comfortable . . ."); *WC*, 317–18.

32. *CCD*, 7:390; DAR 219.1:146; *Power*, 489; *WC*, 318 ("One . . .").

33. DAR 219.1:146.

34. *ED-CFL*, 2:247.

35. DAR 210.3:24 ("marked . . ."); DAR 219.9:277 ("lower . . .").

36. DAR 210.3:21; DAR 219.1:147 ("disgustingly rich" and "reckless . . ."), 9:270 ("enormously rich"); *Tormented*, 655.

37. DAR 158, 59; Power, 490–91 ("driven . . ."); *ED-CFL*, 2:249; L. Huxley, 2:255 ("I take . . .").

38. *Companion*, 244; Romanes, 132 ("the splendid . . .").

39. DAR 158, 60; *Tormented*, 658–59.

40. DAR 219.9:280 ("derangement . . ."), 281 ("perfectly . . ."); Colp, *To Be an Invalid*, 93 ("received . . .").

41. DAR 219.9:282 ("quite comf"), 288; Colp, *To Be an Invalid*, 93; DAR 210.3:40 ("a placid . . ."), 41, 43; DAR 242 (1882); *ED-CFL*, 1:xi.

42. Colp, *To Be an Invalid*, 94 ("excessively depress[ing]"); DAR 210.3:45 ("heart . . ."), 46.

43. DAR 239.1:5.1, 3; M. Keynes, *Leonard Darwin*, 7–8.

44. DAR 239.23:2.7.

45. *Companion*, 115; DAR 219.9:37; DAR 239.23:2.8 ("I have . . ." and "What . . ."); M. Keynes, *Leonard Darwin*, 8.

46. Colp, *To Be an Invalid*, 94–95; DAR 210.9 ("I . . .").

47. *Companion*, 22, 210; DAR 210.9; DAR 245:320 ("a great . . ."); Colp, *To Be an Invalid*, 95–96 ("If . . .").

48. DAR 210.9 ("I . . ."); Colp, *To Be an Invalid*, 95 ("You . . ."); DAR 245:320 ("very . . .").

CHAPTER 19. Life at a Lower Pitch

1. *CCD*, 3:43 ("sudden death"); DAR 242 (1882).

2. DAR 239.23:2.13; DAR 242 (1882); *Times* (London), 21 April 1882.

3. F. Darwin, *Life and Letters*, 2:531; "John Lubbock"; H. Orel, 219; *Tormented*, 664–69 ("the will . . . ," 667).

4. *Power*, 495–96; *Tormented*, 667–68; *Times* (London), 26 April 1882.

5. W/M 579.

6. H. Orel, 219 ("ignored . . ."); *CCD*, 1:334–36 ("Philos"); *Companion*, 87–88, 267.

7. L. Huxley, 2:259 ("a touching . . ."); W/M 579 ("2 months . . ." and "I hardly . . .").

8. DAR 245:56 ("It is . . ."), 321 ("the great . . ."); DAR 219.1:150 ("in the Bath . . ."), 9:289 ("I am . . ."), 295; DAR 239.23:2.14 ("I feel . . ."); *ED-CFL*, 2:256–57 ("flat . . .").

9. Hoppen, 671–73; McCord, 371–73.

10. Jenkins, *Gladstone*, 480–81; McCord, 373.

11. DAR 219.1:150.

12. *Times* (London), 12 May 1882 ("not . . ."); DAR 219.9:289 ("Yesterday . . .").

13. DAR 210.3:50; DAR 219.9:300 ("the best . . ."); DAR 239.23:2.13; M. Keynes, *Leonard Darwin*, 7–8.

14. DAR 245:322 ("Isn't . . ."); DAR 210.3:50; DAR 239.1:6.3 ("I must . . ."); M. Keynes, *Leonard Darwin*, 8.

15. DAR 219.9:300 ("cold . . ." and "They . . ."); DAR 239.1:6.3 ("sit . . ." and "My . . .").

16. DAR 239.1:6.3–6 ("a disappointing . . . ," 3; "quite . . . ," 5; "there . . . ," 6).

17. DAR 239.1:6.9 ("the fatal . . ." and "The natives . . ."); C. Darwin, *The Descent of Man*, 1:201 ("At some . . .").

18. DAR 239.1:6.10 ("It feels . . ."), 12; M. Keynes, *Leonard Darwin*, 8 ("determine . . .").

19. DAR 210.3:49, 50.

20. Bobbitt, 111–12, 125, 177, 181; DAR 210.3:52–53; DAR 219.9:322 ("nooks . . ."); *ED-CFL*, 2:260; Magnusson, 777.

21. DAR 219.9:304 ("care-worn . . ."); DAR 242 (1882); Raverat, 177; Sedgwick, xii–xiii et passim.

22. DAR 210.3:62 ("clapping . . ." and "much . . ."); DAR 239.23:2.19, 20 ("We are"); DAR 242 (1882).

23. DAR 219.9:322; Pine, *Burke's Landed Gentry*, 610; Raverat, 191.

24. DAR 210.3:58 ("sweet . . ."), 69 ("a souse . . ."), 70 ("fidgetty . . ."), 73; DAR 239.23:2.22 ("Grand . . ."); DAR 242 (1883).

25. Cattermole and Wolfe, 35; DAR 210.3:69 ("enormous").

26. DAR 219.1:162; DAR 239.23:2.24 ("the stupidest . . ."), 25 ("the pleasantest . . ."); F. Darwin, "Sir George," ix; M. Keynes, *House by the River*, 34, 39; Magnusson, 285.

27. Bobbitt, 141, 172–83 ("I want . . . ," 172; "the most . . . ," 176; "he could . . . ," 181), 190–91 ("inveterate . . . ," 190), 207; *CCD*, 1:51; *Companion*, 27; F. Darwin, "Sir George," iv; Pine, *Burke's Peerage*, 128.

28. DAR 239.1:6.12 ("a bit . . ."), 14.

29. McCord, 369–71; ExploreLanka.com, "Anuradhapura," www.explorelanka. com/places/nc/anu.htm; DAR 239.1:6.15, 16 ("rather . . ."); DAR 219.1:155 ("better . . ."); DAR 242 (1883).

30. DAR 210.3:77; DAR 219.1:158 ("nice . . . ," "turned . . . ," and "Poor . . ."); DAR 242 (1883); B. Darwin, *The World That Fred Made*, 59 ("special . . ."); Raverat, 191–95.

31. DAR 210.3:73; DAR 242 (1883).

32. *ED-CFL*, 2:261–62 ("It . . ." and "astonished . . .").

33. DAR 219.1:157 ("the quiet . . ."), 158; DAR 210.3:77, 78, 80; *ED-CFL*, 2:262 ("loitered . . .").

34. DAR 210.3:77 ("great . . ."), 80–82 ("that tiresome . . . ," 80; "my back . . . ," 81); DAR 219.1:162; DAR 242 (1883); DAR 245:68–69 ("I want . . ." and "Why . . .").

35. DAR 210.5:35; DAR 242 (1883).

36. DAR 219.9:394 ("about . . ."); DAR 210.3:89 ("a habit . . ."); *ED-CFL*, 2:263–264; M. Keynes, *House by the River*, 44.

37. Raverat, 15–29 ("pretty . . . ," 15); Bobbitt, 173, 190–98 ("brotherly . . . ," 196); Leedham-Green, 168.

38. Bobbitt, 202–7 ("Until . . . ," 203); DAR 210.3:88–90, 93; M. Keynes, *House by the River*, 41.

39. DAR 210.3:96 ("very . . ."), 97 ("A[unt] . . ."), 99 ("a flock . . ." and "I want . . ."), 100 ("When . . ."); DAR 219.9:403; Raverat, 21, 28, 30.

40. Bobbitt, 209–11 ("Maud . . ."); M. Keynes, *House by the River*, 42–43; Pine, *Burke's Landed Gentry*, 610.

41. DAR 210.3:101 ("Maude . . ."), 112 ("Now . . ."), 115; DAR 242 (1884); M. Keynes, *House by the River*, 45–57.

42. DAR 219.1:174 ("all hope . . ."), 175 ("very . . ."); DAR 219.9:434; DAR 242 (1884); Raverat, 13.

CHAPTER 20. *The Life and Letters*

1. Hoppen, 661–62; Jenkins, *Gladstone*, 509–12; Magnusson, 1024.

2. Farwell, 253–81; Hoppen, 658–62.

3. Jenkins, *Gladstone*, 510–11 ("as . . ." and "half . . ."); Chenevix Trench, 203, 247 ("a wild . . ."); Farwell, 278–79; Hoppen, 662.

4. Farwell, 280 ("Gordon . . ."); *ED-CFL*, 2:265 ("I got . . ."); Hoppen, 662; Jenkins, *Gladstone*, 510–12.

5. DAR 219.1:164 ("Gen. . . ."); Hoppen, 663 ("These . . ."); DAR 210.3:113 ("never

. . ."); Jenkins, *Gladstone*, 513–15 ("After . . . ," 514); "William Ewart Gladstone" (see chap. 18, n. 13).

6. DAR 219.9:409, 443 ("painting . . ."); DAR 242 (1885); B. Darwin, *The World That Fred Made*, 28.

7. B. Darwin, *Life Is Sweet, Brother*, 121; Silverman, 15–17 ("in a . . ." and "We . . .").

8. Cattermole and Wolfe, 118; DAR 219.1:175; DAR 219.9:442 ("much . . ."), 444; M. Keynes, *Leonard Darwin*, 9; Spaulding, 54.

9. DAR 242 (1885); *ED-CFL*, 2:269 ("gave up . . ."); Silverman, 7 ("the humble . . .").

10. Gathering the Jewels, "A 'Bath Chair,'" www.gtj.org.uk/en/small/item/GTJ 08567; DAR 210.3:115; DAR 219.1:176 ("Yesterday . . ."); DAR 219.9:447; *ED-CFL*, 2:267–69 ("there . . . ," 267).

11. DAR 219.9:406 ("Nobody . . ."), 432 ("I have . . ."), 463 ("I am . . ."), 526 ("a work . . ."); *ED-CFL*, 2:269 ("made . . ."), 275.

12. *Companion*, 37, 268; DAR 219.1:187; M. Keynes, *House by the River*, 170; H. Orel, 223 ("preserve . . ."); Natural History Museum, "The North Hall Statues," www.nhm.ac.uk/visit-us/history-architecture/architecture-tour/north-hall/north-hall -statues/index.html.

13. DAR 219.9:466 ("avoiding . . ."); DAR 219.1:187 ("he . . ."); DAR 242 (1885).

14. Compare Barlow, 85, with F. Darwin, *Life and Letters*, 1:277.

15. DAR 219.1:178.

16. DAR 219.1:180.

17. Compare Barlow, 86, with F. Darwin, *Life and Letters*, 1:278.

18. Compare Barlow, 87, with F. Darwin, *Life and Letters*, 1:278.

19. DAR 219.1:180.

20. Barlow, 87.

21. Compare Barlow, 90, with F. Darwin, *Life and Letters*, 1:281.

22. Compare Barlow, 92–93, with F. Darwin, *Life and Letters*, 1:282.

23. Barlow, 93–94.

24. DAR 219.1:178 ("not . . ."); *ED-CFL*, 2:173.

25. *ED-CFL*, 2:175 ("vivid"); Barlow, 87 ("very few . . .").

26. Barlow, 85–96; *Companion*, 114.

27. DAR 219.9:442 ("feeling . . ."); M. Keynes, *House by the River*, 42, 57–59.

28. Spaulding, 54 ("looked . . ."); DAR 219.9:481 ("Girl . . ."), 489 ("I shd . . ."); DAR 242 (1885).

29. *Companion*, 112–14; DAR 239.23:4.9 ("dreadful").

30. DAR 239.23:4.3.

31. DAR 219.9:532 ("It . . ."), 537–539 ("know . . . ," 538); DAR 239.23:4.8, 13, 14b, 18 ("a rage . . ."); DAR 242 (1886).

32. DAR 242 (1885); *ED-CFL*, 2:271.

33. *Companion*, 161; DAR 219.9:471 ("Poor . . ."); DAR 242 (1885).

34. DAR 219.9:472.

35. DAR 219.9:485 ("I have . . ."), 489 ("A wretched . . ."), 492 ("Frank . . ."), 495; Pine, *Burke's Peerage*, 2190.

36. *Companion*, 185; DAR 219.9:553 ("Husband . . ."); DAR 242 (1886); *ED-CFL*, 2:xx, xxv.

37. DAR 210.3:134.

38. DAR 210.3:134; DAR 219.9:556 ("had..."), 560; Pine, *Burke's Landed Gentry*, 1727.

39. *ED-CFL*, 2:274; Jenkins, *Gladstone*, 519–38.

40. DAR 219.1:188, 202; DAR 239.23:4.1 ("I am..."); DAR 219.9:526 ("I was..."); Jenkins, *Gladstone*, 536.

41. DAR 239.23:4.13 ("Home..."); DAR 219.1:198 ("some..."); *ED-CFL*, 2:274, 297; Jenkins, *Gladstone*, 554–55.

42. Brendon, 174 ("Bed-Stead"); Jenkins, *Sir Charles Dilke*, 240–43 ("a puritan...," 240); W. T. Stead Resource Site, www.attackingthedevil.co.uk.

43. DAR 219.9:485 ("I..."); Jenkins, *Sir Charles Dilke*, 241.

44. Jenkins, *Sir Charles Dilke*, 160, 214–17 ("vilely..." and "Virginia...," 217).

45. Ibid., 217–19 ("liaison...," 217; "her..." and "taught...," 219), 232–35; Jenkins, *Gladstone*, 542; Newsome, 94.

46. Jenkins, *Sir Charles Dilke*, 235–36.

47. DAR 219.9:522.

48. DAR 219.9:525; Jenkins, *Sir Charles Dilke*, 11, 241–43, 370 ("the victim..."); Magnusson, 419–20.

49. DAR 219.9:524 ("[Frank]..."); F. Darwin, *Life and Letters*, 1:309–10; Desmond and Moore, *Darwin's Sacred Cause*, throughout.

50. L. Darwin et al., 291–93; Magnusson, 1313.

51. DAR 239.1:7.1.

52. DAR 219.9:555.

Chapter 21. Banting, Books, and the Queen's Jubilee

1. Barry Groves, "William Banting," www.second-opinions.co.uk/banting.html.

2. Raverat, 148–49.

3. DAR 219.9:578 ("Bessy..."), 581 ("only..."); Smith, "Charles Darwin's Health Problems," 298.

4. DAR 219.9:593 ("B's..."); DAR 242 (1887).

5. DAR 242 (1887, 1888).

6. DAR 219.9:577.

7. DAR 219.9:578 ("very..."), 81 ("I felt..."); DAR 242 (1887); "Helen Gladstone" (see chap. 18, n. 16).

8. DAR 219.9:580.

9. DAR 219.9:578 ("which..."), 579 ("absurd").

10. DAR 219.9:586 ("Only..."); F. Darwin, "Sir George," xi; Forrest, 55; Trinity College Cambridge, "The Master of Trinity," www.trin.cam.ac.uk/index.php?pageid=172.

11. Forrest, 57.

12. Cartage.org.lb, "Murray, Charles Fairfax," www.cartage.org.lb/en/themes/Biographies/MainBiographies/M/Murra1/Murray.htm; DAR 239.23:5.14 ("He..."); DAR 219.1:208, 9:622 ("Mr...").

13. DAR 219.1:193 ("I..."), 208, 220, 9:622 ("the Pigamy..."; DAR 242 (1887); Spalding, 30 ("impressive..."), 410.

14. DAR 219.9:593 ("I..."); *ED-CFL*, 2:278 ("To-morrow...").

15. Weintraub, 1–24 ("soirées...," 6); DAR 219.9:601 (I...").

16. Weintraub, 11–16.

17. Hudson, 16–19.

18. Cambridge Philharmonic Society, "Sorry, my bees won't let me attend," www.cam-phil.org.uk/history.html; DAR 219.1:229; DAR 239.23:5.10 ("there..."); DAR 242 (1887); F. Knight, 83; Stubbings, 64; DAR 219.9:606 ("at 9...").

19. DAR 219.9:625 ("I have..."); Raverat, 193.

20. *Companion*, 189; DAR 219.1:222, 223 ("in a state...").

21. DAR 199.5:16 ("some..." and "a little..."), 17 ("great..."), 56 ("the highest...."); Magnusson, 416.

22. DAR 219.8:49 ("I..."); DAR 199.5:17, 18 ("delighted").

23. *Times* (London), 19 November 1887.

24. *Companion*, 44, 192; DAR 219.9:628; Pine, *Burke's Peerage*, 587, 605, 1841.

25. DAR 239.1:8.10.

26. DAR 219.9:634.

27. *WC*, 326.

28. DAR 219.9:639.

29. DAR 219.1:224.

30. *WC*, 329 ("I..."); DAR 219.9:670 ("waning").

31. DAR 219.9:677 ("a blessed..."); *Companion*, 291, 294.

32. DAR 219.9:636.

33. DAR 219.9:598 ("Now..."); B. Darwin, *Life Is Sweet, Brother*, 36–48; Raverat, 13.

34. DAR 219.9:631 ("I am glad..."), 629 ("I am sorry...").

35. DAR 219.9:682 ("Help..."); DAR 239.23:5.20 ("Horace...").

36. DAR 219.9:679 ("I am..."); Raverat, 47–59.

37. DAR 219.1:227.

38. Silverman, front cover.

39. DAR 219.9:649; DAR 239.1:9.3 ("At..."); Magnusson, 250.

40. DAR 239.23:6.4.

41. DAR 219.9:687 ("Now..."); DAR 219.1:234 ("Frank..."); Peile, 2:746.

42. F. J. Wedgwood, *The Moral Ideal*, vii–viii ("a History..."); Stawell, 394 ("series...").

43. Stawell, 394 ("an able..."); DAR 219.9:670 ("I have..."), 685 ("read...").

44. Mayr, 306; F. J. Wedgwood, *The Moral Ideal*, 168 ("Accident...").

45. Sandford; James; Walker; Crawford; W. Knight; Murphy; Garibaldi; DAR 219.9:695 ("The Tom..."), 708 ("Don't read *A London*..."), 720 ("We found..."), 730 ("Don't read Principal..."), 743 ("We have...").

46. Levy; Jefferies; Seeley; Main; DAR 219.9:692 ("suits me..."), 712 ("The descriptions..."), 716 ("sharp..."), 750 ("So...").

47. DAR 219.9:742.

48. DAR 219.9:707 ("How..."), 700 ("Huxley..."); A. Desmond, *Huxley*, 566–68; Goodwin, 116, 120–21, 145–46; Michael Gilleland, "The Gadarene Swine," laudatortemporisacti.blogspot.com/2005/05/gadarene-swine.html.

49. DAR 219.9:1194.

50. Clark, 97–98, 108–10 ("melancholia . . ." and "Rationally . . ."); A. Desmond, *Huxley*, 557–58; Luisetta Mudie, "The History of Neurosis and the Neurosis of History," www.scribd.com/doc/21280332/The-History-of-Neurosis-and-the-Neurosis-of-History ("Napoleon . . .").

51. Clark, 110–11; A. Desmond, *Huxley*, 569, 572; NetBible, "Leviticus18:6–29," net.bible.org/passage.php?passage=Leviticus%2018:6–29%23n1#n3.

52. DAR 219.9:712 ("Ethel . . ."), 692 ("so called . . .").

53. A. Desmond, *Huxley*, 569 ("an ageing . . ."), 572; DAR 219.9:690 ("cheap . . .").

54. Campbell, 225 ("Burke . . ."); DAR 219.9:593 ("I . . ."); McCord, 373, 382–83; A. N. Wilson, *The Victorians*, 531–33 ("felonious . . .").

55. DAR 219.9:693 ("How . . ."), 701; Lyons, 369, 391–404, 422, 431; Magnusson, 1127; McCord, 382; *Times* (London), 28 February 1889 ("fabricated . . ." and "sincere . . ."); A. N. Wilson, *The Victorians*, 532.

56. *WC*, 333 ("Thank God"); DAR 219.9:741 ("I wish . . ."); DAR 242 (1889).

57. DAR 219.9:731, 732 ("Gladiolus . . ."), 736 ("This is . . ."), 737 ("brilliant mass" and "The weather. . ."); DAR 242 (1889).

58. DAR 219.9:740 ("The Down . . ."); DAR 242 (1889).

59. DAR 245:141 ("You must . . ."); DAR 210.3:158 ("jolly" and "had had . . ."); DAR 219.9:742; DAR 242 (1889); B. Darwin, *Life Is Sweet, Brother*, 49–66.

CHAPTER 22. The Leos Abroad, and The Last Maerite Left Standing

1. *Companion*, 116; DAR 210.3:160; DAR 219.9:771; DAR 239.1:9.3, 10, 15, 18; M. Keynes, *Leonard Darwin*, 13–14.

2. DAR 239.1:9.16.

3. DAR 239.1:9.17.

4. DAR 219.9:816 ("energy . . ."); M. Keynes, *Leonard Darwin*, 14–15.

5. DAR 239.1:10.10.

6. DAR 239.1:10.9.

7. DAR 239.1:10.14.

8. Old Tokyo, "Yoshiwara," www.oldtokyo.com/yoshiwara.html.

9. DAR 239.23:8.29 ("a curious . . ."), 9.3 ("Your . . .").

10. DAR 219.9:861 ("Another . . ."); DAR 239.23:9.3 ("I shall . . ."); Raverat, 196–97 ("Aunt . . .").

11. DAR 239.23:8.29 ("see . . ."); DAR 210.3:174 ("We enjoyed . . ."); DAR 242 (1891); M. Keynes, *Leonard Darwin*, 15.

12. DAR 219.9:778 ("Maud . . ."); DAR 242 (1890); Speake, 94.

13. DAR 245:159–61 ("wdn't . . ." and "a feeble . . . ," 159; "there . . ." and "a very . . . ," 160; "He's . . . ," 161); DAR 219.9:820 ("undergo . . ."); Magnusson, 1499–1500; Vaughan Williams, 7, 30, 206–7.

14. Walford, W. Besant, and Stanley, DAR 219.9:814 ("a stupid . . ."), 817, 834 ("Mrs Ruck . . ."); Magnusson, 479.

15. DAR 219.9:834 ("So . . ."); Lyons, 150–52, 239, 452, 458–59; Magnusson, 1127.

16. Jenkins, *Gladstone*, 532–34, 567–73 ("would render . . . ," 573); Lyons, 590, 598–602; Magnusson, 1127–28.

17. DAR 219.9:912.

18. DAR 219.9:911.

19. DAR 210.3:175 ("peacefully"); DAR 242 (1891).

20. DAR 210.3:176.

21. DAR 219.1:255.

22. DAR 245:173.

23. DAR 219.9:905–7 ("Grapes . . . ," 905; "a bit . . . ," 906; "mutton . . . ," 907); *ED-CFL*, 2:293.

24. DAR 219.9:905, 908; DAR 242 (1891); DAR 245:178; *ED-CFL*, 2:294.

25. DAR 239.1:9.20.

26. DAR 239.1:12.1.

27. DAR 239.23:10.3, 6, 7; DAR 219.9:963 ("I am . . ."); M. Keynes, *Leonard Darwin*, 15–17.

28. M. Keynes, *Leonard Darwin*, 15–17 ("an unpleasant . . ."); McCord, 383–84.

29. DAR 219.9:963 ("I am rather . . ."), 976; M. Keynes, *Leonard Darwin*, 15–16 ("Mine . . . ," 16; "I'm afraid . . . ," 15).

30. DAR 239.23:10.11 ("I must . . ."); DAR 210.3:183 ("It is . . ."); M. Keynes, *Leonard Darwin*, 15.

31. DAR 219.9:969 ("My theory . . ."); Jenkins, *Gladstone*, 584–85; McCord, 384–85.

32. McCord, 385; DAR 239.1:12.6 ("I expect").

33. Jenkins, *Gladstone*, 605 ("This is . . ."); McCord, 385; DAR 239.23:11.21 ("I think . . .").

34. *Annual Register [for] 1893*, 235–36; DAR 219.9:1053; DAR 239.1:12.12 ("We get . . ."); Wakefield.gov.uk, "Featherstone Massacre," www.wakefield.gov.uk/Culture AndLeisure/HistoricWakefield/FeatherstoneMassacre/default.htm.

35. *Annual Register [for] 1893*, 235–36, 268–71; "Featherstone Massacre," (see n. 34).

36. DAR 219.9:1070, 1079 ("left . . ."), 1098 ("to be . . ."); Magnusson, 96, 286, 773, 1097.

37. DAR 219.9:1018 ("that blessed . . ."); DAR 242 (1893); DAR 245:219 ("It's delightful . . ."); *ED-CFL*, 2:300.

38. Martin; Oliphant; Dougall; A. Besant; Selous; DAR 219.9:1038 ("Don't . . ."), 1040 ("I have . . ."), 1100 ("*What* . . ."), 1104 ("We find . . ."), 1108 ("I am . . .").

39. DAR 219.9:1126 ("You asked . . ."); F. J. Wedgwood, *Message of Israel*, throughout.

40. DAR 219.9:670, 684, 685; DAR 239.23:4.8; DAR 242 (1880s and 1890s); *ED*, 332; *WC*, 340 ("enjoyed . . .").

41. DAR 219.9:1021; B. Darwin, *Life Is Sweet, Brother*, 51–67 ("[I] played . . . ," 57; "a discreditable . . . ," 62; "ecstatic . . . ," 59).

42. *Companion*, 115; DAR 210.3:210; Pine, *Burke's Landed Gentry*, 610; Raverat, 177 ("painfully . . ."), 196 ("care . . ."); DAR 219.9:1010 ("I fully . . .").

43. DAR 219.9:1070, 1072; DAR 245:211; *New York Times*, 13 October 1899; Pine, *Burke's Peerage*, 782.

44. DAR 219.9:1089 ("in her . . ."); DAR 239.23:12.3.

CHAPTER 23. The Last Wind of the Watch

1. DAR 219.9:1157 ("Poor . . ."); F. Darwin, *Childhood*, 4.

2. *Companion*, 228; DAR 219.9:1161 ("I wrote . . .").

3. DAR 219.9:1181; *Power*, 459; *Tormented*, 618.

4. DAR 242 (1895); DAR 245:236 ("Did . . .").

5. DAR 219.9:1130 ("I . . ."); DAR 242 (1894).

6. *Companion*, 123; DAR 219.9:1159, 1160, 1166 ("Poor . . .").

7. DAR 219.9:1167 ("I am . . ."), 1185 ("like . . ."), 1188, 1192; Jennifer Rosenberg, "The Murder of Rasputin," history1900s.about.com/od/famouscrimesscandals/a/rasputin.htm.

8. DAR 219.9:1180.

9. *Times* (London), 25 March 1895.

10. DAR 219.1:282.

11. DAR 219.9:1150 ("whatever . . ."); B. Darwin, *Life Is Sweet, Brother*, 67–74 ("decent . . . ," 74).

12. B. Darwin, *Life Is Sweet, Brother*, 67.

13. Sager, 301 ("conviviality"); B. Darwin, *Life Is Sweet, Brother*, 72 ("There is . . .").

14. DAR 242 (1895); A. Desmond, *Huxley*, 610–11 ("terrible scares"); *Times* (London), 1 July 1895.

15. *Times* (London), 1 July 1895; L. Huxley, 2:359 ("fast . . .").

16. DAR 242 (1895); A. Desmond, *Huxley*, 611–12 ("the last . . ."); *Times* (London), 5 July 1895.

17. Bigham, 330–32; McCord, 385–87 ("short . . ." and "good . . . ," 386).

18. McCord, 384–88 ("uncongenial situation," 387); Bigham, 299, 305; M. Keynes, *Leonard Darwin*, 18.

19. DAR 219.9:1207, 1208, 1215 ("nearly . . ."); M. Keynes, *Leonard Darwin*, 18–19; *Times* (London), 28 February 1896.

20. DAR 219.9:1250 ("a feeble . . ."), 1259 ("drunkards . . . ," "flatness . . . ," and "a very . . ."); M. Keynes, *Leonard Darwin*, 19 ("We could . . ."); *Henry IV, Part 1*, act 5, scene 4; Magnusson, 286; *Times* (London), 28 February 1896.

21. DAR 219.1:284 ("I think . . ."); *Companion*, 188; DAR 219.9:1020, 1115, 1206; DAR 242 (1895); F. Darwin, *Childhood*, 4; Pine, *Burke's Peerage*, 605–6; *Times* (London), 8 December 1900.

22. DAR 219.9:1241; DAR 242 (1895; "youthful . . ."); Raverat, 191.

23. DAR 219.9:1249 ("Fr has . . ."), 1258 ("Romane's . . ."); Romanes, 14–15 ("Perhaps . . .").

24. DAR 219.9:1240 ("at Van . . ."), 1324 ("the wickedness . . ."); DAR 242 (1896); Armenian National Institute, "Hamidian (Armenian) Massacres," www.armeniangenocide.org/hamidian.html.

25. OnWar.com, "British Reconquest of Sudan 1886–1899," www.onwar.com/aced/data/sierra/sudan1896.htm; DAR 219.9:1268 ("I am ..."), 1269 ("I wish ..."), 1272 ("Leo ..."); Farwell, 330–38.

26. "Reconquest of Sudan" (see n. 25); Farwell, 335–38.

27. DAR 219.9:1259, 1265, 1277 ("hearty ..."), 1283 ("allowance"), 1285, 1288; *ED-CFL*, 2:309.

28. *ED-CFL*, 2:308 ("met ..."); DAR 219.9:1274, 1280 ("spunge").

29. DAR 219.9:1325 ("On ..."); DAR 242 (1895, 1896).

30. DAR 219.1:303; DAR 219.9:1298–1301, 1305, 1311, 1315; DAR 219.11:25; DAR 242 (1896).

31. *CCD*, 8:365–66, 9:33–34; DAR 242 (1896).

32. DAR 219.9:1309.

33. DAR 219.9:1310.

34. A Dictionary of Methodism in Britain and Ireland, "Band of Hope," www.spartacus.schoolnet.co.uk/REhope.htm; DAR 219.9:1310 ("see ...").

35. DAR 219.9:1311.

36. *Companion*, 185; DAR 242 (1896).

37. DAR 219.9:1320 ("I hate ..."), 1323 ("I hope ..."), 1324 ("On Wed...."). Emma's visit to Dover with the children may have occurred in October 1844 (DAR 242).

38. *Companion*, 207; DAR 219.11:25 ("younger ..."); DAR 242 (1896).

39. DAR 219.10:35; DAR 219.11:25 ("I arrived ...").

40. *ED-CFL*, 2:205.

41. *Times* (London), 5 October 1896.

42. Downe Parish Records, Centre for Kentish Studies, P123/1/14; Moore, "Darwin of Down," 480.

43. DAR 245:346.

44. Raverat, 176–84 ("a really ...," 181).

45. F. Darwin, "Sir George," xxiv–xxv; Pine, *Burke's Landed Gentry*, 610.

46. Internet Archive, "Frederick William Maitland," www.archive.org/stream/frederickwilliamoofishuoft#page/n9/mode/2up; Pine, *Burke's Landed Gentry*, 610; Raverat, 195 ("when ...").

47. M. Keynes, *Leonard Darwin*, 22–25; Pine, *Burke's Landed Gentry*, 610; Stone, 130–31; *New York Times*, 11 December 1912 ("some ...").

48. Cattermole and Wolfe, 127–30 ("services ...," 129); Pine, *Burke's Landed Gentry*, 610.

49. Pine, *Burke's Landed Gentry*, 610; Raverat, 119–38.

50. *Cambridge Chronicle and University Journal*, 16 June 1926.

51. *ED-CFL*, 2:47.

52. Barlow, 97.

Bibliography

Adler, Saul. "Darwin's Illness." *Nature* 184 (1959): 1102–3.

Agassiz, Louis. *Études sur les glaciers*. Neuchâtel: Jent et Gassmann, 1840.

Anderson, Frederick, Lin Salamo, and Bernard Stein, eds. *Mark Twain's Notebooks & Journals*. Vol. 2, *1877–1883*. Berkeley and Los Angeles: University of California Press, 1975.

Annual Register [for] 1893. London: Rivingtons, 1894.

Arbuckle, Elisabeth Sanders, ed. *Harriet Martineau's Letters to Fanny Wedgwood*. Stanford, Calif.: Stanford University Press, 1983.

Atkins, Hedley. *Down: The Home of the Darwins*. London: Royal College of Surgeons of England, 1974.

Barlow, Nora, ed. *The Autobiography of Charles Darwin, 1809–1882*. New York: W. W. Norton, 1958.

Barrett, Paul H., Peter J. Gautrey, Sandra Herbert, David Kohn, and Sydney Smith, eds. *Charles Darwin's Notebooks, 1836–1844*. Ithaca, N.Y.: Cornell University Press, 1987.

Barthorp, Michael. *The Zulu War: A Pictorial History*. Poole, Dorset: Blandford, 1980.

Besant, Annie. *Annie Besant: An Autobiography*. 1893. Whitefish, Mont.: Kessinger, 2003.

Besant, Walter. *Captain Cook*. London: Macmillan, 1890.

Bigham, Clive. *The Prime Ministers of Britain, 1721–1921*. London: John Murray, 1922.

Bobbitt, Mary Reed. *With Dearest Love to All: The Life and Letters of Lady Jebb*. Chicago: Regnery, 1960.

Bowlby, John. *Charles Darwin: A New Life*. New York: W. W. Norton, 1990.

Bowler, Peter J. *Charles Darwin: The Man and His Influence*. Oxford: Basil Blackwell, 1990.

———. *Theories of Human Evolution: A Century of Debate, 1844–1944*. Baltimore: Johns Hopkins University Press, 1986.

Bradby, H. C., ed. *Tom Brown's School-Days*, by Thomas Hughes. Boston: Ginn, 1918. Originally published in 1857.

Brendon, Piers. *The Decline and Fall of the British Empire, 1781–1997.* New York: Knopf, 2008.

Brent, Peter. *Charles Darwin: "A Man of Enlarged Curiosity."* New York: Harper & Row, 1981.

Bridgeman, Harriet, and Elizabeth Drury, eds. *The Encyclopedia of Victoriana.* New York: Macmillan, 1975.

Browne, Janet. *Charles Darwin.* Vol. 1, *Voyaging.* New York: Knopf, 1995.

———. *Charles Darwin.* Vol. 2, *The Power of Place.* New York: Knopf, 2002.

Burke, John. *A Genealogical and Heraldic Dictionary of the Peerage and Baronetage of the British Empire.* 7th ed. London: Henry Colburn, 1843.

Burkhardt, Frederick, Sydney Smith, et al., eds. *A Calendar of the Correspondence of Charles Darwin, 1821–1882, with Supplement.* Cambridge: Cambridge University Press, 1994.

———. *The Correspondence of Charles Darwin.* Vols. 1–16 (1821–1868). Cambridge: Cambridge University Press, 1985–2008.

Butler, Samuel. *Evolution, Old and New; or, The Theories of Buffon, Dr Erasmus Darwin, and Lamarck, as Compared with That of Mr Charles Darwin.* London: Hardwick and Bogue, 1879.

Campbell, Christy. *Fenian Fire: The British Government Plot to Assassinate Queen Victoria.* London: HarperCollins, 2002.

Cattermole, M. J. G., and A. F. Wolfe. *Horace Darwin's Shop.* Bristol: Adam Hilger, 1987.

[Chambers, Robert]. *Vestiges of the Natural History of Creation.* 9th ed. London: John Churchill, 1851.

Chapple, John. *Elizabeth Gaskell: The Early Years.* Manchester: Manchester University Press, 1997.

Chenevix Trench, Charles. *The Road to Khartoum: A Life of General Charles Gordon.* New York: W. W. Norton, 1978.

Clark, Ronald W. *The Huxleys.* New York: McGraw-Hill, 1968.

Colp, Ralph, Jr. *Darwin's Illness.* Gainesville: University Press of Florida, 2008.

———. *To Be an Invalid.* Chicago: University of Chicago Press, 1977.

———. *"To Be an Invalid,* Redux." *Journal of the History of Biology* 31 (1998): 211–40.

Cook, Hera. *The Long Sexual Revolution: English Women, Sex, and Contraception, 1800–1975.* Oxford: Oxford University Press, 2004.

Crawford, F. Marion. *Greifenstein.* London: Thomas Nelson, 1889.

Crowl, Philip A. *The Intelligent Traveller's Guide to Historic Britain.* New York: Congdon & Weed, 1983.

Darwin, Bernard. *Life Is Sweet, Brother.* London: Collins, 1940.

———. *The World That Fred Made.* London: Chatto & Windus, 1955.

Darwin, Charles. *The Descent of Man, and Selection in Relation to Sex.* 1871. 2 vols. Princeton, N.J.: Princeton University Press, 1981.

———. *The Expression of the Emotions in Man and Animals.* 1872. Chicago: University of Chicago Press, 1965.

———. *The Formation of Vegetable Mould, Through the Action of Worms, with Observations on Their Habits.* New York: Appleton, 1890.

———. *On the Origin of Species.* 1859. Cambridge, Mass.: Harvard University Press, 1964.

———. *The Power of Movement in Plants.* With Francis Darwin. London: John Murray, 1880.

———. *The Variation of Animals and Plants under Domestication.* 2 vols. London: John Murray, 1868.

———. *The Voyage of the* Beagle. Edited by Leonard Engel. Garden City, N.Y.: Doubleday, 1962.

———, ed. *Zoology of the Voyage of H.M.S. Beagle.* London: Smith, Elder, 1839–1843.

Darwin, Francis, ed. *The Autobiography of Charles Darwin and Selected Letters.* New York: Dover, 1958.

———, ed. *The Foundations of "The Origin of Species": Two Essays Written in 1842 and 1844 by Charles Darwin.* Cambridge: Cambridge University Press, 1909.

———, ed. *The Life and Letters of Charles Darwin.* 1888. 2 vols. New York: Basic Books, 1959.

———. "Memoir of Sir George Darwin." In *Scientific Papers,* by George Darwin, 5: iv–xxv. Cambridge: Cambridge University Press, 1916.

———. *Springtime and Other Essays.* London: John Murray, 1920.

———. *The Story of a Childhood.* Edinburgh: Oliver and Boyd, 1920.

Darwin, George. "Note Upon the Article 'Primitive Man—Tylor and Lubbock,' in No. 273." *Quarterly Review* 137, no. 274 (1874): 587–88.

———. "On Beneficial Restrictions to Liberty of Marriage." *Contemporary Review* 22 (1873): 412–26.

Darwin, Leonard, Arthur Schuster, and E. Walter Maunder. "On the Total Solar Eclipse of August 29, 1886." *Philosophical Transactions of the Royal Society of London,* ser. A, 180 (1889): 291–350.

Darwin Papers. Cambridge University Library.

Desmond, Adrian. *Huxley.* London: Penguin, 1997.

———. *The Politics of Evolution.* Chicago: University of Chicago Press, 1989.

Desmond, Adrian, and James Moore. *Darwin: The Life of a Tormented Evolutionist.* New York: Warner, 1991.

———. *Darwin's Sacred Cause: How a Hatred of Slavery Shaped Darwin's Views on Human Evolution.* Boston: Houghton Mifflin Harcourt, 2009.

Desmond, Ray. *Sir Joseph Dalton Hooker: Traveller and Plant Collector.* Woodbridge, Suffolk: Antique Collectors Club; Royal Botanic Gardens, Kew, 1999.

Dictionary of National Biography. 61 volumes. Oxford: Oxford University Press, 2004.

Dolan, Brian. *Ladies of the Grand Tour.* New York: HarperCollins, 2001.

Dougall, Lily. *What Necessity Knows.* London: Longmans, Green, 1893.

Downe Parish Records, Bromley Central Library, Bromley (Greater London).

Downe Parish Records, Centre for Kentish Studies, Maidstone, Kent.

Farwell, Byron. *Queen Victoria's Little Wars.* New York: Harper & Row, 1972.

Ffrench, Yvonne. *The Great Exhibition: 1851.* London: Harvill, 1950.

Finer, Ann, and George Savage, eds. *The Selected Letters of Josiah Wedgwood.* London: Cory, Adams & Mackay, 1965.

Forrest, D. W. *Francis Galton: The Life and Work of a Victorian Genius.* London: Paul Elek, 1974.

Freeman, R. B. *Charles Darwin: A Companion*. Folkestone, Kent: Dawson; Hamden, Conn.: Archon, 1978.

Froude, James Anthony, ed. *Letters and Memorials of Jane Welsh Carlyle*. 3 volumes. New York: Harper & Brothers, 1883.

Garibaldi, Giuseppe. *Memorie autobiografiche*. Firenze: G. Barbera, 1888.

Gerdts, William. "Sculpture: American." In Bridgeman and Drury, *Encyclopedia of Victoriana*, 182–86.

Gilbert, Richard. *The Clerical Guide, or Ecclesiastical Directory*. 3rd ed. London: F. C. and J. Rivington, 1829.

Gill, Gillian. *Nightingales*. 2004. New York: Random House Trade Paperbacks, 2005.

Gillespie, Neal C. *Charles Darwin and the Problem of Creation*. Chicago: University of Chicago Press, 1979.

Golubovsky, Michael. "Unexplained Infertility in Charles Darwin's Family: Genetic Aspect." *Human Reproduction* 23 (2008): 1237–38.

Goodwin, Michael, ed. *Nineteenth-Century Opinion*. Harmondsworth, Middlesex: Penguin, 1951.

Gould, Stephen Jay. *The Mismeasure of Man*. New York: W. W. Norton, 1981.

Gray, Asa. *Darwiniana: Essays and Reviews Pertaining to Darwinism*. Edited by A. Hunter Dupree. Cambridge, Mass.: Belknap Press, 1963.

Greg, W. R. *Literary and Social Judgments*. Boston: James R. Osgood, 1873. At www.archive.org/stream/literarysocialjuoogreg/literarysocialjuoogreg_djvu.txt.

Greville, Charles C. F. *The Greville Memoirs*. Edited by Henry Reeve. 3 vols. London: Longmans, Green, 1874.

Haley, Bruce. *The Healthy Body and Victorian Culture*. Cambridge, Mass.: Harvard University Press, 1978.

Harris, John. *The Gallant Six Hundred*. New York: Mason & Lipscomb, 1973.

Harrison, J. F. C. *A History of the Working Men's College, 1854–1954*. London: Routledge & Kegan Paul, 1954.

Harrison, Roy, and John Wild. *Maer: A Guide to the Village and Church*. Crewe, Cheshire: John Porter, for Maer Parochial Church Council, 1989.

Hartnoll, Phyllis, ed. *The Oxford Companion to the Theatre*. London: Oxford University Press, 1951.

Healey, Edna. *Emma Darwin: The Inspirational Wife of a Genius*. London: Headline, 2001.

Hedley, Arthur. *Chopin*. Revised by Maurice J. E. Brown. London: J. M. Dent, 1974.

Herbert, Sandra. *Charles Darwin, Geologist*. Ithaca, N.Y.: Cornell University Press, 2005.

Herbert, Sandra, and Paul Barrett. "Introduction to Notebook M." In Barrett et al., *Charles Darwin's Notebooks*, 517–19.

Heyck, Thomas William. "Educational." In *A Companion to Victorian Literature & Culture*, edited by Herbert F. Tucker, 194–211. Malden, Mass.: Blackwell, 1999.

Holmes, Richard. Introduction to *Romantics & Revolutionaries: Regency Portraits from the National Portrait Gallery, London*, 10–23. London: National Portrait Gallery, 2002.

Hoppen, K. Theodore. *The Mid-Victorian Generation: 1846–1886*. Oxford: Clarendon Press, 1998.

Hudson, Roger. *The Jubilee Years, 1887–1897*. London: Folio Society, 1996.

Humble, Nicola, ed. *Mrs Beeton's Book of Household Management*. Abridged from the original 1861 edition. Oxford: Oxford University Press, 2000.

Huxley, Julian. *T. H. Huxley's Diary of the Voyage of H.M.S.* Rattlesnake. London: Chatto & Windus, 1935.

Huxley, Leonard. *Life and Letters of Sir Joseph Dalton Hooker*. 2 vols. London: John Murray, 1918.

Huxley, Thomas H. *Man's Place in Nature, and Other Anthropological Essays*. New York: Appleton, 1915. First three essays originally published in 1863.

Iltis, Hugo. *Life of Mendel*. Translated by Eden and Cedar Paul. New York: W. W. Norton, 1932.

Jackson, Lee, ed. *A Dictionary of Victorian London*. London: Anthem, 2006.

Jalland, Pat. *Death in the Victorian Family*. Oxford: Oxford University Press, 1996.

James, Henry. *A London Life*. London: Macmillan, 1889.

Jefferies, Richard. *Wild Life in a Southern County*. London: Smith Elder, 1879.

Jenkins, Roy. *Gladstone*. New York: Random House, 1997.

———. *Sir Charles Dilke: A Victorian Tragedy*. Rev. ed. London: Collins, 1965.

"John Lubbock." Obituary Notices. *Proceedings of the Royal Society of London*, ser. B, 87, no. 599 (1914): i–iii.

Keith, Arthur. *Darwin Revalued*. London: Watts, 1955.

Keynes, Margaret Elizabeth. *A House by the River: Newnham Grange to Darwin College*. Cambridge: Darwin College, 1976.

———. *Leonard Darwin: 1850–1943*. Cambridge: Printed privately at the University Press, 1943.

Keynes, Randal. *Annie's Box: Charles Darwin, His Daughter, and Human Evolution*. London: Fourth Estate, 2001.

Keynes, Richard Darwin, ed. *Charles Darwin's* Beagle *Diary*. Cambridge: Cambridge University Press, 1988.

———. *Fossils, Finches and Fuegians: Charles Darwin's Adventures and Discoveries on the* Beagle, *1832–1836*. London: HarperCollins, 2002.

Kinealy, Christine. *This Great Calamity: The Irish Famine, 1845–52*. Boulder, Colo.: Roberts Rinehart, 1995.

Kirkland, Janice J. "Henry James and the Darwins of Ridgemount." *Henry James Review* 19, no. 1 (1998): 91–93.

Knight, Frida. *Cambridge Music*. Cambridge: Oleander Press, 1980.

Knight, William. *Principal Shairp and His Friends*. London: John Murray, 1888.

Krause, Ernst. *The Life of Erasmus Darwin*. Translated by W. S. Dallas. Introduction by Charles Darwin. London: John Murray, 1879.

Leedham-Green, Elisabeth. *A Concise History of the University of Cambridge*. Cambridge: Cambridge University Press, 1996.

Lerwill, Chris. *The Darwins of Shrewsbury*. East Bergholt, Suffolk: C. J. Lerwill, 1981.

Levy, Amy. *Reuben Sachs*. 1888. London: Persephone, 2001.

Litchfield, Henrietta, ed. *Emma Darwin: A Century of Family Letters, 1792–1896*. 2 vols. New York: Appleton, 1915.

Loeb, Lori Anne. *Consuming Angels: Advertising and Victorian Women*. New York: Oxford University Press, 1994.

Loy, James. "Charles Darwin as Primatologist: A Literature Guide." *American Journal of Primatology* 42 (1997): 53–60.

Lyell, Charles. *The Geological Evidences of the Antiquity of Man, with Remarks on Theories of the Origin of Species by Variation.* London: John Murray, 1863.

Lyell, K. M., ed. *Life, Letters and Journals of Sir Charles Lyell, Bart.* 2 vols. London: John Murray, 1881.

Lyons, F. S. L. *Charles Stewart Parnell.* New York: Oxford University Press, 1977.

MacKenzie, John M., ed. *The Victorian Vision: Inventing New Britain.* London: V&A Publications, 2001.

Mackintosh, Robert James, ed. *Memoirs of the Life of the Right Honourable Sir James Mackintosh.* 2 vols. Boston: Little, Brown, 1853.

Magnusson, Magnus, ed. *Cambridge Biographical Dictionary.* Cambridge: Cambridge University Press, 1990.

Main, Alexander, ed. *Wise, Witty, and Tender Sayings in Prose and Verse, Selected from the Works of George Eliot.* Edinburgh: Blackwood, 1872.

Martin, David Christie. *Bob Martin's Little Girl.* New York: John A. Taylor, 1892.

Martineau, Harriet. *Harriet Martineau's Autobiography.* Introduction by Gaby Weiner. 2 vols. London: Virago, 1983.

Mayr, Ernst. *The Growth of Biological Thought: Diversity, Evolution, and Inheritance.* Cambridge, Mass.: Belknap Press, 1982.

McCord, Norman. *British History, 1815–1906.* Oxford: Oxford University Press, 1991.

Meacham, Standish. *Lord Bishop: The Life of Samuel Wilberforce, 1805–1873.* Cambridge, Mass.: Harvard University Press, 1970.

Millar, Delia. 2001. "Royal Patronage & Influence." In MacKenzie, *The Victorian Vision,* 26–49.

Millhauser, Milton. *Just Before Darwin: Robert Chambers and "Vestiges."* Middletown, Conn.: Wesleyan University Press, 1959.

Mivart, St. George. *Man and Apes.* New York: Appleton, 1874.

———. *On the Genesis of Species.* London: Macmillan, 1871.

———. "Primitive Man: Tylor and Lubbock." *Quarterly Review* 137, no. 273 (1874): 40–77.

Molesworth, William Nassau. *The History of England From the Year 1830–1874.* 3 vols. London: Chapman and Hall, 1874.

Moore, James R. "Darwin of Down: The Evolutionist as Squarson-Naturalist." In *The Darwinian Heritage,* edited by David Kohn, 435–81. Princeton, N.J.: Princeton University Press, 1985.

———. "On the Education of Darwin's Sons: The Correspondence between Charles Darwin and the Reverend G. V. Reed, 1857–1864." *Notes and Records of the Royal Society of London* 32, no. 1 (1977): 51–70.

Morris, R. J. *Cholera 1832: The Social Response to an Epidemic.* New York: Holmes & Meier, 1976.

Morris, Solene, and Louise Wilson. *Down House: The Home of Charles Darwin.* London: English Heritage, 1998.

Mosley, Charles, ed. *Burke's Peerage & Baronetage.* 106th ed. 2 vols. London: Burke's Peerage, 1999.

Mowat, R. B. *A New History of Great Britain.* Vol. 3. London: Oxford University Press, 1926.

"Mr. Darwin at Cambridge." *Nature* 17 (1877): 64.

Munson, James. *Maria Fitzherbert: The Secret Wife of George IV.* New York: Carroll & Graf, 2001.

Murphy, Arthur. *The Life of David Garrick, Esq.* 2 vols. London: J. Wright, 1801.

Newsome, David. *The Victorian World Picture.* New Brunswick, N.J.: Rutgers University Press, 1997.

Nichols, Peter. *Evolution's Captain: The Dark Fate of the Man Who Sailed Charles Darwin Around the World.* New York: HarperCollins, 2003.

Norton, Sara, and M. A. DeWolfe Howe, eds. *Letters of Charles Eliot Norton.* 2 vols. Boston: Houghton Mifflin, 1913.

Oliphant, Mrs. [Margaret]. *The Sorceress: A Novel.* 3 vols. London: F. V. White, 1893.

Orel, Harold, ed. *Charles Darwin: Interviews and Recollections.* New York: St. Martin's Press, 2000.

Orel, Vítezslav. *Gregor Mendel: The First Geneticist.* Translated by Stephen Finn. Oxford: Oxford University Press, 1996.

Orrego, Fernando, and Carlos Quintana. "Darwin's Illness: A Final Diagnosis." *Notes & Records of the Royal Society* 61, no. 1 (2007): 23–29.

Pearson, Hesketh. *The Smith of Smiths: Being the Life, Wit, and Humour of Sydney Smith.* New York: Harper & Brothers, 1934.

Peckham, Morse, ed. *The Origin of Species, by Charles Darwin: A Variorum Text.* Philadelphia: University of Pennsylvania Press, 1959.

Peile, John, comp. *Biographical Register of Christ's College, 1505–1905, and of the Earlier Foundation, God's House, 1448–1505.* Vol. 2, *1666–1905.* Cambridge: Cambridge University Press, 1913.

Perkin, Joan. *Victorian Women.* London: John Murray, 1993.

Pierce, Nathaniel F., and Arabindo Mondal. "Clinical Features of Cholera." In *Cholera*, edited by Dhiman Barua and William Burrows, 209–20. Philadelphia: W. B. Saunders, 1974.

Pine, L. G., ed. *Burke's Landed Gentry.* 17th ed. London: Burke's Peerage, 1952.

———, ed. *Burke's Peerage.* 100th ed. London: Burke's Peerage, 1953.

Plowden, Alison. *The Young Victoria.* New York: Stein and Day, 1981.

Pool, Daniel. *What Jane Austen Ate and Charles Dickens Knew.* New York: Simon & Schuster, Touchstone, 1993.

Porter, Roy. *London: A Social History.* Cambridge, Mass.: Harvard University Press, 1994.

Raby, Peter. *Alfred Russel Wallace: A Life.* Princeton, N.J.: Princeton University Press, 2001.

Raverat, Gwen. *Period Piece: A Cambridge Childhood.* London: Faber and Faber, 1952.

Richards, Evelleen. "Redrawing the Boundaries: Darwinian Science and Victorian Women Intellectuals." In *Victorian Science in Context*, edited by Bernard Lightman, 119–42. Chicago: University of Chicago Press, 1997.

Richardson, John. *The Annals of London: A Year-by-Year Record of a Thousand Years of History.* Berkeley and Los Angeles: University of California Press, 2000.

Ritvo, Harriet. *The Animal Estate: The English and Other Creatures in the Victorian Age*. Cambridge, Mass.: Harvard University Press, 1987.

Romanes, Ethel. *The Life and Letters of George John Romanes*. London: Longmans, 1896.

Sadie, Stanley, ed. *The New Grove Dictionary of Music and Musicians*. Vol. 11. London: Macmillan, 1980.

Sager, Peter. *Oxford & Cambridge: An Uncommon History*. London: Thames & Hudson, 2005.

Sanders, Charles Richard, Kenneth J. Fielding, and Clyde de L. Ryals, eds. *The Collected Letters of Thomas and Jane Welsh Carlyle*. Vol. 10. Durham, N.C.: Duke University Press, 1985.

Sandford, Mrs. Henry. *Thomas Poole and His Friends*. London: Macmillan, 1888.

Secord, James A. *Victorian Sensation: The Extraordinary Publication, Reception, and Secret Authorship of "Vestiges of the Natural History of Creation."* Chicago: University of Chicago Press, 2000.

Sedgwick, John. *In My Blood*. New York: HarperCollins, 2007.

Seeley, L. B, ed. *Fanny Burney and Her Friends*. New York: Scribner and Welford, 1890.

Selous, Frederick Courteney. *Travel and Adventure in South-East Africa*. London: Rowland Ward, 1893.

Shanley, Mary Lyndon. *Feminism, Marriage, and the Law in Victorian England, 1850–1895*. Princeton, N.J.: Princeton University Press, 1989.

Sheehan, William, William H. Meller, and Steven Thurber. "More on Darwin's Illness: Comment on the Final Diagnosis of Charles Darwin." *Notes & Records of the Royal Society* 62, no. 2 (2008): 205–9.

Silverman, Jeff, ed. *Bernard Darwin on Golf*. Guilford, Conn.: Lyons Press, 2003.

Smith, Fabienne. "Charles Darwin's Health Problems: The Allergy Hypothesis." *Journal of the History of Biology* 25, no. 2 (1992): 285–306.

———. "Charles Darwin's Ill Health." *Journal of the History of Biology* 23, no. 3 (1990): 443–59.

Spalding, Frances. *Gwen Raverat*. London: Harvill, 2001.

Speake, Robert, ed. *Betley: A Village of Contrasts*. Keele, Staffordshire: Department of Adult Education, Keele University, 1980.

Stanley, H. M. *In Darkest Africa, or the Quest, Rescue and Retreat of Emin, Governor of Equatoria*. London: Sampson Low, Marston, Searle and Rivington, 1890.

Stawell, F. Melian. "Review of *The Moral Ideal*." *International Journal of Ethics* 18, no. 3 (1908): 394–97.

Stecher, Robert M. "The Darwin-Innes Letters: The Correspondence of an Evolutionist with His Vicar, 1848–1884." *Annals of Science* 17, no. 4 (1961): 201–58.

Stone, Dan. *Breeding Superman: Nietzsche, Race and Eugenics in Edwardian and Interwar Britain*. Liverpool: Liverpool University Press, 2002.

Stott, Rebecca. *Darwin and the Barnacle*. New York: W. W. Norton, 2003.

Stubbings, Frank. *Bedders, Bulldogs, and Bedells: A Cambridge Glossary*. Cambridge: Cambridge University Press, 1995.

Sweet, D. W. "Warfare and International Relations: Britain, Europe and the 'Pax Britannica.'" In *The Cambridge Historical Encyclopedia of Great Britain and Ireland*, edited by Christopher Haigh, 265–68. Cambridge: Cambridge University Press, 1985.

Symons, Julian, ed. *Carlyle: Selected Works, Reminiscences and Letters*. London: Rupert Hart-Davis, 1955.

Temperley, H.W.V. *Life of Canning*. London: James Finch, 1905.

Tennyson, Hallam Tennyson, Lord. *Alfred Lord Tennyson: A Memoir by His Son*. 2 vols. London: Macmillan, 1897.

Thomson, Keith Stewart. *HMS* Beagle: *The Story of Darwin's Ship*. New York: W. W. Norton, 1995.

Trewin, J. C. *Mr. Macready: A Nineteenth-Century Tragedian and His Theatre*. London: George Harrap, 1955.

Turner, James C. *The Liberal Education of Charles Eliot Norton*. Baltimore: Johns Hopkins University Press, 1999.

Uglow, Jenny. *Elizabeth Gaskell: A Habit of Stories*. London: Faber and Faber, 1993.

———. *The Lunar Men: Five Friends Whose Curiosity Changed the World*. New York: Farrar, Straus and Giroux, 2002.

Vaughan Williams, Ursula. *R.V.W.: A Biography of Ralph Vaughan Williams*. London: Oxford University Press, 1964.

Venn, J. A. *Alumni Cantabrigienses*. Cambridge: Cambridge University Press, 1940.

Vries, Leonard de, comp. *Victorian Advertisements*. London: John Murray, 1968.

Walford, Lucy Bethia. *Troublesome Daughters*. Edinburgh: William Blackwood and Sons, 1880.

Walker, Mrs. [Mary A.]. *Untrodden Paths in Roumania*. London: Chapman and Hall, 1888.

Walters, S. M., and E. A. Stow. *Darwin's Mentor: John Stevens Henslow, 1796–1861*. Cambridge: Cambridge University Press, 2001.

Walton, John K. "Home and Leisure." In MacKenzie, *The Victorian Vision*, 50–73.

Weaver, Cora. *A Short Guide to Charles Darwin and Evelyn Waugh in Malvern (Life— and Death)*. Malvern, Hereford and Worcester: Cora Weaver Press, 1991.

———. *A Short Guide to Malvern as a Spa Town (The Water Cure)*. Malvern, Hereford and Worcester: Cora Weaver Press, 1991.

Wedgwood, Barbara, and Hensleigh Wedgwood. *The Wedgwood Circle, 1730–1897: Four Generations of a Family and Their Friends*. Westfield, N.J.: Eastview Editions, 1980.

Wedgwood, Frances Julia. *The Message of Israel in the Light of Modern Criticism*. London: Isbister, 1894.

———. *The Moral Ideal*. 1888. London: Kegan Paul, Trench, Trübner, 1894.

Wedgwood, Henry Allen. *The Bird Talisman: An Eastern Tale*. Illustrated by Gwen Raverat. London: Faber and Faber, 1939.

Wedgwood-Moseley Collection of Wedgwood Correspondence. Keele University Library.

Weinreb, Ben, and Christopher Hibbert, eds. *The London Encyclopaedia*. New York: St. Martin's Press, 1984.

Weintraub, Stanley. *Victoria: An Intimate Biography*. New York: Dutton, 1987.

Willey, Basil. *Darwin and Butler: Two Versions of Evolution*. London: Chatto & Windus, 1960.

Wilson, A. N. *God's Funeral*. New York: W. W. Norton, 1999.

———. *The Victorians*. New York: W. W. Norton, 2003.

Wilson, Leonard G. *Charles Lyell, the Years to 1841: The Revolution in Geology.* New Haven, Conn.: Yale University Press, 1972.

Wood, Horatio C., Jr. *Pharmacology and Therapeutics for Students and Practitioners of Medicine.* Philadelphia: J. B. Lippincott, 1912.

Wright, Robert. *The Moral Animal: The New Science of Evolutionary Psychology.* New York: Pantheon, 1994.

Young, G. M. *Victorian England.* London: Folio Society, 1999.

Ziegler, Philip. *King William IV.* London: Collins, 1971.

Index

Agassiz, Alexander, 263, 321
Agassiz, Louis, 92
Albert, Prince, Consort of the United Kingdom, 133, 134, 144, 242, 325
Albert Edward, Prince of Wales, 205, 221, 306
Allen, Baugh (uncle), 10, 49, 58
Allen, Caroline (aunt), 5, 24. *See also* Drewe, Caroline
Allen, Catherine (Kitty, aunt), 5. *See also* Mackintosh, Catherine
Allen, Elizabeth (Bessy, mother), 5. *See also* Wedgwood, Elizabeth Allen
Allen, Elizabeth Hensleigh (grandmother), 5
Allen, Emma (aunt), 5, 6, 10, 13, 58, 117, 202
Allen, Frances (Fanny, aunt): death, 244; death of family members, 59, 101; and Emma, 58, 125; move to London, 10; and Nightingale family, 147; personality, 6; romantic attachment to James Mackintosh, 47; support for Hensleigh Wedgwood, 42; travel, 13; views on Evangelicism, 46

Allen, Harriet (aunt), 5. *See also* Surtees, Harriet Allen
Allen, Jessie (aunt), 5, 6, 10, 13, 89. *See also* Sismondi, Jessie de
Allen, John Bartlett (grandfather), 5
Allen, John Hensleigh (uncle), 5, 10, 24, 58
Allen, Louisa Jane (aunt), 5. *See also* Wedgwood, Louisa Jane
Animals, humane treatment of, 140, 200, 246
Appleton, D.: publisher, 140; publishing house, 176

Barlow, Nora (granddaughter), 310
Beagle. See HMS *Beagle*
Blyth, Edward, 149, 159
Bonham-Carter, Elinor, 192, 204, 206
Britain. *See* Great Britain
Brown, Robert, 67, 84
Butler, Henry Mantagu, 322
Butler, Samuel, 268–69

Cambridge, Duke of, 68, 151, 331
Cameron, Julia, 212, 213

Carlyle, Jane, 52, 67, 170–71
Carlyle, Thomas, 52, 67, 73, 87–88, 265, 278
Carpenter, William Benjamin, 171, 180
Chambers, Richard, 106–7, 171
Charlotte, Queen of England, 2–3
Clapham Grammar School, 152–53, 159, 168, 174, 210–11
Cobbe, Frances Power, 211, 246
Collos, Madame, 15
Crewe, Frances, 60
Crofts, Ellen (daughter-in-law), 292, 295–96, 297. See also Darwin, Ellen Crofts
Crystal Palace, 133–34, 144

Darwin, Amy Ruck (daughter-in-law), 236–37, 239, 249–51. See also Ruck, Amy
Darwin, Anne Elizabeth (Annie, daughter): birth and childhood, 92, 94, 119, 384n55; decline and death, 124–32, 136; gravesite, 198–99; personality, 114; physical appearance, 225, fig. 9; scarlet fever, 121, 122
Darwin, Bernard Richard Meirion (Babsy/Dubba, grandson): adolescence, 330, 331, 352; birth, 249–51; childhood, 252–53, 256, 261–62, 296–98, 304; education, 338, 352, 357–58; gravesite, 368; love of art, 112–13, 304; love of golf, 304, 352, 357, 358; love of writing, 298, 331; physical appearance, fig. 16; travel, 264, 277, 292, 365–66
Darwin, Caroline (cousin, sister-in-law), 14, 15, 31, 32, 69–70. See also Wedgwood, Caroline Darwin
Darwin, Catherine (Catty/Cath, cousin, sister-in-law), 14, 15, 22, 77–78, 89, 116, 198. See also Langton, Catherine Darwin
Darwin, Charles Galton (grandson), 330, 343
Darwin, Charles Robert (husband, cousin): beliefs (see Religious beliefs of

Charles Robert Darwin); biographies of, 307–10, 317–18, 325–28; careers in science (see Evolutionist, career of Charles Robert Darwin; Naturalist, career of Charles Robert Darwin); death of family members, 116–17, 125–30, 199, 251, 279; education, 23, 34, 40, 42; employees (see Employees of the Darwin family); as father and grandfather, 87, 112, 113, 192, 252; gravesite, 285–86, 296, 307; humane treatment of animals, 140, 200, 246; ill health (see Health issues of Charles Robert Darwin; Water cure facilities); income and finances, 66–67, 76, 110, 117, 136, 176, 279–80; legacy, 285–86, 306–7, 341, 361; life (see Life events of Charles Robert Darwin; marriage (see Marriage relationship of Charles and Emma Darwin); personality, 80, 100; physical appearance, 205, fig. 5, fig. 11, fig. 17; and Rev. Ffinden, 235–36; romantic attachments (see Martineau, Harriet; Owen, Fanny); support for Wallace, 274–75; town in Australia named after, 291; travel, recreational, 31; views on marriage, 71–72, 78, 83
Darwin, Charles Waring (son), 112, 154, 159, 162, 164, 368
Darwin, Elizabeth (Lizzy/Bessy, daughter): adolescence, 172, 189; adulthood, 210, 232, 320–21; birth and childhood, 112, 122, 130; charity activities, 370; Church of England, 206; death, 370; death of sister-in-law Amy Darwin, 251; education, 192, 203; gravesite, 368; ill health, 122, 172, 179, 188; move to The Grove, 291; neurological affliction and behavior, 112, 139–40, 205, 214, 251; personality, 31, 114, 207, 370; physical appearance, 320, fig. 15; surrogate mother to Bernard Darwin, 252, 296; travel, 228, 264, 292, 296
Darwin, Elizabeth Fraser (Bee, daughter-in-law), 290–91, 294–95, 318–19,

339–42, 347, 348, 369. *See also* Fraser, Elizabeth

Darwin, Ellen Crofts (daughter-in-law), 297, 300–301, 304, 311–12, 369. *See also* Crofts, Ellen

Darwin, Emma Cecilia Farrer (Ida, daughter-in-law), 277, 281, 304–5, 311, 353, 369. *See also* Farrer, Emma Cecilia

Darwin, Emma Nora (granddaughter), 311

Darwin, Emma Wedgwood: beliefs (*see* Religious beliefs of Emma Wedgwood Darwin); biography, 101; charity activities, 110, 363, 364–65; dowry, 76; editorial work, 168, 170, 171–72, 219, 307–10, 367; as a grandmother, 112–13, 252, 298, 311; household management, 81–82, 83; humane treatment of animals, 140, 200, 246; ill health (*see* Health issues of Emma Wedgwood Darwin); life (*see* Life events of Emma Wedgwood Darwin); love of music, 83, 113, 141, 144, 148, 151–52, 160, 205–6, 211, 269–70; love of reading, 305–6, 333–34, 343–44, 351–52; marriage (*see* Marriage relationship of Charles and Emma Darwin); personality, x, 8–9, 100, 165, 180, 193–94, 204, 282, 370; physical appearance, *fig. 4, fig. 10, fig. 18, fig. 20*; political views, 87–88, 272, 275–76, 322; portrait, 323; temperance activities, 364–65; travel (*see* London, social visits by Emma Wedgwood Darwin; Travel by Emma Wedgwood Darwin); writing, 18–19, 200. *See also* Wedgwood, Emma

Darwin, Erasmus (father-in-law), 4, 55, 268–69

Darwin, Erasmus (Little Ras, grandson), 281, 292–93, 330

Darwin, Erasmus Alvey (Ras, cousin, brother-in-law): as a city gentleman and idler, 51–52, 61, 98, 135; death, 277–79; death of family members, 116, 273; education, 23, 34; and Emma

Wedgwood Darwin, 51, 52–53, 75; gravesite, 285, 368; ill health, 129; inheritance, 117; physical appearance, *fig. 12*; views on *Origin of Species*, 169

Darwin, Frances Crofts (Piggamy, granddaughter), 311, 312, 323

Darwin, Francis (Franky/Frank, son): academic career at Cambridge, 292, 332, 361; birth and childhood, 112, 119, 130, 172; birth of daughter Frances, 311; building Wychfield, 297; death of wife Amy, 251–52, 268, 300; education, 159, 176, 203, 211, 222, 233, 236; ill health, 172, 188; income, 297; knighthood, 369; physical appearance, *fig. 12*; research with father Charles, 233, 236, 261; travel, 206, 264, 296, 304; wed to Amy Ruck, 217, 236–37; wed to Ellen Crofts, 297; wed to Florence Maitland, 369; during wife Ellen's miscarriage, 300–301; writing, 307–10, 317–18, 325–28, 361

Darwin, George Howard (son): birth and childhood, 107, 109, 119; birth of daughter Gwendolen Mary, 311; death, 369; education, 152–53, 154, 159, 168, 176, 201–2, 203, 211; ill health, 129, 148, 179, 232–33; knighthood, 369; move to Newnham Grange, 300, 304; physical appearance, *fig. 13*; purchase deal of The Grove, 291; scientific and academic life, 202, 233, 261, 293–94, 369; search for a wife, 294; travel, 206, 228, 247, 256, 264, 298–99; wed to Maud Du Puy, 249, 298–300; writing, 233, 239–40

Darwin, Gwendolen Mary (granddaughter), 311, 330–31

Darwin, Henrietta Emma (Etty/Hen, daughter): adolescence and young adulthood, 160, 166–67, 182, 192; birth, 101, 102; childhood, 113, 119, 124–25, 130, 134, 144, 156; death of sister Annie, 130–31; editorial work, 219; ill health, 122, 156–60, 162, 172–75,

Darwin, Henrietta Emma, *cont.*
178, 179, 181; income and finances,
208, 225; personality, 113–14, 166, 194;
physical appearance, 225, *fig. 14*; travel,
203, 204–6, 214, 219, 365–66; wed
to Richard Litchfield, 223, 224–26.
See also Litchfield, Henrietta Emma
Darwin
Darwin, Horace (Skimp, son): birth and
childhood, 112, 132, 185–86, 192; birth
of daughter Emma Nora, 311; birth of
son Erasmus, 281; childhood, 159, 192;
education, 189, 211, 226, 227, 233; ill
health, 188–89, 198, 233; income, 266;
inventions, 233, 246, 369; knighthood,
369; military activities, 369; move to
The Orchard, 293; physical appearance, *fig. 12*; political activism, 305;
scientific instrument design, 261, 293,
369; travel, 190, 206, 228, 239; visit to
Down House, 277; wed to Emma Farrer, 265–66, 267
Darwin, Leonard (Lenny/Leo, son):
advocate of negative eugenics, 369;
astronomy, 238, 282, 318–19; birth and
childhood, 112, 122, 130, 172, 394n43;
education, 176, 211, 222; engagement
to Elizabeth Fraser, 282; at Henrietta's
wedding, 225; honeymoon, 290–91,
294–95; ill health, 172, 190–91; with
Intelligence Division, 304, 318, 331–32;
meeting Col. Gordon, 254–56; member of Parliament, 315, 347–51, 359–60;
as military school teacher, 256, 261;
physical appearance, *fig. 10, fig. 12*;
with Royal Engineers, 232, 237, 245,
282, 289, 339; scientific societies, 369;
travel, 237–39, 244–45, 247, 290–91,
294–95, 318–19, 340–42; wed to Elizabeth Fraser, 289–90; wed to Mildred
Massingberd, 369; writing, 347
Darwin, Margaret (granddaughter), 343
Darwin, Marianne (cousin, sister-in-law),
14. *See also* Parker, Marianne Darwin

Darwin, Mary Eleanor (daughter), 98,
99, 114, 368
Darwin, Maud Du Puy (daughter-in-
law), 300, 304, 310–11, 330, 343, 352,
369. *See also* Du Puy, Maud
Darwin, Robert Waring (uncle, father-
in-law): death, 115–17; death of wife
Susannah, 14; depression, 14; as
doctor to family members, 3, 49, 59,
88, 89, 95; Emma's views on, 73; as a
grandfather, 92, 93; medical career,
4; money management skills, 4, 6, 13,
98, 100, 117; physical description, 4;
political views, 71; sense of humor,
76, 383n77; views on Charles Robert
Darwin, 41, 76, 328
Darwin, Ruth (granddaughter), 311
Darwin, Sara Ashburner Sedgwick
(daughter-in-law), 257–59, 262–64,
292, 353, 369. *See also* Sedgwick, Sara
Ashburner
Darwin, Susan (cousin, sister-in-law):
death, 207; death of father, Robert
Waring Darwin, 116; death of mother,
Susannah, 14, 15; views on Frances
Crewe, 60; visits to the Darwin family, 22, 89, 102, 133
Darwin, Susannah Wedgwood (aunt,
mother-in-law), 3, 4, 13, 14, 117
Darwin, William Erasmus (Doddy/
Willy, son): adulthood, 168, 176,
185; banking career, 181, 184–85, 232,
369; birth and infancy, 86–87, 89,
92; childhood, 94, 119, 124, 130, 135;
death, 369; death of family members,
285, 286, 287, 313–14; education at
Cambridge, 159, 163, 168, 188; education during childhood, 123–24, 136,
137–38, 141, 155; Emma's visit to, 190;
help with family finances, 198, 270,
297, 314, 355; ill health, 148, 188; inheritance, 207–8; personality, 113, 258;
physical appearance, 186, 262, *fig. 12*; at
sister Henrietta's wedding, 225; travel,

239, 262–64; views on marriage, 215; wed to Sara Sedgwick, 216, 257–59

Darwin, William Robert (Billy, grandson), 352

Darwin family, physicians to: Allfrey, Charles, 283; Ayerst, James, 198; Beddoes, Thomas, 3–4; Brinton, William, 200; Brodie, Benjamin, 156; Clark, Andrew, 233, 273, 281, 283; Cockell, Mr., 98; Darwin, Robert Waring, 3, 49, 59, 88, 89, 95; Engleheart, S. P., 179, 188, 189; Gully, James Manby, 117–19, 124, 125, 126, 127, 128, 156; Headland, Edward, 172, 188; Holland, Henry, 117, 124, 173, 174–75, 188; Jenner, William, 201; Lane, Edward, 156, 157, 173; Moore, Norman, 262, 281, 283, 366–67; Moxon, Walter, 283; Robinson, James, 144, 179; Scott, Dr., 366–67; Woodhouse, Mr., 179. *See also* Diseases; Health Issues

Derby, Lady, 360, 363

Dicey, Albert, 315, 326

Dickens, Charles, 67, 68, 185, 213, 295

Dilke, Sir Charles, 303, 316–17, 344

Diseases: Chaga's disease, 65–66, 90–91; cholera, 45, 47, 145; consumption, 5, 14, 24, 61, 129; diphtheria, 162; measles, 172, 244; scarlet fever, 121–22, 142, 148, 161, 174, 190–91; tuberculosis, 128–29; typhus and typhoid fever, 128, 173; whooping cough, 59, 148. *See also* Health issues *under various names*

Disraeli, Benjamin (prime minister), 242, 247–48, 254, 271, 276

Down House: Charles's study, 81, *fig. 7*; description, 97, 296, *fig. 6–8*; family life, 112–13, 149, 337–38, 363–64; help for beggars at, 110, 363; hothouse, 149; purchase, 93–94, 97–98; renovations, 100, 110, 158, 362–63; Sandwalk, 110, 119, 167, 188, 281, 364; servant's ball, 220; spelling of name, 385n1

Down Lodge, 236, 237, 239, 243, 252

Drewe, Caroline (aunt), 14, 24, 33, 58–59. *See also* Allen, Caroline

Drewe, Edward (cousin), 29, 32

Drewe, Rev. Edward (uncle), 5

Du Puy, Ella, 311, 312

Du Puy, Maud (daughter-in-law), 249, 294, 298–300. *See also* Darwin, Maud Du Puy

Du Puy, Nellie, 294

Employees of the Darwin family: Brodie, Jessie, 94, 125, 126; Brooks, William, 267–68; Covington, Syms, 81, 82, 143; Evans, Mrs., 234, 235; Grut, Mrs., 165–67; Harding, Bessy, 92, 93; Jackson, William, 281, 286, 296; Jenkins, Mr., 17; Lettington, Henry, 327, 360; Ludwig, Miss, 188, 189; Parslow, Arthur, 354–55; Parslow, Joseph, 89, 93, 114, 119, 220, 286, 354–55; Parslow, Mary Anne, 360, 363; Pugh, Miss, 154–55, 156, 165, 205; Thorley, Catherine, 117–18, 119, 124, 125, 154, 157, 327

Etruria Hall, 3, 6, 9, 10, 12, 36

Evolutionary theory: of Butler, 268–69; of Chambers, 106–7, 171; of Erasmus Darwin, 268–69; of Gérard, 111; and God or religion, 184, 196, 212, 218–19, 230, 308–9, 334; human, 68, 170–71, 175, 195–97, 218, 240; human emotion, 227–28; of Huxley, 197, 218; of Lyell, 195–97; and Mendel, 191; of Mivart, 218, 240; morals, by George Darwin, 233; natural selection, 157–58, 160, 192, 196, 210, 218–19; species theory development, 103–6, 149–50, 152, 155; transmutation theory development, 67–68, 95–96, 105–6; of Wallace, 155, 160, 161, 219

Evolutionist, career of Charles Robert Darwin: accusations of plagiarism by, 268–69; caricatures in the media, 96, 228; *On the Descent of Man*, ix, x, 218, 227, 264; *The Expression of the*

Evolutionist, career of Charles Robert
  Darwin, *cont.*
  Emotions, 227–28; first species essay,
  103–6; human emotion, 227–28;
  humans, 68, 218; natural selection,
  157–58, 160; *On the Origin of Species*,
  ix, x, 95, 163, 168–72, 175–76, 209, 218;
  species theory, 149–50, 152, 155; transmutation, 67–68, 92, 95, 105–6; *The
  Variation of Animals and Plants Under
  Domestication*, 210, 218; views on *Vestiges*, 107; Wallace's research published
  first, 160; work with Hooker, 102–3

Farrer, Emma Cecilia (Ida, daughter-in-
  law), 265–66, 267. *See also* Darwin,
  Emma Cecilia Farrer
Farrer, Euphemia Wedgwood (Effie,
  niece), 230–31, 353. *See also* Wedg-
  wood, Euphemia
Farrer, Thomas Henry (Theta), 211,
  230–31, 265–66, 277, 353
Ffinden, Mrs., 234, 363
Ffinden, Rev. George Sketchley, 233–36,
  368
FitzRoy, Adm. Robert: captain of the
  Beagle, 41, 64, 65; career, 67, 101, 155,
  204; suicide, 204; wedding, 70
Fox, Eliza Ann, 60
Fox, Harriet, 95
Fox, Louisa Mary, 8, 142
Fox, Mary Elizabeth, 16
Fox, Rev. William Darwin: Charles Dar-
  win chosen as godfather, 94; children,
  60; death of wife Harriet, 95; friend-
  ship with the Darwin family, 117–18,
  119, 121, 123, 149; news of Annie
  Darwin's gravesite, 129; relationship
  with Charles Darwin, 44, 60, 94
Fox, Samuel William, 94
Franke, Hermann, 270–71, 277
Fraser, Elizabeth (Bee, daughter-in-law),
  282–83, 289–90. *See also* Darwin,
  Elizabeth Fraser
Fraser, Tom, 295, 303–4

Galton, Erasmus, 285
Galton, Francis, 230, 260, 285, 322, 369
Galton, Louisa Jane, 322
Gascoyne-Cecil, Robert Arthur. *See*
  Salisbury, Lord (prime minister)
Gaskell, Elizabeth, 150, 151, 277
George III, King of England, 2
George IV, King of England, 17, 36
George V, King of England, 343
Gifford, Harriet (cousin), 35, 42, 53, 72
Gladstone, Helen, 273, 321–22
Gladstone, William E. (prime minis-
  ter): approval of pension for Wallace,
  274–75; and Britain's relationship
  with Ireland, 288–89, 314–15, 344–45,
  347, 349–50; and death of Gen.
  Gordon, 303–4; and death of Samuel
  Wilberforce, 231; elections, 272, 347,
  348–49; and Queen Victoria, 242,
  248; views on the Balkan conflict, 254;
  visit to Cambridge, 322
Gordon, Col. Charles George, 254–56,
  302–4
Gray, Asa: friendship with Lenny
  Darwin, 194; honors, 325; support for
  Charles Darwin's research, 149, 155,
  157–58, 194; support for *Origin of Species*, 169, 171; views on evolution, 184;
  views on the U.S. Civil War, 187, 203;
  visits with the Darwins, 216, 245, 263
Great Britain: abolition of slavery, x,
  54–56; and Afghanistan, 271; anti-
  vivisection legislation, 246; Ashanti
  War, 242; Balkans conflicts and the
  Crimean War, x, 142–43, 144–47,
  158, 254; Battle of Waterloo, 12; and
  Canada, 314; Chartism and the working classes, 87–88, 98, 106; Deceased
  Wife's Sister Bill, 335–36; decline
  in food supply, 87, 109–10, 271–72;
  divorce of Sir Charles Mordaunt,
  220–21; elections, 272, 347–49, 359;
  Emma's homes (*see* Down House;
  Etruria Hall; Grove, The; Macaw Cottage; Maer Hall); First Anglo-Boer

War, 276; and France, 2, 6, 12, 137; and India, 159, 247–49; and Ireland, 37, 58, 62–63, 272, 275–76, 288–89, 314–15, 336–37, 344, 349–50; miners and labor relations, 348, 350, 351, 360; parliamentary reform, 37–39, 46, 54; Peninsular War, 2; Poor Laws, 58, 61–62, 63, 110; Queen Victoria's reign, 68–69, 242, 324–25; Royal Titles Act, 247–48; severe winters, 91–92, 202, 204, 356–57; stamp tax, 63; and Sudan, 256, 302–3, 362; and the U.S. Civil War, 186–87, 194–95, 201; Zulu War, 271

Great Exhibition of 1851, 133–35

Grey, Earl (prime minister), 38, 39, 46, 58, 63

Grove, The, 291, 296, 297, 321–22, 356, *fig. 19*

Haeckel, Ernst, 209–10, 218

Harrison, Lucy Wedgwood (niece), 270. *See also* Wedgwood, Lucy

Health issues. *See* Diseases; Darwin family, physicians to; Health issues of Charles Robert Darwin; Health issues of Emma Wedgwood Darwin; Medical considerations

Health issues of Charles Robert Darwin: caregiving by wife Emma, 89, 91, 157, 202; chronic symptoms, 88–90, 115, 117, 172–73, 199–200, 201; eczema, 90, 197, 281; flu, 188; heart problems, 280–81, 283; loss of memory, 233; possible diagnoses, 65–66, 89–91, 117. *See also* Water cure facilities

Health issues of Emma Wedgwood Darwin: deafness, 305; decline, 305, 321, 351, 366–67; facial surgery, 156; flu, 188; heart problems, 273; and repeated pregnancies, 107, 108, 132, 152; scarlet fever, 191; teeth, 179

Hensleigh, Elizabeth (Bessy, mother). *See* Wedgwood, Elizabeth

Hensleigh, Elizabeth (grandmother). *See* Allen, Elizabeth Hensleigh

Henslow, Frances, 115. *See also* Hooker, Frances Henslow

Henslow, Rev. John Stevens: death, 181; professor at Cambridge, 41, 42, 67; support for Charles Darwin's research, 41, 102, 149, 155; visit to the Darwins, 83, 84

Historical context: 1800s: Peninsular War, 2; 1820s: Battle of Waterloo, 12; 1830s: education for girls, 12; grand tours, x, 13, 25–28; Queen Victoria, x, 68; workhouses, 61–62; 1840s: decline in food supply, 109–10; family planning, 108; infant mortality rate, 100; 1850s: Balkans conflicts, x, 142–43, 144–47, 158; croquet in Britain, 182; Great Exhibition, 133–35; 1860s: International Exhibition, 189, 191; U.S. Civil War, 186–87, 189, 194–95, 200–201, 203; 1870s: Afghanistan, 271; Ashanti War, 242; Balkans conflicts, 254; Franco-Prussian War, 222; penny-farthing bicycle, 245–46; status of the British Empire, 242; Sudan, 255, 256; 1880s: Collier scandal, 335–36; Dilke scandal, 316–17; First Anglo-Boer War, 276; Parnell-Piggott scandal, 336–37; Sudan, 302–3; W. T. Stead scandal, 315–16, 317; Zulu War, 271; 1890s: Hamidian Massacres, 361–62; Parnell-O'Shea scandal, 344–45; Sudan, 362. *See also* Diseases; Great Britain; Medical considerations; Slavery

HMS *Beagle*, 40–42, 47, 53, 56, 64–66, 287

Holland, Sir Henry: connections to the Wedgwood family, 16, 51; dismissal of Charles Darwin's writings, 66, 169; as doctor to Darwin family, 117, 124, 173, 174–75, 188; views on first-cousin marriage, 175; views on Maer household, 11; wed to Saba Smith, 60

Homes of Emma Darwin. *See* Down House; Etruria Hall; Grove, The; Macaw Cottage; Maer Hall

Hooker, Frances Henslow (Franny), 199. *See also* Henslow, Frances

Hooker, Hyacinth Jardine Symonds, 253, 313, 360

Hooker, Joseph Dalton: burglary of home, 190; death of Charles Lyell, 243; death of family members, 199, 204; engagement to Frances Henslow, 115; expedition to India and Tibet, 115, 119–20; Intl. Exhibition juror, 189; knighthood, 261; support for Charles Darwin, 102–3, 143, 149, 155, 158, 175; travel, 232; views on evolution, 103, 107, 111, 169, 171; visits to Down House, 108, 140, 180, 220, 312–13, 360; wed to Hyacinth Jardine, 253

Hooker, Maria Elizabeth, 199

Hooker, Sir William Jackson, 102, 120, 203–4

Horner, Leonard, 71, 84

Huxley, Ethel, 335–36

Huxley, George, 358

Huxley, Henrietta Heathorn (Nettie), 137, 180, 297, 359, 364

Huxley, Joyce, 335

Huxley, Leonard, 180

Huxley, Marian (Mady), 335

Huxley, Noel, 129, 174, 180, 358, 364

Huxley, Thomas Henry: anti-vivisection investigation, 246; articles on religion and science, 334; death, 358–59; at death of Charles Darwin, 285; death of son Noel, 174; *Evidence as to Man's Place in Nature*, 197, 218; ill health and walking holiday, 231–32; opposition to Mivart, 240; statue, 306; support for Charles Darwin, 129, 137, 155, 158, 175–76, 260, 306; views on bishop Wilberforce, 231; views on *Origin of Species*, 169, 171; visits to the Darwin family, 179–80, 297, 312

Innes, Rev. John Brodie, 114, 133, 136, 153, 216–17, 233, 274

International Exhibition of 1862, 189, 191

Jebb, Caroline (Cara), 294, 298, 299, 311

Jebb, Richard, 291, 299

John Murray Publishers, 168, 176, 195, 268, 274, 280

Josiah Wedgwood and Sons. *See under* Wedgwood pottery works

Keynes, Randal, 128, 199

Kovalevsky, Vladimir, 210

Lamb, William (prime minister), 63

Langton, Catherine Darwin (Catty/ Cath, cousin, sister-in-law), 198, 207. *See also* Darwin, Catherine

Langton, Charles (brother-in-law): birth of son Edmund, 95; death, 314; death of son Edmund, 247; finances, 314; ill health, 61, 129, 313–14; move to Maer Hall, 94; wed to Catherine Darwin, 198; wed to Charlotte Wedgwood, 43

Langton, Charlotte Wedgwood (sister), 61, 94, 95, 111, 184–85, 187, 219. *See also* Wedgwood, Charlotte

Langton, Edmund (nephew), 95, 195, 219, 246–47

Langton, Emily Caroline (Lena), 219, 246, 314

Langton, Stephen, 314

Leopold, Prince, 122, 256

Life and Letters of Charles Darwin, The (Darwin), 307–10, 317–18, 325–28

Life events of Charles Robert Darwin (chronological): birth, 4; memory of death of mother, 14–15; young adulthood, 34, 71–72; courtship of Emma, 73–76, 77–82; wed to Emma Wedgwood, 29, 82; move into Macaw Cottage, 81; move into Down House, 93–94; death, 283; funeral and burial, 284–87. *See also* Health issues of Charles Robert Darwin; Marriage relationship of Charles and Emma Darwin

Life events of Emma Wedgwood Darwin (chronological): birth, x, 1–2, 8; childhood and adolescence, 8–23, 24–28 (*see also* Maer Hall); young adulthood, 29–33, 35, 45–53, 55; death of sister Fanny, 48–49, 50; marriage proposals, 50–53; courtship by Charles, 73–76, 77–82; wed to Charles Darwin, 29, 82; birth of son William Erasmus, 86–87; birth of daughter Anne Elizabeth, 92; move to Down House, 97–98; birth and death of daughter Mary Eleanor, 98, 99; birth of daughter Henrietta, 101; birth of son George Howard, 107; birth of daughter Lizzy, 112; death of daughter Annie, 125–28, 130–32, 199; birth of son Francis, 112; birth of son Leonard, 112, 122; birth of son Horace, 112, 132; miscarriage, 144; birth of son Charles Waring, 112, 154; menopause, 176–77; death of sister Charlotte, 187; death of sister-in-law Amy, 251, 268; death of sister Elizabeth, 274; death of husband Charles, 283, 296; widowhood, 284–301, 323; wintering at The Grove, 291, 292, 305; death of cousin Caroline, 329; lost link with old times, 329, 346; death of brother Frank, 329–30; death of brother Hensleigh, 345–46; death, 366–67; obituary and funeral, 368. *See also* Health issues of Emma Wedgwood Darwin; Marriage relationship of Charles and Emma Darwin; Travel by Emma Wedgwood Darwin

Litchfield, Henrietta Emma Darwin (Etty/Hen, daughter): biography by Gwen Raverat, 369; biography of mother by, 101, 369–70; death of family members, 278, 288, 366–67; devotion to Bernard Darwin, 252–53, 338; gravesite, 368; infertility, 232, 249, 252; later years, 369–70; life in Maryle-bone, 232; marriage relationship, 229; move to Kensington Sq., 296, 305; physical appearance, 225, *fig. 14*; poisoning, 346; travel, 264, 277, 346; wed to Richard Litchfield, 223, 224–26. *See also* Darwin, Henrietta Emma

Litchfield, Richard (son-in-law): background, 224; death, 369; life in Marylebone, 232; move to Kensington Sq., 296, 305; support for Charles Darwin's research, 228; travel, 264, 346; wed to Henrietta Darwin, 223, 224–26

London, social visits to by Emma Wedgwood Darwin: 1830s, 45, 52, 53, 57–58, 73; 1840s, 100–101; 1850s, 134, 136, 140, 141, 151–52, 160; 1860s, 181, 195, 205–6, 211; 1870s, 228; 1880s, 269–70

Longfellow, Henry Wadsworth, 212–13

Lubbock, John William, 140, 141, 152, 204, 235, 285

Lubbock, Lady, 154, 180, 204

Lyell, Charles: *Antiquity of Man*, 195; at coronation of Queen Victoria, 69; death, 243–44; knighthood, 121; scientific career, 134, 195; soft voice, 205; support for Charles Darwin's research, 155, 158, 160; views on evolution, 170, 184, 195–97; views on slavery, 317–18; visits to the Darwins, 84, 108, 121, 152

Lyell, Katherine, 317

Lyell, Mary, 84, 108, 121, 152, 230, 243

Macaw Cottage, 81, 82, 83, 89, 94, 98

Mackintosh, Catherine (Kitty, aunt), 5, 10, 35–36

Mackintosh, Fanny (cousin), 16, 42–43. *See also* Wedgwood, Fanny Mackintosh

Mackintosh, Mary (née Appleton, wife of Robert Mckintosh), 213

Mackintosh, Robert (cousin), 42, 46, 51, 61, 64, 80

Mackintosh, Sir James (Mac, uncle): death, 46–47, 380n28; disapproval of Fanny's marriage, 42, 43; East India

Mackintosh, Sir James, *cont.*
Company, 38; *History of England*, 33, 35, 46; life in India, 5, 6; marriage, 35; physical description, 5; political career, 5, 33; support for the Allen sisters, 10, 13, 16

Maer Hall: Charles Darwin's visits to, 23, 89; Charles Langton's move to, 94; description, 1, 23, *fig. 1*; and Emma's parents, 7, 10; family life, 11, 21, 22–23; guests, 21–22, 33, 92; purchase, 4; renovations, 6, 7; sale, 111; and Wedgwood financial difficulties, 9, 10

Maitland, Florence Henrietta (daughter-in-law), 369

Malvern. *See* Water cure facilities, Malvern

Marriage relationship of Charles and Emma Darwin: closeness, x, 105, 128, 164, 253–54, 284, 287–88, 367; Emma as caregiver, 89, 91, 157, 202; pet names, 83; working together, 168, 170, 171–72, 219, 367

Marsh, Anne, 51, 67

Martineau, Harriet: and Charles Darwin, 67, 70–71, 76, 383n77; political activities, 58, 71; romantic relationship with Ras Darwin, 51, 53, 70; spinster, 150

Massingberd, Mildred (daughter-in-law), 365, 369

Medical considerations: amyl nitrate, 283; application of "blisters," 188; Banting Diet, 320–21; bismuth, 89; calomel, 89; chloroform, 122–23, 154, 179, 343; cod liver oil, 179, 182, 262; Florence Nightingale and nursing, 147, 150, 151, 158; hydrotherapy (*see* Water cure facilities); hypnosis, 335; menopause, 176–77; mercury, 89, 152, 154, 173, 175, 181, 203, 249, 351; mineral acids, 156, 200; nux vomica, 273; physicians (*See* Darwin family, physicians to); Prussic acid, 89; quinine, 281

Mendel, Gregor, 191

Mivart, St. George Jackson, 218, 240

Moor Park. *See* Water cure facilities, Moor Park

Moscheles, Ignaz, 31

Moseley, Frances (Fanny, sister-in-law), 43–44. *See also* Wedgwood, Frances Moseley

Napoleon Bonaparte, Emperor of France, 2, 6, 12

Napoleon III, Emperor of France, 136–37, 141, 144, 222

Naturalist, career of Charles Robert Darwin: analysis of *Beagle* specimens, 67–68, 102, 111; barnacles, 136, 141, 143, 147, 167; conferences, 121, 149; *Coral Reefs*, 95; entymology, 42; *The Formation of Vegetable Mould*, 257, 280; *Geological Observations*, 111; Geological Society, 67, 74, 92, 95, 100, 103, 167; insectivorous and climbing plants, 229, 243, 273; medals and honors, 143–44, 167, 209, 247, 259–60; orchids, 182, 184, 364; *The Power of Movement in Plants*, 261, 274–75; reputation, 66, 86, 96, 164–65, 205, 209–10; voyage of the *Beagle*, 40–42, 44, 47, 53, 56, 64–66, 287; worms, 256–57, 280

Newton, Alfred, 220, 297, 321, 326

Nightingale, Florence, 147, 150, 151, 158

Nightingale, W. E., 184

Norton, Charles Eliot, 213, 214, 215, 239, 245, 257, 263

Olmsted, Frederick Law, 201, 263

Owen, Fanny, 8, 34, 44–45, 70

Owen, Richard, 67, 86, 171–72, 306

Parker, Frank, 207, 208

Parker, Henry, 60, 116, 151, 207, 208

Parker, Marianne Darwin (cousin, sister-in-law), 60, 116, 162. *See also* Darwin, Marianne

Parker, Mary Susan, 60
Parnell, Charles Stewart, 272, 288, 314,
  336–37, 344–45
Parson, Arthur, 270
Pets, 17, 27–28, 114, 219, 274, 312, 355–56,
  363
Physicians. *See* Darwin family, physicians
  to
Pottery factory. *See* Wedgwood pottery
  works

Raverat, Gwen, 249, 320, 321, 353
Reed, Rev. G. V., 159, 176, 189, 201–2, 203
Religion: Catholic Apostolic Church,
  46; Catholic Church, 26, 37, 62;
  Charles Darwin (*see* Religious beliefs
  of Charles Robert Darwin); Church
  of England, 21–22, 34, 37, 40, 41, 66;
  and Darwinism, 184, 196, 212, 218–19,
  230, 308–9, 334; Emma Darwin (*see*
  Religious beliefs of Emma Wedgwood
  Darwin); Evangelicism, 24, 45–46,
  334
Religious beliefs of Charles Robert
  Darwin: Church of England career,
  34, 40, 41, 66; hesitancy at being a
  godfather, 94–95; loss of faith and
  Emma's Christianity, x, 79–80, 84–86,
  95, 105–6, 165, 170, 307–8; vestigial
  theism with daughter Annie's illness,
  128, 183; views on God, 95, 184
Religious beliefs of Emma Wedgwood
  Darwin: and the children, 18–19,
  113, 114, 206–7, 282, 330; churches
  and churchgoing, 168, 182–83, 236;
  Church of England, 21–22; decrease
  in religious orthodoxy, x, 282, 334–35;
  edits to *The Life and Letters*, 307–8;
  favorite prayer, 49; and her marriage
  (*see* Religious beliefs of Charles Robert Darwin, loss of faith and Emma's
  Christianity); and Rev. Innes, 114–15;
  skepticism of Evangelicism, 46, 334
Rich, Mary, 35, 42, 43, 45–46, 135
Romanes, George John, 280, 361

Rosebery, Earl of (prime minister), 359
Rossetti, Dante Gabriel, 224, 323
Ruck, Amy (daughter-in-law), 217,
  236–37. *See also* Darwin, Amy Ruck
Ruck, Lawrence, 217, 236
Ruck, Mary Ann, 217, 236, 277
Ruskin, John, 213, 224, 264, 323

St. Chad's Church, 14, 116–17, 207
St. Mary the Virgin, 114, 217, 225,
  233–34, 285, 363, 368
St. Peter's Church, 1, 29, 82, 83, 92,
  384n55, *fig. 1*
Salisbury, Lord (prime minister),
  314–15, 347, 359
Sedgwick, Adam, 42, 64, 106, 169–70
Sedgwick, Arthur, 262, 292
Sedgwick, Maria Theodora (Theo), 258,
  263
Sedgwick, Sara Ashburner (daughter-
  in-law), 213, 215, 216, 299. *See also*
  Darwin, Sara Ashburner Sedgwick
Seymour, Gertrude (aunt), 10, 24
Shaen, Margaret, 276–77, 360
Sismondi, Jean Charles Léonard
  Simonde de (Sis, uncle), 13, 15, 25, 28,
  29–33, 73, 89
Sismondi, Jessie de (aunt): death, 141;
  and Emma Darwin, 74–75, 89;
  heirloom seal, 274; later years, 117;
  marriage, 13; Wedgwood family visits
  to, 25, 28, 29–33, 73. *See also* Allen,
  Jessie
Slavery: abolition in Britian, x, 54–56;
  Charles Lyell's views on, 317–18;
  emancipation medallions, 54; Eman-
  cipation Proclamation, 195; Wedg-
  wood family opposition to, 29, 46,
  63, 187, 194–95, 201, 230
Spencer, Earl John Charles (Lord Al-
  throp), 63, 286
Spencer, Herbert, 67
Spottiswoode, William, 285, 286
Stokes, Adm. John Lort, 41, 286–87
Stonehenge, 256

Sulivan, Bartholomew James, 40, 136, 137, 306, 307
Surtees, Harriet Allen (aunt), 33, 58. *See also* Allen, Harriet
Surtees, Rev. Matthew (uncle), 5

Tait family, 121
Temperance, 360, 364–65
Tennyson, Alfred, 145–46, 212, 213
Tollet, Ellen, 21, 228–29, 343
Tollet, George, 21
Tollet, Georgina, 21, 75, 168, 181, 228
Tollet extended family, 46, 51, 118, 147
Travel by Emma Wedgwood Darwin: Bournemouth, 191–92; Cambridge, 273; Dover, 366, 412n37; Eastbourne, 141, 174, 292; France, 15, 31, 73; grand tour, 24, 25–28; Ireland, 58; Isle of Wight, 162–63, 212; Lake District, 264, 277; London (*see* London, social visits by Emma Wedgwood Darwin); St. Leonard's-on-Sea, 187; Scotland, 72–73, 148–49; Southampton, 190, 292; Stonehenge, 256; Switzerland, 29–33; Torquay, 181–82, 184; Wales, 58, 217
Tylor, Edward Burnett, 228

Vaughan Williams, Arthur, 243
Vaughan Williams, Margaret Wedgwood, 243, 270, 278, 312. *See also* Wedgwood, Margaret
Vaughan Williams, Ralph, 216, 343
Victoria, Queen of England: birth of Prince Leopold, 122; and death of Gen. Gordon, 303; as Empress of India, 247–48; Golden Jubilee, 324–25; in mourning for husband Albert, 242; opening the Great Exhibition, 134, 144; title of Baron to Thomas Farrer, 353
von Humboldt, Alexander, 84, 86

Wallace, Alfred Russel, 155, 161, 169, 219, 274–75, 286

War. *See under* Great Britain; Historical context
Water cure facilities: Ilkley Wells House, 168; Malvern, 117–19, 124–28, 198, 232, 339–40; Moor Park, 157, 160, 163, 167, 168; Sudbrook Park, 173
Wedgwood, Allen (cousin), 13, 29, 82, 92, 129, 278
Wedgwood, Amy (niece), 59, 189, 219
Wedgwood, Caroline (niece), 59, 95
Wedgwood, Caroline Darwin (cousin, sister-in-law): birth of daughter Katherine Elizabeth Sophy, 95; death, 328–29; death of brother Ras Darwin, 278–79; death of daughter Sophy Marianne, 82, 83; death of father Robert Waring Darwin, 116; death of husband Joe, 270; move to Leith Hill Place, 94; response to *Life and Letters*, 328; visits with family, 121; wed to Joe Wedgwood, 69–70. *See also* Darwin, Caroline
Wedgwood, Catherine (Kitty, aunt), 2, 13, 14, 25
Wedgwood, Charlotte (sister), 8, 12, 24, 25–28, 35, 43. *See also* Langton, Charlotte Wedgwood
Wedgwood, Cicely Mary (niece), 59
Wedgwood, Clement (nephew), 195, 314
Wedgwood, Elizabeth Allen (Bessy, mother): anti-slavery activities, 29; background, 5; birth of daughter Emma, 1–2; death, 110–11, 117; death of daughter Fanny, 49; homes, 3, 7, 10; ill health, 25, 35, 38, 53–54, 57, 58, 99; as a mother, 11, 35; physical appearance, *fig. 3*; travel, 24, 25–28; views on Emma's marriage, 82–83; wed to Jos Wedgwood, 5. *See also* Allen, Elizabeth
Wedgwood, Emma: close relationship with sister Fanny, 8, 15–16; close relationship with sister Sarah Elizabeth, 8; education, 11–12, 15, 16–18; life events (*see* Life events of Emma Wedgwood

Darwin); love of politics, 55, 58; love of reading, 21; love of writing, 18–19, 20–22, 377n39; personality, 8–9, 12, 20, 35; physical description, 20; travel (*see* Travel by Emma Wedgwood Darwin). *See also* Darwin, Emma Wedgwood

Wedgwood, Ernest Hensleigh (Erny, nephew), 59, 137, 140

Wedgwood, Euphemia (Effie, niece), 130, 150, 230–31, 253, 353. *See also* Farrer, Euphemia Wedgwood

Wedgwood, Fanny Mackintosh (Fanny Hensleigh, sister-in-law): birth of children, 50, 57, 59; death, 337; death of family members, 59, 202, 278, 279; Emma's views on, 329, 345; friendship with Elizabeth Gaskell, 150; helping Emma, 86, 125; ill health, 329; nickname, 44; with Ras in London, 51, 52; visit to Down House, 133; wed to Hensleigh Wedgwood, 42–43. *See also* Mackintosh, Fanny

Wedgwood, Frances (Fanny, sister): childhood and adolescence, 8, 15–18, 19–20, 22; close relationship with sister Emma, 8, 15–16; death, 47–48; education, 15, 16–18; move to Cresselly, 25; personality, 8, 31, 345; spirituality, 19–20; travel, 24, 25–28, 29–33; young adulthood, 45–46

Wedgwood, Frances Julia (Snow, niece), 50, 150–51, 184, 327–28, 332–33, 352

Wedgwood, Frances Moseley (Fanny Frank, sister-in-law), 44, 50, 59, 240–41. *See also* Moseley, Frances

Wedgwood, Francis (Frank, brother): business aptitude, 24; death, 329–30; political aid to father Jos, 39; travel, 15; unhappy marriage, 240–41; and Wedgwood pottery works, 27, 33, 134; wed to Frances Moseley, 43–44

Wedgwood, Godfrey (nephew), 50, 219, 230–31, 253, 274, 357

Wedgwood, Henry Allen (Harry, brother): *The Bird Talisman*, 113, 313; birth of daughters Louisa and Caroline, 59; death of son John, 221; death of wife Jessie, 229; decline and death, 312–13; education, 9, 12, 13, 16; family visits, 22, 142; as a lawyer, 33; move to Seabridge House, 61; political aid to father Jos, 39; romantic attachment to Jessie Wedgwood, 22; with sister Emma in London, 205; travel, 13; wed to Jessie Wedgwood, 36

Wedgwood, Hensleigh (brother): birth of son Bro, 59; birth of son Ernest, 59; in the civil service, 42–43, 69; death, 345–46; death of family members, 59, 202, 273; education, 12; family visits, 22, 133, 195, 204; ill health, 329; as a lawyer, 33; travel, 15; and Wedgwood pottery works, 134; wed to Fanny Mackintosh, 42–43

Wedgwood, Hope (niece), 182, 253, 357

Wedgwood, James Mackintosh (Mack/Bro, nephew), 57, 59, 150, 202

Wedgwood, Jessie (cousin, sister-in-law), 21, 22, 36, 59, 61, 229

Wedgwood, John (nephew), 221

Wedgwood, John (uncle), 3, 5, 6, 9–10, 13, 24, 33

Wedgwood, Josiah (grandfather), 2–3, 6, 54–55, 376n5

Wedgwood, Josiah, II (Jos, father): anti-slavery activities, 29, 53, 55; approval of son Charles's *Beagle* voyage, 41; death, 101, 117; death of daughter Fanny, 49, 50; as a father and husband, 11; financial difficulties, 6, 9–10, 13; homes, 3, 7, 10; ill health, 99; as a landed gentleman, 3, 6–7, 9; personality, 10–11, 38; physical appearance, 10, *fig. 2*; political career, 38–39, 50, 53, 61–64; spiritual views, 24; travel, 24, 25–28; views on Emma's engagement, 75–76; and Wedgwood pottery works, x, 3, 7, 33, 94; wed to Bessy Allen, 5

Wedgwood, Josiah III (Joe, brother):
death, 270; death of family members,
49, 82, 83; education, 9, 12; family vis-
its, 22, 121, 204; marriage to Caroline
Darwin, 69–70; move to Leith Hill
Place, 94; travel, 13; and Wedgwood
pottery works, 33
Wedgwood, Katherine Elizabeth Sophy,
95, 384n55
Wedgwood, Louisa (niece), 59
Wedgwood, Louisa Jane (Jane, aunt), 5,
6, 9, 10, 24, 59
Wedgwood, Lucy (niece), 195. *See also*
Harrison, Lucy Wedgwood
Wedgwood, Mabel (niece), 270
Wedgwood, Margaret (niece), 216. *See
also* Vaughan Williams, Margaret
Wedgwood
Wedgwood, Robert (cousin), 59, 60
Wedgwood, Rose (niece), 251, 270–71
Wedgwood, Rowland (nephew), 244–45
Wedgwood, Sarah (Sally, grandmother),
2
Wedgwood, Sarah Elizabeth (aunt), 2,
13–14, 21, 25, 111, 153–54, 368
Wedgwood, Sarah Elizabeth (Eliza,
cousin), 59
Wedgwood, Sarah Elizabeth (Elizabeth,
sister): as caregiver for parents, 77, 78,
94, 101; death, 273–74; death of family members, 48, 187; gravesite, 368;
helping sister Emma with births, 92,
122, 132, 154; homes, 111, 187, 212; later
years, 8, 187, 212, 273; personality, 35;
at sister Emma's birth, 8; spine problems, 9, 77; as a teacher, 12; travel, 24,
25–28, 58, 72–73; young adulthood, 45
Wedgwood, Sophy Marianne (niece), 82,
83, 270
Wedgwood, Susannah. *See* Darwin,
Susannah Wedgwood

Wedgwood, Thomas (cousin), 12, 45
Wedgwood, Thomas (Tom, uncle),
3–4, 6
Wedgwood pottery works: emancipa-
tion medallions, 54; family part-
nership, 33; financial difficulties,
6, 9–10; inheritance, 2–3, 376n5;
Josiah Wedgwood and Sons, 33, 50,
94; management, 3, 7, 27, 134; Potter
to Her Majesty, 3; Wedgwood &
Brown, 134
Wellington, Duke of, 2, 12, 37, 141
Westminster Abbey, 285–86, 296, 307,
324–25
Wilberforce, Samuel, 175, 231, 234
Wilhelm I, Kaiser of Germany, 222, 247
William IV, King of England, 36–37, 39,
46, 63, 68
Wollaston, T. V., 154, 155, 158
Wolseley, Gen. Garnet, 242, 331
Working Men's College, 224, 225, 264,
277
Writings of Charles Robert Darwin:
Autobiography, 23, 34, 253; *Coral
Reefs*, 95; *On the Descent of Man*, ix,
x, 218, 227, 264; *The Expression of
the Emotions*, 227–28; first species
manuscript, 103–6; *The Formation of
Vegetable Mould*, 257, 280; *Geological
Observations*, 111; *Narrative* volumes,
86; notebooks, 67–68; *On the Origin
of Species*, ix, x, 95, 163, 168–72, 175–
76, 209, 218; pamphlet on humane
treatment of animals, 200; *The Power
of Movement in Plants*, 261, 274–75;
publishers (*see* Appleton, D.; John
Murray Publishers); travel journal
and *Journal*, 66, 86; *The Variation of
Animals and Plants Under Domestication*, 210, 218; *Zoology of the Voyage
of the Beagle*, 86, 92, 95

JAMES D. LOY is former chair of the Department of Sociology and Anthropology and professor emeritus of anthropology at the University of Rhode Island. He has published more than thirty professional papers, coauthored a monograph on rhesus monkey behavior, *The Behavior of Gonadectomized Rhesus Monkeys*, coedited a collection of primatological essays, *Understanding Behavior*, and coauthored four editions of the introductory human evolution textbook *Humankind Emerging*. James Loy's interest in the Darwin family stems from thirty-five years of teaching courses on human evolution.

KENT M. LOY is a retired audiologist. She has published four professional articles dealing with various aspects of primate behavior and is coauthor of the monograph *The Behavior of Gonadectomized Rhesus Monkeys*.